# DICKENS STUDIES ANNUAL

# DICKENS STUDIES ANNUAL

# Essays on Victorian Fiction

EDITORS

Stanley Friedman
Edward Guiliano
Anne Humpherys
Michael Timko

# DICKENS STUDIES ANNUAL

## Essays on Victorian Fiction

VOLUME
31

*Edited by*
Stanley Friedman, Edward Guiliano,
Anne Humpherys, and Michael Timko

AMS PRESS
NEW YORK

DICKENS STUDIES ANNUAL
ISSN 0084-9812

*International Standard Book Number*
Series: 0-404-18520-7
Vol. 31:0-404-18931-8

*Dickens Studies Annual: Essays on Victorian Fiction* welcomes essay- and monograph-length contributions on Dickens and other Victorian novelists and on the history of aesthetics of Victorian fiction. All manuscripts should be double-spaced and should follow the documentation format described in the most recent *MLA Style Manual*. The author's name should appear only on a cover-page, not elsewhere in the essay. An editorial decision can usually be reached more quickly if two copies of the article are submitted, since outside readers are asked to evaluate each submission. If a manuscript is accepted for publication, the author will be asked to provide a 100- to 200-word abstract and also a disk containing the final version of the essay. The preferred editions for citations from Dickens's works are the Clarendon and the Norton Critical when available, otherwise the Oxford Illustrated or the Penguin.

Please send submissions to The Editors, *Dickens Studies Annual*, Ph.D. Program in English. The Graduate Center, CUNY, 365 Fifth Avenue, New York, NY 10016-4309. Please send inquiries concerning subscriptions and/or the availability of earlier volumes to AMS Press, Inc., Brooklyn Navy Yard, Bldg. 292, Suite 417, 63 Flushing Ave., Brooklyn, NY 11205.

Manufactured in the United States of America

# Contents

# Preface

Like Shakespeare's Cleopatra, Dickens and other Victorian novelists captivate because of their "infinite variety." The articles in this volume reflect the extraordinarily wide range of subjects and techniques found in Victorian fiction, a multifariousness that attracts scholars and critics of many persuasions.

We thank all of those who have submitted manuscripts to us, and we again express our deep gratitude to those specialists who have accepted our invitations to serve as outside reviewers. These readers, who generously contribute their time and expertise, enable us to transcend our own personal preferences and thereby broaden the appeal of *DSA*.

We especially wish to thank Professor David Garlock for his survey of Dickens studies published in 2000, Professor Linda Peterson for her examination of recent work on the Brontës, Professor Robert A. Colby for his discussion of recent Thackeray scholarship, and Professor Susan Hamilton for her essay reviewing recent materials concerning Elizabeth Gaskell.

For encouraging us by providing practical assistance, we are extremely grateful to the following administrators: President Frances Degen Horowitz, Provost William P. Kelly, Ph.D. Program in English Executive Officer Joan Richardson, and Linda Sherwin, Assistant Program Officer, Ph.D. Program in English, all of The Graduate Center, CUNY, and Interim President Russell Hotzler, Dean Tamara S. Evans, and Department of English Chair Nancy R. Comley, all of Queens College, CUNY.

We extend thanks to Professor John O. Jordan, Director of The Dickens Project at the University of California, Santa Cruz, and to JoAnna Rottke, Project Coordinator for The Dickens Project, for placing on the Project's website the tables of contents for volumes 1-27 of *DSA,* as well as abstracts for subsequent volumes. (These materials are included in the Project's Dickens Electronic Archive.) The Dickens Project can be reached at http: //humwww.ucsc.edu/dickens/index.html

We again thank Gabriel Hornstein, President of AMS Press, for his enthusiastic and consistent support, and we once more express our indebtedness to

vii

Jack Hopper, our editor at AMS Press, for his skillful and congenial help in diverse areas. Finally, we thank our editorial assistant, Evan Brier, for his able handling of many complex chores needed to sustain our enterprise.

—The Editors

# Notes on Contributors

RACHEL ABLOW is assistant professor of English literature at the University of Rochester. She is currently completing a manuscript entitled "The Marriage of Two Minds: Reading Sympathy in the Victorian Marriage-Plot."

ERIC BERLATSKY is a PhD candidate at the University of Maryland, College Park. His interests include twentieth-century British and postcolonial fiction, modernism, postmodernism, and narrative theory. He is currently working on his dissertation on representations and theorizations of history, historiography, and memory in postmodern fiction. He also has an article forthcoming on narrative framing in a book project from *The Uses of Popular Culture* conference in Rhode Island.

ROSEMARIE BODENHEIMER is professor of English at Boston College, and the author of *The Politics of Story in Victorian Social Fiction* and *The Real Life of Mary Ann Evans: George Eliot, Her Letters and Fiction.* She is currently working toward a new book on Dickens and autobiographical storytelling.

ROBERT A. COLBY is professor emeritus, Graduate School of Library and Information Studies, Queens College, CUNY. His publications include *Thackeray's Canvass of Humanities: An Author and His Public* (1979) and the *Historical Introduction to Vanity Fair* (1989) in the Thackeray Edition under the general editorship of Peter Shillingsburg. He is currently at work on a study of the background of Thackeray's travel books.

DAVID GARLOCK is an adjunct assistant professor in the Department of Modern Languages and Comparative Literature at Baruch College, the City University of New York. He has published essays on Thomas Hardy and Charles Darwin in prior issues of *DSA*. His forthcoming book is still forthcoming.

JAN B. GORDON, the author of *Gossip and Subversion in Nineteenth-Century British Fiction: Echo's Economies,* is professor of Anglo-American Literature at Tokyo University of Foreign Studies. He is currently working on the role of the "transparent" body in fin de siècle culture in anticipation of his own impending retirement. His work has previously appeared in *DSA 24*.

MELISSA VALISKA GREGORY recently completed her doctoral dissertation, "Domestic Terror in Victorian Culture: Narratives of Psychological Violence," at Indiana University.

SUSAN HAMILTON is associate professor in the Department of English at the University of Alberta. Her publications include *Criminals, Idiots, Women, and Minors: Nineteenth-Century Writings By Women on Women* and articles on Victorian anti-vivisection and Florence Nightingale. She is currently working on a book on Victorian feminism and the periodical press, provisionally entitled "Frances Power Cobbe and the Practice of Everyday Feminism." She is editor of the *Victorian Review,* an interdisciplinary journal in nineteenth-century studies.

EMILY WALKER HEADY is a graduate student in English at Indiana University. This is her first published article.

RICHARD LETTIS, professor emeritus of English at Long Island University, has written several articles and two books on Dickens, and has coedited a collection of essays on *Great Expectations.*

NORMAN MACLEOD is senior lecturer in the Department of English Language at the University of Edinburgh. His main interests are in English grammar, text, and discourse analysis, stylistics, and the language of fiction. He has published articles on Henry James, Graham Greene, William Golding, and Philip Roth, and several articles each on the language and style of Charles Dickens and Kingsley Amis, as well as on the stylistic analysis of poems and on aspects of the textual analysis of the use of pronouns in English.

GRACE MOORE is a lecturer in English at the University of Bristol, U. K. She completed her doctoral thesis at the University of Exeter and has published articles on Dickens, Peter Carey, and Bernhard Schlink. She is at present working on two books, *Dickens's Others*, a study of class, race, and colonialism in the work of Charles Dickens, as well as a study of reworkings of Victorian novels. An edited collection on Victorian crime, *Doing the Police in Different Voices* (with Andrew Maunder) is forthcoming.

LINDA PETERSON is professor of English at Yale University and author of *Victorian Autobiography: The Tradition of Self-Interpretation* (1986), *Victorian Women Artists and Authors* (1994, with Susan Casteras), and *Traditions of Women's Autobiography: The Poetics and Politics of Life Writing* (1999). Her current project is a study of the professionalization of nineteenth-century women of letters.

S. D. POWELL is assistant professor of English at Texas Christian University in Fort Worth, Texas. He is a specialist in Middle English literature. One of his current research projects is to explore eighteenth- and nineteenth-century reception and editing of Middle English didactic romances.

CATHERINE RISING graduated from UC Berkeley in 1987 with a PhD in English and became what the MLA calls an independent scholar. Her published books are *Darkness at Heart: Fathers and Sons in Conrad*, and *Outside the Arch: Kohut and Five Modern Writers*. She has also written for two journals, *Conradiana* and *Psychoanalysis and Contemporary Thought*.

# The Negative's Capability:
# Real Images and the Allegory of the
# Unseen in Dickens's Christmas Books

*Emily Walker Heady*

*In recent years, a wealth of attention has been paid to Victorian visual culture, particularly to the ties between novelistic realism and photography. Published just a few years after the photograph was introduced to England, Dickens's Christmas books complicate this pairing by showing that the nineteenth-century novel is already deeply imbricated in a whole culture of visual discourses, many of which highlight just how easy it is to fool the eye. Using* A Christmas Carol *and* The Haunted Man *as case studies, I argue that Dickens's layering of mutually deconstructive, realist and anti-realist, photographic and phantasmagoric imagery systematically undercuts the power of the image—any image—to make a straightforward truth claim. However, given the allegorical nature of Dickens's stories, it would be misplaced to say that his skeptical spectacles drain his visual effects of meaning; quite on the contrary, these books insist that we need such images—albeit deceptive ones—to structure our vision of the world. We must learn to see past things in order to see into them; we must, Dickens shows, accept our inability to see truth in images not as a limitation but rather as an invitation to interpretation.*

In recent years, literary critics and art historians alike have discussed the simultaneous advent of the photograph and the heyday of the realist novel midway through the nineteenth century. They generally assert that the use of photography in fiction contributes to our sense that the narrative, like the photographic image, is a piece of—and not a statement about—the world and that realist fiction teaches us the rules of photographic seeing and vice versa (Sontag 4, 87). The ties grow stronger yet: Nancy Armstrong has argued that realist novels often give us photographic moments—or at least invoke images that seem ripe for a pose—in order to assure us that the narrative is true; photographic images in these novels, she says, come to stand for physical reality, "as if an adjective were replacing a noun" (27). Jennifer Green-Lewis also points to the tie between the two media, both of which promise to mirror society, to tell true stories, and to make "a statement that this is the way things really are" (6, 19–20, 31). Yet, as both critics point out, Victorian realism's claims to truth rest more heavily on a cultural agreement that realism is real than on the notion that novels can give us objective slices of Oliver Twist's or Dorothea Brooke's or Becky Sharp's life. Similarly, we recognize that photography's claims to truth and authenticity are primarily predicated on a social understanding by which the image is taken as reality, rather than on the dubious notion that photography is an art form whose only author is an *objectif* (Bazin 197). We know that photographs and realist novels alike can (and do) lie (Green-Lewis 2; Sontag 5–7).

The Victorians were no less understanding than we about the ability of the photograph or the daguerreotype (I use the terms interchangeably here for simple convenience) to tell half-truths. Louis Daguerre pointedly marketed as "correct" the images produced by the invention which bore his name (22). On the other hand, the photograph's British inventor, Fox Talbot, saw the camera's ability to disclose things the eye skims over, and his startlingly unrecognizable close-ups and "photogenic drawings" of plant life, body parts, and fabrics combined to make the everyday unfamiliar and, further-more, worth looking at. But even as the photograph on one hand unveiled a hidden reality, on the other, it made possible the creation of *another* reality, as we see in the numerous Victorian photographs that feature people (most often women) disguised as members of other races, classes, or even historical periods. Julia Margaret Cameron, for instance, produced a plethora of images of women dressed as Bible characters; Lewis Carroll dressed young Alice Liddell as a beggar girl; and Arthur Munby photographed his maid (and later wife) Hannah Cullwick as, among other things, a chimney sweep, Mary Magdalene, and her own employer.[1] And at the Exposition Universelle in

Paris in 1855, just a few years after the publication of the last of Dickens's Christmas books, a German photographer created a sudden rage for portraiture by showing just how good a retouched photographic image could look (Sontag 86). Even for Victorians, then, the photograph was fraught with deep contradictions: it could tell half-truths—or lie altogether—and yet, paradoxically, still be real.

Although I do not wish to take issue with the many painstaking critical efforts to link realism to photography, I am concerned that seeing the relationship between the two as natural or inevitable at times causes us to run roughshod over the tensions underlying Victorian vision: by taking photographic moments in novels to be moments of straightforward truth-telling, we assume that photographs in narrative are other than photographs in culture. Further, by assuming that photographic seeing falls directly in line with the grammar of realism, we unfortunately elide the numerous instances in which a novelist uses photographic imagery to *question* the notion that an image can tell the truth, as well as the myriad photographic moments in texts that stand only half (or not at all) under the realist umbrella. Finally, this too common pairing skims over the enormous complexity of pre-photographic visual culture, which more often than not taught Victorians that their eyes could be deceived. Privileging visuality over materiality and the image over the word, the photograph's traffic with the novel, then, may revolve more around structuring *how* we see instead of *what* we see (Green-Lewis 26).

In this essay, I explore the implications of photographic seeing in two texts that combine realist social commentary with ghost story sensationalism: Charles Dickens's *A Christmas Carol* (1843) and *The Haunted Man* (1848). The first and last of Dickens's famous Christmas books, these stories reflect the photograph's widespread visibility and popularity. Indeed, critics as diverse as G. K. Chesterton and Nancy Armstrong have noticed Dickens's tendency to see the world as though it were a photograph, or, conversely, to embed images that seem photographic within the text (Chesterton xvii; Armstrong 86, 126). But, as Dickens demonstrates, the photograph was from its advent seen in relation to other nineteenth-century structures of vision. In the Christmas books, for example, we continually see the photograph in relation to the phantasmagoria. Exploring the strengths and weaknesses of these two forms of visual trickery by putting them into conversation with each other, Dickens privileges surface-seeing as a way of reading the world, while at once undercutting the reliability of his own images; placing the reader in a world that is overwhelmingly—if not entirely—visual, Dickens tells us not to believe what we see.

I read *A Christmas Carol* and the *Haunted Man* as similar texts with similar projects: the construction of a new, more-than-visual way of seeing that collapses memory with vision, sight with touch, and imagined spectacle with lived experience. In *A Christmas Carol*, for instance, Ebenezer Scrooge's visitation by his dead business partner Jacob Marley and spirit-led journey though Christmases past, present, and future make visual memories out of scenes in which he may or may not have been present. While his journey back to childhood only brings to mind buried memories, Scrooge sees the Cratchits' poverty, his ex-fiancée's daughter, and his own impending death for the very first time in his "shadows"—and who knows if they are real? Like the photograph, Scrooge's visions construct memories around visual codes rather than lived experience.

In *The Haunted Man*, similarly, Redlaw's gloomy memories of betrayal at the hands of his fiancée and best friend Mr. Leeford are just as visually real as the ghost who comes with an offer to erase them. Having accepted the ghost's offer, Redlaw finds that his wiped memory makes it impossible for him to observe his fellow men with compassion—even the orphan child whom angelic Milly Swidger and her husband Mr. William adopt, and the sick, unfortunate son of the Leefords' unhappy marriage. He cannot know a reliable image unless it moves him. Spreading his "virus" around and erasing the memories and the feelings of young Leeford, the poor but merry Tetterby family, and Mr. William's eighty-seven-year-old father Philip, Redlaw proves that the images we see are only as reliable as the homegrown sentiment informing them. Although *The Haunted Man* is less hopeful than *A Christmas Carol* about human vision's ability to uncover truth, both texts nonetheless express these doubts by using photographic and phantasmagoric ways of seeing to deconstruct the truth of the image. Putting forward an allegorical model of vision in which we read images both literally and metaphorically, and as both visual and metaphysical truth, Dickens teaches us to think beyond binaristic questions of images' reliability and instead urges us to read his visual effects as *significant* to his moral and ideological project.

While Dickens's undercutting of the image's realism may appear surprising in light of recent critical trends, it ought not to shock us that Dickens's imagery, like Victorian images in general, is inflected with a deep skepticism. Two decades before Dickens wrote the Christmas books, a series of experiments on the eye had begun to prove that perception is not an apprehension of a physical reality but rather a product of a number of physical processes that create—not import—the image. From the eighteenth century onward, crowds had gathered for public unveilings of magic lantern shows, dioramas, and panoramas, all of which worked to place the viewer in a space—in Egypt, or at the Battle of Waterloo, for example—that created the illusion of being in a time and place far removed from a London theater (Crary 112–13).[2] Jonathan Crary reacts against seeing the photograph as a logical next step in a series of visual technologies questing after ever-greater verisimilitude, and Dickens's vexed images back up his claim. More than a way of showing truth, Crary rightly argues, the photograph is a structure of vision, a way of seeing that blurs the notions of inside and outside for the viewer, and, furthermore, that had been a long time coming (24).

The critical tendency to conflate the realist project with photographic seeing, then, proves troublesome within the realm of visual culture as a whole—not just in Dickens's half-realist ghost stories. Indeed, Victorian audiences sought after realist social commentaries wherever they could find them. The panorama and diorama often represented bloody battles of the past and accompanied them with a history lesson, just as historical and narrative painting often gave viewers scenes that had both aesthetic and educational value. The magic lantern, however, was easily the most heavy-handed visual teacher. The rampant didacticism characterizing lantern shows only seemed to increase their popularity, with even the most austerely religious Londoners flocking to the theaters to see narratives about families reduced to poverty by the father's alcoholism (these usually ending with the joyous signing of a temperance pledge), or, just as popular, tales of beggar children who cling to life just long enough to convert to Christianity and then deliver speeches about the evils of poverty to the rescue society women who made their last hours of life warm and comfortable (Horton 14–15).[3] Even the spectre-show of the phantasmagoria, which I will discuss in more detail below, was a story with a moral, as audiences in both Paris and London were told to remember that they, like the loved ones whose ghosts were ostensibly there before them, would return to dust and ashes. As Armstrong suggests, Victorian audiences were more "hailed" by visual representations than verbal addresses (22), and, it seems, Dickens's continual return to the visual—and the Victorians' faithful attendance at the light shows of the earlier nineteenth century—confirm that idea. It is as though they were ready to read a lesson—and a social truth—in any image set before them, "correct" or not.

The central visual image in both *A Christmas Carol* and *The Haunted Man* is a ghost. In *A Christmas Carol*, we encounter four ghosts, Jacob Marley and the Spirits of Christmases Past, Present, and Future, while in *The Haunted Man* we encounter two: the protagonist's and Milly Swidger's spirit-doubles. These maybe-there, maybe-not images fit well within Victorian entertainment culture, in which the vastly popular phantasmagoria of the late-eighteenth and early-nineteenth centuries routinely raised (or produced) the dead and showed them off onstage. Like their phantasmagoric siblings, the ghosts of the Christmas books are empirical impossibilities—and quite possibly projections, as Dickens acknowledges in his assessment of Redlaw in the final paragraphs of *The Haunted Man*:

> Some people have said since, that he only thought what has been herein set down; others, that he read it in the fire, one winter night about twilight time; others, that the Ghost was but the representation of his gloomy thoughts, and Milly the embodiment of his better wisdom. *I* say nothing.                    (472)

Similarly, in *A Christmas Carol*, a fearful Scrooge, confronted with the shade of his long-dead business partner, attempts to convince himself that the ghost is only a side effect of an undigested dinner (19). But digestion aside, Jacob Marley, like Redlaw's double, is still visible. Terry Castle describes the ghost as a reified confusion between inside and outside, as an apparition at once in the mind and in the world: "The magic lantern was the obvious mechanical analogue of the human brain, in that it 'made' illusionary forms and projected them outward. But in another highly paradoxical sense, ghosts now seemed *more real than ever before*—in that they now occupied (indeed preoccupied) the intimate space of the mind itself" (58). Redrawing the boundaries between the mind and the outside world, the phantasmagoric specter questions the idea of a "reliable" image by asking us to believe and to respond to something that we know to be a projection. Thus, in spite of Scrooge's initial skepticism, he soon ceases to question the reality of the phantoms he sees: the ghosts haunt not just his chambers but also his sleeping and waking thoughts.

The phantasmagoria's ghosts, similarly, might as well have been real, for the sight of them unnerved Victorian audiences much as Marley's shade "disturbed the very marrow in [Scrooge's] bones" (19). Indeed, knowing that the phantasmagoria mechanically produced its ghosts did not make them any less real for the audience, who were often terrified enough to flee from the specters (Castle 30). Recalling Crary's description of the photograph as a dismantler of notions of inside and outside, Castle reminds us that visual culture teaches us to read the image as part of the world—and the world as image—whether or not the image ought to be believed (Crary 24).

The ghosts of the Christmas books serve as a good case study for Dickens's complicated assimilation of visual codes, and we can see just this sort of attention to the power of the image on the pages of nearly all his books. His objects seem to glow with some spark of life; characters bear visual stamps that assure they look like no one else does (or could); light and shadow and fog focus and frame his scenes. Dickens's novels are, in fact, so heavily dependent on their own imagery that reading outside of his visual codes is more or less impossible. Could Oliver Twist, who has truth written all over his face, possibly lie? Surely, the shriveled miser Scrooge stoops when he walks. But even as Dickens relies on his images to tell the truth to his readers, he also insists that we must learn to see beyond unreliable human vision. The fog of *Bleak House* obscures our ability—and indeed, *everyone's* ability—to see through the confusion of Jarndyce and Jarndyce. Esther Summerson's facial disfigurement hides her resemblance to Lady Dedlock, yet we know that the truth is hiding just below the image's skin. Dickens has situated us squarely within the paradox at the heart of photographic realism: by highlighting the instability of human vision, he forces us to view all images as potentially unreadable, yet at the same time, his novels rely on the image to speak—they tell that Mr. Sowerberry is his coffin-shaped snuff box, and that Mr. Bumble is his hat.

Beyond this, images structure Dickens's narration: just as light and shadow can be seen as both authors and subjects of the photograph,[4] so also does chiaroscuro figure prominently as a textual grammar in the Christmas books. Indeed, from the opening pages of both stories, Dickens teaches us to read (and fetishize) certain characters and objects by framing them within relations of light and shadow that mirror the moral economy of the book. Scrooge's spirit-filled nephew Fred is characterized, in contrast to the dark sky and frigid weather outside, as "ruddy and handsome" and "all in a glow" (8). Later, returning to Scrooge's boyhood in a vision, we again come face to face with embodied holiday spirit, in the form of the "positive light" issuing from Mr. Fezziwig's calves during the festive Christmas ball he throws for his friends and employees (36). John Leech's full-color frontispiece to the 1843 edition of *A Christmas Carol*, in fact, features Mr. Fezziwig front and center, dressed in bright yellow clothing that seems to serve as a light source for the scene. And just a few pages into *The Haunted Man*, when Mr. William enters, a lamp in his hand, and illuminates Redlaw's murky apartment, Dickens tells us that it is as though "his fresh face and active manner had made the pleasant alteration" (378). Just as the Spirit of Christmas Present becomes a warm light that Scrooge's best efforts cannot extinguish (42), so also does Dickens's slippery syntax equate the bodies of his most positive characters, all of whom he describes as "cheerful" in both manner and voice, with the light that they send out. And these characters' attractiveness makes us desire what they have—an overdose of holiday cheer. We get the sense that without the light Fred and Mr. Fezziwig throw on the scenes at hand, there would be no "Wonderful party, wonderful games, wonderful unanimity, wonder-ful happiness!" (89).

In the Christmas books, warmly glowing faces signal the presence—and the desirability—of Christmas spirit; turning a spotlight on Mr. William, Scrooge's nephew, and Mr. Fezziwig, Dickens uses light to teach us how to see. But if Dickens uses the glow of Christmas spirit to structure our desire for these unequivocally positive characters, he also uses the "dismal light" (15) emanating from Marley's face on the doorknocker to signal again a visual lesson—this time through the shadowy lens of memory. Redlaw's fire matches the dim glow of the doorknocker: too dreary to create Christmas cheer, these flickering images instead bring to light a long series of visual disclosures, not the least of which is the appearance of the ghosts. In parallel annunciation scenes in the two Christmas stories, Redlaw says to his spirit, "I see you in the fire" (390), while Scrooge sees "not a knocker, but Marley's face" (14). In both tales, objects that ought to be homey and inviting dissolve into ghastly, ghostly images, and dismal memories, which Redlaw describes as "pictures that were delusions" (393), obscure the warm glow of Christmas cheer. The dreary light of memory in these scenes differs qualitatively from the glow of Christmas spirit: while Scrooge's nephew's face illuminates the scene at hand, Marley and the fire spend as much time rewriting history as lighting it up, and collapse photographic and phantasmagoric ways of seeing with the delusions of presence conjured by Redlaw's fire. Furthermore, both the spirits and Scrooge habitually refer to the imaginary scenes as "shadows" (40, 68), a term that draws attention not only to their status as projection but also to a complicated web of Victorian discourses of vision. On one hand, that is, the word "shadow" recalls the phantasmagoria with its resonance to the word "shade," as well as the widely known fact that the phantasmagoria was nothing *but* a shadow show. On the other, shadows also point to how Victorians talked about the almost-tactile memories the photograph raises. In 1843, for instance, Elizabeth Barrett, enthralled with the daguerreotype, said, "I long to have such a memorial of every being dear to me in the world. It is not merely the likeness which is precious in such cases—but the association and the sense of nearness involved in the thing . . . the fact of the *very shadow of the person* lying there fixed forever!" (qtd. in Sontag 183).

Calling on the powers of hallucination the phantasmagoria promises and the power of authentication the photograph possesses, then, Dickens uses these shadows to make visual, light-and-shadow memories out of events that Scrooge has never seen—and indeed, that may never occur. Scrooge's tomb-stone, after all, is just as available to his eyes as the already visual scenes from his childhood. Replacing events that have not occurred with images, Dickens privileges the visual over the historical, and surface-seeing, a false memory, over remembered experience. The first shadow—Marley's ghost—even overwrites the stone tiles bordering Scrooge's ancient fireplace:

> The fire-place was an old one, built by some Dutch merchant long ago, and paved all round with quaint Dutch tiles, designed to illustrate the Scriptures. There were Cains and Abels; Pharoah's daughters, Queens of Sheba, Angelic messengers descending through the air on clouds like feather-beds, Abrahams, Belshazzars, Apostles putting off to sea in butter-boats, hundreds of figures, to attract his thoughts; and yet that face of Marley, seven years dead, came like the ancient Prophet's rod, and swallowed up the whole. If each smooth tile had been a blank at first, with power to shape some picture on its surface from the disjointed fragments of his thoughts, there would have been a copy of old Marley's head on every one. (16–17)

Much as a photograph creates a memory of the Sphinx or the Pyramids in the mind of a person who has never gone to Egypt, so also do Scrooge's phantasmagoric shadows freeze knowledge of Christmas Yet to Come as an image that by its very status as memory seems already to have happened. Further, the ghostly image of Marley's face in the tiles of the fireplace shows not just that a shadow can create memories where there were none before, but that it can also rewrite old ones: the ghost, written in air, swallows up the scriptures, written in stone.

At stake here is not just a question of visuality but also one of temporality. If Scrooge's journeys through Christmases Present and Yet to Come locate memory in some time other than the past, Marley's ghostly image in the fireplace tiles rewrites the past—even a scriptural past—altogether, replacing it with an illusory present-tense image. To a large extent, Scrooge's temporal troubles can be traced back to the hybridized, half-photographic and half-phantasmagoric, nature of his visions, for both of these visual media turn time into a hoax (Gilbert 28). By insisting on its power to resurrect the dead, the phantasmagoria gestures at once to long-dead people and to modern-day observers. Early photographs also confound temporality, as they preserve the illusion of a timeless, otherworldly space cleared of humanity by extremely long exposure times.[5] Both apparatuses, in other words, make time meaning-less. The same pattern holds true for *A Christmas Carol*. Scrooge lives the same night three times, his clock striking one o'clock over and over again. Christmas comes multiple times, with celebrations starting and ending before Scrooge has even gotten out of bed, and then starting again when he arrives to take his place at them. Marley, who has been dead for years, stands before Scrooge and talks to him like an especially convincing phantasmagoric spec- ter—he is so convincing, in fact, that he can even sit down. And a well- placed allusion to Hamlet's ghost on the first page of the book tells us that the time is indeed out of joint. Located in no clear temporal frame, the images driving Scrooge's conversion reshape distant memory as in-the-moment expe- rience. And we cannot doubt these images because they only show us what we know already—that Marley's self-interest followed him into the afterlife, and that Bob Cratchit is underpaid. Speaking of the photograph, then, what Barthes would call a "temporal hallucination" (Barthes 115) is the very thing that allows Scrooge to live at once in the Past, the Present, and the Future (84), and to assert that his shadows are past-tense memory, present-tense action, and timeless truths that we already know.

In collapsing the realms of the ghostly phantasmagoria and the reliable photograph, Dickens asserts that memory both produces and is produced by the image. Further, he shows that the confused temporality of memory—its simultaneous pastness and presentness—mirrors that of the photograph and the phantasmagoria, both of which create—and only exist because of—temp- oral ruptures. Nowhere is the vexed temporal status of Dickens's images more evident than in his description of Milly Swidger in *The Haunted Man*. A veritable angel in the house, and an angel of mercy elsewhere, Milly is more a type of goodness than a flesh-and-blood character. At the same time, the apparent flatness of her personality does not keep her from acting throughout the story as a photographic and phantasmagoric producer of memory along the lines of Scrooge's shadows. Milly is associated with the production of memory from the first time we meet her. In her first appearance in the text, for instance, she enters Mr. Redlaw's room only to hang the holly that stirs her father-in-law's eighty-seven years of memory and that later withers in the face of Redlaw's mind-wiping illness. Her conversation continually circles back to her own memories, as she, referring often to the spiritual presence of her deceased child, raises the dead like the phantasmagoria or an old photograph (Barthes 9).

But more significantly, it is Milly who brings healing to the Tetterby family (and to everyone else) after they are infected with Redlaw's virus. Coming among them "like the spirit of all goodness, affection, gentle consideration, love, and domesticity" (457), Milly restores people to themselves by teaching them to subordinate empirical realities to family ties. Mr. Tetterby's words to his wife—"I forgot the precious children you have brought about me, and thought you didn't look as slim as I could wish. I—I never gave a recollection . . . to the cares you've had as my wife . . . and I quarrelled with you for having aged a little in the rough years you've lightened for me" (456)—reminds us that the visual affront posed by Mrs. Tetterby's portly figure has the potential to loosen domestic ties, and the image to overwrite history. Milly's restoration of the characters' memories falls in line with this pattern, as she softens the cruel—albeit reliable—images Mr. and Mrs. Tetterby have of each other by helping them to see through backward-looking eyes; she replaces scientifically correct assessments with visual appeals to lived experience. Mrs. Tetterby's confession to her husband only verifies this: "I thought there was no air about you; but there is and it's the air of home, and that's the purest and best there is, and God bless home once more, and all belonging to it, Dolf!" (456–57). Milly breathes new life into old images by recasting them as experience: just as Scrooge's encounter with Marley's ghost teaches him to read his miserly past in light of daily life, both his own and others', so also does Milly's presence lead the Tetterby family to filter their images of one another through a lens of familial history. In fact, Milly herself *becomes* just such an image when her shadow stands beside that of Redlaw and promises a cure to the virus of forgetfulness with a dose of domesticity. Like a family photograph, Milly's ghost assures Redlaw that home will not be forgotten.

Continually gesturing toward the realms of the photographic and phantasmagoric in order to turn images into experience, Milly puts pressure on the notion that memory can be preserved in any form that is not continually reconstructed, both temporally and visually. But her presence in the book as both body and image also calls into question the notion that the image operates outside the bounds of the flesh. This is further complicated by the presence of the other ghosts, all of whom occupy the realms of the visual and the material at once. Significantly, Dickens insists in both Christmas stories that his protagonists are alone when they see the ghosts (67, 389), an assertion which makes it impossible for us to detach the images we see from the bodies of the protagonists. Describing Redlaw's relationship to his ghost, Dickens says, "As *he* leaned his arm upon the elbow of his chair, ruminating before the fire, *it* leaned upon the chairback, close above him, with its appalling copy of his face looking where his face looked, and bearing the expression his face bore." And when the ghost describes himself as a neglected child who had to battle for affection and success, Redlaw replies, "I *am* that man"

(390–91). Form mirroring form, gaze reflecting gaze, face matching face, and past echoing past, the original and copy—*he* and *it*, body and image—go hand in hand. But the ghosts not only mirror the flesh; they also *have* it. Marley's see-through ghost, we know, can sit down—and does (18). Later, when Scrooge seizes the hand of the ghost of Christmas Yet to Come, it trembles, and, against Scrooge's best efforts, shakes off his grip (83). Similarly, in *The Haunted Man*, the ghost will not permit himself to be touched, saying, "Lay a hand on me and die!" (393), while at once admitting, if only by issuing the warning, that he has some physical reality. In language which curiously echoes Dickens's mirror-image description of Redlaw's ghost (390), Marjorie Garber casts the ghost in terms of photography—both are "original copies" of forever gone people or events (Garber 16). Similarly, Terry Castle calls photography "the ultimate ghost-producing technology of the nineteenth century" (61), which follows from Dickens's description of Redlaw's ghost as "the animated image of himself dead" (390). The echoes we hear in these descriptions suggest that the photographic/phantasmagoric image and the body are not so far apart as we might first believe, and that viewing the image and material reality as opposing terms is a mistake.

This pattern, not surprisingly, squares with the way in which the phantasmagorias of the 1790s launched an apparently *physical* attack on their viewers. Blurring the line between the projected image and the viewer's body, the phantasmagoric specters seem to take on a flesh of their own. This uneasy dialectic between image and body underlies Dickens's continual—almost obsessive—attention to the bodies of his characters throughout the whole of both works. When Scrooge sees Belle's daughter for the first time, for instance, the narrator jumps in with an intensely physical description of both Belle's daughter and himself:

> I wouldn't for the wealth of all the world have crushed that braided hair, and torn it down; and for the precious little shoe, I wouldn't have plucked it off, God bless my soul! to save my life. As to measuring her waist in sport, as they did, bold young brood, I couldn't have done it; I should have expected my arm to have grown round it for a punishment, and never come straight again. And yet I should have dearly liked, I own, to have touched her lips, to have questioned her, that she might have opened them; to have looked upon the lashes of her downcast eyes, and never raised a blush; to have let loose waves of hair, an inch of which would be a keepsake beyond price . . .            (40–41)

This assertion that Scrooge's visions are not divorced from the realm of material reality is matched by a similar discussion of London's waste. The filth in the beetling shop of Christmas Yet to Come, we learn, includes a mass of decaying bodies whose materiality allows them to hide things: "Secrets that few would like to scrutinise were bred and hidden in mountains of unseemly rags, masses of corrupted fat, and sepulchres of bones" (72). Moving between the realms of touch and sight, Dickens recasts Scrooge's shadows as experience by asserting their physical reality.

In *The Haunted Man*, similarly, Dickens continually displaces visual memories into other sensory realms. The "old echoes" in Mr. Redlaw's mind, for instance, mirror the echoes in his hall, which rumble until they are stifled in a forgotten crypt (375); the "incessant whisper" (394) of memory will, we know, torment the protagonist until, in Redlaw's words, "Death idly jumbles all together, and rubs all out" (382). While here the movement of sound mirrors the motion of Redlaw's memory, in Redlaw's own quarters memory and concrete objects gesture toward one another. The bough of holly that Milly mounts on the wall, we learn, was bought by the man whose portrait hangs over the refrain "Lord, keep my memory green!" This prayer, we know, helps Philip Swidger to recall all of his eighty-seven Christmases (385). And, of course, it is only when Redlaw's memory-erasing copy emerges from the shadows that the holly's color fades. Tied financially and symbolically to memory, the bough of holly reifies the immaterial shadows Redlaw sees in his fire. Finally, when Redlaw has learned his lesson and begs for a reprieve, he likens memory to the atom, the loss of even one of which would unbalance the universe: "In the material world, as I have long taught, nothing can be spared; no step or atom in the wondrous structure could be lost, without a blank being made in the great universe. I know, now, that it is the same with good and evil, happiness and sorrow, in the memories of men" (443).

The relationship that Dickens sets up between the material world and the characters' immaterial memories is one in which concrete objects continually stand for and comment on private thought. Leading us to read holly as memory and Redlaw's ghost as Redlaw himself, *The Haunted Man* uses objects and immaterial realities as surrogates for one another, and Redlaw's ringing "I *am* that man" (391) reminds us that the phantom, the Redlaw-as-representation, makes visible the private reality that Redlaw sees in the fire. Similarly, in *A Christmas Carol* Scrooge's shadows turn the material into images, opening up the realms of projection and representation in order to comment on Scrooge's real world. When Fred enters Scrooge's counting-house with an invitation to dinner, for instance, his face not only shows us that we ought to desire his Christmas spirit, but also, blazing with warmth, contrasts mightily with the "last frail spark" of the fire by which Bob Cratchit tries to warm

himself (9). Reducing the counting-house's dreary chill to a light-on-dark
representation, Fred's face shows us how to read the scene at hand. Indeed,
as Audrey Jaffe has shown, it is only a reduction of everything to representation that leads to Scrooge's conversion. Just as Redlaw only learns to value
his bad memories after they have been turned into ghostly representations,
so also does Scrooge prove that he has become his better self when he pur-
chases a reified version of peace on earth and goodwill to men—a giant
turkey.[6] This pattern, one in which the material is only worth having or seeing
when it is turned into an image, is brought to a logical conclusion by the
disappearance of the materially real ghosts at the end of the stories (Jaffe
333). Thus Scrooge and Redlaw, left without visible copies of themselves
with which to identify, must learn to identify with the set of representations
that is culture if they are to continue to operate within the visual order put
forward by Dickens's Christmas books. It is as though they must exit the
realm of photography and metonymy—which would forever attach the image
and the referent—and enter the realm of the metaphor, where seeing correctly
is predicated on seeing difference—the space between a turkey and Christmas
spirit, or between a glowing face and a smoldering coal—as metaphysical
truth. Indeed, it is the ideological project of the books to bring the protagonists
in line with the metaphorical grammar of seeing that Dickens calls culture
(Jaffe 328).

I argue that Dickens's use of both phantasmagoric and photographic ways
of seeing the world opens up our ability to read beyond glossy surfaces: like
photographs, the ghosts and the turkeys in the window are surface truths, but
like the phantasmagoria, their significance is as much in the viewer's mind
as in the world. Paradoxically, then, we must read the image's surface in
order to see beyond it. And even as the plots of the Christmas books teach
the protagonists to read their image-based society metaphorically, so also do
the books themselves bring the reader into the realm of realism by undercutting our ability to read literally. Realism, what Armstrong calls "the entire
problematic in which a shared set of visual codes operated as an abstract
standard" (11), seems at first to stand at odds with Dickens's fantastic ghosts
and metaphorical turkeys.[7] At the same time, however, seeing realism as
a shared cultural code predicated on metaphor—*not* reliable photographic
images—allows us to resituate realism's visual complexities within the didactic ideological project of Victorian image culture. Just as phantasmagoric
specters could teach real lessons about life and death, so also can ghosts—or
turkeys—act as mouthpieces for Dickens's social commentary. Reading the
underside of images, then, allows the fantastic or the illusory to serve the

same critical function as *Oliver Twist*'s gritty street scenes or a narratorial diatribe against the abuses in chancery. Indeed, our ability, 150 years later, to read peace and joy in the Christmas books' images suggests that in some sense, Dickens's ubiquitous texts have *already* done their ideological work. Furthermore, we know that our twenty-first-century Christmases still bear the mark of Dickens's London—and if we forget, we can count on Hallmark cards to remind us that it is our civic duty to have "a Dickens of a Christmas."

But if the Christmas books' realism wants to teach us to read visual codes metaphorically, how do we interpret those moments in which our vision fails us? Indeed, Dickens's attention to the gaps in human vision continually reminds us that we cannot always count on our eyes. When faced with Marley's ghost for the first time, for instance, Scrooge explains that he doubts his senses because "a little thing affects them. A slight disorder of the stomach makes them cheats" (19). Scrooge goes on to say that seeing Marley could be a side effect from a meal that did not agree with him, and, given that food so often serves as a vessel for Christmas spirit, the joke could, not accidentally, be a literal truth. Later, we learn that vision is not at all necessary for Scrooge's journey to his boyhood home, for he "could walk it blindfold" (29), just as the blindfold that Scrooge's nephew's friend Topper dons for a game does not keep him from seeing well enough to propose marriage to the sister in the lace tucker (63–64). The most consequential visual gap in *A Christmas Carol* occurs in the Christmas Yet to Come scene. Scrooge cannot tell the ghost from the scenery—he sees only a "dusky shroud" and "a spectral hand and one great heap of black"—though he does sense that the spirit is watching him intently (69). Leech's illustration for this scene, in fact, is so dark that it is almost indecipherable. Scrooge's journey through Christmas Yet to Come is shrouded throughout—the scene at the beetling shop, for instance, occurs behind a screen of rags, and the smoking lamp, like the fire, produces no light (73). Later, we see a bed "on which, beneath a ragged sheet, there lay a something covered up" which we cannot make out because the room is too dark (76). But even though Scrooge has not the power to remove the shroud (77), we know this is his corpse; bound up in Dickens's ideological vision, we do not need to see to *see*.

The scenario in *The Haunted Man* is quite similar, and throughout Redlaw is taught, like Scrooge, to see beyond his empirical blindness. When Redlaw first accepts the ghost's offer to wipe his memory, he says that he feels as though his "mind is going blind" (417). The same blindness fills his house as well, as the shadows steal around the corners, distorting vision but prompting memory (376–77). But Redlaw's inability to see signals not a withdrawal from society but rather an entrance into it. Just as Scrooge only completely converts when he *doesn't* see his own corpse, so also does Redlaw's prayer of thanksgiving for his memory of Christ on the cross demonstrate that he now lives by faith and not by sight. The notion that blindness produces insight complicates the relationship of memory and history, word and image, in a way that none of the hypervisual scenes can. When Christmases Past and Present freeze memories as full-color scenes unfolding in mid-air, as we have seen, they unavoidably produce—not reproduce—the event as we remember it. But the visual gaps at the center of Christmas Yet to Come and Redlaw's quarters, on the other hand, assure us that what we are (not) seeing is real: we don't know what some future Christmas may look like; we know only that Scrooge will some day die because the words written on his tomb tell us so. The image we can't see is the reliable one.

Placing us firmly in a double bind, Dickens undercuts the reliability of the image while at once using it to point arbitrarily to deeper truths. Paradoxically, blindness produces insight, but we cannot see into the life of things without the things themselves. The overwhelmingly enthusiastic response of Dickens's audiences to the Christmas books—above all their willingness to "see" their truth in London daily life[8]—suggests that audiences, like post-conversion Scrooge and Redlaw, and like us, already spoke a social language predicated on metaphor. Thus, when embodied metaphors take the stage—the children Want and Ignorance—as part of Dickens's realist project, we ought not to be surprised. On the contrary, these children exemplify the Christmas books' way of seeing the world, as they both turn flesh into image and, more importantly, demonstrate that metaphor has come to depend on the very illusions of materiality the image constructs. Their bodies serve as interpretive frames for our reading of the world—without them, there is no reality to see.

At the same time, however, we must read this material reality as symbol, and their flesh as language, if we are to interpret correctly. That is, we must see the world in a way that is other than—but predicated on—the visual. Indeed, even from the first pages of *A Christmas Carol*, Dickens's metaphors embody a way of reading that is both visual *and* verbal. We learn in the first paragraph, for example, that Marley is not just dead but "dead as a doornail." This pun rings true as both wit and reality, for Marley does, in fact, *become* a doorknocker—or vice-versa—in front of Scrooge's eyes (14). Later, we learn that Tiny Tim was "as good as gold" (53) at church, which reminds us both of his angelic behavior and of his ability to move Scrooge to spend his money on the Cratchit family. His plight and his impeccable behavior become a source of income for his family. Most obvious among the metaphorical moments in *A Christmas Carol*, of course, is the scene I already alluded to, in which the children Ignorance and Want peek from beneath the skirts of Christmas Present—such children are discreet individuals with bodies of their own, but they also point in true allegorical fashion to the plight of hundreds and thousands of other bodies. The ghost tells Scrooge (and Dickens's audience) how to read these children: just as the photograph represents and replaces memory itself, the children's bodies both stand for and are the state of England (Patterson 175).

If in *A Christmas Carol* reading the image as both body and metaphor provides access to the truth of the narrative, *The Haunted Man* moves one step further, inviting us to read the story itself as allegory in which Redlaw plays out a conversion story that could belong to anyone who has "gloomy thoughts" and "better wisdom" (472). Beyond this, however, we can also read the whole story as a commentary on the state of England—and the allegory here, as in *A Christmas Carol*, is centered in the figure of a child. Prowling the pages of the book as though they were winding streets, the hungry child whom Milly adopts is so typical of London orphans that he doesn't even have a name. The boy embodies the necessarily materially bound existence of London's poor, as he "bound[s] at the table like some small animal of prey, and hug[s] to his breast bread and meat" (398–99). Later, when Redlaw pays the boy for guiding him to a poor neighborhood, the child, literalizing hand-to-mouth street living, transfers the coins from his palm to his mouth and back again (430). The allegory spreads to the protagonist as well, as we learn that Redlaw, looking at the boy during their trip into the slums of London, notices that "the expression on the boy's face was the expression on his own" (431). Together failing to respond to cemeteries with proper tenderness or to the moon and music with proper poetic emotion, Redlaw and the boy stand for those whom life has turned into beasts that can only read the world materialistically. Later, they again mirror each other's unnaturalness, as we learn from Redlaw's phantom that they together represent "the two poles of the immaterial world": Redlaw stands for human presumption, the boy for human indifference (448). Hearing from the mouth of a ghost that Redlaw's world is an allegory, we have no choice but to read the images Dickens gives us as *both* realist commentary upon England and as phantasmagoric ghost story—and indeed, it is only allegory that allows the flesh and the image, substance and meaning, to co-exist symbiotically.

Dickens's use of allegory—a visual and metaphysical truth that can be read both literally and metaphorically—to further the social commentary of his

Christmas books obviously creates problems for analyses which would reduce the truth the realist novel tells to photographic surface-seeing. Jennifer Green-Lewis says that the photograph "implied metaphorical ways of seeing" (25) that helped to define what we think of as real, and Dickens's Christmas books illustrate this, as they incorporate photographic and phantasmagoric structures of vision to teach us ways to peel back the image's deceptive skin. At the same time, as we have seen, the photograph was in some sense *already* metaphorical, as it cast an enormously wide—and sometimes contradictory—net across culture within just a few years of its advent. In spite of its clear tie to consumer culture, for instance, the photograph was often taken to be a democratic art form which would allow all classes and peoples to see themselves on a level plain (Lalvani 18; Green-Lewis 73). And even though people knew that photos could validate untruths, in the later nineteenth century the camera would be used repeatedly to catalogue and capture the look of such disorders as criminality or mental illness (Green-Lewis 161). This series of paradoxes—the ability of the photograph to both hide and reveal truth, to mine interiority and yet authenticate surface-seeing—is the product of the same tensions in nineteenth-century seeing that allow Dickens to use the image to so many varied ends in his realist allegories.

The tensions underlying Dickens's images carry through into our present-day readings of these texts, as his conflation of the image with word and the word with flesh announces a style of realism predicated on an extremely paradoxical definition of "real"—and one that we do not often adopt. Furthermore, his texts urge the readers into an equally paradoxical conversion predicated at once on faith and sight: the visual experience of reading the Christmas books brings us to reaffirm our blind faith in charity and memory; the image teaches us to see the world beyond its frame. I do not wish to put forward the notion that the realist vision we see in the Christmas books carries over into other Victorian—or even Dickensian—texts. However, many of the same visual tensions on which Dickens predicates his allegorical way of seeing—the unreliability of the photographic, the otherworldliness of the phantasmagoria, the didacticism of the magic lantern, and so on—ought to be brought to bear on other texts, realist or not, simply because they are so firmly entrenched within the history of Victorian image culture. A more in-depth reading of realist fiction with these tropes in mind is, of course, beyond the scope of this study, as is a detailed analysis of visuality in other allegorical texts. However, by reading allegory as realism, we expand on the notions of what images can do in texts and, further, what texts can do in culture.

# NOTES

1. See Carol Mavor's excellent study *Pleasures Taken: Performances of Sexuality and Loss in Victorian Photographs*, which contains several chapters on dress-up photography.
2. Richard Altick's *The Shows of London*, an enormously detailed history of English visual culture, traces the history of Daguerre's diorama from its earliest days to its vast popularity in the 1820s and 1830s in London and eventual demise in 1848, and of the magic lantern, which, though in existence from the 1600s onward, found new life in the 1700s with the advent of better projection systems.
3. For transcripts of magic lantern shows, see G.A. Household and L.M.H. Smith's collection, *To Catch a Sunbeam: Victorian Reality through the Magic Lantern.*
4. André Bazin (197) says that the photograph and cinema "satisfy . . . our obsession with realism" by writing the notion that a human authors a photograph or a film out of the equation. Along these lines, in an 1874 memoir of her first days as a photographer, Julia Margaret Cameron said of one model, "I felt as if she entirely had made the picture" (qtd. in Green-Lewis, *Framing*, 64).
5. Daguerre's famous *Boulevard du Temple* (1838), for instance, shows a busy city street that appears deserted except for the one person who stood still long enough to match the exposure time—a man getting his shoes shined. For more examples of similar early photographs, see Shelly Rice's *Parisian Views.*
6. See Audrey Jaffe's "Spectacular Sympathy: Visuality and Ideology in Dickens's *A Christmas Carol.*" Jaffe, using Althusser's discussion of interpellation, shows that Scrooge shows himself to be already a part of the charitable (albeit capitalist) project of *A Christmas Carol* by hearing the call of the "speaking commodities" in the shop windows. Scrooge's and Redlaw's willingness to learn from the ghosts, then, could be viewed in much the same terms: because they see themselves in the shadows, they can be seen as already within the realm of the image.
7. For opposing discussions of the truthfulness or verisimilitude of realism, see George Levine's *The Realistic Imagination* and Roman Jakobson's *Language in Literature.*
8. See Paul Davis's *The Life and Times of Ebenezer Scrooge*, which shows how *A Christmas Carol* held (and holds) a unique place in culture as "secular scripture" (14). Dickens's text lends itself particularly well to this sort of reading, as it was designed, Davis suggests, as a response to the findings of the Children's Employment Commission (43). Dickens, horrified by the grisly conditions of factories in which children worked, declared himself "perfectly stricken" and made known his plans to write a pamphlet on behalf of the children. He changed his mind a few days later, saying that at the end of the year "a Sledge hammer" would "come down with twenty times the force." See also Kathleen Tillotson, "A Background for *A Christmas Carol*," 166.

# WORKS CITED

Altick, Richard. *The Shows of London*. Cambridge: Harvard UP, 1978.

Armstrong, Nancy. *Fiction in the Age of Photography: The Legacy of British Realism*. Cambridge: Harvard UP, 1999.

Barthes, Roland. *Camera Lucida*. New York: Hill and Wang, 1981.

Bazin, André. "The Ontology of the Photographic Image." *Film Theory and Criticism: Introductory Readings*. Eds. Leo Braudy and Marshall Cohen. New York: Oxford UP, 1999. 195–211.

Castle, Terry. "Phantasmagoria: Spectral Technology and the Metaphorics of Modern Reverie." *Critical Inquiry* 15 (1988): 26–61.

Chesterton, G.K. *Appreciations and Criticisms of the Works of Charles Dickens*. New York: E. P. Dutton, 1911.

Crary, Jonathan. *Techniques of the Observer: On Vision and Modernity in the Nineteenth Century*. Cambridge: MIT P, 1990.

Daguerre, Louis. *An Historical and Descriptive Account of the Various Processes of the Daguerréotype and the Diorama*. 1893. New York: Kraus, 1969.

Davis, Paul. *The Lives and Times of Ebenezer Scrooge*. New Haven: Yale UP, 1990.

Dickens, Charles. *The Christmas Books*. Ed. Ruth Glancy. New York: Oxford UP, 1988.

Garber, Marjorie. *Shakespeare's Ghost Writers*. New York: Methuen, 1987.

Gilbert, Elliot. "The Ceremony of Innocence: Charles Dickens' *A Christmas Carol*." *PMLA* 90 (1975): 22–31.

Green-Lewis, Jennifer. *Framing the Victorians: Photography and the Culture of Realism*. Ithaca: Cornell UP, 1996.

Horton, Susan. "Were They Having Fun Yet?: Victorian Optical Gadgetry, Modernist Selves." *Victorian Literature and the Victorian Visual Imagination*. Eds. Carol Christ and John Jordan. Berkeley: U of California P, 1995. 1–26.

Household, G.A. and L.M.H. Smith, Eds. *To Catch a Sunbeam: Victorian Reality through the Magic Lantern*. London: Michael Joseph, 1979.

Jaffe, Audrey. "Spectacular Sympathy: Visuality and Ideology in Dickens's *A Christmas Carol*." *Victorian Literature and the Victorian Visual Imagination*. Eds. Carol Christ and John Jordan. Berkeley: University of California Press, 1995. 327–44.

Jakobson, Roman. *Language in Literature*. Eds. Krystyna Pomorska and Stephen Rudy. Cambridge: Harvard UP, 1987.

Lalvani, Suren. *Photography, Vision, and the Production of Modern Bodies.* Albany: SUNY P, 1996.

Levine, George. *The Realistic Imagination.* Chciago: U of Chicago P, 1981.

Mavor, Carol. *Pleasures Taken: Performances of Sexuality and Loss in Victorian Photographs.* Durham: Duke UP, 1995.

Patterson, Arthur. "Sponging the Stone: Transformation in *A Christmas Carol.*" *Dickens Quarterly* 11 (1994): 172–76.

Rice, Shelly. *Parisian Views.* Cambridge: MIT, 1997.

Sontag, Susan. *On Photography.* New York: Farrar, Straus and Giroux, 1977.

Talbot, Fox. *The Pencil of Nature*, vol. I. 1844. New York: Da Capo, 1964.

Tillotson, Kathleen. "A Background for *A Christmas Carol.*" *The Dickensian* 89 (1993): 165–69.

# Labors of Love:
# The Sympathetic Subjects of
# *David Copperfield*

## *Rachel Ablow*

*This essay argues that in* David Copperfield *(1850), the identificatory model of sympathy often associated with Charles Dickens is characterized as an almost inevitably inaccurate act of projection: as David's misunderstandings of James Steerforth and Dora Spenlow suggest, whatever such a form of sympathy might reveal about one's own feelings, it says little about other people's. In place of identification, therefore, Dickens's novel reproduces a model of sympathy organized around the ethically valuable desire for another person's love and approval—a model often associated in the nineteenth century with relationships between husbands and wives. Within the novel the object of this desire for sympathy is ''Agnes,'' the woman so impossibly good that she makes real an ideal of femininity. In relation to the reader, its name is* David Copperfield, *the fiction that overcomes the opposition between the real and the ideal by constituting a new kind of reality in and of itself.*

Recent critical discussions of sympathy in Charles Dickens's novels have tended to agree that the novelist sought to make readers identify with his principal characters. For some critics, this attempt is most significant as a way to alter readers' understanding and treatment of real persons.[1] For others,

*Dickens Studies Annual,* Volume 31, Copyright © 2002 by AMS Press, Inc. All rights reserved.

it is interesting insofar as it represents an attempt to alter readers' understanding of themselves; identifying with a character, they have claimed, covertly trains one in how to experience oneself as a subject.[2] In this essay, I argue that in *David Copperfield* (1850), the identificatory model of sympathy critics have so often taken for granted is characterized as an almost inevitably inaccurate act of projection: whatever it might say about one's own feelings, it reveals little about other people's. In place of identification, therefore, Dickens's novel valorizes and seeks to reproduce a model of sympathy organized around the ethically valuable desire for another person's love and approval, a model of sympathy most consistently associated in the middle of the nineteenth century with relationships between husbands and wives. Hence, by contrast with those critics who have insisted on the novel's investment in the acts of generosity that might result from the experience of identification, I argue that *David Copperfield* posits such gestures as secondary effects of the work that love encourages one to perform on oneself. And by contrast with those who have claimed to reveal the novel's previously-concealed interpellative effects, I argue that this novel not only calls attention to its disciplinary agenda, it defines it as the principal source of its literary and ethical value.

The notion that *David Copperfield* seeks to encourage love in its readers rather than identification significantly alters how we understand this text. Most importantly, it suggests that rather than a bildungsroman organized around David's acquisition of the ability to understand his fellows accurately, the novel constitutes an investigation into the kind of character able to make questions of accuracy irrelevant. In my account, *David Copperfield* is less committed to describing the development of a mature epistemology, in other words, than it is to defining the object that cannot be mistaken. Within the novel the name of this object is "Agnes," the woman so impossibly good that she makes real an ideal of femininity. In relation to the reader, its name is *David Copperfield*, the fiction that transcends the distinction between the real and the ideal by claiming to constitute a new kind of reality in and of itself.[3] This redefinition of the novel's focus suggests, in turn, a new conception of its intended function. Rather than seeking to establish the domestic woman's jurisdiction over "the most basic qualities of human identity," as Nancy Armstrong has argued of the domestic novel, I argue that in *David Copperfield* Dickens seeks to install the novel-form itself in this privileged position of disciplinary power (3).[4]

From the outset, *David Copperfield* seems as if it should be committed to a model of sympathy that relies on empirical accuracy. Throughout his childhood and young adulthood, David repeatedly mistakes the people and events he observes. And consistently, those errors have dire consequences for himself and for those he loves. As a result, it is hardly surprising that so many critics have described David's history in terms of his development of the ability to understand his fellows; his epistemological difficulties are so destructive as to constitute a problem the novel will necessarily have to resolve.[5] Yet David's errors are both more intractable and more productive than critics have acknowledged. His misunderstandings of Steerforth and Dora Spenlow, for example, have some terrible results. In neither instance does the novel offer any indication as to how his mistakes might have been avoided, however. Further, in both cases, his errors also provide him with objects around which to organize his ambitions. As a result, his mistakes come to seem as profitable as they do inevitable.

David's relationship with James Steerforth establishes the pattern for all his love affairs. As in each of his subsequent relationships, the younger boy becomes attached to his friend well before he knows him—that attachment effectively preventing him from acquiring any further information about its object. Initially attracted to Steerforth because of his "nice voice, his fine face, and his easy manner, and his curling hair," David's interest in the older boy is described in almost exclusively erotic terms.[6] "I thought of him very much after I went to bed," we are told after their first day together, "and raised myself, I recollect, to look at him where he lay in the moonlight, with his handsome face turned up, and his head reclining easily on his arm. He was a person of great power in my eyes; that was, of course, the reason of my mind running on him" (140). However one understands the "power" referred to in this passage, it is clearly closely associated with the boy's "handsome face" and inviting posture. Yet, as J. Michael Léger has pointed out, the libidinal nature of this boyhood crush is never made to seem like a problem in the novel; it is described with a straightforwardness that suggests that such attachments can be taken for granted (301).[7] Instead, the problem with David's affection for his friend derives from his failure to recognize the true nature of his feelings: his deluded insistence on attributing it not to Steerforth's beauty, but instead to his virtuousness. The difficulties he encounters in this relationship thus arise not from the fact that he loves his friend for the "wrong" reasons, but instead from the fact that he thinks he loves him for the "right" ones.

David's idealization of Steerforth requires an enormous amount of effort to maintain. Repeatedly, the younger boy witnesses examples of his friend's selfishness and arrogance. And repeatedly, he refuses to accept the most obvious implications of what he sees. When Steerforth tells him that he has been making covert visits to Yarmouth and that he has bought a boat he intends to christen the "Little Em'ly," for example, the reader is well aware that these acts are signs of his intention to seduce David's childhood friend. David, however, refuses to recognize the obvious. "'Now I understand you, Steerforth!'" he exclaims as soon as he has formulated a theory to explain what he has been told:

> "You pretend to have bought [the boat] for yourself, but you have really done so to confer a benefit on [Mr. Peggotty]. I might have known as much at first, knowing you. My dear kind Steerforth, how can I tell you what I think of your generosity?"
> "Tush!" he answered, turning red. "The less said, the better."
> "Didn't I know?" cried I, "didn't I say that there was not a joy, or sorrow, or any emotion of such honest hearts that was indifferent to you?"
> "Aye, aye," he answered, "you told me all that. There let it rest. We have said enough!" (383)

David's misunderstanding in a scene like this is so improbable as to verge on the incredible. Yet, however perverse David's mistakes may seem, the novel makes it difficult to regard them as criminal.[8] Not only are the errors he makes about Steerforth's designs on Emily similar to those he makes on many other occasions—in the context of the older boy's abuse of Mr. Mell and Tommy Traddles, for example—the novel also explicitly shuts down the question of David's guilt for his childhood friend's seduction. After revealing that Emily has run away, Ham insists that David is not to blame for having introduced her to the agent of her downfall: "'[I]t ain't no fault of yourn,'" Emily's fiancé tells him, "'and I am far from laying of it to you'" (515). David quickly accepts this absolution: "[W]hen I heard [Mr. Peggotty] crying, the impulse that had been upon me to go down upon my knees, and ask their pardon for the desolation I had caused, and curse Steerforth, yielded to a better feeling. My overcharged heart found the same relief, and I cried too" (516). While it remains unclear why weeping represents a better feeling than self-recrimination, we are clearly asked to accept the shift in David's feelings as legitimate. His errors are the result of an innocent conviction of his friend's virtuousness, rather than from any malicious intentions towards Emily.

David's mistakes are only further excused by their enormous productivity. Regardless of the dubious value of its object, his love for Steerforth is effective, encouraging him to transform himself from an ignorant, cowed, diffident child into an accomplished storyteller, a respectable scholar, and a brave young man willing to fight the butcher's boy in order to win his friend's love and approval. These achievements stand him in good stead throughout his life. His labors as a storyteller, in particular, yield an immediate profit in the form of the help Steerforth gives him with his schoolwork. They also help train him for his eventual career as a novelist. Because his efforts are motivated solely by love for Steerforth, however, any suspicion that his labors might be the result of greed or personal ambition are effectively cancelled. As he explains of his storytelling, "I was moved by no interested or selfish motive, nor was I moved by fear of [Steerforth]. I admired and loved him, and his approval was return enough. It was so precious to me that I look back on these trifles, now, with an aching heart" (145). Whatever material benefits he receives from his efforts are nothing more than an incidental consequence of his desire to please his beloved; all he ever seeks is the love of one he perseveres in imagining to be worthy of his devotion.[9] David's perceptual "errors" or idealizations thus not only motivate change, they also obscure whatever benefits that change might yield.

The personal and economic productiveness of David's habit of idealizing those he loves is even more apparent in his relationship with his first wife. As in the case of his attachment to Steerforth, David's love for and consequent inability to understand Dora Spenlow causes considerable problems. Most importantly, it leads him to marry a woman unsuited to be his wife. At the same time, however—again, as in the previous example—David's conviction of his beloved's virtuousness is also useful, for it provides him with an object for his ambitions. Because he loves her, he must work to be worthy of her. And in the process of laboring to this end, he remakes himself into an aspiring and then a successful member of the professional middle class.

Even before David meets her, it is clear that much of Dora's appeal lies in her ability to function as the object of his ambitions. The first time he visits her father's home, for example, his raptures begin well before they are introduced:

There was a lovely garden to Mr Spenlow's house; and though that was not the best time of the year for seeing a garden, it was so beautifully kept, that I was quite enchanted. There was a charming lawn, there were clusters of trees, and there were perspective walks that I could just distinguish in the dark, arched over with trellis-work, on which shrubs and flowers grew in the growing season. "Here Miss Spenlow walks by herself," I thought. "Dear me!"

We went into the house, which was cheerfully lighted up and into a hall where there were all sorts of hats, caps, great-coats, plaids, gloves, whips, and walking-sticks. "Where is Miss Dora?" said Mr Spenlow to the servant. "Dora!" I thought. "What a beautiful name!"

We turned into a room near at hand (I think it was the identical breakfast-room, made memorable by the brown East Indian sherry), and I heard a voice say, "Mr Copperfield, my daughter Dora, and my daughter Dora's confidential friend!" It was, no doubt, Mr Spenlow's voice, but I didn't know it, and I didn't care whose it was. All was over in a moment. I had fulfilled my destiny. I was a captive and a slave. I loved Dora Spenlow to distraction!      (450)

The anatomy of beauty performed in this passage has an ambiguous relationship to the woman who supposedly constitutes its central object. The charms of the garden and house purport to point to the woman who occupies them. Because David has not yet met her, however, he seems intoxicated less by her than by the world she inhabits. The "lovely" and "beautifully kept" garden that "enchants" him, the "charming" lawn, the "cheerful" house, and the "beautiful" name Dora's parents have given her thus seem to serve less as mementos for her than as the sources of her allure. Only at the end of the passage does Dora appear, and by this point the conclusion is inevitable: "I had fulfilled my destiny . . . . I loved Dora Spenlow to distraction!" "Dora Spenlow" has come to serve as the signifier for a house, a class position, and a universe of inanimate and highly attractive objects.

David is never described as seeking to marry Dora for her money, however. It may be difficult to accept his claim that, "As to marriage, and fortune, and all that, I believe I was almost as innocently undesigning then, as when I loved little Em'ly" (454). But by the time they marry, Dora's father has died and her fortune has disappeared. Rather than a source of income, therefore, David's first wife constitutes the means by which he can imagine himself as—and so make himself into—an upwardly mobile member of the middle class. Initially, his transformation is undistinguished: "Within the first week of my passion, I bought four sumptuous waistcoats—not for myself; *I* had no pride in them; for Dora—and took to wearing straw-coloured kid gloves in the streets, and laid the foundations of all the corns I ever had" (458). After David's aunt loses her fortune, however, he alters the terms of his self-making. No longer able to inhabit the role of a fop, he re-imagines himself as an industrious young man, striving with all his might towards the object of his affections. "I was not dispirited now," he explains after having decided on a course of action:

What I had to do, was, to turn the painful discipline of my younger days to account, by going to work with a resolute and steady heart. What I had to do, was, to take my woodman's axe in my hand, and clear my own way through the forest of difficulty, by cutting down the trees until I came to Dora. And I went on at a mighty rate, as if it could be done by walking. . . .

> I got into such a transport, that I felt quite sorry my coat was not a little
> shabby already. I wanted to be cutting at those trees in the forest of difficulty,
> under circumstances that should prove my strength. I had a good mind to ask
> an old man, in wire spectacles, who was breaking stones upon the road, to lend
> me his hammer for a little while, and let me begin to beat a path to Dora out
> of granite.                                                                    (582)

Neither walking at a "mighty rate" nor wearing a shabby coat yields any
material gain. But rather than simply earning money, David is committed to
being able to think of himself as one who works his way up from the bottom,
conquers adversity, and so eventually wins the hand of the woman he loves.

Whatever his intentions, David's exertions are highly profitable. Taking
on several jobs at once, he quickly earns enough money to marry. And once
he does, he is confronted with the mistake he has made, for having constructed
a narrative of progress around winning his beloved, once he has achieved this
goal, he has nothing left to do. "It was a strange condition of things," he
explains, "the honey-moon being over, and the bridesmaids gone home, when
I found myself sitting down in my own small house with Dora, quite thrown
out of employment, as I may say, in respect of the delicious old occupation
of making love" (701). David may have been thrown out of "employment"
in the matter of "making love," but since his courtship has largely consisted
of his labors in the marketplace, he has also been thrown out of work in a
more literal sense. Without any sentimental object for his efforts, his work
comes to seem like nothing more than a way to make money. This state of
affairs is reflected in subsequent descriptions of his labors. Although prior to
this point in the novel we are often told that he works, we almost never see
him doing it. Once he is married, by contrast, he is repeatedly shown engaged
in time-consuming, physically exhausting, money-making labor.[10] The pages
become littered with the material details of his working life—from his tools
("'Please let me hold the pens,'" Dora pleads [715]), to his work habits
("Sometimes, of an evening, when I was at home and at work—for I wrote
a good deal now, and was beginning in a small way to be known as a writer—I
would lay down my pen" [712]), to his income ("when I tell my income on
the fingers of my left hand, I pass the third finger and take in the fourth to
the middle joint" [693]). Without any greater object, David's labors become
degradingly and hopelessly material.

This situation is only exacerbated by Dora's inability to provide David
with a new goal towards which to strive. As Chris R. Vanden Bossche has
pointed out, Dora's inept housekeeping never endangers the couple's financial
security (98). Nevertheless, her errors do pose a problem for they make it

impossible for David to imagine that he labors in the service of any domestic ideal. Spending "one pound six" for salmon they cannot finish (704), using the "immense account-book" as a toy for Jip (712), and failing to notice the items on their accounts that they have not purchased (708) may not threaten the household's stability, but such mistakes do serve to keep their finances constantly and disturbingly visible. This situation culminates with the arrest of one of their servants for stealing. Although the losses they sustain are considerable, David's concern is less for the money than for the way the servant's confessions call attention to the economic basis of their household. As the servant reveals one theft after another, David admits that "I got to be so ashamed of being such a victim, that I would have given him any money to hold his tongue, or would have offered a round bribe for his being permitted to run away" (760). Had Dora been more competent, we are led to believe, David would never be subjected to such exposure. Combined with her failure to produce a child, Dora's domestic ineptitude makes it impossible for David to organize a new set of ambitions around their life together.

As I mentioned at the outset of this essay, in the mid-nineteenth century, the kinds of benefits attributed in *David Copperfield* to David's desire for Steerforth's approval and for Dora's hand in marriage tended to be associated with the relationships between husbands and wives. Particularly for those who claimed the effectiveness of "female influence," married men's desire for the sympathy, approval, and affection of their supposedly more virtuous wives constituted a powerful means by which to insure their sustained industriousness and integrity.[11] As Sarah Lewis claimed in her popular treatise, *Woman's Mission* (1839), for example, "The man carries with him to the forum the notions which the woman has discussed with him by the domestic hearth. His strength there realizes what her gentle insinuations inspired" (38). As a result, she concluded, "Woman, at present, is the regulating power of the great social machine" (46).

For Lewis, as for many commentators of the 1830s and early '40s, female influence was the result of an ongoing dialogue between husbands and wives. Married women were able to preserve their husbands' integrity, they claimed, because of the therapeutic effects of their conversation, their example, and the watchful eye they kept on the other members of the household. By the later 1840s and '50s, however, a different model of female influence began to emerge: one which relied less on married women's ameliorative interactions with their husbands than on *un*married women's status as the object of their future husbands' ambitions. In his poem, "The Angel in the House" (1856), for example, Coventry Patmore provides a particularly vivid account

of the power women have over the men who seek to marry them. Scolding
the woman who gives her love too easily, he insists that she relinquishes
what may be a unique opportunity to reform the man she will marry:

> Ah, wasteful woman, she that may
>     On her sweet self set her own price,
> Knowing he cannot choose but pay,
>     How has she cheapen'd paradise;
> How given for nought her priceless gift,
>     How spoil'd the bread and spill'd the wine,
> Which, spent with due, respective thrift,
>     Had made brutes men and men divine.        (107–08)

Couching the woman's love as the object of her future husband's ambition,
Patmore encourages her to make the most of this singular opportunity. It is
up to her to dictate the terms of the engagement; it is thus up to her to demand
that her partner embody a certain moral standard.

Such a model of female influence bears a strong resemblance to the effects
of David's attachments to both Steerforth and Dora. As in these fictional
cases, the "power" that Patmore describes revolved around the lover's desire
for and idealization of his beloved. And, as in these cases, the danger of such
idealizations is that once the lover achieves his object, he will be disappointed.
As Patmore warns the lover, although during the courtship the beloved may
seem perfect ("she's so simply, subtly sweet/My deepest rapture does her
wrong" [39]), after the marriage, she can easily lose her charm:

> The lover who, across a gulf
>     Of ceremony, views his Love,
> And dares not yet address herself,
>     Pays worship to her stolen glove.
> The gulf o'erlept, the lover wed,
>     It happens oft, (let truth be told,)
> The halo leaves the sacred head,
>     Respect grows lax, and worship cold.        (93–94)

Patmore attempts to resolve this problem by chastising husbands who experience such disappointment: "Unless her choice of him's a slur," he insists,
"He never enough can honour her/Who past all speech has honour'd him"
(94). In his "Of Queens' Gardens" (1865), Ruskin offers another solution,
exhorting married women to behave so as always to command their husbands'
respect. In order to merit the power she wields over her husband, Ruskin

asserts, the woman "must—as far as one can use such terms of a human creature—be incapable of error. . . . She must be enduringly, incorruptibly good; instinctively, infallibly wise" (Ruskin 1865, 98). Whether one encourages husbands to maintain an idealized view of their wives, or wives to embody those ideals, however, the problem remains the same: the equation of love with a form of idealization that threatens to obscure the nature of the beloved.

Although rarely couched as a solution to the problem of how to enable future spouses to see one another clearly, many commentators claimed that the novel-form was particularly well suited to promote understanding between persons more generally. As Elizabeth Rigby Eastlake wrote in 1848, for example, "We are a particularly shy and reserved people. . . . We meet over and over again . . . but mutually and honourably . . . forbear lifting those veils which each spreads over his inner sentiments and sympathies" (599–600). Yet "there are ways and means for lifting the veil," she continued, "and a new and remarkable novel is one of them—especially the nearer it comes to real life" (599). Critics regularly repeated this understanding of the function of the novel. Novels have the power, they argued, to show us aspects of our neighbors that we otherwise would never see.[12] As John Ruskin argued, for example, in reading a novel, "We hold intercourse with an infinite variety of characters, and that under peculiarly favourable circumstances, for their thoughts and the motives of their actions are laid open to us by the author; we perceive where they mistake and where they do wrong, we behold the workings of their feelings and the operation of their reason " (Ruskin 1836, 365). Unlike relationships in real life, moreover, in reading a novel, we are predisposed to think well of those we come to understand: as Ruskin continued, "no one ever envies the hero of a romance; selfishness is put entirely out of the question" (Ruskin 1836, 365). As a result, "We become, for the time, spirits altogether benevolent, altogether just, hating vice, loving virtue, weeping over the crime, exulting in the just conduct, lamenting the misfortune, rejoicing in the welfare of others" (Ruskin 1836, 366).[13]

Accounts such as Eastlake's and Ruskin's were not without their critics, of course. Both religious and utilitarian commentators often asserted the absence of any useful relation between literature and life. As the anonymous writer of "Cheap Literature" (1859) insisted, for example, since "The machinery [of the story] is entirely in the hands of the author, and is at his absolute disposal for good or evil. . . . it is easy to see that the author can conduct us to any given conclusion with the greatest possible certainty; but it is equally clear that his conclusion, whatever it may be, is mere smoke".

(332). As a result, the critic concluded, "That fiction . . . should have ever become an instrument to illustrate or enforce moral or religious truths, or even practical lessons in the life it professes to delineate is incomprehensible" (332). While this critic indicts all fictional representations, according to some proponents of realism, only some fictions should be accused of misleading readers. As George Eliot argued in "The Natural History of German Life" (1856), for example, idealist fictions *are* dangerous. But the solution is not to condemn fiction, but instead to distinguish between realism and idealist texts. "The thing for mankind to know is, not what are the motives and influences which the moralist thinks *ought* to act on the labourer or the artisan, but what are the motives and influences which *do* act on him. We want to be taught to feel, not for the heroic artisan or the sentimental peasant, but for the peasant in all his coarse apathy, and the artisan in all his suspicious selfishness" (111). Picturesque representations of the poor may be aesthetically appealing, Eliot insisted, but rather than encouraging readers to understand and feel affection for real people, they encourage only a sense of disappointment when reality fails to live up to the illusion — hence the importance of ensuring that fictions are accurate rather than just attractive.[14]

As I have already begun to suggest, Dickens, too, describes idealization as dangerous. But while Eliot holds out hope for a form of realism able to encourage both love and understanding, in *David Copperfield* Dickens makes the opposite claim, advocating instead a kind of fiction that can serve as the object of one's affection without claiming any empirical accuracy.[15] Dickens does not solve David's epistemological problems by providing him with a new, more accurate way of seeing, in other words. Instead, he provides him with a new object to observe. In relation to Agnes Wickfield, the epitome of female virtue, appearance and reality are invariably the same. It is thus impossible to over-idealize her; she is the embodiment of every ideal.

Agnes has been the object of much critical disdain in the twentieth century. According to John Lucas, for example, Agnes is a "bit of a bore, even if not actually unbearable" (198). Michael Slater has asserted that "it would be a bold critic indeed who would claim this character to be a success" (250). And Michael Léger has described Agnes's "preternatural calm and goodness and her ill-developed character" as making her seem "non-human" (319). However accurate descriptions like these might be to the experience of reading about Agnes, they do not take into account the consistency with which she is explicitly described in *David Copperfield* as a literary character. She is never posited as a model for a person, in other words; she is not a representation of a woman who could exist in the real world. Instead, she constitutes the end-point of a narrative of the production of a new kind of object for David to understand.

The narrative of the emergence of Agnes as the infinitely virtuous and hence the endlessly desirable object of David's love can be broken down into three stages. In the first, David recognizes the distinction between his idealistic visions of Steerforth and Dora on the one hand, and the real persons who actually exist on the other. In the second, the impossibility of deciding between the real and the ideal generates a psychic crisis. And in the third, he reorganizes his subjectivity around a new kind of object, able to unite the real and the ideal in a single being. Taken together, these three stages reproduce a narrative of the experience of the sublime. As Neil Hertz describes this narrative, "Typically the posited relationship of attenuated subject and divided object reveals its inherent instability by breaking down and giving way to scenarios more or less violent, in which the aggressive reassertion of the subject's stability is bought at some other subject's expense" (223). This narrative is of particular use in describing David's trajectory, for it provides a model for a psychic crisis that arises as a result of an undecidability within an object rather than as a result of a problem that originates entirely within the subject. It is also useful insofar as it reveals the violence that constitutes the necessary condition for the re-consolidation of the subject.

In the first of the three stages that enable his recognition of his love for Agnes, David identifies the discrepancies between the versions of Steerforth and Dora he had loved and the real persons who actually exist. Contrary to what one might expect, neither of these recognitions is couched in terms of his acceptance of the errors he has made. Instead, they are framed as acknowledgements of the discrepancies between different kinds of objects: the real and the ideal. In the passage in which David describes his response to Steerforth's seduction of Emily, for example, he claims that:

> What is natural in me, is natural in many other men, I infer, and so I am not afraid to write that I never had loved Steerforth better than when the ties that bound me to him were broken. In the keen distress of the discovery of his unworthiness, I thought more of all that was brilliant in him, I softened more towards all that was good in him, I did more justice to the qualities that might have made him a man of a noble nature and a great name, than ever I had done in the height of my devotion to him. Deeply as I felt my own unconscious part in his pollution of an honest home, I believed that if I had been brought face to face with him, I could not have uttered one reproach. I should have loved him so well still—though he fascinated me no longer—I should have held in so much tenderness the memory of my affection for him, that I think I should

have been as weak as a spirit-wounded child, in all but the entertainment of a
thought we could ever be re-united. That thought I never had. I felt, as he had
felt, that all was at an end between us. What his remembrances of me were, I
have never known, they were light enough, perhaps, and easily dismissed—but
mine of him were as the remembrances of a cherished friend, who was dead.

(516)

At the beginning of this passage, the object of David's love and the person
who existed are described as different aspects of the same person: Steerforth
is both brilliant and unworthy; a man with great potential who polluted an
honest home. As the passage continues, however, the distinction between
Steerforth's positive and negative attributes widens until they appear to belong to different characters. The figure David holds in his imagination, whose
qualities "might have made him a man of a noble nature and a great name,"
remains the object of his affection: if they could have been re-united, "I
should have loved him so well still." Such a reunion is inconceivable, however, for his memories are of a "cherished friend, who was dead." Mean-
while, the person who exists is probably still alive, but any encounter with
him would be meaningless: in David's mind, the real Steerforth is merely the
phantom of his fictional other.

David's recognition of the discrepancy between his fantasy of Dora and
the real woman he marries takes a similar form. As in the case of Steerforth,
when confronted with his error, David defines it less as one of perception—seeing one thing when he should have seen another—than as one of
conception—imagining that the ideal and the real were contained in a single being.

I loved my wife dearly, and I was happy; but the happiness I had vaguely
anticipated, once, was not the happiness I enjoyed, and there was always something wanting. . . . What I missed, I still regarded—I always regarded—as something that had been a dream of my youthful fancy; that was incapable of
realization; that I was now discovering to be so, with some natural pain, as all
men did. But that it would have been better for me if my wife could have
helped me more, and shared the many thoughts in which I had no partner; and
that this might have been; I knew.                                 (765)

When confronted with what might look like an error about the nature of
his beloved, David claims instead to have made a mistake about her status.
Distinguishing between the "happiness [he] enjoyed" with Dora and the
"something" he had dreamed of but had missed, David does not simply
dismiss the illusion. Instead, as in the case of Steerforth, he allows that illusion
to linger as a kind of Platonic ideal of which the reality is only a shadow.

The second stage of the narrative that results in David's recognition of his love for Agnes is staged as a confrontation between real and ideal objects. In the "Tempest" chapter in which Steerforth and Ham are killed, the conflict between the real and the ideal begins even before David arrives to witness it. As a result, he is made to seem entirely passive in relation to the chaos: an innocent bystander bewildered by the battle he witnesses.

> The tremendous sea itself, when I could find sufficient pause to look at it, in the agitation of the blinding wind, the flying stones and sand, and the awful noise, confounded me. As the high watery walls came rolling in, and, at their highest, tumbled into surf, they looked as if the least would engulf the town. As the receding wave swept back with a hoarse roar, it seemed to scoop out deep caves in the beach, as if its purpose were to undermine the earth. When some white-headed billows thundered on, and dashed themselves to pieces before they reached the land, every fragment of the late whole seemed possessed by the full might of its wrath, rushing to be gathered to the composition of another monster. Undulating hills were changed to valleys, undulating valleys (with a solitary storm-bird sometimes skimming through them) were lifted up to hills; masses of water shivered and shook the beach with a booming sound; every shape tumultuously rolled on, as soon as made, to change its shape and place, and beat another shape and place away; the ideal shore in the horizon, with its towers and buildings, rose and fell; the clouds fell fast and thick; I seemed to see a rending and upheaving of all nature. (858–59)

In this scene of impending carnage, the "ideal shore in the horizon," with its virtual "towers and buildings" undermines and threatens to replace its real counterpart on shore. The result is a rending of nature exceeded only by what might happen next: at the point when the ideal displaces the real, all lives on land will be lost.

In response to this undecidable opposition between two different kinds of objects, David becomes hopelessly disoriented. "There was that jumble in my thoughts and recollections," we are told, "that I had lost the clear arrangement of time and distance" (859). Such confusion builds until he is unable to see anything beyond himself: "I looked out . . . but could see nothing, except the reflection in the window-panes of the faint candle I had left burning, and of my own haggard face looking in at me from the black void" (861). As in Hertz's account of the experience of sublime "blockage," at this moment David is unable to resolve an "unsettling and indeterminate play between two elements . . . that themselves resist integration" (44). He thus remains suspended between them, unable to recognize either himself or anything that lies beyond. And as the ship carrying Steerforth breaks up off-shore, this confusion intensifies to the point that he becomes unable to differentiate between himself and other people: "The agony on the shore increased. . . . Some ran wildly up and down along the beach, crying for help where no help could be. I found myself one of these" (863–64). David regains his lucidity only after Steerforth's body has been salvaged from the water:

> [On] that part of [the shore] where she and I had looked for shells, two chil-
> dren—on that part of it where some lighter fragments of the old boat, blown
> down last night, had been scattered by the wind—among the ruins of the home
> he had wronged—I saw him lying with his head upon his arm, as I had often
> seen him lie at school.                                                    (866)

As Garrett Stewart points out, in Steerforth's dead body "we find . . . a death pose that epitomizes not only the young rogue's careless posture in life but by displacement also replays the narrator's own earlier vision of a perfect self" (Stewart 1983, 202). By identifying the dead body on the shore with the person he first loved at school, in other words, David collapses the man Steerforth eventually becomes with the boy who had yet to disappoint him. He brings together the real and the ideal and so, too, is able to bring together the Peggotty home as it was when "she" (Emily) and he were children with the "ruin" it becomes; the innocence of his early love for Emily as they played together on the shore with the illegitimate sexuality she comes to represent; and, most importantly, the Steerforth he thought he knew, with the person he turns out to be. The ideal and the real are thus united in the form of a beautiful dead body lying on the shards of his past.

However useful this dead body may be in enabling David to reconsolidate his subjectivity, it fails to offer him any new object for his labors. He thus wanders aimlessly around Europe until he receives the letter that instigates the third stage of this narrative, in which he reorganizes his sense of himself around a new kind of object.

> [Agnes] gave me no advice, she urged no duty on me; she only told me, in her
> own fervent manner, what her trust in me was. She knew (she said) how such
> a nature as mine would turn affliction to good. She knew how trial and emotion
> would exalt and strengthen it. She was sure that in my every purpose I should
> gain a firmer and a higher tendency, through the grief I had undergone. She,
> who so gloried in my fame, and so looked forward to its augmentation, well
> knew that I would labour on. She knew that in me, sorrow could not be weak-
> ness, but must be strength. As the endurance of my childish days had done its
> part to make me what I was, so greater calamities would nerve me on, to be
> yet better than I was; and so, as they had taught me, would I teach others. She

commended me to God, who had taken my innocent darling to His rest; and in
her sisterly affection cherished me always, and was always at my side go where
I would; proud of what I had done, but infinitely prouder yet of what I was
reserved to do.                                                        (888)

Agnes's letter both redefines David's work and provides a crucial model for
it. Couching his labors as an act of generosity rather than as a form of
entertainment (as it was in his relationship with Steerforth) or as a kind of
alienated labor (as it was in his relationship with Dora), she provides her
future husband with a mission of which he can be truly proud. Writing may
be both pleasurable and profitable, but these things are incidental to its fundamental status as a form of kindness and care.

Such a model of the labor of writing suggests, in turn, a new model for
the relationship between readers and texts. In claiming that David's fictions
have the potential to help his readers in much the same way that her letter
helps him, Agnes suggests that readers will be similarly inspired by what
they read, strengthened by it, and encouraged to do what they know to be
right. But further, this model implicitly suggests that they, like he, will become
attached to the one whose words they read. "I put the letter in my breast,
and thought what had I been an hour ago! When I heard the voices die away,
and saw the quiet evening cloud grow dim ... [I] felt that the night was
passing from my mind, and all its shadows clearing, there was no name for
the love I bore her, dearer to me, henceforward, than ever until then" (888).
The letter is thus imagined as the signifier for an object of love as well as for
a source of inspiration. And, in relation to David, at least, it is extremely
effective. Inspired by her words and impelled by his desire to please her,
David immediately gets back to work. After answering Agnes's letter, "I
worked early and late, patiently and hard. I wrote a Story, with a purpose
growing, not remotely, out of my experience, and sent it to Traddles, and he
arranged for its publication very advantageously for me; and the tidings of
my growing reputation began to reach me from travelers whom I encountered
by chance" (889). The fact that David is paid for his story is couched here as
both an appropriate recompense for his exertions and as a fortunate accident,
negotiated by someone else with only implicit sanction from him. His principal goal is only ever to be worthy of Agnes's opinion of him by reproducing
the kinds of effects her text has had on him, encouraging his readers' virtuous ambitions.

At the end of the novel, then, we are offered an image of both marital and
of readerly attachment. "O Agnes, O my soul, so may thy face be by me

when I close my life indeed; so may I when realities are melting from me, like the shadows which I now dismiss, still find thee near me, pointing up- ward!'' (950). Agnes's upward-pointing finger indicates a narrative of endless progress and self-improvement. And it leaves us with an image of the ideal wife that is also an image of the ideal text, providing the reader with the inspiration for and a model of endless self-improvement. Hence, in Agnes's and David's relationship, Dickens argues for according the novel-form a role that is not just analogous to that of the wife, but that may serve as a substitute for it. Like her, the novel encourages a self-reflexiveness equivalent to the internalization of discipline. Like her, it serves as an object around which to organize one's values and ambitions. And like her, it constitutes the object of love.

It is worth noting that this is a conclusion to which nineteenth-century critics appear to have come to as well. Again and again, reviewers described their affection for both the novelist and his characters in terms that were explicitly familial. According to the critic for the *Sunday Times*, for example, ''The creations of [Dickens's] genius were our companions. . . . dear to our hearts for themselves, and making their parent dearer for the elevated plea- sures they have afforded us'' (1). The *Saturday Review* agreed: ''To a degree unequaled by any other novelist except perhaps SCOTT, [Dickens] had the power of making the reader feel thoroughly at home in an imaginary world, and of being and living and moving in it naturally'' (760). Dickens's great achievement, these critics suggest, lay in his ability to generate emotional bonds between readers and characters—bonds that made those readers feel part of a family comprised of the writer as well as of the products of his imagination. Upon his death, therefore, the eulogists proclaimed that his loss was like that of a close personal friend or even a member of the family. ''The loss of such a man is an event which makes ordinary expressions of regret seem cold and conventional,'' asserted the leading article in the *Times*, for example. ''It will be felt by millions as nothing less than a personal bereave- ment'' (9). *Fraser's Magazine* agreed: ''When the sad news was made public it fell with the shock of a personal loss on the hearts of countless millions, to whom the name of the famous author was like that of an intimate and dear friend'' (130). Dickens was more than just a writer or a leader, articles like these asserted; he was an ''ever-welcome friend and companion of [readers'] leisure'' (639). ''He lived not only before our eyes,'' the *Sunday Times* proclaimed, ''but in our very hearts. He not only had a place there, but a home—a home, too, which he continually occupied, and his presence made too glad and happy for memory to lose or eloquence to explain'' (1).

The similarities between accounts like these and David's descriptions of his relationship to Agnes only confirms the extent to which the end of *David Copperfield* functions as an allegory of the production of a new kind of literary character and hence, too, of the development of a new kind of relationship between readers and texts. As in David's final love-affair, for all these readers, Dickens and his characters constituted the objects of love. And for all these readers, such love served as the impetus behind their efforts to be ever better than they were before.

# NOTES

1. See, for example, Thomas Laqueur's description of Dickens's novels as "humanitarian narratives": works that attempt to make "details about the suffering bodies of others engender compassion" in their readers (178). "Anyone who has read about . . . the prolonged death . . . of Paul Dombey," he argues, "is affected by [this report] of the death of others. A common body, a shared organic nature, bonds reader and character" (181). Hence, according to Laqueur, Dickens's appeal resides in his ability to make readers understand and even experience suffering that has some correlation to that of real people in the real world.

2. According to Mary Poovey, for example, the "structural patterns and transformations that are written into [*David Copperfield*] as the very conditions of its intelligibility . . . . construct the reader as a particular kind of subject—a psychologized, classed, developmental individual" (Poovey 1988, 89–90). Insofar as we read and understand this novel, in other words, we necessarily experience ourselves in the terms its structure dictates. Even though he ultimately characterizes the subjective product of the novel in very different terms, D. A. Miller agrees that interpellation constitutes the condition of the novel's intelligibility. "For a moment in *David Copperfield*," he writes, "the text raises the possibility that David might be any David; for a moment, it so happens, it invites me to imagine that he might be myself" (192). Although their essays are now more than twelve years old, Poovey's and Miller's readings of *David Copperfield* continue to set the terms for discussions of the interpellative effects of Dickens's fictions.

3. Although Dickens struggles elsewhere with the questions raised in this text about the effects of reading and its relation to the effects of love, in *David Copperfield* he is unusually explicit in defining the nature and ethical value of the novelist's labors. This novel also represents the first time that Dickens specifies an analogy between readers' and spouses' sympathy. I am interested in this novel not just because it is centrally concerned with the nature and effects of writing, therefore, but because those concerns are articulated in terms that were already associated with questions about love, sympathy, and ethical reform.

   Dickens's prefaces serve as a useful index of his changing ideas about the relationships between himself, his readers, and his characters. In the preface to

*The Pickwick Papers* (1837), for example, Dickens describes himself as an entertainer whose object "was to place before the reader a constant succession of characters and incidents . . . and to render them . . . life-like and amusing" (xxiv). In the preface to *Nicholas Nickleby* (1839), he identifies himself instead as a "correspondent" whose relationship to the reader might be based on friendship as well as commercial exchange. "[T]he Author of these pages," he writes, "flatter[s] himself . . . that on the first of next month [readers] may . . . think of the papers which on that day of so many past months they have read, as the correspondence of one who wished their happiness, and contributed to their amusement" (47). In the preface to *The Old Curiosity Shop* (1841), Dickens compares himself to the host of a public house, and his readers to guests, thus couching the novel as a kind of commercial version of a home. And in the preface to *Dombey and Son* (1843), he describes himself as his readers' fellow traveler, referring to the novel as "the journey we have just concluded" (41). Here, for the first time, Dickens claims to have an emotional attachment to his characters equivalent to what his readers might experience. Referring to the death of Paul Dombey, he writes that "I may claim to have felt it, at least as much as anybody else; and I would fain be remembered kindly for my part in the experience" (41). Only in the preface to *David Copperfield*, however, does the novelist produce a fully formed account of the novel as a kind of domestic sphere. Referring to his "love" for the reader, and to the characters as his "companions," he claims that in completing the novel he felt "as if he were dismissing some portion of himself into the shadowy world, when a crowd of the creatures of his brain are going from him for ever" (45). The notion that Dickens's characters constitute some portion of himself is dramatized even more fully in the 1867 version of the preface, in which he posited himself, his characters, and (however ambiguously) the text as members of the same happy family: "It will be easily believed that I am a fond parent to every child of my fancy, and that no one can ever love that family as dearly as I love them. But like many fond parents, I have in my heart of hearts a favourite child. And his name is DAVID COPPERFIELD" (47).

4. Both Janice Carlisle and Garrett Stewart have noted Dickens's association of fictional with domestic spaces. Carlisle's claim that "The imaginative home that Dickens and his reader come to inhabit is . . . another ideal model of the relation that should obtain between all men," for example, is similar to my own (43). But while Carlisle emphasizes fiction's role as a *model* for inter-personal relationships, I argue that Dickens regards the novel as a kind of supplement to the inevitable limitations of such relations. In that sense, my claims are closer to Garrett Stewart's assertion that Dickens's narratives function as a way to "compensate" readers for "the unknowable nature of source and destination, speaker and listener, teller and reader. What we can never know of or reveal to others, even the secret we may *be* (as well as keep) to ourselves, is what we often cannot help but know in responding to fictional narrative" (Stewart 1996, 206). While Stewart describes Dickens's commitment to the articulation of the experience of an inexpressible interiority, however, in my account, *David Copperfield* is more interested in exploring how that interiority comes into existence in relation to others as a form of desire, which is also the basis of ambition.

5. Gwendolyn Needham initiated critical interest in the novel's disciplinary narrative when, in 1954, she argued that David's failure to understand his fellows reflects a weakness that he overcomes by the end of the novel. Similar claims have been made by critics ever since. See, for example, John Lucas's discussion of the "great number of people whom David learns properly to estimate" as he learns to discipline himself (170). Or else, see Gareth Cordery's claim that the perspective David has at the end of the novel reflects his internalization of the "covert and internal" form of discipline associated with Agnes (71). By the end of the novel, Cordery argues, "All characters are subject to David's disciplinary gaze: he controls, observes, and allocates roles in the prison that is his novel within which his characters (and himself) are trapped" (80).

6. According to Martha Nussbaum, the fact that David's erotic attraction to Steerforth represents a form of love that "simply *happens* to us" means that it serves as a model for "the posture of the heart . . . [that] is best for morality—most vivid, most gentle and generous, most active in sympathy" (336). Both "more susceptible and less judgmental than Agnes' heart is," David's way of seeing Steerforth is bound, Nussbaum argues, "in its mobile attention to particulars, to fall in love, and to feel for the object that it loves a non-judgmental loyalty that no moral authority, however judicious, can dislodge" (360). What Nussbaum fails to note is the fact that David's love is characterized not by forbearance but by misunderstanding. He does not tolerate the other boy's faults; he is unaware of them.

7. As Léger points out, in *Between Men: English Literature and Male Homosocial Desire*, Eve Kosofsky Sedgwick provides a useful account of the relative acceptability of attachments between boys at school prior to the medicalization of homosexuality in the 1890s (Sedgwick 173–79).

8. See, for example, John O. Jordan's claim that David sacrifices Emily in order to encourage Steerforth to treat him as a social equal (85). Or else, see Robert Higbie's assertion that David's relationship with Emily is marked by "physical, potentially guilty desire" (99).

9. As Leonore Davidoff and Catherine Hall have pointed out, in the early- and mid-nineteenth century, male ambition was often regarded with ambivalence. On the one hand, since the ability to support a family was central to almost all common definitions of masculinity, "economic failure was often seen as personal failure entailing a loss of respect and thus manhood in a man's own as well as his children's eyes" (334). On the other hand, too exclusive a focus on material success was often regarded as a threat to one's spiritual and moral well being (90–91). David's attachment to Steerforth helps him escape both dangers.

10. The only other moment in the novel when we see David working is when he is employed at the blacking factory. During this period of his life, his labor is oriented exclusively towards his physical maintenance. As a result, the mass of detail we are given of his life during this period revolves around earning and spending money: "My own exclusive breakfast of a penny loaf and a pennyworth of milk, I provided myself. I kept another small loaf, and a modicum of cheese, on a particular shelf of a particular cupboard, to make my supper on when I came back at night. This made a hole in the six or seven shillings, I know well; and I

was out at the warehouse all day, and had to support myself on the money all the week''(214).

11. This model of self-cultivation had not always been identified with domestic relationships: in the eighteenth century, sympathy's disciplinary effects were much more commonly associated with relationships between men. As Adam Smith argued in *The Theory of Moral Sentiments* (1759), for example: ''nothing pleases us more than to observe in other men a fellow-feeling with all the emotions of our own breast; nor are we ever so much shocked as by the appearance to the contrary'' (54). So strong is the desire for this pleasure, Smith claimed, that we tend to determine our actions on the basis of what we imagine others will approve. By the late eighteenth century, the sentimental conviction that feeling constitutes a reliable basis for the regulation of society had been undermined by (among other factors) the excesses of the French Revolution, the rationalization of the legal system, the institutionalization of poor relief, and the individualism and competitiveness encouraged by laissez-faire economics (Todd 128–46; Davidoff and Hall 199; Perkin 319–39; Poovey 1995, 1–24). The result was that by the early nineteenth century, competition and rational self-interest had come to replace sentiment and sympathy as the principal grounds on which civic order was understood to rest. At the same time that sentiment lost its centrality to notions of the public sphere, however, it gained importance to notions of the private one—an arena often defined by its immunity to the values of the marketplace (Davidoff and Hall 149–92).

12. Recent critics have tended to emphasize the novel's role in helping members of different classes understand one another. (See, for example Jaffe, Born, Childers, and Bodenheimer.) Such a function was clearly important; critics often noted writers' ability to expand middle-class readers' sympathy for the poor. At the same time, the forms of understanding made possible by novels were considered to be at least as important for members of the same class.

13. In her account of Humean sympathy in *Nobody's Story: The Vanishing Acts of Women Writers in the Marketplace, 1670–1820,* Catherine Gallagher describes one rationale for claims like Ruskin's. In describing the relative ease of sympathizing with characters as opposed to people, Gallagher claims that ''The body of the other person, although it conveys the original sense data and serves as the basis for all the modes of relationship that supposedly allow sympathetic identification, is also paradoxically imagined to be a barrier. It communicates but it also marks out the sentiments as belonging to somebody else and hence as being simply objective facts'' (171). Fiction, by contrast, ''freely dispenses with [the problem of the body]; by representing feelings that belong to no other body, fiction actually facilitates the process of sympathy'' (171).

14. In *The Ethics of Reading*, J. Hillis Miller calls attention to the tension between Eliot's commitment to realism and her desire to encourage sympathy. Arguing that her desire to regard people who are '''in fact' ugly, stupid, inconsistent'' as lovable is ''just as baseless as to call them . . . 'a poor lot','' Miller concludes that ''George Eliot's loving reverence for commonplace people'' is premised on a fiction, albeit one that has real effects in the real world (74, 76).

15. It is worth noting that Eliot singled Dickens out for his deceptive idealizations. Describing him as a "great novelist who is gifted with the utmost power of rendering the external traits of our town population," she criticized his failure to "give us their psychological character . . . with the same truth as their idiom and manners" (111). If he did, she claimed, "his books would be the greatest contribution Art has ever made to the awakening of social sympathies. But while he can copy Mrs. Plornish's colloquial style with the delicate accuracy of a sun-picture . . . he scarcely ever passes from the humourous and external to the emotional and tragic, without becoming as transcendent in his unreality as he was a moment before in his artistic truthfulness" (111).

# WORKS CITED

"The Announcement." *Sunday Times* (12 June 1870): 1.

Armstrong, Nancy. *Desire and Domestic Fiction: A Political History of the Novel.* Oxford: Oxford UP, 1987.

Bodenheimer, Rosemarie. *The Politics of Story in Victorian Social Fiction.* Ithaca: Cornell UP: 1988.

Born, Daniel. *The Birth of Liberal Guilt in the English Novel: Charles Dickens to H. G. Wells.* Chapel Hill: U of North Carolina P, 1995.

Carlisle, Janice. *The Sense of an Audience: Dickens, Thackeray, and George Eliot at Mid-Century.* Athens: U of Georgia P, 1981.

"Charles Dickens." *Fraser's Magazine* (July 1870): 130.

"Charles Dickens." *The Times* (18 June 1870): 9.

"Charles Dickens and *David Copperfield.*" *Fraser's Magazine* (Dec. 1850): 698.

"Cheap Literature." *The British Quarterly Review* (April 1, 1859): 313–45.

Childers, Joseph. *Novel Possibilities: Fiction and the Formation of Early Victorian Culture.* Philadelphia: U of Pennsylvania P, 1995.

Cordery, Gareth. "Foucault, Dickens, and David Copperfield." *Victorian Literature and Culture* (1998): 71–85.

Davidoff, Leonore and Catherine Hall. *Family Fortunes: Men and Women of the English Middle Class, 1780–1850.* Chicago: U of Chicago P, 1987.

"The Death of Mr. Dickens." *Saturday Review* (June 11, 1870): 760–61.

Dickens, Charles. *David Copperfield.* New York: Penguin Books, 1985.

————. *Dombey and Son.* New York: Penguin Books, 1970.

————. *Nicholas Nickleby.* New York: Penguin Books, 1978.

————. *The Old Curiosity Shop.* New York: Penguin Books, 1972.

————. *The Pickwick Papers.* Oxford: Oxford UP, 1986.

Eastlake, Elizabeth Rigby. "*Vanity Fair*—and *Jane Eyre*," *The Quarterly Review* 84 (December 1848): 153–85.

Eliot, George. "The Natural History of German Life." 1856; *Selected Essays, Poems, and Other Writings.* Eds. A. S. Byatt and Nicholas Warren. London: Penguin, 1990.

Gallagher, Catherine. *Nobody's Story: The Vanishing Acts of Women Writers in the Marketplace, 1670–1820.* Berkeley: U of California P, 1994.

Hertz, Neil. *The End of the Line: Essays on Psychoanalysis and the Sublime.* New York: Columbia UP, 1985.

Higbie, Robert. *Dickens and Imagination.* Gainsville: UP of Florida, 1998.

Holcombe, Lee. "Victorian Wives and Property: Reform of the Married Women's Property Law, 1857–1882." *A Widening Sphere: Changing Roles of Victorian Women.* Ed. Martha Vicinus. Bloomington: Indiana UP, 1977.

Jaffe, Audrey. *Scenes of Sympathy: Identity and Representation in Victorian Fiction.* Ithaca: Cornell UP, 2000.

Jordan, John O. "The Social Sub-Text of *David Copperfield.*" *Dickens Studies Annual* 14 (1985): 61–92.

Laqueur, Thomas. "Bodies, Details, and the Humanitarian Narrative." *The New Cultural History.* Ed. Lynn Hunt. Berkeley: U of California P, 1989.

Léger, J. Michael. "Triangulation and Homoeroticism in *David Copperfield.*" *Victorian Literature and Culture* 23 (1995): 301–25.

Lucas, John. *The Melancholy Man: A Study of Dickens's Novels.* Sussex: Harvester, 1970.

Lewis, Sarah. *Woman's Mission.* Boston: William Crosby, 1840.

Miller, D. A. "Secret Subjects, Open Secrets." *The Novel and the Police.* Berkeley: U of California, P, 1988,

Miller, J. Hillis. *The Ethics of Reading: Kant, de Man, Eliot, Trollope, James and Benjamin.* New York: Columbia UP, 1987.

Needham, Gwendolyn. "The Undisciplined Heart of David Copperfield." *Nineteenth Century Fiction* 9:2 (1954): 81–107.

Nussbaum, Martha. *Love's Knowledge: Essays on Philosophy and Literature*. Oxford: Oxford UP, 1990.

Patmore, Coventry. *The Angel in the House*. Boston: Ticknor and Fields, 1856.

Perkin, Harold. *Origins of Modern English Society*. New York: Routledge, 1969.

Poovey, Mary. *Making a Social Body: British Cultural Formation, 1830–1864*. Chicago: U of Chicago P, 1995.

———. *Uneven Developments: The Ideological Work of Gender in Mid-Victorian England*. Chicago: U of Chicago P, 1988.

Ruskin, John. "Essay on Literature—1836." *Victorian Fiction: A Collection of Essays from the Period*. Ed. Ira Bruce Nadel. New York: Garland, 1986.

———. "Of Queens' Gardens." *Sesame and Lilies: Three Lectures*. 1865. New York: Merrill and Baker, 1894.

Sedgwick, Eve Kosofsky. *Between Men: English Literature and Male Homosocial Desire*. New York: Columbia UP, 1985.

Slater, Michael. *Dickens and Women*. Stanford: Stanford UP, 1983.

Smith, Adam. *The Theory of Moral Sentiments*. 1759. Indianapolis: Liberty Classics, 1969.

Stetson, Dorothy. *A Woman's Issue: The Politics of Family Law Reform in England*. Westport, CT: Greenwood, 1982.

Stewart, Garrett. *Dear Reader: The Conscripted Audience in Nineteenth-Century British Fiction*. Baltimore: Johns Hopkins UP, 1996.

———. "The Secret Life of Death in Dickens," *Dickens Studies Annual* 11 (1983): 177–207.

Todd, Janet. *Sensibility: An Introduction*. New York: Methuen, 1986.

Vanden Bossche, Chris R. "Family and Class in *David Copperfield*." *Dickens Studies Annual* 15 (1986): 87–109.

# The Subject of David Copperfield's Renaming and the Limits of Fiction

## S. D. Powell

David Copperfield *is notable for the range of names used for the titular hero, a fact remarked on by a series of critics. What has not generally been noticed is the narrator's decision to record those renamings, yet neither to consider directly the reasons young David is so willing to be renamed nor to editorialize those renamings. This essay considers those topics by examining both the narrative and Dickens's more directly autobiographical writings. In the narrative's logic, I argue, the pliability in David's name is symbolic of his unstable identity and his search for surrogate parents from whom he might draw a more stable personhood. Dickens's other writings, notably his autobiographical fragment on the blacking factory period and "Gone Astray," moreover, suggest that Dickens used the renaming of David as a way of keeping himself removed from the autobiographical implications of his narrative, which the initials of the hero otherwise would suggest.*

"I have in my heart of hearts a favourite child. And his name is DAVID COP-PERFIELD."
Preface to the Charles Dickens Edition of *David Copperfield* (1867)[1]

Notwithstanding the insistence of Dickens himself about the name of his "favourite child," the hero of *David Copperfield* is seldom shown using that name. Called everything from Brooks of Sheffield to Doady, from Mas'r

Davy to Trotwood, young David oddly never comments on his lack of a fixed name—nor on the plethora of temporary names he is given throughout the text. "He takes his names as they come," as A. E. Dyson has neatly put it (119).[2] The adult David, narrating the formation of his identity, is not much more forthcoming about the instability of his name; Dickens has him record but not editorialize the renamings. This essay seeks to explain the young hero's silence and, inextricably linked to it, the older narrator's unremarked persistence in recording all of the provisional names. Both the record of renaming and the narrator's uncharacteristic decision to silence both his own and his youthful alter ego's responses to the renaming are worth understanding. For, although David Copperfield's initials mirror the author's, and his life details are similar, David passively rejects his own name, that link to his textual progenitor, reminding the reader again and again that he is doing so. What, I ask, does this unexplained rejection say about Dickens's understanding of his creative enterprise in this novel, typically seen as one of his most autobiographical?

The immediate but not uncomplicated narrative explanation of David's renamings is probably to be sought in his immaturity. Throughout the novel, Dickens hints at the incompleteness of David's development, signaled, for example, by his unabated reverence for Steerforth and his infatuation with Dora. David's unremarked willingness to take on the names of those around him bespeaks a reason for that incompleteness: his unfilled need for the kind of parental care bestowed by the namers. Through much or perhaps all of the book, he is unable to identify himself except in terms of those around him. By allowing and even encouraging his many companions to name him—and through his adult failure to consider the full implications of that renaming, David reinforces our impression that he is, even as an adult, still in search of a parent to care for him. He is, to use Dyson's terms, more clay than potter (119), though as an adult he is complicit in the efforts of his renamers to mold him.

It should also be noted that David's nicknames advance the characterization of those around him and thus, as Sylvère Monod has argued, contribute "both firmly and subtly to creating the unity of the novel" (303).[3] Some critics have worked their way mechanically through David's many names, delineating the significance and symbolic effect of each one.[4] Norman Talbot has analyzed the entire novel, finding three plots (concerning the search for spouse, Steerforth and Emily, and Aunt Betsey and Uriah) and suggesting that in each of these plots David is given a good name (David Copperfield, Mas'r Davy, and Trotwood, respectively) and an ill name (Doady, Daisy, and Master

Copperfield). "The three ill names all try to imprison David in a childish or blissfully childlike state, rendering him impotent where he should be heroically constructive and mature," Talbot writes (268).

What must be added to this approach, however, is that David permits these intrusions on his development. In fact, initially, at least, he welcomes almost all of the alternatives. And, except for Uriah's name for him, Master Copperfield, he never overtly rejects any of them. In short, David repeatedly has a chance to assert his own identity by insisting on proper forms of address, but the older David almost never shows his younger self taking this crucial step toward adulthood. His reluctance to do so allows Dickens to reveal David's continuing uncertainty about the stability of his personhood.[5]

Beyond that, I argue that David's willingness to be renamed must also be related to Dickens's larger mimetic goals. Specifically, it must be considered in light of his decision, as he planned the novel, to rename the hero—initially to be called David or Thomas Mag—David Copperfield, a clear echo of his own name.[6] For in renaming Mr. Mag, Dickens reverses his own initials, but he then refuses the hero the uncomplicated use of those initials. This paradox reflects Dickens's ambivalence towards autobiography, a genre he seems eager to approach, yet from which he also holds himself firmly away. If we see David's naming and renaming in this light, the novel may be read, internally, as a complex meditation on David's quest for parental care and, externally, as Dickens's deliberate consideration of his own personal and authorial identity, his bifurcated role as the textual creator of his favorite child and the autobiographical recorder of his own life story.

Dickens's trial titles for the novel, along with Hablot K. Browne's famous design for the cover of the serialized parts of the novel, neatly hint at the complexity of the relationship between creator and created, both textual and biological.[7] Externally, the assignment of the name David Copperfield to his hero allows Dickens to imply a direct relationship to his own life; internally, calling his memoirs those of "David Copperfield the Younger of Blunderstone Rookery" gives the older David a chance to reclaim his patrimony. Browne's rendering of the title, then, which was surely inspired by the trial titles, emphasizes Dickens's desire for a child, a symbolic offspring or an idealized projection, a desire that is disrupted by the continual renaming, which serves to obscure the genetic link between himself and David. Similarly, the title implies that David's life story is in part a reflection of his desire to associate himself with his dead father.[8] But just as Dickens is uncertain about his relationship to David, so, too, is David ambivalent about his father, whose name he bears only intermittently and whose station in life is lost to him. In short, David's internal ambivalence about his parentage echoes Dickens's own ambivalence about his relationship to David. And the fake insistence that the work was "never meant to be Published on any Account," a phrase that recurs in the trial titles and survives in Browne's engraving, only adds to the sense that this work is, and is not, autobiographical; and is, and is not, a public recounting of private deeds.

David's original naming is only the first of a number of more or less problematic christenings, each a sort of "re-parenting" of the growing boy and young man. Indeed, *David Copperfield* may be read, on one level, as the record of David's serial attempts to find suitable substitutes for his parents.[9] These substitutes, some chosen and some thrust upon him, almost all exercise the parental prerogative of naming their child. David allows these new names to be granted and used, for he wishes, at some level, to see himself as a product of his namers, their surrogate son, and, even as an adult, he feels the need for their formative influences on his life. By changing David's initials or at least by obscuring the association of biological parent with named offspring, moreover, each new name also complicates the equation of Dickens with his favorite child, distancing Dickens from David. That distance is a subject to which I return at the end of this essay.

Naming—specifically the failure of naming—is, in many ways, the major topic of the novel's first chapter, just as it figures so prominently in Browne's design. The name of the family home, Blunderstone Rookery, is one of the first things Betsey Trotwood remarks on. As Aunt Betsey later will with young David's name, she shows little patience for the father's naming: "David Copperfield from head to foot! Calls a house a rookery when there's not a rook near it, and takes the birds on trust, because he sees the nests" (I.5).[10] Peggotty's name is also a subject of Betsey's scorn (I.6).

In this context, which foregrounds naming, the narrator's expression of his acute awareness of his father's absence takes on a new meaning. With dual time references showing that the narrator shares young David's feelings, the narrator reveals the way in which his father's role in his naming is excluded from his perception. "There is something strange to me, *even now*, in the reflection that he never saw me," he writes, "and something stranger yet in the shadowy remembrance that I have of my first childish associations with his white grave-stone in the churchyard, and of the indefinable compassion *I used to feel* for it lying out alone there in the dark night, when our little parlor was warm and bright with fire and candle, and the doors of our house were—almost cruelly, it seemed to me sometimes—bolted and locked against it" (I.2, my emphases). These recollections show that, even much later, David feels in some way complicit in that absence and responsible for its effects; his passive safety behind the bolted doors is transmuted into an active rejection of every kind of paternal influence. The result is that the father's posthumous "involvement" in his son's naming is correspondingly and paradoxically overlooked. Indeed, as if to emphasize and foreshadow the name's failure, the actual naming is placed to the side of Betsey's failed effort to name the goddaughter she is anticipating, a prominent portion of the chapter, and is relegated to the void of early infancy between chapter I, "I am born" and chapter II, "I observe." No more is made of his name, until he begins to be addressed by Peggotty as Master Davy (II.14).

But if the narrator foregrounds Betsey's attempt to name him (or his unborn sister), he also feels similarly complicit in that naming's failure, for, by being born a boy, he drives her (seemingly) permanently out of his life, "like a discontented fairy" (I.10). "From the moment of this girl's birth, child," she had told Clara Copperfield, "I intend to be her friend. I intend to be her godmother, and I beg you'll call her Betsey Trotwood Copperfield . . . . She must be well brought up, and well guarded from reposing any foolish confidences where they are not deserved. I must make that *my* care" (I.6). When Betsey's attempted naming fails, so too does her plan to begin early the control she hopes to exert over her niece's life. Chapter I, then, records the loss of two parental figures, implicitly relating each loss to the topic of David's naming and to the loss of influential figures who might have helped to form his identity.

Chapter I's double sorrow—the loss of father and of godmother—nevertheless leaves David with a good name and in loving hands. Yet, unhappy as he quickly becomes about his mother's remarriage, it is surely indicative of his wish to have a father that it is he who brings the matter up, however obliquely (and even though prompted by Murdstone's accompaniment home from church the previous Sunday). He asks, "if you marry a person, and the person dies, why then you may marry another person, mayn't you, Peggotty?" (II.14). The account of his mother's courtship is necessarily tinged with knowledge of what came later, but young David is not altogether opposed to it, perhaps because he desires a stronger influence on his identity than his delicate mother: for Clara, unlike Betsey, lacks the gumption or flair to make his name stick. And the name Clara gives reflects another person's identity, rather than her own. Given all of this, David is at least taken with the idea of accompanying Murdstone to Lowestoft (II.17), and his complexion made him think Murdstone, "in spite of my misgivings, a very handsome man" (II.18).

It is at this point that David receives his next name, Brooks of Sheffield, a name of which young David is not even aware. The narrator uses this naming to signal the reader that Murdstone's intentions are less than fatherly, for this name assures that Murdstone can keep David in the childish state of ignorance that Talbot describes, rather than assisting constructively in his development. It does not take much longer for young David to realize that this surrogate father will be no happy substitute for his dead one, as he may initially have hoped.

Only a little later, Murdstone, halfheartedly attempting to fill the role of father, bestows a new name on his new stepson. Although he greets David's return from Yarmouth with a controlled, but possibly friendly "Davy boy" (III.34), the next morning he begins imposing on him the grown-up version of his name (IV.36), rejecting the name his mother uses. Again, naming serves as a shorthand commentary on Murdstone. Already then David recognizes Murdstone's cruelty, but his awareness has become more acute since (note again the double time reference): "I had little doubt *then*, and I have less doubt *now*, that he would have knocked me down without the least compunction, if I had hesitated" (IV.36, my emphases). Just as "Brooks of Sheffield" imprisons David in ignorance, "David" catapults him into a premature (and violent) adulthood. Hawes points out, "Mr Murdstone wants to emphasize to David and his mother that David is a boy and not a baby, and that he is not to be treated any longer as a mother's darling" (85), but young David is not ready for such treatment. Murdstone picks the one name, horrible as it is when he uses it, that David will not, may not reject, the name that his dead father had borne and that is, undeniably, his actual name. Yet Murdstone is virtually the only person in the book to call him David (Monod 302), and the narrator uses this fact to emphasize the cruelty of the naming. Ironically, then, by not using a nickname, Murdstone reveals his final rejection of the paternal role in which David had originally imagined him. For the rest of the novel, each conferring of a new name will signal the possibility of a new parental figure.

David's two forays away from Blunderstone Rookery, to Yarmouth and then to school, bring with them new father figures, more agreeable to him. The first of these, the kindly Mr. Peggotty, however, turns out to be, to David's surprise, no father, for, as Mr. Peggotty tells him in their first conversation, he had never given Ham his name, "his father giv it him" (III.26). Here again, the narrator equates naming with fatherhood, an equation that is complicated by the parental care Mr. Peggotty does in fact provide to Ham. In any case, David relates well to Mr. Peggotty's oddly-assembled family, for he is drawn to it by the orphanhood (partial at first, but soon complete) he shares with Ham and Em'ly (see III.27). But their kinship is always incomplete. Em'ly points out the difference between them: "your father was a gentleman and your mother is a lady; and my father was a fisherman and my mother was a fisherman's daughter, and my uncle Dan is a fisherman" (III.27). David never does become another adopted son for Mr. Peggotty, and so throughout his stay at Yarmouth and in later years, he retains the name that Peggotty uses, Master Davy (or Mas'r Davy). Hawes believes that name "nicely combines [the family's] affection with a proper respect" (85), and Talbot characterizes it as "good." John O. Jordan is right, however, to point out the social condescension that is implicit in David's relations with the Peggottys and that ultimately leads to their tragedy (see 70–76).

In his quest for a family (and thanks to his upbringing and society), young David is oblivious to the implications of the reverential, if affectionate, title the family uses for him. He does not consider why they call him what they do. He is only too willing to let them mold him into an honored part of the family. But the name reveals that he never does assume a place in the family and remains, instead, an intruder, adored even after he betrays them by introducing them to their downfall. In fact, in the novel's world, his failure to incorporate himself fully into the Peggotty family is signaled precisely by their reluctance to give him a new name, to mark him as one of their own instead of as a cherished outsider, whose naming reveals not familial or parental but rather social duty. In that respect, they are like Murdstone, but more kindly and wisely refusing to parent David. The naming shows all of that, but the narrator, embarrassed, perhaps, by his betrayal of the family, or bitter that they did not or could not adopt him, will not make the connections explicit.

David's sojourn at Salem House, on the other hand, leads him to a very different sort of father figure—one who, at last, willingly takes on that role. Although his fascination with Steerforth may strike readers today as homoerotic, it is worth considering David's reverence in other lights, as well. Indeed, his attempts to emulate the suavely elegant Steerforth suggest as strongly the relationship between a younger and an older brother as between lovers. Steerforth's command and manliness, moreover, also cast him in the role of surrogate father. One of the first things David does upon their meeting is yield to him the governance of all his worldly possessions, all of his seven shillings (VI.67). Steerforth controls other aspects of David's life, as well, including his sleeping and waking (see VII.73–75), and protects him from

other boys: "nobody dared to annoy one whom he honored with his countenance" (VII.73). Steerforth also commands David's unquestioning affection,
a fact made clear time and again through the novel.

None of this necessarily means that Steerforth fills anything more than a
fraternal role, but later Steerforth moves definitively into the paternal role
when he names David. "Daisy" is not a juvenile nickname, at least in the '
way Steerforth uses it, although it might be considered to be so if its usage
were strictly mocking, if David were being called a sissy. But Steerforth does
not hit upon this name until he is a young adult, "an Oxford man," while
David has finished his schooling (XIX.235), and the name is not directly
mocking or, at least, not perceived by David to be so. Steerforth asks, "'Will
you mind my calling you Daisy?' 'Not at all!' said I. 'That's a good fellow!'"
(XX.237). David's love for Steerforth, of course, will permit no other answer,
although he blushes when Rosa Dartle asks about the name: "Is it—eh?—because he thinks you young and innocent?" (XX.242). Steerforth trespasses
so on David's affections, then, as to impose on him a name as irrevocable as
the one a parent bestows. This is a name, however, unlike his own, which
"must have a touch of contempt," for it symbolizes David's innocence,
which Steerforth "admires and violates" (Dyson 122). In short, recording
the naming allows the narrator, on the one hand, quietly to show the extent
to which his personal identity is controlled, not as lover but as parent, for
good and ill, by Steerforth. The narrator's failure to editorialize the naming,
on the other hand, is tantamount to young David's blush, a tacit but unspoken
acknowledgment of an uncomfortable truth.

Upon leaving Blunderstone for good, David begins his new life as a child-
laborer, lodging with the Micawber family. The Micawbers, so clearly mod-
eled on Dickens's own parents, nevertheless remain a respectful distance
away from David with their forms of address. Mr. Micawber's "Copperfield"
or Mrs. Micawber's "Master Copperfield," Hawes points out, would not
have been unusual forms of address at the time (85), but they do show that
David maintains a greater distance from the Micawbers than he does from
the Peggottys. And the contrast in their naming of David echoes the unsuitability of the Micawbers as parents. David says of his time as their lodger,
"From Monday morning until Saturday night, I had no advice, no counsel,
no encouragement, no consolation, no assistance, no support, of any kind,
from any one, that I can call to mind, as I hope to go to heaven!" (XI.129).[11]
Despite their mutual affection, the relationship remains based on the household economics that are the subject of Mrs. Micawber's first discussion with
David and that remain an issue throughout the novel: he is first their boarder,

eventually their pawning expert, then their financial adviser and, at the end of the Heep affair, (along with Tommy Traddles) their financial rescuer. Indeed, it seems that David is often the member of the household most in charge and most to be respected. For this reason, perhaps, David's identity is stronger in this period than it has been before. He knows what he wants; he knows what he can do for others. The Micawbers' naming signals, and also reinforces, this stronger self-awareness.

We might imagine that David's maturation is complete. The Micawbers' use of his real name and their failure to take on parental roles at least points in that direction. More importantly, young David never sees the Micawbers as potential surrogate parents, and he assumes adult, and even parental, responsibilities in their household. At this point, then, the narrative search for parents appears to have ended.

But it is at most replaced by Dickens's autobiographical renegotiation of the betrayal of children by adults, for if young David does not see the Micawbers as potential parents, the narrator surely does. That larger concern transcends the absence of his parents through death, pointing up the not so humorous failure lying behind the Micawbers' humorous treatment of their youthful lodger. As do Dickens's own parents, the Micawbers fail their charge, rendering him toughened and seemingly mature but still in need of parental guidance. They are good to him, then, but not good enough, for they fail to treat him as a child. The narrator's emphasis on the Micawbers' name for David quietly reveals his sense of betrayal by them and his insistence that David is not yet ready to retain one and only one name, to achieve independent adulthood. Simultaneously, the Micawbers' failure to name David allows for Dickens's excoriation of the Victorians for their refusal to protect children.

When David is taken under the wing of his great-aunt, the theme of children's betrayal is tied even more directly to his search for parents who will name him. Betsey, again displaying her sensitivity to naming, tells him Mr. Dick's true name. "He can't bear his name," she says. "That's a peculiarity of his. Though I don't know that it's much of a peculiarity, either; he has been ill-used enough, by some that bear it, to have a mortal antipathy for it, Heaven knows" (XIV.164). Her recognition of the maltreatment of Mr. Dick at the hands of those who should have protected him and the consequences of it—his desire for a different name—lead Betsey to declare that David, too, must be renamed.[12] Having decided that she and Mr. Dick will care for him as surrogate parents, she works to erase the betrayals he has suffered, declaring, "I have been thinking, do you know, Mr. Dick, that I might call him

Trotwood?'' (XIV.175). She has, after all, reassumed the role she forfeited when David was born, as protector of her nephew's child, as that child's godmother. And so David observes, ''Thus I began my new life, in a new name, and with everything new about me'' (XIV.175). As Harry Stone puts it, ''The fairy godmother who presided imperiously at his original birth presides with equal imperiousness at his rebirth'' (193), though my reading of Betsey's motivations is more favorable than Stone's.

C. A. Bodelsen claims, ''There is an air of bustle and goings to and fro about Trotwood, and also a touch of good-natured eccentricity, perhaps because one is reminded, via 'trot', of a little pony'' (46). But ''Trotwood,'' of course, is not an original coinage for Aunt Betsey. It is her own name and was to have been part of the name of his unborn sister. By accepting Trotwood as a name, then, David is defining himself, not only in terms of his aunt, but also in terms of his alter ego, the girl he was not.[13] His acceptance of the name means he has not just a new name, but a new family of sorts, a father and mother who name him, and a sister whose presence is murkily alluded to by the name (as it will be again by Steerforth's name, Daisy). Aunt Betsey has at last fulfilled her role as godmother, and she provides him a family in which he may safely grow up. The name also suggests that she has bestowed on him a new identity, one less sturdy and predictable, more eccentric than ''David'' could ever be.[14]

It is from this new family that David ventures forth, coming into his own academically and personally. Nearly all of his new acquaintances in Kent call him Trotwood, significantly including Agnes, who retains this name for him right up to their mutual declaration of love (see LXII.706) and presumably after their marriage. But Dora does not, perhaps because she is unable to understand the eccentricity and quick wit in David, which ''David'' so nicely conceals but which ''Trotwood'' lays bare. Dora's usual name for him is ''Doady,'' ''which was a corruption of David'' and may be an attempt to simplify David's personality even further (XLI.491). Monod calls this name ''charming'' (302), and Dyson declares it ''as affectionate as 'Daisy' and far more innocent: a beautiful instance, in the tone surrounding it, of Dora's love, trust, tenderness and unfitness for life'' (126). It is a mistake, however, to follow these critics in examining this name from the point of view of the namer, rather than the named. Dora certainly means no harm in calling David Doady, just as she never means any harm in anything she does or does not do. His willing acceptance of this name, however, and the narrator's refusal to criticize himself for it, should be an immediate tip-off that his attraction to Dora is wrongheaded, that the narrator recognizes, as we do, that ''Doady'' represents a step back from the mature freedom of "Trotwood" and the family that bestowed that name.

It would be too blunt to say that David is attracted to Dora only because she reminds him of his dead mother. Instead, once again, he is still in search of a surrogate parent, even despite his relationship with Betsey Trotwood. Thus, he is willing to be renamed—however inappropriately—by this new "mother," and, while Clara's affectionate "Davy" was acceptable for a young boy, Dora's new corruption of "David" strikes one as very wrong for a young man, just come of age. "Doady" allows David to imprison himself in a blissfully ignorant state, as Talbot points out, and thus in a wretchedly inappropriate and immature love and marriage.[15] These are subjects the narrator will leave the reader to figure out.

David is rescued from this marriage, however, as he is from so many other disasters, and he eventually enters a much more fulfilling and appropriate marriage with Agnes, who never finds it necessary to name David. She does not see herself as a shaper of his life and identity, and what shaping she does is unconscious. When he tells her, " . . . all my life long I shall look up to you, and be guided by you, as I have been through the darkness that is past," she shrugs off the praise: "She put her hand in mine, and told me she was proud of me, and of what I said; although I praised her very far beyond her worth" (LX.688). Agnes, in other words, does not aspire to shape David as a mother would, and her strength not to do so is symbolized by her not giving him a new name. Again, though, it is important not to focus too exclusively on the motives of the namer. What is more interesting is David's reaction to the lack of naming. It is Agnes's strength, not his, that makes him start to see her as more than a mother figure. And he becomes more of a husband than a son to her. Yet the incompleteness of that development is signaled by the two names with which he ends the novel, David and Trotwood, and the fact that Agnes uses the latter name.

As he matures, of course, David's many names cease to have a formative effect on him. The hurtfulness, even of Uriah's scornful "Master Copperfield," diminishes, and, as he gains assurance about his maturity, Miss Murdstone's "boy" (VIII.93), Mr. Murdstone's "Brooks of Sheffield," the waiter's "six-foot" (V.53), the factory boys' "little gent" (XI.131), and the "six-penn'orth of bad ha'pence" used by the young man who steals David's trunk (XII.143–44), all seem far less painful, and even a source of merriment for the narrator. That it takes him so long to reach the state of maturity in which sticks and stones hurt worse than names, however, is made clear by the effect that names given by those in his adopted families have on him, his willingness to accept new names from these families, and his later reluctance to explore the names more fully.

In a book full of orphans, David Copperfield is the one orphan who is in many ways not an orphan. He has many sets of parents, and many adults who take him into their protection and treat him as much like a son as they can. But even the older David searches for more fulfilling parental relationships, and his story may thus be read as the story of a quest for replacements for the family which he has lost but not forgotten at Blunderstone Rookery and for the identity which that family never could give him. That he ends the novel with two names just as he had begun it—as Betsey and David—suggests that this quest is not yet complete, that his identity remains only partially formed. His personal life as Trotwood Copperfield remains separated from his public life as David Copperfield. He must still identify himself in terms of another, though the narrator's acknowledgment of that fact is only glancing. As he writes at the end of his story, Agnes is "the dear presence, without which I were nothing" (LXIV.717). His need for Agnes "pointing upward," we can see, is yet the need of a child for a guiding mother.

Much earlier in the novel, Mr. Murdstone's actions have foreshadowed David's state of perpetual bifurcation. When his mother remarries, David is both a Copperfield and a Murdstone. Indeed, Murdstone even makes a fleeting attempt to change David's last name, when his dinner on the way to school is paid for in the name Murdstone, not Copperfield (see V.52). The confusion that results is symbolic of the confusion he feels about his own identity and his parents'.

Yet this episode—and thus the novel's close—may be read in a different way, too. If Murdstone drops his attempts to rename David, "because Murdstone hates the thought of him far too much by now to persevere," as Dyson argues (121), then we have here a textual acknowledgment of the ways in which names and renaming can be used both to achieve intimacy and to create distance. Murdstone's renaming of David implies a paternal relationship that, from hatred, Murdstone almost immediately aborts by renaming him Copperfield again. Similarly, the narrator uses his many renamings as a way of signaling his newfound maturity and his distance from his younger self, a distance that is belied by his own continuing need for Agnes's parental care, not to mention Agnes's use of Trotwood rather than David to name her husband. Even as an adult, then, the narrator embraces his nickname as suitable for his interior life and rejects his birthname as appropriate only for the outside world. In doing so, he opens a space in his identification with the younger David Copperfield, rejecting, at a fundamental, personal level, his association with the life story he is in the process of writing. Dickens's feelings toward David are considerably kinder than Murdstone's, but they are as complex as David's about his younger self; his use of David's multiple names performs a function similar to the one sought by the narrator, the creation of distance. Dickens's emphasis on the consistent renaming of David invites us to see his feelings towards David as less warm than his own statements imply.

Indeed, the renaming suggests that Dickens wants his public life as a famous author to remain separate from the fictional and yet, clearly, also autobiographical projection of that life onto David. Both internally and externally, however, the novel remains deeply ambivalent about that split. The reasons for this complication, manifested in part by the narrator's failure to editorialize in the face of David's renaming, are to be found in Dickens's own life story. Specifically, I believe that Dickens is uncomfortable with the romanticization of his childhood that *David Copperfield* implies. Although both David and Dickens are betrayed by their parents' failings, the key difference cannot have escaped the author: the betrayal of young Charles was real, his degradation in the blacking factory was real, his parents' failure to educate him properly was real, his poverty and shame were real. They were, in fact, so real and so painful that he hardly wrote about them, and he kept many of the details even from his wife. In this semi-autobiographical novel, then, which editorializes almost every aspect of David's life, the fundamental fact of David's incomplete quest for parental figures and his concomitant inability to achieve fully adult relationships, even with Agnes, are effaced, hinted at only by his perpetual renaming.

And so it is with Dickens writing about himself: the author's reluctance to confide his most intense life details, which, like David's, stem from parental betrayal and affect marital relations, is a constant theme of the long autobiographical fragment about the blacking factory period woven into John Forster's *Life of Charles Dickens*, which was published shortly after Dickens's death. This fragment describes the time his father spent in debtor's prison, when Charles was a child laborer. As Dickens writes, "The deep remembrance of the sense I had of being utterly neglected and hopeless; of the shame I felt in my position; of the misery it was to my young heart to believe that, day by day, what I had learned, and thought, and delighted in, and raised my fancy and my emulation up by, was passing away from me, never to be brought back any more; cannot be written." (Forster 1:22). And, again, "From that hour until this at which I write, no word of that part of my childhood . . . has passed my lips to any human being . . . I have never, until

I now impart it to this paper, in any burst of confidence with anyone, my own wife not excepted, raised the curtain I then dropped'' (Forster 1:32–33). Although there is some indication that Dickens did in fact tell his wife about his experience as a child laborer,[16] even within marriage, Dickens, like his narrator, hesitated about confiding his true feelings about his parents. But the fact that he stresses this hesitation so fully suggests the depth of his desire to tell all.

Dickens also knew the inadequacy of autobiography to relay such details, to capture the horror he had experienced. As he writes in the concluding sentence of the autobiographical fragment (or so it appears in Forster), "[This writing] does not seem a tithe of what I might have written, or of what I meant to write." Moreover, Dickens abandoned autobiography after writing this fragment, choosing fiction instead. As Forster explains, it was "when the fancy of *David Copperfield* . . . began to take shape in his mind, that he abandoned his first intention of writing his own life" (1:20). In fiction, then, Dickens hoped finally to tell his story. But even fiction must not have seemed safe or sharp enough, and so he subverts the equation between his autobiography and his fiction that Forster and subsequent biographers have all taken for granted.[17] To take only one comparatively straightforward example, Charles's experiences as a boarder remind one of David's with the Micawbers, and both end the same way: with a return to a more conventional, though not unproblematic, childhood, David with Betsey, Charles with his parents. Yet the real and tragic failings of his real parents are displaced onto the Micawbers' fictional and risible failings as landlords.

In less fictive writings, Dickens's awareness of childhood's terrors is much more sharply delineated, though it is still veiled. In "Gone Astray," an ostensibly autobiographical story about being inadvertently abandoned on an outing to St. Giles, for example, eight or nine-year-old Charles's anxieties about the need to support himself are so much in the forefront that he never stops to imagine that he might be able to rely further on his own parents. "To the best of my belief," Dickens writes, "the idea of asking my way home never came into my head . . . I have a serious conviction that in the wide scope of my arrangements for the future, I had no eyes for the nearest and most obvious course" (381–82). Instead, he planned to make his own way in the world, if necessary "to go into the army as a drummer" (382). The retrospective recollection of both his childhood panic and his melancholy sense that he would have to provide for himself was surely colored by his parents' more serious, later failure to provide for him. Indeed, the ferocity of the impressions may plausibly be thought to stem from that later period in his life. But, as the older David does in *David Copperfield*, the older Dickens resists making such connections overt or permanent.

Like his novel's narrator, he only intermittently hints at parental duties and parental betrayals. The true causes of his disappointment in his parents are conveyed only in private, autobiographical jottings and rare, confidential conversations with Forster and other close friends. His disappointment and the secrecy of it are especially evident in his comments on his removal from the blacking factory, following his father's release from debtor's prison. It is not till quite some time after that release that Dickens stops working and returns to school, a change that seems to have been a belated paternal expression of support for the boy. But Dickens knew well that his mother opposed the change, and he confides to his autobiography, "I do not write resentfully or angrily: for I know how all these things have worked together to make me what I am: but I never afterwards forgot, I never shall forget, I never can forget, that my mother was warm for my being sent back [to the factory]" (Forster 1:32).

Forster records a number of Dickens's other disappointments. When they had first moved to Camden Town (before his father's bankruptcy), for example, Charles had not been sent to school, as he had hoped to be, and, as he tells Forster, his father "appeared to have utterly lost at this time the idea of educating me at all, and to have utterly put from him the notion that I had any claim upon him, in that regard, whatever" (1:13). Having confided such betrayals to Forster, and having recollected the depth of his miseries, Dickens retreats to fiction and leaves it to his biographers to fill in the connections. But he complicates that task.

The work began with Forster's *Life*, and his assessment of the blend of fact and fiction in *David Copperfield* is still pertinent and forms an implicit basis of many critical and biographical treatments of Dickens, even today. Forster argues: "many as are the resemblances in Copperfield's adventures to portions of those of Dickens, and often as reflections occur to David which no one intimate with Dickens could fail to recognise as but the reproduction of his, it would be the greatest mistake to imagine anything like a complete identity of the fictitious novelist with the real one . . . or to suppose that the youth, who [in the factory] received his first harsh schooling in life, came out of it as little harmed or hardened as David did. The language of the fiction reflects only faintly the narrative of the actual fact . . . Here was but another proof how thoroughly Dickens understood his calling, and that to weave fact with fiction unskilfully would be only to make truth less true" (Forster 2:105).

But my study shows that Forster's emphasis is wrong. It is not that Dickens is spicing his fiction with carefully selected facts, as Forster would have it, but rather that he uses fiction to cancel or blunt fact: he *does* want to make truth either less true or at least more open to revision.

By writing a semi-autobiographical novel, Dickens might have hoped to renegotiate his parents' failures and his childhood deprivation, to understand them better, to come to terms with his own rise from childhood degradation (that is, at least, Forster's implicit argument). But the insistence on the renaming of David, which breaks the stated and implicit bond between him and "his favourite child," shows that the renegotiation is only partially complete. Dickens does not so much weave fact with fiction as he hides fact behind the veil of fiction, rendering fact both commercially viable and personally comfortable. And though he decides to lift that veil a bit in the title of the novel and in the hero's real name, the pains lingering from childhood are still too powerful to be easily repackaged as fiction. Like his narrator, in short, Dickens is drawn to tell his life story but works to break the bonds between his youth and his adult self.

Dickens acknowledged the problems with and limitations of his artifice, though only glancingly, in his preface to the 1850 edition: "I do not find it easy to get sufficiently far away from this Book, in the first sensations of having finished it, to refer to it with the composure which this formal heading [i.e., "Preface"] would seem to require."[18] The continuation might make us think that Dickens is going to confess to the autobiographical element: "My interest in it, is so recent and strong . . . that I am in danger of wearying the reader whom I love, with personal confidences, and private emotions." But this impulse is stopped quickly in the next sentence, set aside, as if for emphasis, in its own paragraph: "Besides which, all that I could say of the Story, to any purpose, I have endeavoured to say in it." And, again, a few sentences later: "I have nothing else to tell . . . " These statements, in their alternation between confession and defense, between openness and secrecy, between truth and fiction, confirm that David Copperfield must—and, equally, must not—be seen as a reflection of Charles Dickens.

# NOTES

1. See *David Copperfield*, ed. Nina Burgis (Oxford: Clarendon, 1981) 752.
2. Dyson and most other commentators on the novel treat the broad range of naming practices as more unified in kind than they actually are. I will follow this practice

here, though I am oversimplifying social conventions, for example, in calling "Mas'r Davy" a new name. Nevertheless, the general critical tendency to consider Mas'r Davy and Brooks of Sheffield as analogous is justified by the similarity of their artistic effects; both names, and all the others, are used by Dickens to reveal the nature of David's interaction with the rest of his world. It is more important to show the variation in these interactions, as revealed by different forms of appellation, than to categorize each of the names as nickname, diminutive, honorific, or the like.

3. Monod builds on a long history in Dickens criticism. In 1917, Elizabeth Hope Gordon was among the first to attempt to categorize Dickens's names, which she called "the last noteworthy appearance in fiction of names that pertinently distinguish the characters" (4). Gordon identifies four categories of names: those whose originals have been identified (6–9), "directly-descriptive names" (10–21), "vaguely suggestive names" (21–32), and those which are neutral (32–34). She concludes, "Names are with him not mere tags for puppets serving but to prevent confusion in the assemblage of characters. Rather they partake of the nature of the people to whom they belong" (34). The next year, however, E. de Laski, studying the surnames in *Pickwick Papers*, *Nicholas Nickleby*, and *Our Mutual Friend*, found that fully seventy-four percent of these names were "British or derived from British family names," while many others are English words or derived from English words. Fewer than a tenth of the names (only four percent in *OMF* ) are "original" coinages. This, de Laski reasons, "raises a strong presumption that Dickens was not as original in his selection of surnames as is ordinarily supposed" (341). Lionel Stevenson assumes the source of Dickens's names is of minor importance: "whether he adopted an existing name or coined a new one, the artistic effect is less in the source than in the application" (242).

   Dickens's use of names remains a source of interest to more recent critics. Kelsie B. Harder points out that his names, in context, "obviously type a character or object, or they give tone and atmosphere to the situation. Individually, they reflect an Al Cappish sort of waggery, often vulgar and grotesque. But when they are placed in clusters they exemplify something more serious, an unconscious attitude that works out and repeats itself over and over" (42). C. A. Bodelsen is also interested in the role of the unconscious in naming in Dickens's novels. Bodelsen claims that "'symbolic' names are inventions of Dickens and form part of a general symbolic technique that permeates his work. What happens is that the sound, or spelling, of the name directs the reader's mind towards certain associations, which in their turn impart their own overtones to the name . . . Even the writer is no doubt often ignorant of how the effect is produced." Harry Stone writes of Dickens's naming: "That there was a right name he had no doubt. It was the name that conveyed the outward show and inward mystery of a character of a book, the name which revealed and yet concealed" (191).

4. See, for example, Dyson 119–26, one of the most complete treatments of the subject, or Hawes.

5. My argument here builds on Joseph Bottum's examination of the novel's naming and his claim that Dickens uses naming in order to examine the philosophical underpinnings of fiction. Bottum writes, "The order of names has caught his

attention, and he does more than use it to express rank and sentiment. Dickens shows both the origin of abuse in extrinsic denomination and the power of names to mark that abuse. And he claims at the novel's end both the possibility of intrinsic denomination and the power of true names to speak the unity of concept and thing'' (454).

6. For a complete record of Dickens's trial titles, see Burgis's edition of *David Copperfield*, 753–55. Two early titles have the hero's name as Charles Copperfield.

7. See Burgis's edition, frontispiece [ii].

8. John O. Jordan notes that ''the title emphasizes that he [David] is well-born, that he has a father whose name he is proud to bear, and that he has an estate with a rather grand-sounding name'' (67). Jordan supposes this reveals David's social ambivalence, but it also shows, more directly, that he wishes to associate himself with his dead father, to show clearly that it is his father who has conferred a name on him, however indirectly.

9. See Hochman and Wachs, especially 55–85, for a more complete consideration of this reading of the novel. Such a reading, admittedly, runs the risk of simplifying complex and multifaceted motivations. That risk seems justified here, given the trial titles and the centrality of problematic parenting in Dickens's own life story.

10. References to *David Copperfield* are to Burgis's edition, and are given parenthetically by chapter and page number.

11. Dickens's autobiographical recollection of his parents' abandonment during the blacking factory period is strikingly similar: ''I certainly had no other assistance whatever . . . from Monday morning until Saturday night. No advice, no counsel, no encouragement, no consolation, no support, from any one that I can call to mind, so help me God'' (Forster 1:27).

12. Herbert Barry has pointed out to me that, in this context, the echo of Dickens's surname in ''Mr. Dick'' provides further evidence of the author's interest in the relationship of the novel's names to his own life story.

13. Monod expands on the significance of this identification with Betsey Trotwood Copperfield, arguing that she ''is something like the embodiment of the feminine side of David's personality'' (323).

14. Hawes is especially thorough in his analysis of David's real first and last names. Pointing out that David was a fairly unusual name in Victorian England, Hawes suggests ''the name 'David' was likely to convey impressions of fallibility as well as strength—impressions, that is, of a hero with certain flaws—to nineteenth-century readers with their ready and knowledgeable acquaintance with the Bible'' (84). After describing the component parts of ''Copperfield,'' Hawes writes, ''The complete name . . . can . . . suggest not only the hero's essential but not extraordinary worthiness, durability, and malleability, but also the area and scope relating to the exercise and development of those personal qualities; there are, in addition, suggestions of familiar Englishness and perhaps . . . of characteristics that can loosely be called natural and Wordsworthian'' (83).

15. The name is only one indication of this, of course. David's over-reliance on Dora manifests itself in the kind of complete and utter trust which a child has for a

parent: "Her idea," he writes after Emily and Steerforth are lost to him, "was my refuge in disappointment and distress, and made some amends to me, even for the loss of my friend. The more I pitied myself, or pitied others, the more I sought for consolation in the image of Dora . . . I don't think I had any definite idea where Dora came from, or in what degree she was related to a higher order of beings; but I am quite sure I should have scouted the notion of her being simply human, like any other young lady, with indignation and contempt" (XXXIII.387). The unsuitability of the marriage is recognized by Aunt Betsey, who calls Dora and David "a pair of babes in the wood," although she is, on the whole, much less scornful than she had been of Clara, whom she had, in similar fashion, dismissed as "a wax doll" (XLIV.522, I.3). Betsey comes to love Dora very much, as perhaps she would have come to love Clara.

16. In the 1892 edition of *David Copperfield*, Charles Dickens, Jr. reported that his father had shown the autobiographical fragment to Catherine. See Ackroyd's biography *Dickens*, 553 and 1118n. See also Michael Slater's essay "How Dickens 'Told' Catherine about His Past." Slater points out that in 1835, Dickens presented Catherine with a copy of the volume of *Lives of the English Poets* that contained Johnson's life of Richard Savage. By calling her attention to Savage's life, Dickens signaled a parallel between the poet's childhood miseries and his own. Slater's conclusion about the presentation to Catherine is similar to my own about his representation of David Copperfield: "Dickens wanted his Desdemona's pity for the perils he had passed but wanted also to conceal the sordid, inglorious nature of those perils" (3).

17. There are notable connections. For two twentieth-century understandings of these connections, see Edgar Johnson's *Charles Dickens: His Triumph and Tragedy* and Peter Ackroyd's *Dickens*, both of which return frequently and justifiably to *David Copperfield* and other novels to fill in details from Dickens's life.

18. See Burgis's edition, [lxxi].

# WORKS CITED

Ackroyd, Peter. *Dickens*. London: Sinclair-Stevenson, 1990.

Bodelsen, C. A. "The Physiognomy of the Name." *Review of English Literature* 2.3 (July 1961): 39–48.

Bottum, Joseph. "The Gentleman's True Name: *David Copperfield* and the Philosophy of Naming." *Nineteenth-Century Literature* 49 (1995): 435–55.

Brook, G. L. *The Language of Dickens*. London: André Deutsch, 1970.

de Laski, E. "The Psychological Attitude of Charles Dickens toward Surnames." *American Journal of Psychology* 29 (1918): 337–46.

Dickens, Charles. *David Copperfield*. Ed. Nina Burgis. Oxford: Clarendon, 1981.

Dickens, Charles. "Gone Astray." *The Works of Charles Dickens.* Vol. 18. New York: Bigelow, Brown and Co., n.d. 380–92.

Dyson, A. E. *The Inimitable Dickens.* London: Macmillan, 1970.

Forster, John. *The Life of Charles Dickens.* Ed. A. J. Hoppé. 2 vols. London: Dent, 1966.

Gordon, Elizabeth Hope. "The Naming of Characters in the Works of Charles Dickens." *University of Nebraska Studies in Language, Literature, and Criticism* 1 (1917): 3–35.

Harder, Kelsie B. "Charles Dickens Names his Characters." *Names* 7 (1959): 35–42.

Hawes, Donald. "David Copperfield's Names." *The Dickensian* 74 (1978): 81–87.

Hochman, Baruch, and Ilja Wachs. *Dickens: The Orphan Condition.* Madison, NJ: Fairleigh Dickinson UP, 1999.

Johnson, Edgar. *Charles Dickens: His Tragedy and Triumph.* 2 vols. New York: Simon and Schuster, 1952.

Jordan, John O. "The Social Sub-text of *David Copperfield.*" *Dickens Studies Annual* 14 (1985): 61–92.

Monod, Sylvère. *Dickens the Novelist.* Norman: U of Oklahoma P, 1968.

Slater, Michael. "How Dickens 'Told' Catherine about His Past." *The Dickensian* 75 (1979): 3–6.

Stevenson, Lionel. "Names in *Pickwick.*" *The Dickensian* 32 (1936): 241–44.

Stone, Harry. "What's in a Name: Fantasy and Calculation in Dickens." *Dickens Studies Annual* 14 (1985): 191–204.

Talbot, Norman. "The Naming and the Names of the Hero: A Study in *David Copperfield.*" *Southern Review* (Adelaide) 11 (1978): 267–82.

# The Names of David Copperfield

## *Richard Lettis*

*Dickens's concern for names may be seen in those chosen for the protag-
onist of his eighth novel, both by him and by most of the characters
in the work itself. In selecting David Copperfield, from a long list of
possibilities, Dickens invited comparison and contrast with the biblical
king, and may have linked his hero to several negative connotations;
he also associated his character with several qualities of the metal.
More importantly, he revealed, through the names his characters substitute for David Copperfield, the various qualities they saw or pretended
to see in him, in some cases using their nickname to achieve selfish
ends. These namings may be arranged in a moral order, from the loving
nickname given by the nurse Peggotty to the cold appelation of the
deadly stepfather, Murdstone. In some degree, it is in dealing with these
names lovingly bestowed or malignly forced upon him, that David comes
to realize his own identity.*

When God permitted Adam to name the beasts of the field, he gave man the
great gift of shaping reality to his own understanding; we came to call that,
among other things, art. Unless a new world is found, no one will ever
challenge Adam's designative accomplishment, but perhaps the artist who
has come the closest so far on earth is Charles John Huffam Dickens.

Names are important to all of us, but Dickens's life overflowed with them.
He always underscored his signature with a flourish of several lines. He gave
himself additional names: ''Boz,'' ''The Inimitable,'' ''T. Sparkler.'' He

*Dickens Studies Annual,* Volume 31, Copyright © 2002 by AMS Press, Inc. All
rights reserved.

named his ten children (his wife had no say in the matter), then devised
nicknames for them, working his way up to such extravagances as "Plornish-
maroontagoonter." And, as Donald Hawes tells us, "for sheer quantity and
exuberance of invention, Dickens's fictional names stand apart" (81). These
names, created with the help of actual names which, as Fred Kaplan shows,[1]
Dickens carefully collected, include some of the most famous cognomina in
literature: Scrooge, Miss Havisham, Little Nell, Oliver Twist, Samuel Pickwick, Fagin, Tiny Tim, Sam Weller—more unforgettable names, one may
think, than offered by any other artist since Adam.

Dickensian names, says Harry Stone, "are quintessential embodiments of
what one sees everywhere in his art, a fusion of the wild, the portentous, and
the fantastic with the rational and the everyday." Like all his work, a name
"distorts, intensifies, and transcends reality in order to be profoundly true to
reality" (203). But in *David Copperfield,* as several writers have argued,
Dickens improved his fictional names over those in preceding novels, where,
as Sylvère Monod says, names showed "awkwardness and hesitation"; now
there was a "greater certainty," a "masterly" creation of names. Instead of
distracting attention from the unity of the novel, as earlier naming had done,
the names now contributed to a unified whole.[2] Dickens learned from early
mistakes, Joseph Bottum suggests, such as Verisopht in *Nicholas Nickleby,* a
name that ceases to apply as the character improves.[3] In *David Copperfield*
there is, as Monod notes (301), but one weak name: Paragon, the too-obvi-
ously ironic designation for David and Dora's maid. Finally, as Bottum observes, Dickens's interest in names is, in *David Copperfield,* "translated into
the story. The characters themselves feel the tension of naming and explore
with the author what their names are for" (437).

Certainly, no work on a novel began with a more thorough search for and
testing of names than did Dickens's preparation for *David Copperfield.* "The
names were now the important thing," Peter Ackroyd says. "Without the
names, he could not begin" (557). John Forster said that Dickens had
"doubts" (6:vi, quoted by Hawes 82) as he began, but if the doubts included
names, it was owing only to the multitudes of possibilities from which he
had to choose. In his "eager search of names" (242), as Fred Kaplan puts
it, Dickens came up with many of his best-known: Micawber, Heep, Trotwood—and, of course, David Copperfield. And to underscore for us the
significance of these and other names in the novel, Dickens endowed some
of its characters with almost as much concern for each other's names as he
had taken in creating them. One notes the frequency of naming, for example.
Almost no one talks to the protagonist without addressing him by name—not

once, but many times: Uriah Heep twenty-two times in one scene, Betsey Trotwood nine times in four pages, along with less frequent but continual naming by Mr. Peggotty, Ham, Mr. Spenlow, Mr. and Mrs. Micawber, and Tommy Traddles. In addition to drawing our attention to names, this frequent usage focuses attention upon our hero (who in places is necessarily reduced to a narrative voice), and also shows what Dickens can do by *not* using names: Agnes rarely calls DC—which we will now call the protagonist, for economy and the easier distinguishing of his birth name from all the others we will consider—by name: she may say "Trotwood" once or twice in an extended conversation, but almost never more often. There are two reasons for this. First, Agnes must be the modest maiden of her time, and may fear that frequent addressing of a young man by name bespeaks a certain untoward familiarity. Second, Agnes loves DC but, unable to shower him with the sort of affectionate terms that Peggotty and his mother use (e.g., "Davy," "darling," "pet"), she neither names him often nor devises a special name for him, perhaps feeling that her love holds him within her precisely and entirely as he is, so that she need not, like the others, develop her own particularizing nickname. DC, failing to understand his own feelings for Agnes, has no such problem, and calls her more frequently by name than he does any other character—a nice irony, for though he appreciates Agnes and understands her goodness, it is not until the end of the story that he sees what "Agnes" really means to him.

The characters who frequently address DC by name also emphasize the importance of naming by giving him so many different appellations:[4] in *David Copperfield,* David Copperfield is almost never referred to as "David Copperfield"—"his name," as Dyson says, "presents problems from the start" (119). There are probably more substitute names for this hero than for any other fictional protagonist—so many, indeed, that one almost suspects a conspiracy to deprive him of his own name, and with it his own, complete, identity. If so, this is attempted, of course, with no universal maliciousness: many of the nicknames given are affectionate, even loving. But in the aggregate the effect is to replace what "David Copperfield" may mean with names that convey what others think DC to be or wish that he were, and though he rarely expresses resentment, and even enjoys and benefits from some of the substitutes (e. g., "Trotwood," with which Aunt Betsey adopts him), he is, it sometimes seems, in danger of losing his name, and his actual self, amidst the flood (so much so that Bottum is prompted to say that DC "must at last overcome every attempt to name him."[5] Seeing this phenomenon from the perspective of the other characters—who, as has been said, are by no means united in any wish to diminish him—the effect of the many names is an extension of the novel's opening question: it is uncertain not only whether DC is a hero, but whether he possesses, at least to those who know him, any consistent identity.

Like their creator (who, as we will see, mulled over several possibilities before choosing "David Copperfield"), the characters among them make up a list of other names, each picking one that he or she feels to be right—though rarely the one Dickens chose from the list of possible names he had made. Dickens once said that he felt himself to be merely writing down what he heard his characters say, and that often he could not control their actions; here he appears to record their disagreement with his choice of name for his fictional self. Certainly, at least, they desire to narrow DC down from all his name comes to entail, as we watch him grow, to some limited aspect with which they desire to be concerned. In the process, of course, Dickens conveys to the reader the many sides he has found in his protagonist's—and sometimes his own—nature, splitting DC not only in two, as with Jekyll and Hyde, but into many facets, leaving the reader to decide the validity and value of each namer's contribution, and to restore him to a whole before his story ends. Bottum, then, is not quite right in his assertion that DC is no more than "a victim of naming" (447).

Finally, some characters also attest to the importance of names by commenting on them: Betsey shrewdly assesses the sinister significance of the Murdstone name (though Victorian primness apparently forbids her to connect "Murd" with "merde"), and takes great exception to "Peggotty," insisting on calling DC's nurse "Barkis," instead (thus she reacts negatively to the names of perhaps the most hateful and the most loving characters in the novel). "It's a most extraordinary world," she says. "How this woman ever got into it with that name is unaccountable to me. It would be much more easy to be born a Jackson or something of that sort, one would think" (527).[6] As Dickens makes DC real for us by naming him, so Betsey Trotwood creates an illusory niece, Betsey Trotwood Copperfield, and often alludes to her as DC's "sister." (Betsey also assigns names to Mrs. Markleham and Dora.) Mr. Dick, on the other hand, eschews the reality of his actual name; his assumed one is an attempt to escape from the unhappy life of his former self (212–13). And Barkis is almost as fascinated by Peggotty's first name as Betsey is disgusted by her last. At first Barkis seems unconcerned about Peggotty's name: he proposes to her without even learning it. But when he attempts to inform her (through DC) that he awaits her answer, the necessity of calling her something occurs to him.

"You might tell her, if you would," said Mr. Barkis, with another slow look at me, "that Barkis was a-waitin' for a answer. Says you—what name is it?"

"Her name?"

"Ah!" said Mr. Barkis, with a nod of his head.

"Peggotty."

"Chrisen name? or nat'ral name?" said Mr. Barkis.

"Oh, it's not her Christian name. Her Christian name is Clara."

"Is it though?" said Mr. Barkis.

He seemed to find an immense fund of reflection in this circumstance, and sat pondering and inwardly whistling for some time.                                                      (114)

Half an hour later, Mr. Barkis wrote Peggotty's full name inside the tilt of his cart, "apparently as a private memorandum" (115). Dickens, we might note, has just done the same thing, as a public one. And, of course, all this fuss about Peggotty's name adds weight to her role in the novel, just as the many names given DC focus our attention upon him.

Littimer's name is also commented upon. The fact that "no one knew his Christian name" (314) helps make this odious servant of Steerforth appear, as DC thinks, the more reputable because there is no first name to object to: "Peter might have been hanged, or Tom transported, but Littimer was perfectly respectable" because, DC adds, of "the reverend nature of respectability in the abstract," which makes DC feel "particularly young in this man's presence." Indeed, Littimer always produces this effect: he calls DC "young innocence," and in one scene, a nod from him is interpreted by DC as "but you're young" (706). All this has implications well beyond our present concern, but if DC has come to think of first names as a handicap, he may have done so because by this point he prefers his last name to his first. "David" was his father's name before it became his, and, in addition to the possible desire to distance himself from his father (of which we will soon speak), DC as teenager is ready to break away from all parentage and be on his own. Adult males in his world are all addressed by their surnames, so at about this time in the novel most men begin to call him "Copperfield" (and those who do not almost never call him "David"; as A. E. Dyson [119] notes, few people who really like him ever do). Aunt Betsey has replaced "David" with "Trotwood," and he and almost everyone else seem to prefer it. Perhaps it is worth noting that Dickens, though he did not dislike his own first name—it was not his father's, and he passed it on to his first son—never used the two middle names his parents chose for him, and never forgave them for doing so. The first of these two names *was*, of course, his father's.[7] We may note, too, that in his letters, as Butt and Tillotson[8] confirm, Dickens never mentioned his hero's first name: except for public utterance, as in the Preface to the Charles Dickens Edition of 1867, it is then and later always "Copperfield." In leaving "David" behind, then, DC actually joins those in the novel who would alter his name; it seems that Dickens cannot even control his own fictional stand-in. But then he seems in his earlier novels not to have cared greatly for "David": Hawes points out that he gave it to Cheerybles' butler, to a gravedigger in *The Old Curiosity Shop,* and to the wicked Montague Tigg's associate in *Martin Chuzzlewit.* "David was not a popular name in England in 1850." (33–34) Hawes adds, because of its associations with Scotland and Wales. Is it possible then that "David" is a counterbalance to Dickens's unconscious linking of himself to DC by his reversed initials—an equally unconscious effort to create a distance? In any case, there seems room for the idea—at least the conjecture—that Dickens chose "David" partly for its negative associations and connotations.

*Does* DC resent having his father's name, as Dickens seems to have done? DC's father died before he was born, and cannot have alienated his son as John Dickens did his. But if DC does not dislike his father, he does have reason to desire separating himself from his memory. All sons do to some extent, of course—it is a part of growing up, and surely many a "Junior" wishes that he had his own individualizing first name. The title of this novel tells us that DC is David Copperfield "the Younger," which is to emphasize that his name was not so much given to him as duplicated in him. (The title also points to one of the novel's themes: DC has trouble throughout in convincing himself that he is ever older.) The early pages show DC carrying this burden. His name has gone before him, in two senses: someone before his birth possessed his name, and that someone is now gone, leaving him an appellation to which particular identity has already been attached (e.g., by Betsey Trotwood) before he can begin his own affixing. And the inherited identity is in good part negative, as Betsey characterizes it. It is not surprising then that DC never calls himself "Junior" in the novel: his legacy is a name that has been sneered at, and that only his helpless mother weakly defends. Omitting pronouns, the first two things DC calls himself in the novel are "posthumous child" (2) and "fatherless little stranger" (4).

Many things both in and outside *David Copperfield,* then, urge us to consider its hero's numerous names carefully. (We should note that it is not DC alone who bears multiple names in his novel: Joseph Bottum lists thirteen others who have two or more (435). To begin, how did Dickens decide upon "David Copperfield"? It took him a long time to settle upon that name: he started with Thomas Mag (Monod, 278) (the novel to be called *Mag's Diversions*), then changed to David Mag, either of them to be of Blunderstone House, though this was for a while changed to "Copperfield House." Perhaps the "D" of David and the "C" of Copperfield caught his ear (though not his consciousness, as we will soon see), for he soon moved on to David Copperfield, having also considered "Wellbury," "Magbury," "Topflower," "Copperboy," and "Copperstone." (Mag was wisely saved for Abel Magwitch of *Great Expectations;* "to magg" at that time meant "to pilfer," though it also could mean "to trick or frolic"[9]—neither was right for DC); he probably also decided that "Diversions" was too light and easy a word for his novel. But why did he choose "David Copperfield" over the others on the list? If he fixed on the name "Murdstone" for DC's first enemy before deciding on "Copperfield," he may have felt that "stone" (and the other names that had death in them, like "Wellbury" and "Magbury") would link his hero too closely to the deadly stepfather.[10] (As it is, "Murdstone" makes a nice contrast to "Copperfield": the latter contains a metal of value and an area where things grow, the former a mineral of death, murder, and defecation. But Dickens did also put "stone"—he liked the word, and used it in the names of characters in other novels—into the name of DC's birthsite, possibly to infuse a touch of mortality into the place where both parents and DC's half-sibling die.) "Topflower" placed too much emphasis on one aspect of DC's nature, that which Steerforth was to identify by his nickname for DC; "Copperboy" was also too limited for the adult protagonist of the latter part of the novel. Then, too, the name Dickens picked is certainly more euphonious than any of the other choices, with its five vowel and seven consonant sounds, the three solid "d's" opening, dividing, and closing the whole. And, as his friend John Forster pointed out, to Dickens's initial surprise, the name supplied his own initials, reversed ("Charles Copperfield" had been one of his early considerations [(278)], doubtless abandoned as too blatant a hint of autobiography). Fred Kaplan says that, "Soon after beginning (the novel), he confessed that he had stuck to that fictional name throughout the exploration of alternatives because he had, even at the earliest stage, recognized that he was writing about himself—'Why else should I so obstinately have kept to that name when once it turned up?' Dickens said" (243). But another important reason for choosing "David Copperfield" lay in the several significances Dickens surely found in his final choice. In selecting "David," he must have at least thought of the great Hebraic king; Hawes says that "for all, or nearly all of his principal characters, . . . he extracted his 'Christian names' from the Bible" (84). Possibly the royal association hinted at an answer to the novel's opening question of whether the protagonist is or is not the hero of his story. In the novel, Mr. Dick and Barkis would seem to agree with the positive answer: Mr. Dick calls David "Phoebus" (213) and Barkis calls him "a young Roeshus,"[11] by which, DC says, "I think he meant prodigy" (156). Mr. Dick's usual innate genius—which is probably why he is called "Dick"—selects the better name: "Phoebus" offers the word-play of "sun-son," and alludes to David's creative capacity. While the differences between the Biblical figure and the English orphan are obvious—the young shepherd needed no Micawber to vanquish his enemy; he tainted his own great name, etc.—the two are alike in a surprising number of ways: both are writers, are threatened by a father figure, rise from humble to high positions; form strong friendships; deal with a sexual rival named "Uriah"; smite their foes, and triumph over them. Probably Dickens did not know that "David" in Hebrew means "beloved"—he disliked the Old Testament, and at the time of writing *David Copperfield* his anti-Semitism was in full force—but the definition is fortuitous, as is the fact that some legends of King David show him vitally concerned with understanding his own nature.[12] Hawes finds attempts to compare the biblical and Dickensian Davids "far-fetched" (84), and perhaps he is right, though it is interesting to consider that Dickens may have played with altering the David-Uriah story to his own use, making the Bible's innocent victim into the nineteenth-century aggressor, replacing the simple David-Jonathan relationship with the more complex David and Steerforth pairing, and changing David from a lustful peeping Tom into a man who cannot recognize the woman he loves until the end of the story.

"Copperfield" also offers interesting possibilities. "Copper" has several meanings, the most useful of which may be "coin"[13] and "container": DC is an item of value, and he contains all that he pours out in his great narrative. We cannot know whether Dickens was aware of the properties of the metal, but some are pertinent: copper is an "excellent conductor" (DC conveys his story to all generations), and it is "corrosion resistant" (unlike King David, DC, despite his guilty feelings about several misdoings, remains relatively untarnished). Hawes points out that the metal is "malleable" and, as opposed to "gold" or "silver," suggests "a fitting plainness and honesty" (83). Even the slang use of "copper" (policeman, from "cop: to seize") is appropriate, for though DC arrests no one, he is, as the title of the second chapter notes, a talented observer—a detective's best quality—and he sees and seizes for his story all the people and the actions of his life; the word "Observation" was included in the title Dickens originally decided upon. "Field," of course, as Salinger uses it in "Holden Caulfield," simply tells us that DC is the place in which all these qualities exist—and some, in DC, grow. (It may also be worth noting that in Holden's last name, Salinger uses "caul"; DC is born with a caul.) Monod aptly suggests that "field" connects Agnes to David—but also that "Wick" connects her to Dickens himself, since Pickwick was the name of his first great character,[14] an idea which must be somewhat weakened by the fact that, as Harry Stone (191) mentions, Dickens considered "Pick," "Wick," "Flick," and "Flicks" for the repulsive Spottletoe of *Martin Chuzzlewit.*

"David Copperfield," then, would seem an appropriate name for Dickens's hero, but as has been said, many characters in the novel disagree, and DC sometimes has to struggle to retain his name. The first time we see him taken from the safety of his own home, by Mr. Murdstone as he visits friends, DC has his first alias thrust upon him.

> "And who's this shaver?" said one of the gentlemen, taking hold of me.
> "That's Davy," returned Mr. Murdstone.
> "Davy who?" said the gentleman. "Jones?" (24)

This is merely a joke, but its connotations are grave,[15] and it starts the long list of substitute names for DC. It is followed at once by a second alias, the clearly more serious "Brooks of Sheffield," which Murdstone uses so he and his friends can talk about DC without his understanding them. Soon they compound the offense by obliging DC to drink "Confusion to Brooks of Sheffield" (25); confusion is certainly what he gets. The episode, Dyson says, "sets up echoes through much of the tale" (121).

The "Brooks" alias is a conventional English term used to avoid speaking an actual name, but "Sheffield" may also have suggested itself to Murdstone because of the association with honed steel: he has just said that DC is "sharp." The name appears again later as it helps to introduce the worst incident in DC's (and Dickens's) life: the wine (or blacking) warehouse period. In this scene Murdstone's friend, Mr. Quinion, jocularly addresses DC as "Brooks," and DC tries to insist upon his own name. Quinion persists with "Brooks," and the conversation leads to his offer to procure the degrading employment for DC—the worst assault on his sense of self-worth (especially in terms of social status) in the novel. Elsewhere, Murdstone also attacks DC's identity by giving the name "Master Murdstone" (69) when he prepays for DC's meal at an inn. Little wonder that, when DC escapes to his Aunt Betsey and she tries to shoo him away, he responds by declaring, for one of the few times in the novel, his full name: "I am David Copperfield, of Blunderstone, Suffolk" (202). He sounds like another young artist, Stephen Dedalus, who tried to assert his identity not only by name but by school, county, country, continent, world, and universe.

As has been noted, DC is not often called "David." Monod properly says that "Practically every character has his or her own way of addressing him," (302) but though these ways often include "Copperfield," they almost never use "David," except in the form of nickname (more evidence that "David" is not a well-liked name). DC is "Mas'r Davy" to Mr. Peggotty and to Ham, and "Master Davy" to Peggotty (when he is not "my pretty poppet," "my pet," "my precious," or "my life"; years after their long separation, DC, though now a man, is still her "darling boy"); Dyson points out that the "Mas'r" of the two men differs from Peggotty's in giving "a kind of added breeziness" (119) to their address, and also that both are important to DC in confirming his social status. To his mother, Clara, DC is also "Davy"—though only a few times— and an assortment of endearments: "dear boy," "precious treasure," "her own boy," and, significantly, as she is dying, "my fatherless boy," her admission that she had got a husband for herself but not a father for her son. Except for the Murdstones (whom we will soon discuss), and Steerforth (once), DC is called "David" only incidentally—by a worker at the blacking warehouse (172), and by Mrs. Markleham (691), for example. Mrs. Markleham condescendingly calls her son-in-law's employee by his first name (instead of "Mr. Copperfield," as Mrs. Micawber properly does), but the warehouseman is one of the few people in the novel to use "David" in friendly fashion—"when we were very confidential," DC explains. But DC is also called "little gent" there, which in this instance is an ironic reference to his gentlemanly pretensions, and, as Bottum suggests, "maintains a space around David" (441).

The simple use of "David" or "Davy" sometimes tells us something about the user. Murdstone calls DC "Davy boy" twice—once in the first "Brooks" scene, as he pretends to some familiarity with his stepson before his friends (and so Dickens can use the "Jones" joke), and once to please Clara (45)—but otherwise calls him only "David" in a cold and formal manner. Bottum calls this merely "disheartening" (437), but surely it is much more than that. For Dyson it is a "sinister use, measured and cruel, and intended to degrade [DC] like a dog" (120); Hawes sees it as an attempt to "emphasize to David and his mother that David is a boy and not a baby" (81). Surely it also supplies further evidence that the name is unsavory, and no doubt helps DC to welcome another first name. (Bad as this is, however, Jane Murdstone's refusal to give him a name at all is worse: for her DC is "boy"—a common, not a proper, noun.) As Dyson says, Murdstone tries to affix his last name to DC, but this "fails to stick—perhaps because Murdstone hates the thought of his face too much by now to persevere" (121).

Steerforth also calls DC "David" on one occasion. When he shows some anticipatory regret for his coming seduction of Emily, Steerforth drops his usual gay nickname for DC and calls him, more seriously, "David" (338); as he recovers his careless mood he reverts to the lighter name again. When Miss Murdstone encounters DC as a man, she calls him only "David Copperfield," as cold and formal as her brother's "David" was to the boy, and denying him the title of "Mr.," as Bottum points out (442). It is ironic that when someone finally gives DC his complete name, it is in an offensive tone.

It is worth pausing for a moment to consider the ongoing use of "boy," as applied to DC. Given lovingly by the two Claras, as we have seen, the word takes on another tone when employed by Miss Murdstone: it is the only thing she calls him (until she meets him as an adult), and it seems to be the worst name she can think of for anyone (perhaps the idea is that spinsters "don't like boys," as she says, because they grow up to be the men who do not propose). When Aunt Betsey first encounters DC, she holds the same negative opinion—"No boys here" (202) she cries—for her wretched marriage has left her with a Havisham-like abhorrence of males (perhaps she associates donkeys with men?). But hatred is not in her true nature, as it is in Miss Murdstone's, and that same night as she watches him sleeping she calls him "pretty fellow," "poor fellow," and "the child" (208). Before Betsey, Mr. Mell had, at Salem House, called DC "new boy," (82) with far less harsh connotation than Miss Murdstone's, though the adjective still makes it hardly an enviable designation. "Boy" recovers something of its better flavor when DC becomes "head boy" at his school (283)—which is also an indication that DC will not be a boy much longer: the next time he is called so it is by Miss Larkin, for whom he is a "bold boy" (285) for evincing his sexual interest in her. This has been foreshadowed by a scene in which Emily called DC a "silly boy" (155) when his feelings for her began to change. In his adult years, DC is occasionally called "boy," but always affectionately—by Traddles, for example ("my dear boy" [816]), and by Dora, even when DC is her "naughty boy" (572). Dora, however, as we will see, has more in mind than affection. Except for Dora (partly), such characters are the antitheses of both Miss Murdstone (they *like* the boy in DC, and hang on to it), and of Uriah Heep, who (like Dora, but worse) has selfish reasons for wanting DC to remain young.

No doubt it has been noticed in all of this that the names given to DC by the characters in his story usually tell us (at least) two things: something about DC himself, as Hawes has said (87), and something about the person who bestows the name upon him. It is possible to see these names in a kind of pattern, roughly ranging from the best and most loving (Peggotty's) to those which mix love and selfish intent, and ending with those designed to reduce DC for the benefit of the namer (the worst of these perhaps a toss-up between Murdstone and Uriah Heep). The pattern shows that Bottum oversimplifies when he argues that it is only "the villains" in *David Copperfield* who use names ("language") to "abuse," (442) for some characters high on the list also name DC to their advantage and not his. (Bottum's mention of villains in this regard, however, supports the idea of such a morally-oriented list.) This ordering of characters by the names they use for DC will for the most part simply support the understanding we have of them through their actions and conversation, but it will also, it is hoped, demonstrate how carefully Dickens employed these namings to emphasize their individual relations to DC. There will be difference of opinion about who goes exactly where in the pattern, but let us make a beginning.

Peggotty, as I have suggested, tops the list.[16] Perhaps DC's mother loves him just as much, but surely not as well, for her love is tainted by the selfishness she shows in taking a husband, a thing Peggotty will not do until she is certain Barkis will not interfere with her attentions to her boy. Aunt Betsey also deserves consideration here, but it takes her some time to come to love David, while Peggotty loves him always, and without reservation. It is appropriate, then, that Peggotty's nickname for DC—the simple and unvarying "Davy"—in no way attempts to change, limit, or appropriate him: its expression of affection and closeness is all she desires. (And though it is close, it is not the possibly disliked "David.") The only gap between them is the social one, which as Bottum mentions is indicated by her "Master" to him and his titleless "Peggotty" to her (440).

Peggotty's own given name, Clara, is the same as DC's mother's, surely done to suggest to us that both are one as mothers to David. But Clara Copperfield, though she calls her son by many affectionate appellations, does not find a steady nickname for him, neither one that could show her easy intimacy and affection, as with Peggotty (as said, Clara uses Peggotty's "Davy," infrequently), nor one that could suggest any insight into his character. Dyson helpfully suggests that "after her second marriage, . . . 'Davy' is always edged with reproach or fear" (119). No doubt Clara loves her son, but the implication is that she loves herself more, and cannot possess him by the naming of names.

As we have seen, Aunt Betsey comes close to rivalling Dickens in the matter of names; like him, as Monod says, she is "keenly alive to the subtle relationship between sounds and ideas or feelings."[17] In addition to what has already been said, she beats out the field by naming DC prenatally: "Before his birth," A. E. Dyson reminds us, "David is Betsey Trotwood Copperfield."[18] Depriving DC of his name and even his sex (and setting the pattern for all who would alter DC to their own liking), Aunt Betsey makes a poor beginning for a fairytale figure, made worse when she abandons him and his mother when he disappoints her. But she later learns to love him deeply, and though she hangs on to her dream of him as her female namesake by calling him "Trotwood," this, as affection increases, shortens to the endearing "Trot." "Trotwood"—her last name—suits her, of course: a busy, active woman, nemesis of donkeys, she would trot, not walk, through life. By giving her name to David perhaps she not only marks her love for him but hopes to instill in him something of her energetic nature (which not a few scenes suggest he could use; here is one of the major differences between DC and his maker); she not infrequently urges him to action. If so, she is partly successful, for though DC is never aggressive in personal relations, he does become a hard-working writer (*like* his maker). As Barkis signals his attempt to possess Peggotty by writing down her first name, so Aunt Betsey takes possession of DC by having "Trotwood" sewn into his clothes. Perhaps the love all this reveals should rank Betsey above DC's mother, but I place her third because she is the first (on our list) to give DC a name that clearly serves her own purpose: as said, it is as close as she can come to her wish that he were his sister. It is interesting to note that, as we will see, she shares the wish for femininity with Steerforth (but one of several connections between characters made by naming, as the reader will perceive), though, of course, for quite a different reason: since Betsey's bad marriage has set her against men, it is only slowly that she can accept the fact that DC is both male and good, a change she signals by calling DC "my nephew" and "my grandnephew" (232). "Trotwood" becomes Agnes's (and Dr. Strong's and Mr. Dick's) name for DC. For the reasons suggested above, I believe, "David" is all but left behind, even though DC does use "David" as his first name for his published works, as we learn from Micawber's public letter at the end of chapter 63.

Perhaps next in line on our tentative love-hate scale for naming DC is Dora, too much like DC's mother to care for him as Peggotty and Betsey do, but loving him as much as her nature allows. Her nickname for him is "Doady," which Dawes (86) says is a corruption of "dote," also then spelled "doat," as it is in chapter 41. The name is not merely "cloying," as Bottum (437) says, but, as DC himself sees, "a corruption of David." (633) On one level it may be as "innocent" as Dyson claims—"a beautiful instance . . . of Dora's love, tenderness, and unfitness for life" (126)—but it also indicates that she would see him as a kind of upgraded pet, a humanized Jip (her dog; this is one of several connections DC has to canines in the story). "Doady" reduces David—who, again, as much else in the novel shows, is struggling to convince himself that he is an adult—to an acceptable place in her small and girlish world: a Doady could never, for example, oblige Dora to learn how to manage a household, as DC ineffectually tries to do.

Like Dora, Steerforth devises an affectionate name for DC—"Daisy"—but with much more complex effects. Though Bottum finds it merely "diminishing" (437), the nickname actually points to two, fairly distinct, qualities Steerforth would find in DC. The first is complimentary, of course: "Daisy" is an English colloquialism meaning "tops," or "of high quality." This is Steerforth's ostensible intention: he likes DC, and gives him an approving nickname. But the appellation is a rather suspicious exaggeration: there is little to suggest that Steerforth really considers DC to be superior, and so the name seems slightly mocking, however affectionately it may be intended. The second implication, though, is clearly darker: "Daisy" is also a woman's name, and, as Dora's "Doady" deprives DC of his maturity, so "Daisy" would rob him of his masculinity: Dyson points out that Steerforth applies it to DC only when he is an adult (122). In contrast to his first meaning of "Daisy," Steerforth's intention here is unambiguous, for he has wishfully feminized his friend early on in their relationship (93), saying that he hopes DC had a sister just like him, one he (Steerforth) could get to know, presumably as he comes to "know" Emily. It is possible that Dickens indicates here a latent homoerotic impulse in Steerforth—not at all uncommon in English schools; in any case, the feminization is appropriate in the broader sense of desire to use, as a man may "use" a woman to her sorrow, for Steerforth puts David to bad use, disastrous to those he loves, and therefore painful to him.

Rosa Dartle makes the feminine implications of "Daisy" clear when she asks DC why Steerforth uses it—"because he thinks you young and innocent?" (313). Of course, she knows quite well this is the case, and is snipping at DC: she joins the rather long list of those who would see him as young and feminine (not even Victorian males considered it manly to be naïve). DC blushes to admit to Rosa the interpretation of girlishness (thereby confirming it verbally and physically), and declares it to himself shortly thereafter: Steerforth "had a way of treating me like a plaything" (316)—which, of course, is the way he treated Emily. Like many others who characterize DC by their nicknames, Steerforth is certainly right about DC's innocence (if not his lack of manliness), as his victimization by such individuals as the waiter at the inn and Mrs. Crupp demonstrate. But Dickens also suggests that youth and innocence in a young man are not entirely negative qualities: several people call DC "child" and "boy" and "young'un" to the end of the novel, with positive implications. On one occasion, even Steerforth defines "Daisy" as something more than hyperbolic affection and feminization. During the period in which he is seducing Emily, he calls DC by the nickname, and then explains, "for though that's not the name your godfather and godmother gave you, it's the name I like best to call you by—and I wish, I wish, I wish you could give it to me" (458). If Daisy for Steerforth is usually a girl-like plaything, at times he is also a man whose innocence is to be envied. (And we remember that Dickens thought of naming his hero "Topflower.") Still worse than Steerforth, though, is his mother, who, as Dyson says, would deprive DC of his name (124), which she claims to have forgotten since the last time her son mentioned it to her.

As Betsey is the first to change DC's name partly for her own purposes, so Steerforth is the last to do so partly out of affection; after him, we dip into those characters who name DC solely to victimize him. His landlady, who wrings every penny she can from her tenant, calls him "Mister Copperfull"—"first, no doubt," DC explains, "because it was not my name; and secondly, I am inclined to think, in some indistinct association with a washing day" (419). The explanation is pertinent—it is one more instance of someone depriving DC of his name; and Dickens liked to use washing women to put men in their place (think of Mrs. MacStinger, Captain Cuttle's landlady in *Dombey and Son*)—but clearly the name has other meanings, as well. Dyson thinks of it as merely "the nearest concession to his identity she can make" (124), but actually it is a doubly ingenious appellation since, as we have seen, "copper" can mean both penny and pot: if his innocence is abused enough, "Copperfull" can be a copper full of coppers for Mrs. Crupp. It is not clear why the mature DC settles for the partial explanation—perhaps so we may "get it" on our own (Dickens did not like to spell things out for his reader), perhaps because Dickens wants us still to see innocence in the adult DC.

Uriah Heep is, of course, candidate for the worst namer of DC, though his appellation is merely the apparently inoffensive "Master," used before DC's last name. Mr. and Mrs. Micawber also call DC "Master," but only when he is a child; as we have heard Dyson say, Peggotty uses it to recognize DC's social status (123). But Uriah hangs on to the word into DC's adulthood, for, unlike Miss Murdstone's negative and Traddles's positive thoughts about DC as a youth, he wants to keep DC young, and calls him "Master" Copperfield almost to the end of the story, because as a minor DC could neither aspire to the love of Agnes nor rival Uriah in Wickfield's business. (Jack Maldon, by comparison and contrast, wishes to make Dr. Strong appear too ancient to seem an appropriate mate for Annie, and so repeatedly calls him "the old doctor" [243].) Several critics have wondered why DC hates Heep so much, and have offered such reasons as class snobbishness; perhaps, but surely the strongest reason is that Uriah attacks DC at the very point at which he is now most vulnerable: his great difficulty in believing himself to be an adult.

One would expect Uriah to call DC "Master" in front of the Wickfields, to impress them with DC's juvenile nature, but in fact he does this most of the time when he and DC are alone. Before Aunt Betsey he addresses DC as "Mister"—though he soon falls back on "Master," almost as much it seems by habit as for any useful purpose. Probably Uriah's intention is not so much to make others think of DC as a child as to make him think so himself—DC is certainly pregnable to the idea—but one suspects as well that the usage may also be a kind of comic vocal wishing. In any case, as with Steerforth's use of "Daisy" to mark DC's innocence, Uriah is not far wrong in seeing DC as young and rather helpless: we have already noted how several other characters join Heep in undermining DC's shaky struggle to think of himself as an adult (and certainly much else in the novel other than naming does the same). When he is addressed by a porter as "T. Copperfield, Esquire," DC says, "I told him I was T. Copperfield, Esq., and he believed it" (243; note DC gladly accepts the "T"—for "Trotwood.") Aunt Betsey and a few others help DC here: she once calls him "boy" when he is grown but immediately corrects herself: "I suppose I must say 'young man' now" (537; see also Dr. Strong, 548).

Upon occasion, Heep affords DC his last name without the "Master" (he never calls him "David"). But the surname does not in his mouth convey the easy familiarity usually intended between men at that time (women, of course, call DC "Mr. Copperfield"). The usage occurs three times: first, after DC has struck him for having involved DC in the problems of Dr. Strong and Annie; second, in the scene of Heep's exposure; and third, when DC encounters him in jail. In the first two scenes, DC is too clearly acting as adult (and, *pace* Steerforth, male) to be called "Master," and by the third there is no longer need for the ruse—except possibly to hurt him, which Uriah attempts more cleverly through his reacquired humility: instead of being a child, DC is now, in contrast to the "reformed" Uriah, a corrupt adult.

Perhaps Heep belongs at the bottom of our list, the naming character who most hates and threatens the happiness of DC. But surely a close second to, if not rival of, Uriah for this honor is Mr. Murdstone. Uriah has an understandable self-interest at work in his opposition to DC, whom he fears as sexual and business rival; Murdstone has, it would seem, only the lion's brutal desire to rid himself of the cubs of the previous king of the pride. (Even his sister's malevolence is somewhat more understandable: as we have noticed, nineteenth-century spinsters were supposed not to like boys.) As Butt and Tillotson say, she merely dislikes DC, while her brother resents "his very existence" (xxxvii). Without ever actually using the word, Murdstone calls DC a dog, and, as Hawes (88) reminds us, has him so labeled at school; the significance of the only nickname he gives DC comes not from the name itself—it tells us something about Murdstone, but nothing about DC—but from its cruel intention to speak about DC's mother without his understanding. The scene is the more painful because DC is indeed, as Murdstone says, sharp, at least enough to sense uneasily that something he would not like is being said, and that he cannot know what it is. And it is Murdstone, not Heep, who in the next scene involving the "Brooks" nickname plays fictional counterpart to Dickens's own father as he dooms DC, like Dickens, to his worst experience, the hated warehouse. Dickens had just finished a portrait of this kind of father in Dombey of the preceding novel, but Dombey has a change of heart, while Murdstone remains a walking symbol of feces and the sepulcher to the end of the tale. The first cause of an alias forced upon DC, he is also the worst.[19]

In his story, David Copperfield's two great triumphs are his success in his profession and his discovery of his love for Agnes Wickfield. But rather little is made of the former, and the latter is accomplished only in the last few pages of the story. Throughout the novel, however, David both suffers and profits (the two experiences of most heroes) from the many names he is given, and it is surely a third triumph that though some of the names are derogatory (one of his victimizers calls him "sixpenn'orth of bad ha'pence" [188], the only one to make him a worthless copper), the majority are, even when they imply some defect, expressive of attachment. J. Hillis Miller remarks that "the center of David's life . . . is the search for some relationship to another person who will support his life, fill up the emptiness within him, and give him a substantial identity" (156–57; quoted by Hawes, 81). With all respect to Agnes, David has also searched for his identity by working his way through the names with which others would identify him, rejecting some and accepting others. The derogatory association with his father's failings is far behind; the disturbing "David" has been almost entirely replaced with the more positively connotative "Trotwood" of Betsey and Agnes, and the man of many appellations knows who he is, and possesses his name.

# NOTES

1. *Charles Dickens' Book of Memoranda.* Kaplan notes that names used in several novels are to be found in the parish register of St. Andrew's Church, Holborn, and that Dickens would have known these names when he resided there, if not by personal contact then by seeing them in "shops, gates, and houses" (82: the quotation is taken from a 1912 newspaper clipping). But, of course, Dickens collected names all his life, as Peter Ackroyd illustrates: "In the petty cash book of Ellis and Blackmore (the law office in which Dickens briefly worked) there are such names as Weller, Mrs. Bardell, Corney, Rudge, and Newman Knott," 118. The twentieth and twenty-first centuries frequently attest to the enduring appeal of Dickensian names by employing them for various purposes: a kind of trout is called "Dolly Varden" (from *Barnaby Rudge*), and a current magician bills himself as "David Copperfield."
2. Sylvère Monod 301. But see also Harry Stone, who argues that in all his names Dickens strove both to reveal and conceal (191ff.).
3. 436; Bottum suggests that Dickens was forced by his first-person narration to choose names more carefully, but admits that this is not borne out by Esther Summerson in *Bleak House*. A better explanation, I believe, is that the autobiographical nature of *David Copperfield* prompted Dickens to work out his names more precisely, just as he did in the partly autobiographical *Great Expectations*.
4. For other Dickens characters with multiple names, see Stone 193–94.
5. 437; Bottum argues that DC must even overcome Betsey's "Trotwood" in order to "reclaim his usurped patrimony," but I see no resistance on his part to that name, and the two people he loves best—Betsey and Agnes—call him by it to the end of the story.
6. All references are to The Modern Library Edition (New York: Random House, 1950); for the use of "little" to augment the meaning of names, see Monod, 335ff.
7. Dickens's resentment of his mother is better known than his animosity toward his father, but even before the aging John Dickens annoyed his son by attempting to profit from his fame, Charles had held him almost equally responsible for sending him to the blacking warehouse; for more on the subject of Dickens and his father, see Ackroyd 2, 13. Ackroyd points out that Dickens in part identified with his father, as well (see also 117), which may explain why some of DC's qualities are comparable to those Betsey finds in David Copperfield, Sr.

8. xlvii. Butt and Tillotson also are critical of David Copperfield, Sr. (xv), and mention an incident in which Dickens "had spoken with undue harshness of his father . . . " (xxi).

9. Butt xxiv; Dickens had previously used "Mag" in a piece in *Household Words* *("Our Vestry"),* and would use it again in "Magson" of his Christmas story, "Going into High Society," in 1858; "Magwitch" was also on the list of title names made in 1849 for *David Copperfield.*

10. Dickens first thought of "Harden" for Murdstone, which could have left "Copperstone" as a consideration until he settled on the final name; "Harden" is also on the list made in 1849, but was never used. Butt and Tillotson show that Dickens did change some names in the course of his writing (xxvi), but Murdstone is not included in their examples. Dickens found "Blundeston" on a signpost near Yarmouth, which he visited for background for the Peggotty family's part of the story. The change to "Blunderstone" was apt: both David Sr. and Jr. can blunder, and "stone" was, as mentioned, both apposite and a favorite with Dickens.

11. The name is a corruption of "Roscius," the Roman comic actor. Barkis probably would not have known Roman performers, but apparently did hear of William Henry West Betty, an early nineteenth-century actor called the "Young Roscius." DC is not performing in the scene: Barkis seems to be simply picking out a complimentary famous name.

12. See Groopman 47.

13. "Copperboy," which we remember was considered for DC, confirms the sense of "coin" in "copper," for "boy" could mean "penny." "Mag," another of Dickens's choices, also could mean "copper half-penny," as Hawes tells us (83).

14. 302–03; Hawes adds to the meanings of "field" the "air of normality" it gives DC, since it is so common in English names. (83)

15. Because "Davy Jones' Locker" is a watery grave.

16. I do not put Agnes in the list for reasons given above (3). Micawber gives DC no special name, though perhaps his constant "Copperfield" is not only the usual appellation for an adult male but also, as Bottum suggests (440), helps him feel that DC is "someone for whom he need not be responsible." If so, this forms an interesting comparison/contrast to Heep's use of "Master." And surely any desire of Micawber's to relieve hmself of responsibility is balanced by the support the name gives to DC's struggle to think of himself as adult.

17. 301: Monod points out that Betsey gives names to Murdstone, Jane Murdstone, Peggotty, Mrs. Markleham, and Dora.

18. 119; Dyson supports my placing Betsey third on the list by saying she is "the very kindest of the novel's non-innocents" (124).

19. Stone perceptively notes that Murdstone's name connects him with DC's father, represented to the protagonist only by the gravestone he can see through his bedroom window. Stone adds much more on this connection (195).

# WORKS CITED

Ackroyd, Peter. *Dickens*. New York: HarperCollins, 1990.

Bottum, Joseph. *"The Gentleman's True Name: David Copperfield* and the Philosophy of Naming." *Nineteenth-Century Literature,* 49 (1993): 435–55.

Butt, John, and Kathleen Tillotson. "Introduction" to the Clarendon Edition of *David Copperfield.* Oxford: Oxford UP, 1981.

Dickens, Charles. *David Copperfield.* New York: Random House (Modern Library ed.), 1950.

Dyson, A. E. *The Inimitable Dickens.* London: Macmillan, 1970.

Groopman, Jerome. "Decoding Destiny," *The New Yorker* (2/9/98): 47.

Hawes, Donald. "David Copperfield's Names." *The Dickensian* No. 385; vol.74, part 2.

Kaplan, Fred. *Charles Dickens' Book of Memoranda.* New York: The New York Public Library, 1981.

———. *Dickens* New York: William Morrow, 1988.

Miller, J. Hillis. *Charles Dickens: The World of His Novels.* Cambridge, MA: Harvard UP, 1958.

Monod, Sylvère. *Dickens the Novelist.* Norman, Oklahoma: U of Oklahoma P, 1968.

Stone, Harry. "What's in a Name: Fantasy and Calculation in Dickens." *Dickens Studies Annual,* 14 (1985): 81–87.

# Dickens's Favorite Child: Malthusian Sexual Economy and the Anxiety over Reproduction in *David Copperfield*

*Eric Berlatsky*

*Numerous* Copperfield *critics have observed how David's sexual desires are directed inappropriately (in Victorian terms) towards incestuous/ sisterly, homosexual, and other somehow inappropriate targets. Simon Edwards further shows how these dangerous sexual desires are "repressed," "disciplined," and twisted into a viable, acceptable, middle-class, heterosexual relationship with Agnes. This assessment of the novel as a reflection of the Victorian need to repress "deviant" sexuality and replace it with a normative heterosexual reproductive substitute is common in Dickens criticism, but it is one which underplays contemporary discourses that worked not only to repress "deviant" sexuality, but also reproductive sexuality. While eighteenth-century sexual discourses often did repress any mode of sexuality that did not lead to reproduction, by 1850 the concurrent discourses of Malthusianism were simultaneously working to discourage the practice of reproductive sexuality as well. While* David Copperfield *may then discipline or "repress" deviant sexual practices, it also encodes fears of reproductivity and reflects Malthusian concerns about the dangers of reproductive sexuality itself. This paper explores how the discourse of Malthusianism contributes to the highly disciplined and socially constructed sexuality displayed particularly in* David Copperfield, *and more generally in Victorian sexuality, and Victorian sexual discourse.*

It is commonly asserted that *Tristram Shandy* is one of the most easily identifiable precursors to Charles Dickens's *David Copperfield*. As Simon Edwards observes, Sterne's meandering autobiographical narrative is specifically called to attention by David's assertion of his intent not to "meander" (50) and by David's tears at the moment of his birth. These tears coincide not only with the striking of the twelve o'clock bell but also with Tristram's own midnight tears (Edwards 70–71). Tristram's story, as Edwards observes, begins at the moment of conception (both literary and sexual), while David's story begins at the moment of birth (physically) and the moment of "recording" (literarily). For Edwards, " . . . this historical moment may coincide with an act of repression, in a novel where the sexual basis of conception cannot be discussed" (71). Here, Edwards suggests that the presentation of the sexual act between Walter and Mrs. Shandy in the latter half of the eighteenth century cannot be "reproduced" in its literary descendant of 1849–1850. He indicates that the infamous Victorian taboos on the representation and discussion of sexuality prevent the open presentation of the moment of conception. However, Foucault has taught us not to trust this "repressive hypothesis" and it is my intention in this essay to explore and reveal how this elision of the moment of conception is discursively produced by a particular Victorian sexual discourse, as opposed to being silenced by Victorian "repression."

Numerous *Copperfield* critics have observed how David's sexual desires are directed inappropriately (in Victorian terms) towards incestuous/sisterly (Little Em'ly), homosexual (Steerforth, Heep), and other somehow inappropriate targets (Dora Spenlow). Edwards further shows how these dangerous sexual desires are "repressed," "disciplined," and twisted into a viable, acceptable, middle-class, heterosexual relationship with Agnes.[1] This assessment of the novel as a reflection of the Victorian need to repress "deviant" sexuality and replace it with a normative heterosexual reproductive substitute is common in Dickens criticism, but it is one which underplays contemporary discourses that worked not only to discourage "deviant" sexuality, but also reproductive heteronormative sexuality. As we shall see, while eighteenth-century sexual discourses often did discourage any mode of sexuality that did not lead to reproduction (and these discourses remained in circulation in the nineteenth century),[2] by 1850, the concurrent discourses of Malthusianism were simultaneously working to discourage the practice of reproductive sexuality as well. Throughout this essay, I intend to show that while *David Copperfield* may then discipline or "repress" deviant sexual practices, it also encodes fears of reproductivity and reflects Malthusian concerns about the dangers of reproductive sexuality itself. It does so by employing and reflecting the proliferation of sexual discourses that Foucault identifies as typifying the Victorian era not strictly by silencing them.

In this context, we can see more clearly just what *David Copperfield*, in its relationship with *Tristram Shandy*, does *not* discuss. Tristram's parents (much to the disappointment of Mrs. Shandy) engage in sexual intercourse once a month and are familiar with the "family planning" technique of the "withdrawal method." The Shandys engage in *coitus interruptus*, the interruption of which (by Mrs. Shandy's ill-timed and unplanned speech) is what allows for Tristram's conception. Dickens's novel, of course, provides none of these details of the actual sexual act of conception, and we can only assume that David has been conceived voluntarily by consenting adults (or, at the metafictional level, by Dickens himself). Nevertheless, the Shandean parallel provides a window into a Victorian (and, in the presence of *Shandy*, obviously pre-Victorian) discourse that plays a significant role in the telling of *David Copperfield*: that of family planning, birth control, and anxiety over the fruits of reproductive sexuality.

### "The Regulation of Populations"

Michel Foucault, in *The History of Sexuality, Volume 1,* identifies four "great strategies" employed in the nineteenth century to create, regulate, and control the disciplinary production of sexuality: the sexualization of children, the hysterization of women, the specification of the perverse, and the regulation of populations. He observes that all of these "strategies" are founded within the Victorian family structure. The family, in Foucault's conception, does not "prohibit" these modes of sexuality, but rather functions as an agent that produces the discourses that regulate sexuality (114). It is not, at first glance, difficult to identify the reproductive, heterosexual, nuclear, Victorian family's central role in the "regulation of populations." Families produce children after all. Nevertheless, the goals of this regulation (if there are "goals" to be found) are unclear. Foucault presents for discussion the possibility that these four strategies that revolve around "genitally centered" sexuality may be "motivated by one major concern: to ensure population, to reproduce labor capacity, to perpetuate the form of social relations" (37). The somewhat ambiguous "ensure population" can mean, at times, the need to produce a larger population in order to provide enough "hands" for labor, or it can mean the reduction of population in an effort to allow for fewer mouths to feed. Foucault discusses both of these possibilities, but his references to the "Malthusian couple" provide a useful entry point to the Dickensian sexual economy of *David Copperfield*.

As is well known, Thomas Malthus's 1798 *Essay on the Principle of Population* became a lightning rod for discussion and disagreement over the role of birth control and family planning in Victorian sexuality. Malthus's oft-misinterpreted and exaggerated thesis that populations tend to increase geometrically while food supplies ("the means of subsistence") tend to increase arithmetically (Malthus 12) triggered an intense amount of anxiety over the dangers of excessive reproduction and discourse surrounding these anxieties. Malthus argued that population would self-regulate because of the two principle "checks" on the rise of population, "misery or vice" (Malthus 17) implicit in overpopulation.[3] However, large numbers of nineteenth-century thinkers and citizens were understandably opposed to these natural controls (most significantly that of starvation), especially within their own family. While Malthus used this principle as the occasion for arguing for the elimination of parish relief and for the practice of "moral self-restraint" in the delaying of marriage (and therefore sexual intercourse), his Malthusian, neo-Malthusian, and anti-Malthusian followers extended, argued, and contradicted his basic assumptions over the course of the century. People like William Godwin, William Hazlitt, Thomas Doubleday, Alexander H. Everett, Archibald Alison, and William Edward Hickson explicitly denied Malthus's ratios, while W. F. Lloyd, John Wade and others championed Malthus's viewpoint. These political economists were augmented by still other, less genteel, elements who acknowledged the existence of Malthus's ratios but denied his suggested methods of population control in favor of less conventional means. Although the application of Malthusian doctrine was widely debated in many social circles, the overwhelming presence of the discourse reveals anxieties over an increased population, an anxiety which undoubtedly existed before Malthus's own work, and that was manifesting itself in the industrialization of England that continued over the course of the nineteenth century. These discourses, of course, eventually led to discussions not only of quantity of births but also quality, and by the end of the nineteenth century, had turned, frighteningly, to the discussion of eugenics.

Roy Porter and Lesley Hall see this Malthusian discourse as the most significant one in producing what became standard notions of Victorian prudery.

> Malthus's *Essay* . . . in effect rewrote the agenda of sexual debate. Plagued by fears of overpopulation, moralists swayed by Malthusian arguments no longer

saw the slightest reason for advertising the pleasures of procreation; instead
they emphasized the irresponsibility and immorality of procreation and hence
of sex, except under the most stringent conditions (moral principle, financial
security). The long shadow of Malthus made dissemination of traditional sexual
advice rather akin to toying with a loaded pistol.                            (127)

Of course, contemporary commentators on Victorian sexuality place more or
less emphasis on the importance of Malthusian discourse in the regulation of
sexuality during the period (as virtually all assertions about Victorian sexuality are hotly contested). However, as we shall see, the debates about overpopulation, the economic dangers of reproductivity, and the strategy of delayed
marriage to improve economic conditions for middle class and working class
alike (which, for convenience, I tie together here under the banner of "Malthusianism") are clearly reflected in the sexual politics of *David Copperfield*.[4]

In the quotation above, Porter and Hall indicate the effects of Malthus's
call for "moral restraint," or the delay of reproductive sexuality until it
becomes economically feasible. John Wade, an ardent Malthusian, argued in
1833 that " . . . without a reasonable prospect of being able to support his
offspring, no man can have any more right to marry, than he has to contract
a debt he has not a reasonable prospect of being able to pay" (331). Malthus,
Wade, and similar conservative Malthusians suggested that, although sexual
desire was itself unavoidable, it was necessary for such desires to be suppressed in order to reduce populations and improve the quality of life of the
people remaining. They refused to acknowledge the possibility of artificially
improving the quality of living through poor relief, or of artificially preventing
reproduction through contraceptive practices. As Angus McLaren indicates
in his history of birth control in the nineteenth century, "Malthusians did not
seek to abolish population pressures. At the very heart of their doctrine lay
the belief that such a force was necessary to drive man—at least working-
class man—from his naturally lethargic state" (51). This suppression of reproductive sexuality was then meant to increase "discipline" among the
laboring classes, strengthen morality, and, as a byproduct, improve the quality
of life. It was for this reason that the threat of alternative modes of population
regulation seemed so dangerous to Malthusians. Rather than improving "morality," Malthusians feared that "unnatural" checks to reproduction would
lead instead to increased amorality. Dr. Michael Ryan, one of the first doctors
to address this topic directly, voiced this concern in 1837:

None can deny that if young women in general, of the lower class of society,
were absolved from the fear of consequences, the great majority of them . . .
would rarely preserve their chastity from the depravity of licentious men: illicit
amours would be common and seldom detected— . . .          (Ryan 19–20)[5]

Although Malthus and his followers, like Ryan, stressed the "natural" controls of restraint on population and at no time advocated birth control, neo-Malthusians (as they came to be called) increasingly insisted on taking the matter of population control into their own hands. Radicals, socialists, and utilitarians were unmoved by the more elitist elements of Malthusian doctrines. They largely adopted the notion that overpopulation (and thus reproductive sexuality) was dangerous to a healthy society, but refused to support the idea that contraception would lead to increased immorality and sexual license. Richard Carlile's *Every Woman's Book or What is Love?* (1828), Robert Dale Owen's *Moral Physiology* (1830), Charles Knowlton's *Fruits of Philosophy* (1832), and Francis Place's *Illustrations and Proofs of the Principle of Population* (1822), along with Place's distribution of myriad handbills advocating "methods of contraception—sponge, sheath, withdrawal" (Weeks 46), provided the opening barrage of the campaign to limit birthrates through unconventional means. George Drysdale's *Elements of Social Science* (1854), a popular and initially anonymous tract, provided an overview of the Malthusian doctrine, sexual physiology, venereal diseases and "briefly analyzed preventive intercourse" (Weeks 46). These groundbreaking works were followed by the founding of the Malthusian League in 1877 (linked to the trial of Charles Bradlaugh and Annie Besant for publishing Knowlton's book). In the Malthusian league, neo-Malthusianism found an institutional center. As Jeffrey Weeks observes, " . . . at no time after 1877 was birth control propaganda hindered by law" (46–47).

Although the beginnings of neo-Malthusian birth control and Malthusian anti-reproductive practices were nominally aimed at working-class concerns (the danger of starvation and of available resources being outnumbered by hungry mouths), as we shall see, the middle class also (if not more so) became increasingly concerned with maintaining control over family size in order to maintain a middle-class standard of living. While Owen, Carlile, Place, and Knowlton seem to have been genuinely preoccupied with the concerns of the working classes (Knowlton, in particular, is concerned with making his advice affordable for all readers), Drysdale and members of the Malthusian league drifted more towards Malthusianism's conservative beginnings while ignoring the social movements that supplanted population concerns.[6] In either case, the discourse of contraception found a stronghold in 1877 in the Malthusian League and may have eventually helped to reduce the birthrate and the size of a population that had gradually and inconsistently increased throughout the early nineteenth century.[7] In advocating contraception the neo-Malthusians and the Malthusian League attempted to separate the act of sex from its reproductive role, an attempt frowned upon by medical men and sexual theorists throughout the larger part of the nineteenth century, but which gained popularity as the century progressed.[8] Carlile makes clear the desire to separate sex from conception when he writes, "—what a dreadful thing it is, that health and beauty cannot be encouraged and extended, that love cannot be enjoyed without conception, when conception is not desired, when it is a positive injury to the parties themselves, and to society at large" (22–23).

Porter and Hall acknowledge other contributors to what came to be associated with Victorian "repression," but their focus on the avoidance of sex because of the economic danger of reproduction (i.e., conservative Malthusianism), rather than the avoidance of any sex alternative to reproduction, is an important concept, and one that implicitly contradicts the notion of Victorian "spermatic economies" explored by the likes of G. J. Barker-Benfield (initially in "The Spermatic Economy" and later in *The Horrors of the Half-Known Life*) and Steven Marcus (in *The Other Victorians*). If, as Henry Abelove speculates, the eighteenth-century population boom can be largely attributed to the "increase in the *incidence* of cross-sex genital intercourse (penis in vagina, vagina around penis, with seminal emission uninterrupted)," at the expense of alternative modes of sexuality (Abelove 126), it is possible to see Malthusianism creating a backlash to this increase in the incidence of this type of intercourse.

In constructions of Victorian masculinity and sexuality consistent with the spermatic economy, sperm is seen as a life force, the expenditure of which will lead to sickness, weakness, and degradation. The "spermatic economy" discourages the "waste" of semen, particularly in the form of masturbation, but also in any form of sexuality that is not "productive." Spermatic "male energy" can be saved up and put to work in the field of masculine labor,[9] but its only allowable usage within the realm of sexual intercourse is for purposes of reproduction. Barker-Benfield's analysis of the spermatic economy is largely confined to American subjects, but Marcus's argument rests largely on Dickens's contemporary, William Acton, whose *The Functions and Disorders of the Reproductive Organs , in Childhood, Youth, Adult Age, and Advanced Life, Considered in their Physiological, Social and Moral Relations* first saw publication seven years after *David Copperfield* (S. Marcus 12–13). The disease resulting from spermatic profligacy, known as spermatorrhoea, was said to have diverse and horrifying symptoms, to be avoided at all costs (and was not limited to Acton's account of sexuality. Its currency in the Victorian public imagination is still, however, a matter of debate). In Acton's construction of sexuality, sex within marriage can also lead to spermatorrhoea, but intercourse for procreational purposes is allowable, while female sexuality, where existent at all, is a necessary extension of the maternal instinct (Marcus 29–31). Whereas in previous centuries, female arousal and orgasm were linked explicitly to conception, " . . . near the end of the century of Enlightenment, medical science and those who relied on it ceased to regard the female orgasm as relevant to generation" (Laqueur, "Orgasm, Generation . . . " 1). This does not, of course, mean that popular opinion did not still often associate female orgasm with the possibility of conception, but nevertheless indicates a movement towards the disassociating of the two. Furthermore, for Acton, pregnancy and reproduction are not (as in the Malthusian conception) undesirable results of libidinal desire, but are rather useful ways of sublimating, eliminating, or channeling that desire. "Pregnancy and childbearing seem to be the only reliable means of stifling sexual desire" (Marcus 30).

As Acton says,

> If the married female conceives every second year, during the nine months that follow conception she experiences no great sexual excitement. The consequence is that sexual desire in the male is somewhat diminished and the act of coition takes place but rarely. And again, while women are suckling there is usually such a call on the vital force made by the organs secreting milk that sexual desire is almost annihilated. Now, as all that we have read and heard tends to prove that a reciprocity of desire is, to a great extent, necessary to excite the male, we must not be surprised if we learn that excesses in fertile married life are comparatively rare, and that sensual feelings in the man become gradually slowed down.                                            (qtd. in Marcus 30)

Here, then, reproduction becomes a desirable means of curbing sexual energy, rather than a danger to be avoided for economic reasons.

It is worth noting here that both Barker-Benfield's and Marcus's accounts now seem dated and lack nuance. Barker-Benfield, in particular, associates the spermatic economy with notions of scarcity (i.e., the "saving" of sperm as if there were a limited amount to be disseminated) that are convincingly rejected by Thomas Laqueur ("Masturbation, Credit, and the Novel"). Likewise, the whole notion of spermatorrhoea has been challenged by Michael Mason and others, as being largely associated with the "quack" trade and was often rejected by licensed physicians (see Mason 295–98).[10] Furthermore, Acton's account of female sexuality (which includes a widespread denial of female sexual desire at all, until a woman is first corrupted by a man) contradicts a large body of discourse that suggests that women were seen as desiring beings, much like men (see, for instance, Mason 203 and Gay 135–44). Nevertheless, as we have seen, the notion of the need to discipline any form of sexuality that is not reproductive has been useful in the study of *David Copperfield* and other Victorian texts. However, as Laqueur, Porter and Hall, and Mason all discuss, while the specific term and "disease" of spermatorrhoea may have been largely a production of nineteenth-century quacks, the phobia over masturbation and the spillage of semen finds its roots in the eighteenth century rather than the nineteenth.

*Onania* (1712), *Onanism* (translated to English in 1769), and the copious works of James Graham (see Porter and Hall 106–21 and Mason 205–15) all preceded the late comments by Acton. The phobic discourse surrounding masturbation and the waste of sperm thus precedes Malthus and largely precedes widespread industrialization. In this context, the goals of Foucault's "regulation of populations" were still largely aimed at *increase* of population, rather than at decrease, as in the Malthusian formulation. As Porter and Hall indicate, "Self-abuse was the enemy of generation, wasting semen and sapping vigour" (115). Graham believed that semen carried the "vivifying elementary fire" (qtd. in Porter and Hall 115) that gave the fetus life and that the waste of such precious fluid was nothing short of evil. Acton and a large group of his contemporaries, including quacks, lay people, and some physicians, then, build primarily on the tradition of a previous time, a time when the possible results of reproductivity (i.e., children) were not something to be feared, but rather to be welcomed. This is not to say that Acton was a man out of his time or that the moral sanctions against wasted semen or non-reproductive sexuality did not carry over into the nineteenth century (as Mason puts it, " . . . what *was* very widely accepted [was] . . . that male masturbation was an evil" (210), but it is rather to suggest that concurrent with and, in some ways, resistant to this discourse, was the simultaneously emergent discourse of Malthusianism, in which seminal reproductivity was not necessarily to be treasured, but rather to be feared.

In this context, Catherine Gallagher notes that the Malthusian discourse inverted old assumptions about the relationship between the physical (human) body and the social body. Traditionally, the two were seen to be in a direct relationship with one another: the stronger the body, the stronger the social body. Barker-Benfield's model of the spermatic economy is consistent with this construction. Human vitality, as maintained through the conservation of semen for reproductive purposes, led to a healthy society, as the ability to create or conceive children was a signifier of physical health. In this way, the social body's health could be determined by the witnessing of increased population. As Gallagher relates, the social utopians (Godwin and Condorcet) that Malthus explicitly confronted in his *Essay*, laid much of their hopes upon the "possibility of biological perfectibility" (83). Malthus, on the other hand, advances the notion that the more virile and "healthy" the individual human body, the more endangered the social body became. Reproduction becomes something to be feared, rather than an indicator of social vitality. "The spirited health and strength of the utopian body leads within two generations to social chaos, want, warfare, and, finally, starvation" (Gallagher 85). It is perhaps this newfound fear of reproduction that can lead William Cohen, in another context, to note of Dickens's *Great Expectations:* "Not only are female domination, male homosexuality, onanism, and sadomasochism eliminated, but genitally oriented maritally legitimated heterosexual monogamy itself comes to seem impossible" (70).

### "I . . . Have Done Enough For My Country's Population"

If we chose to read *David Copperfield* purely within the discourse of the anti-onanistic discourse of Graham and Acton, we would once more be led into a study of *David Copperfield* that focuses on David's famous "undisciplined heart" (first substantially explored in Gwendolyn Needham's classic essay). Such a study might position David's libidinal desire for such inappropriate objects as Steerforth and Uriah Heep alongside the desire for Dora that is motivated by sexual pleasure (rather than by reproductive urges). These desires can be seen to be tending towards an "undisciplined" spermatorrhoeic sexuality (that is, desires which "waste" spermatic energy). David's familial (positioned as unrelated brother and sister) reproductive relationship with Agnes Wickfield at the close of the book shows David, then, disciplining his incontinent tendencies and focusing his sexuality for (literarily) productive and reproductive purposes within the spermatic economy.

In (indirect) support of this theory, Alexander Welsh observes that David "married [Dora] only for sex" (136) (and presumably sex for pleasure rather than for reproduction), and Kelly Hager pursues this logic in her discussion of *David Copperfield* as a novel meant to explain, defend, and authorize divorce. Hager positions Dickens as showing the folly of marrying for sexual pleasure (David and Dora), and, in turn, correcting this error with the more platonic, reproductive (a perhaps oxymoronic construction) relationship with Agnes. Certainly David's attraction to Dora is largely physical. To borrow

Hager's example, David is seen to be distracted by Dora's physical attractiveness even at the most serious of moments, when she expresses her concerns over Agnes as a competitor.

> . . .her bright eyes shining very brightly, and her little right hand busying itself
> with one of the buttons of my coat . . . I glanced in admiring silence at the little
> soft hand traveling up the row of buttons on my coat, and at the clustering hair
> that lay against my breast, and at the lashes of her downcast eyes, slightly
> rising as they followed her idle fingers.                    (*Copperfield* 677)

Within the spermatic economy Steven Marcus and Barker-Benfield identify, one might expect sexual erotics to be sublimated in favor of utilitarian sexual (re)productivity. In this schematic, Dora could undergo a clitoridectomy, while David might need one of J. Laws Milton's contraptions to prevent sexual excitement and spermatorrhoea.[11] Autoeroticism and David's aroused sexuality are impossible to deny in this scene, but it would be limiting to label Dora's inappropriateness as a wife as purely tied to her sensuality. Rather, I mean to suggest that Dora's inappropriateness rests largely on an anti-reproductive (Malthusian) framework, rather than within a purely anti-onanistic (spermatic) economy. Within the logic of the novel, it is Dora's capacity for reproduction (not merely for sex) combined with her economic imprudence that makes her an insufficient (and eventually erased) wife. Despite the central importance of Dora's pregnancy as a cause for her death, it is elided and displaced so remarkably that her term lasts somewhat less than one paragraph:

> I had hoped that lighter hands than mine would help to mould her character,
> and that a baby smile upon her breast might change my child-wife to a woman.
> It was not to be. The spirit fluttered for a moment on the threshold of its little
> prison, and unconscious of its captivity, took wing.               (766–67)

This barely articulated description of Dora's pregnancy and miscarriage lead eventually to Dora's death (a universally agreed upon boon for David and his economic fortunes, although his mourning for her is quite real). In the model of "spermatic economy," we would expect reproductive sexuality to occupy a place of privilege. Here, it is instead shunted into a marginal position and causes death for Dora.[12] This elision encapsulates the general thematizing of the novel's expression of reproductive sexuality; it, for the most part, does not exist. While within an anti-onanistic sexual economy we expect non-reproductive sexuality to be disciplined and marginalized, it is

more surprising that reproductive sexuality is similarly repressed. The exceptions are, of course, the relationships of David and Agnes and of Mr. and
Mrs. Micawber—the first of which does not find expression until the end of
the novel and follows economic stability, the second of which illustrates the
dangers of reproduction which Malthus and his followers enumerate.

Dora's pregnancy is only one of numerous elisions, obfuscations, and
displacements of reproductive sexuality. There is, of course, nothing more
Dickensian than an orphan, and in *David Copperfield* we are presented with
more than our fair share. George H. Ford lists David, Emily, Traddles, the
Orfling, Mrs. Copperfield, Martha Endell and Rosa Dartle as ''full'' orphans,
who have lost both parents. ''Half'' orphans include Steerforth, Uriah Heep,
Annie Strong, Agnes Wickfield and Dora Spenlow (she eventually becomes
a full orphan) (Goldfarb 115). Russell Goldfarb adds Ham Peggotty to the
list of full orphans (115). Another at least half-orphan is David and Dora's
servant who ''had no mother'' (*Copperfield* 759). Even those heterosexual
couplings that do not produce children are either configured as irrevocably
platonic (Betsey Trotwood and Mr. Dick), doomed to separation (Betsey
Trotwood and her husband) or prone to the loss of one half of the possibly
reproductive equation (Mr. and Mrs. Barkis). Where there are children, then,
the reproductive sexual participants (parents) that took part in their conception are not to be found, and where there are both parents, there are no
children (again, as we shall see, the Micawbers are the primary exception to
this rule). These representations, like the burgeoning discourse surrounding
birth control (or neo-Malthusianism) in the mid-nineteenth century, separate
children from the sexual act that produced them and in so doing, separate sex
from reproduction. Dickens's familial representations function as metaphorical birth control; parents do not produce children, or at least are not identifi-
ably seen to do so. More often, they are erased entirely.[13]

This construction of the non-reproductive family is seen most explicitly
and most convincingly in David's first stay in Yarmouth. David misinterprets
the ''family'' of Mr. Peggotty, Ham, Little Em'ly and Mrs. Gummidge as
something of a standard reproductive family, but Mr. Peggotty is forced to
explain the ''drowndead'' fates of Em'ly and Ham's fathers and the similar
fate of Mrs. Gummidge's ''old one'' for whom she continually pines (82–83).
As John Jordan says in his analyses of the class dynamics of the novel,
''Ostensibly a happy, working-class family, they are in fact neither a family
nor happy'' (63). Jordan concentrates on what he perceives to be David's
misinterpretation of the family's happiness, but it is the fact that they are not

a family at all that is most interesting in considering the Malthusian reproductive anxiety reflected in the novel. If David misinterprets the Peggotty's happiness, he is insensitive to class difference, argues Jordan, but David's misinterpretation of the familial structure is hard to attribute to such a pejorative causality. It is not strange that David assumes the Peggottys to be within the reproductive "norm" that Victorian discourse (at least publicly) values so highly. It is rather odd that every member of this strangely incestuous composite has been removed from their reproductive partner. It is hard to blame David for his "reading" of this family; the reader instead wonders where all the parents have gone.

Even the happiness of David's youth is not constructed on the basis of a reproductive nuclear family, but rather on the homosocial representation of his two mothers, Claras Copperfield and Peggotty.[14] Standard interpretations of Dickens's work operate under the assumption that "Dickens the parent seems to have little direct relevance to Dickens the novelist" (Collins *Education* 29). These oddly constructed families are most often seen to be either representative of Dickens's anxiety over his abandonment in the "blacking factory" or of his repressed sexuality in relationship to his own mother (the autobiographical nature of the novel has led to numerous and fruitful psychoanalytic readings). Nevertheless, it is true that at the time of the writing of *David Copperfield*, Dickens was firmly ensconced in his own remarkably reproductive marriage (eight children already delivered, with the ninth to be born during the writing of *Copperfield*—and a tenth to follow). It is possible, then, to see these remarkably non-reproductive families as a reflection of a Malthusian (or neo-Malthusian) discourse that attempts to avoid the reproductive consequences of sex. These consequences, as expressed by Malthusian and neo-Malthusian thinkers in the face of increasing populations, threatened the lower classes with poverty and starvation and threatened a rising middle class with the possibility of downward class mobility.

Philip Collins has confidently declared that Dickens was anti-Malthusian both in his books and in his life (*Education* 26). In terms of his books, although there is little if any direct commentary by Dickens on Malthus's work (and no evidence that I have discovered that he read Malthus firsthand), what little there is seems to reflect an anti-Malthusian bias. In the 1844 Christmas Book, *The Chimes*, Dickens portrays the possible negative repercussions of Malthusian "moral restraint" in delaying the age of marriage. In the story, Trotty Veck's daughter Meg is scheduled to marry the young smith Richard on New Year's Day. Meg is discouraged from doing so by Alderman Cute, a clear parody of a political economist and Malthusian, who advises:

You are going to be married, you say. . .Very unbecoming and indelicate in one
of your sex! . . . After you are married, you'll quarrel with your husband and
come to be a distressed wife. You may think not; but you will, because I tell
you so. Now, I give you fair warning, that I have made up my mind to Put
distressed wives Down. So don't be brought before me. You'll have children—boys. Those boys will grow up bad, of course, and run wild in the streets,
without shoes and stockings. . .Perhaps your husband will die young (most
likely) and leave you with a baby. Then you'll be turned out of doors, and
wander up and down the streets . . .                    (*Christmas Books* 98–99)

These dire warnings are a reflection of Malthusian concerns about the poor
marrying young and not being able to care for their children. Likewise, the
"check" of misery is in plain view, while the "check" of vice is only dimly
hidden behind the image of a woman wandering the streets (a clear vision of
the vice of prostitution that reappears in *Copperfield* in the form of Martha
Endell). The Alderman's affection for statistics and mathematics[15] at the
expense of human compassion is also an obvious mockery of the utilitarian/
political economist strain that Dickens was known to distrust and oppose.

Trotty's dream/vision of the horrific results of the delayed marriage of
Richard and Meg (the corruption of Richard, the death of the child Lillian,
the jailing of Will Fern, the eviction of Meg from her house) serves as a
chilling warning of the results of a working-class world run under strict
Malthusian principles (i.e., a world without poor relief in which misery and
vice are left to check population). Instead, familial love and societal compassion are offered as a reparative for the dangers of overpopulation. Nevertheless, the anxiety over overpopulation that is parodically ventriloquized
through the mouth of Alderman Cute is clearly a very real concern and
something Dickens saw as worthy of confrontation. Implicit in *The Chimes*
is not so much Dickens's objections to the very possibility of overpopulation
and scarcity of resources, but rather his objections to the strict Malthusian
solution to this problem (the withholding of a solution and the trust in the
natural "checks" of misery and vice to deal with overpopulation and scarcity
of resources). Dickens's anti-Malthusian social conscience and argument for
philanthropy towards the lower classes does not eliminate the anxiety over
overpopulation (and therefore reproduction) that Alderman Cute voices.
Rather, as we have seen, this anxiety over reproduction continues to be reflected, particularly in *Copperfield*, and, as we shall see, the doctrine of
"moral restraint" also receives more sympathetic treatment, at least for the
middle classes in his later novel.

In terms of Dickens's life, the hyper-reproductivity of Dickens's family
certainly shows the unlikelihood that he practiced any of the birth control

techniques the neo-Malthusians advocated. Nevertheless, Collins and others have been quick to notice the application that Malthusian discourse had for Dickens's domestic situation. While Dickens's public face was certainly anti-Malthusian (or at least opposed to the very discourse of political economy), he was known to preach Malthusian ideas in a purely domestic context with some regularity. As Phyllis Rose observes, for Dickens, " . . . a variation on the Malthusian principle seemed true. It was as though his dependents increased geometrically and his resources only arithmetically" (162). As early as 1843 (when the Dickens children numbered only four), Dickens was complaining in a letter of the addition of a dependent to his family. " 'We think of keeping the New Year, by having another child. I am constantly reversing the Kings in fairy tales, and importuning the Gods not to trouble themselves: being quite satisfied with what I have. But they are *so* generous when they *do* take a fancy to one!' " (qtd. in Rose 162). As Fred Kaplan observes, Dickens became "increasingly ambivalent" about the birth of his children. In 1865, in a letter to Mrs. Fred Lehmann, he advised, "'don't have any more children'" (qtd. in Kaplan 222). This attitude preceded the date of the letter and increased with each additional child. Dickens's listing of his children "as if adding up the ledger of his domestic woes" (Kaplan 272) in a letter to L. H. Sigourney in 1851 illustrated his concern about the maintenance of his home in the face of increasing economic responsibility: "'Charley, about aged 14, at school at Eton. Mary 13. Kate 11. Walter Landor 10 (going to India bye and bye). Francis Jeffrey 7. Alfred Tennyson 5. Sydney Smith 4. Henry Fielding 2'" (qtd. in Kaplan 272). By this time, Dora, born during the writing of *Copperfield*, had passed away, while Plorn, the final Dickens child, was yet to be born. In the same year, Dickens considered having "a little service in St. Paul's beseeching that I may be considered to have done enough for my country's population" (qtd. in Collins *Education* 26). Kaplan identifies Dickens's "bemused disgust with [the] fecundity [of Dickens and his wife, Catherine]," (272) and regardless of Dickens's personal feelings for any one of his children, their presence en masse seemed to be a burden to him. Dickens's well-known disaffection with his wife (well-advanced by the time of the writing of *Copperfield)* can be at least partially tied to what he perceived to be her hyperfecundity. It seems Catherine had become the repository for Dickens's Malthusian anxieties.

None of this is to suggest that Dickens was somehow impoverished by the intrusion of his ever-expanding family. By 1847 he "had become independent, at least in the sense that his earning power was enormous" (Kaplan 221). Nevertheless, Dickens harbored "exasperation . . . bitterness" that the material evidence of success could not wholly eliminate. Although the assumption of a "upper-middle-class" lifestyle was a choice Dickens made for himself and his family, he still felt the responsibility and difficulty of maintaining that lifestyle with a burgeoning family (Kaplan 221). In addition to the dependents arising from Dickens's own reproductive activity, he was hampered by the economic demands of his own biological mother and father. He had become, by 1850, the sole provider for at least 13 people. This multiplication of mouths to feed may not have outrun Dickens's incredible ability to produce money and food, but the anxiety over the seemingly geometric advance in population was undoubtedly present in his domestic circle. Like many of his contemporaries, Dickens was preoccupied with his economic production and the troubling possibilities his astonishing production of children had on his bountiful resources. The constantly available discourse on Malthusianism was part of Dickens's own experience, as well as that of his readers. Although, as we can see in *The Chimes*, Dickens was publicly anti-Malthusian, the pressures of population and the anxieties over reproduction that the discourse suggests were certainly present both in Dickens's books and in his life.

### Domestic Malthusianism, the Micawbers, Tommy Traddles, and Uriah Heep

Despite the fact that the average mid-Victorian family had something approximating 5.5 to 6 live births (Weeks 45),[16] the only characters in *David Copperfield* who consistently rival the fecundity of the Dickens family are the Micawbers. Not coincidentally, it is also the Micawbers whose debts and "pecuniary emoluments" almost invariably outstrip their earnings. Mr. Micawber's own sense of his inadequacy as a provider is, in turn, almost always tied to his status as a father. David's first meeting with Mrs. Micawber enacts the Malthusian tendency to see "children" as nameless numbers who literally "eat" through a family's economic and physical well-being. Mrs. Micawber is a " . . . thin and faded lady . . . with a baby at her breast. This baby was one of twins; and I may remark here that I hardly ever, in all my experience of the family, saw both the twins detached from Mrs. Micawber at the same time. One of them was always taking refreshment" (212). Here, and throughout the novel, the Micawber twins are merely a number, "two." Neither of them have names and they are depicted not merely as consumers but as perpetual and never satisfied consumers. It is perhaps significant that the first child, Wilkins, Jr., is named and individualized to a degree, while with each successive child, and subsequent weight upon the Micawber family fortune, the children become less and less "people" or agents and more and more numeric consumers, additional weights to be born by the Micawbers—Miss Micawber, the twins, the baby.

David sees the Micawbers as "elastic" personalities in the sense that they are able to confront difficulty and resurrect themselves into cheerful cartoon personalities once again.

> I have known [Mrs. Micawber] to be thrown into fainting fits by the king's taxes at three o'clock, and to eat lamb chops, breaded, and drink warm ale (paid for with two tea-spoons that had gone to the pawn-brokers) at four. On one occasion . . . I saw her lying (of course with a twin) under the gate in a swoon, with her hair all torn about her face; but I never knew her more cheerful than she was, that very same night, over a veal cutlet before the kitchen fire . . .
>
> (214–15)

The "elasticity" of Mrs. Micawber loses some of its comic appeal when she is lying under a gate, baby in hand, disheveled and unconscious. The state of disarray would not be complete (and might be somewhat mitigated) without the presence of the "consuming" Malthusian child who also needs to be fed. It is not surprising that Mrs. Micawber is happy while eating and unhappy in the presence of the child who quite literally consumes her. Despite the seemingly steady supply of food into the Micawber household, Dickens is here careful to identify the means of their sustenance (the pawning of the spoons), as he continues to do in his representations of David's own trips to the pawnbroker to aid his adoptive family (trips that eventually result in the selling of all of the family furniture).   It is traditional to see the strong repressive instincts of David's experience at Murdstone and Grinby's[17] as a reenactment of Dickens's own childhood trauma at the blacking factory. Certainly the passage endnoted below was part of the autobiographical fragment recounting Dickens's days as a youth, and Mr. Micawber is rightly seen as an analog of Dickens's own profligate and irresponsible father. Nevertheless, at the time of the writing of *David Copperfield*, Dickens was a parent of many, like Micawber, not a deserted child, and it is clear through the comments of both Micawber parents that children are not only configured as abandoned and vulnerable, but also as hungry consumers of economic solvency.[18] David's incredible anxiety over his London experiences are not merely a result of the display of his working-class existence in the window of the labeling factory, but also of his membership in a family that is simply too large to feed itself. The Micawbers were once members of the bourgeoisie, a status David desperately strives for throughout the novel, and it is their reproductivity that dooms them to their new status as impoverished lower-class citizens in search of pecuniary recompense. As Chris Vanden Bossche observes, ''David's anxiety has a real social basis, for social mobility runs in both directions: even as many were arriving in the middle and upper classes others were being proletarianized, their position as lower gentry threatened by the changing structure of economic relations'' (35). Malthusian discourse placed birth rate and reproduction in a central role in the fluidity of class structures, and David's incorporation into the reproductive family plays a significant part in his own fear of proletarianization. If David is truly an autobiographical reflection of Dickens himself (as is universally acknowledged), it is not then surprising that *David Copperfield* most often avoids the representation of reproductivity. While the Micawbers display anxiety over reproduction because of the dangers of starvation, David reveals a class anxiety, a fear of becoming the fallen bourgeoisie that the Micawbers represent.

Mrs. Micawber is tempted to leave Mr. Micawber and retreat to the safety of her (supposedly) more affluent family, but '''He is the parent of my children! He is the father of my twins!'' (227). Here, the fruits of reproduction become anchors to impoverishment. As the novel continues and Mrs. Micawber once again becomes pregnant, Mr. Micawber's attention to his children as consumers of his income increases. He acknowledges that it is only because he must feed his ever-burgeoning family that he is forced to gain employment with the despicable Uriah Heep. Even at his moment of greatest triumph, the ''explosion'' of Heep, Micawber cannot but think of the danger his lack of employment will bring to his children: ''It merely remains for me to substantiate these accusations; and then, with my ill-starred family, to disappear from the landscape on which we may be an incumbrance. That is soon done. It may be reasonably inferred that our baby will first expire of inanition, as being the frailest member of our circle; and that our twins will follow next in order'' (825).

Micawber's employment at Wickfield and Heep allows him briefly to overcome his domestic difficulties. When he no longer has this employment, despite the obvious moral superiority of his actions, he may not be able to feed his children.

It is useful here to note that Mr. Micawber's opposite in terms of both the Malthusian (anti-reproductive) and the spermatic (anti-onanistic) sexual economies at work in the novel is Heep himself. As Steven Marcus first noted in *The Other Victorians*, and as several critics have elaborated upon since (including D.A. Miller and Simon Edwards), Heep exhibits all of the classic symptoms of spermatorrhoea, and of being a chronic masturbator. Where Micawber is robust, jocular, humorous, and sexually potent within the domestic reproductive sphere, Heep is thin, sniveling, serpentine, 'umble, and wasteful of his spermatic energies in his onanism.[19] In a purely spermatic (again, anti-onanistic, pro-reproductive) economy one would expect nothing but profligacy, expenditure, and dissipation from Heep, but instead, in the context of Malthusian economy, it is Heep who is able to rise socially and economically (at least initially), while Micawber is left feeding his children.

It is here that we can most clearly see the existence of the competing and concurrent discourse of both spermatic *and* Malthusian economies. Morally, Dickens is clearly operating within a tradition that privileges reproductivity and disdains onanism. That Heep is morally despicable is incontrovertible. At the same time, however, and perhaps less consciously, the novel reveals the *dangers* of sexual fecundity and the *advantages* of non-reproductive sexual options in the polar opposites of Micawber and Heep. Where Micawber is morally superior, he is economically endangered by his reproductive status. At the same time, while Heep is morally bankrupt, his actual economic success can, at least partially, be tied to his (probably involuntary) Malthusian prudence.[20]

This split between material success and moral sanction reveals both strands of the competing spermatic and Malthusian economies. Because Heep cannot be morally sanctioned, he is destined to fail, but even Heep's undoing portrays a continuity with Malthusian sexual economy rather than a complete discontinuity. Micawber has, after all, committed himself to working and meeting the economic needs of his hyper-reproductive family (at the expense of the personal closeness of his relationship with Mrs. Micawber; a closeness, we can only assume, that has produced all of the children in the first place), while Heep has begun to have reproductive, heterosexual desires of his own; he desires to marry Agnes Wickfield. Heep's desire for Agnes triggers David's jealousy and hatred (and, in some readings, latent homoerotic attraction) and Micawber's momentary suspension of reproductive urges allows him to unveil Heep as a fraud and a cheat. Reproductive familial sexuality is here suppressed (by Micawber for economic solvency and by the novel in its treatment of Heep), it is not doing the suppressing. As long as Heep remains purely masturbatory, his economic and social mobility are maintained. When he turns to hopes for the standard Victorian reproductive family (with Agnes), his machinations collapse. What this reading reveals is how sexuality, in all of its guises, is suppressed by the conjunction of these competing sexual discourses. If anti-reproductive and particularly onanistic sexuality is frowned upon as morally reprehensible (Heep) while reproductive sexuality is not economically viable within the Malthusian framework (Micawber), sexuality itself seems to be foreclosed.[21]

What then of Heep's mirror, the similarly upwardly striving adult, David, who is busily trying to "discipline" his heart, and, perhaps more importantly, gain economic solvency and upper middle-class status? Why is it that when David turns to reproductive sexuality with Agnes it does not end unhappily as it does for Heep (or as it does for David and Dora whose sex for pleasure, as we have seen, becomes reproductive and fails)?

As I have touched upon, when Malthusian principles were extended to the middle class, fears were no longer couched in terms of starvation, but in terms of maintaining a standard of living. While with the Micawbers, David's fear of reproduction is configured as a class anxiety, but even as he moves firmly into middle-class status, working for Jorkins and Spenlow, practicing stenography, and working as an assistant to Dr. Strong on the dictionary, we can see his anxieties over reproduction transforming into those of the typical bourgeois subject.

Malthus's program of "moral restraint" increasingly became adopted by a number of bourgeois social theorists over the first quarter of the nineteenth century. Like John Wade, they began to "thrust home the moral to the poor of postponing marriage as a way to avoid pauperism" (Banks 29). That is, the poor were advised to avoid the expense of children, only present via reproductive married sexuality (in theory), by simply delaying marriage until the couple (particularly the man) could afford the consequences (this is the precise advice we see Alderman Cute giving in *The Chimes*). As Joseph Banks (and myriad others) show, however, this advice to the poor (like most advice) originated in the practice that the middle class was already enacting. "For the young middle-class man and woman, marriage implied a family, even perhaps a large family. It was therefore sensible to postpone it until the optimum income was actually achieved" (30). This postponement was not instituted to avoid poverty, but to maintain the accustomed "standard of living" (Banks 198). The extent to which this recommendation was actually enacted (see Mason 48–64 for a detailed analysis of marriage rate statistics) is still under debate, but it is clear that it was a significant recommendation. Certainly, this concept was wedded to certain types of Victorian "morality" that refused contraception as an option and preferred the "family planning" model of delayed marriage (again, this may well have been the public face of couples who did use contraception). Within this discourse, at least, it therefore became "immoral" to marry before the ability to maintain a family was achieved (Banks 47). While Dickens may, as we have seen, practice metaphorical contraception in his separation of parents from children in the novel, his middle-class Victorian morality would not allow for an overt alignment with radicals like Owen, Carlile, and Place either in fiction or in his own sexual behavior. Instead, Dickens's anxieties over reproduction appear more explicitly in representations of traditionally conservative Malthusianism and the "moral restraint" of the delay of marriage. Although Dickens appears opposed to this option for the poor in *The Chimes*, *Copperfield* seems to offer it as a necessary alternative for the upwardly striving, middle-class David.

Dickens's constant appreciation of the dangers of debt and economic insolvency came most appreciably from his profligate father whose insolvency forced Dickens into the world of hard labor at a young age. As he reports in his autobiographical fragment, his father gave him counsel on the danger of debt: " . . . if a man had twenty pounds a year, and spent nineteen pounds, nineteen shillings and sixpence, he would be happy; but that a shilling spent the other way would make him wretched" (Forster 16). This advice was of course transposed into *David Copperfield* by the hyper-reproductive Mr. Micawber when he advises David, "Annual income twenty pounds, annual expenditure nineteen and six, results happiness. Annual income twenty pounds, annual expenditure twenty ought and six, results misery" (231). Tracts such as *The New System of Domestic Economy* , published initially in 1823 and updated in 1857 and 1870, translated these common fears explicitly into Malthusian anxieties over reproduction by presenting charts showing the relationship of family size to the amount of household expenses. A series of letters in the 1858 *Times* addressed similar concerns, debating the possibility of maintaining a family on £300 a year. "A Happy Man" declared "'that magnificent income hardly suffices to keep [a man] going'" (qtd. in Banks 41). Fear of debt and tracts such as these drove home the Malthusian recommendation of delaying marriage until the prospect of children was economically viable.

The best middle-class Malthusian, in these terms, in *David Copperfield* is, of course, Tommy Traddles, renowned illustrator of skeletons. His willingness to wait until the end of time to marry Sophy is predicated not only upon the necessity of "making his way" in the world first, but also on Sophy's incredibly large hyper-reproductive family no longer needing her services. The Traddles' "moral restraint" is obvious when Tommy tells David, "'Wait and hope!' We always say that. 'Wait and hope,' we always say. And she would wait, Copperfield, till she was sixty—any age you can mention—for me!"

(466). It is only through the fact that Sophy is "an extraordinary manager" (897), and that the Traddles are willing to settle for Britannia metal (a concession David is unwilling to make on behalf of Traddles when David insists on Tommy's future purchase of silver) that they are able to get married at all (898). However, Tommy's destiny to be a judge is clear by the time he has married, and he is also able to sustain several of Sophy's sisters at a time. The success of Tommy's delayed marriage can be contrasted with the failure of the hypothetical delayed marriage in *The Chimes.* In *Copperfield,* Malthusian "moral restraint" seems essential for achieving middle-class ambitions.

Tommy's resoluteness in practicing Malthusian "moral restraint" and waiting for the right time to marry is contrasted with the imprudence of young David's marriage to Dora. David comments that the £140 that his family will make at the time of his hiring by Dr. Strong will double his family's income (which, by then, also has to support Betsey Trotwood and Mr. Dick). This new income, in the initial days of his courtship of Dora, is a far cry from A Happy Man's £300. Nevertheless, David attains a job working for a newspaper and begins working on small works of fiction (much like Dickens himself), and it is in the chapter detailing David's nuptials that we learn his income has increased to £350 a year.[22] This sum, according to the readers of the *Times,* should be more than sufficient to support the young lovers (at least as long as they do not reproduce), but, as several onlookers at the wedding whisper, they are a "youthful couple" (699) and Dora's domestic skills do not equal those of Sophy Traddles. Malthus's concept of "moral restraint" is here violated by the youthful marriage and the lack of domestic economy.

The reader is never led to believe that David and Dora are in any danger of starving because of their economic imprudence, but David is nevertheless concerned that they are a "contagion" (761), infecting their domestics with the inability to hang on to money. This anxiety rests on middle-class desires to maintain or, more likely, improve their middle-class standard of living. As Chris Vanden Bossche has investigated, the middle-class domestic "pastoral" is tied to the image of the "cookery" book that David tries to force Dora to learn. This explicitly foregrounds the notion of "feeding" the family, a possibility that, as any book of domestic economy would advise, is more difficult with an increase in family size. As David has aspirations for class mobility up the social scale deriving from the success of his writing, the anxiety over reproduction seen in the Micawbers and the threat of hunger configured in the inability to master the cookery book, show that there is still the anxiety over possible class mobility down the social scale as well. We can see this anxiety in David's unrealistic insistence on domestic prudence, even if the reality of David's income makes this unwanted downward mobility almost impossible (again, there are parallels here to Dickens's own life).

We can see, then, the results of reproductivity when combined with domestic imprudence. Dora's inability to maintain a household and to make her "figures" add up (a problem Clara Copperfield, who meets a similar fate, also has) makes the introduction of children into the Copperfield household seem unwise and, in the terms we have seen Wade use, immoral. We have seen that David's class anxiety is tied to the reproductive anxiety of both David and the novel in general. From this perspective, Dora must (in Malthusian terms) be written out of the novel (by Dickens if not by David himself) when she threatens to give birth.[23] The central drama of David's private autobiography is of his rise to fame, security, and upper middle-class status. Therefore, when the reproductive romantic subplot that Dora provides threatens to subvert that rise (and the threat is not fully formulated until the romance does become reproductive), this threat is removed, and David is soon provided with a "suitable" replacement in order to fulfill the conventions of the Victorian novel. Here it is possible to see that in the novel, as in Dickens's assessment of his own wife, women (particularly Dora, Clara and Mrs. Micawber) become the repository for Malthusian anxieties. Where men have the economic and social mobility to, at times, overcome Malthusian scarcity of means, the women are consigned to death for their imprudence and reproductive "transgressions." Clearly here, Dickens, in conjunction with much Victorian discourse, relegates women to the domestic space and then punishes them for their domestic (re)production.

Dora's replacement, however, is not imprudent or cavalier in her domestic duties; Agnes has been taking care of her father's home and has also been making "figures" add up for her whole life. It is difficult within this Malthusian context to take David's analysis of his "undisciplined heart" or of "the unsuitability of mind and purpose" that he borrows from Annie Strong at face value. The ambiguity of these formulations have been discussed thoroughly elsewhere, but it is clear that at least some of the "unsuitability" that exists between David and Dora originates with economics and these economic disjunctions find expression in the threat of reproduction. This is not to say that we must find David guilty of eliminating Dora (he loves her, after all, until the very end), but rather that the novel's Malthusian logic cannot allow David to be brought down by Dora's economic imprudence, which is exacerbated by her reproductivity.

Despite the fairly consistent difficulties, anxieties, and elisions associated with reproductive sex and reproduction, the novel does close with a "happy" representation of David and Agnes as reproductive Victorian couple. What then do we make of Agnes's remarkable fecundity with which the novel closes? Although it would be impossible to deny that the conclusion of *David Copperfield* is meant to be a happy one, the representation of David's children has interesting similarities to the representation of the hungry Micawber brood. Like the Micawbers, the Copperfield children are all but nameless (the eldest, we know, is named Agnes) and they are seen as a "group" rather than as individuals. " . . . three of our children . . . " are playing in the room when Mr. Peggotty returns from Australia to visit, and "One of our boys laid his head in his mother's lap [the boy remains nameless]" (939). The number of children they have produced is not specified, but we know that there are more than three. This conventional domestic pastoral that occurs ten years after the previous chapter refuses to make the family concrete and personal, but rather, as Phyllis Rose says, they are a mythologized family "dividing and subdividing like bacteria in a Petri Dish" (151). In the following chapter, the reader learns that there are additional daughters named Betsey Trotwood and Dora (among, possibly, others) and that there are several boys as well (947), but the exact number of children is never clear.

What allows for this sudden bountiful reproductivity within the conservative Malthusian sexual economy is David's economic status. After Heep's "explosion" and David's Wordsworthian trip to Switzerland to write another novel, David's fame and fortune rapidly increase. Both Mr. Omer and Mr. Chilip have read his work and word of his fame has reached their provincial neighborhoods. Mr. Omer has read every word and not felt a bit sleepy (801). Like Dickens, David achieves literary fame and fortune (although the representation of his actual literary productions are also elided). Within the bourgeois Malthusian framework, then, he has waited long enough to marry and replaced the economically profligate wife with the ideal "Angel of the House." His fear of sliding into proletarianism can be safely put to rest (or so it would seem, although Dickens's own experience suggests that David's unqualified enthusiasm for his virility may be short-lived) along with his anxiety over reproduction.

Similarly, the Micawber family's ability to overcome the burden of reproductivity fits largely into a Malthusian model. Malthus himself discussed the possibility of emigration as at least a partial relief to the population problem. He saw the need for emigration as a signifier of "misery" in the mother country, but acknowledged the short-term bounty a thinly populated destination (like America or Australia) could provide.[24] While some of the more conservative Malthusians saw emigration as a red herring that avoided the more important measure of discipline and self-restraint, others like John Wade saw it as an opportunity for population reduction. Additionally, as Jeffrey Weeks observes, "some sections of the working class, especially where child labor is a necessity ... still had need of a large family" (60–61). In this context, children can become producers, rather than simply consumers. As the Micawbers prepare to embark on their new life as farmers in Australia, the young Wilkins, Jr. has already begun to learn how he can help his family.[25] The Micawbers are off to a land where the resources are available, even to feed a family that grows as rapidly as their own. As Micawber exhorts triumphantly, "'Enough of delay: enough of disappointment: enough of limited means. That was in the old country. This is the new. Produce your reparation. Bring it forward'" (880). Micawber's rhetoric here is certainly that of the optimistic Malthusian (like Wade) and just as his debts are derived within a Malthusian context, they can presumably be paid within the same context.[26] Trevor Blount observes the enthusiasm for emigration which Dickens and others felt at mid-century. Much of this enthusiasm was based around economic opportunity and the hope for new resources (Dickens 35), new resources that can feed the expanding hunger of hyper-reproductive families.

## Unwanted Children, Desired Children

In the wake of Foucauldian social critique, it is a commonplace to remind ourselves that "natural" sexuality is not "natural" at all, but rather an intricate construction of social discourses. It is important to see the discourse of Malthusian anxiety over reproduction not only in *David Copperfield,* but as a contributor to any construction of Victorian sexuality. Where David seems to have a "natural" or "moral" inclination to redirect his sexual energies away from Dora and toward Agnes, it is possible to see this not only in terms of the "repression" associated with spermatic economies, but also within this Malthusian sexual economy. I would argue that it should be seen in both of these contexts, not one or the other. The fact that these two discourses can provide conflicted and divided readings (as we have seen with Micawber and Heep) does not preclude their coexistence. David's "undisciplined heart" can be seen to be undisciplined economically in this reading. As Welsh and Hager have shown us, David's desire for Dora is attached to sexual pleasure, and not familial or reproductive desire. Nevertheless, David's attempt to separate his sexual desire and his reproductive function, as we have seen, is unsuccessful. Dora, therefore, becomes an inappropriate love object not merely in the spermatic economy that disciplines libidinal urges but also in the Malthusian framework that silences reproductivity.

Where David has failed to make the separation of sex and reproduction, we have seen how Dickens has narratively managed to do so (outside of the economically unsuccessful Micawber family). While Edwards and others have sufficiently noted how non-reproductive or "deviant" sexuality is repressed in the novel, the Malthusian schematic allows us to see how reproductive sexuality is repressed as well. The non-reproductive constructions of families (seen most clearly in the Peggottys), the tacit economic (if not moral) approval of onanism (Uriah Heep), and the removal of one or both parents (in the cornucopia of orphans) remove access to either sex or to reproduction and remove the connection between the two.

The Malthusian sexual economy further allows the investigation of one of the most puzzling and interesting ways in which the novel works to elide reproduction and to confuse the sexual producer/product relationship of parent to child. Children are, of course, the clearest signifier of heteronormative sexuality, but, in *David Copperfield,* they also become the object of sexual desire. We have seen how reproductive families tend to treat their children as numbers without names, mere consumers in danger of starvation. As James Kincaid reminds us, " . . . in 1856 . . . nearly half the children born [in England] die before they are five years old" (75). Nevertheless, the population increased by approximately 11% per year during the nineteenth century and there were more than enough new babies to replace the old (Kincaid 75).[27] Children were, as they were by the Micawbers, mass-produced, and if *David Copperfield* and Dickens's own domestic ledger are any indication, a certain amount of depersonalization was inevitable. Nevertheless, where children of identifiable and represented reproductive parents are seen as impersonal industrial productions, in *David Copperfield* orphans and half-orphans (that is children separated from their reproductive progenitors) become objects of sexual desire in addition to its products.

Dora Spenlow, after all, does demand to be referred to as a "child-wife," while Betsey Trotwood's construction of Clara Copperfield as a "poor baby" is irresistible to the "firm" Mr. Murdstone. David has a child-love in Little Em'ly, a love that fades when she begins to have aspirations to be a "lady," wishing not only to improve her class status, but also to "grow up." Steerforth is attracted to "David/Daisy's" childlike innocence, while David refuses to remember his homoerotic hero Steerforth as anything other than a child, at his best, and "lying with his head upon his arm" (866). James Kincaid

explores the nature of desire for children in Victorian culture and its relationship to contemporary pedophilia in his *Child-Loving* and suggests that in
addition to these constructions of desire for children, the reader is invited
into a voyeuristic sexual desire for David in his childhood innocence (an
impulse the adult David shares with us) (Kincaid 306–09).

Kincaid places the sexual attractiveness of children in something of a Lacanian absence, ''Little David is so pure, so insistently empty, that we might
have trouble not occupying him, taking him over'' (306). Children are empty
of experience and sexuality and therefore can be erotically ''filled'' or ''entered'' by the pedophile or sexual desirer (which Kincaid universalizes to a
degree in his depiction of the reader as voyeur). Continuous with this absence
is the tempting flirtation of the inevitable brevity of childhood, ''the prosaic
fact that children do not stay children'' (Kincaid 226). Accompanying the
desire for the child is the desire for lost childhood (an inevitable result of the
passage to adulthood), the nostalgia Kincaid sees so clearly in works like
*Peter Pan, Alice in Wonderland,* and, of course, *David Copperfield.*

If we keep this conception of desire for children in mind, and take the
widespread Victorian impulse to deny children's own sexual desire into account, it is possible to see anti-reproductive traces in the pervasive (sexual)
desire for children in Dickens's novel. Within Acton's pro-reproductive, anti-
onanistic spermatic economy, the necessity of denying children any sexual
feelings at all is important, ''In a state of health no sexual impression should
ever affect a child's mind and body'' (qtd. in S. Marcus 13) and, although
he acknowledges the dangers of sexual temptation in children, he advocates
measures being taken to monitor and prevent these dangers. Parents are to
''watch their children'' (qtd. in S. Marcus 17), circumcision is to be considered and children must sleep in separate beds (S. Marcus 17–18). Acton's
plea to ''watch your children'' seems continuous with Kincaid's description
of adult voyeuristic desire for children, but as Steven Marcus observes, Acton
presents us with what seems to be ''a contradictory consciousness'' (15).
''On the one hand, children are spoken of as pure and innocent and sexually
quiescent; on the other, they are described as constantly threatened by horrid
temptations, open to stimulation and appetite'' (S. Marcus 15). Marcus here
(perhaps unintentionally) prefigures what Foucault elaborates in *The History
of Sexuality* as the Victorian tendency to ''hide'' or conceal in order to
produce or reveal. While children's sexuality is publicly claimed to be a
secret, the injunction to protect this secret actually discursively produces the
notion of the sexually perverse child.[28] Likewise, what Kincaid shows us
about Acton's double consciousness is that the impulse to deprive children

of sexuality may itself be a sexual desire for the child. It is the innocence and the "absence" of sexuality that makes children sexually attractive to adults (because, ironically, of its simultaneous construction of children as inherently perverted); parents must "watch" their children not only to make sure that they maintain their innocence, but also to desire voyeuristically that innocence (and to construct its opposite, perversion).

The sexual attractiveness of children, then, is in pre-pubescent sexual innocence and the absence of experience. Victorian anxiety over childhood masturbation and sexuality (and its modern equivalent) can be seen in this light not merely as fears of forming bad habits and becoming spermatorrhoeic adults, but also as fears of losing the desired innocent object. Clearly the desired innocents in *David Copperfield* lose their attractiveness (at least temporarily) when they lose their innocence. This loss of innocence in the novel is tied explicitly to reproductivity and recovered only in death.

It is interesting to note that the model for the "child-bride" that never loses her innocence is Annie Strong. Annie is constructed as the child figure of Dr. Strong's parental desire. The doctor is explicitly described as Annie's "father figure" whose change to "lover" status takes the innocent Annie by surprise. Dr. Strong's sexual desire for Annie is predicated (in our model of sexual desire for children) on her childlike innocence, an innocence that is threatened by Jack Maldon. The threat of the intrusion of adult/adult sexual desire onto the parent/child sexuality displayed by the Strongs is dispersed by Annie in "Mr. Dick Fulfils My Aunt's Predictions" (716ff.) when she denies any involvement with Jack Maldon. Annie's innocence is then maintained, not only in terms of sexual desire outside of marriage, but perhaps within the marriage as well. It is hard to imagine Annie and Dr. Strong involved sexually and there is no clear indication that they are. One thing is certain, the only clear signifier of heterosexual intercourse, the production of a child, is not attached to the Strongs. This parent/child, possibly chaste and definitely not reproductive marriage is held as the model for David's own life. It is Annie who suggests the "unsuitability of mind and purpose" and "the first mistaken impulse of an undisciplined heart" that become David's catch phrases throughout the remainder of the novel.

Despite the fact that unlike Annie Strong, Clara Copperfield is clearly not a sexual innocent (as she has given birth to David before Murdstone encounters her), Mr. Murdstone, like Betsey Trotwood, sees her as a "baby" and although he professes to want to turn her into a "firm" adult, it is clear that, like Dr. Strong, he would prefer she remain childlike. When given the chance, he chooses another child-wife to desire and abuse. When Clara publicly reveals her capacity for sexual desire and sexual production (for the second time) by giving birth to David's brother, like Dora, Clara dies and is replaced. Where Annie's chastity and perpetual innocence are affirmed by her lack of ability to reproduce, Clara's innocence, like Dora's, is lost in the act of giving birth. Further, like Clara, Little Em'ly is desired by Steerforth in her innocence, and like Clara, when she loses that innocence, she is abandoned. The sexual desire for children is here clearly depicted although its results remain problematic. While an eternal child may be the ideal sexual object (as with Annie), it is clear that such idealization is unrealistic and damaging. The consummation of the desire for sexual innocence leads, of course, to the loss of that innocence. This results in the inevitable "fallen woman" trope that is seen in Little Em'ly or in the death of the desired object that is seen in Clara and Dora Copperfield.

Whereas childhood innocence and the desire for children can be lost when children grow up or reproduce, some measure of innocence can be restored in death. As James Kincaid succinctly observes, "The good child is patient, quiet and submissive; the best child is eternally so . . . " (234). The absence or Lacanian "lack" that one desires to fill in children is only increased by the eternal absence that occurs in death, especially when the dead are remembered as children. David's insistence on remembering Steerforth at his best, as a schoolboy, asleep, with his head on his arm, keeps Steerforth anchored as a desired subject, eternally innocent, removed from his transgressions upon Little Em'ly. David self-consciously wishes Em'ly had died in her innocence,[29] rather than grow up to live (fairly happily) in Australia. Dora can be remembered with love as a child only if she dies, while David's love for his mother is presented vividly after her death when she can revert to being the unattached innocent Mrs. Copperfield of his youth, and not the distant Mrs. Murdstone of his later childhood.

We have observed how reproduction, babies, and death are associated in the novel, tied together by the fear of Malthusian economic deprivation. It is possible, then, to see some relationship between the fear of reproduction and the clinging to non-reproductive sexual innocence that Kincaid suggests. If, as Roy Porter and Lesley Hall have proposed, Malthusianism was at the root of Victorian "repression," (or at least played a substantial role in the disciplining of sexuality) the disavowal of reproduction can lead to the eroticization of the child who is not sexually reproductive. While children produce anxiety and fear as the signifiers of overpopulation, they remain "desired" sexually at least partially because they can produce no more children. Death, then, can simultaneously become an undesired economic reality from which to escape and a way to immortalize and eroticize childhood innocence. Additionally, the depiction of dead children becomes the ultimate means of addressing and repressing the fears of overpopulation that reproduction brings to the surface. Death, like the child, is both undesired and infinitely desirable. It is, perhaps, this perverse analogizing of childhood and death that could lead Dickens to name his ninth child Dora, just as he was planning to "kill" Dora within the course of the novel. It is ironic and sad that Dora Dickens was to die shortly thereafter, following her fictional sister into the annals of canonized innocents. Dickens echoed David's comments on Little Em'ly by voicing a desire for perpetual innocence at the death of his own Dora; "if, with a wish, I could cancel what has happened and bring the little creature back to life, I would not do it" (*Letters* 355). Although several of Dickens's letters suggest that this platitude functioned as a mask for a more deeply felt loss, it was a platitude that he repeated and that sheds some light on the thematics of eternal innocence explored in *Copperfield*.

## Literary Production and Reproduction

In the figure of the novel itself, the ideal "innocence" of the dead child can be reconciled most clearly with Malthusian economics. In the well-known preface to the 1869 edition of *Copperfield*, Dickens writes: "Of all my books, I like this the best. It will be easily believed that I am a fond parent to every child of my fancy, and that no one can ever love that family as dearly as I love them. But, like many fond parents, I have in my heart of hearts a favorite child. And his name is DAVID COPPERFIELD" (47).

Fred Kaplan writes, "The novel was more precious to him than his own children, because the favorite child was himself," (250) but it is also the novelistic production, and not strictly the autobiographical character that Dickens identifies as his most treasured offspring. In this interesting and provocative metaphor, Dickens creates an alternate family to the one causing him so much reproductive anxiety. By 1869, Dickens had ten living children, as well as an estranged wife and a possible mistress to support. Mary Poovey has investigated the ways in which Dickens attempts to build a masculine subjectivity out of the role of the writer and how his ability to turn writing into an economically productive profession (both in life and in his fiction) became central to that project. Building on this conception, we can see that the novels are favored children within the Malthusian economy because, unlike his biological creations, they produce resources and money rather than consume them.

This is not, of course, the full story of Dickens's impulse to replace his family with a shelf full of books.[30] Rather, as we have seen, the novel (and especially the autobiographical *bildungsroman*), like death, provides the opportunity, to freeze and eternalize all that is desirable in innocence and childhood. Likewise, in *David Copperfield* , it allows Dickens to present a frozen moment in which economic security is ultimately achieved and fears of reproductive sexuality and class angst can be abandoned. In the mythologized domestic pastoral of the home of David and Agnes, children can be produced without economic repercussions (principally because the novel comes to a conclusion), while the happily reproductive Micawbers can find enough resources to feed their hungry children. The finished and commercial novel (and for Dickens it is commercial despite his protestations that David never wished to publish it on any account) can then defeat the logic of Malthusian economics both by generating income and by eternally representing that defeat in its depictions of childhood innocence, economic security, and (eventually) reproductive happiness. Where *Tristram Shandy* opened with an unplanned reproductive moment, *David Copperfield* closes with the successes of Malthusian family planning: an economically buoyant family unit, and a completed literary production. It is no wonder that *David Copperfield* was Dickens's favorite child.

# NOTES

1. Here, Edwards' account is not, in fact, so different from Foucault's conception of discursive sexuality. Edwards reviews the historical and social changes in mid-Victorian Britain that generate a new kind of Victorian masculinity, essentially documenting the discursive production of a type of sexuality, as Foucault does. Likewise, as always, Foucault is concerned with the disciplinarity created by "power," the very type of discipline that Edwards discusses in terms of the disciplining of "deviant" sexualities. For Foucault of course, the "specification of the perverse" discursively creates types of individuals, rather than (necessarily) repressing certain types of sexual activity.
2. This anti-reproductive discourse, which in the nineteenth century become tied to spurious medical maladies like spematorrhoea will be more thoroughly examined later in the essay.
3. Throughout this essay, where I refer to Malthus I explicitly use the 1798 *Essay*. This version contains the first hints of his arguments favoring "moral restraint"

and ambiguously condemning birth control practices (the term birth control, according to Angus McLaren (15), was not introduced until the twentieth century, but it remains convenient here for the sake of analysis). Here, Malthus never explicitly mentions "moral restraint" as a preventive check but does continually refer to early marriage as a dangerous contributor to increased population. The 1803 version placed "moral self-restraint" more clearly at the center of its argument by proclaiming it as a new type of "preventive check," while the initial version concentrated more centrally on the "checks" of misery and vice and on the "ratios" that lead to overpopulation. See Mason, pp. 265ff. for an interesting discussion of Malthus's more explicit move towards "moral restraint" and the contemporary critical reaction to it. As Malthus's *Essay* progressed and expanded over the years, these themes were expanded upon and explored more thoroughly. Malthus's arguments, however, remained largely the same.

4. While Dickens may not have read Malthus directly or commented on his work, Malthus's name was consistently circulated as the central figure in the debates about overpopulation and the dangers of reproductivity I discuss in this essay. It is for this reason that I use "Malthusian" throughout the essay as a means of signifying those in the debate who believed in the dangers of overpopulation and discouraged youthful marriage and excessive reproductivity. I also occasionally use the term to refer to the debates themselves, letting context dictate the signification of the term. I use "neo-Malthusian" (in consistency with contemporary discourse) to refer to those who advocated birth control as a means to curbing overpopulation.

5. This passage is also cited in McLaren's *Birth Control in Nineteenth-Century England* (82). As McLaren discusses, Ryan was himself censured by the medical community for even discussing the possibility of contraception.

6. See Angus McLaren's *Birth Control in Nineteenth-Century England* for a further exploration of this topic.

7. The degree to which contraception had an appreciable effect on population statistics is a matter of some debate by McLaren and Chandrasekhar, among others. Michael Mason expresses his belief that the use of birth control devices and techniques did have an appreciable effect on lowering the population during the latter half of the nineteenth century: " . . . awareness of new barrier methods of contraception was an extremely important part of the explanation of the late-nineteenth-century fertility decline" (64). Mason bases this assertion partially on the decreased illegitimacy fertility rates that preceded the more general decrease in fertility rates, indicating (possibly) premarital contraceptive practices that eventually expanded to conjugal sexuality (see Mason 64–65ff.) Nevertheless, Mason calls his own views "unfashionable" and, like most elements of Victorian sexuality, this is a topic of much debate. Peter Gay agrees with Mason by proclaiming that nineteenth-century population figures point to the efficiency of contraception (265).

8. Again, this is a matter of some debate, although most scholars agree that most officially licensed medical practitioners discouraged contraception or simply refused to mention it for the greater part of the nineteenth century. This did not mean, however, that private individuals were not embracing the new possibilities

afforded to them by effective contraception. Peter Gay posits that reliable condoms were widely available by 1850 and that by the mid 1880s their use was fairly widespread, at least among the middle class (256–58). Michael Mason is more skeptical about the widespread use of condoms, but agrees that birth control itself, including the sponge, douche, pessary, etc. had a clientele by mid-century and was increasingly popular after 1877 (57–58). These particular dates can (and have been) challenged, of course, but it seems likely that portions of the public embraced contraception before the medical community began officially to sanction it.

9. See Herbert Sussman's *Victorian Masculinities* for a further exploration of this possibility.

10. Mason and others assert that Acton is, perhaps, not a representative choice for representing Victorian sexual discourse, as he moved dangerously close to quackery as his career progressed. Although his book was popular, it did not necessarily reflect the beliefs of the "official" medical community. I believe it is important to note here that for my purposes it matters little whether or not spermatorrhoea was an "officially" sanctioned medical disease (it probably was not by mid-century), but rather that spermatorrhoea was still largely a part of the cultural imagination and a threat to at least a portion of the "lay" public. It seems to be clear that the practice of quacks undoubtedly kept spermatorrhoea in the public imagination and the distaste for masturbation was maintained even by a large percentage of licensed physicians.

11. See Ornella Moscucci on clitoridectomies and Porter and Hall (141–5) on Milton's preventive techniques. Milton is described by Mason as similar to Acton in his movement through a career that began legitimately "but moved toward the borderline with the illegitimate" (189) through his fascination with spermatorrhoea.

12. Birth is consistently associated with death throughout the novel, most clearly elsewhere in the birth of David's brother, a reproductive act that results in the deaths of both the baby and David's mother—also referred to as "baby" by Betsey Trotwood.

13. This reading of the Dickensian "family" as a reflection of or parallel to contemporary anti-reproductive discourse does not necessarily obviate or displace the more traditional (and psychoanalytic) reading of Dickens propensity for portraying orphans. This tendency is often seen to be a reflection of Dickens's own sense of isolation from his own family and a general sense of parental abandonment. As Fred Kaplan writes, "Whereas Dickens felt like an orphan, David *is* one" (252). Although this certainly would explain David's isolation and alienation from his mother in *Copperfield*, I believe that the more general suppression of reproductivity is a reflection of the contemporary discourses of Malthusianism that I have identified.

14. I use the term "homosocial" here to indicate a same-sex familial pairing, rather than in the more circumscribed context Eve Sedgwick delineates in *Between Men*.

15. Alderman Cute's companion, Mr. Filer, comments specifically on Meg and Richard's ignorance of "the first principles of political economy," (97) and asserts that people like Meg and Richard (i.e., the poor), "have no earthly right or

business to be born. And *that* we know they haven't. We reduced it to a mathematical certainty long ago'' (*Christmas Books* 98). This is a clear mockery of the Malthusian ratios along with a more general critique of the anti-humanism of political economy. See Collins's *Dickens and Crime* for a specific analysis of Alderman Cute's real-life analog, Sir Peter Laurie (183–88).

16. Again, as with most statistical information on Victorian sexuality and/or population, there is some debate among historians on this issue. In addition to Weeks, Michael Mason has some useful comments on the subject (48–72).

17. As David recounts (taken directly from Dickens's 1847 autobiographical fragment), ''The remembrance of that life is fraught with so much pain to me, with so much mental suffering and want of hope, that I have never had the courage even to examine how long I was doomed to lead it'' (272).

18. Again, I do not wish here to reject the psychoanalytic possibilities of seeing David's abandonment as Dickens's repressed trauma to be reintegrated through narration (as we can see in a reading like Ned Lukacher's in *Primal Scenes*, for instance), but rather that this episode can also be viewed through the prism of Malthusian anxiety over reproduction and scarcity of resources.

19. Neither character's sexual proclivities are shown explicitly, of course, but Micawber's children serve as effective signifiers of his virility while Heep's physical appearance marks him as a masturbator—his moist hands, his undulations, his sallow complexion. As Steven Marcus says, '' . . . masturbation was unquestionably at the bottom of all of Uriah Heep's troubles'' (19).

20. This is not to say that masturbation was sanctioned completely (or even partially) in neo-Malthusian (pro-contraceptive) discourse, but merely that there is a tacit separation of the sexual act and the reproductive consequence.

21. This, of course, can lead us once again to the anti-Foucauldian notion of Victorian ''repression'' of sexuality as such. Here I am willing to go as far as Michael Mason, who observes that what Foucault denies is the repression of sexual discourse, not the repression of sexual practice (Mason 172–73). In this context, I suggest that both anti-onanistic and anti-reproductive discourses contribute to the proliferation of the discussion of sexuality that Foucault notes, while attempting to restrict the actual practice of sex itself. In this way, as Foucault himself asserts, discourses (like the anti-onanistic and Malthusian discourses) produce discipline and control human subjectivity and behavior. I decline here to comment on the effect these discourses had on actual sexual behavior (although Foucault is more likely to see discursive ''prohibitions'' as incitement to transgression and clearly Dickens himself was not unduly affected by the anti-reproductive discourse that his novel plays out), but rather point to how these discourses are reflected in Dickens's novel and how they contribute to a highly disciplined notion of Victorian marriage and ''family.''

22. This amount is ambiguously alluded to in David's '' . . . when I take my income on my fingers of my left hand, I pass the third finger and take in the fourth to the middle joint'' (693).

23. I believe it is possible to see David's choice of Dora as being disciplined both by Malthusian (anti-reproductive) and by ''spermatic'' (pro-reproductive, anti-nonreproductive) sexual economies. Dora is overtly sexual beyond what is necessary

for strictly reproductive purposes, making her less "moral" a choice than the sisterly Agnes. Simultaneously, she is reproductive when it does not appear to be economically viable to reproduce. As with the encounter of Heep and Micawber discussed above, Dora's duality encapsulates the novel's tendency to discipline all sexuality, by morally reproaching excessive non-reproductive sex (as in the case of Heep's onanism) and by indicating the economic perils of reproductive sexuality not governed by Malthusian "moral restraint." David never consciously identifies Dora's reproductivity as part of her inappropriateness, but within the sexual logic of the novel, undoubtedly part of her "unsuitability of mind and purpose" lies in her inability to manage their household in such a way as to comfortably support their expanding family.

24. Malthus consistently uses America as an example of a land where population has yet to catch up to resources, but he additionally cites America's incredibly rapid population growth as a sign that his ratios are correct. See for example, Malthus pp. 40–42.

25. Dickens presents the possibility of child as producer rather than consumer at the moment of emigration: "Both Mr. Micawber and his eldest son wore their sleeves loosely as being ready to lend a hand in any direction . . . " (874).

26. The phrase "optimistic Malthusian" may seem, of course, to be a bit of an oxymoron. Most of what Dickens seemed to dislike (at least in the example of *The Chimes* I allude to above) was the tendency of economists like Malthus to be too pessimistic, not allowing for the possibility for relief of "misery and vice" through philanthropy and social intervention. Nevertheless, here I refer to the economists, like Wade, who embraced Malthus's ratios as fact, but were willing to consider employing means of relief like emigration. Malthus's own concession to "moral restraint" as a possible relief made his 1803 edition more optimistic than his 1798 original *Essay*. For Malthus himself, both emigration and moral restraint were merely species of "misery," only desirable as the least of two evils to avoid starvation.

27. Again, these numbers are open to interpretation and are much debated by Victorian sexual historians. Certainly, despite what may well have been a general increase in population for the majority of the century, by the last third of the 1800s populations seem to have been declining, perhaps under the influence of neo-Malthusian birth control techniques (see notes 7 and 8 above).

28. Marcus and Foucault, of course, seem to be strange bedfellows, as part of Foucault's project is the deconstruction of Marcus's binaries between the "repressed" sexual discourse of someone like Acton and the "liberated" discourse of something like *My Secret Life*. Nevertheless, in this instance, I see Marcus's configuration of Acton as productive in seeing how Foucault's assertion that the supposedly repressive warning against child perversion is actually constructive (through discourse) of that perversion. Likewise, as I do throughout this article, I think Marcus's description of Acton is easily seen as merely one in a proliferation of sexualized discourses, rather than as a repression of sexuality. Acton, Malthus, and the author of *My Secret Life* all participate in the discursive proliferation around sexuality, although they all participate in different registers with the possibility of different results. Marcus's assertion of the double-sided nature of

children's sexuality is mirrored in Foucault's assessment of the "pedagogization of children's sex" (104), referring to the "dangerous and endangered sexual potential" (104) of children's sexuality.

29. David reflects, " . . . would it have been better for Little Em'ly to have had the water close above her head . . . Yes, it would have been" (86).

30. Dickens's penchant for naming his children after authors (Henry Fielding, Alfred Tennyson) or characters in his own novels (Dora) reflects his tendency to see his children (at least metaphorically) as books and his books as children.

# WORKS CITED OR CONSULTED

Abelove, Henry. "Some Speculations on the History of Sexual Intercourse During the Long Eighteenth Century." *Genders* 6 (Fall 1989): 125–30.

Acton, William. *The Functions and Disorders of the Reproductive Organs , in Childhood, Youth, Adult Age, and Advanced Life, Considered in their Physiological, Social and Moral Relations.* London: J. Churchill, 1857.

Alison, Archibald. *The Principles of Population and Their Connection with Human Happiness in Two Volumes.* Edinburgh: Blackwood, 1860.

Allbutt, H. Arthur. *The Wife's Handbook: How a Woman Should Order Herself During Pregnancy, in the Lying-Room, and after Delivery with Hints of the Management of the Baby, and on Other Matters of Importance, Necessary to be Known to Married Women, Eighth Edition.* London: R. Forder, 1888.

"Anti-Marcus." *Notes on the Population Question.* London: J. Watson, 1841.

"Art. IV.—*An Essay on the Principle of Population; or, a View of its past and present Effects on Human Happiness; with an Inquiry into our Prospects Respecting the Future Removal or Mitigation of Evils Which it Occasions. By R. T. [sic] Malthus, A. M. late Fellow of Jesus College, Cambridge and Professor of History and Political Economy in the East India College, Hertfordshire. The Fifth Edition, with Important Additions. Three Vols. 8vo. London. 1817.*" *Quarterly Review* 17 (July 1817): 369–403.

"Art. VI.—*Of Population. An Inquiry Concerning the Power of Increase in the 'Numbers of Mankind, Being an Answer to Mr. Malthus's Essay on That Subject. By William Godwin. London. 8vo. 1821. pp. 626.*" *Quarterly Review* 26 (July 1821): 148–68.

"Art. VI.—*An Inquiry Concerning the Power of Increase in the Numbers of Mankind. Being an Answer to Mr. Malthus's Essay on that Subject. By William Godwin. London, 1821.*" *Edinburgh Review* 35 (July 1821): 362–77.

Banks, Joseph A. *Prosperity and Parenthood: A Study of Family Planning Among the Victorian Middle Classes.* London: Routledge and Kegan Paul, 1954.

Barker-Benfield, G. J. "The Spermatic Economy: A Nineteenth-Century View of Sexuality." *Feminist Studies* 1 (1972): 45–74.

———. *The Horrors of the Half-Known Life: Male Attitudes Toward Women and Sexuality in Nineteenth-Century America.* New York: Harper & Row, 1976.

*Birth Control and Morality in Nineteenth Century America: Two Discussions.* Includes Charles Knowlton's *Fruits of Philosophy* (1878 edition) and Robert Dale Owen's *Moral Physiology* (1859 edition). New York: Arno Press, 1972.

Butt, John and Kathleen Tillotson. *Dickens at Work* (1957). London: Methuen, 1982.

[Carlile, Richard]. *Every Woman's Book or What is Love? Containing Most Prudent Instructions for the Prudent Regulation of The Principle of Love and The Number of a Family.* London: R. Carlile, 1828.

Chandrasekhar, Sripati. *"A Dirty Filthy Book:" The Writings of Charles Knowlton and Annie Besant on Reproductive Physiology and Birth Control and an Account of the Bradlaugh-Besant Trial.* Berkeley: U of California P, 1981. Contains complete texts of Knowlton's *Fruits of Philosophy*, Besant's *The Law of Population*, and Besant's *Theosophy and the Law of Population*.

Cohen, William A. *Sex Scandal: The Private Parts of Victorian Fiction.* Durham: Duke UP, 1996.

Collins, Philip. *Dickens and Education.* New York: Macmillan & Co. Ltd., 1965.

———. *Dickens and Crime.* New York: St. Martin's, 1994.

Dickens, Charles. *David Copperfield* (1850–51). London: Penguin, 1985.

———. *The Letters of Charles Dickens* (1850–52). Vol. 6. Ed. Graham Storey, Kathleen Tillotson and Nina Burgis. Oxford: Clarendon, 1988.

———. *Christmas Books.* London: Oxford UP, 1954.

Doubleday, Thomas. *The True Law of Population Shewn as Connected with the Food of the People* (1847). New York: Augustus M. Kelley, 1967.

Edwards, Simon. "*David Copperfield:* The Decomposing Self." *New Casebooks: David Copperfield and Hard Times.* Ed. John Peck. New York: St. Martin's, 1995. 58–80. Originally published in *The Centennial Review* 29:3 (1985): 328–52.

Everett, Alexander H. *New Ideas on Population with Remarks on the Theories of Malthus and Godwin* (1826). New York: Augustus M. Kelley, 1970.

Forster, John. *The Life of Charles Dickens* (1872–74). Vol. 1. London: Dent, 1966.

Foucault, Michel. *The History of Sexuality Volume I: An Introduction* (1978). Trans. Robert Hurley. New York: Vintage, 1990.

Gallagher, Catherine. "The Body Versus the Social Body in the Works of Thomas Malthus and Henry Mayhew." *Representations* 14 (Spring 1986): 83–106.

Gay, Peter. *Education of the Senses.* New York: Oxford UP, 1984. Vol. 1 of *The Bourgeois Experience: Victoria to Freud.* (I also consulted Vol. 2: *The Tender Passion,* 1986, but all citations above are from the first volume).

Goldfarb, Russell M. *Sexual Repression and Victorian Literature.* Lewisburg, PA: Bucknell UP, 1970.

Hager, Kelly. "Estranging *David Copperfield:* Reading the Novel of Divorce." *English Literary History* 63 (1996): 989–1019.

Hazlitt, William. *A Reply to the 'Essay on Population' by the Rev. T. R. Malthus in a Series of Letters to Which are Added Extracts from the 'Essay' with Notes* (1807). New York: Augustus M. Kelley, 1967.

Hickson, William Edward. *Malthus. An Essay on the Principle of Population in Refutation of the Theory of The Rev. T. R. Malthus.* London: Taylor, Watson, and Maberly, 1849.

Holyoake, Austin. *Large or Small Families: On Which Side Lies the Balance of Comfort?* London: R. Forder, 1892.

Houston, Gail Turley. *Consuming Fictions: Gender, Class and Hunger in Dickens's Novels.* Carbondale: Southern Illinois UP, 1994.

Jordan, John O. "The Social Sub-Text of *David Copperfield.*" *Dickens Studies Annual: Essays in Victorian Fiction* 14 (1985): 61–92.

Kaplan, Fred. *Dickens: A Biography.* New York: William Morris, 1988.

Kincaid, James R. *Child-Loving: The Erotic Child and Victorian Culture.* New York: Routledge, 1992.

Laqueur, Thomas. "Masturbation, Credit and the Novel During the Long Eighteenth Century." *Qui Parle* 8.2 (Spring/Summer 1995): 1–19.

———. "Orgasm, Generation, and the Politics of Reproductive Biology." *Representations* 14 (Spring 1986): 1– 41.

Lloyd, W. F. *Two Lectures on the Checks to Population Delivered Before The University of Oxford in Michaelmas Term 1832.* Oxford: S. Collingwood, 1833.

Lukacher, Ned. *Primal Scenes: Literature, Philosophy, Psychoanalysis.* Ithaca, NY: Cornell UP, 1986.

Malthus, Thomas R. *The Works of Thomas Robert Malthus: Volume One: An Essay on the Principle of Population: The First Edition (1798) with Introduction and*

*Bibliography.* Ed. E. A. Wrigley and David Souden. London: William Pickering, 1986.

"Marcus." *On the Possibility of Limiting Populousness.* London: John Hill, 1838.

Marcus, Steven. *The Other Victorians: A Study of Sexuality and Pornography in Mid-Nineteenth Century England.* New York: Basic Books, 1974.

Mason, Michael. *The Making of Victorian Sexuality.* Oxford: Oxford UP, 1994.

McLaren, Angus. *Birth Control in Nineteenth-Century England.* New York: Holmes and Meier, 1978.

Miller, D. A. "Secret Subjects, Open Secrets." *The Novel and the Police.* Berkeley: U of California P, 1988. 192–220.

Moscucci, Ornella. "Clitoridectomy, Circumcision, and the Politics of Sexual Pleasure in Mid-Victorian Britain." *Sexualities in Victorian Britain.* Ed. Andrew H. Miller and James Eli Adams. Bloomington: Indiana UP, 1996. 60–78.

Needham, Gwendolyn B. "The Undisciplined Heart of *David Copperfield.*" *Nineteenth-Century Fiction* 9:2 (September 1954): 81–107.

Newman, Francis William. *The Corruption Now Called Neo-Malthusianism.* London: The Moral Reform Union, 1889.

Place, Francis. *Illustrations and Proofs of the Principle of Population* (1822). Ed. Norman Himes. New York: Augustus M. Kelley, 1967.

Porter, Roy and Lesley Hall. *The Facts of Life: The Creation of Sexual Knowledge in Britain, 1650–1950.* New Haven: Yale UP, 1995.

Poovey, Mary. "The Man of Letters Hero: *David Copperfield* and the Professional Writer." *Uneven Developments: The Ideological Work of Gender in Mid-Victorian England.* Chicago: The U of Chicago P, 1988. 89–125.

Rose, Phyllis. *Parallel Lives: Five Victorian Marriages.* London: Hogarth, 1984.

Ryan, Michael, M.D. *The Philosophy of Marriage in its Social, Moral, and Physical Relations; with an Account of the Diseases of the Genito-Urinary Organs, Which Impair or Destroy the Reproductive Function and Induce a Variety of Complaints with the Physiology of Generation in the Vegetable and Animal Kingdoms; Being Part of a Course of Obstetric Lectures Delivered at the North London School of Medicine, Charlotte Street, Bloomsbury, Bedford Square.* Philadelphia: Barrington and Haswell, 1848.

Smith, Kenneth. *The Malthusian Controversy.* London: Routledge and Kegan Paul, 1951.

Sterne, Laurence. *The Life and Opinions of Tristram Shandy, Gentleman* (1759–1767). Ed. Ian Campbell Ross. Oxford: Clarendon, 1983.

Sussman, Herbert. *Victorian Masculinities: Manhood and Masculine Poetics in Early Victorian Literature and Art.* Cambridge: Cambridge UP, 1995.

Vanden Bossche, Chris R. "Cookery Not Rookery: Family and Class in *David Copperfield.*" *New Casebooks:* David Copperfield *and* Hard Times. Ed. John Peck. New York: St. Martin's, 1995. Originally published in *Dickens Studies Annual* 15 (1986): 87–109.

Wade, John. *History of the Middle and Working Classes with a Popular Exposition of the Economical and Political Principles Which Have Influenced the Past and Present Condition of the Industrious Orders.* London: Effingham Wilson, Royal Exchange, 1833.

Weeks, Jeffrey. *Sex, Politics and Society: The Regulation of Sexuality Since 1800.* London: Longman, 1989.

Welsh, Alexander. *From Copyright to Copperfield: The Identity of Dickens.* Cambridge, MA: Harvard UP, 1987.

# Which Hand? Reading *Great Expectations* as a Guessing Game

## Norman Macleod

*The frequency of references to hands in* Great Expectations *(1860–61) has been recognized by a number of commentators, who have tended to take these references, reasonably enough, as working both mimetically and symbolically—grounded in realism but significant besides. But these references may have an additional diversionary function, by entering cumulatively into a covert textually-established scheme whereby, in apparently off-hand references, Dickens continually teases the reader as to which hand—left or right?—any particular character employs. Quite natural patterns of just sufficiently egregious wording and idiom reveal a possible cryptic scheme when attended to closely: certain linguistic features seem to show that Joe Gargery is right-handed, Mrs. Joe left-handed, that the ambiguous Pip is left-handed but pretending to be right-handed, and that the text is always teasingly inexplicit about the handedness of Estella. Furthermore, a character's dominant handedness interacts with that character's manual habits when accompanying speech and other behavior, so that characters like Joe and Mrs. Joe, respectively seen at first as straightforwardly "good" and "bad," come to be distinguished (and related) in a more complex scheme that perhaps reflects a deeper understanding of them as characters.*

Near the end of chapter 7 of *Great Expectations* (1860–61), Pip tells us of the evening when his sister, Mrs. Joe Gargery, and Uncle Pumblechook come with the news that Miss Havisham wants Pip to go and play at her house. The plan is that Pip will go off that evening with Pumblechook, who is to deliver him to Miss Havisham's the next morning, and so Mrs. Joe begins to get Pip (whom she describes as "grimed with crock and dirt from the hair of his head to the sole of his foot") ready for his imminent departure:

> With that she pounced upon me, like an eagle on a lamb, and my face was squeezed into wooden bowls in sinks, and my head was put under taps of water-butts, and I was soaped, and kneaded, and towelled, and thumped, and harrowed, and rasped, until I really was quite beside myself. (I may here remark that I suppose myself to be better acquainted than any living authority, with the ridgy effect of a wedding-ring, passing over the human countenance).[1]

Pip's description does not seem to be taken up specifically with the forcible ablutions of that particular night, but becomes instead a generalized and whimsical account of what it always must have felt like to have his face and hair washed by Mrs. Joe. The mixture of accuracy and amused excess in the description expresses a distanced, grown-up acceptance that the young Pip could not have felt at the time, and this quality of humorous and nostalgic tolerance is carried through to—and underwritten by—the indulgent and light-hearted self-mockery of the bracketed para-diegetic aside: "(I may here remark that I suppose myself to be better acquainted than any living authority, with the ridgy effect of a wedding-ring, passing unsympathetically over the human countenance)." But behind the distracting whimsy of Pip's remarks it is possible to miss an implication, embedded in the playful and throw-away parenthesis, and whose import seems to be belittled by those quarantining brackets—the point apparently sidelined by a writer easily finding another way of signalling his playful tone. Not only that, but the implication—once it has been drawn—seems both obvious and insignificant, and therefore additionally discountable. But, following from the culturally given fact that the wedding-ring hand is the left hand, the implication is there—namely, that Mrs. Joe's preferred or active hand is her left hand.[2] The implication is that this is the hand that she does things with (such as washing Pip's face and hair while his head is apparently held pinioned by her static right arm—indeed, held "under her arm, as a boot would be held in a boot-jack" (44), as Pip has earlier described another instance of Mrs. Joe holding his head under her arm so as to administer a pint of the dreaded Tar-water). Now if this business of the wedding-ring hand were the only covert and seemingly dismissible reference to hands in *Great Expectations*, one could and would let it go: the possibility of something being stealthily signalled (rather than slipping unseen into the text, or being over-keenly picked out) would hardly arise.

In fact, *Great Expectations* is full of references to hands, and a number of them are like the instance unpacked above—individually carrying an implication that could easily be taken as stray in any single case, but seeming, when considered alongside other similar instances, to belong to a deliberate and covert scheme whose factitious patterns seem to correlate very closely with any reader's likely responses to different central characters in the novel. Indeed, this is a central argument of what follows—that at least in relation to the presentation of the leading characters introduced in the early chapters of *Great Expectations* it is possible to pick out marginal and circumstantial references to hands which, over the piece, seem to coexist as a fugitive system. This system or scheme is one which can be said to match with the reader's sense of characters as favorable or unfavorable, but at the same time it is not something that consciously prompts these responses. The possibility of the scheme, in fact, could most easily be handled by dismissing it as unlikely—merely a caprice of the narrative if it is there at all; novels, after all, deal with people and their everyday lives and activities, and having hands is a fact about people, and people's constant use of their hands is a necessary feature of their domestic, social, and commercial existence. So it is simply inevitable that novels should mention people's hands and what they do with them. All this is taken as read: but alongside it the argument that follows adopts an additional and more contentious assumption—namely, that in *Great Expectations* references to hands have an import in the fictionality of the text alongside their function in creating the realism of the world of the novel. The claim is that references to hands in *Great Expectations* are both realistic and at the same time involved in a textually contrived pattern—one that is factitious but not, I believe, adventitious, and which corroborates but does not directly express things conveyed in other ways about the purported realism of the world of the novel, and particularly its chief inhabitants and personalities.

The frequency of references to hands, and to actions involving hands, in *Great Expectations* has been observed more than once before, and along with such observations there have come various suggestions of significance, some of them dealing with issues of textual fictionality as well as with more immediate concerns of fictional realism.[3] Charles R. Forker, the first commentator to pursue the matter in detail (although acknowledging the prompting of an earlier brief aside of J. Hillis Miller), sees the recurrent references to hands in a standard literary way, "as a *leitmotif* of plot and theme—a kind of unifying symbol or natural metaphor for the book's complex of human interrelationships and the values and attitudes that motivate them" (281). And Forker notes that the frequent and systematic character of hand references in *Great Expectations* makes them an especial part of the novel's significance: "As strokes of characterization, hands are always important in Dickens, and *Great Expectations* is merely the one novel that puts them to the most consistent and meaningful use" (293).

The majority of those other commentators who, later than Forker, have also drawn attention to the consistency of references to hands in *Great Expectations* have equally readily assumed their function to be essentially symbolic and/or mimetic. Accordingly, Jack B. Moore, pointing out that "hearts" and "hands" are two key words in *Great Expectations*, observes: "Care is taken by Dickens to focus on his characters' hands, and thereby to inform the reader of the nature of the character" (52). Moore then concludes: "Communication with hands also symbolises throughout the novel the sincerity and depth, or superficiality and fraud, of various characters" (54). More recently, Jerome Buckley has commented on the cohesively symbolic function of hand references in *Great Expectations*: "Throughout the novel even the simplest gesture . . . is likely to have symbolic import, for the whole is as much unified by recurrent symbols and chains of imagery as by solidity of structure" (47). And Buckley suggests that although references to hands are "reproduced with a literal accuracy, it is the logic of poetry and not of a workaday realism that accounts for their presence and the design into which they are woven" (47).

In 1980 and 1981, two other scholars separately made significant comments on hand references in *Great Expectations*. First, Harry Stone pointed (the italics are mine) to an "intricate web of hand imagery that surrounds Pip to give his most ordinary handshakes, hand injuries, and hand gestures the symbolic force and potency of ritual. That ritual, in turn, is part of an elaborate network of hand imagery that links half the characters in *Great Expectations* in a secret freemasonry of hands. One is constantly astonished by this magical ceremony of hands, for *though plain to view, it is virtually invisible; it merges with—one might almost say it loses itself in—the book's compelling realism*" (334). Next, Walter L. Reed separately observed (again, the italics are mine) that in *Great Expectations*—citing it as a "common example" of semiotic transformation in fiction:

> a whole prototextual sign language is generated simply by attention to the physical detail of hands. These manual markers in the novel are not simply

metaphors, a pattern of imagery in the traditional sense where literal phenomenon and figurative expression are relatively distinct. They are rather an example
of the physically literal world shaping itself into rudimentary patterns of meaning, creating a primitive version of language which characters may speak
and—occasionally—comprehend. *They are part of the represented world presenting itself back as text."*                                    (269–70)

And now, very recently, Nicola Bradbury has also drawn attention to references to hands in *Great Expectations* as one of a range of different motifs
which "are included in the language of the whole novel, but [which] each
have their own idioms, their own tone, and different degrees of obviousness
or abstruseness: . . . they are all themselves, but also signals of something
else" (58). Bradbury then goes on to remark perceptively about these systems:
"They make up the recognisable world of the novel, but they also point to
its fictive quality. They bring Pip's history to life, and they obstruct our simple
wish to believe it. Instead they ask us to read, to interpret, to understand"
(58). Most recently of all, William A. Cohen focuses on manual conduct in
*Great Expectations* in developing an argument that "One of the nineteenth-
century novel's principal accomplishments is to formulate a literary language
that expresses eroticism even as it designates sexuality the supremely unmen-
tionable subject" (220). For Cohen, *Great Expectations* is a novel which
"encrypts sexuality not in its plot or in its announced intentions, but in its
margins, at the seemingly incidental moments of its figurative language,
where, paradoxically, it is so starkly obvious as to be invisible" (221). Cohen
reads the novel in terms of a "manual semiotics" of masturbation, claiming
to identify an indirectly and covertly signalled "pattern that runs throughout
*Great Expectations*, a pattern which figures the sexual caress not in the geni-
tals that are handled but in the hands that do the touching" (221).

   There is a common tendency and direction to almost all these interpretations—namely, that Dickens uses references to hands in *Great Expectations*
both mimetically and symbolically, endowing references that are grounded
in the reportage of literal and everyday realism with a figurative and textural
consistency that underlines various aspects of characterization, plot, and
theme. No one would want to say that these qualities of reference and significance are not there in any proper reading of *Great Expectations*, but I want
to suggest that there is an additional—and overlapping—scheme, which exists
textually as well as mimetically, and whose textual role is as much ludic or
diversionary as functional, serving to distract and disconcert the reader as
much as it confirms or supplements the reader's natural understanding of
characters and events—though it does that, too. All in all, I would like to argue

that the references to hands in *Great Expectations* provide an interpretative sideshow, a subtextual and distracting puzzle that seems to have meaning and to that extent to be palpably in the text, but which at the same time exists in the text in such a fugitive manner as to seem, not just factitious, but adventitious.

In a sense, without adopting any view about the reading intriguingly developed by William A. Cohen, I too see the references to hands in *Great Expectations* as being interesting in a textual rather than simply representative way, and (like Cohen) as being fugitive, covert, semiotic, but I do not read them at all as portentously or lubriciously. Instead, they seem to me to be references that turn one aspect of the reading of *Great Expectations* into a diverting kind of guessing game. And, like Harry Stone and Walter L. Reed, I am struck by the apparently designed invisibility and artifice of the pattern of these references. Indeed, insofar as the central claim of this argument links with any of those that have preceded it, it seems to me to find the clearest resonances in Reed's finely discriminated observation, that ''These manual markers in the novel are not simply metaphors'' but are also '' . . . part of the represented world presenting itself back as text''—an instance of what others (as Reed notes) have seen as a transforming semiotic characteristic of written fiction (270). In Nicola Bradbury's words, ''They make up the recognisable world of the novel, but they also point to its fictive quality'' (58).

There is an unusual (or, at least, a noticeable) quality of idiom, expression, and style in some of the manual references in Pip's narrative in *Great Expectations*. Pip sometimes tends, in references to hands, to use phrases and other kinds of expressions which it is possible to take in two quite distinct ways: either one can see them as idiomatic, as expressions that have a meaning that is conventional and indirect, and distinct from the natural and directly compositional meaning that the expression—*as constructed*— could bear; or one can see these expressions literally, seeing them as meaning exactly what they say, even if this more basic meaning has implications or undertones not borne by the phrase in its more usual idiomatic function. Indeed, looked at as transparently having the meaning its overt form potentially conveys, such an expression can appear to have a meaning that is quite comic or unnatural. An example—merely the handiest, being one that occurs very prominently in the text and that is well enough recognized not to be controversial—would be the early reference to Mrs. Joe having brought Pip up ''by hand'' (39), which conventionally means by bottle-feeding but which, as Jerome Buckley indicates, also suggests ''by systematic cuffing''—literally by use or action of the hand (47). Indeed, Buckley's secondary interpretation merely echoes Pip's own youthful incomprehension regarding the meaning of this phrase.

As Nicola Bradley notes, in Pip's inexperienced interpretation of this particular idiom, "Literal and metaphorical are comically locked together" (58).

The literal underside of an idiomatic expression used by Pip can come to the fore alongside the more germane idiomatic sense in various ways: sometimes it is brought into prominence by some other constructional device in Pip's narrative; sometimes the expression used is one where the idiomatic sense can be grasped only by also registering the facilitating literal meaning. Whatever the case, and whatever the particular circumstances, the reader of Pip's narrative, particularly in the early stages, can distractingly—and sometimes comically—be made aware of the literal meaning of an expression that has already become established as the vehicle of a figurative and idiomatic meaning.[4] This is the case when Pip tells us of his sister's boast of having brought him up "by hand" and of his own childish misunderstanding of that idiomatic Victorian gentility:

> Having at that time to find out for myself what the expression meant, and knowing her to have a hard and heavy hand, and to be much in the habit of laying it upon her husband as well as me, I supposed that Joe Gargery and I were both brought up by hand.       (39)

The fact that Mrs. Joe's hands are coarse, tough, unfeminine, and punitive is expressed idiomatically in a singular hackneyed phrase ("to have a hard and heavy hand," which is equivalent to saying she was hard- and heavy-handed), with the attributive adjectives functioning non-restrictively, not to identify a particular hand but to characterize a quality of the hands—and, thereby, the nature of Mrs. Joe's handedness. But Pip takes or treats the phrase as if it were literally meant in the singular and as if the adjectives were restrictive in function, specifying and identifying the particular hand indicated: thus the phrase "a hard and heavy hand" is pronominalized by Pip with *it*, suggesting that it is as if the earlier noun phrase functioned referentially rather than attributively in making a specific rather than a generic reference to Mrs. Joe—picking out one particular hand of hers rather than simply sketching an aspect of her manual nature. But here we can recall that other detail from the description of Mrs. Joe's characteristic way of conducting Pip's evening ablutions—that it sounds there as if she is characteristically left-handed. Taking these two references to Mrs. Joe—references that are at one and the same time egregious and transient, carrying clear implications but with nothing said definitely and outwardly—and allowing them to rebound suggestively upon each other in our minds, prompts the speculation that when

Pip speaks of his youthful sense of his sister as having "a hard and heavy hand" he means us to understand that he thought or took it that the phrase identified and perfectly described Mrs. Joe's very (and singularly) active left hand, rather than simply being an idiomatic way of referring to the most prominent and memorable characteristic of her hands.

There are other examples which involve a comically literal precision in the use of an idiomatic phrase in reference to hands, and where we can again be led to see a particular but unstated contextualization for an otherwise irrational or supererogatory literalism. Furthermore, such contextualizations regularly fit in with others in a wider and ironic scheme of references to hands which can, at best, be appreciated only as a shadowy quality of the text, pervasively there but never explicitly conveyed—something covert, subtextual, almost subliminal, but (once sensed) diverting enough to become consciously part of what one registers as one reads. Fully recognized, this scheme turns out to correlate in an intriguing way with any ordinary wholehearted reading of the novel. The scheme allows us to see that, in *Great Expectations*, a good or sympathetic character like Joe is right-handed, an initially unattractive or unsympathetic one like Mrs. Joe left-handed, and where a character is complex, or ambiguous, or cannot be seen clearly, either by the reader or by Pip, then the hand references are unclear. But further than that—better yet, indeed—Pip is left-handed, like his sister, but strives (and in the end largely manages) to conceal his handedness. And overlapping with such an apparently simple system (which at least seems to be in touch with natural and/or conventional notions) is a second, seemingly more contrived system, which additionally differentiates (1) an initially unsympathetic character with a potential for good (such as Mrs. Joe), from (2) a fundamentally very attractive character who may have a slight potential for humbug or snobbery, or who may betray some awareness of social position or class (such as—belatedly—Joe). Thus, Mrs. Joe is someone who *supplements* speech with some simultaneous and emphatically underlining action of her *single* characteristic hand; while Joe has a preferred but not uniquely characteristic hand and *substitutes* two-handed signalling actions for speech, or—when speaking—*accompanies* his speech with *two-handed* dissembling actions which nevertheless somehow betray his unreliable wordings. And overlapping with these two systems there may be others—for instance, one which separates those characters whose two-handed actions are deliberate and/or self-conscious from those whose same actions are instinctive and/or unconscious.[5]

Several early references to Joe Gargery make him out to be involved with Pip in a private non-verbal system of signalling their responses and attitudes to Mrs. Joe—especially when she is on the rampage. Thus, we are told about Joe, variously:

> (1) Joe, who had ventured into the kitchen after me as the dust-pan had retired before us, drew the back of his hand across his nose with a conciliatory air when Mrs Joe darted a look at him, and, when her eyes were withdrawn, secretly crossed his two forefingers, and exhibited them to me, as our token that Mrs Joe was in a cross temper. This was so much her normal state, that Joe and I would often, for weeks together, be, as to our fingers, like monumental Crusaders as to their legs. (53)

> (2) "Well," said Joe, passing the poker into his left hand, that he might feel his whisker; (79)

> (3) My sister catching him in the act, he drew the back of his hand across his nose with his usual conciliatory air on such occasions, and looked at her. (81)

> (4) "No, Joseph," said my sister, while Joe apologetically drew the back of his hand across and across his nose, . . . (82)

The significant reference here is in (2), where we are told that Joe passes the poker into his left hand, thus freeing his right hand for stroking his whisker. Pip constructs his narrative report so as almost to make it seem that Joe's action is deliberate and intentional, with the consequence of his earlier act ("that he might feel his whisker") reported almost as if it were the purpose behind that earlier act (of "passing the poker into his left hand"). One says "almost" advisedly since Pip's carefully constructed sentence remains so delicately poised that it can also be read as establishing a simply sequential (rather than consequential) relationship between the events it describes in these contiguous clauses: thus it would be very difficult to specify whether these two clauses are connected paratactically or hypotactically (that is, as equals, or with one dependent on the other), and accordingly it must remain uncertain whether Pip is talking of what Joe does as part of Joe's conscious intention or as something characteristic and habitual, and so done without reflection. But the suggestion of intentionality and awareness (rather than abstracted and musing unconsideredness) is sufficently registered for us to be predisposed (as Pip's wording allows, and indeed perhaps prompts) to consider that Joe's movement is part of a covert, non-verbal signal expressing a particular attitude to Mrs. Joe. Certainly, this is how Pip tends to see it, and at least his suspicion that this is so is sufficiently communicated by the sentence structure with which he chooses to describe it. But once we take (2) like that, it next seems to be part of Joe's deliberateness to ensure that his signal is performed with his right hand. And that leads us to a more definite contextualization of the other tantalizingly inexplicit references in examples (1), (3), and (4), so that we now also take the hand that is talked about in these cases as Joe's right hand, rather than as his left, or as not possibly identifiable either way. These less definite references do not exclude being treated on a par and in terms of (2), and we are drawn to see Pip's talk of Joe drawing "the back of his hand" across his nose, not as an idiomatically legitimate way of talking (equivalent to saying "the back of a hand"), with Joe using one or other hand thoughtlessly and unconsideredly, but as a literally-meant specific reference (equivalent to "the particular hand that the reader and I are presumed to know he regularly and characteristically used in this way").

If there is significance in the various references to hands along the lines being sketched here, then the most prominent feature of each and every example is the fugitive nature (and at the same time the tantalizingly relevant quality) of each example's contribution to the perception of the scheme of which it seems to be a part. The scheme seems to be sketched so elusively that its observation seems always to risk being capriciously missed. The scheme (in keeping with many more general aspects of Pip's whole narrative) is privative, secret, ironic, revealed as much through its being concealed as through being expressed. But at the same time as it is easy to see the scheme as nebulous, there is always some inescapable and linguistically salient feature which provides the first indication or suggestion of some particular and more-than-expected significance in what is said. Thus, in example (1) above, Pip talks of Joe crossing "his two forefingers" and not simply "his forefingers" (nor, less simply, but still more obviously than what he does say, "both his forefingers"). What Pip means is also underlined—indeed, once you think you have worked out what he does mean, seemingly corroborated—by the typically sidelined and potentially distracting reference to Pip and Joe being "as to our forefingers, like monumental Crusaders as to their legs." It is not the forefinger (or index finger) of each hand, but the paired forefingers of a single hand, that—to Pip's view of things—Joe uses in any non-verbal signal regarding Mrs. Joe. The comparison to monumental Crusaders tantalizingly enriches the challenge of interpretation at the same time as it clarifies: though it fits with one view clearly, one almost simultaneously sees that it could also fit with the alternative.

What ultimately matters is that the alternative but eschewed phrasing of "both his forefingers" would certainly have conveyed a clear and opposite meaning (of the index—or whatever—finger of each hand), while the phrase

Pip does use ("his two forefingers") seems an alertingly redundant version of its inexplicit synonym (namely, "his forefingers"). The question arises, and prompts us to seek an answer—why say "his two forefingers" when you could, apparently just as efficiently, say "his forefingers"? Once again, and once more not explicitly but, indeed, in a form of words that has the potential to contradict the seemingly inescapable meaning that it itself at first prompts, we are told something about a character—this time Joe Gargery—which can lead us to believe that one preferred, more active, hand—on other evidence, as well as that above—is alone involved in making (or in seeming to Pip to make) a covert signal to Pip. Without advisedly careful reading here we could take it that both hands are involved, just as in other cases we could easily assume—or not become concerned over thinking—that each hand is variously involved. But each time, in each instance, a very specific interpretation, consistent from case to case, can be glimpsed, all regularly allowing a contextualization to the effect that Joe uses his right hand for signalling things to Pip, or at least to do things that Pip regards or takes as signals. Accordingly, when we come on a remark about Joe such as the following, the otherwise circumstantial locative detail (about the position of curls and whiskers) does not seem at all pointless or insignificant: "After that, he sat feeling his right-side curls and whisker, and following Mrs Joe about with his blue eyes, as his manner always was at squally times" (42).

The examples we have been considering are, of course, not the only significant references to Joe and actions involving his hands. In the early chapters of *Great Expectations*, Joe's great habit is to sit by the hearth, holding the poker and stirring the fire in the grate. Thus, at various points we are told of Joe:

> (1) "That's what she did," said Joe, slowly clearing the fire between the lower bars with the poker and looking at it; "she Ram-paged out, Pip."          (40)

> (2) "Well, Pip," said Joe, taking up the poker, and settling himself to his usual occupation when he was thoughtful, of slowly raking the fire between the lower bars: . . .          (76)

> (3) "Which you see, Pip," said Joe, pausing in his meditative raking of the fire, looking at me, "were a drawback on my learning."          (77)

> (4) "Though mind you, Pip," said Joe, with a judicial touch or two on the top bar, . . .          (77)

> (5) Joe's blue eyes turned a little watery; he rubbed, first one of them, and then the other, in a most uncongenial and uncomfortable manner, with the round knob on the top of the poker.          (77)

(6)"Whatever family opinions, or whatever the world's opinions, on that subject may be, Pip, your sister is," Joe tapped the top bar with the poker after
every word following, "a—fine—figure—of—a—woman!"                    (78)

(7) I broke out crying and begging pardon, and hugged Joe round the neck:
who dropped the poker to hug me, and to say "Ever the best of friends: an't
us, Pip? Don't cry, old chap!"                                        (78)

(8) "And why on the sly? I'll tell you why, Pip."
He had taken up the poker again, without which, I doubt if he could have
proceeded in his demonstration. "Your sister is given to government."   (79)

(9) "Well," said Joe, passing the poker into his left hand, that he might feel
his whisker; and I had no hope of him whenever he took to that placid occupation; "Your sister's a master-mind. A mastermind."                    (79)

Only the last (and already partially-cited) instance of these, (9)—and that
indirectly—gives any indication of which hand Joe uses to hold the poker,
and indeed also suggests that that hand is his preferred hand for all conscious,
deliberate, directed, intentional actions. A major implication of (9), applied
generally and with nothing stated or indicated elsewhere to contradict it, is
that Joe holds the poker in his right hand, transferring it to the left—as in (9)
above—only when he embarks on what Pip regards as some private and
meaningful gesture prompted by something said by Mrs. Joe. Example (5)
above suggests that with any other distraction, as long as it does not involve
covert response to Mrs. Joe, the poker is held to in the same hand, the right
hand, as is normally used for manipulating it, no matter how inconvenient
such retention is or how unnatural the resultant action may seem to an outsider, or how discomfiting to oneself. Only when retention is quite impossible
or impractical or against the spirit of another activity—example (7)—is the
poker dropped. And, it is hinted, Joe finds fireside talk almost impossible
without (example 8) the accompaniment of the poker—well, he is a blacksmith, after all: its use, or at the very least its retention, seems a necessary,
though perhaps an unconscious, accompaniment for everything he says to
Pip. Indeed, in one case (example 6), the poker is important as the means of
Joe's underlining of his words. Putting everything together, we can read example (6) by imagining Joe holding the poker *in his right hand* and emphasizing
every word by striking the poker on the grate.
    When, later in the novel, we find out that Joe has learned—after a fashion,
perhaps a blacksmith's fashion—to write, it is no surprise, all things considered, to be told of his style or behavior as a writer, and to discover that he
uses his right hand to write (but with his left hand called into play in a

supporting role): "It was necessary for Joe to hold on heavily to the table with his left elbow, and to get his right leg well out behind him, before he could begin, and when he did begin, he made every downstroke so slowly . . . " (474). Now, in his (blacksmith's) writing style, also pinioning something firmly with his left arm while working on it actively with his right hand, Joe is suddenly seen as akin (but still as opposite) to Mrs. Joe when she takes firm hold of Pip or a loaf of bread. It is even a late feature of Joe's scribal antics that he " . . . removed a finishing blot from the paper to the crown of his head with his two forefingers . . . " (474). Clearly this time (and perhaps in tantalizing corroboration of the point at issue in the example about Crusaders and their legs considered earlier) what is meant are the two forefingers of just one hand—Joe's right (and writing) hand.

Joe, then, seems to be presented as someone who is naturally right-handed, so naturally so in fact that he prefers to transfer the much-handled poker to his left hand when (but only when) he wants to use his right hand communicatively in some private or abstracted signal or gesture: so that while he is talking to Pip, the poker is constantly available to be brought into play, and can be used—and on one occasion is used, with vigorous, right-handed emphasis—to underline each separately uttered word.

As I have briefly indicated already, there are also interesting references involving Mrs. Joe and her hands, and some of these references seem both tantalizing and contrived in the way they are expressed. The most tantalizing of all references to Mrs. Joe regarding her handedness is found in the wonderful and much remembered description of her slicing bread for Joe and Pip:

> My sister had a trenchant way of cutting our bread-and-butter for us, which never varied. First, with her left hand she jammed the loaf hard and fast against her bib—where it sometimes got a pin into it, and sometimes a needle, which we afterwards got into our mouths. Then she took some butter (not too much) on a knife and spread it on the loaf, in an apothecary kind of way, as if she were making a plaister—using both sides of the knife with a slapping dexterity, and trimming and moulding the butter off round the crust. Then, she gave the knife a final smart wipe on the edge of the plaister, and then sawed a very thick round off the loaf: which she finally, before separating from the loaf, hewed into two halves, of which Joe got one, and I the other.          (42)

On its own, this must seem straightforward and untroublesome, at least as far as knowing what it says is concerned. But when looked at from the perspective taken here, and with other more obviously significant (and perhaps more puzzling) references in mind, *and giving close but relevant attention to details of its language and structure,* this passage reveals several uncertainties. Key linguistic details show that Dickens can be seen as going to some pains to tease rather than to direct the disconcerted reader, by seeming to point things unambiguously towards a direction that turns out not to be the only one available. The fond detail of the description can be seen straightforwardly as capturing Mrs. Joe's unwaveringly characteristic way of slicing bread. But at the same time the exuberant and affectionate minutiae can take our attention away from muted uncertainties over how to take some of the things that are said alongside. Thus, although one might think that it is, it is never clearly stated—never established in an out-and-out manner—which hand Mrs. Joe is so very actively using here: first, to spread the butter and trim it, then to cut, divide, and finally serve the individual portions of bread. What *is* made clear is the dexterity and efficiency of the whole business ("using both sides of the knife with a slapping dexterity"; "a final smart wipe"; "a trenchant way"), even to the final implication that the bread is sliced, the slice halved, and then each half-slice fluently served all with the same single knife-wielding hand (and all virtually in the same movement) that has achieved the preparatory buttering and spreading.

The fact that we have to describe the whole thing as done with dexterity—and that Dickens nudges us thitherwards by himself using the word *dexterity*—need not be seen as decisive nor as an etymologically-based clue, since in describing manual action *dexterity* is not limited to an etymologically permitted meaning but has become the neutral, general, and unmarked term for any kind of manual skill or adroitness. In fact, its use by Dickens may be a kind of false light or misleading clue, since the etymological idea of dexterity (that it applies to the right hand) may seem to fit, without trouble, with what comes across as a clear implication of the first descriptive clause of the extract: "First, with her left hand she jammed the loaf hard and fast against her bib." That clause seems to say, without making any bones about it, that Mrs. Joe used her left hand to hold the loaf firmly against her bib, thus freeing her right hand (the link with *dexterity*) for doing all the—well, dexterous—things that follow. This is clearly the obvious way to read the sentence—that it mentions the left hand as part of the fixed (or firm, or at least temporarily maintained) environment into which the loaf was jammed, with the consequence that only the right hand was free to do other things with. But while that is the obvious way it is not the only way to read the clause "First, with her left hand she jammed the loaf hard and fast against her bib," and there are various factors in the language of the clause which, individually and severally, can be seen—once considered—to work against that easy (and seemingly unquestionable) reading. In fact, it is just as legitimate (and almost as obvious idiomatically) to read the sentence in the opposite way—with the left hand being mentioned as the hand which projects the loaf into the space in which it is jammed, that space being formed in the gap between the rigid right hand (and arm) and the bib.

The crucial factor here is that the hands form a pair—so that when only one is mentioned in circumstances where the other is involved, then the other is implied. In a sentence or clause with the main verb *jam*, where one phrase specifies part of the environment into which something is jammed ("against her bib"), then a phrase mentioning one hand can identify that hand *either* as the other part of the environment (with the implication that the other hand is free as the means of projecting and jamming something into this environment), *or* as the means of projection (with the other, unspecified, hand now being implied as the other part of the environment). Thus "with her left hand she jammed the loaf against her bib" is semantically quite ambivalent (although it tantalizes by looking clear, and becomes fugitive in being so easy to read unreflectively in that apparently clear way). In such a construction, "with her left hand" can specify the hand mentioned either as part of the environment or as the means of projection: and it all depends on how you take the explicit phrase as to what the remaining correlative implication is—either that the right hand is free for doing other things, or it is not. It just is not as clear as it looks from the sentence used by Pip exactly what is being conveyed by that sentence.

There is another, wider, factor to draw out here. Quite apart from particular cases where *jam* occurs with a *with*-phrase mentioning one out of a pair of hands (as in "with her left hand she jammed the loaf against her bib"), other cases show that the colligation of *jam* and a *with*-phrase is generally and inherently ambiguous (though, of course, always with a predisposition to see only or first of all—or most easily—the unmarked or idiomatically most encountered meaning). Thus a sentence like *John jammed the jar with pencils* can be used to say either that John filled the jar brimful with pencils or—conceivably—that John used pencils (placed and pressed tightly around the jar) to jam the jar, perhaps pressed into service as a makeshift mousetrap, into a hole that otherwise was too big. This ambivalence is even more clear when we compare plural and singular forms of the same sentence—*John jammed the jar with pencils* and *John jammed the jar with a pencil*. The first (plural) form favors an interpretation where pencils are put into the jar, the second (singular) form does not at all easily mean that but instead strongly suggests that jar and pencil were together put into the same, larger, hole. But in appropriate circumstances either sentence can have either meaning.

There is a final, and more immediate, point. In terms of well-formedness in a grammar—that is, in terms of constraint by grammatical rules—there is no *grammatical* restriction against a sentence like *With her left hand she jammed the loaf against her bib with her right hand*. Such a sentence is a touch inelegant, of course—perhaps sufficiently maladroit stylistically as always to prompt replacement or revision. But that does not affect the force of the theoretical point being made here—and, indeed, does not mean that such a sentence, once cited, cannot be seen as possibly meaningful. As far as linguistic form is concerned, the occurrence in such a sentence of two *with*-phrases, fulfilling different functions and yet overlapping in their area of reference, is not in any way restricted grammatically—that is, by the rules of sentence construction in the language: such a sentence structure is available in the language for anyone who can find a way to use it without sounding too inelegant. So given the strict grammaticality of a single sentence involving two *with*-phrases in different senses and identifying different hands—a sentence that may be potentially unrealizable pragmatically but that is not excluded structurally—it follows that any related sentence (such as the one in the text), using only one such *with*-phrase, can be using that phrase in either of two distinct senses: there is no necessary priority of one sense over the other—or if there is one in practice, that does not mean that the other possibility is excluded in fact or theory.

Given all this, one may claim that the opening clause of the sentence used by Pip ("First, with her left hand she jammed the loaf hard and fast against her bib") could mean either (a) that she enclosed the loaf in the space between her bib and her left hand using her right hand to project the loaf; or (b) conversely, that her right hand bounded the space and her left hand was the projecting hand. Of course, an ordinary reading need not be detained by the possibility of this ambivalence. But the possible relevance of the ambivalence increases markedly once this clause comes to be regarded in relation to the tantalizing-and-covert-but-still-just-detectable-quality that constantly turns up in relation to references to hands in *Great Expectations*. One then has to consider that here Dickens may be exploiting an idiomatic expectation that a *with*-phrase accompanying the verb *jam* will normally have an obvious and single interpretation whereby the *with*-phrase is part of the description of the space into which something is jammed. The naturalness of such a reading will hardly register as anything other than inevitable *unless* one has begun to suspect that Mrs. Joe is characteristically left-handed. But crucially, the clause has that other possible and opposite interpretation, which may be what Pip means or wants to say (and for his own purposes to say indirectly, marginally, and covertly, but to say in a way sufficient for the intrigued reader to pick up and not to be surprised by).

An interesting final but important observation to make here regarding the whole issue of the interpretation of this particular clause is that Dickens departs from the usual positional syntactic order associated with the more idiomatic sense, where the *with*-phrase typically comes after, not before, the main verb *jam*. It may be significant (or at least no accident) that what Dickens writes is "with her left hand she jammed the loaf against her bib," a more marked and topicalized structure than the more usually encountered form associated with conveying the standard idiomatic reading—namely, *she jammed the loaf against her bib with her left hand*. Of course, this marked and topicalized rearrangement in the text has carefully been "naturalized" by the resourceful Pip. The fronting of *with her left hand* both facilitates and is prompted by the way the remainder of Pip's sentence then proceeds after the opening clause—with, after a dash, a parenthetic and appositional aside commenting on the final reference of the opening clause, *her bib*. To have left *with her left hand* in a more usual final position in its clause would have disrupted and obscured the fluency of what the continuation of the sentence goes on to say about *her bib*—and distractingly would have allowed the remark "where it sometimes got a pin into it" to apply fleetingly and inelegantly to any normally positioned post-verbal occurrence of *her left hand*. But the interesting (and concealed) pay-off is that the repositioned phrase *with her left hand*—now initial and not final in its clause—is then in a position more appropriate to its having the sense of identifying the projecting rather than the environing hand, and that is precisely the meaning we want to argue for as appropriate to a proper description and understanding of Mrs. Joe's manual actions.

The various arguments considered above allow us to see that the clause "First, with her left hand she jammed the loaf hard and fast against her bib" may still be read as in keeping with an idea that Mrs. Joe is left-handed—this being, on other evidence, her characteristic hand and the one she always uses more actively. Of course, the clause concerned can still also be read in the opposite way, and is more obviously and slightly less self-consciously read in that way—but what has now to be allowed is that this is not the *only* way to read the clause. There are two interpretative possibilities, and their coexistence in the same expression (and the associated obscurity of what is being said) reflects a situation that is very generally typical of references to manual actions in *Great Expectations*. At very first sight a seemingly out-and-out and very straightforward contradiction of the idea that Mrs. Joe is left-handed, prominently placed in the opening of Pip's memorable and egregious description of his sister slicing bread, turns out to be yet another instance of a seemingly simple reference to hand actions that intercalates covert and elusive counter-indications.[6]

There are still other interesting indirect references to Mrs. Joe's use of her hands. Mrs. Joe's bib is always "stuck full of pins and needles" (40): indeed, when Mrs. Joe jammed the bread against her bib "it sometimes got a pin into it, and sometimes a needle" (42). Paralleling Joe and his poker, Mrs. Joe tends to be "sat with her head bending over her needlework" (45). And the question of just how she does this needlework becomes significant when we come on instances such as these:

(1) "That's the way with this boy!" exclaimed my sister, pointing me out with her needle and thread, and shaking her head at me. (46)

(2) . . . "Now, you get along to bed!"
I was never allowed a candle to light me to bed, and, as I went upstairs in the dark, with my head tingling—from Mrs Joe's thimble having played the tambourine upon it, to accompany her last words—I felt fearfully sensible of the great convenience that the Hulks were handy for me. (46)

In these instances there is almost an implication (part of what draws one's attention to them in the first place) that there is no need to be specific about which hand Mrs. Joe has used. Metonymy will do; it seems to be assumed that the identity of the hand involved will follow from our being told about the needle and thread, and about the thimble. At the same time we have to consider a possibility that warns us not to treat these examples too straightforwardly—that is, by assuming that the truncated references involved are simply an aspect of skilful metonymic writing, figurative and descriptive at the same time, intending no covert implication regarding the use of the hands. But such exquisitely-poised readerly uncertainty is as usual where *Great Expectations* is concerned—the technique of all these manual references seems to be to raise or allow (and at the same time to make it possible to miss, dismiss, or discount) the possibility of covert or side-lined reference. The key factor is that once it has been noticed that Mrs. Joe's preferred, active hand could be her left hand, and when examples like those above can be read in that light *without being contradictory or contradicted*, then they too can be assimilated with other supporting evidence and can become part of a richer context of expectation into which other and subsequent (and equally tantalizing) references can come to be fitted.

Making all these points about Mrs. Joe's handedness must not be taken as meaning that she is not two-handed—simply that there is evidence of a preferred hand. And even that evidence derives from two-handed activities.

Where the need to indicate something as being done with a single or particular hand does not arise, Mrs. Joe is shown as using both hands equivalently—indeed, complementarily—and (dare one say it?) dexterously. Accordingly, she customarily ties her apron strings "fastened over her figure behind with two loops" (40), can be provoked so that on one occasion "she pounced on Joe, and, taking him by the two whiskers, knocked his head for a little while against the wall behind him:" (43), and reacts to Orlick's verbal abuse of her "with a clap of the hands and a scream together" (142), going on to "beat her hands upon her bosom and upon her knees" and later to "clench her hands in Joe's hair" (142–43).

In the early chapters of *Great Expectations*, then, one can make out a pattern where Mrs. Joe, who is characteristically left-handed, uses only that hand as her active hand—and, in a further refinement, uses that hand to accompany and underscore simultaneously expressed *speech*. Mrs. Joe predictably seems quite the opposite of Joe—he is characteristically right-handed, always with the poker in his right hand, but transferring it to *his* less active left hand whenever he needs to free his right hand for signalling what Pip takes to be private *unspoken* reactions to things said by Mrs. Joe: furthermore, when Joe does speak out, he underscores what he says by striking the grate with his poker, retained in his right hand, as he speaks.

These observations emerge from the identification of patterns of expression and reference in the opening chapters of *Great Expectations*. Suddenly, at the end of chapter 4 and into chapter 5, Dickens interpolates (not as covertly as elsewhere, but still not in an obvious way) references which may reveal a norm against which the habits of various different characters—Joe and Mrs. Joe, for instance—can be measured. The sergeant in charge of the soldiers who come to the Gargery household in pursuit of convicts is shown as very disciplined in his military bearing—something partly borne out by various references to how he disposes his hands. For once, in the second of these cases listed below, the text is not tantalizingly inexplicit—indeed, this time, against the prevailing practice shown in other examples, it seems to be perfunctorily and robustly over-explicit, as if taking on a disciplined "military" bearing of its own:

(1) But, I ran no farther than the house door, for there I ran head foremost into a party of soldiers with their muskets: one of whom held out a pair of handcuffs to me, saying, "Here you are, look sharp, come on!"        (61)

(2) It was the sergeant who had spoken to me, and he was now looking round at the company, with his handcuffs invitingly extended towards them in his

right hand, and his left on my shoulder.                                              (61)

(3) "Because," returned the sergeant, clapping him on the shoulder, "you're
a man that knows what's what."                                                         (63)

(4) There, we were stopped a few minutes by a signal from the sergeant's hand,
while two or three of his men dispersed themselves among the graves, and also
examined the path.                                                                     (65)

(5) "You can say what you like," returned the sergeant, standing coolly looking
at him with his arms folded, "but you have no call to say it here."        (70)

There are just these five references to the sergeant and his hands, all of
them capable of being interpreted in the light of the most (and redundantly
over-) explicit second instance, example (2). In (2), we are shown the sergeant
using his right hand communicatively (but non-verbally—signalling with his
handcuffs) and reserving his left hand for doing something inactive or non-
dynamic (applying control or restraint—this time to another person). So,
when we come to (3), where restraint is involved but where the text is now
more characteristically inexplicit, we are led to take it (he is a disciplined
soldier, after all!) that his left hand is used; and correlatively we assume, in
(4), involving a non-verbal signal, that it is his right hand that is meant.
Significantly (and underlining the sergeant's self-controlled use of his hands),
when we find him not doing typically sergeantly things, neither controlling
people, nor signalling to them, we find him, in (5), with his arms folded.

The sergeant, a trained, military man, establishes—or rather references to
his disciplined bearing do—a norm: right hand for communication via non-
verbal signals, left hand for manipulation, control, and restraint: and when
he does speak neither signalling nor other-directed restraint is simultaneously
involved. This is a norm against which other characters can be assessed. Joe,
for instance, is partly like him, partly unlike him: he uses his left hand for
restraint, and his right hand for non-verbal signalling (of a private rather than
a public kind), but he is more markedly right-handed, using his right hand
by preference for all sorts of actions; and he prefers to be doing something
with his hands (with that Cohen-esque poker of his!) rather than to just sit
or stand with his arms folded: and, if anything, he prefers silence to verbaliza-
tion.[7] Predictably, when contrasted with the sergeant, Mrs. Joe emerges as
very much the mirror image of her husband. Mrs. Joe is left-handed, for both
action and signal, with either of these capable of being accompanied by
simultaneous speech, and it is her right hand that she prefers for acts of
pinioning or restraint (be it a loaf of bread or Pip's cranium), freeing her left

hand for activity. And in all these ways she seems the opposite of her husband, Joe. And neither of them is quite like the sergeant.

When Mrs. Joe, after the attack on her, can no longer speak, there are interesting variations introduced into the pattern identified above, and here we have as good an example as any that could be found of how, in *Great Expectations*, developments in the real or everyday world of the novel have an effect on the rudimentary patterns of meaning that show up in the text's presentation of itself as fictive. Now, after the attack, Mrs. Joe has to rely on very indirect means of communication. Pip has "to keep my slate always by her, that she might indicate in writing what she could not indicate in speech. As she was (bad handwriting apart) a more than indifferent speller, and as Joe was a more than indifferent reader, extraordinary complications arose between them, which I was always called in to solve" (149). Another development of course is that Mrs. Joe is now driven to replace speech (previously supported with decisive and energetically demonstrative manual action) with the manual action of writing—or rather, of laboriously "[tracing] upon the slate a character that looked like a curious T" (150), something which she goes on to do repeatedly. In these new circumstances, Mrs. Joe—writing or tracing, one would like to think, with her left hand—now signals far-from-clear significances non-vocally via exclusively manual action, and in these respects is suddenly more like the poker-wielding, moustache-stroking Joe (just as Joe is momentarily more like her when he emphasizes his words by striking the poker on the grate, or when he holds down the paper on which he writes).

Alerted by the apparently differential treatment of Joe and Mrs. Joe in terms of references to their hands in the early chapters of *Great Expectations*—and noting how this scheme becomes a triangle of referential forces with the entry of the disciplined sergeant—one is on the alert for such differentiation in relation to other characters, and especially to intriguingly complex, distant or ambivalent characters like Estella and Pip.

The treatment of Estella is perhaps the most teasingly ambivalent throughout the entire scope of the novel. Although hand references to Estella are frequent, she is absolutely undifferentiated as to handedness anywhere in the text. From the moment of her first appearance, "[coming] across the courtyard, with keys in her hand" (85), no real and ultimately reliable clue is given as to which hand that might have been. All references are similarly singular like that first "her hand," or occasionally plural ("her hands"—377, and once "her two hands"—93, or "her fingers" in reference to her knitting—372). The very few cases that involve adjectival attribution are appropriately attitudinal rather than descriptive—"a taunting hand" (94), or when

descriptive hardly specific—"her white hand" (259), or can become tinged
with irony for the hand-fixated reader—"the friendly touch of the once insen-
sible hand" (491). There are some references to Estella which are intriguing
simply for the way they serve to avoid a differentiation that other, perhaps
more immediate, expressions might establish: "Her handsome dress had
trailed upon the ground. She held it in one hand now, and with the other
lightly touched my shoulder as we walked" (260). Of course, the way things
are correlatively said here (" . . . one hand, . . . the other . . . ") is naturally
how they can and should be put, but it is not the only way that things could
or might have been stated.

When we come to look at references involving Pip, the plot may—or may
not—thicken. Mentions of his own hands made by Pip in the early chapters
(alongside those already considered involving Joe and Mrs. Joe) show a
noticeable restriction to undifferentiated forms in the plural, and in the one
instance which is singular there is also a palpable and self-advertised oddity.
These are the relevant plural examples:

(1) I was dreadfully frightened, and so giddy that I clung to him with both
hands, and said, . . .                                                    (37)

(2) . . . the remorse with which my mind dwelt on what my hands had done.
                                                                          (54)

(3) I held tight to the leg of the table under the cloth, with both hands, and
awaited my fate.                                                          (59)

(4) Always holding tight by the leg of the table with my hands and feet, I saw
the miserable creature finger his glass playfully.                       (59)

(5) I looked at him eagerly when he looked at me, and slightly moved my
hands and shook my head.                                                  (69)


These five cases all have noticeable characteristics: the phrase involved
*may* be idiomatic in its function—(1), (2); or plural in emphasizing intensity—(1), (3), (4); or perhaps indicative of some covert signal—(5); but what
they all have in common, somewhat unexpectedly, is their plurality: Pip makes
no reference explicitly mentioning *hand* in the singular in this section of the
novel. When a singular reference is, or may be, intended, it is left to be
carried by implication, what is said apparently avoiding explicit singular
mention of *a hand*, *the hand,* or *my hand.* Thus we find:

(1) At this dismal intelligence, I twisted the only button on my waistcoat round
and round, and looked in great depression at the fire.                   (40)

(2) I leaned over Joe, and, with the aid of my forefinger, read him the whole
letter.                                                                    (76)

(3) Therefore, I naturally pointed to Mrs Joe, and put my mouth in the form
of saying 'her?'                                                           (45)

Again, these are natural things to say, but they do not disturb the arguable
tendency—that when Pip makes hand references about himself either they
are in the plural, or he generally avoids being specific or explicit.

There *is* one striking occasion, in fact, where Pip—at least in these early
chapters—makes a manual reference using *hand* in the singular, and it is an
instance that is unmissably odd, one that seems inescapably contrived, based
as it is on a sylleptic coalition of literal and idiomatic meanings which cannot
but catch the attention. The instance in question arises on the night Pip
inscribes his wonderful letter to Joe, and involves particularly the crucial
reference in the final sentence of the following extract:

> One night I was sitting in the chimney-corner with my slate, expending great
> efforts on the production of a letter to Joe. I think it must have been a full year
> after our hunt upon the marshes, for it was a long time after, and it was winter
> and a hard frost. With an alphabet on the hearth at my feet for reference, I
> contrived in an hour or two to print and smear this epistle:
>     'M I DEER JO i opE U R KRWITE wE LL i opE i sHAL soN B HABELL 4 2 TEEDGE
> U JO AN THEN wE sHORL B sO GLODD AN wEN i M PRENGTD 2 U JO woT
> LARX AN BLEvE ME INF XN PIP.'
> There was no indispensable necessity for my communicating with Joe by letter,
> inasmuch as he sat beside me and we were alone. But I delivered this written
> communication (slate and all) with my own hand, and Joe received it as a
> miracle of erudition.                                                    (75)

This scene provides us with the first instance in the novel of Pip referring
to, but not specifying, a particular hand of his in the singular, and the reference
is underlined on the very next page with another singular reference (already
quoted above in connection with an earlier stage of the argument) implying
but again not identifying a particular hand: '' I leaned over Joe, and with the
aid of my forefinger, read him the whole letter'' (76). Presumably, the hand
with which Pip points is still the same one as Pip has just previously referred
to (in the extended extract above) as ''my own hand.'' It is worth noticing that
the two references being focussed on here occur in a scene that is additionally
distinguished by being the first in the novel when Pip and Joe are alone
together: it is an occasion of great intimacy wherein one senses a mutual

sympathy between Pip and Joe that is—curiously but inescapably—under-lined rather than destroyed by Pip's choosing to write Joe a letter. One senses a deeply private occasion wherein Pip is secure, relaxed, unburdened, affected by the sincerity of the other and himself moved to a responsive sincerity. It is the kind of occasion where Pip can be himself, and can behave with a natural and free sentiment towards the other. And it is of this occasion that Pip, in his narrative, for the first time speaks distinctively—and, in the closing sentence of the above extract, doubly distinctively—in reference to himself and his hands.

The key remark is "I delivered this written communication (slate and all) with my own hand. . . . " Pip puns or equivocates on the word *delivered*, and makes sure by his parenthetical interpolation ("slate and all") that we do not miss the now egregious duality of meaning—that *delivered* fits with two senses, "expressed, communicated" and "handed over." But that pun makes prominent another verbal quibble, one involving literal and idiomatic mean-ings of the phrase *my own hand*: the idiomatic meaning, namely "in my own handwriting or script," which goes with "expressed, communicated," and the more literal sense, fitting with "handed over," of "using one of my own hands." The whole thing is so intricate and contrived that the artifice of the almost-laboured witticism cannot be missed. But one's acceptance of the legitimacy of the whole of Pip's rather creaking pun depends on taking *my own hand* as being a phrase that can be used literally as well as idiomatically. One might say that *my own hand* is and has to be always idiomatic, its literally descriptive counterpart being *my hand* or *a hand*. But things seem otherwise for Pip: *delivering* both the slate (handing over) and its message (expressing or communicating) works as a pun only if *with my own hand* is also a pun, equivocal between an idiom and a literal description. One is led, or allowed, to assume that *with my own hand* is something that Pip can literally say where others might simply say *my hand* or make no manual reference at all, along-side a verb like *delivered*. And for that to be the case, the phrase has to mean for Pip something like "my characteristic or preferred hand."

But if that is the case—which hand is that, left or right? The labored and non-fluent character of Pip's epistle could suggest that it is not the hand he usually uses—hence perhaps the need to draw attention to its doubly being pressed into play here—except that Pip's labored inscribing is best seen as simply that of an untrained, unpractised, and very youthful hand. Neverthe-less, such an answer may indeed turn out to be possibly relevant, if it can be suggested that, on this auspiciously private occasion, it is with his left hand that Pip inscribes his message to Joe. And this is indeed the speculation that

I will try to demonstrate with an examination of references elsewhere in the text: namely, that Pip may be left-handed like his sister, with this being something he keeps hidden or suppressed or that he unconcernedly allows when alone with Joe, or something that—wanting to be like Joe—he strives to correct, but which he can be seen ultimately to betray in a few instinctive or unconsidered moments. Some such covertness may lie behind the otherwise noticeable absence of any simple singular reference such as *my hand* when talking of himself, at least in the early chapters—the references that do turn up being plural, or in the striking instance that we have been considering, provocative and potentially revealing as well as singular. The claim here is that Pip is left-handed (like Mrs. Joe) but pretends or strives to be right-handed (like Joe), presenting himself as always two-handed, hardly mentioning or using his preferred or characteristic hand except at relaxed and totally secure moments (such as in the case discussed above, where he is alone at home with Joe), or when he behaves instinctively or without forethought.

The most revealing references to Pip and his handedness are, as might by now be expected, indirect and implicative rather than unarguably inscribed, and are liable to be seen as significant only to the extent that one has already become alert to the possibility of covert reference and hidden indication. Such references arise at points where Pip's narrative is at pains to establish a perhaps untypically instinctive or rash or impromptu or improvised quality in his conduct or action. One such occasion is the fight with Herbert Pocket near the end of chapter 11. At first, Pip responds helplessly to Herbert's comically theatrical pugilism, being "secretly afraid of him when I saw him so dexterous" (119) and observing that "My heart failed me when I saw him squaring at me with every demonstration of mechanical nicety" (120). So it thus comes as a surprise to the reader as much as to Pip "when I let out the first blow, and saw him lying on his back, looking up at me with a bloody nose and his face exceedingly fore-shortened" (120). Herbert is back "on his feet directly" and "with a great show of dexterity" so that "The second greatest surprise I have ever had in my life was seeing him on his back again, looking up at me out of a black eye" (120). The summary of the rest of the fight, which goes repeatedly and finally against the consummately dexterous Herbert, is never again as explicit concerning the specifics of Pip's involvement: but these two instances are sufficient for the reader to understand that, for once, Pip is doing things instinctively and in an almost unconsciously reactive way. The question is, which hand might have delivered these decisive, instinctive, knock-down blows?

We do not find out, although the little information that is gleanable reveals characteristically interesting indirectness. At the start of chapter 12, immediately following the conclusion of the fight with Herbert, Pip is driven to rueful and anxious reflection about the whole incident and its consequences for himself. Among these he notes that ''I had cut my knuckles against the pale young gentleman's teeth'' (122). Again, a term is used— ''knuckles''—that can cover every likely possibility: both sets of knuckles, or the knuckles of one or other of the left and right hands. But one is forced to wonder just how ambidextrously two-fisted (and equally, how unlucky) Pip would have had to have been to emerge from the fight with Herbert having cut the knuckles of *both* of his hands. A surely more reasonable conclusion would have to be that, while both fists may well, indeed must, have been used, one particular fist is more likely to have been stronger and more natural, and used more often, and it is the knuckles of that fist that have been cut and bloodied. But which hand, which fist—right or left?

Things are clearer on the next—and very prominent—occasion when Pip behaves (and uses his hands) in a headlong and instinctive fashion. This comes in the crucial scene in chapter 49 where Pip rescues Miss Havisham from the fire. Throughout its entire extent the description of the rescue is most marked by one repeated feature—an emphasis on how instinctive and almost unconscious were Pip's actions and reactions. The express reiteration of this point is carried in particular by the various phrases now highlighted in italics in the extract below:

> I had a double-caped great-coat on, and over my arm another thick coat. That I got them off, closed with her, threw her down, and got them over her; that I dragged the great cloth from the table for the same purpose, and with it dragged down the heap of rottenness in the midst, and all the ugly things that sheltered there; that we were on the ground struggling like desperate enemies, and that the closer I covered her, the more wildly she shrieked and tried to free herself; *that this occurred I knew through the result, but not through anything I felt, or thought, or knew I did. I knew nothing until I knew that we were on the floor by the great table,* and that patches of tinder yet alight were floating in the smoky air, which, a moment ago, had been her faded bridal dress.
>
> Then I looked round and saw the disturbed beetles and spiders running away over the floor, and the servants coming in with breathless cries at the door. I still held her forcibly down with all my strength, like a prisoner who might escape; *and I doubt if I even knew who she was, or why we had struggled, or that she had been in flames, or that the flames were out, until I saw the patches of tinder that had been her garments, no longer alight but falling in a black shower around us.*

> She was insensible, and I was afraid to have her moved, or even touched. Assistance was sent for and I held her until it came, as if I unreasonably fancied (*I think I did*) that if I let her go, the fire would break out again and consume her. When I got up, on the surgeon's coming to her with other aid, *I was astonished to see that both my hands were burnt; for, I had no knowledge of it through the sense of feeling.*     (414)

It is no surprise to us, given what has happened, that "both [Pip's] hands were burnt," but it is interesting (given that he has been oblivious of anything to do with his hands in these moments of panic) for us to be told by Pip, just afterwards, at the opening of chapter 50, and with direct and emphatic clarity, that

> My hands had been dressed twice or thrice in the night, and again in the morning. My left hand was a good deal burned to the elbow, and less severely, as high as the shoulder; it was very painful, but the flames had set in that direction, and I felt thankful it was no worse. My right hand was not so badly burnt but that I could move the fingers. It was bandaged, of course, but much less inconveniently than my left hand and arm; those I carried in a sling; and I could only wear my coat like a cloak, loose over my shoulders and fastened at the neck. My hair had been caught by the fire, but not my head or face.
>                                                                    (416)

Apart perhaps from the quibble about the direction the fire had presumably taken (and how could Pip, already by his own testimony distracted from all but the rescue of Miss Havisham, have observed that tendency, other than as an a posteriori assumption?), what Pip offers is factual and pointed testimony; and it shows very clear evidence from which can be deduced the conclusion that, when he is not thinking about it, Pip will tend to use both hands to the extent that he has to, but his left more than his right.

In the period of recovery from his manual injuries Pip faces a new situation—willy-nilly, his natural hand and arm are now the bandaged right hand and arm ("the bandaged arm under my coat"—432; "my arm"—420, 424); there is no doubt, for instance, as to which is "the arm I could use" (457), nor as to which hand has now to be involved when Pip tells us (433–34) that "[I] knocked at the door with my hand" or "[The latch] rose under my hand" or "[I] had taken up the candle in my hand." And Pip's manual state is not lost on Jaggers, who very pointedly draws attention to his manual limitations, in several ways, when he concludes his advocate's urging that Pip not reveal what he knows of Estella's parentage by saying:

> . . . then I tell you that you had better—and would much sooner when you had thought well of it—chop off that bandaged left hand of yours with your bandaged right hand, and then pass the chopper on to Wemmick there, to cut *that* off, too.          (426).[8]

Following the climactic scene of the death of Magwitch, there are only very few other manual references in the remainder of Pip's narrative. Among these is one that recalls the starting point of this entire discussion. It comes in chapter 59 when Pip returns after his eleven year absence, and comes on Joe and Biddy and the new, young Pip:

> Biddy looked down at her child, and put its little hand to her lips, and then put the good matronly hand with which she had touched it, into mine. There was something in the action and in the light pressure of Biddy's wedding ring, that had a very pretty eloquence in it.          (490)

This incident is open to being correlated with other references in the novel in various ways. Biddy is left-handed, it would seem, like Mrs. Joe, but using characteristic manual action instead of words (like Joe, and just as Mrs. Joe finally had to) to communicate feelingly with others; and so on. Finally, what are we to make of the closing and most significant incident of all, as Pip and Estella make their way out of the ruined place?

> I took her hand in mine, and we went out of the ruined place; and, as the morning mists had risen long ago when I first left the forge, so, the evening mists were rising now, and in all the broad expanse of tranquil light they showed to me, I saw no shadow of another parting from her.          (493)

Which hand is "her hand"? And which is "mine"? And how are the hands clasped—*droit-à-droit*, or right to left, and—in the latter case—from whom to whom? Are Pip and Estella parting civilly with a handshake, as in the original ending, or are they going to marry? Right to the very end, it seems, *Great Expectations* continues to involve the reader in its sophisticated literary version of an old-established guessing game: which hand?

# NOTES

1. *Great Expectations*, ed. Angus Calder (Harmondsworth: Penguin, 1965), 82. Subsequent references to the novel will be to this edition, and will be indicated parenthetically in the text.

2. Culturally-given nowadays, and perhaps in general, but not everywhere. In Germany, for instance, the wedding ring is worn on the right hand, and this may be the case in Iceland too. Might there have been some long-lost practice, different from ours, in the Kent of the early nineteenth century? If so, all the arguments that follow would have to be put into reverse—and at the same time the covert quality of Pip's narrative might be seen to have an additional feature.

3. Another major Victorian novel has recently been seen as making significant and extensive use of hand references. Discussing *Middlemarch*, Daniel Karlin speaks of "the predominance, in the novel's system of representation, of hands and everything associated with them," mentioning that he has "seventy pages of extracts, . . . , in which hands are mentioned: either directly, or by association with the actions and gestures they perform, or in a multitude of figurative expressions" (30).

4. Over and above such cases, one also notices various fixed phrases, idioms, tags, and grammatical metaphors, where the lexical item *hand* is now frozen in a non-literal usage that is now part of the fabric of the language, as in such cases as *single-handed, like a child in his hands, a skilled hand, some unknown hand, on the other hand, wash his hands of her, have a hand in, red-handed, near at hand*, etc., etc. There are close to one hundred such expressions throughout the text, and with only one or two particular phrases ever recurring, it is as if *Great Expectations* diffusely incorporated a virtually complete thesaurus of English *hand*-idioms: OED, for instance, lists no more than seventy main senses and uses for the item *hand*.

5. Among various possibilities, which I do not further consider or detail, is a recurrent scheme which identifies characters in terms of a single hand and some appropriately-associated metallic object held or carried therein: Joe and his poker, the army sergeant and his handcuffs, Estella and her keys, the man in the pub with his swizzle-stick file, Mrs. Joe with her needle and thimble (and her bread-knife), Orlick with his gun *and* hammer—and perhaps Miss Havisham with her walking stick?

6. Another side-lined indication of the possible scheme is that we come across one single (and notably contrasting) reference to Joe cutting bread: "'Mr and Mrs Hubble might like to see you in your new gen-teel figure, too, Pip,' said Joe, industriously cutting his bread, with his cheese on it, in the palm of his left hand, and glancing at my untasted supper . . .'" (171).

7. At least one other individual, like the sergeant occupying and performing a professional role, is referred to elsewhere in *Great Expectations* as characterized, in that professionalism, in terms of the use or disposition of the hands, identifying right and left. Early on (in chapter 4–indeed, just before the appearance of the sergeant and his party of soldiers), Pumblechook—contributing to a comically pointless dinner-table discussion of the moral instructiveness for young people of contemplating pigs and pork (!)—suddenly and cruelly observes to Pip about his likely different fate had he been born "a four-footed Squeaker": " 'You would have been disposed of according to the market price of the article, and Dunstable the butcher would have come up to you as you lay in your straw, and he would have whipped you under his left arm, and with his right he would have tucked

up his frock to get a penknife from out of his waistcoat-pocket, and he would
have shed your blood and had your life. No bringing up by hand then. Not a bit
of it!' '' (58).

8. In my observation, there seems to be just one instance in the novel (prior, of
course, to the developments that emerge after Pip's ordeal by fire in chapter 49)
where Pip can be identified as making a singular and explicit manual reference
using the phrase "my right hand." And on reflection, this instance does not seem
all that surprising, occurring as it does in the narration of a scene where Pip
shows himself behaving in an extremely self-conscious and dissembling way as
he confronts Pumblechook and Mrs. Joe with his extravagant account of the
marvels he claims to have found at Miss Havisham's—as Pip himself admits, it
is all lies, helpfully conveyed with an accompanying insouciant miming: " . . . I,
with an obtrusive show of artlessness on my countenance, stared at them, and
plaited the right leg of my trousers with my right hand" (98). As far as I can
see, this is the only such instance. But invoking a useful principle once formulated
by David Lodge, aware that "laborious methods . . . do not claim 100% accuracy," I have to point out that "Any errors . . . will not in general have assisted
my arguments: I may have missed some occurrences of a particular linguistic
element in a particular text, but I have not invented any" (85).

# WORKS CITED

Bradbury, Nicola. *Charles Dickens' "Great Expectations."* London: Harvester
Wheatsheaf, 1990.

Buckley, Jerome H. *Season of Youth: The Bildungsroman from Dickens to Golding.*
Cambridge, MA: Harvard UP, 1974.

Cohen, William A. "Manual Conduct in *Great Expectations*." *ELH* 60 (1993):
217–59.

Dickens, Charles. *Great Expectations.* Ed. Angus Calder. Harmondsworth: Penguin,
1965.

Forker, Charles R. "The Language of Hands in *Great Expectations*." *Texas Studies
in Literature and Language* 3 (1961–62): 280–93.

Karlin, Daniel. "Having the Whip-hand in *Middlemarch*." In *Rereading Victorian
Fiction.* Ed. Alice Jenkins and Juliet John. London: Macmillan, 200, 29–43.

Lodge, David. *Language of Fiction: The World of His Novel.* Cambridge, MA: Harvard
UP, 1958.

Moore, Jack B. "Hearts and Hands in *Great Expectations*." *Dickensian* 61 (1965):
52–56.

Reed, Walter L. *An Exemplary History of the Novel: The Quixotic versus the Picaresque.* Chicago: U of Chicago P, 1981

Stone, Harr. *Dickens and the Invisible World: Fairy Tales, Fantasy and Novel Making.* London: Macmillan, 1980.

# Dickens and the Identical Man: *Our Mutual Friend* Doubled

## Rosemarie Bodenheimer

*This essay examines the obsessional nature of Dickens's attention to characters who are or who might be "somebody else," as well as the pattern of betrayed partnerships that runs through* Our Mutual Friend. *Dickens's letters during the years between the staging of* The Frozen Deep *and the composition of* Our Mutual Friend *suggest the preoccupations with false identities, broken partnerships and money-making that shaped the novel in ways that distinguish it from his earlier work. Whereas doubled characters had previously split up aspects of a single syndrome, the male doubles in* Our Mutual Friend *are fused with one another in displays of intimate otherness that create, in this novel, the very condition of identity.*

No long-buried secrets fuel its plots, no abandoned orphans walk its streets, no fallen or frozen women advertise their shame, no illegitimate children seek their origins, no parents abuse and neglect their children onstage. No state institutions loom; no prisons threaten; the police detective is a philosopher, the lawyers are virtually unemployed. "The Harmon Murder" is a misnomer; the suicide-murder of Bradley Headstone and Rogue Riderhood is a relief. With the exception of the Boffin fraud, *Our Mutual Friend*'s numerous plots and deceptions are conducted in the present and managed by the characters in full view of·the reader. To be sure, Bradley Headstone has a silenced pauper past, but that past is empty, a place of pure possibility. Something new has happened in Dickens's work; the elaborate plot wiring that distributes and displaces the ancient burden of authorial class anxiety has been short-circuited. Despite the dust, despite the money—or maybe just because of them—this novel has a certain lightness of being, expressed in the skittery wackiness of what its characters often get to say.

Of course *Our Mutual Friend* has its own obsessions. "It is questionable whether any man quite relishes being mistaken for any other man," the narrator says early on (OMF I, 2),[1] but the novel is all about men who are, and men who arrange to be, mistaken for others. John Harmon is not identical with the Man from Somewhere whose story ends in drowning, but he and his double George Radfoot meet because each has been mistaken for the other from behind. The "horrible old Lady Tippins" carries her title only because her late husband was "knighted in mistake for somebody else by His Majesty King George the Third" (OMF I, 10). In fact, claims the narrator, the wrong ideas of the present time are "generally some form of tribute to Somebody for something that never was done, or, if ever done, that was done by Somebody Else" (OMF II, 11). Bradley Headstone "in his own schoolmaster clothes . . . usually looked as if they were the clothes of some other man," but dressed to imitate Riderhood's; "he now looked, in the clothes of some other man or men, as if they were his own" (OMF IV,1). In the novel as a whole there are only a few scenes in which at least one of the characters in a dialogue is not impersonating someone else or present under false pretences. Much of the pleasure in reading the novel comes from watching those impersonations at work. Clearly Dickens is revelling in variations on this theme, quite as if he were playing out the act of character-making, and especially his own lifelong interest in "t'Other one," as Jonas Chuzzlewit had put it many novels back.

It's difficult to find a proper name in *Our Mutual Friend* that is not subjected to elaborate questioning, multiple renaming, or obsessive repetition, as if all the characters partook of the plight of poor Sloppy, who "has no right name" (OMF I, 16). "Speaking correctly." Miss Peecher instructs her pupil, "we say that Hexam's sister is called Lizzie, not that she is named so. Do we not, Mary Anne?" (OMF II, 11). The narrative treats us to innumerable versions of her distinction, until it becomes clear that, in a world of absent fathers and evaded marriages, there is no particular authority on which a given name is based. Much is made of introduction scenes between one character and another, which are fraught with the potential for mistake—or worse, for recognition. Once mistakes are cleared up, Veneering becomes

"Veneering as Veneering"; Twemlow is "Twemlow a̲
I, 2). Even identity, then, is a condition of impersonati̲
the prolonged name-dance of his introduction to Mr. B̲
seeing him before from behind: it's "you as you identicall̲
self-same stick under your very same arm, and your very same b̲
us" (OMF I, 5). The move between mistaking someone from behind, and
meeting him face to face, will become a prominent motif later in this essay.

As for that enigmatic title phrase, "our mutual friend" it is generally used
between two people who want to refer to an absent third party without pro-
nouncing a proper name. It conjures up an aura of conspiratorial secrecy, a
partnership of private knowledge. And partnerships abound in this novel,
each set mirroring other partner pairs and splitting into secret trios. The young
heroes appear in classic double pairs, which also destabilize and triple. As
readers, we're reduced to the condition of Twemlow at the Veneerings, mut-
tering, "Oh, then there are two-three-four of us, and *he's* the other!" (OMF
I,10). It's not just "t'Other Governor" but "t'otherest Governor" that this
novel imagines, as though there were a superlative of identical otherness that
Dickens wanted to push to the very edge.

What are we to make of all this delightful, if obsessional, identity-play?
We all reach somewhere else for terms that will help light up the novel, and
I will reach first for Dickens's letters, during the five-year period before he
began to conceive this story. It was the most dramatic period of Dickens's
life since his famously shame-inducing stint as a working boy in a blacking
warehouse at the age of twelve. Full of theatrical enterprises, broken partnerships, double lives, and an urgent need for money, this turbulent period of
adulthood exploded in the breakup of the Dickens marriage, and generated
many of the figures that were to saturate the text of *Our Mutual Friend.*

During the autumn of 1856, the Dickens household was temporarily transformed into a theater company. The play in rehearsal, suggestively titled *The
Frozen Deep,* had been imagined by Dickens and co-written and acted with
his younger friend and collaborator Wilkie Collins.[2] *The Frozen Deep* was
inspired by the controversy surrounding the 1845 disappearance of Sir John
Franklin's expedition to find a northwest passage through the Arctic. In the
face of rumors that the crew had succumbed to cannibalism, it meant to assert
the ultimate triumph of English self-discipline over the extremities of both
physical and mental suffering. The play featured Dickens in the role of Richard Wardour, an explorer with a longstanding passion for Clara, the fiancee
of one of his shipmates. Wardour transforms his murderous jealousy into
self-sacrifice, carries his failing rival to safety across the wasteland of frozen

deep, gives him back to his betrothed, and then—having infused the other man with his own energy—dies nobly at Clara's feet. Dickens created and played this role with a realistic passion that stunned his audiences and led one reviewer to rave that Dickens "has all the technical knowledge and resources of a professed actor; but these, the dry bones of acting, are kindled by that soul of vitality which can only be put into them by the man of genius and the interpreter of the affections" (*Leader*, 10 January 1857; qtd in *Letters*, 8, 254n). It was Dickens's opportunity to perform himself both as the caged wild beast he often imagined himself to be, and as the man of self-sacrificial love. Violating all the rules of drama, *The Frozen Deep* features a gun, brandished about by Dickens, that does not go off in the third act.

Although Dickens had always involved his family and friends in amateur theatricals, *The Frozen Deep* was a project on an altogether different scale. Dickens built a special room to extend the family schoolroom at Tavistock House, which was turned into a theater with a 30–foot stage, professionally painted sets, and special effects, including special gas fittings to light a sunset and and a high platform from which two little boys could produce snow (to John Deane, 23 June 1857; *Letters* 8, 358). As co-author, actor, and manager, Dickens allowed himself a complete revel in the stage, which had always both compelled and frightened him. In letters to his respectable friends, he assured them that the project "has been a remarkable lesson to my young people in patience, perserverance, punctuality, and order" (to Sir James Emerson Tennent, 9 January 1857; to Lady Eastlake, 10 January 1857; *Letters* 8, 256–57). He was determined to rid theatricals of any unsavory lowlife aura which might compromise not only the family women who were acting in the play, but the hard-won respectability of the famous author himself. Yet Dickens's own Frozen Deep, the ferocious self-discipline which had created and maintained his bourgeois status and his good name, was on the verge of meltdown.

After the Tavistock House performances, the play moved to a public space, the Gallery of Illustration, and featured a private performance for Queen Victoria. When the queen asked Dickens to receive her personal thanks at the end of the performance, he begged off, asking her "to excuse my presenting myself in a costume and appearance that were not my own' " (to John Forster, 5 July 1857; *Letters* 8, 366). He had no intention of being mistaken for an actor—another man—when he was not onstage. The third set of performances took place at the Free Trade Hall in Manchester, with professional actresses substituting for the Dickens women in this large and very public setting. As replacements for his sister-in-law and daughters, Dickens hired

Mrs. Frances Ternan and two of her three actress-daughters. By the end of the three Manchester performances, he was in love with eighteen-year-old Ellen Ternan, and on his way to becoming the male protector of a new, theatrical family.

Dickens found it as difficult to deny himself the emotional catharsis of public acting as he found it impossible to stay away from Ellen. "I have just come back from Manchester, where I have been tearing myself to pieces, to the wonderful satisfaction of thousands of people," he wrote to an acquaintance at the end of the Manchester performances (to Mrs. Brown, 28 August 1857; *Letters* 8, 421). He immediately took a restless trip with Collins to pursue the Ternans on tour, under the guise of a collaborative journalism project for *Household Words*. Collins sprained his ankle on a mountain that Dickens insisted on climbing, and Dickens dramatized the episode in comic detail: "C.D. carrying C., melodramatically (Wardour to the life!) everywhere" (to John Forster, 9 September 1857; *Letters* 8, 440). "As to the Play itself," he had written earlier, "I derive a strange feeling out of it, like writing a book in company. A satisfaction of a most singular kind, which has no exact parallel in my life" (to James Emerson Tennent, 9 January 1857; *Letters* 8, 256). A week after *The Frozen Deep* closed, he was trying out on his old friend and advisor John Forster a plan to approximate the satisfaction of writing books in company without quite becoming a professional actor: he floated the idea of doing readings from his books in public, for money.

Forster was horrified. "It had so much of the character of a public exhibition for money as to raise, in the question of respect for his calling as a writer, a question also of respect for himself as a gentleman," he wrote (qtd *Letters* 8, 435n). Dickens persisted, testing the idea on other upper-class friends like his fellow-philanthropist Angela Burdett-Coutts. "She was for a moment tremendously disconcerted," her reported to Forster, "*under the impression that it was to lead to the stage'*!! . . .That absurd association had never entered my head or yours . . . " (19–20 March 1858; *Letters* 8, 535). But once the reading tours were launched, he was more honest with his partner in bohemia, Wilkie Collins. From a hotel on his first national tour, he wrote Collins, "I miss Richard Wardour's dress, and always want to put it on. I would rather, by a great deal, act" (11 August 1858; *Letters* 8, 624). Perhaps he felt more emotional range disguised as Richard Wardour than he did in his staged impersonation of the famous author Charles Dickens.[3] Dickens's determination to move out of a bourgeois marriage, toward the stage and a family of actresses suggests that in his late forties he could not prevent himself, Bradley

Headstone-like, from drawing closer to the netherworld he had worked so hard to deny.[4]

Dickens's readings did work to channel the manic energy released by acting in *The Frozen Deep,* allowing him to tear himself to pieces in public more often than even he required. At the same time they constituted a scheme for making large sums of money by recycling his books. Throughout this period he represented himself as desperate for money. "I carry through life as long and as heavy a train of dependents as ever was borne by one working man," he told a Dr. Gill in 1864; and one need only to count up the number of establishments he was supporting to see how that might be (11 January 1864; *Letters* 10, 338). His exuberance about the success of his readings centered on the emotional response of the audience, on the numbers who had to be turned away from each performance, and, above all, on the money he took in. Arthur Smith, his first business manager and tour partner, became a double figure in his letters—the one who stood in for Dickens's own propensity to turn audiences into money. "Even Arthur could not squeeze more than £75 into the room," Dickens wrote to his sister-in-law Georgina Hogarth (5 August 1858; *Letters* 8, 617). "What Arthur's state has been tonight . . . you cannot imagine. They turned away hundreds, sold all the books, rolled on the ground of my room knee deep in checks, and made a perfect Pantomime of the whole thing" (to Georgina Hogarth, 20 August 1858; *Letters* 8, 629). And, to Edmund Yates a day later, "Arthur bathed in checks—took headers into tickets—floated on billows of passes—dived under weirs of shillings—staggered home, faint with gold and silver" (*Letters* 8, 631). The world of *Our Mutual Friend,* with its schemes for making money by impersonation, recycling old material, and reading aloud, was always quite close to home.

By 1862, however, reading was a wearier-looking enterprise. In that year Dickens considered the offer of a reading tour to Australia that would, as he put it, "make me more independent of the worst" (to John Forster, 5 October 1862; *Letters* 10, 134). He could not bear to contemplate the discomfort of travel and the exertion of the readings; it was a question of going to Australia for money or writing a book at home (to Thomas Beard, 4 November 1852; *Letters* 10, 153). He had not written a big book since *The Frozen Deep,* only the two shorter fables—*A Tale of Two Cities* and *Great Expectations*—that ran weekly in his magazine *All the Year Round. Our Mutual Friend,* a big book full of ingenious and shady ways to make a living, was itself written under a special pressure to bring in a lot of money.

Dickens's separation from Catherine in 1858 catalyzed a chain of other breaks with long-standing partners. Several colleagues were involved in the prolonged separation negotiations, and some of them turned to enemies in Dickens's eyes during the difficult period when true and false rumors were circulating about the demise of the marriage. He dissolved his partnership with his publishers Bradbury and Evans after Evans, who had helped Catherine, failed to publish Dickens's self-vindicating "personal" statement in *Punch*. Abruptly breaking off relations, Dickens wrote to Evans: "I have had stern occasion to impress upon my children that their father's name is their best possession and that it would indeed be trifled with and wasted by him, if, either through himself or through them, he held any terms with those who have been false to it, in the only great need and under the only great wrong it has ever known" (to F.M. Evans, 22 July 1858; *Letters* 8, 608). When Bradbury and Evans went to court over the terms of the dissolution of partnership, Dickens was happy to conspire with his new editor, Frederick Chapman, and his other cronies to outwit and outbid his former partners in the auction which put *Household Words* up for sale. By the end of 1859, Dickens had also split up with his illustrator Hablot Browne, who had continued to work with Evans. His relationship with Browne's replacement, Marcus Stone, who illustrated *Our Mutual Friend*, was less an intense partnership than a kind of mentorship or patronage.

By the time he began to work on *Our Mutual Friend*, Dickens's imagination had had time to absorb his life crisis, and to transform its elements and its anxieties in characteristic ways. In June 1862, according to Forster's biography, he made an explicit connection between the trauma of his late forties and his childhood suffering. "Ask yourself whether it is natural that something of the character formed in me then, and lost under happier circumstances, should have reappeared in the last five years," he entreated Forster. "The never-to-be-forgotten misery of that old time bred a certain shrinking sensitiveness in a certain ill-clad, ill-fed child, that I have found come back in the never-to-be-forgotten misery of this later time" (qtd. in *Letters* 10, 97–98). If the plot of *Our Mutual Friend* is less dependent on a hidden past than other Dickens novels, it is probably because the miseries of the present had displaced the old obsessions with newer ones. Dickens was now living a double life, moving between his own family and his shadow family, the theatrical Ternans. He was renting cottages for himself under false names in order to see Ellen. Her name never appeared in his letters; even to those who knew her, she was, so to speak, only to be referred to as Our Mutual Friend. He was recycling and impersonating his own characters in public readings. He had broken several partnerships that had in his view become betrayals. He was anxious about the compromise of his good name. And he was exhausting himself with the need to make money. All of these situations were played out and inventively multiplied in the texture of *Our Mutual Friend*.

"I have been swallowing too much of that word, Pardner," says Gaffer Hexam to Rogue Riderhood in chapter one; and by the end of the novel we have swallowed that word more times than we can count. What is at stake in this much-multiplied set of variations? What connects the corpse-robbers with the predatory Lammles, the anti-Semitic fiction that constitutes the Fledgby-Riah partnership, the klutzy machinations of the friendly movers Wegg and Venus, and even that sweetly domestic pair, Mortimer Lightwood and Eugene Wrayburn? This question has usually been treated by making a set of distinctions between the treacherous bad partnerships formed to make money, and the trusting good partnerships in which one character helps redeem the other. In a major article on this topic, John Farrell does a rich investigation of the intricate interlocking of partnerships and doublings *in Our Mutual Friend*. He is especially interested in the way that authentic selfhood is created through dialogical mutuality between and within character. Such an approach can also highlight what is to me the most stunning formal feature of this novel—that so much of what's important takes place in theatrical dialogue rather than in the familiar Dickensian self-performing narration. Ultimately, however, Farrell takes the familiar ground of separating the sheep from the goats, the damned from the saved. Coming at the subject from another angle, I am interested in the ways that Dickens imagined multiple forms of the relationships among making money, collaboration, impersonation, and maintaining a good name. I would like to propose a Dickens who beams his troubling preoccupations through a fictional prism that refracts a whole spectrum of figurative self-recognitions.

To varying degrees, the partnership pairs feature a division between a skilled one who is the front person and a manipulative one who covertly works the scene. Mrs. Lammle does the onstage work while watching for signs from her husband just as Riah plays his mock-fictional role as the representative of another while watching Fledgby's face for instruction. Wegg needs Venus, as Riderhood needs Gaffer, for his technical expertise. Lightwood is the working lawyer on the case as well as the feminized partner who founds himself on Eugene, only to be abandoned in Eugene's secret nocturnal wanderings in search of somebody else. All of the partnerships are dissolved, betrayed, or at least threatened by secret alliances with a third party. The unequal, shifting dynamics of power between the partners gets at least as much dramatic attention as the business of their plots. In fact, partnerships collapse not because they are formed to make money in devious ways, but through the instabilities of their internal power structures.

Most of the partnerships are intimate alliances of distrust, in which suspicion of the partner is hardly different from suspicion of the self. Venus and Wegg call each other "partner" or "brother" when each is most intent on keeping his secret plans from the other. Gaffer casts off Riderhood in order to keep his name clear from association with a man who robs live bodies, and Riderhood returns the favor by blackening Gaffer's reputation and later by accusing him of the murder to which Riderhood himself may have been an accessory. "I know more of the ins and outs of him than any person living does," says Riderhood to Abbey Potterson, "Notice this! I am the man that was his pardner, and I am the man that suspects him." "Then," retorts Miss Abbey, "you criminate yourself," and she proceeds to blackball the both of them (OMF I, 6). In the great scene which ends the second book, Mrs. Lammle betrays the design on Georgiana Podsnap as "a partnership affair, a money-speculation," as if the partnership in question were the one between her husband and Fledgby. The portraits she shows Twemlow to cover up their secret dialogue are all judged on degrees of "likeness"—that is to say, difference—between the self and its representation: "So like," she says of one, "as to be almost a caricature" (OMF II, 16). She might be talking about herself, or Riah: in Dickens's most demonic twist on the subject, Fledgby plays the part of the stereotypical designing Jewish bill-broker, but he keeps his own name clean by forcing Jewish Riah to act that very caricature in public. As he puts it to himself, he pays Riah for the use of his bad name as an old Jew. (OMF III, 13). When Riah recites his lines "I am but the representative of another, sir . . . I do as I am bidden by my principal" (OMF III, 1), he is of course telling the truth, a truth which, Fledgby makes sure, is read as artful fiction. The interlocking of Fledgby's actual character with what Riah calls "the character which it is your policy that I should bear" (OMF III, 1) suggests an intimate association between a hidden truth and its displaced representation that Mrs. Lammle understands all too well. It is of course only Mrs. Lammle, herself the representative of another, who understands intuitively that "Pubsey and Co., St Mary Axe" is not Riah but Fledgby (OMF III, 17). Hovering over it all we can hear the words of poor depressed Georgiana Podsnap, who gets to articulate an underlying animus in the novel's conception of partnership: "If I was wicked enough—and strong enough—to kill anybody, it should be my partner" (OMF I, 11).

In these and innumerable other ways the novel's partnerships echo and comment on one another, raising the question "Who is speaking for whom?" or asking us to watch as one character attempts to clear his name by casting his guilt and desire upon another. There is very little distance between the economically motivated partnerships and the more classic psychological doublings in this text. Dickens had spent his fiction-making career creating doubles, others, substitutes and scapegoats, but in this novel he seems to be writing *about* them. He's on to himself. He had been in the habit of creating doubles by fission—separating aspects of a single syndrome into the good hero and the declassed villain, as he had done with David Copperfield and Uriah Heep, or into the good woman and the fallen one, as with Esther Summerson and Lady Dedlock in *Bleak House*. Such splits vigorously protect the middle-class virtue of their protagonists by insulating them from their own fears of falling—into shamingly lower-class and overtly sexualized positions. In *Our Mutual Friend*, however, the major male characters—like the self-doubled Dickens—seem to be overcome with the desire to fall, away from their earned or inherited status, away from the normative marriage plot and the fallen women who siphon off that plot's excess energy. Now Dickens begins to create doubles by fusion: they become inseparable, dependent, even identical.[5] The man who exists in violent intimacy with "another man" sits at the heart of the tale, in the paired stories of Eugene Wrayburn/Bradley Headstone and John Harmon/Rokesmith.

Dickens had told the Wrayburn-Headstone story before—notably through the Richard Wardour-Frank Aldersley pair in *The Frozen Deep*. In the play, Wardour lives his life in fear of, and desire for, what will happen when "I and that man shall meet, face to face" (Brannon, 34). The story was told again in a beatified version, the Sydney Carton-Charles Darnay substitution in *A Tale of Two Cities*. In each story, two men are intimately connected through their rivalrous love for the same woman; as Eve Sedgwick famously pointed out, the Girardian triangle of desire exists to create a homosocial and/or homosexual bond between the men (Sedgwick, ch. 9). It was only in *Our Mutual Friend* that Dickens created a Wardour-figure who acts on his murderous attraction to his rival lover—allowing the gun to fire in the third act. He did so by adding the old, charged factor of class difference to the erotics of the Headstone-Wrayburn rivalry.

Bradley Headstone is given Richard Wardour's energy, his violent, unrequited love and his conflict-ridden murderous hatred. Eugene Wrayburn is given Sydney Carton's indifference, his inability to strive for himself, and his courting of death. Both men, fleeing the word "wife," are galvanized by the words "sister" and "daughter." Neither man is bland; neither is innocent; neither is good, neither is a rescuer, neither sacrifices himself—all of those qualities are instead invested in Lizzie, the elusive object of their desire. The contest that ensues is remarkable because Dickens manages to keep the alternating current vividly crackling between the two men. As the narrator puts it at the opening of their great dialogue scene, "There was some secret, sure perception between them, which set them against one another in all ways" (II, 6). What happens between them is a fusion that expresses itself as animosity.

As their dialogue scene unfolds in book two, chapter six, it reads as an intensely uncomfortable humiliation of a lower-middle-class man by an upper-class man. Over and over Headstone plays into Wrayburn's hands by delivering the lines that Wrayburn twists and returns, like a series of poisoned darts. In this way, Wrayburn penetrates Headstone's motives, negates Headstone's being, and reveals nothing himself. But he can only do so—he only bothers to do so—because he is a man who, in relation to Lizzie, occupies a ground identical to Headstone's. For his part, Headstone refuses to give up; though unable to conceal his feeling and his class resentment, he is quite capable of condemning Eugene's moves in return, and of insisting on the seriousness of his threats. One has the class assurance, one the emotional drive that the other lacks, yet they recognize each other; each says to the other "I see who you are and what you're doing." The wordless nocturnal chase scenes around London dramatize this same dynamic in dumb-show. Eugene, the goader, seems to have the upper hand, but hunter and hunted are confounded in the chase, and both men are equally compelled to rehearse, and to defer, the moment when they might turn and meet "face to face." Eugene knows that tormenting Bradley is a way of defending himself from, and attacking himself for, the emotional situation they share. As he puts it, "I own to the weakness of objecting to occupy a ludicrous position, and therefore I transfer the position to the scouts [Bradley and Charley]" (III, 10). The process of self-projection down the social scale is transparent, in this novel. And for the first time in Dickens's work, class difference itself is not the eroticized issue. Fear of excessive feeling is more charged than fear of falling.

Eugene's crisis is his face-to-face encounter with his murderer. As the narrator tells it, the murder attempt is an intimate event in which the bodies of the two men are fused in an embrace of assault and dependence. When they fall on the river-bank together, it is not entirely clear who has gone into the river: "he fell on the bank with him, and then there was another great crash, and then a splash, and all was done'' (IV, 6). Through the infusion of this identity exchange, Eugene gets what he needs: enough of Bradley's primal energy to survive, and a blurring of class status that allows him to do what Bradley would have done: to marry Lizzie. As in *The Frozen Deep*, this infusion of energy flowing from one man to another is eroticized but not specifically sexual—it is not, for example, anything like the anal rape Eve Sedgwick talks about (Sedgwick, 169). The sheer energy of released desire, rather than a specific sexual object, is the valued product of male identity exchange.

Bradley Headstone continues the chain of self-projection down the social scale when he doubles with the pure aggressiveness of Rogue Riderhood, hoping to throw suspicion on the Rogue for his own assault on Eugene. Their final, mortal, intimate embrace echoes the Headstone-Wrayburn exchange: Headstone like Eugene before him leads Riderhood on a back and forth wild goose chase until the moment when he turns and closes with him, face to face in death. In that gesture Headstone both takes charge of his own split self, and achieves a violent release from the straitjacket of his self-proclaimed role as ''a man of unimpeachable character'' (OMF II, 14). Dickens awards him with the novel's strongest exit, first in the wonderful gesture of erasing his own public name, and then in the final willed and murderous mastery of his own projected aggressiveness.

In the John Harmon-Julius Handford-John Rokesmith story, the themes I have been sounding are gathered together within the boundaries of a single body. Otherness becomes the explicit condition of identity. John Harmon's soliloquy—if that is the right name to attach to it—recovers a recent memory of trauma and dissociation, but it is also an investigation of the splits that occur when memory is transformed into autobiographical narrative (OMF II, 13). Dickens situates the soliloquy so that it rises beautifully from a scene of impersonation. John Rokesmith has disguised himself in the clothes of his dead double, George Radfoot, and announced that death to Rogue Riderhood as part of his effort to get Riderhood to clear Gaffer Hexam's name. In this guise as ''the man'' he releases an aggressive, threatening power that we rarely see in any of his other manifestations. Dressed up in Radfoot's coat and armed with Radfoot's knife, Harmon-Rokesmith can act out a manhood that seems an essential precondition of his appearance onstage as himself.

Reviving Radfoot returns him to the scene of his trauma for the first time, and when he is through with Riderhood he tries to revisit that scene—the wall, the dark doorway, the flight of stairs, the room. As if caught in Freud's dream of the uncanny, he cannot find the place; he can only go in confused circles that bring him back to the point he started from. The sense of disorientation in space pervades the memory of his trauma. Radfoot had taken him through turns and doubles in city streets, making him literally lost. (Here, as in the Wrayburn-Headstone chase, the cityscape serves as psychic territory). Harmon can never figure out how he landed on the opposite side of the river from where he started. Against that sense of confusion he builds his narrative as he walks away from Limehouse Hole, still dressed in George Radfoot's coat.

Harmon's story is about another difficult return, to the England of his father, with its "miserable associations" and the childhood feelings they elicit—shrinking, mistrust, self-division, fear of himself and others. This section resonates with Dickens's two "never-to-be-forgotten" miseries, the adult turmoil that stirs up the "shrinking" sensitivity of the child. As Harmon tells it, the revival of those uneasy and most unwelcome feelings leads him to take up with his double Radfoot, in a plot to snoop on Bella and defer the paternal injunction of marriage. Like Wrayburn and Headstone, Harmon evades the predictable marriage plot by mediating his desire through another, "identical" man. After their partnership is double-crossed, the soliloquy dramatizes the process of reinvesting doubleness in the self.[6] John Harmon has to create himself through a tale that asserts a continuity of self despite his experience of gaps in memory, consciousness and time. But as he does so, his narrative regularly raises the question of just who is talking, who is the subject of the discourse, and who is being addressed.

Dickens, we know, had always been interested in the phenomena of memory and amnesia. He maintained a lifelong friendship with Dr. John Elliotson, who had taught him to practice mesmerism. In *A Tale of Two Cities*, he had created, in Dr. Manette, a case of amnesia that revives when Manette is faced with disturbing memories that bear on his long trauma of imprisonment. Harmon's story is told as a struggle to incorporate trauma while not being sucked back into its circular disorientation. He is determined to "pin himself" to his perplexity, to "think it out" in a way that asserts a straight path from beginning to end. The dangers he sees lie in the movements of mind that inevitably occur in retrospective telling. He is afraid of succumbing to swirls of affect, mixing up the present with the past, or falling into retrospective "speculation" about motives he had not suspected at the time of the events themselves. He chastises himself for any of those deviations from factual and temporal linearity, as though he were preparing a court case that will turn on the question, "What did he know and when did he know it?"

Harmon's telling is a self-disciplinary action that asserts a victory over childish self-distrust and the dissolution of boundaries. Truth-claims are continually made: the facts, when Harmon stops to check them, are always right. His concern with reconstructing the temporal order, and accounting for the exact period when the sense of time was lost, also evokes later nineteenth-century anxieties about the potential for loss and error in the sequencing of memory. What the Victorian psychologist James Sully called "illusions of memory" are closely bound up with easily fractured illusions about the continuity of the self.[7]

In the story itself, Harmon suffers a major breach of self-continuity: he passes through a state of identity dispersion and dissociation, which is reversed by his immersion in the Thames. While he is drugged the "men wrestling violently all over the room" create a hallucinatory multiplication of his own aggressive struggle with Radfoot; when he hears blows, they are alienated from his body, which is likened to a felled tree in a forest. The drug impairs his ability to use language, and he falls "into a silence of weeks, months, years." Only in this retrospective narrative can he use the word "I" for a symbolizing entity that had ceased to exist. When he and Radfoot are dumped into the river together, the return to his own name is figured as the falling away of a "heavy horrid unintelligible something." This abjected prelinguistic formlessness will return to traumatize Julius Handford when he sees the "horrible, horrible sight" (OMF I, 2)—the decomposed, borderless body of his dead double. It's no wonder he can't "identify" that corpse.[8]

The speaking of this soliloquy seems designed to sew Harmon-Rokesmith together, minus the spooked and stuttering Julius Handford. But its rhetoric keeps him in pieces. The narrating "I" is not John Harmon, but a voice in dialogue with somebody else he calls John Harmon, someone with whom he checks the accuracy of facts, or whom he warns against straying from the straight path of narrative. John Harmon is more spoken to than speaking, never more so than when he is drowning and someone—but who?—says "This is John Harmon drowning! John Harmon, struggle for your life!" The "This" would seem to be the body of John Harmon, not fully identical with the "I" who now "cried it aloud in a great agony." It's as if John Harmon were being reintroduced to himself, in a recognition scene where a physical body and a capacity for speech and feeling converge, but do not fully merge.

In the latter part of the narrative, the "I" refers to the names John Harmon and John Rokesmith in the third person; "I" is both identical to and alienated from both of them. John Rokesmith is identified with duty: he must clear Gaffer's name and clean up the other moral messes caused by his deceit. John

Harmon is identified with the aggressive and sexual feeling that must be buried under piles and mounds of earth that recall the father's crushing legacy. Thus, despite the straight and narrow path of narrative, this character ends up circling back to where he began. In effect, Harmon-Rokesmith's story ends with a deliberate repetition of the self-drowning which he has just narrated himself out of. Returning to his impersonation as secretary and agent of another, he chooses a role that is hardly different in kind from Bradley Headstone's "Schoolmastering" or from the secret agencies of the partnership pairs. The only real distinction is that Harmon-Rokesmith gets to cast himself in both parts and to control the staging.

In this highly theatrical novel, engaging "face to face" with a double figure, whether it's projected outside or within the solitary mind, seems to be a necessary condition for a selfhood that can endure either life or death. The characters who exist, in the full sense of that word, are the ones who fight their way to a recognition of their own self-estrangement. From this point of view the whole novel begins to look like a "violent wrestling of men all over the room"—men who can, at best, save themselves by embracing themselves as Somebody Else.

## NOTES

This essay was first presented as a lecture at the Dickens Universe, University of California at Santa Cruz, August, 2000.

1. All quotations from *Our Mutual Friend* (OMF) will be designated by book and chapter.

2. For a detailed study of the collaboration of Dickens and Collins, as well as a recreated text of the original play, see Brannan.

3. John Glavin makes a fruitful distinction between Dickens's sense of a theatricality that could at best "actually generate self," and his fear of theater as a locus of shame and destruction (67).

4. It is worth remembering in this context that Dickens associated his fellow-workers in the blacking factory with theater life: one in particular had a father who worked in the Drury Lane theatre, and a little sister "who did imps in the Pantomimes" (Forster 26).

5. For a fine account of the general development of doubling in Dickens, see Gillman and Patten, who read doubling in the late fiction as a Freudian conflict: a "fundamental internalized warfare between the demonic energies of the unconscious and the civilizing repressions of the conscious" (448). Along similar lines, Taylor Stoehr sees *Our Mutual Friend* as a work with an easier, more open relationship with the old conflicts.

6. MacKay has done a study of the speech as a hybrid of Romantic and Victorian ideas of the self, in which she discerns a gradual transition from Romantic to Victorian modes as the soliloquy proceeds.
7. In chapter 10, "Illusions of Memory," Sully spends a large portion of his essay discussing the distortions of time-lengths and time-sequences that occur when people try to remember their pasts. He wants to make it clear that the memory is no infallible calendar of events, and seems to have felt the need to dwell on this matter in detail.
8. Harmon's time calculations suggest that Radfoot's body would have been in the river for two weeks before being brought in by Gaffer Hexam.

# WORKS CITED

Brannan, Robert Louis. *Under the Management of Mr. Charles Dickens: His Production of "The Frozen Deep."* Ithaca: Cornell UP, 1966.

Dickens, Charles. *The Letters of Charles Dickens*. Pilgrim Edition. Ed. Graham Storey and Kathleen Tillotson Vols. 8–10. Oxford: Clarendon, 1995–1998.

———. *Our Mutual Friend*. Ed. Adrian Pool. Harmondsworth: Penguin 1997.

Farrell, John. "The Partners' Tale: Dickens and *Our Mutual Friend.*" *ELH* 66 (1999): 759–99.

Forster, John. *The Life of Charles Dickens*. Ed. J. W. T. Ley. London: Cecil Palmer, 1928.

Gillman, Susan K. and Robert L. Patten. "Dickens: Doubles: Twain: Twins," *Nineteenth-Century Fiction* 39 (1985): 441–58.

Glavin, John. *After Dickens: Reading, Adaptation and Peformance*. Cambridge: Cambridge UP, 1999

MacKay, Carol Hanberry. "The Encapsulated Romantic: John Harmon and the Boundaries of Victorian Soliloquy" *Dickens Studies Annual* 18 (1989): 255–76.

Sedgwick, Eve Kosofsky. *Between Men: English Literature and Male Homosocial Desire*. New York: Columbia UP, 1985.

Stoehr, Taylor. *Dickens: The Dreamer's Stance*. Ithaca: Cornell UP, 1965.

Sully, James. *Illusions: A Psychological Study*. New York: Appleton, 1881.

# Swarmery and Bloodbaths: A Reconsideration of Dickens on Class and Race in the 1860s

## Grace Moore

*This essay offers a reappraisal of Dickens's stances on class and race in the 1860s and examines his reactions to the Jamaican rebellion of 1865, the American Civil War, and growing working-class agitation for suffrage; it also touches briefly upon his engagement with the Irish Question. The article argues that rather far from being a vehement supporter of Governor Edward Eyre's draconian attempts to quell the uprising in Morant Bay, Dickens was in fact ambivalent to events in the West Indies. Far from displaying the type of vitriolic and public fury that characterized his reaction to the Indian "Mutiny" of 1857, Dickens's involvement with the Eyre Defence League was nominal and resulted largely from loyalty to Thomas Carlyle. By juxtaposing Dickens's responses to events in the public sphere with Carlyle's more polemical outbursts, the piece attempts to extricate Dickens's perspective on events at home and abroad from that of his mentor.*

> "The Jamaican story, is characteristic of the beastliness of the 'true Englishman' "[1]

Along with the Indian Mutiny, the Jamaican insurrection of 1865 became one of the most controversial race-related incidents of the nineteenth century.

Coinciding as it did with both the ethnography debate between the poly-genecists and monogenecists and the reconfiguration of race relations in the reconstructed American South, the event elicited vehement responses from both supporters and detractors of Governor Edward Eyre (see figure 1 for the interconnections between these events). The uprising in Morant Bay was just one of a string of rebellions which had peppered the history of British involvement in the Caribbean, probably, as Gad Heuman has argued, as a result of the high ratio of slaves (or, by 1865, ex-slaves) to white masters (151).[2] The first slave revolt had occurred in 1673, and by the eighteenth century, according to Mary Turner, revolts took place on average once every five years (153). Unsuccessful plots had been discovered in 1823 and 1824, while on December 27, 1831, up to 20,000 slaves rose up in the last major rebellion before the abolition of slavery. The turbulence did not abate with abolition, indeed, it often arose in response to fears that slavery would be re-established. There were riots in 1839, 1848, and 1859, yet none of them were repressed as brutally as at Morant Bay, and certainly, none of them had the same impact upon such a broad cross-section of the British public.

Most of the nineteenth-century unrest involved damage to property only. However, the second of the two disturbances of 1859 was less restrained and involved bloodshed. The riot was sparked by the arrest of a man of mixed race, Theodore Buie, along with a number of his supporters in response to a desire on the part of Buie's white Scottish aunt to evict him from the Florence Hall Estate, where he lived. The sixty prisoners taken were released by a large, violent crowd before they could be brought to trial, and the Falmouth police station continued to be stoned even after they had been freed. When police fired on the crowd, two women were killed instantly and another person died from wounds several days later. In addition, eight or nine others were wounded. As Heuman points out, the events were even more politically charged by the fact that they took place on August 1, the twenty-first anniversary of the granting of full freedom. He argues that this event, although insignificant to the British public at the time, may be read as a precursor of the more bloody events six years later:

> The riots of 1859 highlighted some of the issues which profoundly affected post-emancipation Jamaica and would prove crucial six years later at Morant Bay. High taxes [the cause of the first riot in 1859], whether in the form of assessments or of toll-gates, were a serious problem for the mass of the people, especially as the Legislature had shifted a heavy proportion of the taxes onto the ex-slaves and away from the plantocracy. The lack of justice, which was an important element in the Buie case, was one of the leading factors in the outbreak at Morant Bay.          (161)

This absence of justice heightened racial tensions by demonstrating that the law was far from impartial and was in place, not to guarantee law and order for all, but to protect the economic interests of white settlers and their descendants. While these events may have paved the way to Morant Bay, they were certainly not regarded with any particular significance in the mother country when they took place.

The regular succession of easily quelled revolts does not appear to have had any effect whatsoever on Dickens, who seems to have regarded the West Indies in the same way as he perceived Australia. The Caribbean was a useful place to exile problematic characters in need of a swift change of fortune, such as Walter Gay in *Dombey and Son*—it could also provide a plausible source of wealth and refuge for characters like Monks/Leeford in *Oliver Twist*.[3] In 1859, the pages of *Household Words* were far too concerned with a reassessment of its editor's stance on events in India to be concerned with what seemed to be a relatively insignificant uprising in Jamaica. The rising at Morant Bay was, in itself, not remarkably different from any of the other demonstrations which had, by the very nature of the inequality of the two groups, characterized black-white relations both before and after emancipation. It was not the uprising itself that was responsible for the considerable controversy that dominated public debate from 1865 to 1868, but rather the manner of its suppression.

In brief, the immediate catalyst for the activity was, just as in 1859, a court case, although relations between the planters and the former slaves had been particularly tense for a long time, largely as a result of a long period of economic depression. Over the previous ten years Jamaica had been subject to epidemics of cholera and smallpox, both drought and floods had affected crops and many sugar planters had been bankrupted. The American Civil War had exacerbated the situation since 1861, as cheap food imports from the U.S. were no longer available, thus leading to higher prices. Blockades of Southern ports also prevented the importing of American cotton garments. As Thomas C. Holt has noted,

> By 1865 not only had the cost of cotton trebled but osnaburgh, the hempen substitute that had clothed workers since slavery had more than doubled in price. The price of fish doubled. Cornmeal went up as much as 75 per cent. Flour was up 83 per cent. . . . According to one recent calculation the overall cost of living on the island rose 60 per cent between 1859–61 and 1865.
>
> (264–265)

So appalling had living conditions become, that in February, 1865, the secretary of the Baptist Missionary Society of Great Britain, Dr. Edward Bean

Underhill, who had visited the island in 1859 to study the standard of living, wrote to the British Colonial Office to draw attention to the plight of the Jamaicans. It was left to Edward Eyre (who had been appointed governor of the island the year before, having been acting-governor since 1862) to respond to this letter, which he did in an extremely public and insensitive manner. Rather than conceding that problems existed, Eyre repudiated all of Underhill's allegations and took no ameliorative steps. The planters of the St. Ann district responded by circulating a petition to the queen complaining of their impoverished state and requesting that crown lands be opened up to the peasantry to allow them to cultivate food. Eyre passed the letter to the Colonial Office, along with a number of his own unfavorable observations on the sloth of the Jamaican and what he regarded as Underhill's subversive intentions. The resulting reply, known as *The Queen's Advice*, was penned by Henry Taylor of the Colonial Office, who seems to have been woefully ignorant of the hardships suffered in Jamaica and to have unquestioningly accepted Eyre's repudiations. Taylor's response—neatly described by Holt as taking the form of "a lecture in classical political economy" failed to engage with any of the complaints put forward by the petitioners and urged the people to work harder instead of depending upon the charity of others (277). Eyre had this deeply insensitive and factually inaccurate reply reproduced and displayed across the island. It was, however, widely believed that the queen would not have permitted such a letter to have been written in her name unless she had been severely misled, and it was realized that Eyre was the guilty party.[4]

Eyre's actions generated further unrest throughout the island and heightened resentment against the plantocracy, who were determined that crown lands would not be turned over to the people. After a period of political rallying—much of which took place in native Baptist chapels and meeting houses—rebellion erupted on October 11, 1865, when several hundred people attacked the police station at Morant Bay following a court case on October 7. The ensuing confrontation between the local police and the crowd resulted in eighteen deaths in the ranks of the militia, and a further thirty-one people were wounded. In the next few days two planters were murdered and many others were threatened, leading Eyre to declare a state of emergency and to place the district under martial law. At this point, it would seem that Eyre panicked, and by misjudging what had begun as a local insurrection—albeit one resulting from more widespread discontent—he exacerbated the crisis by bringing in troops and in the inevitable clashes which followed this act, nearly five hundred people were killed. Reports filtering back to Britain rather exaggerated the figures, with *Lyons' Newspaper* observing, "It is supposed that in little more than a week, more than 2000 people have been either shot or hung, whilst the number flogged is enormous. It is commonly reported that more than 300 women and young girls have been catted" (Jamaica 28). A writer to the *Birmingham Post*'s letters column went even further by questioning Eyre's judgment on November 13, 1865, just ten days after his dispatch requesting military assistance was received in London:

> No one attempts to do anything but condemn the savage outbreak; yet none of us can believe there was a wide-spread intention to murder the white and coloured (people) at Christmas, form a republic, burn Kingston &c, &c. These are the false and foolish assertions of men who are alarmed, and conjure up to themselves the most dreadful things.        (Jamaica 26)

Some of the troops involved in putting down the rising had served in India during the Sepoy Rebellion, and this factor undoubtedly influenced their behavior, which seems have been tempered by a lust for revenge rather than a desire to restore peace. Indeed, the orgy of gratuitous violence initiated by the British is demonstrated in the following extract from the despatch of Captain Ford, who commanded the St Thomas-in-the-East Irregular Troops:

> On our march from Morant Bay we shot two prisoners and catted five or six, *and released them as these latter were only charged with being concerned in plundering, not murders.* This morning we made raid with thirty men, all mounted, and got back to head-quarters at four p.m., bringing in a few prisoners, and having flogged nine men, and *burned three negro houses, and then had a court martial on the prisoners, who amounted to about fifty or sixty.* Several were flogged without court-martial, from a simple examination; nine were convicted by court-martial: one of them to a hundred lashes, which he got at once, the other eight to be hanged or shot. . . . This is a picture of martial law. The soldiers enjoy it—the inhabitants have to dread it. If they run on their approach they are shot for running away. The contents of all the houses we have been in, except only this very house, but including the barracks, have been reduced to a mass of broken and hacked furniture, with doors and windows smashed by the rebels.        (Jamaica 21)

It is a telling fact that the Jamaica Committee, who wished to prosecute Eyre for his draconian and reactionary behavior, included this extract in its collection of *Facts and Documents*. The behavior of the troops is marked by a complete disregard for human suffering, and the account clearly points to the brutality of the forces of law. While Captain Ford's references to the damaged property are obviously intended to draw attention to the barbarity of the rebels, their juxtaposition with accounts of wholesale floggings simply emphasize the excessive British conduct.

Eyre himself certainly played upon memories of the recent Indian Mutiny in an attempt to defend his actions. As he declared to the Jamaican Assembly on November, 7 1865:

> One moment's hesitation, one single reverse, might have lit the torch which would have blazed in rebellion from one end of the island to the other; and who can say how many of us would have lived to see it extinguished? It is my duty to point out to you that, satisfactory as it is to know that the rebellion in the eastern districts has been crushed out, the entire colony has long been, still is, on the brink of a volcano, which may at any moment burst into fury. There is scarcely a district or a parish in the island where disloyalty, sedition, and murderous intentions are not widely disseminated and, in many instances, openly expressed.[5]

The reasoned and reasonable observations of the *Birmingham Post* and *Lyons*'s offer a direct contrast to Eyre's assertions of savagery and brutality. They also demonstrate the type of emotional response elicited by the Jamaican controversy, and when pitted against the latent fears and prejudices against native peoples that lingered in the wake of the Sepoy Rebellion, a fierce public debate soon began to rage in Britain. On the one side, figures like John Stuart Mill, Huxley, Darwin, and Lyell called for Eyre to be prosecuted as a murderer, while on the other, men like Carlyle, Charles Kingsley, and John Ruskin demanded that he be recognized as a hero. What was already an incredibly complex and factionalized debate assumed a complicating class dimension with the involvement of the radical John Bright, and the ensuing alignment of the working classes with Mill's Jamaica Committee, which was a logical step after their support for the North during the American Civil War. Fears of working-class unrest were exacerbated by the demonstration held in Southampton by the working men of the city to protest against the Eyre's reception at a banquet held in his honor once he had been recalled to Britain. The debate continued well into 1868, with a Royal Commission being set up to investigate Eyre's actions and various attempts on the part of the Jamaica Committee to prosecute him for murder and then for high crimes and misdemeanours.

Having responded so vocally to the Indian uprising of 1857, one might expect Dickens to have been equally outspoken on the subject of the Morant Bay Rebellion of 1865, especially with the sensationalist press coverage that the event attracted. Rumors of a bloodbath abounded, as the *Jamaica Papers* display:

> The *Morning Journal* says that "It has been stated in the House of Assembly that the number of 'rebels' executed under sentence of the courts-martial, exclusive of those destroyed in the bushes by the soldiers and the maroons, amount to over 2,000." We have heard it rumoured that the number actually destroyed in every way amounts to about 3,000, but we do not vouch for its correctness.
>
> (Jamaica 28)

Exaggerated though this account is, when compared to stories appearing in reliable sources like *The New York Herald* telling of "EIGHT MILES OF DEAD BODIES," it seems rather tame (Semmel 22). These narratives of hysteria were clearly out of control, and Malchow draws attention to the parallels—both conscious and subconscious—between the suppression of events at Morant Bay and the tall stories that circulated during the Indian Mutiny:

> [T]he most available resonance was, of course, that with the presumed sexual and sadistic depravity of the Indian Mutiny. An actual Indian connection was perhaps implied in allusions in the press to the fact that since 1860 Indian "coolies" had been introduced into the West Indies as laborers. Although there was no suggestion that these had been involved in the revolt, this created the sense of a general mobility of racial threat throughout the empire.     (213)

Yet, Dickens failed to exhibit the same public fury with which he had responded to events in India. While his public support for Governor Eyre is frequently cited as further evidence of a persistent and entrenched racism, Dickens's response to the unrest in the West Indies was, typically, far more complex. Critics like Brantlinger and Oddie have regarded Dickens's involvement with the Eyre Defence League as an almost natural progression from his outbursts against the Indian race in the early stages of the Sepoy Rebellion. In an attempt to trace neatly an aversion to non-white races first manifested in "The Niger Expedition" and sustained throughout his career, the fact that Dickens's involvement with the league was only nominal is all too conveniently overlooked.

Dickens had surprisingly little to say on the subject of events in Jamaica, and while historians invariably list him as a supporter of Eyre, his endorsement seems only to have extended to a signature on a petition. Whereas his anger at the Indian Mutiny had dominated his correspondence for several months, Dickens refers to the occurrence at Morant Bay only once in a letter to W. W. F. de Cerjat, with whom he was always particularly candid.

Admittedly, by the 1860s Dickens's correspondence was less voluminous than in previous decades. Having burned all the letters he had ever received on September 3, 1860, he was becoming increasingly self-conscious about what he consigned to paper and how it could be used by future biographers. Overall, though, he was less emotive in his reactions that he had been in 1857, although, as the de Cerjat letter demonstrates, he remained prone to accumulate crises and connect them to one another. The letter is worth quoting at length, since George Ford—one of only two other critics to have attempted to deal with Dickens's stance on Jamaica in any depth—has referred only to excerpts, thus negating the cumulative effect of Dickens's rhetoric:

> If the Americans don't embroil us in a war before long it will not be their fault. What with their swagger and bombast, what with their claims for indemnification, what with Ireland and Fenianism, and what with Canada, I have strong apprehensions. . . . The Jamaican insurrection is another hopeful piece of business. That platform-sympathy with the black—or the native, or the devil—afar off, and that platform indifference to our own countrymen at enormous odds in the midst of bloodshed and savagery, makes me stark wild. Only the other day, here was a meeting of jawbones of asses at Manchester, to censure the Jamaica Governor for his manner of putting down the insurrection! So we are badgered about New Zealanders and Hottentots, as if they were identical with men in clean shirts at Camberwell and were to be bound by pen and ink accordingly. So Exeter Hall holds us in mortal submission to missionaries, who (Livingstone always excepted) are perfect nuisances, and leave every place worse than they found it.
>
> Of the many evidences that are visible of our being ill-governed, no one is so remarkable to me as our ignorance of what is going on under our Government. What will future generations think of that enormous Indian Mutiny being ripened without suspicion, until whole regiments arose and killed their officers? A week ago, red tape, half-bouncing and half pooh-poohing what it bounced at, would have scouted the idea of a Dublin jail not being able to hold a political prisoner. But for the blacks in Jamaica being over-impatient and before their time, the whites might have been exterminated without a previous hint of suspicion that there was anything amiss. *Laissez aller*, and Britons never, never, never!          (Letters 114–16)[6]

The letter continues with a series of grumbles about the railway boom and the influence of shareholders in the companies in the House of Commons. Yet Dickens almost catches himself slipping into the state of mind which had so nearly overwhelmed him in the previous decade and ends by observing half-ironically, "I seem to be grumbling, but I am in the best of humours" (Letters 115). This letter is particularly interesting in that it demonstrates the interconnectedness of events both across the Empire and beyond—links that Thomas Carlyle was later to emphasize in his anti-working-class suffrage tract, *Shooting Niagara*. It also shows the way in which Dickens still connected misrule at home with misplaced priorities overseas and an "indifference" to the English working classes. His language, when discussing the Jamaicans is certainly derogatory, with its references to "bloodshed" and "savagery," but when compared to his previous calls for vengeance one can see that it has become comparatively moderate. Most importantly, the letter does not conflate the public and private anxieties which combined to produce the crisis of the 1850s. By the 1860s, however, his new life without Catherine seems to have enabled him to untangle his public and private concerns, just as his fiction had moved on from the intersecting worlds of *Bleak House* to the rigidly demarcated public and private existences of Wemmick in *Great Expectations*. As a result of having successfully separated these anxieties, events in the public domain must have appeared to be more distant and therefore more manageable. In addition, as his correspondence attests, by the '60s Dickens had become increasingly apolitical and seems no longer to have been able to respond with the same passion to events not directly affecting him. His priorities now lay primarily with his reading tours, his deteriorating health, his writing and, to a lesser extent, with the welfare of his family.

When analyzing the part of the above letter dealing specifically with Jamaica, George H. Ford stated, "Dickens is an interesting example. Although he did not play a prominent part, his views were identical with those of Carlyle. He was one of the first to applaud Eyre as a hero" (227). Having cited an extract from the letter dealing specifically with Jamaica, Ford continues,

> This was written by the so-called "friend of the common man," the great reformer, the writer whom Macaulay had once considered a dangerous socialist. It is sometimes forgotten that Dickens was not so much the friend of the common man as the friend of the common Englishman. (227–28)

Ford's assertion that Dickens's views were the same as Carlyle's is a curious one, and he offers no evidence to support it, other than some flimsy parallels between "The Nigger Question" and "The Noble Savage" (220, 227–28).[7] In fact, Dickens's tone in the letter is far less impassioned than that of any of the 1857 correspondence. It is certainly far removed from Carlyle's predestinarian assertions that both race and class boundaries have been divinely ordained and should therefore not be tampered with. Carlyle felt able to argue:

> One always rather liked the Nigger; evidently a poor blockhead with good dispositions, with affections, attachments,—with a turn for Nigger Melodies,

and the like:—he is the only Savage of all the coloured races that doesn't die out on sight of the White Man; but can actually live beside him, and work and increase and be merry. The Almighty Maker has appointed him to be a Servant. Under penalty of Heaven's curse, neither party to this pre-appointment shall neglect or misdo his duties therein.                                            (5)

While Carlyle's stance may be a difficult one for the modern reader to grasp, it is a consistent one, and in my opinion, critics like Ford seem to be challenged by the lack of consistency in Dickens, a figure so resolute in every other way. For Carlyle with his vision of a rigidly ordered hierarchy, it is the white man with his "swarmery," or ideas on democracy and equality, who is ultimately responsible for the bloodbaths in America and Jamaica, and the ensuing anarchy that he foresees as the result of working-class suffrage in Britain. He regards both the Southern slave and the emancipated Jamaican as child-like workers, who should remain in their places for both their own good, and the good of society as a whole. Abhorrent though his arguments may seem today, one can trace a logic to them that is conspicuously absent from Dickens's sporadic outbursts of prejudice against non-whites. Carlyle evidently gave a great deal of thought to his view of a chain of being wherein it was the white man's duty to ensure that the former slave was forced to continue to work, rather than succumbing to what he saw as an innate idleness. Dickens, on the other hand, does not seem to have considered racial issues in any depth: his comments are reactions grounded in the rhetoric of scientific racism, but lacking the force of a coherent argument. By 1865, Dickens's viewpoint was far removed from that of Carlyle and there is no evidence to suggest that he adopted the type of systematic racial program developed by Carlyle. It is for this reason perhaps more than any other that Dickens had virtually nothing to contribute to the debate on Governor Eyre.

Just as Dickens himself had little to say about the revolt in Jamaica, so *All the Year Round* is conspicuous for the paucity of its coverage of an event which had proved so divisive to all classes in Britain.[8] "Black is not *Quite* White," the sole article to be published on the Eyre controversy appeared on March 3 1866, although interestingly a short piece on the Indian Mutiny, "Under Fire" was published on February 17, 1866.[9] The tone of "Black is not *Quite* White" is somewhat deceptive. The article begins by lamenting the events that had occurred in Jamaica and the author purports to be able to see the argument from both sides:

The late melancholy events in Jamaica have naturally called forth a burst of feeling; on one side, of sympathy and commiseration for our "poor oppressed

brethren'' (whose only crime is their colour); on the other, of wrath and indignation against a race for which so much has been done, and which has so ungrate-
fully turned on its benefactors and attempted to destroy them.

Without pretending to prejudge the merits of the late rebellion, or of the
means which were adopted to suppress it—questions which will, no doubt, be
fully and fairly investigated—it may be suggested that both these extreme
expressions of feeling are unreasonable and exaggerated. The first is the result
of a total want of knowledge of the real character of the negro, and the second
arises from the absence of reflection in a moment of excitement as to the causes
which may have produced that character.                                    (173)

On a superficial level the author may seem to be taking the path of moderation,
with his expressions of sympathy. However, the fact that the words ''poor
oppressed brethren'' are placed in quotation marks suggests that the writer
is simply quoting and does not share these sentiments, while the language
used to describe the ingratitude of the race is far more emotive and is, significantly, not reported speech.

The liberal tone is rapidly dropped after the opening paragraphs as the
author offers a series of case studies based upon his own experiences in the
Caribbean. These individual character sketches depict a whole host of deceptive Jamaicans who have attempted to outwit or dupe the writer, and who are
shown to have a strong propensity toward vengeance when detected. The
figures depicted bear a more than passing resemblance to Carlyle's pumpkin-
eating Quashee of The Nigger Question, as stock racial stereotypes are brought
into play, and the discourse of scientific racism is employed to argue for a
natural inferiority:

> Naturally improvident and indolent, he sought a fresh scope for his hereditary
> cunning in sharp-witted schemes to meet his wants and gratify his appetites
> and vices. When, failing in this he was satisfied barely to exist, he gradually
> fell lower and lower in the scale of humanity: not, however, without crying out
> against the oppressors who would not feed him in idleness, and not without
> repeated attempts at rebellion, in the senseless hope that by murdering those
> oppressors and seizing their property he would at last attain the goal of affluent
> indolence.                                                                (174)

Having asserted that ''the original African negro is not a high moral type of
nature,'' the writer goes on to observe that an innate barbarism and duplicity
have been cultivated by the conditions of slavery and servitude to which the
Jamaican has been subjected (173). Although here we see a recognition that
the white man is responsible for these flaws which have developed in response

to conditions of oppression, the article's author seems unable to acknowledge his own complicity in the process. Indeed, despite the succession of anecdotes, which are given as exemplars of the behavior of an entire race, at no point does the narrator stop to wonder whether his servants behave disloyally for the simple reason that he is not a good master. Some of the conclusions drawn from the "evidence" that is offered require rather a leap of logic on the part of the reader. We are, for instance, offered an account of a dispute between John, a faithful servant, whose sole failing is an inclination to drink, and Francis, a vicious new cook who arms himself and ambushes John, apparently without provocation. Having defeated Francis by biting through his finger, John declares, "I tank de Lord who give me de victory over my enemy!" at which point the narrative voice interjects and observes, "After the butchery at Morant Bay, is it not recorded that the assassins met together and sang songs of praise for their victory?" (175). This curious juxtaposition of a personal vendetta with events at Morant Bay is clearly the result of its author's belief that the uprising is far from an isolated event, but rather the manifestation of a far deeper animosity. As I have explained, the riots were certainly not a spontaneous outburst, but the result of months and years of discord. Yet the constant barrage of racial generalizations serves to undermine the assertion at the beginning of the piece that the behavior of the Jamaicans has been shaped by their systematic oppression at the hands of the white plantocracy. Instead, the Jamaicans are depicted as hypocritical, bloodthirsty, and volatile, and in spite of initial protestations, responsibility seems to have been shifted decidedly onto the former slaves. Thus, according to the title, morality is reduced to a manichean allegory whereby skin color becomes a marker of right or wrong, an inevitable result of the fact that they are black, not *quite* white.

While Dickens did not pen "Black is not *Quite* White," we must conclude from its presence in *All the Year Round* that he is likely to have concurred with the views it expounded. There is nothing within the journal's pages to which the piece may be compared or contrasted, and indeed, *All the Year Round*'s negligence of the Eyre case is so extraordinary that it warrants a little speculation. It is possible that by this time of his life Dickens simply no longer cared about events in far-flung locations like the Caribbean, and that his less-than-active support for Eyre was rather backing for Carlyle instead. Nevertheless, the sheer newsworthiness of the ongoing skirmishes between the Eyre Defence League and the Jamaica Committee would have warranted a significant number of articles. Some other factor must, therefore, have made Dickens hesitant about becoming embroiled in the discussion. Although

reactions may have been blown out of proportion by none too distant memories of events in India, there was no occurrence in Jamaica to match what
came to be perceived as the assault on British womanhood, committed at the
Bibighar. Indeed, after the rapid about face on his initial impulsive reactions
to the Sepoy Rebellion in the wake of revelations about British conduct
towards Indians, Dickens would certainly have exercised caution in dealing
with so controversial a racial issue as the Jamaican uprising in his journal.
Finally, from a business perspective, excessive enthusiasm for and promotion
of the Eyre Defence League would easily have alienated a large sector of
Dickens's readership, had he used the journal as a platform for championing
the former governor.

Bernard Semmel has commented that the divisions on the prosecution of
Eyre were actually already in place before 1865. He regards the American
Civil War as the pivotal event in establishing the two factions, and it is
therefore worth briefly looking backward to examine Dickens's responses to
the hostilities. Like many members of the middle class, Dickens took the side
of the South. Although it is tempting to read his support as a logical progression along the way from his outbursts against the sepoys in the late 1850s,
to his support for Eyre in 1865, his championing of the Southern states
resulted from his belief in free trade, rather than a desire to see slavery
upheld. He wrote, with a good deal of political astuteness, to his friend W.W.
F. de Cerjat in March 1862:

> I take the facts of the American quarrel to stand thus. Slavery has in reality
> nothing on earth to do with it, in any kind of association with any generous or
> chivalrous sentiment on the part of the North. But the North having gradually
> got to itself the making of the laws and the settlement of the Tariffs, and having
> taxed the South most abominally for its own advantage, began to see, as the
> country grew, that unless it advocated the laying down of a geographical line
> beyond which slavery should not extend, the South would necessarily recover
> its old political power and be able to help itself in the adjustment of commercial
> affairs. Every reasonable creature may know, if willing, that the North hates
> the Negro, and that until it was convenient to make a pretence that sympathy
> with him was the cause of the War, it hated abolitionists and derided them up
> hill and down dale. For the rest, there is not a pin to choose between the two
> parties. They will both rant and lie and fight until they come to a compromise;
> and the slave may be thrown into that compromise or thrown out of it, just as
> it happens.                                                    (Letters 53–54)

In other words, for Dickens, those who reduced the war to a question of
Abolition were mere humbugs seeking support for the North and using the

slave as a political pawn. What is also clear from this extract, is that Dickens at this time held a keen interest in the developments in America and was well acquainted with the debates surrounding the conflict. In the early 1860s he had been deeply depressed by the prospect of a war, viewing it in catastrophic terms and writing with feeling to his American friend Captain Morgan, "I wish to God, in the interests of the whole human race, that the War were ended" (Letters 190). By 1865, however, his concern with American politics seems to have fizzled out; his letters showed no interest in Reconstruction and *All the Year Round* was concerned primarily with the war's impact on Britain's economy.[10] Dickens's reaction to the Civil War was, though, markedly different to that of his friend and mentor, Thomas Carlyle, who insisted in his customary high-flown rhetoric:

> To me individually the Nigger's case was not the most pressing in the world, but among the least so! America, however . . . felt that in the Heavens or the Earth there was nothing so godlike, or incomparably pressing to be done . . . . A continent of the earth has been submerged, for certain years by deluges as from the Pit of Hell; half a million (some say a whole million, but surely they exaggerate) of excellent White Men, full of gifts and faculty, have torn and slashed one another into horrid death, in a temporary humour, which will leave centuries of remembrance fierce enough: and three million absurd Blacks, men and brothers (of a sort), are completely "emancipated"; launched into the career of improvement,—likely to be "improved off the face of the earth" in a generation or two.                                                     (7)

While Dickens is saddened by the war, Carlyle clearly regards it as a type of apocalypse—the chaos that will ensue when attempts are made to tamper with the world order. His reference to improvement "off the face of the earth" certainly echoes Dickens's observations at the end of his "Noble Savage" essay, yet this is where the parallels between the two writers end. Dickens adamantly refused to reduce the conflict to the type of racialized binary that it had become for Carlyle and would not accept the slaves as scapegoats for the massive destruction and loss of life, which evidently posed a challenge to his friend's notion of what constituted a civilized race.

Despite Dickens's negation of the race element involved in the American conflict, *All the Year Round* did allow the debate's rhetoric to permeate its articles, particularly once the war had ended. One of the most noteworthy articles, "Slavery in England," appeared in June, 1867, and harked back to some of the harrowing accounts of cruelty against slaves appended to Harriet Beecher Stowe's novel, *Uncle Tom's Cabin*. The piece observes that while measures have been taken—albeit devastating ones—to redress the social inequalities in the United States, the conditions endured by many a British worker remained remarkably similar to those of the slave:

> High-born English ladies, it will be remembered, formally remonstrated with their American sisters on the horrors perpetrated with the sanction or through the indifference of the gentlemen slaveholders, and received a tart retort, telling them to look at home, and to give up girding at their neighbours until their own social anomalies were redressed. The sufferings of milliners and work-girls, the extremes of poverty and wealth to be witnessed in our cities, and the selfish indifference of fashionable life, were all aimed at in the reply; and disinterested readers of the correspondence probably thought, with Sancho Panza, that "a good deal might be said on both sides." Were any similar controversy to arise now, the American ladies could quote facts from a recently published blue book, which go far to show that some of the worst evils of the slavery they have abolished flourish among us, and that in many of our English counties bands of children of tender years are handed over bodily to brutal and irresponsible tyrants, who corrupt and maltreat with as much efficiency as any Southern overseer. (585)

This invective against poor working conditions and exploitation was prompted by the sixth report of the Children's Employment Commission, which made a number of shocking revelations to undermine British feelings of superiority. With its analogies between the state of the child laborer and that of the Southern slave the piece aims to manipulate the righteous indignation the reader would have expressed on reading *Uncle Tom's Cabin* by presenting the children's condition so as to make it more interesting and appealing. The everyday nature of this form of exploitation has rendered the underclass invisible, in the geographical sense that isolated the upper and middle classes from the living areas of the proletariat. The public had also become so habituated to the idea of child labor that it had not occurred to them to question its morality. "Slavery in England" therefore seeks to raise the visibility of child labor by defamiliarizing it and couching the issue in the discourse of a popular—and more exotic—cause like Abolition. The article takes no account of the reader's sensibilities and deliberately aims to shock, as is exemplified in this account of the degradation that the system has bred:

> Of the ways in which our white slaves are housed, we read: They live like pigs; great boys and girls, mother and fathers, all sleeping in one room in many instances; and a policeman, writing of the gross immorality of the young girls, says: "Their boldness and shamelessness I never saw equalled during some years of police life and detective duty in the worst parts of London." Nor is

this wonderful when the character of their masters and mistresses is considered.
One old gang-master of seventy-two is convicted of an indecent assault upon
a girl of thirteen, who worked under him; and the member of parliament who
forwards the particulars, adds: "I am afraid such cases would come oftener
before the magistrates if the children dared to speak."                    (588)

Accounts like the above would indubitably have alarmed the comfortable
middle-class readers, and perhaps even prompted them to action, just as
novels like *Oliver Twist* had done in the 1830s. Yet the interplay between the
discourses of race and class was by no means a one-way process. Since the
issue of slavery was now entangled with the devastation wreaked by the Civil
War, the transposition of British class tensions into North American terms
would undoubtedly have planted misgivings in many minds. Thus, an analogy
that was intended to incite sympathy, empathy, and action resulted also in
fears of revolution, class conflict, and the construction of the disenfranchised
working classes as barbarous, volatile, and irrational.

Working-class leaders were quick to recognize the similarities between
their state and that of the black slaves overseas, and registered their support
for the North (and its economic policies) in the Civil War. At home, Trade
Union activity had been stepped up after 1859 and widespread support for
campaigns like the Builders' Union's strikes led to fears of working-class
insurrection. Such anxieties were further aroused by calls for universal male
suffrage, which led the likes of Carlyle to speak of those demanding it as
"delerious" and to declare that the measure was too much too soon. Carlyle
believed that a working-class electorate with the ability to vote would be
uncontrollable. Dickens, on the other hand, responded in a much more moderate manner:

> As to the Reform question, it should have been, and could have been, perfectly
> known to any honest man in England that the more intelligent part of the great
> masses were deeply dissatisfied with the state of the representation, but were
> in a very moderate and patient condition, awaiting the better intellectual cultiva-
> tion of numbers of their fellows. The old insolent resource of assailing them
> and making the most audaciously hardy statements that they were politically
> indifferent, has borne the inevitable fruit. The perpetual taunt "Where are
> they?" has called them out with the answer, "Well then; if you *must* know,
> here we are."                                                      (Letters 292)[11]

Dickens sees "the masses," as he refers to them, as a reasoning and reasonable body who have waited patiently for electoral reform. Later in the letter
he continues, "I have a very small opinion of what the great-genteel have

done for us, that I am very philosophical indeed concerning what the great vulgar may do: having a decided opinion that they can't do worse'' (293). This comment is illustrative of how Dickens—who had throughout his career drawn comparisons between the working classes at home and the colonized abroad—managed to disentangle the knotted concerns of race and class, at a time when for most, the issues were becoming completely inseparable. Indeed, with its simple faith in the innate good nature of the working man, Dickens's observation reveals a belief on his part in the nobility of the proletariat even when misgoverned. There is no scope in his vision of the loyal but thwarted workforce for the allegations of savagery that were becoming a feature of class discussions, with the proletariat being reconfigured as a separate and inferior race, incapable of improvement. This is not to suggest that he abandoned his discourse of colonialism altogether, but that it remained static, disregarding the racialization of class, and continuing as a useful tool for drawing attention to the neglect of domestic issues and the less exotic others. As his interest in political events beyond the British Isles waned, Dickens appears to have become more tolerant of demands for reform at home, and even of the at times menacing manner of calling for them.

Once Dickens's growing insularity in the years following the Sepoy Rebellion has been registered, his lack of involvement in the Eyre case comes as less of a surprise. It is rather astonishing, though, that in the light of the numerous parallels made by the likes of Bright and Mill between responses to the insurrection in the West Indies and those to the increasing political agitation in Ireland, that Dickens had so little to say about Britain's nearest colony.[12] Semmel has stressed the links between the two colonies in the public mind with his observation that:

> The Eyre case. . . posed an important imperial question, and opinions on the matter were closely related to what was happening in the most troublesome part of the Empire—Ireland. . . . In 1867 and 1868, the British newspapers were filled with stories of Fenian disturbances. After the parliamentary extension of the suffrage, Fenian raids replaced Reform riots as a chief source of worry. The possibility of insurrection in Ireland was real—and frightening. Governor Eyre had crushed a Jamaica insurrection and had kept that island within the Empire. If Eyre were convicted, would that not place an obstacle in the path of those entrusted with the task of keeping the peace in Ireland—and keeping an Ireland, more and more bent on Home Rule, within the United Kingdom?
> (133)

While it can be argued that events in the Caribbean had no impact whatsoever on him, the same may not be said of the Fenian agitation, which increased throughout the 1860s. The unrest was no longer a distant concern and spread to the mainland with the unsuccessful raid on Chester arsenal by over a thousand London Fenians on February 11. One would therefore imagine that Dickens would have responded to the activities of the Fenian movement in a style akin to the outbursts of the late 1850s. Certainly, with an increasingly hostile portrayal of the Irish in the media such a reaction would hardly have been unexpected, nor would it have appeared to be extreme. The precedents for denigrating the people of Ireland were already in place, and just as the English working classes were being compared to primitive peoples and even gorillas, so the Irish were subject to the same comparisons on an even greater scale. *Punch* was one of the forerunners in the depiction of the Irishman—or more accurately the Fenian—as an ape, particularly after the failed campaign to invade Canada (November 1865) and the heightened violence of the republicans [see figure 2, detail from "A Great Time for Ireland," *Punch,* 14 December 1861, and figure 3 "How Not to Do It," *Punch*, 23 October 1869]. Indeed, as Curtis has commented:

> The student of Anglo-Irish relations in the nineteenth century is bound to encounter sooner or later enough evidence to establish that the fall of the stereotypical Irishman from a state of disgrace in Anglo-Saxon eyes took him further down the scale of mankind or, rather, the Hominoidea so that by the 1860s the "representative Irishman" was to all appearances an anthropoid ape. Among the forces that accelerated Paddy's degeneration was the assumption that there were qualities in Irish Celts which marked them off as a race or breed quite distinct in looks or behaviour from those who claimed Anglo-Saxon, Danish, or Norman ancestry in the British Isles.                                (1–2)

While Curtis correctly charts the rise of the belief that the Irish were a lower race, his assertion that they were regarded as a race apart fails to take account of the growing fears of atavism and the anxiety that the English working classes were capable of sliding backwards. The Irish were constantly aligned with other colonial groups, like the rebellious Jamaicans and Indians. Imagined resemblances between the Irish and other non-white races, or even gorillas, could serve both those who wished to point to Irish inferiority and those who were more sympathetic to the rule of subject races. Moderates like the Irish war correspondent William Howard Russell had seen similarities between the Irish peasants and the Indian ryot-class during the Indian Mutiny. Even John Stuart Mill remarked on the "many points of resemblance between the Irish and the Hindoo character" in a curious call for Ireland to be governed in the same way as India (Mill, 22).

As a result of Fenian calls for the workforce on the mainland to join with them, coupled with memories of alliances between the Chartists and the Irish Nationalists in the 1840s, it became difficult for many people to avoid considering the two groups in combination. Dickens, however, resisted these comparisons, just as he rejected the view of the Irishman as belonging to a lower race.[13] Although he considered the Irish Question as one of the catalogue of domestic and imperial disasters he listed in the letter to de Cerjat cited above, he seems to have successfully avoided falling into the trap of pigeon-holing the Irish as troublesome colonials who could be dealt with according to a set of generic rules for governing others. Again, just as with Jamaica, he seems to have had remarkably little to say on the subject of Ireland, which is particularly surprising when one considers that he undertook two reading tours there during the politically turbulent years of 1867 and 1869. As Leon Litvack points out, his first visit of 1858 served to dispel a number of preconceptions about stereotypical Irish behavior, and the sensitivity of reactions to his readings forced him to re-evaluate the people (297–98). Thus, unlike many of his contemporaries, he is able to separate the ordinary Irish from the Fenians, and he is even able to view the latter's cause with a degree of sympathy. He went so far as to remark in January 1869, "these are not times in which other powers would back our holding Ireland by force, unless we could make our claim good in proving fair and equal government."[14] Such a statement, referring to American support for the Irish, is particularly noteworthy when we consider that Dickens had direct experience of the growing troubles. His reading tour of 1867 was very nearly cancelled in response to political events in Ireland, and the tone of his correspondence of the time is rather dismissive, treating the unrest as an inconvenience that will disrupt his plans. Moreover, the fact that he was writing to reassure those at home who were concerned for his well-being must be considered when assessing the tone of his letters. Dickens was undoubtedly less politically engaged by this time of his life and most of the letters from the 1867 tour merely describe events without endeavoring to analyze or judge them. Writing to Mrs. Bernal Osborne in March 1867 he reveals that the situation has an almost unreal feeling for him:

> When, when, when, will you be at peace in Ireland and sit under your vines and fig-trees without hanging revolvers and Enfield rifles on the branches? I feel as if I were in a more than usually incomprehensible dream when I am shown a hosiery establishment in Sackville Street here, from which some scores of young men decamped in the last wretched "risings" to starve in wildernesses or pine in jails. So the notion of your being guarded in your house, and of our

getting involved with America (as we shall at last) on this mad head, has a
grim absurdity in it of such nightmare breed that I half believe I shall wake
presently and wonder how I ever came to invent in my sleep the word "Fenian."

(Letters 336)

While he might protest the absurdity of the situation, it certainly did possess
a nightmarish quality that increased throughout the 1860s. Following the
catastrophe in the Crimea and the devastation that had swept across America,
the prospect of a civil war could not be ruled out, nor could American intervention. Dickens was, then, evidently more bewildered than angered by the
state of affairs in Ireland, and his belief that England should deal with her
own affairs before interfering overseas unquestionably served to increase his
understanding for demands for Home Rule.

*All the Year Round*'s strategy for dealing with the Fenians was far more
straightforward, although it underwent an alteration in 1867. In the early
1860s, the journal simply did not take the movement seriously. As in the case
of India during the Mutiny, several historical articles appeared, depicting the
long-term animosity between landlords and tenants and dealing with the history of Fenianism. This process is neatly demonstrated by the article, "Thugee
in Ireland," the very title of which is something of a misnomer as there is
nothing remotely ritualistic about the murder it discusses.[15] Yet the word
"thugee" is immediately evocative of India and all the connotations of insurrection that now attached themselves to the subcontinent. The piece narrates
the history of the murder of a clergyman, the reverend Mr. Snipe some sixty-
five years before by a band of misguided men. In the years before 1867 the
potential threat posed by the movement was frequently defused by resorting
to humor, and this article attempts to undermine the dangerous leader of the
gang by rendering him absurd. We are informed that,

In a retired place . . . a force of no less than three hundred men had been silently
collecting, all well armed with swords, blunderbusses, and pistols. They were
all under the command of a person who enjoyed some lawless reputation, under
the denomination of Captain Fearnought, but whose real name was Taite.

(374)

Having deflated the heroic qualities of the captain by exposing his true (and
rather mundane) identity, the author continues to suggest that the members
of the band were beguiled by hyperbole. This time it is wild exaggeration
which makes the loyalty of the followers seem ridiculous, as their initiation
is juxtaposed with a series of wild rumors:

All these men had been sworn to a very strange oath "to God and the world, to certify the truth"; also, "to dethrone all kings, plant the tree of liberty in Ireland, and *be* a republic like America." And their leader had further inflamed their animosity with a stirring and appropriate speech, in which he reminded them of the rumours then abroad that the Reverend Mr Knipe was shortly to be placed at the head of one hundred thousand men, whom he would lead in person to exterminate the innocent Irish peasantry.          (375)

This unquestioning commitment to the overthrow of *all* kings further reveals the way in which the author believes the men to have been seduced unthinkingly by empty rhetoric, while the allegations about Mr. Knipe point to their gullibility. The piece goes on to recount several similar murders, presumably with the intention of showing the reader that revenge killings had been going on for generations and that the perpetrators have always been caught and punished for their deeds.

Another important tactic in the pre-'67 articles was to negate the actual cause of the republicans. The "Thugee in Ireland" piece achieves this aim with an account of the murder of another religious figure, this time a Catholic priest noted for his benevolence, who is killed for guessing that a gang of men he meets are Fenians. The authorial voice intervenes after the murder has been narrated:

It will be observed how little sectarian animosity had to do with this awful crime—how little that deep reverence for the priestly character, which signally characterises the Irish peasantry, availed to save this unfortunate gentleman from the consequences of his dangerous knowledge.          (377)

Thus, the peasantry, who have already been dismissed for the "artful disguise of their real feelings" are sweepingly categorized as bloody, warlike, vengeful and unthinking (375). The author sets the tone for these generalizations at the beginning of the piece by observing that, "[a] sort of wantonness gets into a *nation's* veins" (374, my italics). Significantly, no attempt is made to differentiate the ordinary Irish peasant from the minority who have succumbed to the rallying-cry of the Fenian leaders. Implicit in this move is the belief that if they had not been fighting to free themselves from English hegemony, then the Irish would be fighting among themselves for some other reason, according to what the writer refers to as the "wild code of the place" (376). Disunity among the Irish is further emphasized in a subsequent article ironically entitled "The Fenian Brothers," which begins by drawing attention to opposition to the erection of a statue in memory of Prince Albert on the college green in Dublin before moving on to a discussion of the Irish National Fair in Chicago. The essay registers a sympathy akin to that of Dickens for the Irish Catholics when it asserts of the Catholic Church:

> Oppressed as their Church truly is by a dominant Protestant establishment, which is the genuine cause of more than half the bad blood of the country, its honest efforts to check the ''Young Irish'' party in its wild course of sedition have been unintermitting, and made at some sacrifice of popular influence.
>
> (392)

Unlike its predecessor, this piece manages to separate the ordinary Irish from the Fenians, but nevertheless it resorts to the same ridiculing tactics by taking swipes at ''Fenian spelling'' and ''Irish sense'' (392). In spite of the fact that this article registers the oppression that Catholics have had to contend against, its author goes on to attempt to vindicate Britain's conduct during the potato famine and suggests that the peasantry has been wilfully misled through a ''love of fighting somebody or anybody'':

> [T]here is a tragic side of it, not, indeed, for England, but for the warm-hearted people among the untaught masses of Ireland, who are thus misled. The Fenian chiefs are themselves no better taught than the majority of sharpers. They write about ''blessings and boquets'' [sic] and ''auxilliary entertainments'' [sic] and everywhere, in distorted ill-spelt language, scatter their wicked perversions of the truth. What Irishman of moderate intelligence does not know how heartily England strove to allay the distress of the Irish famine of 1847–8, yet thus a ''smart'' Fenian ventures to play on the credulity of his victims        (392).[16]

The piece then continues to recount the speech of a Fenian who had adopted the Swiftian view that the English hoped to eradicate the Irish by allowing them to starve to death. However, once again, rather than endeavoring to empathize with the Irish or to discover why they felt this way, the article merely seeks to discredit the Fenians as undereducated and dishonest.

*All the Year Round*'s attitude towards Ireland underwent a radical alteration in 1867 as Fenian activity escalated and fears of an uprising grew. Dickens was, between January and May, involved in a particularly gruelling schedule of public readings (including his visit to Ireland during March). Whereas in the past American Fenians had been little more than a joke, after the attempted rising in Dublin on March 5, they were now regarded as dangerous conspirators. As I have demonstrated, Dickens was unusual in his unwillingness to condemn the Irish, but he was—as is exemplified by his 1866 letter to de Cerjat [see above]—very much afraid of the consequences of American involvement in the Irish Question, and feared that a war would ultimately ensue. Fenian disturbances ceased to be matters for humorous treatment as activity on the mainland was stepped up and they came to pose a very real threat. Pieces like "Fenian James Fitzpatrick" and "Curragh Camp," which sought to reassure the public by pointing to a long history of detection of Fenian plots, began to appear with greater frequency.[17] American Fenian supporters are shown to be treacherous even to their own comrades, as in "Fenian James Fitzpatrick" where an American murders the eponymous subversive anti-hero for knowing too much. Equally, "The Fifth of March in Dublin" highlights the American role in the conspiracy without any of the humour or caricaturing displayed in pieces like "The Fenian Brothers."

Dickens's colonial discourse thus underwent an extraordinary revision in the 1860s, enabling him to separate class and race issues that were increasingly being conflated by both science and the media. His thought process was completely reconfigured in the aftermath of the Indian Mutiny, and thus by refusing to allow public and private occurrences to merge he was able to respond to each individually, rather than allowing his anger to accumulate and finally erupt. By this time of his life Dickens had become totally disillusioned with the governing classes, and his sympathies were with the working man, with whose frustration he identified and whose self-restraint he admired. He was therefore able to resist the analogies that were made by those around him and could deal with each domestic or colonial dilemma individually, and thence more moderately.

# NOTES

I am particularly grateful to Chris Brooks and Regenia Gagnier of the University of Exeter for feedback on this article. I should also like to thank Leon Litvack of Queen's University, Belfast for his generosity in sharing his extensive knowledge of Dickens and the Irish Question, and for preventing several errors from slipping through the net.

1. Karl Marx to Friedrich Engels. Quoted in James (Jan) Morris. *Heaven's Command: An Imperial Progress* 1973. (Middlesex: Penguin, 1979) 316.
2. Heuman asserts that the ratio of black to white had increased from ten to one in the eighteenth century, to thirteen to one.
3. See Paul Sharad "Speaking the Unspeakable: London, Cambridge and the Caribbean." In *De-scribing Empire: Postcolonialism and Textuality*. Eds. Chris Tiffin and Alan Lawson (eds) (London: Routledge, 1994) 201–18. Sharrad argues that while Monks's association with the Caribbean is illustrative of the moral degeneracy that Dickens identified with the slave-owning colony, the "shadowy but

inarticulated'' (208) presence of the West Indies reveals an early sign of the limitations in Dickens's sympathies toward non-white races. As Sharrad observes, ''Dickens's later condemnation of slavery in the emotive tales with which he castigates the oppression of London's deserving poor accuses his audience of double standards, but his basic rationale for opposing the barbarities of institution-alized slavery is that it corrupts the whites involved in it, and therefore demeans white civilization as a whole'' (209). Compelling though Sharrad's argument is, I think that it is rather reductive of Dickens's opposition to slavery in the 1830s. Although Monks undoubtedly belongs to a tradition of the ''imperial gothic'' whereby his evil is identified with his otherness, to suggest that Dickens is only concerned with the moral implications for the white man is to undermine his essential compassion for all human suffering. Sharrad attempts to display a con-tempt towards black people in the 1830s, by citing references to ''a rascally bunch of Negurs'' (208) in correspondence that was not penned until 1865. He continues to insinuate that an absence of references to the abolitionist crusade in letters written before *Oliver Twist* (1837–38) and full abolitionism in the colonies reveals some kind of indifference to the plight of the slave. In fact, both *Sketches by Boz* and *The Pickwick Papers* abound with allusions to the abolitionist cause. Some of these references are, admittedly, negative, in that they suggest the need to focus upon white slaves closer to home before looking overseas. However, even satirical accounts such as ''Our Parish,'' which shows the cause becoming more attractive after a missionary has imitated a dialogue between two slaves, demon-strate an interest in the issue and a concern that the public may not be committing to it for the right reasons. The distress that Dickens revealed in his brief foray into the American South in the 1840s is surely evidence of his genuine abhorrence for the institution.

4. Throughout the disturbances, according to Heuman, Paul Bogle, one of the men identified by Eyre as a ringleader, maintained that he was not rebelling against Victoria. See Gad Heuman. *The Killing Time: The Morant Bay Rebellion in Jamaica* (Warwick University Caribbean Studies. Basingstoke: Macmillan. 1994) 37–38.

5. Philip D. Curtin. *Two Jamaicas: The Role of Ideas in a Tropical Colony 1830–1865* (Cambridge, Mass: Harvard UP, 1955) 197–98.

6. The only other critic to deal with Dickens and Jamaica is K.J. Fielding, see K.J. Fielding. ''Edwin Drood and Governor Eyre.'' *The Listener*. December 25, 1952: 1083–84.

7. For a reassessment of the polemical ''Noble Savage'' article see Grace Moore. ''Re-appraising Dickens's 'The Noble Savage.' '' *The Dickensian* (forthcoming, 2002).

8. As a *weekly* publication, priding itself on its contemporaneity, *All the Year Round*'s neglect of the Eyre controversy is extremely surprising, particularly when set alongside the plethora of references to the uprising in *Punch*. It would seem, however, that the Jamaica debate was largely carried out through pamphlets and speeches. The leading *quarterly* and *monthly* journals were, by and large, more interested in mulling over events in India in the 1850s and discussing the more pressing concerns of the American Civil War, the Irish Question, and British

electoral reform. The table below reveals the small number of articles dealing with Jamaica during the 1865–1868 period, while its contents draw attention to the larger number of pamphlets dealing with the issue. The articles listed below are much lengthier than the single *All the Year Round* offering.

| Journal | Number of articles | Details of articles |
|---|---|---|
| *Blackwood's Edinburgh Magazine* | 2 | **Volume 99, May 1866.** 581–597. "The Negro and the Negrophilists." **Volume 104, July 1868**. 106 "Cornelius O'Dowd: Political Prize Courts—Jamaica Committees—A Hint for the 'House.' " |
| *The Edinburgh Review* | 0 | |
| *The Quarterly Review* | 1 | **Volume 120, number 239.** Review of: —*Papers relating to the affairs of Jamaica presented to both houses of parliament by command of Her Majesty, February 1866.* —*Papers relating to the disturbances in Jamaica presented to both houses of parliament by command of her majesty. Parts I, II, III, February 1866.* —*Report of the Jamaica Royal Commission, 1866 presented to both houses of parliament by command of Her Majesty. Parts 1&2.* |
| *The Westminster Review* | 2 | **Volume 32, July-October 1867.** Review of: —George Price. *Jamaica and the Colonial Office: Who caused the crisis?* —Thomas Harvey & William Brewin. *Jamaica in 1866: A Narrative of a Tour through the Island.* —J.M. Ludlow. *A Quarter Century of Jamaican Legislation.* —John Gorrie. *Illustrations of Martial Law in Jamaica.* —*Report of the Jamaica Royal Commission.* Parliamentary Paper 15589. **Volume 33, January-April 1868**. Review of Thomas Carlyle. *Shooting Niagara.* |

9. Given the marked change in attitudes toward India and the Indians which had been a part of the journal's campaign for investment in the Indian cotton industry, the presence of this article is somewhat incongruous. It is clearly a result of

Edward Eyre's parallels between events in India and those in Jamaica, although
the piece itself is a rather unremarkable account of a soldier's experiences while
serving under Sir Colin Campbell.

10. The only two references to the American Civil War in Dickens's correspondence
of 1865–67 are "To Mrs Kemble, March 1, 1865" and "To W.W.F. de Cerjat,
November 30, 1865," both of which are cited here. See *The Letters of Charles
Dickens.* Volume 11. 21, 114–16.

11. As the editors of the Pilgrim edition point out in a footnote, Dickens is here
responding to a mass meeting of between 22,000 and 25,000 people held by the
Trades' Societies in the grounds of Beaufort House, where it was declared that
the only Reform Bill that would satisfy would be one that would enfranchise
all men.

12. For a thorough survey of Dickens's engagement with Ireland and the Irish both
at home and abroad, see Leon Litvack. "Dickens, Ireland and the Irish." *The
Dickensian* (forthcoming, 2001).

13. Dickens was certainly still au fait with the evolutionary debate in the 1860s, as
demonstrated in his letter to the naturalist Professor Richard Owen thanking him
for a copy of his *Memoir of the Gorilla*—which he claimed to have read for "the
twentieth time." See: To Professor Richard Owen, July 12, 1865. *The Letters of
Charles Dickens.* Volume 11. 69–70. It is likely that this awareness was the very
factor which made such parallels so unappealing to him. Indeed, Semmel has
pointed out the paradoxical behavior of the evolutionists with reference to the
Eyre controversy with his observation that, "[I]t was the evolutionists, the theorists of the struggle for existence and survival of the fittest, who protested against
the operation of just these principles in Jamaica, while the opponents of evolutionary doctrine turned out to be advocates of a primitive 'social-Darwinism.' "
Bernard Semmel. *The Governor Eyre Controversy.* 120.

14. To W.W.F. de Cerjat, January 4, 1869. Walter Dexter (ed.). *The Letters of Charles
Dickens 1858–1870.* Volume III (Bloomsbury, London: The Nonesuch Press,
1938) 698.

15. See also "The Fenians." *All the Year Round.* October 21, 1865. 300–304. This
article undertakes an historical quest for the real Ossianic Fenians of fourteen
hundred years before, and demonstrates how they differed from the movement
of the 1860s. The piece undermines the latter-day Fenians by demonstrating how
their plots are always uncovered before they may be carried out and generally
implying that recruits are misguided in their allegiances.

16. Of course the debate surrounding England's role in exacerbating the effects of
the famine still continues to this day. See, for example, Cormac O'Gráda. *Black
'47 and Beyond: The Great Irish Famine in History, Economy and Memory* (New
Jersey: Princeton UP) 1998. O'Gráda argues that famine relief was inadequate
and was discontinued too soon, but suggests that a combination of bureaucracy,
misinformation, and a poor transportation system was responsible for the lack of
aid, rather than an absence of compassion for the Irish. In many ways this state
of affairs can be compared to the Crimean disaster and the way in which Britain's
construction of itself as a great colonial power was severely undermined by the

mismanagement of the war. It would seem that the rhetoric of empire far outstripped the practicality of crisis management and simple organization.
17. See *All the Year Round*, May 18, 1867: 488–92 and May 25, 1867: 520–24. Also "The Fifth of March in Dublin," *All the Year Round*, April 6, 1867: 342–45.

# WORKS CITED

"Black is not *Quite* White." *All the Year Round.* March 3, 1866: 173.

Carlyle, Thomas. *Shooting Niagara: And After? Reprinted from Macmillan's Magazine for August 1867 with some additions and corrections.* London: Chapman & Hall, 1867.

Curtin, Philip D. *Two Jamaicas: The Role of Ideas in a Tropical Colony 1830–1865.* Cambridge: Harvard UP, 1955.

Curtis, L. Perry. *Apes and Angels: The Irishman in Victorian Caricature.* Newton Abbot: David & Charles, 1971.

Dickens, Charles. *The Letters of Charles Dickens.* Ed. Madeline House and Graham Storey. 12 vols. New York: Oxford UP, 1965–2001.

———. *The Letters of Charles Dickens 1833–1870.* Ed. Mary Dickens and Georgina Hogarth. London: Macmillan, 1893.

———. *The Letters of Charles Dickens.* Ed. Walter Dexter. 3 vols. Bloomsbury, London: Nonesuch, 1938.

"The Fenian Brothers." *All the Year Round.* June 4, 1864: 392.

Ford, George H. "The Governor Eyre Case in England." *University of Toronto Quarterly* (April 1948): 17.

Heuman, Gad. "From Slave Rebellions to Morant Bay: The Tradition of Protest in Jamaica." In Ed. Wolfgang Binder. *Slavery in the Americas.* Wurzburg: Könighausen & Neuman, 1993.

Holt, Thomas C. *The Problem of Freedom: Race, Labor, and Politics in Jamaica and Britain, 1832–1938.* Baltimore: Johns Hopkins UP, 1992.

*Jamaica Papers Number One. Facts and Documents Relating to the Alleged Rebellion in Jamaica, and the Measures of Repression; including notes on the trial of Mr Gordon.* London: The Jamaica Committee, 1866.

Litvack, Leon. "Ireland and the Irish." In *The Oxford Reader's Companion to Dickens.* Ed. Paul Schlicke. Oxford: Oxford UP, 1999.

Malchow, H.L. *Gothic Images of Race in Nineteenth-Century Britain.* Stanford: Stanford UP, 1996.

Mill, John Stuart. *England and Ireland.* London: Longmans, Green, Reader & Dyer, 1868.

Morris, James (Jan). *Heaven's Command: An Imperial Progress.* Middlesex: Penguin, 1979.

O'Gráda, Cormac. *Black '47 and Beyond: The Great Irish Famine in History, Economy and Memory.* New Jersey: Princeton UP, 1998.

Semmel, Bernard. *The Governor Eyre Controversy.* London: MacGibbon & Kee, 1962.

Sharad, Paul. "Speaking the Unspeakable: London, Cambridge and the Caribbean." In *De-scribing Empire: Postcolonialism and Textuality.* Ed. Chris Tiffin & Alan Lawson. London: Routledge, 1994.

"Slavery in England." *All the Year Round.* June 15, 1867: 585.

"Thugee in Ireland." *All the Year Round.* June 28, 1862: 374.

"Under Fire." *All the Year Round.* February 17, 1866: 125–27.

# Dickens and the Transformation of Nineteenth-Century Narratives of "Legitimacy"

## Jan B. Gordon

*One paradoxically secures some interior legitimacy only by denying another assumed patriarchal legitimacy that, through three-quarters of* Bleak House, Great Expectations, *and* Our Mutual Friend, *successfully mimes the real thing. Yet, one becomes authentically legitimate only by renouncing the pretense of legitimacy, thereby preserving the right to self-determination. The denial of any foundational idea of legitimacy alone can make the law, the criminal, or the orphan—similar discontinuities—narratively, but not necessarily "legally" legitimate. The conversion from narratives of judgment to narratives of detection in Dickens's last novels enables legitimacy to be self-generated, whereby "internal consistency" (of the plot) and authenticity (of character) become synonymous. Only then, can justice become more than an institutionally-mandated procedure for the recovery of precedent, and come to be intricated, as with the plots of novels, in the distribution of belief-formation, both among the characters and between those characters and the reader.*

> "I hate," said Eugene, putting his legs up on the opposite seat, "I hate my profession."
> "Shall I incommode you if I put mine up too?" returned Mortimer. "Thank you. I hate mine."

*Dickens Studies Annual*, Volume 31, Copyright © 2002 by AMS Press, Inc. All rights reserved.

"It was forced upon me," said the gloomy Eugene, "because it was understood that we wanted a barrister in the
family. We have got a precious one."
"It was forced upon me," said Mortimer, "because it
was understood that we wanted a solicitor in the family.
And we have got a precious one."

(*OMF* I, iii. 19–20)

Early in Dickens's last complete novel, *Our Mutual Friend*, his two representatives of the legal profession confess in a moment of candor that they were
not exactly "called" to the bar, but had it thrust upon them as an historical
"expectation," in this case patriarchially instantiated. Like the creaky tradition of Common Law itself—at least until Blackstone's partially successful
critique—they too bear the privileged weight of *precedence* which has "set
them up" in shared chambers. Over-determining, Eugene Wrayburn's father
"in the clearest manner provided (as he called it) for his children by pre-
arranging from the hour of the birth of each, and sometimes from an earlier
period what the devoted little victim's calling and course of life should
be"(*OMF* I, xii, 193). If the numerous orphans and semi-orphans in Dickens's
work—Oliver Twist, David Copperfield, Pip, Esther Summerson—are em-
blems of historical discontinuity from some metaphysical Origin which must
be either recuperated or fictionally supplied (in an age when Darwin, Newman, expeditions to discover the sources of the Nile, and perhaps even Henry
Murray's *Oxford English Dictionary* project were all dedicated to the recovery
of some foundational moment of ideological or geological descent which was
vulnerable to "tracing"), then the individual whose place has been chosen
*for* him could be conceived of as a kind of counter-orphan, the victim of *too
much* rather than a *lack of* antecedence.

    In the case of the orphan-figure, the ontic restlessness and curiosity of
Dickens's waifs surely owes something to the competing jurisdictions which
pursued him, each with a separate agenda. As Sir Leon Radzinowicz has
reminded us, mendacity included a vast array of real or imagined offenses,
ranging from thieves, to the seasonally (or chronically) unemployed, to alco-
holics, and even those like abandoned spouses or children with no fixed
domicile. Because of the reluctance of localities to incur any increase in rates,
vagrants were traditionally involuntarily returned to the parish from whence
they came: invisibility becoming for a long period an entirely acceptable
remedy for dealing with the "genealogically discontinuous."[1] Informers who
supplied the names and locations of the homeless were paid a fixed rate, a
practice which, though it led to rampant abuse, was later adopted by the

Metropolitan Police in criminal cases. Those in pursuit of the socially abandoned included then, informers, the parish constable, civil magistrates, The Church of England, various voluntary associations like the Society for Bettering the Conditions and Increasing the Comforts of the Poor, a Penal Poor Law administered by Poor Law Commissioners, and later, of course, the Metropolitan Police. Made a philosophical subject by so many competing bureaucracies, the orphan-figure—small wonder—when we encounter it in Dickens's novels, should always be under pursuit. Jo the Crossing-Sweeper, Betty Higden, Oliver Twist, and Pip are invariably weary with a fatigue attendant upon being constantly "moved on," as objects of institutional or individual surveillance.

Although this enforced vehicularity will occasionally bring them in contact with the law or its representatives, attorneys themselves offer a contrasting image: the individual with too much rather than too little time on his hands. Were it not for the riparian cycles of death and rebirth which draw their energies to the Thames's more violent reaches and waterside characters, the two attorneys of *Our Mutual Friend*, one suspects, would have symbolically "float[ed] with the stream through the summer and Long Vacation," (*OMF* I., xii, 191), as they appear to float with neither self-direction nor purpose through life, represented as a predetermined narrative. Mortimer Lightwood and Eugene Wrayburn furnish their chambers with tea pots, sherry glasses, a cooking stove, and other accoutrements of genteel domesticity, even as the "suppress[ion] of . . . domestic destiny"(*OMF* I, xii, 193) becomes an integral part of their legal partnership. Clearly, freeing oneself from the law—imagined both as a patriarchally-determined profession and as a profession whose narratives and judgments are based upon precedent—is difficult, even as it brings the attorneys into contact with the orphan-figure. No wonder that Wrayburn expresses a wish for self-sufficiency, imagined in this instance as a lighthouse where "there would be no Precedents to hammer at, except the Precedent of keeping the light up . . . to look out for wrecks" (*OMF* I, xii, 192). The figure of speech is so noteworthy precisely because what is being maintained is no longer the continuous "family name," but the illumination of the discontinuous social flotsam which has been unable to heed the geographic marker. The metaphor of the law as a lighthouse is, however, rich in hermeneutic potential. As in some sense a repository of narratives which collectively enunciate the historical irrelevance of its mission, the law-as-lighthouse is both a guardian of the shallows and a warning that others have been unable to stay away from its reaches. Often what the lighthouse in fact illuminates is its own impotence: the wreck. To be sure, there were a "string" of lighthouses constructed over time—one of the great navigational projects of early nineteenth-century Britain—but the seriality is not of immediate relevance to the endangered, for whom any sequence of priority and succession must often appear either irrelevant or "always-already" too late.

In other words, Dickens's lawyers, in contradistinction to their compliant reputations, early on represent some *resistance* to the law imagined as a "received" profession or body of knowledge and as a narrative with a recuperable foundation to be "traced up," in the manner recommended by Blackstone. The struggle of the justice system to free itself from a metaphoric model of the law itself as a narrative entirely dependent upon patriarchal precedent defines the efforts of remarkable attorneys in *Bleak House*, *Great Expectations*, and *Our Mutual Friend* who liberate themselves from "family interests" as well as the legal interests and practices imagined as a collateral family of knowledge, by creating alternative, a-filiative family narratives, embodying an altogether different model of legal praxis. At the same time that a belief that the recuperation of legal precedent yields justice comes to be compromised, the law's frequent ward in Dickens, the orphan-figure, equally compelled to "trace up" the missing antecedent, finds either a willfully absent biological precedent or a plurality of possible precedents. Any socially-reproducible meaning (of the law) and any biologically-reproducible meaning (of the putative heir) are "stained" in tandem by an increasingly elusive precedent whose attempted recovery yields only recovery. The possibility of discontinuities in an unbroken succession of the law—and thereby an unfaithful distribution of justice—on the one hand is matched by the potential for an equally unfaithful distribution of the familial "good name" (and the transitive estate which it bears) on the other. In some double sense, then, lawyers are often the guardians of orphans in Dickens, both sharing the nineteenth-century fetish of the ubiquitous Precedent.

This essay will attempt to show that Dickens's involvement with a certain crucial transformation in legal narrative and its analysis transcended his early exposure to the justice system, represented in his father's incarceration for debt and his own expérience as a court reporter, by now well-known biographical details. Although the law, like the life of the orphan-figure caught up in it, may appear to be irrational or arbitrary, nineteenth-century legal theory proclaimed the law to be an internally coherent and unified body of rules, accessible to historical recuperation in the same way as Darwin had demonstrated to be true of the biological sciences. The putative coherence and unity of the law stemmed from the fact that the discipline was imagined to be informed by a permanent group of foundational precedents from which, upon the application of logical procedures, formal rules and principles developed over time. Were this the case, whole subject areas within the law—say torts and contracts—would have their boundaries fixed by these commonly shared principles of descent and the established techniques of, simultaneously, *recuperation* and *adaptive application.* Policing the boundaries within and between these distinctive, and ever more highly individuated "branches" of the law, comes to constitute a major activity of the so-called rule of law, just as policing boundaries between and among remote family members in Dickens's convoluted plots ensures that the "progression" of the estate through time is properly maintained despite the claims of the odd usurper, facsimile precedent, or fictional author(ity) to credibility.

Secondly, the essay will explore the ways in which Dickens, by subtly challenging what David Sugarman has termed the "black letter" tradition, with its privileging of Precedent and closed model of rationality (in the interests of protecting individual freedom), was illuminating the contradictions, inconsistencies, and omissions which jurisprudence had sought to strategically repress until the end of the nineteenth-century and perhaps beyond (22–61). Assuming that this subtle critique imbedded in Dickens's plots is directed toward a specific set of historical assumptions that shaped legal institutions, practices, and ultimately the shape of legal education in nineteenth-century Britain, his novels must be read as part of the prolonged debate involving the respective autonomy (and domain) of written and unwritten law. Along with Blackstone, Bentham, Mill, Austin, and Dicey, Dickens's late novels collectively comprise part of the sustained critique of the idea of a foundational, univocal concept of historical precedent in the transition from the pre-modern to the modern in the notion of an English legal system and constitution. As we shall see, however, the inability to "refer back" to an antecedent authority which purportedly lent the system its rationality and autonomy (the two being often equated), eventually comes to constitute in a double sense the historical amnesia that characterizes one aspect of the history of legal narrative. For it results in the return to a pre-modern idea of legal autonomy as residing in "custom," a consensual continuity which transcended the call for an identifiable, authorizing Beginning.

Finally, this essay will suggest that the so-called liberation from a legal system metaphorically imagined to be structured as antecedent and successive "branches" to be "traced up" until a specific application to a specific case is realized, paradoxically enables the law to assume the omnipresence of a fatherless transcendence. The constitutional order no longer has the idea of a limit or potential for critique built into it. As a consequence, its extraordinary

vitality comes to be defined by an "everywhere-ness" of coordinated recognition and consent, resembling that afforded "custom" under the pre-modern
regime of Common Law courts in Great Britain. What had previously been
the rational *content* of the law comes to be resolved by interpretation, in a
somewhat hermeneutical gesture. This is signalled in Dickens's oeuvre by a
metaphoric extra-territoriality which comes to define what passes for the unity
and internal consistency of a system of jurisprudence. The law is given a full
*presence* indistinguishable from the elusive penumbra of surveillance and ad
hoc public intrusion. Rather than having its content determined by the appeal
*to* and recovery *of* foundational moments and principles, authoritative interpretation will come to privilege the location and perception of the interpreter
in Dickens's novels. The figure of the attorney imperceptibly shades into or
becomes indistinguishable from the detective-figure with his corollary interest
in the criminal and social *circum*stances of legal transgression, the everywhere-ness of crime which imaginatively corresponds to that of the legal
system itself, insofar as it is publicly perceived.

By now, Dickens's comic critique of nineteenth-century legal practice in
*Bleak House* is very familiar, his words having found their way into numerous
briefs. Yet, the analogy by which legal *precedent* is problematized along with
more tangible "informing patriarchies" warrants closer attention. Because
*Jarndyce and Jarndyce* involves a contested legacy, the attempt to reach a
judgment becomes symptomatic of the difficulties inherent in recuperating
any precedent whose "will" has been obscured over time. As early as the
opening chapter of *Bleak House*, the Court of Chancery is made to resemble a
more familiar enclosure wherein judgments are rendered; behind a "curtained
sanctuary," enshrined in a room with "stained-glass windows" dimly lighted
by "wasting candles" (*BH* 1, 50), petitioners like poor Gridley stand before
a lord high chancellor to be ritually "purged" of contempt in a markedly
clerical setting. The ability of the courts to reach anything like a final judgment
is continually foreclosed, however, as a consequence of the misplaced privilege accorded inscription. For it is the systematic commitment to writing
which entails some collateral repression of voice:

> "On such an afternoon, if ever, the Lord High Chancelor ought to be sitting
> here—as he is—with a foggy glory round his head, softly fenced in with crim-
> son cloth and curtains, addressed by a large advocate with great whiskers, *a
> little voice*, and an *interminable brief.* . . . On such an afternoon, some scores
> of members of the High Court of Chancery bar ought to be—as they are—mis-
> tily engaged in one of the ten thousand stages of an endless cause, tripping one

another up on slippery precedents, groping knee-deep in technicalities, running their goat-hair and horse-hair warded heads against *walls of words.*"

(BH 1, 50, italics added)

With its clerical trappings and presiding officer cowled with a foggy aureole, Dickens's Chancery seems a logical extension of the seventeenth-century idea that justice was secularized theology, a notion at least as old as Part III of Hobbes's classic *Leviathan* (*Of A Christian Commonwealth*). In the first chapter (actually chapter 17 of *Leviathan*) of his work, Hobbes had defined the polity as a reduction of the plurality of wills to one will, and it is precisely this notion of political unity that forms the basis of a seamless identification between the crown in parliament and the commonwealth itself. That identification, however, restricted any possible development of either a tradition of natural rights or the separation of powers. In the *Civil Commonwealth* Hobbes extended his argument to a crucial theological question: who has the authority to interpret laws, given that "All Laws, written and unwritten, have need of interpretation"(322). He wishes above all to subordinate the law to the question of who interprets it. The law is *binding* (a word with theological resonance) for Hobbes because, even if it is historically or by virtue of specific application somewhat removed from relevance it nonetheless remains "the Sovereigns sentence"(323). Law can only be the expression of unity of a single commonwealth. In considering the possibility of appeal to divine law, Hobbes remains faithful to traditional Anglican political theology. "Sinne being nothing but the transgression of the Law," any distinction between temporal and spiritual realms is impossible:

> . . . if men were at liberty to take for God's Commandments, their own dreams and fancies, or the dreams and fancies of private men; scarce two men would agree upon what is God's Commandment; and yet in respect of them, every man would despise the Commandments of the Commonwealth. I conclude therefore, that in all things not contrary to the Morall Law (that is to say, to the Law of Nature,) all Subjects are bound to obey that for divine Law, which is declared to be so, by the Laws of the Commonwealth.          (333)[2]

Although individuals can dissent from the law as a private, individual act, if they did so in large numbers, the commonwealth ceases to exist. Hence any constitution which would limit sovereign power is impossible, given the "naturally unified" nature of the polity. This would be tantamount to privileging precedent:

It is therefore in vain to grant Sovereignty by way of precedent Covenant. . . . But when an Assembly of men is made Sovereign; then no man imag-
ineth any such Covenant to have past in the Institution; for no man is so dull
as to say, for example, the People of Rome made a Covenant with the Romans,
to hold the Sovereignty on such and such conditions, which not performed, the
Romans might lawfully depose the Roman People.                    (231)

Anticipating the potential of both comparative judgments and demands to
guarantee individual rights, Hobbes is adamantly opposed on the grounds that
each would divide a sovereign power which had been a priori consensually
*author*ized. He blames both doctrines upon "men . . . , that making profession
of the Lawes, endeavour to make them depend upon their own learning, and
not upon legislative Power." Although stopping short of condemning all
independent intellectual activity, the author of *Leviathan* cautions that the
profession of "Lawes" threatens to establish a shadow authority against the
polity by "working on men's minds, with words and distinctions, that of
themselves signified nothing, but bewray (by their obscurity) that there wal-
keth (as some think invisibly) another Kingdome . . . in the dark" (370). The
commonwealth must resist a specific class with its will-of-the-wisp nomi-
nalism which creates divisions within a previously unified sovereignty. A
particular weapon of these men who would create the shadowy "Kingdome
of Fayries" is "precedent Covenant," upon which the parties in Dickens's
*Jarndyce and Jarndyce* hammer away.

   Hobbes—along with Richard Hooker's *Of the Laws of Ecclesiastical Polity*—was crucial to the advent of the idea of a strange, univocal institutional
sovereignty indistinguishable from the will of the people. Eventually, this was
to become part and parcel of the notion of an Establishment against which
resistance was procedurally (and one suspects, intellectually) very difficult.
For Hooker, church and commonwealth form a continuum, as properties and
actions of a univocal subject, which bears a resemblance to Hobbes's:

So albeit properties and actions of one kinde doe cause the name of a Commonwealth, qualities and functions of another sort the name of a Church to be given
to the multitude, yet one and the self same multitude may in such sort be both
and is so with us, that no person appertayning to the one can be denied to be
also of the other.                                               (319)

As Hobbes's denial of the power of precedent Covenant had an egalitarian
purpose which has only recently been fully recognized, so with Hooker's
equation of church with civil society.[3] If Hooker's unity would deny special

authority to a clerical class which had a history of independent agendas in European politics, then Hobbes's would have the effect of making any attorney-at-law by definition a representative of the crown, potentially limiting, if not foreclosing, any totally independent "representation" of others. We must also note, however, that this unity of crown, courts, parliament, and church is traditionally, even when discussed by its advocates and participants, almost mystical, entirely in harmony with that foggy combination of court and church with which *Bleak House* commences. A presumably consensually binding, quasi-transcendent precedent which defines the commonwealth forestalls, at least temporarily in the early history of British jurisprudence, the privileging of a strictly legal concept of precedent. These two radically different concepts of "precedent," as we shall see, come to share a dialectical relationship.

As early as 1616, when Sir Edward Coke, chief justice of the Court of King's Bench, had sought to determine whether a court of equity could grant relief after (or against) a judgment handed down by a court of common laws, the relationship between law and equity had been the subject of abundant judicial commentary. Like most pre-nineteenth-century scholars of the law, Sir William Blackstone (1765–1769) strongly maintained that the application of abstract knowledge alone in the settlement of civil disputes was not a sufficient guarantee of good legal judgments since, were such to be the case, "the least variation from established precedent will totally distract and bewilder" the student of the law (33). Like many of his successors, Blackstone feared any divergence from a system which privileged law as historically descendant, even while recognizing the logical inconsistency of such a model. Hence, in one breath, he would urge the legal practitioner or judge to "trace" up the principles and grounds of the law, even to the original elements (37). Thus, the determination of judgment necessitated the continually renewed "beginning over and over again"(*BH* 8, 146), just as it does in the practice so successfully parodied by Dickens. In Blackstone's analysis, moreover, the tradition of common or statute law comes to be metaphorically identified with the *letter* of the law, whereas its more elusive *spirit* resided in the "inner self" of western liberalism, the conscience or "heart" of an often arbitrary judge (Taylor 24–36).

Blackstone's defense of the privileged precedent was partially a consequence of his fear that the more liberal or "softer" *interpretation* (rather than application) of the law mandated by courts of equity, insofar as they came

to consider the individual *circumstances* of each particular case, could lead
to the empowerment of judges as legislators:

> Equity thus depending upon the particular *circumstances* [italics added] of each
> individual case, there can be no established rules and fixed precepts of equity
> laid down without reducing it to a positive law. And, on the other hand, the
> liberty of considering all cases in an equitable light must not be indulged too
> far, lest thereby we destroy all law, and leave the decision in the heart of the
> judge. And law, without equity, though hard and disagreeable, is much more
> desirable for the public good than equity without law which would make every
> judge a legislator.                                          (I, 62)

Equity, because it threatened to reduce law to a determination from an un-
forseeable set of individual circumstances, would erase the law, considered
as an historically transmitted body of inscription, just as surely as Krook, the
paralegal cursitor in *Bleak House*, must erase each letter J-A-R-N-D-Y-C-E A-
N-D J-A-R-N-D-Y-C-E, before inscribing the next. Remarkably, Blackstone's
analogy bears an affinity with the way in which some traditionalists greeted
equally highly individualized interpretations of the New Testament among
both scholars dedicated to the so-called "higher criticism" and dissenting
sects in nineteenth-century England. The random application of equity, like
those who would advocate private interpretations of Holy Writ, would, for
Blackstone, legally enable the "breast of the judge" to "rise above the law,
either common or statute" (III, 433).

On the other hand, though, Blackstone was only too aware that, unlike the
courts of equity in classical antiquity, the British institution which went by
that name was vulnerable to paying too much homage to the tradition of
tracing the precedent which had earlier conspired to make common law virtually indistinguishable from statutory law. Like Hobbes and Hooker, Blackstone was convinced that the best laws, as measured by longevity and the
unanimity of a community's acceptance, were identical with custom. These
were narratives "used so long that the memory of man runneth not to the
contrary" (I, 77). And custom is precisely that condition of lacking the very
precedent which legal practice had dedicated itself to tracing: "So that if
anyone show the beginning of it, it is no good custom."[5] How could a "common law," the general wisdom of whose application was defined by its *lack*
of a beginning, become part of a judicial system dedicated to its opposite, the
location of a precedent having as its object the clarification of a "beginning?"
The fear, common to many scholars of British law, of a written constitution

guaranteeing individual rights, may represent another side of the same hermeneutical problem: if the law is genuinely *common* to all as a collective consensual narrative, why should it demand the constant recuperation implicit in
appeals to foundational precedents? For once any dispute is imagined to be
amenable to *referential* resolution, the argument could be made that it could
no longer be *equitably* decided.

To his credit, Blackstone is sensitive to the twin perils that beset good
legal judgments: an over-determining historical record which demands recuperation of the applicable precedents (law-as-application) and the arbitrary
determination of an interpreter considering the individual circumstances and
objective of a criminal act (law-as-intention). Yet, the trajectory of the *Commentaries* would ultimately narrow the gap between the two traditions, for in
Blackstone's prescient analysis, courts of equity in Britain have ultimately
become something entirely different, retaining only the name. For the fate of
"common law," which became less customary as it was solidified into trace-
able statutes, is similarly destined for British courts of equity:

> a court of equity is not bound by rules or precedents, but acts from the opinion
> of a judge, founded on the circumstances of every particular case. Whereas the
> system of *our* [italics added] court of equity is a laboured connected system
> governed by established rules and bound down by precedents.     (III, 432)

Though Chancery was initially designated as a court of equity, separable from
Common Pleas, the Exchequer, and the King's Bench, which collectively
constituted the courts of law, shortly after the end of Dickens's career, their
consolidation into a "unitary system of jurisprudence" was formalized by
the Judicature Act of 1873. This "creeping" codification with its corollary
intrusion of the identification and recuperation of precedence is a subtext of
both Blackstone's *Commentaries* and Dickens's novels where, to borrow from
Eugene Wrayburn's rhetoric in *Our Mutual Friend*, life itself came to be
defined as "getting in the way of the law" (*OMF* I: 3, 63).

The hegemony of legal practice is suggested in two ways in Dickens's
work: the law, Blackstone's "laboured connected system," is a dense family
of interests competing with other biological and social models of the family
and secondly, it operates so as to leave no space outside of itself. Just as
there is a "fashionable tree" (*BH* 2, 57) to which Lady Dedlock socially
belongs as part of a distinctive class, represented in the "family tree" of
portraits in descending chronological order which grace the mantelpiece of
Chesney Wold and a genuine family tree whose branches consist of remote

cousins hoping for inclusion in bloated pension lists, so there is a comparable tree of the law whose interrelated branches of parasites proliferate in the damp climate which has historically fostered the massive oaks of Chesney Wold. Some are higher, some lower, but collectively, this arboreal tribe threatens to block out light altogether. For in Dickens's world, courts and law chambers are notorious for having limited access to sunlight, perhaps best illustrated in Jaggers's "eccentrically patched . . . skylight"(*GE* 20, 187) which looks down upon the easily frightened Pip on his first trip to London. Whereas *Bleak House*'s solicitor, Tulkinghorn, carries "secrets in every limb of his body," the appropriately named young Smallweed, though a relative newcomer and, as a clerk, very marginal to the profession, is nonetheless already regarded as an "old limb of the law"(*BH* 20, 327).

If both procedurally and in the "light" shed upon their practice, barristers and solicitors are metaphorically members of a preternaturally old, yet somewhat less than distinguished family of interests in Dickens, they often appear as genuine appendices to the families they putatively represent. Not unlike the figure of the orphan again, Tulkinghorn, for example, leads a kind of double-life, common in Dickens to those touched by illegitimacy, no matter from what side of the law. Though initially introduced as the "butler of the legal cellar" (*BH* 2, 59), and therefore part and parcel of the extended Dedlock family and its assorted retainers, the reader is later informed that the solicitor is "only in a manner part and parcel of the place" (*BH* 7, 137), being most often a repository of silence. Yet, this equally appropriately named encloser of speech "represents" his patron socially, as well as legally (the two being interchangeable), "at *corners* of dinner tables in great country houses and *near doors* [italics added] of dressing rooms" (*BH* 2, 59), even "standing in" as a substitute patriarch during those occasions of Lord Dedlock's "diplomatic" as well as physical indisposition. As a guardian of the family secrets, Tulkinghorn is a kind of "second" or surrogate father, to whom, as is often the case with Dickens's attorneys, the presence of an *illegitimacy* is entrusted, willingly or unwillingly.

Similarly, the Jaggers of *Great Expectations* serves as a surrogate father for two radically different commodities which Dickens elides in the operational dynamics of the novel's plot. He distributes Abel Magwitch's newfound wealth to the Pip who assumes he has come into his "expectations," and distributes the "abandoned" infant, Estella, to the genuinely abandoned Miss Havisham. In other words, the law and its agents, transform the badly flawed or "interrupted" biological families in Dickens, into a-filiative families the law would appear to allegorize. Yet, assuming that at least early on in *Great*

*Expectations*, Jaggers *is* the law, its efficiencies seem largely operational, shuffling money and babies between donors and adopted or adopting recipients who remain unknown to each other. The law *distributes*, identifying "matches" of sorts, but clearly no more productive of social harmony than arrangements dictated by love, economic interest, or proximate convenience. Finding a home, even one that imperfectly ministers to the needs of his provisional wards, it is Jaggers in his capacity as an *instrument* of the law who creates these ad hoc families informed by perceived intention, fictive obligation, or arbitrary necessity rather than legal or biological precedent.

Instead of the parent who wills his passive offspring to the law, as do Wrayburn and Lightwood in *Our Mutual Friend*, the law functions in *Great Expectations* as a surrogate antecedent who "stands in" for the absent parent or institutional precedent. But the peculiar feature of the law's operational efficiencies is that it simultaneously *creates* orphans (in removing Estella from her mother and hence, beyond the "reach" of the law) and becomes their guardian. Jaggers both *orphans* and symbolically *adopts*, and these apparently contradictory maneuvers enhance the law's ethically (legally?) neutral status. Insofar as it arranges an imaginary relationship among those whose *il*legitimacy is defined by the same absentee precedent (Magwitch as the "father" shared by Estella and Pip, thereby symbolic siblings), the law enables an incestuous narrative of their affection. This generation of operational "self-sameness"—a-filiative families, incestuous romance, simultaneously donating and receiving money and children—would seem to leave no activities, contradictory though they may be, *outside* the law, endowing it with its extraordinary range. And yet, as we shall see, legal gaps do surface.

This extraterritoriality of the law extends even unto its insinuation into the domestic sphere, where Jaggers dispenses an allotted portion of food and drink from a dumbwaiter, a controlled nurturing and sharing like that of Fagin. But, if he is a surrogate father, Jaggers surely has much more at stake than merely "standing in" for an absentee patriarch. Pip is at one point in the evening amazed to learn that Jaggers takes a rather special albeit not precisely defined, interest in the splotchy Bentley Drummle for whom the lawyer confesses, "I like the look of that fellow" (*GE* 26, 234). In a novel filled with sexual abuse, domination, and even masochism, Jaggers has an intriguing sexual identity, blurring as he does the barrier which traditionally separates the roles of legal, protective guardian and lover. The "law" seems to belong to two different families or familial "interests" simultaneously, even as it would seek to disclaim any intimacy for the sake of an imaginary objectivity, re-enforced in Jaggers's habitual use of a protecting subjunctive register in his speech. Like the residence in which Jaggers dwells, the law seems paradoxically overly solid and heavy in its furnishings, yet at the same time containing large areas which are shut away, apparently, from both obvious functionality and access.

Similarly, the Tulkinghorn of Bleak House seems to hint at the potential of any historical secret or enclosure to be released to a wider, more public "circulation." Though an "oyster of the old school whom nobody can open" and in whose domain "everything that can have a lock has got one" (*BH* 10, 182), the "old-fashioned" attorney who, like Jaggers with his mourning rings and vest chains, already seems a bit sartorially dated when we initially encounter him, appears to be entirely dedicated to preserving the historical family "tree" with the branches of the legal forest. He is entrusted with drawing up wills and their successive codicils, arranging the shape of "entailments," and designing restrictive easements which protect Chesney Wold from the access of the neighboring rabble who would trample its paths. His work largely consists of distributing authentic claims by family members, defending the family against spurious claims, and "representing" the estate at civic and social functions. If the illegitimate child is a synecdoche for a kind of unintended "accident" in the Victorian novel, an interruption of authorized descent, the solicitor might be conceived of as a kind of post facto birth control device, through whose agency the patriarch, at the last possible moment, would attempt to posthumously control the size of the family tree by admitting an indiscretion here, or cutting off a wayward offspring there, and for all we know admitting the historically extraneous "member." Hence, when Tulkinghorn gains confirmation of the existence of Lady Dedlock's illegitimate child and attempts extortion as the price of preserving the family secret, he is symbolically disassociating himself from monopoly *by*, and it could be argued, *as*, a single family of interests and practices.

In other words, Tulkinghorn's decision to extract an additional commission from a patriarch to whom he is ostensibly loyal, might suggest the emergence of the law from an essentially family practice dedicated to the maintenance and enclosure of secret narratives, into another set of interventions, publicly and openly negotiated beyond effective control of the family. This change might suggest either or both of two crucial transformations: the slow decline of the landed family as a lineal continuity with specific legal heeds, or perhaps new demands of a banking, commercial, and insurance sphere which competed with the landed oligarchy for the representational services of the attorney-at-law. Jacques Attali's persuasive argument vis-à-vis the way in which the stockpiling of the social reproduction of music came to be inextricable from its meaning, could apply equally to the evolution of the medical and legal professions in the nineteenth century.[6] Just as the exclusively *family* doctor became an anomalous practice identified with the resistance to professional independence and disciplinary progress (in say, George Eliot's *Middlemarch*, to name one example), so the solicitor kept on exclusive retainer by a single, powerful family, becomes as old-fashioned as the suspenders and silk stockings worn by the preternaturally old Tulkinghorn. The law can no longer be retained or contained in the family.

Despite conservative appearances and trappings, Dickens's lawyers often struggle to escape their antecedent family and its expectations (Lightwood and Wrayburn of *Our Mutual Friend*), to "open" a seam in an outwardly continuous, closed family of interests (Tulkinghorn of *Bleak House*), or to blur the boundaries between discreet categories of families to whose preservation or maintenance they had been ostensibly appointed (Jaggers of *Great Expectations*). This "opening"of a narrative succession surely illuminates the dangers inherent in either tracing up the genealogically unsullied precedent, or, in the case of Lady Dedlock, presuming that the sullied precedent might be obliterated by historical or moral amnesia. If the orphan-figure resembles one model of the law insofar as it might be hypostasized as the vestigial "trace" looking for a pre-existent applicable context determined by an otherwise absent, unidentifiable, or irrelevant precedent, we might expect them to share similar modes of representation.

The trope by which Dickens "relates" the crisis in the history of legal interpretation to the dispossessed family member, is the *copy*. As the orphan is often de-nominated (in the sense of being "written down" as opposed to "speaking up") as a kind of composite or palimpsest of his assumed guardians, so the procedures of Chancery are entirely dependent upon precise transcription of an historical record by the numerous scribes who inhabit the warren of back streets adjacent to the court, a transcription that as we shall see, is prey to considerable drift. The author-copyist of legal documents, like other surrogate fathers and legal guardians in Dickens's novels, both signifies and does not signify simultaneously, much as do those other place-holders of the legal family tree, John Doe and Jane Roe. In fact, the plot of *Bleak House*, like so many of Dickens's plots, revolves about the question and status of a representation: whether or not one Nemo's transcribed record is faithful to an original (in the same way that a proper heir is faithful to his antecedent) or is inadmissible because it has sustained, well, "corruptions" in transmission. The illegitimate *copy*, be it orphan or legal brief—and they are often syntagmatically interchangeable since both are somewhat mechanically

"brought up by hand," to borrow from Mrs. Joe's description of Pip's upbringing in *Great Expectations*—are marked by a metaphorically disfiguring
stain, not dissimilar from that "blot upon the family name"(*BH* 19, 290) in
which Esther Summerson exists in the speech of her first guardian, the religious Miss Barbary dedicated to the "letter" as opposed to the "spirit."

If, however, we were to read this blot literally rather than figuratively, as
a smudged inscription, then the orphan-figure would exist analogously to
the imperfect copy, a stain upon the presumptive precedent, in a socially
reproductive process which demands the faithful repetition (as a kind of repetition) of an historically continuous "good name." As a stain, the orphan
is vulnerable to being *read* as a quasi-transparency, like the law, seen *through*
to the meaning which he simultaneously represents and displaces. The visibility of the orphan's genealogical opacity is *like* that which Tulkinghorn encounters when he attempts to discover the real name of the scribe whose
"law hand" (*BH* 2, 61) has been recognized by her former lover, Lady
Dedlock. Like the copied legal documents and the child whose detachment
from the presence of the father raises the spectre of an error in the transmission of a "line" of descent, Nemo *né* Captain Hawdon, has a kind of double-
life like that of Tulkinghorn and Jaggers , the life of *a differential same*ness.
As with the affidavits, petitions, and motions which he transcribes, and like
the history of the law as a discipline in the nineteenth century, the precedent
is only reproducible as an (elusive, but foundational) absence.

> "Nemo !" repeats Mr Tulkinghorn. "Nemo is Latin for no one."
> "It must be English for some one, sir, I think," Mr Snagsby submits with his
> deferential cough. "It is a person's name. . . . "                    (BH 10, 185)

Behind the presumably orderly transcriptions of the law is a "nothingness"
which nominates in the same gesture by which it *de-nominates*, depending
upon whether it is read as naming a subject or that subject's absence. Like
the Krook of the rag and bone shop who can read (serially) only by erasing
one character in an inscripted series before writing the next, legal practice in
Bleak House "goes on constantly, beginning over and over again" (*BH*
8, 146).

Reading itself is a provisional activity in much of Dickens's work, given
the deflection from *propriety* (considered as self-sameness) which defines the
historically and socially discontinuous as equivalent. Esther Summerson of
*Bleak House*, for example, assumes a number of nicknames in the course of
the novel—"Dame Durden" and "Mother Hubbard" among them—as if to

remind the reader that, absent an identifiable paternity, she is a palimpsest of successive over-inscriptions. Similarly, Pip, after initially inventing the fiction that he has named himself in the graveyard (the repressed fantasy of the lower classes, that of the self-made man?), ultimately acquiesces to Herbert Pocket's scheme to rename him "Handel." That name would signify only to one so familiar with the composer's music as to associate the name with the musical score about a blacksmith. In effect, Herbert Pocket rewrites Pip's dubious metaphorical "family" as a *metonymic* one, randomly constituted as a more or less arbitrary, lateral association, rather than a genealogically prescribed, linear succession which typically characterizes the *metaphoric* register. [7] A corollary to this experience of successive re-writing often occurs when a foundational precedent is finally recovered only to reveal itself as either internally divided or a plurality. This is but one technique by which presumably metaphysical antecedents (of the law or unclaimed offspring) resist the appeal of its "derivatives." As it turns out, for example, there is not just one will, but two in *Bleak House*, just as in fact there are two dwellings to which the name "Bleak House" is applicable. Similarly, there is not one "Pip," despite the appeals of his uniqueness, but a second "Pip" (born to Joe Gargery and Biddy) who resists adoption by his namesake late in the novel, so as to avoid a "duplicated life." Along with acquiring a surplus of names in use, as it were, often an a priori diversion of/in the originary calls attention to the ease with which the potential for dissimulation makes of every antecedent authority something very provisional indeed.

The deflection from a unitary and antecedent authority exhibited both by the law and those caught up in it in Dickens's work goes a long way toward explaining a recurrent form of violence which mimes the act of reading or attempting to read through a copy to its precedent. Typically, an adult, like Jaggers on the stairs at Miss Havisham's Satis House, seizes a child and holds its head and face as close as possible to his own in a terrorizing gesture. Yet, rather, than a prelude to physical violence, the menacing gaze or stare is revealed as a futile attempt on the part of the law to ""read"" the orphan so as to determine what it genealogically ""represents:""

> "Whom have we here?" asked the gentleman, stopping and looking at me.
> "A boy," said Estella.
> He was a burly man of exceedingly dark complexion, with an exceedingly large head and a corresponding large hand. He took my chin in his large hand and turned up my face to have a look at me by the light of the candle.
> (*GE* 11, 111)

The attempt to read "back" (metaphorically) to what lies *behind* the face or picture, as we have seen with Tulkinghorn's attempted resurrection of "someone"[8] from "Nemo," is never adequate. To so privilege inscription is to always risk betrayal in a culture which so values "letters." Perhaps the best instance of this futility is to be found in the opening scene of *Great Expectations* in that infamous episode wherein the frightened Pip strives to read behind the tombstone inscriptions on the graves of his deceased parents to arrive at a determination of their physical appearances: " . . . my first fancies regarding what they were like, were unreasonably derived from their tombstones. The shape of the letters on my father's, gave me an odd idea that he was a square, stout, dark man, with curly black hair" (*GE* 1, 35). Language is being called upon to perform a task for which it is entirely unsuited: to be consistently representational and univocally self-verifying.

Typically then, at least as regarded inscriptively, the law, like the parentless child is socially perceived as either filled with gaps or absences in continuity that impede familial or genetically authorized restoration or, conversely, is incessant, procedurally self-consuming, albeit without ever proceeding to judgment. In this latter model, both the law and the orphan would correspond to Stanley Fish's notion of the irrepressible nature of the discontinuous which is called upon to continually furnish the grounds for its own interpretation (328–31).[9] Like Dickens's fathers, then, the law is either *never fully present* in the lives of those it touches or, is thoroughly dissimulated in the form of spurious copies which are the basis for a virtual industry dedicated to the representation, reproduction, and interpretation of antecedents by surrogates and pretenders.

In the first instance, the language of the law exhibits the same curious "squeezing" of voice as that so often experienced by its defendants—the Pip choked in the graveyard, or the Gridley charged with contempt as he unsuccessfully tries to represent himself in his own voice, or for that matter, even the Esther Summerson who can represent herself to herself only through the radical gesture of the diary with which she has a fully inscripted "dialogue." The repetition of briefs, affidavits, rejoinders, and filed motions are all dedicated to denying the "com-*plaint*" as a first step in "standing in" for it, as one of Jaggers's unfortunate clients discovers:

> "We thought, Mr Jaggers"—one of the men began, pulling off his hat.
> "That's what I told you not to do," said Mr Jaggers. "*You* thought! I think for you; that's enough for you. If I want you, I know where to find you; I don't want you to find me. Now I won't have it. I won't hear a word"
>
> (*GE* 20, 191).

This repression of voice by/in its various legal representations is even more graphic in *Bleak House*: absence is "represented" in Dickens's own text. In response to her periodic "state of the orphan" letters to her legal guardians, Esther Summerson always receives by return post "exactly the same answer, in the same round hand with the signature of Kenge & Carboy *in another writing . . .* " (*BH* 3, 73, italics added). On closer scrutiny, however, her correspondence with the law betrays its characteristic drift: it only *seems* to be a unitary repetition; inscriptively, her correspondence reveals the divided authority which characterizes the presence of the law. Along with "walls of words" and "banks of advocates"(*BH* 1, 50), such discursive mediators deny any access to the "fountainhead" of jurisprudence which remains virtual rather than real. In the words of Jaggers during an early meeting with a Pip curious to know the name of his mysterious benefactor, "I have curious business to transact with you, and commence by explaining that it is not of my originating"(*GE* 18, 164). In a similar vein, Esther Summerson's early correspondence with Kenge & Carboy further confuses by a curious compression which transforms ordinary discourse into a rather specialized legal dialect which stifles aspiration in any phonetically sensitive reader:

> Old Square, Lincoln's Inn
>
> Madame ,
>    Jarndyce and Jarndyce
>    Our clt Mr Jarndyce being abt to rece into his house, under an Order of the Ct of Chy, a Ward of the Ct in this cause, for whom he wishes to secure an elgble compn, directs us to inform you that he will be glad of your secres in the afsd capacity.                                         (*BH* 3, 74)

In the narratives in which its procedures are conveyed, the law is simultaneously both resistant to recovery as an instantiating voice (which exists only as a nebulous "aforesaid capacity," abbreviated) *and*, almost paradoxically, is replete with gaps and absences which foreclose the possibility of any historical continuity and, when reproduced in official documents, is often as smudged, stained or inscriptively illegible as Dickens's orphans.

No wonder those associated with the "black letter" tradition as agents, clerks, attorneys, scribes, and judges, are similarly "smudged"—literally or figuratively—by the ink which is the medium of their work. Like orphans with runny noses and dirty hands, courts and their associated "dirty hangers on and *disowned relations* of the law" (*BH*, 5, 99, italics added), to borrow from Esther Summerson's appraisal, are among the dirtiest of the denizens of Dickens's numerous underworlds. Even when they self-consciously attempt to rid themselves of the filth of criminal association, as does the Jaggers of *Great Expectations* with his perfumed scent and frequently washed hands, the sites of lawyering present the prospective client with a truly "dismal atmosphere" where even the walls are made "greasy"(*GE* 20, 188–89) either by the demands of the unwashed or the demands of inscription. Guppy, the clerk at Kenge & Carboy, for example, is initially encountered by Esther Summerson as someone who had "inked himself by accident"(*BH* 3, 75), even before he proposes marriage by announcing that he wishes "to file a declaration"(*BH* 9, 175). Krook's dramatic death at the hands of spontaneous combustion, which operationally resembles the self-consumption of the entire bequest of *Jarndyce and Jarndyce* in legal fees, reduces him physically to the greasy, inky blackness which, as a copyist, has all along defined his marginal existence. Jo the Crossing-Sweeper verbally alters Nemo's inquest, a rational, abstract enquiry into the cause of death, into an "Inkwhich" (*BH* 16, 216), a delightful malapropism which participates in the very process it purports to describe—the exposure to the law, experienced as a submission to some "inking" through which a subject is brought to "book." Chesney Wold itself has been the subject of so many legal petitions and applications of easement on behalf of the neighboring Boythorn, that, at least in the eyes of Dickens's omniscient narrator, it has long ago been flattened into a mere "view in India ink"(*BH* 2, 56). Nor apparently does death offer relief from the plague of inscriptive iteration. Nemo's untimely demise in the hovel adjacent to *Cursitor* Street, occurs amidst "a bundle of pawnbroker's duplicates" (BH 9, 194); even *negation* lives and dies the life of the *copy*.

This parody of the filthy duplicate detached from its origin in Dickens's judicial novels may in fact reflect a crucial feature of legal practice in nineteenth-century Britain. Interminable legal suits were one consequence of the need, prior to 1852, to copy each legal document for every party to a suit with costs to be borne by the estate. With the Chancery Procedure Act of 1852, manual copying was replaced by commercial printing houses. One consequence was a considerable increase in unemployment among unskilled (and largely illiterate) scribes. In fact, one prominent social historian has deduced that fully twenty percent of the lowest paid laborers in the London of the 1840s were employed in the printing and copying trades, a truly massive underground (Jones 21–22, 28–35).[10] Because affidavits were used in lieu of personal appearance or direct oral testimony (and cross examination) until the Act took effect, there is some sense in which at least in terms of its material reproductions, Dickens was entirely faithful to the historical institutionalization of that plethora of "law hand[ s ]"(*BH* 2, 61) and their enlarged grasp in obscuring both precedent and the uninscribable voices of those without access to this extra-mural machinery. With the taking of direct testimony, a kind of "voice" must establish its own "credibility," as it were, in legal transactions, although, as we shall see, it is not immediately clear that this orality displaces the metaphysical precedent, as it so obviously does in, say Jacques Derrida's controversial project.

To be sure, Dickens's sustained critique of a system dedicated to equating the rationality of jurisprudence with the recuperation and application of historical precedent echoes Blackstone's fears that the judgments of so-called courts of equity—presumably given over to the arbitrary, albeit equitably applied opinions of a court officer on an ad hoc basis—were being slowly codified in such a way as to be virtually indistinguishable from a system so dependent upon identifying the appropriate legal antecedent. The history of jurisprudence in nineteenth-century Britain is replete with imaginative attempts to escape or otherwise subvert a system that so identified reason with an historical appeal. John Austin had intended his classical *The Province of Jurisprudence Determined* as a preface to his expanded *Lectures on Jurisprudence*, reconstructed by his widow and students from his notes, which appeared in 1863. Although the author had presumably intended ultimately to demonstrate the relations of positive morality to law, his prefatory work alone comprises Austin's (largely abridged) legacy, as an author of legal textbooks. Austinian jurisprudence today is read largely as a defence of historical jurisprudence: the recovery and elucidation of the law of the land and its application defines good jurisprudence. In the words of his editor, Jethro Brown, "justice . . . accord[ s] to a law which the judges make and apply retrospectively"(181).

In a similar vein, Frederick Harrison, professor of jurisprudence at the Inns of Court, went a step further and cautioned against any slackening of the ties that defined "recuperative" justice:

> It is so great a strain upon the mind to build up and retrace the conception of a great body of titles reducible to abstract and symmetrical classification, and capable of statement as a set of consistent principles—and this is what I take jurisprudence to be—that we are perpetually in danger of giving to law a literary instead of a scientific character, and of slipping in our thoughts from what the law is into speculating upon the coincidences which made it what it once was.
> (121–22)

The emphasis upon establishing precedent and a symmetrical, orderly descent according to historical principles was obviously subsidized by the growth of empire and the need to bring (pedagogical) order and the civilized rule of law to places like India which lacked such a tradition.

Occasionally, trained nineteenth-century legal minds did question the predominance accorded historical tradition in the determination of justice in specific cases before a court. A. V. Dicey warned his readers that

> antiquarianism is not law and the function of the trained lawyer is not to know what the law was yesterday, still less what it was centuries ago, or what it ought to be tomorrow, but to know what are the principles of law which actually and at the present day exist in England.                                    (14)

Yet, despite his apparent modernity in attempting to moderate antiquarianism with formalism, Dicey too worries that English constitutional law has no foundational origins, in contradistinction to the Founding Fathers' 1789 Constitution for America. As a consequence, the British scholar is torn between his willingness to promulgate a critique of the overdetermining *precedent*—and hence crucial to Dicey's reputation as a modernist—and the need to find some way by which basic or foundational enactments can be discriminated from the operations of ordinary law. Dicey achieves this by a truly extraordinary maneuver: in place of the absent foundational principle, he substitutes something like an ''operational beginning'' which smacks of the arbitrary: the notorious Septennial Act. At the beginning of the Hanoverian succession, the crown and the ministry were convinced that an appeal to the electorate was fraught with the potential for destabilizing Britain's domestic tranquillity. Hence a sitting parliament prolonged its own life from three years to seven, even though that exceeded their function as delegates. This act of parliamentary self-authorization breaks the tradition by which a legal precedent had informed a chronologically linear ''succession'' of dependent statutes and is co-terminal with it:

> Parliament made a legal though unprecedented use of its powers . . . That Act [the Septennial] proves to demonstration that in a legal point of view Parliament is neither the agent of the electors nor in any sense the trustee for its constitutents. . . . The Septennial Act is at once the result and the standing proof of such Parliamentary sovereignty.                              (Dicey 47–48) [12]

A unique incident at a singular chronological moment is simultaneously both the proof of a legal argument and the consequence of the same argument. Modern principles of popular sovereignty and democratic participation by an electorate is being made subordinate to a heretofore unexplored domain of parliament.

At no point in Dicey's analysis is the unlimited sovereignty of parliament a matter of concern. The judiciary cannot stand in a relationship of extraterritoriality to parliament because the will of England *is* parliament, the sole external limit on any sovereignty being disobedience by the majority of its subjects:

> the essential property of representative government is to produce co-incidence between the wishes of the sovereign and the wishes of the subjects; to make in short, the two limitations on the exercize of sovereignty absolutely co-incident.
>
> (Dicey 84)

Dicey's historical amnesia—his willingness to accept the absence of a foundational moment in the history of British jurisprudence (save the metaphoric seduction of parliament by the crown and the ministry)—leads directly to the metaphysics of coincidence between the wishes of a sovereign and its subjects. More about this philosophy of coincidence later—but, given the relationship of "representation," one might with reason ask why they are not one and the same? This is to suggest that the notion of coincidence endows the law with an omnipresence, an "everywhere-ness" which has neither internal limitations (in the trajectory of reversing a line of historical descent) nor external limitations (by an appeal to some "outside" authority sufficiently detached to judge the law).

In one sense, this "everywhere-ness" or *always-already* "thereness" of the law can be coaxed from Blackstone's earlier work, despite its historically conservative reputation. For between the "letter of the law"—that familylike "connected system . . . bound down by precedents" which he feared to be the ultimate fate of courts of equity—and the "spirit of the law," heretofore centered in the arbitrary "breast of the judge," the jurist posits a *via media* which also has neither internal nor external limitations which leave it open to critique. Blackstone advances the radical claim that "the fairest and most rational method to interpret the will of the legislator is by exploring his *intentions* [italics added] at the time when the law was made, by signs the most natural and probable"(I, 59). Among these signs, strangely enough, are "either the words, the context, the subject matter, the effects and consequence, or the spirit of the law" (I, 59). The "spirit of the law" is now determined by the "spirit of the law," but imagined as a *sign*, fully equivalent to other signs. The intention of the legislator, so Blackstone's argument continues, is accessible by recourse to these *circumstantial* signs, literally, those found "around" (either spatially or chronologically?) the enactment of a statute rather than any occluded foundational moment. Since the regime of signs to be read by those rendering judgment is simultaneously "natural and probable," even the accurate tracing up of the antecedent would by no means guarantee certainty. The "natural and probable" patriarch of the law, deducible only *circumstantially* (after the fact) would remain forever probable. For it is precisely the probability of error which serves to limit the arbitrary nature of what had previously been the provenance of equity, with its tendency to rise above the common law. The legal concept of *intentionality*, as articulated in Blackstone, is some "spirit" (yet accessible as a circumstantial sign) which might precede the often irrecoverable historical precedent, which garners so much of his attention. Conceptually, if one might pardon the pun, it has proved extraordinarily seductive.

As literary critics understand only too well, and as Frederick Harrison justifiably feared, *intention* is an origin before the slippery Origin. If the ordinary, patriarchally-hypostasized precedent is often resistant to recovery for Dickens's orphans and lawyers, the positing of some presumably antecedent "state of mind" which precedes engendering (of children or the law) would, at least superficially, appear to be even more difficult. Because intention is not as directly readable as patriarchy would presume to be—in the blood, facial features, or worldly effects of its offspring—the deductive determination of its presence requires the use of abstract reasoning, not mere tracing. And this very process could conceivably rearrange Blackstone's ubiquitous "circumstances" into a variety of patterns or structures in competition with that privileged "connected system . . . bound down by precedent" which so closely resembles that of the traditional family. The putative "naturalness" of the signs from which intentionality is to be deduced really cuts two ways: like a "natural" child, its precise relationship with its precedent is disguised or postponed as an "expectation."

Once the intellectual consequences or contemporary relevance of retracing the legal precedent is effectively challenged, the very notion of precedence is folded into two remarkably similar *operational*, as opposed to metaphysical, beginnings. The omniscience of Dicey's arbitrary Septennial Act, which leaves no possibility of separation between the law (even historically) and its subjects, and Blackstone's *intention*, which would achieve consensuality by eliding an a priori "spirit" of the law with its post facto claims through a common regime of signs, have identical effects. The *ground* of the law is made continuous with its *force*. This is, above all, the crucial narrative transformation which impacts both nineteenth-century jurisprudence and Dickens's (only scarcely fictional) narrative responses to it.

Although we habitually comprehend a given narrative under the assumption that it is narrated by some "one" with an a priori specific interest, agenda, or attitude, the consumer can never recover intention from utterance or inscription alone. That would be possible only if the narrative was meaningful in such a way that it could be self-verifying, a clear impossibility. Because heeding a certain set of signals rather than others entails taking that particular set as meaningful for a variety of often indeterminate reasons, the mere act of selecting *which* signal, in order to gain credence, is often attributed to an author. This is one reason why Stanley Fish has consistently argued that the intention is always constructed by the interpreter, absent the self-validation attempted by Pip in the graveyard (395).

Nonetheless, most of us have thoughts that are never overtly expressed, even though they have a demonstrable content. If my intention when addressing or writing you—as I am at this very moment—is solely constituted by intentions that the addressee constructs for me, then it would have no content independent of those constructions. To maintain this hypothesis, everyone's thoughts would have to be constructed by someone else. Since, however, in order to do any constructing at all, we must *always-already* have (some) thoughts, one could not hold a constructivist view of intentionality without incurring the risk of infinite regress.

Is it possible that debates regarding the recovery of intention could be restated as debates about *relational properties*—environmental, structural, historical, economic—of a given syntagmatic order? The interpreter, be he literary critic, judge, or even translator, gives varying responses, depending upon which relational property is privileged at that historical moment and for what reason. Although some critics might determine intention in terms of some relational property involving an author's expressed will, others, influenced by institutions, ideologies, or demands from his consumers, might advance an argument that the same text is dependent upon say, cultural distinctions; systems of class, race, or gender; or, in the case of reader-response criticism, upon the "horizon" of possible encounters. This might explain why the consumer of a text in literary criticism often foregrounds his reading (and some fictional attribution of intention to an author) by identifying the particular ideological affinities to which the author might adhere, given his education, the frequency of certain allusions, or even, the occasion and format of social reproduction. It is not only that what is selected *as* a relational property partially determines what is deduced as intention, but that some of these relational properties are in conflict with others. [14]

But, in jurisprudence, as distinct from literary criticism, once the *ground* of the law comes to be indistinguishable from the *force* of the law, the potential for displacement begins to arise. Whereas the *ground* of the law would include those circumstances in which particular legal propositions would be regarded as verifiable, the *force* of the law defines the relative power of any applicable legal proposition to justify coercion under widely differing circumstances. Once the general public is perceived of as being impacted by the force of the law, as opposed to what grounds it, they establish a variety of relationships to it which, paradoxically, come to define their individuality. Although various nineteenth-century legal commentators, including Dickens have challenged the importance of recuperating precedence as a necessary step in arriving at humane judgments, legal minds have traditionally had more difficulty in determining *how* we *value* both experience and socially censurable behavior.

In this respect, Jeremy Bentham, despite his reputation as a pragmatic utilitarian, was crucial to the development of legal narratives less dependent upon an increasingly inaccessible precedent or on intention, that ephemeral precedent in situ. Even in his early work, Bentham dedicated himself to a critique of another a priori contractual consent arrived at in the absence of precedent: Rousseau's eighteenth-century notion of the General (inalienable) Will, which all citizens shared as a natural right.[15] Convinced that governments must do more than insure security in return for the loss of individual autonomy once removed from a state of nature, Bentham chose to emphasize *verifiable* reciprocity between the law and its subjects. Only collective associations could remind the individual that no rights exist without corresponding duties, given the condition that no right could be imagined without imagining a corresponding duty not to infringe upon it. The importance of "organic form," then, for Bentham lay not in any presumed natural-ness of the law, as it surely did for those who imagined the history of the law as miming the patriarchal structure of biological families (or trees with descendant branches), but rather in its potential for assembling arrangements sufficiently flexible to allow different outcomes (the adequacy of which could be measured by testing) and simultaneously self-organizing (any tested application would produce a relative, albeit changing order for each of the parties to it). [16]

In extending this paradigm to a calculus of moral transgressions and corresponding punishments, the force of the law was suddenly imagined to be capable of grading or assigning a specific value, depending upon the *organizational family* which the offense in some sense belonged. The consequence was the creation of an *economy* wherein a similar sentence is meted out to presumably similar transgressions in a system involving substitution. One act is defined *in terms of* or *in relation to* another, with contributing "circumstances" entering into the equation in a transaction. Unlike "tracing up" the legal precedent in order to determine the applicable "parent" in a specific case, a legal code in which transgressions were graded so as to correspond with putatively equivalent sentences, emphasizes the distribution of justice rather than the maintenance of the law as an historically-acquired legacy. The law is suddenly a *force* to be applied rather than a "find" to be discovered; hence any obligation to obey cannot effect its ontic status.

It remained for Bentham's ( occasionally adversarial ) disciple, John Stuart Mill, to extend the range of what constituted a legal *fact*: "the whole of the present facts are the infallible result of all past facts and more immediately of *all the facts* which existed at the moment previous [ital. added]" (VII, 379). Although Mill continues to enlist precedent in his logic, it is a more immediate presence, potentially encompassing all facts (with the privileged precedent merely one more fact among many) than was the case when it constituted a foundational fact. To borrow from a new, contemporaneous discipline, the earth sciences, Mill deploys the logic of uniformitarianism to replace that of the instantiating moment which is analogous to a kind of legal catastrophism. There could be no better illustration of the strategies by which the *ground* of the law is being systematically dispersed as part of its *force* on the way to becoming "circumstances." This change is reflected procedurally as well; whereas in Blackstone's time, "direct testimony" had been narrowly defined as admissible only from a witness to a crime, by the 1850s, even those geographically or personally remote from the actual criminal act could offer testimony, widening the range of those caught up in its narratives and enlarging dialogic *respons*-ibility.

The transformation of the law and its discourses into organic narratives, more like those of fiction, can be easily discerned in Thomas Starkie's remarkable *A Practical Treatise on the Laws of Evidence*. There, the representation of crime and those laws which would attempt its control and punishment, though it continues to include relations of descent, has broadened to comprehend other organizational models which are not necessarilly dependent, but involve the possibility of horizontal "connections:"

> All human dealings and transactions are a vast context of circumstances, interwoven and connected with each other, and also with the natural world, by innumerable mutual links and ties. No one fact or circumstance ever happens which does not owe its birth to a multitude of others, and which is not connected

on every side by kindred facts, and which does not tend to the generation of a
host of dependent ones, which necessarily co-incide and agree in their minutest
bearings and relations, in perfect harmony and concord, without the slightest
discrepancy or disorder.                                              (I, 560)

Although the "generation of dependent" circumstances remains, evidentiary
relations as well as the law itself are "connected on every side by *kindred*
facts," potentially making of "all human dealings and transactions" a later-
ally-organized, a-filiative "family." There are various ties which bind individuals into associations—some voluntary, some not. Co-incidence and/or
agreement in their minutest interrelationships can be checked, because the
myriad circumstances can be interpretively interwoven and rewoven, so as
to generate alternative patterns in the same *text*(ile).

The deductive solving of criminality by reducing acts and motives to an
interrelated text is a democratizing gesture. Any act, human agent, or law is,
at least potentially, relatable to any other, given an imaginative interpreter.
Whereas the traditional biological family is replete with gaps, seams, and
spurious offshoots, deductively-induced associations can be tested for ele-
gance or harmony. One literary critic has advanced the theory that it is
precisely this newly realized potential for a (structurally) infinite displacement
within some model of "co-incidental facticity" which informs the shift to
narrative realism in the novel in the second half of the nineteenth-century. [17]
Assuming that anyone is at least potentially connected (as co-incidental) with
a crime and that many statutes may be applicable in determining the degree
or gradation of responsibility, even a complete abstraction, like "social conditions"—at least after the creation of special Parliamentary Commissions to
investigate the so-called "condition of England question"—could have a
"share" in criminality. This enhanced range of "relational responsibility"
or authorship would imply that a variety of contributing circumstances heretofore unidentified or anonymous might impinge upon intentionality; in fact
the *force* of the law might be the name applied to the dispersal of its *ground*
throughout the social order.

The revision in Pip's attitude toward Jaggers in the course of *Great Expectations* might reflect this change. In the beginning of their association, Pip is
shocked to discover that Jaggers's vaunted legal reputation is partially due
to a propensity to "invent" witnesses to a crime and to pay them for their
services. Throughout the first half of the novel, Jaggers appears as the consummate shyster, constructing fictional legal defenses, all the time washing
his hands from the moral and inscriptive "staining" which is the life of his

profession. Only later in the novel is Jaggers's system of substitution seen to be part of a larger scheme in which the legal order is being subtly redefined as a model of competing (and hence exchangeable) narratives: victims do not have to be "caught up" in it. In removing Estella from the reach of a court which has charged her mother with murder, the lawyer substitutes a private system of justice for the publicly mandated one. He will not "trace up the precedent," either metaphorically or literally in his arguments before the court, but will displace the accused from one narrative "family" to another, with a virtual rather than real precedent.

This displacement from one discursive order to another will come to constitute the operation of justice. In the process, Jaggers reimagines society, as he will "revise" the law, into a *network* of interdependent relations rather than as some descendent "line" whose attachments must be maintained :

> "Put the case that he often saw children solemnly tried at a criminal bar, where they were held up to be seen; put the case that he habitually knew of their being imprisoned, whipped, transported, neglected, cast out, qualified in all ways for the hangman, and growing up to be hanged. Put the case that pretty nigh all the children he saw in his daily business life, he had reason to look upon as so much spawn, to develop into the fish that were to come to his net—to be prosecuted, defended, forsworn, made orphans, bedevilled somehow."
>
> "I follow you, sir."
>
> "Put the case, Pip, that there was one pretty little child out of the heap, who could be saved; whom the father believed dead, and dared make no stir about; as to whom, over the mother, the legal adviser had this power: 'I know what you did and how you did it. . . . I have tracked you through it all, and I will tell you all. Part with the child, unless it should be necessary to bring you off, and then it shall be produced. Give the child into my hands, and I will do the best to bring you off. If you are saved, your child is saved too; if you are lost, your child is still saved.' Put the case that this was done, and that the woman was cleared."  (*GE* 51, 424–25)

In this truly remarkable dialogue, Jaggers imagines the law operates so as to socially reproduce its victims while disclaiming any responsibility for them, exactly like absentee patriarchs;[18] in the process, the law just keeps on "spawning." In removing Estella from the range of this legal machinery to his own "private" system (in which her mother, Molly, will serve her time not in a public jail, but as Jaggers's own, equally brutalized domestic servant), Jaggers reveals crucial features of the operational dynamics of the law as it is experienced by both its subjects and its agent/representatives.

Although the law is publicly perceived as sacred, even quasi-divine in the respect accorded it, the arbitrarily, self-reproducing nature of its operational efficiencies can be easily mimed, privatized by others, a strategy which, at least on the surface, appears to offer relief. Its representatives and agents can on occasion take it into their own hands (even as they wash their hands of its effects). In "appropriating" the discontinuous and thereby criminalized orphan-figure and re-distributing her to another family of interests under the guise of saving her from the social reproductions of the law, Jaggers is repeating the law's own strategies for self-maintenance, as if providing a measure of immunity from its reproductive efficiencies. If to be either acquitted or "saved" from the justice juggernaut, is merely to be *transferred* to Jagger's jurisdiction, then the student of both narrative and the law might be expected to ask what, if any, *equity* has been achieved, save securing subjective rights free of objective law?

For, although Jaggers succeeds in liberating her from the (literal and figurative) "brambles" which characterize the circumstances of her birth, he merely delivers her into the similar "brambles" which characterize the overgrown, ruined garden of Satis House. As her mother's heart was broken, and as her "second mother," Miss Havisham, had her heart broken, so Estella will initially break hearts only to have her own ultimately broken by a misogynistic husband who habitually beats her late in *Great Expectations*. If, as is the case with both Estella and her mother, to be rescued from the reaches of the law is but a further immersion in its consequences, appropriately disguised, then the operation of the law ultimately leaves nothing outside of itself. The law would have a continuous presence, just as it did in the "consensual" strategies by which the British judicial system has habitually identified the law with some a priori will of parliament which historically, cannot be resisted. If to be shifted to another quasi-familial order does not really deliver one from the law so much as it re-inscribes the reach of the law, "under cover," as it were, then its representations, in the innumerable scribes, clerks and repetitions which stain hands and generate dubious inscripted supplements in *Bleak House* does not seem off the mark. One way or another, the law operates as a vast machinery dedicated to its own social reproduction. The unverifiable "copy" serves as an appropriate synecdoche precisely because everyone seems to participate, willingly or not, in a de facto inscription in which they are denied any voice. Yet, surely, Jaggers's resistance to the law is ethically, structurally, and I would argue, historically significant.

The subtle change symbolized in Jaggers's attempt to shift the jurisdictional "responsibility" for Estella might best be described as being *like that* which attends upon the change from *transcription*, the writing *down* of that which is prior, to *translation*, a related, albeit dissimilar form of reproduction. From one perspective, of course, both are copies. But one presumes to be a verbatim recovery, whereas the other admits to either a provisionality or constructs an imaginary faithfulness to an originary after an act of interpretation. When a court reporter "takes down" the proceedings of a case (as Dickens did during his apprenticeship as a writer), there is never an allusion to the "intention" of the participants. Translation, however, moves the *apparently discontinuous* child, circumstances, or narrative into another provisional relationship, often, as is the case with Jaggers's "transportation" of Estella to Miss Havisham, for a specific interpretational agenda which serves to subvert any exclusively referential status. The resistance of the lawyer, detective, or literary critic to the "dangling sign" in the rush to interpretational judgment (which we often disguise as authorial intention) bears a striking resemblance to the orphan's psychological resistance to his own detachment from patriarchy. Absent a recuperable precedent (or patriarch), we assign an authorial intention which lies *behind* or under the missing antecedent, yet which enforces similar demands: "organic wholeness," "cohesion," "internal consistency," "referential authenticity," so familiar to those of us who practice literary criticism and evaluate the practice of others.

Because any group of signs, *read* as related by a designated audience, could conceivably come to constitute a "coherent family" (given enough faith), there is a corresponding urge among members of these professions to look for *any* connections, symbolic or virtual, where they might not exist at all: Jaggers's "what have we here?" being a perfect instance. To reappropriate an earlier metaphor whereby the last will and testament was compared, only slightly facetiously, to a post facto contraceptive by which a patriarch attempted to make his *real* family identical to his *intended* family, so we interpreters too, eschew "accidents," particularly after we have the associations we want.

The danger may be that we create, wittingly or unwittingly, a *relation*, perhaps even a kinship, between narrative justice and political justice. Dickens's lawyer/detectives, like we literary critics—a likeness which draws us to them—are in effect co-conspirators in the effort to keep a family of apparently *discontinuous circumstances*, to invent a phrase which might encompass unacknowledged children and unrelatable events which surround a crime against the public, *together*. If to be judged guilty is no longer a question of being physically, socially, or legally/procedurally stained by precedent, as was the young Dickens forced to work at Warren's Blacking Factory, affixing in-scripted labels to inky polish for gentlemen's boots in order to redeem his father's indebtedness, but rather to be moved into a narrative "association," then one could conceivably be judged innocent by virtue of participation in a different narrative. There would be nothing permanent about the syntag-matic order into which one was born, if he could be metonymically translated to a different associational pattern. The truly discontinuous child (or clue) could belong to a plurality of associations, depending upon the surrogate author(ial) skill—read "ingenuity"—of a lawyer, novelist, or critical reader, given some freedom to move syntagms in and out of a potentially infinite number of "plots."

The Victorian multi-plotted novel would, efficiently, enable the socially or historically discontinuous "member" to be re-constituted within a more or less arbitrary association.[19] Such a fate, though not quite that of the dreamed-of "self-made man" (the desire for whom is perhaps unconsciously intimated in the Pip who fictionalizes "naming" himself in the opening pages of *Great Expectations*), figuratively his own precedent, might nonetheless be a step in that direction. Any social position is constructed, and this arbitrary construc-tion, after the fact, is made purposive by endowing it with intentionality. It is as if the precedent-as-patriarch were being subtly replaced by that of say, the precedent-as-artist. The logic by which this shift in legal *mentalité* is effected, is suggested in Wills's *Essay*:

> A profound knowledge of comparative anatomy enabled the immortal Cuvier, from a single fossil bone, to describe the structure and habits of many of the animals of the antediluvian world. In like manner, an enlightened knowledge of human nature often enables us on the foundation of apparently slight circum-stances, to follow the tortuous windings of crime, and ultimately to discover its guilty author, as infallibly as the hunter is conducted by the track to his game.                                                                    (27)

Wills alludes to the relatively new discipline of *comparative anatomy*; an interpreter must "track" development by moving laterally, *between* organic structures, taking note of their similarities and differences. In order to *relate* two or more designs, habits, or functions across generic boundaries, any differences are as important as similarities, which is not true when one is merely recovering "foundations" of either the law or a succession of criminal motives and acts—which in Wills's analysis, are often merely supplementary "slight circumstances."

In assisting this openness to a transaction between two superficially dissimi-lar orders, Dickens, through Jaggers, is extending the metaphoric family. He becomes the vehicle, as it were, of a *translation* which permits the reader of *Great Expectations* to consider how the social betrayal of the impoverished is like (unlike) the sexual betrayal of the rich Miss Havisham. Most sensitive critics would argue that the legal persecution and ultimate social abandonment of Magwitch to prison ship and Australia is different from the sexual abandonment of Miss Havisham to the oppressive monotony and darkness of Satis House, even though their betrayals share the same metaphoric precedent in Compeyson. We might, for example, argue that society as a whole makes a promise to "love, honour, and respect" its individual members—at least as a speech act—in the same way as does a partner in the betrothal ceremony. Feminists might argue that sexual abandonment involves emotions of personal defilement or, even worthlessness, which are exclusive to intrusive physical acts and the promises which accompany them and differ from the common expressions of low self-esteem which characterize other social and legal outcasts. And yet, Jaggers's actions, those of the less-than-respectable lawyer in carrying money and babies so as to redistribute each in a novel which creates an "economy" in which the past (inheritance) is the future (expectations), forces the reader to compare and contrast each form of (traditionally) patriarchal investment in the future. As the agent of an exchange system, Jaggers allows the reader not merely to become cognizant of the "connections" between varieties of families and their specific abuses, but to argue about their differences.

In *Justice as Translation*, James Boyd White has argued that no translation can achieve, nor should it aim at bringing about, the "same effect" as the original in a different language or register. Whereas a theory of law which privileges the antecedent and the necessity of its restoration in the determination of legal judgments has its claims, the history of law is, for White, the progressive dilution of a recuperative model in favor of a transactional one:

> There is no position outside of culture from which the original can be experienced or described. It is read by one of us, translated by one of us speaking to the rest of us. The meaning and identity of the original are defined in the differences we perceive in it, in what makes it strange to us. To another, it will present a different set of differences, and thus be a different text with a different meaning.    (252) [20]

Any translation or sophisticated interpretation (and Jaggers's actions are nothing if not interpretive) exists in its own right. That is one reason why the best of both forms of social reproduction come to constitute not commentary *upon*, but part of some "body" which collectively constitutes the history of literature as identical to the history of responses *to* and readings *of*, it. This would be entirely synchronous with Ronald Dworkin's suggestion that useful theories of the law are no longer semantically-based, but are rather interpretive of a particular stage of an historically-developing practice (101–04). Yet, as anyone familiar with Ezra Pound's translations from Japanese literature realizes, a translation may acquire value as independent art ("every judge a legislator") in direct proportion to its deconstruction of an ostensible precedent. White's (and Jaggers's) model of the history of jurisprudence as a succession of translations or "adaptations to changing circumstances" makes no room for the introduction of an independent legal element into the legal order *which would be recognized as legal.*

Even if we accept White's analogy with translation, there is no guarantee that the operation of the law is any different from that of society at large wherein a multiplicity of autonomous sub-systems conduct their own discursive practices detached from any *internal* relations to morality or politics. Even a good translation would not put an end to a recursively closed circuit of communication that self-referentially delimits the law from even its immediate environment with which it has contact only through incomplete observations or discontinuous "adaptations" that pose as applications. Jaggers experiences the world only through a patched skylight and engages it only through hands washed clean of every previous encounter—experientially, each contact is its own precedent. As an autopoietic activity, the legal system is like a monad, simultaneously closed and open insofar as it describes its own components as legal categories, employs these self-thematizations for the sole purpose of constituting and reproducing legal acts, and even, as Dickens's Chancery operatives illustrate, finances itself from resources which it alone produces in an apparently closed economic circuit.

Once it becomes autonomous the legal system can no longer maintain any *direct* exchange with its intrasocial environment save in some derivative sense: by altering itself, it presents another "face" to other systems which in turn react in a quasi-dialogical sense in an attempt to recover a "reflective equilibrium" *that is disguised as justice.* Throughout *Great Expectations* Jaggers is really an operator ranslator who (1) somewhat hermeneutically delivers his own anonymous justice as compensation for the gaps which he has exploited in the traditional justice system and (2) enables us to elide biological and economic orders of investment and dis-investment (social abandonment). But, by describing the conflict-resolving capacity of the law as a purely *systemic* capability, social integration by means of the law is assimilated to the model of a balancing, objective, unintentional coordination dedicated to achieving social equilibrium. His work enables people to have access to the false foundations of the law, symbolized in the sets of false patriarchs and matriarchs with whom he deals, but can never go beyond that to genuine interdependencies that are necessary if the law is to be an instrument of social action. On the one hand, his legal discourse is trapped in an autonomous subsystem conducting its own (often incompatible) constructions of reality, so exaggerated in Jaggers's grammatical use of the passive voice and subjunctive mood or the "law hand" from Kenge & Carboy in *Bleak House*. At the same time, however, the law is being called upon as an agent of "general social communication," to borrow from the German legal scholar, Gunther Teubner, thereby influencing other discursive worlds, in its transforming capacity (727–57).[21]

Law, then, would appear to belong to two orders simultaneously: it is a system of knowledge and a system of action. The law is a composite text, composed of legal propositions and their successive historical interpretations, but also an institution, a complex of normatively governed activity. Insofar as it incorporates doctrinal knowledge, highly systematized, and hence, separable from any quasi-natural institutional orders, there is a procedural as well as a substantive aspect of the law, both of which are subject to rationalizations. Although historically related, as we have seen in the evolving of courts of common law and equity, they must ultimately be separated analytically. This takes place in tandem with the slow secularization of the foundation of the law, as it shifts from principles that transcend the law to an *activity* inherent in the law which is nonetheless resistant to any reductive subsystemization. As we have seen, in the early chapters of Dickens's later novels, the law is as directed toward self-interest and self-maintenance as were his characters, defensively bundled up against socialization in the stagecoach ride of *A Tale of Two Cities*, who drew the following comment from an omniscient narrator:

> A wonderful fact to reflect upon, that every human creature is constituted to be that profound secret and mystery to every other. A solemn consideration when I enter a great city at night, that every one of those clustered houses encloses its own secret; that every room in every one of them encloses its own secret; that every beating heart in the hundreds of thousands of breasts there, is in one of its imaginings, a secret to the heart nearest it! Something of the awfulness, even of Death itself, is referable to this.          (*TTC* 3, 44)

The Tulkinghorn of *Bleak House* is in some sense *always-already* dead, even before his murder, and that death of the "old school" is an Allegory of the Death of the Law, in one of its incarnations, as an inaccessible appendix.

In order to be liberated from the prison-house of its code-specific social subsystem, two conditions must be fulfilled. First, some *general* communication medium must exist beneath the threshold of functionally specific codes. As we shall see, in Dickens's work this medium will come to resemble nothing so much as ordinary language. With its large capacity and range of circulation, ordinary language is superior to special codes insofar as it allows some reckoning of the costs incurred by more highly differentiated subsystems, while remaining sensitive to problems that affect the whole of society in ways which Jaggers's spatial, sexual, and linguistic isolation will not permit. Ordinary language is not tied to a single code, but is inherently multilingual. The specialized language of the law differentiates itself *only within the boundaries* of a multifunctional language, while nonetheless remaining *intertwined* with other, equally highly differentiated, coded systems through it. Ordinary language allows operations to hive themselves off, but cannot itself be thought of as a systemic, highly-coded system. Law would then function as a hinge between an only intermittently recoverable system of descendant precedents (some of which clearly have fictitious claims) and the politics of everyday life. Ordinary language forms a universal horizon of understanding and at least in principle, can translate from a number of different discursive media. But it cannot operationalize its messages for all potential addressees. For *adoption* into some special code, it remains dependent upon the law that communicates with "directing" agendas dictated by economics, culture, or simply administrative power. The law would then be neither foundation nor force, but a "transformer" which guarantees a socially integrated network of communication *across social life*.

And secondly, but perhaps concomitantly, there must be a paradoxical emergence of *legitimacy*, defined by rights that secure for citizens the exercize of political autonomy, out of what had previously been hypostasized as mere *legality*. Even in the absence of a determinable patriarchal foundation of the law, there must be some other way of creating the sense of "belonging;" otherwise, lawful behavior is only a duty, leaving open any motive for conforming to social norms. Given the ease with which, at least historically, the autonomous will of the individual has been co-opted by an antecedent consensual collusion with a quasi-transcendent legislative and judicial Establishment in Great Britain, this is no easy task. In the last half of the nineteenth century, as we have seen from Austin and Dicey, there grows the suspicion that private law can be legitimated from its own resources only as long as it could be assumed that a legal subject's private autonomy had a foundation in his moral autonomy. But with the waning of any idealist grounding of the law, at least under a positivist perspective, the law can assert itself only in a particular practice which furnished specific decisions and powers with the force of a de facto bindingness. Individual rights were in some sense "secondary reflections" of an established legal order which transferred to individuals the power of will objectively incorporated *only* in law.

Although private autonomy was secured in various legally protected spheres in the nineteenth century (primarily those involving contract or property rights in Dickens's novels), the bond between freedom of choice and a subject's autonomous will, like that elucidated in Kant's "principle of right," had been progressively eroded over time. Right was a power or rule of will conferred only by the legal order, as we have seen. Once the moral and/or natural person has been severed from the legal system in this way, by an appeal to some higher legitimacy and normative independence from the political process of legislation, there is nothing to impede the abstract subordination of "subjective rights" to "objective law" where the latter's legitimacy finally exhausted itself in the legalism of political domination articulated in positivist terms. The Bentham who imagined the judiciary system as an efficient means for maximizing the satisfaction of human interests is really not so different from the Jaggers who, not unlike the established legal system as it turns out, shuffles the discontinuous "member" in and out of his own alternative "jurisdictions," preserving only the vestige of an autonomous will, but in effect, reproducing its judgments.

In Dickens's, as in Jurgen Habermas's work, genuine *legitimacy* can emerge only when subjects who had previously been defined by (natural?) rights based upon some autonomous will, make a rationally motivated transition from a state of permanent conflict (or defensive self-protection) to cooperation under a coercive law that demands a partial renunciation of freedom for everyone.[22] In order for this to occur, all parties would have to understand what a social relationship based upon reciprocity involves since nothing in nature prepares them for it. They would have to learn how to "take the perspective of the other" and, *self-reflexively*, perceive themselves *from the perspective of a second person*. Legitimacy is to be *constituted* through a mutual recognition (not the oppressive gaze or stare of the law nor Chancery proceedings with its repetitively indifferent legalese)—a socio-cognitive framework of "perspective taking" between counterparts. Only in this way could a single human right, no matter how radically based in the individuated will, differentiate itself into a "system of rights" through which both the freedom of every subject as a human being as well as the equality of each member with every other (as a subject) assume a positive shape. Admittedly, the operations of the law would still have the force of consensuality, but it would be a derivative consensuality, involving pluralizing projections, rather than, as in the historical bias of British jurisprudence, an a priori consensuality in lieu of a shared patriarchal foundation.

This change in the ontological status of the force of the law (and the narratives of its institutional practices) is nowhere better reflected than the displacement of Tulkinghorn by Inspector Bucket in *Bleak House* and the near revolutionary transformation of Eugene Wrayburn in *Our Mutual Friend*. Perhaps we should also add the wily Jaggers to this list of make-overs, for in the concluding chapters of *Great Expectations*, he finally physically leaves the metaphorical and literal staining of the law courts and his greasy office to actively involve himself in Magwitch's attempted flight from legal prosecution. His highly conditioned and hedged legal discourse is ultimately abandoned—along with defensive posture—for a more transactive presence in the life of someone who is no longer merely a client. In each case, an attorney or one ostensibly dedicated to protecting, conveying, or negotiating family secrets is transformed into or replaced by an individual who, in projecting himself into new, a-familial associations, becomes a detective. Self-reflexive identification of a self, entailing some sacrifice, with another is crucial to his discoveries and the new social relationships which arise as a consequence will inaugurate a new model of *legitimacy*.

Bucket initially appears to work in league with the legal butler, even referring to the lawyer as a "partner" (*BH* 53, p. 770) at the latter's funeral. And indeed, the ease with which Bucket's skeleton key allows him access to Tulkinghorn's law chambers (at which time he discovers the murder) gives the Inspector a kind of dual identity, both inside and outside the secrets of the law. He can strategically ally himself with another as a partner, or detach himself from the law to identify a guilty partner. For he quickly separates himself from Tulkinghorn (and the law's) methodical taciturnity by a new "velocity . . . of interpretation" (*BH* 56, 820), not at all dependent upon faithfully tracing up precedents through chronological layers of inscriptive enclosure: Tulkinghorn's cramped law library and the Dedlock library with its "family lists," "the little library within the larger one" (*BH* 53, 771), between which legal life oscillates. Whereas Tulkinghorn's self-enclosed life, like the symbolic "life" of the law in the nineteenth century one suspects, is organized, like *Jarndyce and Jarndyce*, around the proxemics of infinite regress, the progressive interiority which defines an absentee, hidden, or inaccessible authority from which legal, genetic, or financial bounty is imagined to flow, Bucket eschews petitions and repetitions, favoring the oral/aural register:

> He is no great scribe; rather handling his pen like the pocket-staff he carries about with him always convenient to his grasp; and discourages correspondence with himself in others, as being too artless and direct a way of doing delicate business.                                    (*BH* 53, 771)

Bucket maintains a vast network of informants, in a world where even the unwashed subalterns, like Jo the Crossing-Sweeper, are equal to the rich as *carriers* of information (for which disease, the smallpox which is so upwardly mobile in *Bleak House*, may be a synecdoche). Bucket's networks are largely affiliations of voice, testimony to the Inspector's skill as a listener and discriminator of sounds. He is a great ventriloquist, having trained his ear to precisely duplicate Hortense's French accent. Although he confesses to a deficiency in the (auto?) poietic mode (*BH* 57, 832), Bucket easily and in perfect harmony joins in the vocal accompaniment at Mrs. Bagnet's birthday party. This talent at vocal accommodation is matched by a remarkable ear which discerns the onset of Sir Leicester Dedlock's cerebral hemorrhage almost before its victim or Dickens's omniscient narrator, as "an unusual slowness in his [Sir Leicester's] speech, with now and then a curious trouble in beginning which occasions him to utter inarticulate sounds" (*BH* 54, 784). Given the surplus of highly systematized (and largely autopoietic) legal inscription and the proliferation of parasitical agents entrusted with its transmission, Inspector Bucket's dedication to voice is remarkable. The oral register is clearly as conjunctive in the last half of *Bleak House* as writing had been disjunctive in the novel's earlier chapters. It is precisely Bucket's use of *ordinary language* which enables him (as the force of the law) to gain access to private as well as public life. No family is foreclosed to his participation, given his remarkable skills at social assimilation: even the screaming, unruly Bagnet children delight in playing upon his knees. Whereas Jaggers shuffles his clients in and out of ad hoc families in order to achieve a merely provisional freedom and rigidly maintains control of his own privacy during social occasions, Bucket's relationship with Mrs. Bucket is so accommodative and flexible as to allow the criminal, Hortense, to become a temporary appendix to their own domestic arrangements: "As he says himself, what is public life without private ties? He is in his own way a public man, but it is not in that sphere that he finds happiness. No, it must be sought within the confines of domestic bliss" (*BH* 49, 732).

The Inspector's "adaptability to all grades"(*BH* 53, 777) surely stems in part from the fact that his own father "was first a page, then a footman, then a butler, then a steward, then an innkeeper"(*BH* 53, 777), exhibiting a remarkable talent—given mid-nineteenth-century England—at upward social mobility, as ultimately unconfined to class as Bucket himself is. Although ostensibly one of the new breed of civil servants, so competent compared to the Bow Street Runners who investigate the assault upon Mrs. Joe in *Great Expectations*, Bucket's skills can nonetheless be privatized on an ad hoc basis by the very rich, like the Sir Leicester Dedlock in search of the absent Lady Dedlock. Although derivatively a member of the lower classes, Inspector Bucket, be he partaking of fine sherry from the Chesney Wold cellars, or "moving on" Jo the Crossing-Sweeper, is at home virtually everywhere, not unlike the ordinary language which defines his discursive posture. To his companion, Esther Summerson, on the midnight ride in search of the missing Lady Dedlock, he appears as an individual man, but simultaneously, always in conference:

> "He had gone into every late or early public-house where there was a light (they were not a few at that time, the road being then much frequented by drovers), and had got down to talk to the turnpike keepers. I had heard him ordering drink, and chinking money, and making himself agreeable and merry everywhere; but whenever he took his seat upon the box again, his face resumed its watchful steady look...."    (*BH* 57, 829)

Toward the end of *Bleak House*, the life of the written copy, prone to such reproductive "drift" in its early pages, is given the velocity of speech, as Bucket uses technology to wire a "wanted" poster to all corners of the Kingdom. For only oral information so circulated can keep up with the "train of circumstances"(*BH* 54, 781), the progressive de-centering of evidence making the rounds as circumstantial. The high velocity of information combined with Bucket's enhanced associational capacity truly transforms the nature of space in *Bleak House* by opening up "clearings" in a text which had previously been overdetermined by patterns of infinite inscriptive regress: " 'I know so much about so many characters, high and low, that a piece of information more or less, don't signify a straw. I don't suppose there's a move on the board that would surprise *me* ... ' " (*BH* 54, 782). One consequence, though perhaps not our primary interest, is the transformation of Dickens's novel into a kind of anti-museum opposite to the recovery of precedent which had maintained closed arenas of accumulation, like Krook's rag-and-bone shop, Tulkinghorn's old-fashioned demeanor, or the first Bleak

House, with its *demodé* curios and knickknacks in hidden corners, tucked away from view. Political life is now, more than metaphorically, imagined by Bucket as a "board"—a game of connections defined by rules as opposed to being maintained by a myth of origins. Political space is defined by operations that orient it, situate it, and abet or impede its functioning in a polyvalence of conflictual programs or contractual proximities and agreements. Assuming that Bucket represents some new *force* of the law as opposed to the law as a repository of inherited knowledge, then this force "marks" the country in the same way as do other new constructive energies which are addressed simultaneously in Dickens's novel, as an informational "grid:"

> Railroads shall soon traverse all this country, and with a rattle and a glare the engine and train shall shoot like a meteor over the wide night-landscape, turning the moon paler; but, as yet, such things are non-existent in these parts, though not wholly unexpected. Preparations are afoot, measurements are made, ground is staked out. Bridges are begun and their not yet united piers desolately look at one another over roads and stream, like brick and mortar couples with an obstacle to their union. . . .                                 (*BH* 55, 801)

If this ubiquitous force of the law is indeed, as Jo the Crossing-Sweeper alleges, "in all manner of places all at wunst"(*BH* 46, 690), it is perhaps too easy to assume, along with so many critics, including the writer of this essay, that an omniscient detection and surveillance which leaves no corner unexposed, is law's lifeblood.[23] For Bucket *apparently* has no real objective existence separable from the social incarnations of power. His curious polycentrism is surely a crucial feature of the burgeoning state bureaucracy which, insinuating itself within certain institutions, works to prevent the formation of class unity. Although an "opening" in a system of written inscription that has over-saturated people and places in *Bleak House* with signification has been achieved as a consequence of Bucket's "social circulation," any genuine systemic reform would appear to be limited. For, from one perspective, the state bureaucracy is simply allowed to disguise itself as yet another (comparably) benign "guardian" holding the future in trust. Inspector Bucket, in this view, is not really so dissimilar from Jaggers, as he freely authorizes different associations, not with the desire to maintain a shaky concept of freedom, but nonetheless enforcing arbitrary a-filiations in which he acts for the *state's patriarchal interests*. Bucket would be merely an instance of Althusser's *I*nstitutional *S*tate *A*pparatus, interpellating the socially non-purposive individual.[24]

Yet, Dickens is surely more subtle, as he suggests, to the contrary, that such a patriarchal guardian is merely another *formalism* in *Bleak House*.

For, at the moment when Bucket departs from the deceased Tulkinghorn's chambers, watched over by the embossed Allegory on the ceiling, the law, now as a force, has been dislodged from its customary socio-political position to become, at least potentially, a *transformative* power. Although Bucket is a police inspector, his "moving along" of Jo the Crossing-Sweeper, is ultimately purposive, for he subtly directs the urchin to be treated by Dr. Allan Woodcourt, Esther Summerson's suitor, who thereby becomes a public health officer rather than a family physician. The law apprehends anti-social behavior, but also comprehends communicative diseases which threaten the commonwealth, and for which individual responsibility is waived. Although the force of the law is derived from the people, with which it must stay in touch for re-validation, there is no rigid line separating the abstraction from its particularity as an ultimately derivative force: "Time and place cannot bind Mr Bucket. Like man in the abstract, he is here today and gone tomorrow—but, very unlike man indeed, he is here again the next day" (*BH* 53, 769) . Even though lacking a privileged or even a socially identifiable origin, Bucket is enmeshed in the people, especially in his perambulations in *Bleak House*, where he "pervades a vast number of houses and strolls about an infinity of streets"(*BH* 53, 768). Yet, Bucket's complex ontology is such that, at least visually, he seems detachable from any a priori purposiveness; when walking in a straight line, he often suddenly "wheels off, sharply at the very last moment"(*BH* 22, 363). His own reciprocating gaze similarly appears to participate in two visual planes simultaneously: "he takes in everybody's look at him, all at once, *individually and collectively*, in a manner that stamps him a remarkable man"(*BH* 49, 728, italics added).

This *division* in Inspector Bucket's posture, personality, and aspect toward a variety of constituents is the most characteristic feature of the law's presence: it is the individual perceiving himself from a collective perspective, the perspective of the Other. Bucket is both an abstraction, potentially transparent (nowhere more so than when he looks across London from on high), but also immanent, of the people, both in his social origins and tastes. Moreover, there is in his conduct none of the tension between the transcendent, impersonal rule of law founded on innate human rights (or positioned like that of Dickens's omniscient narrator) and the spontaneous, autonomous self-organization of a community that makes its law through the sovereign will of the people (like Esther Summerson's quasi-vocal diary). Furthermore, this force of the law relies neither on political virtues residual in the ethos of small, relatively homogenous communities with which he has contact, nor really on state coercion (his "bull's eye" does not coerce but only illuminates), but rather on the appeal of a better argument. Bucket's socially transformative solution does what other institutions and practices—foggy Chancery, gloomy and chill provisional guardians, family lawyers, social and religious missionaries—can never achieve: discursive "resolution" in a society whose map is characterized by autonomous pockets of self-interest.

In other words, the substantive legal equality that the history of British jurisprudence attempts to place at the heart of any legitimacy claims of the law, can be satisfactorily explained neither by any *semantic properties* ties inherent in the law nor to the *historical development of general laws*. The evolving form of universal normative propositions has nothing to say about their validity. Rather, the claim that a norm lies equally in the interest of everyone implies a sense of rational acceptability. But this is clarified—and the process of progressive clarification will become crucial to the nineteenth-century mystery novel or novel of detection—only under *pragmatic* conditions set by rational, competing discourses. Suddenly, all that really matters is the compelling force of the better argument based upon relevant information which encompasses the largest quantity of previously dispersed circumstances. The "playing field" of competing discourses allows the force of the law to be metaphorically imagined as a *contest* among alternative discourses: hence the quickened pace and temporal urgency which pervades the penultimate chapters of *Bleak House*, *Great Expectations*, and *Our Mutual Friend*, novels which begin with scenes saturated by too much, rather than too little, time. The internal connection between consensual, popular sovereignty and individual autonomy lies in the normative content of *exercizing* political autonomy, which is entirely independent of the grammatical form or the historical legacy of the law, to deploy a redundant pun in keeping with the spirit of Dickens's own.

In *Our Mutual Friend*, Eugene Wrayburn, having had his precedent privileging profession chosen *for* him by a patriarch desirous of a family lawyer, struggles throughout Dickens's narrative to (doubly) avoid a life spent tracing the precedent. But, in a paradox like that of the *force* of the law itself, he can achieve this only by conceiving of his own life as having a precedent in the life of another. As it so happens, this is precisely the subject of Eugene Wrayburn's first legal case. John Harmon has similarly chosen to escape from a betrothal to the spoiled Bella Wilfer, willed by his own father's last will and testament in the same way as was Wrayburn's future profession, by feigning his violent death in the Thames. Figuratively reborn under the assumed name of John Rokesmith, he is thereby able to alter the confinement of patriarchal precedent not by absolutely denying it—which makes for bad filial as well as legal judgments—but by re-positioning himself "outside" his patronymic. He achieves this by anonymously changing his once and future fiancee's selfish behavior by constituting himself as an "imaginary," the impoverished secretary to her father; in his fiancee's words, "you repress yourself, and force yourself to act a passive part" (*OMF* III, ix, 521). Assuming that, as Euguene Wrayburn's originary "legal subject" as well as the ultimate model for the attorney's own adaptive resistance, Harmon-Rokesmith's hyphenated identity is significant, it would surely represent the simultaneous obedience to precedent and an attempt to force social change by projecting itself beyond historically antecedent determinations.

When one of the waterside characters of *Our Mutual Friend* who gains his livelihood by harvesting bodies and their personal effects from the Thames (historically suspected of subsidizing the yield during times of scarcity) appears at Wrayburn's chambers to file an affidavit against a former business associate, the lawyer at last has a precedent upon which to hammer away. But, as is often the case in Dickens, the precedent assumes the form of the recovered, but incompletely identified body of death, in this instance, the man who had been Harmon's surrogate. As in *Bleak House*, the lawyer's precedent is irrecoverable, save as spawned copies of irrelevant reproductions at police stations. As Wrayburn desultorily presses his nefarious client's case, he discovers that his legally adversarial family, despite illiteracy, poverty and the low status of their literal undertaking, nonetheless wish to recuperate the "good name" of the father, Gaffer Hexam. Incredibly, the subaltern classes so often caught up in the law accept the myth of the noble patronymic, the sacred precedent, even when there is nothing save death itself attached to it.

Ultimately, Lizzie Hexam moves from an existence in the family of the "accused," to an object of Wrayburn's sympathy, to a student taught by a lawyer, and finally to the lawyer's spiritual life—as a wife. And like his own legal precedent, John Harmon, the law, symbolized in Eugene Wrayburn, must be dislodged from its customary, somnolent chambers. With his life's work (the law) patriarchally pre-determined, Wrayburn imagines himself, like those "engaged orphans" of *The Mystery of Edwin Drood*, Edwin and Rosa Bud, as an "embodied conundrum" forced "to find out what I *meant*"(*OMF* II, vi, 286, italics added). The law's characteristic homage to antecedent authority is reproduced as chronic boredom, that "loading of time" which has been addressed critically by Walter Benjamin. [25] Wrayburn's is the life of postponed engagements and appointments. In discussing money owed to the upholsterers of their shared law chambers, the dialogue of Lightwood and

Wrayburn evokes the spectre of some fulness of *intention* that nonetheless can never mean:

> "I mean to pay him, Eugene, for my part," said Mortimer, in a slightly injured tone.
>
> "Ah! I mean to pay him, too," retorted Eugene. "But then I mean so much that I—that I don't mean."
>
> " Don't mean?"
>
> "So much that I only mean and shall always only mean and nothing more, my dear Mortimer. It's the same thing."          (*OMF* II, vi, 283)

Wrayburn's counterproductive life of vague incapacity resembles that of the law, insofar as *expression* gives way to the communication of *expressivity* in its stead. Akin to allegory insofar as it calls out for translation, an expressiveness that is never resolved into the particularity of a specific expression "says" not *what* it means, but only *that* it means—remarkably like the finger of Allegory on Tulkinghorn's ceiling or the clerk, Wemmick's open and shut (but often silent) "post-office mouth" in *Great Expectations*. This might be one representation of "pure intentionality," with its evacuation of determinate meaning. Eugene Wrayburn distances himself from any antecedent purposiveness that might lend itself to articulate expression as an act of subjective consciousness when questioned about his "designs" on Lizzie Hexam by his law partner: "My dear fellow, I don't design anything. I have no design whatever. I am incapable of design. If I conceived a design, I should speedily abandon it, exhausted by the operation" (*OMF* II, vi, 294). Having been vocationally abandoned (an orphan of over-determination) by his father, Wrayburn-as-the-law is metaphorically sterile, unable to *conceive*!

This errant intransitivity, unable to transcend its own indolent physicality, is precisely what comes to characterize the operations of the law in *Our Mutual Friend*. Speaking in indeterminate sentences, pauses, and ellipses of incompletely articulated speech or—as in Wemmick's "get portable property," in aphorisms which have dictatorial effect only in repeated iteration—the utterances of the law are remarkably resistant to shared communication. This status of the law is nowhere better illustrated than during Wrayburn's slow recovery (alive, but barely) from the depths of the Thames whose superficial margins have heretofore marked the limits of his idyllic gentleman's life. As a consequence of a vicious beating about the head, he entirely loses the power of continuous, coherent speech which might communicate meaning. Unable to be understood, he exists, like allegory, as an incompletely shared *expressivity*, and thereby suddenly entirely synchronous with what he has always ontologically, *been*. He is the law, bound by precedent, yet lost in the *maze* of his *praxis*, no less than the assorted barristers and solicitors, similarly exhausted, who exhaust the proceeds of *Jarndyce and Jarndyce* in *Bleak House*, desirous of a foundational self-consciousness :

> "If you can give me anything to keep me here for only a few minutes—"
> "To keep you here, Eugene?"
> "To prevent my wandering away I don't know where—for I shall begin to be sensible that I have just come back, and that I shall lose myself again—do so, dear boy!"                                             (*OMF* IV, x, 737)

Eugene Wrayburn can paradoxically become "free" of the law only when he comes to be completely identified with *both* its ideological and human adversarial subjects, equally vulnerable to "drift." This progressive identification with the wandering orphan-figure ultimately enables Eugene Wrayburn's marriage to Lizzie Hexam, so symbolic of the ease by which the law, like Wrayburn's own observation of the "legal mind," comes to resemble "the dyer's hand, assimilating itself to what it works in,—or would work in, if anybody would give it anything to do"(*OMF* III, x, 541). Wrayburn's life, like the law itself as narrated by Dickens, punishes only through some seemingly arbitrary ambiguity, dissolving social and ideological categories, and, like the evanescent Inspector Bucket, often intangible in its brutal formlessness. Apparently, the law is not at all some semantic reservoir modelled upon human consciousness, but rather its allegorical blindness (like that of Wrayburn, seeing only stars after his beating), forever drifting beyond the limits of any legal ground. Traditional representations of legality, as we have seen in brief vignettes of British legal history, rest upon some identification of the law with its own "self-given-ness." Miming practical reason, justice would be imagined to be a consequence of some representational continuity or correspondence between the law-making powers of some sovereign will and the performative powers which command *in accordance with* the law.

In Dickens's late novels, however, as if in a preemptive response to Dicey's labored attempt to locate what is only a fictional continuity, the law is seen to arise *from the point* where such a progression from legislation to execution is inevitably interrupted or otherwise fails. Guilt is no longer a question of assigning one punishment among myriad possibilities. Instead, legality derives its extraordinary power from the formlessness and ambiguity of an *indistinction*, its judgments illegible, unreasonable, or the function of some amnesia. Guilt suddenly appears as the consequence of the very exhaustion of the legal order itself, its incapacity to extricate itself from some universal culpability to which it is "wed." By the conclusion of *Our Mutual Friend*, this obscured distinction between the sovereign will and the performative force of the law is suggested by the existence of an inextricably shared narrative register. Mortimer Lightwood, Wrayburn's equally errant law partner, reveals himself as not merely the participant in a "legal case," but the quasi-omniscient narrator of Dickens's novel, *Our Mutual Friend*, which is inseparable from his presence. His comments have *always-already* been internalized within the master-narrative; grammatically his existence is a citation *within* an everyday exchange, for the entire "story" is part of his dinner conversation at the table of the duplicitous Veneerings. The narrative of the law is inseparable from ordinary language in which and by which it is reproduced. In deploying the convention of "framing narratives," Dickens has liberated normally institutionalized legal narratives into what in Bakhtin's last work is defined as some *answerability*—"the un-indifferent participation [of assorted parties] in a once occurrent act"(39). All actors are free to believe or to "drop out" of dialogic participation, for the force of the law is now its ability to compel belief among potential addressees, agents, and authorizing institutions. In this respect the determination of legitimacy would really be no different from other (normative) narrative claims insofar as it must engage the un-coerced consent of participants in an evolving *explanatory process* that appears to its participants as *judgment*.

With his "discourse principle," Jurgen Habermas has recently reminded, even if Pip's penultimate renunciation of a legally-mandated "expectation" did not, that legally-granted liberties entitle one to recuse himself from communicative action, thereby denying illocutionary obligations. Legitimate law is compatible only with those modes of legal coercion that do not destroy the rational motives for obeying the law. In spite of its coercive character the law must not compel its addressees, but must offer them an option, in each case, of abrogating the exercise of their communicative freedom and *not* taking a position on the legitimacy claim of the law, just as do the discursive addressees at the Veneerings' tables. They must remain, without being reduced to the moral self-legislation of *individual* persons, entirely free to surrender the performative attitude toward law (in a particular case) in favor of the objectifying attitude of an actor who decides on the basis of utility calculations (152–57). [26]

This new definition of *legitimacy*—the self-conscious, consensual acknowledgement of the parties to a law that *only* they can create law and only in so authorizing it, remain bound to it—is nowhere better symbolized than in the peculiar concluding pages of *Great Expectations*. From the perspective of Pip, as one "caught up" in the law (quite literally, given Jaggers's gesture of holding Pip's diminutive head between his hands on the stairs of Satis House), the concluding chapters reverse the trajectory of the novel's legal narratives. For it is only upon Magwitch's death, that the idea of legitimacy (with all of its peripheral implications) is seen to arise at the point of some exhaustion of the law, a vanished potential for self-validation. Throughout the novel, Magwitch continues to trust the law to distribute his money to Pip, even as the law holds the convict in a trust (never to return to England). By law, the return of a transported felon was punishable by loss of freedom as well as property through a court-mandated forfeiture of assets. Informers, in this case Magwitch's former partner in crime, could claim a share of the accumulated assets as a reward. In *Great Expectations*, the informer dies, rendering any claim, moot.

In a remarkable gesture, however, the Pip who would normally have expected to come into his full "expectations" upon his benefactor's death, is freed on a "technicality" which leaves the larger part of Magwitch's Australian assets in place, in harmony with Pip's newly found spirit of material renunciation which assumes the form of an "opting out": "I was not related to the outlaw, or connected with him by any recognizable tie; he had put his hand to no writing or settlement in my favour before his apprehension and to do so now would be idle. I had no claim . . . " (*GE* 55, 458) . The law "holds" Magwitch's life earnings as a repository of *intentionality*, against which are lodged a plethora of claims: those of the state (forfeiture); Compeyson (the informer's reward); Jaggers (as a legal retainer); perhaps Estella (his sole surviving biological heir); and of course Pip (his entirely self-designated heir apparent).

Yet, in a remarkable reversal in a novel which recovers extremely remote familial "connections," Pip voluntarily renounces an extra-familial relationship which had been legally-mandated through Magwitch's agent, Jaggers, but which is ultimately as provisional (i.e., from Provis) as other ties. Although fully cognizant of the *intention* of Pip's fictive father (and entirely in keeping with precedent, Magwitch's antecedent behavior), there is nonetheless no legal claim binding Pip to his benefactor once Pip has so affirmed its absence. Apparently, money (capital investment in Pip's future) no more establishes real legitimacy than does sperm (biological investment in a son's future) absent the consensual recognition and acknowledgment of all the parties.

Magwitch's mysterious largesse is thereby preserved as a spontaneous "gift" rather than the contractual obligation to one whose file and food might have freed him from being "caught up" in the law. The law may "make" gentlemen, but these relationships can be unmade when one of the parties opts out in an act which makes him a co-author of the arrangement. Upon Magwitch's death, there will ironically be a discontinuance of the "expectations" over which the law might have exacted some punitive "share;" as in *Bleak House*'s Chancery proceedings, the state exacts an enormous commission for *interpreting intentionality* and recuperating obscure antecedents, thus becoming a fully equivalent party not a mere agent of legitimation. Dickens's strategy of subverting an idea of legitimacy based upon precedent, an idea so crucial to the history of British jurisprudence, is filled with irony.

For paradoxically, the law (an anonymous, unsigned *intention* which assumes the periodicity of a social *practice*) as interpreted by Pip restores him at last to a precedent which turns out to be—the absence of precedence, metaphorically and psychologically represented as *il-legitimacy*. Without extant biological antecedents in the opening graveyard scene, the youth is ultimately severed from his equally fictive "ancestor," Magwitch, by a similar highly literal interpretation of inscription or its absence. His "ends" are existentially indistinguishable from his orphaned "beginnings:" discontinuous. Only with some doubling of illegitimacy (the confrontation with a recovered absence) will enable Pip to derive a new, partially self-authorized *legitimacy*: the somewhat euphemistically addressed "self-made" man who, as Pip announces, "became a third in the Firm"(*GE* 58, 489) of Clarriker and Company, a counting house. In noting that "we had a good name, and worked for our profits, and did very well"(*GE* 58, 489), a more mature Pip acknowledges that one's figurative legitimacy, his good name, is a plurality, a "we" derivative of one's interactive efforts rather than a "given" of history known as an expectation.

But this recognition can occur only after the characteristic exhaustion of the law that appears a recurrent vulnerability in *Bleak House*, *Great Expectations*, and *Our Mutual Friend*. In each, a judicial system imagined to be dependent for its judgments upon recovering a foregrounding precedent, is seen to be without foundation in tandem with its most frequently interpellated subject, the orphaned. This exhaustion is often experienced as either a self-forgetfulness, like that of the barristers groping their way through a maze of copies in Chancery proceedings, or alternatively, as some radical deficiency of full presence, signalled by a failure of speech. Pip's recurrent losses of (verbally expressed) consciousness after the return of Magwitch; the blood rather (rather than speech) which gushes forth from Richard Carstone's mouth as he awaits legal judgment; and the Eugene Wrayburn restored to his originary "life," speechlessly adrift first in the Thames, and then, dependent upon the dialogic translation of his asyntagmatic utterance by Lizzie Hexam, would all be instances of vocational, vocal, and legal drift. If a chronically errant inscriptive order which spawns unauthorized counterfeits in *Bleak House* would render the life of the law as some undisciplined *excess* which forever reopens (by supplementing) what the Rogue Riderhood of *Our Mutual Friend* falsely believed to be the legally "binding powers of pen and ink and paper"(*OMF* I, xii, 149), then Wemmick's empty "post-office mouth" of *Great Expectations* reveals any independent "voice" of the law, to be but an empty envelope, an entirely adequate synecdoche of hollow intention.[27]

Hence, law conceived of as either a descendant body of inscripted statutes informed by antecedence (the common law tradition) or law conceived of as some arbitrary voice in the breast of the judge or his agents (equity) share a similar weakness—which justifies as much as anything else, their consolidation in the mid-1850s. Neither tradition is informed *by* or derived *from* the consensual acknowledgment of those under its judgments. Jaggers's office whose greasy walls are smudged and stained with the ink of legal cursitors and the near catatonic clerk, Wemmick, who speaks only in repeated aphorisms, are initially, the two sides of the law in *Great Expectations*; similarly, Cursitor Street which harbors Nemo (and his descent toward greasy blackness) and the vocally closed "oyster," Tulkinghorn, are the equivalent operations of the law in *Bleak House*. This shared resistance to the "voice" of the other, be it plaintiff or defendant, is nowhere better illustrated than in the continuous contempt citations which descend upon the poor Gridley of Bleak House who desires nothing, save to speak for himself in everyday language, that is, without the legal representation that would "squeeze" it *à la* Kenge & Carboy's letters to Esther Summerson.

In moving from either the occupational, social, or thematic "position" of the attorney to that of the detective, Bucket, Jaggers, and Eugene Wrayburn all traverse the existential attitudes schematized below:

| ATTORNEY | DETECTIVE |
|---|---|
| 1. Obedient to precedent | 1. Precedent as one component among many |
| 2. Faithful to representation | 2. Privileges non-representational |
| 3. Physically static | 3. Physically ambulatory |
| 4. Dependent upon familial systems or models | 4. Embraces *ad hoc* relationships |
| 5. Bound to inscription | 5. Orally/Aurally sensitive |

| | |
|---|---|
| 6. Uses passive voice to enforce detachment | 6. Active voice engages connections |
| 7. "Maze" of documents and procedures | 7. "Maze" of potentially related people |

In processing this transformation of narrative interests, each of Dickens's texts comes to produce its own truth through the realization (as opposed to the recovery) of a series of predictions; the repetition of crucial scenes; and the redoubling of narrative events which collectively allow the narrative to *operate* a constant confirmation of its own premises. Truth is a progressive unfolding of potential relationships rather than an historical recovery, surely one consequence of the way in which referentiality is suddenly seen to *pass through* experience.[28] Hence, the conversion of the attorney-figure to the detective energizes Dickens's text in a variety of ways.

More a *career* than a *calling*, the detective must incorporate a range of disparate learning from apparently unrelated branches of knowledge—which is perhaps why Watson, like Mortimer Lightwood of Wrayburn, is always puzzled by Holmes's not so "elementary" knowledge in Arthur Conan Doyle's work. Empirical observation, social "contacts," and affective memory are all equally counted as resources for a Jaggers (in the novel's penultimate pages) or Inspector Bucket. There is a certain self-indulgent, even joyful attitude which comes to possess the lawyer-turned-detective, in marked contrast to the earlier spatial and discursive defensiveness in their attitudes and activities. The "meaningful relationships" which these figures pursue and assemble, insofar as they come to resemble a "game," like Bucket's aforementioned moves on a "board" (*BH* 54, 782) are at least partially provisional. The law operates to determine "winners" and "losers," but there is always the suggestion that a different narrative strategy could generate different results.

As ever larger numbers of people are touched by criminality in one way or another in Dickens's later novels, there emerges a circularity, not unlike that which characterizes the arguments which, as we have seen, have historically, accompanied debate regarding the origins of the so-called legitimacy of the British legal system. This circularity might assume the following rhetorical assertion: "there are no criminals, because it is after all only an intellectual game, because there are no criminals." It would appear that anyone can be procedurally "related" irrespective of their biological, historical, or social "related-ness." The Bucket who temporarily harbors Hortense for a larger strategic purpose in *Bleak House* might suggest that the law is merely *instrumental*, insofar as it forms alliances with its putative antagonists. It would seem as if we really have not gained much in this transformation of "illegiti-macy" from a biological notion of discontinuity to some *assignment* (post facto) of guilt by virtue of being placed in a narrative family by state officers: in both instances, "illegitimacy" is socially constructed as a response to the realization that British law endows it too with only a provisional legitimacy, absent some a priori notion of collective consent.

But we must take care—Dickens's care—lest we reduce *justice* (fairness of the outcome) to merely *procedural justice* (fairness). Both kinds of justice embody certain values: of the outcome on the one hand, and of the processes and procedural guarantees by which the outcome is achieved on the other. And yet, Dickens, as does John Rawls and Stuart Hampshire, intimates that the justice of the procedure always depends upon the justice of its likely outcome.[29] Although fair procedures are crucial to justice—such as say, giving all parties equal access to judicial institutions—the procedure of a trial would not be just unless it was so intelligently drawn up as to give the correct decision much of the time. If a procedure failed to result in a fair outcome, it would not be a procedure for justice, but for something else. Although procedurally unorthodox to put it mildly, Inspector Bucket subsidizes what, for Frank Kermode novel readers always do anyway, notably "to read for the ending."[30] Previously unrelated social activities and discourses are made to appear so unified as to compel a "readerly" notion of belief which simulta-neously subverts the procedural oversaturation of *Bleak House,* which throughout, is made to appear as part and parcel of the general overdetermina-tion of precedent.

Initially, Dickens's novels commence as *narratives of judgment*: one either awaits judgment as does the Miss Flite of *Bleak House,* faithfully attendant upon the interminable *Jarndyce and Jarndyce,* awaiting the opening of the "seals" only to be disappointed in the exhaustion of the law in a material self-referentiality or, like Eugene Wrayburn, laconically fulfils the judgments (as expectations) of another. Similarly, those who would put their faith in *procedural justice* discover that its narrative distributions, like those of Jag-gers with Molly's baby or Magwitch's money, often reproduce the same injustices that ostensibly dictated the initial intervention of the law. But *Bleak House, Great Expectations,* and *Our Mutual Friend* all end, as one suspects the late nineteenth-century discourse of the law did, as *narratives of explana-tion.* The readers of the novel are surprised, as are many parties to it, by constructed patterns which explain disparate acts and facts which the law as a discipline can never achieve. These narratives, like the fiction of which they are an inseparable part, must ultimately compel our belief rather than distributing judgments, with all of the ethical implications, so disturbing to legal commentators who imagine a "vacated" judgmental role as some missing antecedent in the rise of "illegitimacy."[31]

Just perhaps, this very *vacancy* is already contained *within* Dickens's account of the operations of the law, thereby limiting a *foreseeable* extraterritoriality. For like Bucket, the law can acquire knowledge only by straying from some historically prescribed trajectory, "in some undefinable manner to lurk and lounge" even while he "pretends to have a fixed purpose in his mind of going straight ahead"(*BH* 22, 363–64). Like the law in whose behalf he acts and the criminal whom he would apprehend, the inspector as well as most of Dickens's other agents of the law, are loiterers. And like other expressions of loitering—parentheses, footnotes, appendices—these digressions mark certain discursive material as, albeit not quite illegitimate,[32] secondary, insofar as they are both not entirely relevant, yet admissible. This characteristic digression is simultaneously a critique of an earlier legal model as well as the manifestation of another law operating *within* that earlier tradition and tarrying (loitering?) there: notably, that the tolerance extended to the digressions of the agents of the law as well as its prey has its ground in the law's self-conscious recognition of its lack of recuperable legitimacy. The law has no dry earth to stand upon, even as it "moves on" and, in the case of Jo the Crossing-Sweeper, moves other waifs on.

Jaggers's representations of the law's efficiency, had made the law operationally analogous to a fishing net, perhaps even a "drift net," to be faithful to the riverine imagery and activity of *Our Mutual Friend* and its two attorneys, professionally and occasionally physically, adrift. Like Bucket's similarly structured board game whose every "move" he presumes to know, there nonetheless remain gaps and seams in the law's inclusiveness, so dissimilar from the arboreal model with its convoluted descendant legal "branches" which informs the procedures and geography of Chancery and its environs in the first half of *Bleak House*. Through these openings, lies both the possibility of escape (for the criminal classes) and of "opting out" for those who resist either the law's pre-sumptions or any independently authorized hegemony. The law's efficiency *is* its (strategic) deficiency.

No wonder, then, that the law presents those caught up in it in Dickens's work with such a unique experience: that of exposure to a Being in force without significance. Jean-Luc Nancy has identified the effect of this exposure as analogous to that of *abandonment*, but a curious abandonment which remains *inside* the force of the law:

The destitution of abandoned Being is measured by the limitless severity of the law to which it finds itself exposed. Abandonment does not constitute a sub-poena to present oneself before this or that court of law. It is a compulsion to appear absolutely under the law, under the law as such and in its totality. In the same way—it is the same thing—to be *banished* amounts not to coming under a provision of the law but rather coming under the entirety of the law. Turned over to the absolute of the law abandoned one is abandoned *completely outside its jurisdiction* [ital. added].                              (149–50)

To be abandoned *to* the law is therefore in some sense, to be abandoned to a ban, an exclusion. The law is simultaneously open and closed, insofar as it enables the exclusions of its prey from its own injunctions, considered as a continuity. If the law itself is abandoned—in the sense of lacking an historically foundational moment and persisting in an absence of signify-ing—there is some in which the law is the antecedent abandoned, conspiring in the unique exceptionalism which clings to the accused in Dickens.

These openings in the legal net, the absent antecedent displaced now onto the body of the law and marking the parties to its procedures, enable the transformation of Dickens's otherwise determining or determined legal narra-tives into narratives of discovery by those otherwise trapped in it. Among those so caught up is the Molly of *Great Expectations*, whose body is that text, the woven "tex-tile" of the simultaneously open and closed nature of the law and of so many cases brought before it: "She brought the other hand from behind her, and held the two out side by side. The last wrist was much disfigured, deeply scarred and scarred *across and across*"(*GE* 26, 236, italics added). As the double "subject" of the law, now on display, Molly is the ever-amended legal text, compelling diverse beliefs, even as she is simultane-ously free and not free—to "move on."

# NOTES

Citations from the work of Charles Dickens are designated by abbreviations followed by chapter and page number which refer to the following editions:
    *BH Bleak House*—Edited by Norman Page with an introduction by J.
    Hillis Miller. Harmondsworth: Penguin, 1987.
    *GE Great Expectations*. Edited by Angus Calder. Harmondsworth: Penguin, 1965.
    *OMF Our Mutual Friend*. With an introduction by E. Salter Davies. Oxford: Oxford
    UP, 1967.

1. The competition among custodial guardians for a publicly recognized jurisdictional responsibility would suggest that in effect, these guardians were "producing" the very image of the discontinuous, orphaned outcast that they were supposedly charged with "taking in." See Sir Leon Radzinowicz and Roger Hood, *The Emergence of Penal policy in Victorian and Edwardian England* (Oxford: Clarendon, 1990), 28–42. This paradox may be acknowledged in Dickens's novels by the way in which the discontinuous orphan is often "propelled," given a perpetual motion, by legal institutions and and their representatives either "at rest" or overly domesticated.

2. It is perhaps noteworthy that violations of laws of nature ("Morall Law") alone, among all potential transgressions, are potentially in conflict, in Hobbes's scheme, with Divine Law. This doctrinal "moment" of separation comes to define the Hobbesian state as a kind of artificial Providence. In the same way that the state of nature neutralizes sin by naturalizing it, Leviathan's absolute power neutralizes grace by making it artificial: the natural individual is the soul of the artificial individual that is the body politic. The absolute sovereignty of the body politic which is nonetheless founded on and deduced from the state of nature in Hobbes's thought is well articulated in Chapter 3 of Pierre Manent, *Histoire intellectuelle du liberalisme: Dix leçons* (Paris: Calmann-Levy, 1987).

3. The seamless unity of Church with civil society in Hooker in part rests upon a belief that the original power to make church law resides in the "whole body" of that very Church for which they are made. Hence, in the interpretation of the law there can be no disunity, because all conflicts would return to the condition of being the "property of" that alone which has the power of making law—notably, the commonwealth. There would be no question of the "force" of the law, for there is really no distinction between *giving* and *interpreting* the law in Hooker's work: judgment is a reflection of consensual interpretation.

4. Taylor attributes this "split" between an internalized "voice" of western liberalism, exempt from institutional coercion and/or collusion, and some outer loyalty, to Herder's *Ideen.* What is remarkable about Blackstone's somewhat earlier reflections on a similar theme, is the way in which an arbitrary "voice," perhaps like Wordsworth's "still, small voice of humanity," is imagined as a potential "balance" (the equalizations of equity?) to the dependence upon precedent which is imagined to be inherently inequitable in its results. The "voice" of the judge, no matter how arbitrary, is for Blackstone at least potentially a principle of equality: justice would have a discursive component.

5. Ibid. A bit later in the same section, Blackstone reveals his awareness of this anomaly: the peculiar capacity of the law to compel obedience depends upon the fact that it really does not need to, since it is inseparable from the "custom" of the people. It is not a field of knowledge (which would be dependent upon the discovery of a Beginning, a moment when the law separated itself from other discourses) so much as it, in Blackstone's rhetoric, is a re-cognition, an "acknowledgment." See pp. 79–82 for this distinction.

6. Jacques Attali, *Bruits: Essai sur l'economie de la musique* (Paris : Presses Universitaires dè France, 1974), would analyze this change as that which often occurs with the historical shift from *representation* to *reproduction* (in this specific

instance, of music). The shift from a quasi-familial agent (like say, a minstrel) playing what his lord commanded him to play (and hence a representation of social conflict) historically yielded to the music of one who sells his labor to clients rich enough to pay, but no longer rich enough to monopolize his skills, might also apply to the status (and ultimately perhaps, the interests) of the family lawyer in Britain during the 1840s. Tulkinghorn's discovery in *Bleak House* can never have an "added value" unless he exacts his own price, like that achieved by an evolving concept of copyright law, for maintaining control over its reproduction as gossip. In Anthony Trollope's *Doctor Thorne* (1858) a similar shift from a model of familial "representation" to "reproduction" (as the compounder of his own prescriptions) is seen in the unsteady career of a country medical practitioner.

7. The frequency of catachresis, the slippage of a "given" name into ever mutating appellations or nicknames, would suggest that one's "good name" is no longer to be easily recovered historically, but rather by comprehending a lateral "field" as opposed to a descendant "line." Metonymy would privilege this kind of lateral substitution, as opposed to metaphor, which would attempt a recovery of some presumably primary, informing "ground." Proper names in Dickens's novels—"Hav-i-sham," Jaggers (the "Jaggah" or guardian of private property in the India of the Raj), "Ded-lock" (he of the enclosed secrets), even "Buck-et" (who takes everything in)—all seem as proper/improper denominations of what the characters *do*, as if character were defined by contextual "role" rather than historical lineage.

8. Mieke Bal, "De-Disciplining the Eye," *Critical Inquiry* 16 (spring, 1990), 506–32, argues that *metaphoric* readings such as those we literary critics favor, tend to erase the systemically disturbing or extraneous that do not "fit" some informed (and presumably transcendent) recuperative model of reading. If so, the shift from attorney to detective-figure in Dickens's narratives involves nothing less than a new way of reading, one which "makes room" for the arbitrary, systemically "orphaned," or otherwise non-informed. *Metonymy* tends to be ideologically more tolerant, because it is at least potentially more inclusive of that which is not syntagmatically (re)cognizable. For a specific application to Dickens's *oeuvre*, see my "Dickens and the Political Economy of the Eye," *Dickens Studies Annual* 24 (1996): 1–35.

9. Fish argues that, though the law can never "catch up" with its own justifications, in a pragmatic sense its efficient, functional machinery renders the identification of any philosophical "ground" largely irrelevant.

10. Because of the authority which accrued to such easy "textualization" of human wishes and acts, resistance to the power of the law is often represented in Dickens as a besieged "voice." A prime example might be Esther Summerson's diary (the closest writing comes to monologue), smuggled into the gaps in Dickens's own omniscient narrative as well as the legal proceedings of Chancery.

11. Although Sarah Austin maintained that her husband had long contemplated a "wider" work, Austin's *Lectures* were abridged into truncated versions in order to suit the demands of the fledgling discipline of legal education. Hence relationships between say, morality and utility, are absent in favor of the equation of the

law with normative concepts. The demands of the legal "text" here too, as in Dickens's narratives, comes to shape the discursive course which law in some larger sense, will assume in the nineteenth-century. See David Sugarman's analysis of this "black letter" tradition in "'A Hatred of Disorder:' Legal Science, Liberalism, and Imperialism" in Peter Fitzpatrick (ed), *Dangerous Supplements: Resistance and Renewal in Jurisprudence* (Durham: Duke UP, 1991), 34–67.

12. Intriguing here is Dicey's subtle critique of the so-called "evolutionary" bias which characterizes so much of the ideology of the law in nineteenth-century England. In place of the essentialism which required an idea of the law as "progressing" or evolving through ever higher degrees of individuation (by means of which the law is always accompanied by a continually enhanced social integration), Dicey would find the "origin" and the consequences in the same (extra-legal?) Act.

13. Fish may leave himself open to questioning when he argues that, since there is "no alternative to interpretive construction," the fact that critics and lawyers are always doing it "is neither here nor there." Such clearly smacks of an antinomianism: we wander in the desert conscious of our errors, but always thinking of it as truth. In confounding literary and legal interpretations, Fish may be losing sight of the ways in which unlike literary criticism, legal interpretation does often prescribe precisely *which* and *what* kinds of errors lead to reversals of judgments.

14. See Alfred R. Mele and Paisley Livingstone, "Intentions and Interpretations," *Modern Language Notes*, 107 (1992): 931–49, for a median position between those who would disavow all attempts to identify intention as a fallacy and those who would regard *meaning* as being entirely dependent upon identifying intention.

15. Bentham argues that there could not be a person (as an individual) without the simultaneous existence of society as a clear response to the Rousseau who described the relation between the first person (in nature) and society or language by positing that Other as a giant or a large abstraction.

16. Foucault's Bentham—who foregrounds the equation of the assignment of stereotypical classes to the penalties of the quotidian—surely neglects another Bentham for whom social classification was an instrument of individuation. Even in the Panopticon, changing groupings of prisoners—like Jaggers's in *Great Expectations*—makes all individuals appear as social reproductions of their ongoing relationships of resemblance to and difference from their companions. For an essay which attempts to illuminate this other, less familiar Bentham, see Frances Ferguson, "Canons, Poetics, and Social Value: Jeremy Bentham and How to Do Things with People," *Modern Language Notes* 110 (1995), 1148–64.

17. The case for such a relationship, as far as I know, was initially made by Alexander Welsh, *George Eliot and Blackmail* (Cambridge: Harvard UP, 1985).

18. Dickens's model wherein the law continues to reproduce its offspring both procedurally and in those "touched" by it even as its foundational authority remains transcendent bears an uncanny relationship with Jacques Derrida's, "Force of the Law: The 'Mystical Foundation of Authority,'" *Cardozo Law Review* 11, no. 5–6. (1990) 48ff. Whereas in Derrida, the law's forceful presence is guaranteed by its genealogical absence, Dickens's judicial narratives would include suggestions of voyeurism as common to both forms of patriarchal control. The discontinuous is subjected to the "gaze" or surveillance of a surrogate parent who cannot

resist returning to see what it has "made" (Magwitch's return or Miss Havisham's habit of bedecking Estella with jewels, both of which subject the subject
to a "look" which admires in the same gesture by which it controls). In Dickens's
model, the law does not merely "keep on coming" as a force, but returns as a
checking observer indistinguishable from any interpellative posture.

19. Peter Garrett, *The Victorian Multi-Plotted Novel: Studies in Dialogic Form* (New
Haven: Yale UP, 1980) has argued that in the nineteenth-century novel generally,
a "relatedness" is projected among the superficially "unrelated" in such a way
that a collective narrative gains hegemony over any narrative of private life.

20. White's model—in which a common text presents a different set of differences
to succeeding generations of interpreters—is inadequate to explain a unique features by which the law is, in its *applicable force*, often extended into entirely
different *domains*. A translation of Homer by Pope, Robert Fitzgerald, or Robert
Fagles presents a different set of differences depending upon a number of vari-
ables: enhanced knowledge of Greek culture; different agendas of their respective
audiences or publication format; or even a different reading of the Greek equivalent of the "wily" Odysseus. But the "drift" of legal narratives can reach beyond
the subject: a case which appears to hinge upon the question of say, equal access
before the law, can as in Roe vs. Wade, come to be applied to legal questions
regarding a so-called "right to privacy," as in subsequent decisions regarding
informed consent of parents. Additionally, by often embodying dissenting opinion, implicitly or explicitly, legal narratives can often mime the dialogic, even as
it pretends to judgment. In some sense this constitutes an anticipation of later
dissent or even reversals, which is seldom "contained" in translations.

21. Teubner's model here, as elsewhere in his work, imagines a completely decentered
society which nonetheless can communicate with itself through a concept of some
"life-world."

22. See Jurgen Habermas, *Between Facts and Norms: Contributions to a Discourse
Theory of Law and Democracy*, trans. William Rehg (Cambridge: MIT Press,
1996), especially 104–20, where the German philosopher elaborates the differences between morality and law as different discursive possibilities.

23. D.A. Miller, "Discipline in Different Voices: Bureaucracy, Police, Family, and
*Bleak House*." In *The Novel and the Police* (Berkeley: U of California P, 1988)
55–106 applies Foucault's paradigm of institutional control of the family to the
emergence of Bucket whose presence allows for the existence of a field outside
the dynamic of power and immune from its political effects. Similarly, in my
earlier "'In All Manner of Places All at Wunst:' Writing, Gossip, and the State
of Information in *Bleak House*," in *Gossip and Subversion in Nineteenth-century
British Fiction: Echo's Economies* (Basingstoke and New York: Macmillan, 1996)
156–236, the shift from a legal "case" to one of detection was imagined to be
incompatible with individual political or spatial autonomy. Both essays fail to
recognize the extent to which Bucket's actions endow so many characters with
a new kind of autonomy, as self-reflexive "clues" who have a share (and hence
a "voice") in a "life-world."

24. In separating the concept of the *ISA* from the Althusser *oeuvre*, many critics forget
that even in *Reading Capital*, the knowledge process is viewed as a process of

the production of "intellectual instruments." Any reading which would substitute "vision" (as would Bucket's remarkable inductive powers) would run the risk of falling under the category of a "religious myth." The operations of the law as imagined by Dickens surely produces such "instruments," but as clues to a mystery, they have a more unified relationship to a master narrative than any relationship to judicial institutions alone might produce. See Louis Althusser, *Reading Capital* (London: Verso, 1970).

25. In *Our Mutual Friend*, Eugene Wrayburn's boredom is overcome when he discovers that time, presumably an agent in the carriage of secrets, cannot be stored any more than the "meaning" of the law can be exclusively held in its institutional practices. A marvellous discussion of this issue is to be found in Walter Benjamin, *Gessamelte Schriften* , ed. Rolf Tiedemann and Herman Schweppenhauser (Frankfurt: Suhrkamp, 1972–85), 5: 162–64.

26. Habermas argues that the logic of discourse must never be too quickly identified with constitutional (or judicial) procedure. As soon as codes of law and power are set up, deliberation and decision-making assume the differentiated form of political opinion- and will-formation. Law imposes a certain form on conflict-regulating norms. The meaning of "ought" remains unspecified as long as the relevant problem and the aspect under which it can be solved are indeterminate. From this perspective, the transformation from legal narratives to those of detection which occurs late in Dickens's novels, introduces an element of indeterminacy (perhaps the indeterminacy of fictions?) which mimes the "mystery" resolved by a Bucket or Eugene Wrayburn, each of whom seems to escapes certain limits of the law.

27. Christopher Diffee, "Postponing Politics in Hawthorne's *Scarlet Letter,*" *Modern Language Notes* III (December, 1996) 835–71, addresses the similar way in which Hester Prynne, by her response to a community's law, evacuates its intention. Through her empty naming of Pearl's paternity ("I will not speak"), Hester's penance ironically preserves a relationship between law and transgression. The scarlet letter itself thereby becomes an allegory of the law, like those detached letters which Krook erases before continuing on to the next ones in *Bleak House*, forever drifting beyond any legal grounds. The law speaks only in fractures, disarticulated speech, which becomes the mark of guilt.

28. Marie-Christine Leps, *Apprehending the Criminal: The Production of Deviance in Nineteenth-Century Discourse* (Durham: Duke UP, 1993) sees this gesture as crucial to the production of social deviance in later novelists (i.e., Zola) the movement of referentiality *through* experience in such a way as to produce a near transparency is the subject of John T. Irwin's critique of Barbara Johnson's critique of Derrida's critique of Poe's "The Purloined Letter" in *The Mystery to a Solution: Poe, Borges, and the Analytical Detective Story* (Baltimore: Johns Hopkins UP, 1994), wherein a letter remains hidden because it is too open.

29. See especially Rawls's reply to Habermas in John Rawls, *Political Liberalism* (New York: Columbia UP, 1996) 420–33. See also Stuart Hampshire, *Innocence and Experience* (Cambridge, Mass: Harvard UP, 1989).

30. Assuming that Bucket's actions redirects the reader's attention to "endings" as opposed to patriarchal "beginnings" through the techniques elaborated in Frank

Kermode's *Sense of an Ending*, there nonetheless remains a crucial problematic. Though any narrative-field corresponds to a segment of space excerpted from a larger whole, the conception of the world as ultimately obedient to law would imply that it is bound in a relationship of single elementary components, yet open, unbounded, and contingent when considered as a totality. This "two-sided" nature of the law would imply that it can never be reduced to a narrative field. This problematic resistance to reduction, applied to a different narrative field, is the subject of the work of Meyer Schapiro, *Theory and Philosophy of Art: Style, Artist, and Society*, Selected Papers IV (New York: Braziller, 1994).

31. James Q. Wilson, *Moral Judgment* (New York: Basic Books, 1997), has argued that the increased use of "diminished capacity" as an accepted legal defense, has created an acute moral paralysis, that makes sound legal judgment impossible. In arguing for the return to some "original" spirit of the law (centered in *judgment* rather than *explanations* of say, abuse excuses), Wilson would ally himself with those sociologists and politicians who plead for a more authoritative (simultaneously privileging the father-figure as well as legal antecedent) legal environment.

32. Ross Chambers, *Loiterature* (Lincoln and London; U of Nebraska P, 1999), has argued that because the dividedness of attention is what really makes digression possible, the loiterly subject becomes a socially marginal figure to the extent that social or historical centrality is defined in terms of stability, permanence, and closure. In suggesting, by virtue of both the double-mindedness of its representatives and its resistance to resolution that the law is not a genuine discipline, Dickens in some sense is converting it to a narrative—one more among many. See especially chapter 3 of Chambers's book, "Loiterly Subjects or *Ça ne dessin pas*," 56–66.

# WORKS CITED

Althusser, Louis. *Reading Capital.* London: Verso, 1970.

Attali, Jacques. *Bruits: Essai sur l'economie de la musique.* Paris: Presses Universitaires de France, 1974.

Bakhtin, M.M. *Toward a Philosophy of the Act.* Trans. Vadim Liapunov. Ed. Vadim Liapunov and Michael Holquist. Austin : U of Texas P, 1993.

Bal, Mieke. "De-Disciplining the Eye." *Critical Inquiry* 16 (1990).

Benjamin, Walter. *Gessamelte Schriften.* Ed. Rolf Tiedemann and Herman Schweppenhauser. Frankfurt: Suhrkamp, 1972–1985.

Bentham, Jeremy. *A Fragment on Government.* Ed. J. H. Burns and H. L. A. Hart Cambridge: Cambridge UP, 1988.

Blackstone, Sir William. *Commentaries on the Laws of England.* Vols. I-III. Ed. William C. Jones. San Francisco: Bancroft-Whitney Co., 1915.

Brown, W. J. "The Jurisprudence of M. Duguit." *Law Quarterly Review.* Vol. 32 (1916).

Chambers, Ross. *Loiterature.* Lincoln: U. of Nebraska P., 1999.

Derrida, Jacques. "Force of the Law: the 'Mystical Foundation of Authority.'" *Cardozo Law Review* 11 (1990).

Dicey, A. V. *Introduction to the Law of the Constitution*, 7th edn. Ed. E.S. Wade. London: Sweet & Maxwell, 1957.

Diffee, Christopher. "Postponing Politics in *Hawthorne's Scarlett Letter.*" *Modern Language Notes* 111 (1996).

Dworkin, Ronald. *Law's Empire.* Cambridge: Harvard UP, 1986.

Dickens, Charles. *Bleak House.* Ed. Norman Page. Introd. J. Hillis Miller. Harmondsworth: Penguin, 1987.

———. *Great Expectations.* Ed. Angus Calder. Harmondsworth: Penguin, 1965.

———. *Our Mutual Friend.* Introd. E. Salter Davies. Oxford: Oxford UP, 1967.

Ferguson, Frances. "Canon, Poetics, and Social Value: Jeremy Bentham and How to Do Things with People." *Modern Language Notes* 110 (1995).

Fish, Stanley. *Doing What Comes Naturally: Change, Rhetoric, and the Practice of Theory in Literary and Legal Studies.* Durham: Duke UP, 1989.

Garrett, Peter. *The Victorian Multi-Plotted Novel: Studies in Dialogic Form.* New Haven: Yale UP, 1980.

Gordon, Jan B. " 'In All Manner of Places All at Wunst:' Writing, Gossip and the *State* of Information in *Bleak House.*" *Gossip and Subversion in Nineteenth Century British Fiction: Echo's Economies.* New York: Macmillan, 1996.

Habermas, Jurgen. *Between Facts and Norms: Contributions to/a Discourse Theory of Law and democracy.* Trans. William Rehg. Cambridge: MIT Press, 1996.

Hampshire, Stuart. *Innocence and Experience.* Cambridge: Harvard UP, 1989.

Harrison, Frederick. "The English School of Jurisprudence III." *Fortnightly Review*, Vol 21 (1879).

Hobbes, Thomas *Leviathan.* Ed. C. B. McPherson. Harmondsworth: Penguin, 1968.

Hooker, R. *Of the Laws of Ecclesiastical Policy.* Book VIII. Ed. P. G. Stanwood. Folger Library Edition. Cambridge: Harvard UP, 1981.

Jones, Gareth Stedman *Outcast London: A Study of the Relationship between Classes in Victorian England.* Harmondsworth: Penguin, 1971.

Leps, Marie-Christine. *Apprehending the criminal: The Production of Deviance in Nineteenth-Century Discourse.* Durham: Duke UP, 1993.

Manent, Pierre. *Histoire intellectuelle du liberalisme: Dix leçons.* Paris: Calmann-Levy, 1987.

Mele, Alfred and Livingstone, Paisely. "Intentions and Interpretations." *Modern Language Notes* 107 (1992).

Mill, John Stuart *A System of Logic Ratiocinative and Inductive* in *Collected Works.* Ed. James M. Robson. London and Toronto : Routledge & Kegan Paul and U of Toronto P, 1976.

Miller, D.A. "'Discipline in Different Voices:' Bureaucracy, Police, Family, and *Bleak House.*" *The Novel and the Police.* Berkeley: California UP, 1988.

Nancy, Jean-Luc. *The Birth of Presence.* Trans. Britain Holmes. Stanford, CA.: Stanford UP, 1993.

Radzinowicz, Sir Leon and Hood, Roger. *The Emergence of Penal Polity in Victorian and Edwardian England.* Oxford: Clarendon Press, 1990.

Rawls, John. *Political liberalism.* New York: Columbia UP, 1996.

Schapiro, Meyer. *Theory and Philosophy of Art: Style, Artist, and Society.* IV. New York: Braziller, 1994.

Starkie, Thomas. *A Practical Treatise on the Laws of Evidence.* 3rd edn. London: Stevens and Norton, 1842.

Sugarman, David. "Legal Theory, the Common Law Mind, and the Making of Text-book Tradition" In *Legal Theory and Common Law.* Ed. W. Twining. Oxford: Basil Blackwell, 1986.

———. " 'A hatred of Disorder:' Legal Science, Liberalism, and Imperialism." *Dangerous Supplements: Resistance and Renewal in Jurisprudence.* Durham: Duke UP, 1991.

Taylor, Charles. *The Ethics of Authenticity.* Cambridge: Harvard UP, 1985.

Teubner, Gunther. "How the Law Thinks: Toward a Constructivist Epistemology of the Law," *Law and Society Review* 23 (1989).

Welsh, Alexander. *George Elliot and Blackmail.* Cambridge: Harvard UP, 1985.

White, James Boyd. *Justice as Translation*: *An Essay in Cultural and Legal Criticism*. Chicago and London: U of Chicago P, 1994.

Wills, William. *An Essay on the Principles of Circumstantial Evidence*, 3rd edition. Philadelphia: Johnson, 1857 rpt. of 1850 edn.

Wilson, James Q. *Moral Judgement*. New York: Basic Books, 1997.

# The D. Case Reopened

## Catharine Rising

*This paper employs Kleinian theory to suggest that what Felix Aylmer dismissed as the "ostensible plot" of* The Mystery of Edwin Drood—*John Jasper murders his nephew—is the plan most likely to have met Dickens's psychological needs. Of the various theses in* The D. Case *(Dickens, Fruttero, and Lucentini), only this one would have enabled him both to enjoy the murderous impulses of Jasper, a character closely identified with himself, and to escape the onus of them. Jasper is a split personality, not guilty by reason of insanity. According to the aesthetic theory of Klein's colleague Hanna Segal, such defensive splitting is bad art or no art at all. Nevertheless, readers have continued reading* Drood. *Kleinian theory can readily explain their persistence: Jasper's split offers them as vicarious murderers the same gratifications it afforded Dickens.*

Of the various solutions to *The Mystery of Edwin Drood* proposed by the Rome work group in *The D. Case* (Dickens, Fruttero, and Lucentini), Kleinian theory would indicate as the only possible finding the group's Thesis A: John Jasper, the opium-smoking cathedral choirmaster of Cloisterham, murders his nephew Edwin Drood out of jealousy that Drood is engaged to the delectable Rosa Bud. From a Kleinian standpoint, only this plot would offer Dickens optimal relief from the guilt of murderous impulses of his own. Thesis B, the unknown hired assassin who muffs his job, and Thesis C, the student Neville Landless as a murderer set on by his Lady Macbeth of a sister, would not

---

*Dickens Studies Annual,* Volume 31, Copyright © 2002 by AMS Press, Inc. All rights reserved.

have met Dickens's needs with the same psychic neatness. B and C offer less scope for the Kleinian defense mechanisms of identification/introjection and projection, in the use of which Dickens shows a remarkable ingenuity. [1] These tactics result in what Kleinians would call an aesthetic failure; yet as we shall see, Kleinian theory can also account for the novel's continued popularity.

We might begin by noting Dickens's consuming need, shortly before his death, to read—and keep reading—in public the murder scene from *Oliver Twist*. His biographer Peter Ackroyd comments that people were reluctant to join him after the performance of such lines as " . . . he beat it *twice* upon the upturned face *that almost touched his own . . . seized a heavy club*, and *struck her* down!! . . . *the pool of gore that quivered and danced in the sunlight on the ceiling . . .* but *such* flesh, and *so much blood*!!! . . . *The very feet of his dog were bloody*!!!! . . . *dashed out his brains*!!" (Ackroyd 1041, 1031). Dickens's manager George Dolby believed that audiences "might in part be alarmed by the demonstration of what Dickens himself called (apparently jokingly) his 'murderous instincts'" (1041). Despite this levity, however, Ackroyd notes the "attraction of repulsion" that the act of murder held for him, and the "terrible threnody" of his fiction from Sikes's murder of Nancy through Jonas Chuzzlewit's murder of Montague Tigg and into the butcheries of *A Tale of Two Cities* and *Barnaby Rudge* (518, 519). We might add that the dirge continues through his last three major works, *Our Mutual Friend* (1865), *No Thoroughfare* (1867), and the unfinished *Drood* (1870).

How then might Dickens have dealt with the murderous instincts with which Ackroyd has credited him? The orthodox Kleinian answer to this question—Dickens could wiggle out by splitting—has been anticipated by a literary critic. In a recent attempt to rehabilitate the novelist's seemingly insipid portrayals of good women, G. D. Arms has located the rage of an abused child, the self-effacing Esther Summerson, in the fiery Mademoiselle Hortense of *Bleak House*, and Esther's split-off self-respect in her haughty mother, Lady Dedlock. Arms suggests that Dickens, unable to let go of a delusive belief in perfect human beings, could deal with such ugly traits as murderous rage only through "the device of dismemberment" (95).

From a Kleinian perspective, the usefulness to the author of such simplified or flattened characters lies in the ease with which he can introject/identify with the good ones and project unwanted parts of himself onto the bad ones. Such behavior toward real objects marks Klein's paranoid-schizoid position of early infancy, a phase in which the child's sense of guilt is minimized, since both self and object are split into good and bad parts and the reprehensible aspects of the self can be projected onto the (m)other. In contrast, heavy and inescapable guilt attends Klein's "depressive position," which is reached when the child in the second quarter of its first year perceives the mother and other objects, on whom it has phantasied greedy and sadistic attacks, as whole persons—good and bad, loved and hated (61–93). In an ideal maturation, the self-righteous paranoid would wholly yield to the self-accusing depressive. But as Freud reminds us, "in mental life nothing which has once been formed can perish" (*SE* 21:69). Since the paranoid-schizoid position can never be fully and finally transcended, but survives to fluctuate with the depressive, we should not be surprised to find Dickens returning through his fiction to the irresponsibility of earliest childhood.

A character flattened even as *Drood* progresses is Helena Landless, whose exotic origin and even more exotic capabilities at the outset would have seemed to bear out the work group's Thesis C. This hypothesis maintained that Dickens, stung by the success of Wilkie Collins's *The Moonstone* in 1868, undertook in *Drood* to beat Collins on the latter's own ground, the sensational detective novel. C required Dickens to plagiarize a pair of suspiciously dark Ceylonese immigrants from the homicidal Brahmans of *The Moonstone*. The murder and disposal of Drood—motivated, according to C, by an insult offered Islam by Drood's father in Egypt—are urged by Helena on her twin or partner Neville. When she first appears in Cloisterham, she is possibly capable of all this activity, including the dissolution of Drood's body in quicklime. Powerful, feral, gypsylike, reportedly able to tear out her own hair when frustrated in one of the escapes she had planned to free herself and Neville from their brute of a stepfather, she also communicates telepathically, without the need for a word or look, with the youth she calls her brother. She not only feels what he feels but knows what he is doing (*MED* 7:91). Moreover, she does not fear Jasper's hypnotic power—an omission signifying either that she is not susceptible or that she exercises a power akin and superior to his. But after chapter 7, which ends with a "slumbering gleam of fire" in her "intense dark eyes" and the authorial admonition, "Let whomsoever it most concerned look well to it!" (is this the moment, asks C, when Neville is murdering Drood?), the uninhibited Helena vanishes from the novel.

A new one appears in chapter 10: a spiritual guide to Neville in the control of his passions and a model that Minor Canon Crisparkle, his other mentor in self-restraint, can hold up to him. "What you have overcome in yourself, can you not overcome in him?" Crisparkle asks her. "Who but you can keep him clear of it?" (10:130). She in turn reveres the Minor Canon, *mens sana in corpore sano*, as the polestar an unfortunate duo had missed in childhood: "Follow your guide now, Neville, and follow him to Heaven!" (14:174,

10:129). If Helena dissembles in her role as the twinship's better half, subduing the rage of two abused children, she deceives not only Crisparkle but the rest of Cloisterham.

She is so sharply diminished, however, that such a masquerade appears unlikely. The new Helena lacks paranormal communication with her brother, so that he must explain to her in detail the reason for his solitary walking tour, "a healthy project, denoting a sincere endeavor, and an active attempt at self-correction" (14:174). And if Crisparkle in teaching one teaches two (10:122), this result follows mundanely from the fact that the twins study together. But if Helena Two is not telepathic, neither is she mesmeric. By chapter 21 she reveals a jealous fear that her timid protégée Rosa, who has repeatedly consulted Crisparkle on the details of an escape from Jasper, might lure the canon away from her. On the brink of another conference, Rosa is "sedately" informed: " . . . you needn't disappear again" (21:250). This second, domesticated Helena leaves the *Macbeth* references of chapter 14, "When Shall These Three Meet Again?"—at some point of which the murder might be expected to occur—stranded without a Lady Macbeth, although chimneys topple, rooks caw, and the witchlike Princess Puffer foretells harm to someone called Ned. [2]

The advent of a Helena whose chief trait is the long-suffering goodness de rigueur for Dickens's ideal woman [3] would suggest a revision of his plan for the novel, an abandonment of sensational detective fiction for a psychological drama in which the characters serve his rather specialized needs for identification/introjection and projection. Helena Two is an avatar of Dickens's idealized sister-in-law Mary Hogarth, an angel in the house whom he took to represent the best part of himself—a guiding spirit who is, like the tireless Agnes Wickfield at the close of *David Copperfield*, "pointing upward."

Since Dickens has dropped the exotic Helena, we may safely dispense with the other exotics proposed by Sir Felix Aylmer, the principal source for Theses B and C: Jasper as a Eurasian half-brother of Drood, Jasper as a Thug carrying out a ritual sacrifice of Drood to the goddess Kali, unnamed Arab emissaries who pursue a blood feud in Cloisterham, and the Princess Puffer as their English grandmother bent on revenging herself on yet another of her grandsons, Jasper. Let us confine ourselves to what Aylmer (4) dismisses as the "ostensible plot," which the work group designated Thesis A: Jasper dispatches his nephew out of jealousy. On this psychological fiction Klein's theory of defensive splitting will throw some light.

Along with his ideal woman, whom he had managed to locate within himself, Dickens in *Drood* provided an ideal man for another felicitous self-image. Tartar, the ex-naval lieutenant who seems destined to win Rosa and, together with her guardian Grewgious, to penetrate the mystery of Drood's disappearance, matches Virginia Woolf's description of Dickens himself: "He has to perfection the virtues conventionally ascribed to the male; he is self-assertive, self-reliant, self-assured; energetic in the extreme" (Woolf 76). Forster describes the "eager, restless, energetic" look of his face, "that seemed to tell so little of a student or writer of books, and so much of a man of action and business in the world" (1:70). Such was Dickens's self-image, for he lamented to Angela Burdett-Coutts that his eldest boy, Charley, had "less fixed purpose and energy than I could have supposed possible in my son" (Ackroyd 687).

In contrast to Helena and Tartar, a character not very helpful to Dickens in his quest for blamelessness is the complex Neville, who ably illustrates Klein's depressive position. Neville loves Rosa and feels the urge to kill her titular fiancé Drood but fights against his own violent impulses. Having merely breathed his hatred to his spiritual guides, Crisparkle and Helena, he is abject, "repentant," "wretched"; "I beg your forgiveness for my miserable lapse"; " . . . I do want to conquer myself" (*MED* 10:128, 10:129, 14:174). An authorial identification with the guilt-ridden Neville would clearly impinge on Dickens's innocence, yet points of similarity between the two exist. In place of Dickens's stint in the blacking factory we have Neville's miserable childhood with a "miserly," "cruel," and "grinding" stepfather (7:88). And obviously author and character share a longstanding interest in murder. Neville tells Crisparkle: "It was well [my stepfather] died when he did, or I might have killed him" (7:88). Dickens had, however, an appropriate defense against Neville. According to the plan divulged to Forster (2:407), this troublesome, "tigerish" (*MED* 7:90) youth was to die at the end of the novel. Here the moral requirements of Dickens's readers coincided with the needs of his own psyche. If splitting was his defense in paranoid-schizoid phases, a fictional burial, akin to repression, shielded him from depressive guilt.

But repression, which requires for its maintenance energy needed elsewhere, is not an ideal defense. Dickens needed to live as productively as possible with his violent impulses. In *Drood* he formulated his most daring, or most puerile, solution to the problem of self-identification with murderers: he anticipated Stevenson's novella of 1886 by creating in John Jasper a Jekyll-Hyde.[4] In Forster's account (2:407) of his intentions, Jasper in a condemned cell was to regard the murder of Drood as committed by someone else. Dickens presents the artist, choirmaster, and devoted uncle of Drood, his "dear boy" (*MED* 19:227, 228), as peacefully coexisting with the meticulous killer who smokes opium to enjoy visions of a planned murder; drugs Neville and

Drood into a quarrel that will throw suspicion on the outsider; cultivates the fatuous Mayor Sapsea, who believes he knows what to think of Neville's blackly un-English looks; gets the cathedral mason, who can tell him the uses of quicklime and crypts, drunk in order to plan the disposal of Drood's body; has never sung better in the cathedral than when he wears around his neck the black scarf with which he will presumably strangle his nephew; and afterwards regrets only that in a later dream the deed is "too short and easy. . . . No struggle, no consciousness of peril, no entreaty" (22:271). With the possible exception of the moment in which Jasper—having learned that the murder was unnecessary because Drood and Rosa had broken their engagement—falls in a heap on the floor, not enough communication exists between his two selves for one to reproach the other. The fear for Drood's safety, previously expressed in Jasper's diary, was not attributable to a Jekyll's knowledge of a Hyde in his own body. Rather, the threat was always portrayed as coming from "the demoniacal passion of this Neville" (10:132), who makes himself an easy mark for projection: "[Drood] goaded me . . . beyond my power of endurance. . . . I would have cut him down if I could, and I tried to do it" (8:104). The haggard choirmaster who swears revenge—"That I never will relax in my secrecy or in my search. That I will fasten the crime of the murder of my dear dead boy upon the murderer. And That I devote myself to his destruction" (16:201)—betrays no awareness that the man he seeks is himself. Jasper is a paranoid-schizoid who has cleanly projected his violence. [5]

Dickens identified himself with the bifurcated Jasper more freely than with any of his other murderers. Like Dickens, the choirmaster, though darkish, is perceived as English (he escapes the racial slurs aimed at Neville). Like Dickens, he exercises enough mesmeric power over a woman to worry somebody (Marcus 347–48, *MED* 7:95–96). Also like Dickens, he has, despite his artistic success, "some stray sort of ambition, aspiration, restlessness, dissatisfaction" (2:49). Dickens gave Jasper at twenty-six his own crisis at midlife. When he was nearing forty, he lamented David Copperfield's "unhappy loss or want of something"; when he was forty-five and on the point of dismissing his wife, he was writing to Forster: "Why is it, that as with poor David, a sense comes always crushing on me now, when I fall into low spirits, as of one happiness I have missed in life, and one friend and companion I have never made?" (Forster 2:218, 219). Now let us observe Jasper's reaction to a youth on whom youth is wasted—the languid Drood sauntering into his birthright: marriage to Rosa and a place in the family engineering firm, from which he is "going to wake up Egypt a little" (*MED* 8:96). "The world is all before him where to choose," cries his uncle (8:100).

> See how little he heeds it all! . . . It hardly is worth his while to pluck the golden fruit that hangs ripe on the tree for him. And yet consider the contrast, Mr. Neville. You and I have no prospect of stirring work and interest, or of change and excitement, or of domestic ease and love. You and I have no prospect . . . but the tedious, unchanging round of this dull place.          (8:101)

Jasper is Dickens in the full bitterness of climacteric.

Another similarity lies in the fact that Jasper reaches his creator's psychological bedrock, which is not Neville's Freudian and oedipal struggle with the (step)father but the earlier struggle with the mother. Dickens has left Jasper's childhood a blank, but a piece of Dickens's own can be inferred from Jasper's relation to a female persecutor, the hag called Princess Puffer. She tracks him to Cloisterham from her London opium den, where she calls herself a "mother" (22:266) to customers. And so she is—at least to Jasper, the bad mother split off from the angel in the house. This shrewd addict is perhaps a blackmailer, the counterpart of Headstone's nemesis Riderhood in *Our Mutual Friend*. Having long concocted the drug to send Jasper on his murderous "journey," she rejoices that "practice makes perfect. I may have learned the secret how to make ye talk, my deary" (22:270, 272). From Jasper under the influence she has made out a threat to the person he calls Ned. Her inability so far to extract the further information that would put him wholly in her power may account for the fist she shakes at him in the cathedral. Like Riderhood in a close watch on Headstone at the Thames lockhouse, she has sated her victim's appetite in the den and put him to bed, but in *Drood* the assignment of perverted maternal functions to a woman suggests that Dickens is coming nearer to suppressed material—his projection of disowned traits upon his earliest object, the mother.

It might be argued that Dickens's view of his mother was not, as Kleinian theory would have it, necessarily a projection of himself. Even paranoids, it is said, have enemies. Is his fictional witch (22:272) not the objectively bad parent who would have sent him back to the blacking factory after his father had set him free, and in his years of prosperity tried to use him as a perpetual treasury for herself and her improvident husband? He reported that in her "senile decay," while her daughter-in-law and younger daughter "were poulticing her poor head . . . the instant she saw me . . . she plucked up a spirit and asked me for 'a pound'" (Slater 15). This resilient figure appears to have been a source for the Princess, coughing from opium smoke, looking senile even if she is not, [6] lamenting "my poor head" (*MED* 1:38), begging from both Drood and the mysterious Datchery. Kleinians insist, however, that the young child's frightening view of the mother is in fact shaped by the projection of its innate evil. How else could Klein's own children have regarded her as a monster? [7]

Dickens's relation to the murderous Jasper may be further clarified by a look at the problem of guilt in a second art form in which he engaged while writing *Drood*: his public readings. Superficially his obsession with a man's murder of a woman in *Oliver Twist* might indicate revenge on one or more of the women in his life on whom he had, according to Kleinian theory, projected his own unsatisfactory traits: the mother he never forgave for wishing to extend his child labor in the blacking factory; the sister who accepted from debt-ridden parents an expensive education at the Royal Academy of Music while he was menially employed; the wife he wrote off as incompatible after she had borne him ten children; the once-loved flirt, Maria Beadnell Winter, who had refused to marry him and whom he mercilessly shunned when she was twenty years older and much fatter; Ellen Ternan, nearly thirty years his junior, with whom he was having a frustrating affair. (Jack Lindsay describes him as "a man entangled with a woman whom he could not wholly subdue" [347]). But the ebb and flow of his identity in the Sikes-Nancy scene, in which he took all the parts, points to an underlying search for traits, not whole persons, which he could readily utilize for identification/introjection or project onto others. He was not in any simple way Sikes, a man killing a woman, but he knew what Sikes's murderous rage was; we must assume he left it with Sikes. Hence perhaps his exultation in this particular performance of all his public repertoire. It was accompanied by a strange excitement in the performer and preceded, when he gave it for the last time, by his lament or boast, "I shall tear myself to pieces" (Ackroyd 1065). His peculiar delight in what would ordinarily be a psychic trauma, the loss of identity, [8] implies the existence of a compelling covert gain. A piece of himself to which he could cling free of guilt was the victim. The role he relished most may have been Nancy's, for he bubbled that he was being "nightly murdered by Mr W. Sikes" (Ackroyd 1032). Socially degraded, loving, and wronged, Nancy resembles Oliver Twist and Dickens's self-image of the abandoned child. The pathos he invariably saw in his own past is, if anything, enhanced by the change of gender. [9]

According to Lindsay, Dickens, though verging on schizophrenia in his public readings, somehow gave up the defense mechanism of splitting in his portrayal of Jasper, the artist and frustrated lover who so closely resembled himself. The change was linked in *Drood* with a shift from a botched murder to a successful one. On the evidence of such rejected titles as *The Flight of Edwin Drood* and *Edwin Drood in Hiding*, he first toyed with the idea of bringing back alive a supposed victim to confront his would-be killer. Soon, however, Dickens turned from "a melodramatic device to one of spiritual significance; the risen man was now to rise [only] in the driven soul of the murderer" (397). At the bottom of the frontispiece drawing made by C. A. Collins to Dickens's order, Jasper holds a lantern up to a motionless young man who probably represents Drood's ghost—the sight of which effects a "spiritual resurrection . . . the advent of the murdered man marks the break into a new level of consciousness, a new pang of growth" (397). But this comforting theory is undercut if we look closely at Collins's frontispiece; Jasper appears keenly interested in the undead (who would not be?) and nothing more.

From a Kleinian standpoint, it would appear that in the last work Dickens attempted, his reputation stands or falls on his treatment of Jasper. However irrelevant to the facts of *Drood* Lindsay's theory of a Jasper finally unified may be, it does happen to satisfy Hanna Segal's Kleinian definition of art as a means of restitution—the need for which arises in the depressive position. The artist recreates whole objects lost to him/her by phantasied attacks, which trigger guilt and a fear of losing the object, both in the external world and internally. At this juncture, " . . . the whole internal world feels destroyed and shattered" (Segal 205). In a carryover from the paranoid-schizoid position,

> bits of the destroyed object may turn into persecutors, and there is a fear of internal persecution as well as a pining for the lost loved object. . . . The memory of the good situation, where the . . . ego contained the whole loved object . . . [engenders] the wish to restore and re-create the lost loved object outside and within the ego. (205–06)

If so, what motivated Dickens to create his theater of part characters must be for Kleinians something quite different, the desire to avoid guilt by creating easy targets for identification and projection. But since, unfortunately for Dickens, Segal defined great art as that which achieves wholeness, his many two-dimensional characters would fail her test. And since she defines art as a means of making restitution by the recreation of whole objects now ruined and lost, would these more limited characters even qualify as art? Segal does not tell us. She does not have to.

We can now reconstruct a Kleinian dilemma in which Dickens's identification with murderers had placed him at the end of his life. He may have sensed, in anticipation of Segal, that the greatness of art lies in its grasp of wholeness. But if he treated Jasper as a whole, the guilt of this virtually autobiographical killer would become his own. What then was his escape route? He made of Jasper a man both good and bad, physically united but not guilty by reason of dissociation, insanity. This loophole would not have been provided by Neville, Drood's self-accusing killer in Thesis C, nor by Thesis B's Arab assailant, of whom nothing is known. Dickens was bound to Thesis A—the only one in which the killer could plausibly be exonerated. While Dickens in life might admit guilt to his daughter—he wished he had been "a better father—a better man" (Ackroyd 1075)—his last act in literature was to preserve his innocence. As Freud well knew, art compensates us for the defects of our reality (*SE* 9:143–53).[10]

But Kleinians would argue that Dickens's "solution," or sleight of hand to escape guilt, is aesthetically as well as morally and psychologically deficient. Jasper is not a whole in the sense intended by Segal: psychological, not physical. (Siamese twins, physically joined, mentally going their separate ways, would not be a whole either). Jasper is two part characters, not one whole. Doubtless Dickens in a textbook paranoid-schizoid case identified with the Jekyll and projected murderous impulses onto the Hyde; he failed to attain the maturity of the defensive stance, which would have united them. But since Jasper is not seen as a psychic unity, *Drood* in Segal's sense is not great art and perhaps not art at all.

If this view is correct, the novel's popularity requires some explanation. Defensive splitting, which enabled Dickens to enjoy Jasper's murderous impulses while escaping Jasper's guilt, gives the same opportunities to homicidal readers—who are, according to Klein, legion; she fully upheld Freud's belief in a death instinct.

# NOTES

1. The work group's Thesis D, Wilkie Collins as the murderer of Dickens himself, is peripheral to Kleinian theory, which focuses on internal rather than external evil. Klein's move to exclude external reality has been analyzed by Maria Torok, Barbro Sylwan, and Adèle Covello.
2. The name by which Drood is known only to Jasper.
3. Dickens also hints at a future Rosa smaller than the unrepentant "Miss Impudence" (*MED* 2:50) who, like Bella Wilfer of *Our Mutual Friend*, resents a fiancé to whom someone else has consigned her like a sack of potatoes. The

chastened Rosa to come is already visible when she persuades Drood to break the engagement their fathers made for them; Drood is disarmed by his momentary glimpse of "woman's nature in the spoilt child" (3:61). The depths of her "exhaustless well of affection" have not yet been moved; when they are, "what developing changes might fall upon the heedless head, and light heart" will be revealed (9:106). But we can guess.

4. As many critics have noted, Dickens in his account of the two Miss Twinkletons, the stony educator and the sexy gossip, has already asserted his belief in the possibility of a split personality. "As, in some cases of drunkenness, and in others of animal magnetism, there are two states of consciousness which never clash, but each of which pursues its separate course as though it were continuous instead of broken (thus, if I hide my watch when I am drunk, I must be drunk again before I can remember where)" (*MED* 3:53).

5. It is not only Jasper who succeeds in thrusting his ferocity onto Neville: in Dickens's mockery of projection (of which he probably knew a great deal), most of Cloisterham does the same. The cook at Rosa's school amplifies the wine Neville threw at Drood into a "bottle, knife, fork, and decanter (the decanter now coolly flying at everybody's head, without the least introduction)" (9:107). When Drood's watch and shirt-pin turn up in a weir, it is bruited that but for his sister's good influence, Neville "would be in the daily commission of murder. Before coming to England he had caused to be whipped to death sundry 'Natives'—nomadic persons, encamping now in Asia, now in Africa, now in the West Indies, and now at the North Pole," but invariably black and virtuous. "He had repeatedly said he would have Mr. Crisparkle's life. He had repeatedly said he would have everybody's life, and become in effect the last man" (16:198). Given the foreign-looking Neville as a receptacle for violence, the plain Englishness of the urchin Deputy, who stones man, beast, and headstone for pure pleasure, can be overlooked.

6. The original of the Princess Puffer was probably a famous London opium-eater called "Lascar Sal," who appeared to be about eighty years old when she was actually only twenty-six (*MED* 314n4).

7. Nicholas Wright has offered a solution to this puzzle in his play *Mrs. Klein.*

8. Nevertheless, trauma is trauma. Both Dickens's son Charley and his manager George Dolby, without recognizing a psychic cause of his exhaustion, blamed his fatal stroke in 1870 on the strain of this one endlessly repeated killing (Ackroyd 1040).

9. His facility in reverting to an abused childhood appears in the stark detachment of this father of ten children from "his poor wife's fecundity, the rueful jokes in letters to his friends about her being in 'an uninteresting condition,' 'favouring me (I think I could have dispensed with the compliment) with No. 10,' and so forth. As editor of *Household Words* Dickens must have relished Wilkie Collins's joke in a 1858 sketch describing a Mrs. Bullwinkle: "About a month since, my wife advanced me one step nearer to the Court for the Relief of Insolvent Debtors, by presenting me with another child" (Slater 352). Slater notes a possible parallel in Dickens's own mother's contribution of a fifth and sixth child (Alfred, born 1822, and Augustus, born 1827) after the family had got into financial straits

with four (352). The adult Charles, though no friend of contraceptives, absolved himself of any role in procreation by reverting to the child who had not been responsible for babies, and who had seen his gifts eclipsed and prospects threatened by their relentless arrivals.

10. Can we assume that if Dickens had lived to finish *Drood*, he would have needed to bury the technically innocent Jasper as he did culprits like Headstone, Obenreizer, and Sikes in prior works? A killer in the condemned cell in which Forster locked him is not a killer at the end of a rope. One can imagine an appeal, a plea of insanity, a stay, a commutation. Dickens told Forster (2:407) of "a very curious and new idea" for the novel, "not a communicable idea" but "a very strong one, though difficult to work."

# WORKS CITED

Ackroyd, Peter. Dickens. New York: Harper Collins, 1990.

Arms, G. D. "Reassembling *Bleak House*: 'Is there *three* of 'em then?'" *Literature and Psychology* 39.1–2 (1993): 84–96.

Aylmer, Felix. *The Drood Case*. London: Rupert Hart-Davies, 1964.

Dickens, Charles. *David Copperfield*. New York: Signet-New American Library, 1962.

———. *The Mystery of Edwin Drood*. Harmondsworth: Penguin, 1974. Designated as *MED*.

———. *No Thoroughfare*. New York: Peter Fenelon Collier, 1900. 7–173. Vol. 30 of *The Works of Charles Dickens*. 30 vols.

———. *Oliver Twist*. New York: Signet-New American Library, 1961.

———. *Our Mutual Friend*. Harmondsworth: Penguin, 1971.

Dickens, Charles, Carlo Fruttero, and Franco Lucentini. *The D. Case: The Truth about the Mystery of Edwin Drood*. Trans. Gregory Dowling. San Diego, CA: Harcourt-Harvest, 1993.

Forster, John. *The Life of Charles Dickens*. Ed. B. W. Matz. Philadelphia: Lippincott, n.d. 2 vols.

Freud, Sigmund. *The Standard Edition of the Complete Psychological Works of Sigmund Freud*. Trans. and Ed. James Strachey. 24 vols. London: Hogarth, 1953–74.

Klein, Melanie. *Envy and Gratitude and Other Works*. New York: Macmillan-Free, 1984. Vol. 3 of *Writings*. 4 vols.

Lindsay, Jack. *Charles Dickens: A Biographical and Critical Study*. London: Andrew Dakers, 1950.

Marcus, Steven. *Dickens from Pickwick to Dombey*. New York: Basic, 1965.

Segal, Hanna. "A Psychoanalytic Approach to Aesthetics." In *Reading Melanie Klein*. Ed. Lyndsey Stonebridge and John Phillips. London: Routledge, 1998. 203–22.

Slater, Michael. *Dickens and Women*. Stanford: Stanford UP, 1983.

Torok, Maria, Barbro Sylwan, and Adèle Covello. "Melanie Mell by Herself." Trans. Ian Patterson. In *Reading Melanie Klein*. Ed. Lyndsey Stonebridge and John Phillips. London: Routledge, 1998. 51–80.

Woolf, Virginia. "David Copperfield." *The Moment and Other Essays*. San Diego, CA: Harcourt, 1975. 75–80.

# The Unexpected Forms of Nemesis: George Eliot's "Brother Jacob," Victorian Narrative, and the Morality of Imperialism

*Melissa Valiska Gregory*

*This essay uses George Eliot's "Brother Jacob" (1864) to suggest that a central preoccupation of Victorian narrative, the figure of the nemesis, is sometimes raised by nineteenth-century writers in relation to the psychology of British colonialism. The sudden appearance of a character from the past who forces a moral reckoning, and who reveals that past wrongs always resurface in the present, has a particular cultural resonance when it comes to imperial ideology. Eliot's story, which features a racialized nemesis figure, can be interpreted as illuminating the moral evasions that sustain imperialism. Indeed, in mid-century Victorian narrative, the figure of the nemesis often poses (if only indirectly) profoundly troubling questions about the moral integrity of imperial authority.*

I

This essay investigates how a central preoccupation of Victorian narrative, the nemesis, is raised by nineteenth-century writers persistently, if obliquely, in relation to the psychology of British colonialism. Even in its most generic form, the return of the unexpected nemesis often provides the energetic center of many mid-Victorian narratives. As Peter Brooks has demonstrated, the inevitable reentry of previously repressed or banished characters drives the plots of some of the most famous Victorian novels. Those characters who are expelled at the beginning always come back, and no attempt to keep them out of the story will succeed. Magwitch's return in Charles Dickens's *Great Expectations* (1860–61), for instance, precipitates a complex chain of revelations, and Raffles's reappearance in George Eliot's *Middlemarch* (1872), acts as an explosive catalyst for exposure and retribution. In fact, Dickens's ostensible efforts at resolving Magwitch's disappearance early in the novel fail, because (remarks Brooks) "as readers we know that there has been created in the text an intense level of energy that cannot be discharged through these official plots" (122). Pip's attempt to repress his memory of the convict on the moor only guarantees Magwitch's reentry into his life, which, in turn, forces upon Pip a new self-awareness and sense of moral obligation.

Indeed, for those nineteenth-century novelists especially concerned with foregrounding the theme of moral responsibility, the figure of the nemesis proves an important narrative device for illuminating the moral implications of one's conduct. The nemesis's plotted return suggests that all human actions carry inescapable moral consequences, consequences which are exposed particularly when the actions of a former life or identity are unexpectedly brought to bear on the present. The narrative dynamics of the nemesis thus closely resemble the Gothic energies of repression and return, but with a subtle and crucial difference: the mid-Victorian nemesis of Dickens or Eliot is inherently bound to specific social and ethical considerations. As F. R. Leavis observes of *Felix Holt* (1866), "Nemesis has a face corresponding to . . . moral quality" (54). This is not to say that Gothic narratives cannot accommodate moral questions, of course, but to suggest that the nemesis works as a particular and important narrative tool for Victorian writers preoccupied with questions of moral accountability. In mid-nineteenth-century literature, the unexpected nemesis reveals the inevitable and powerful repercussions of human agency.

This concern with agency and accountability, and its attendant dynamics of displacement and apprehension, absence and return, have strong affinities with the political forces and cultural anxieties surrounding nineteenth-century British imperialism. If, as Brooks observes, "the return of the repressed—the repressed as knowledge of the self's other story, the true history of its misapprehended desire—forces a total revision of the subject's relation to the orders within which it constitutes meaning" (120), then the return of the nemesis in Victorian literature bears a startling correlation to those social energies which threatened the authority of colonial power in real life. The sudden appearance of a character from the past who forces a moral reckoning, and who reveals that one's past mistakes always emerge to disrupt one's present life, has a particular cultural resonance when it comes to ideology of imperial domination.

Ultimately, I propose that the literary trope of the nemesis provides mid-Victorian writers with a metaphor and narrative structure for posing, if only indirectly, profoundly troubling questions about the moral integrity of imperial authority. A closer look at this narrative device, then, both enlarges our understanding of the range of literary responses to the Empire, and considers, more generally, how a formalist literary approach might be productively conjoined with the analysis of imperial dynamics so crucial to the literary and cultural criticism of the Victorian period over the past two decades.

My investigation begins with George Eliot's "Brother Jacob" (1864), a story that exposes the moral evasions which sustain colonialism through a nemesis figure, thus strongly suggesting a connection between the tropes of mid-century literary narrative and a moral critique of imperial ideology. Although Eliot considered it only "a slight tale" (Harris and Johnston 86), its comparatively simple plot revolves exclusively around the reappearance of a nemesis (the title refers to the nemesis himself), revealing Eliot's use of the device in its most concentrated form.[11] "Brother Jacob" was never—and is not—one of Eliot's more popular texts, but Jacob's return at the end of the story prefigures, in important ways, a major narrative trope of her later and more significant work.

Eliot returned to the idea of the nemesis throughout her career, and her repeated use of the nemesis figure as a moral agent was noted both by her contemporaries and by later readers, from Marcel Proust to Leavis to, more recently, Alexander Welsh.[2] Eliot's own identification of the story as a fable, moreover—a genre that both foregrounds moral consequences and employs metaphorical characters who represent specific human types and social values—also makes it ideal for investigating the relationship between the nemesis and its larger symbolic associations.[3] More specifically, of all of Eliot's works, "Brother Jacob" is distinctive in its explicit attention to the colonies, insofar as it prominently satirizes England's bourgeois ignorance about its own imperial space. Indeed, the moral effect of the nemesis's return depends heavily on this ignorance, and lends the story's colonial allusions an importance they might not otherwise have.

Finally, that Eliot's 1860 writing of "Brother Jacob" occurred virtually on the heels of the Indian Mutiny of 1857–58, a crisis that rocked British faith in the Empire's stability and cleared the way for more serious and sustained critiques of colonial rule (as well as for more serious oppression of colonial subjects), further invites an interpretation of it as a text with the capacity for illuminating the relationship between mid-Victorian literary narrative and colonial psychology.[4] While there is no way to tell whether the Mutiny and the urgent questions it raised regarding imperial authority and British failure were actually in the forefront of Eliot's consciousness as she composed "Brother Jacob," the story nevertheless resonates with suggestive allusions to the Empire, and invites a close scrutiny of the ignorance and selfishness that underscore colonial domination. My reading is thus indebted both to the work of postcolonialist literary scholars like Edward Said, who asserts that "the novel . . . and imperialism are unthinkable without each other" (71), and also to historians such as Antoinette Burton, who suggests that the project of "civilizing" the colonies permeated British culture even on the most local levels. I also try, however, to complicate Said's powerful analysis of Victorian novels as the ultimate consolidations of imperial author-ity. Since the publication of *Culture and Imperialism* in 1993, many literary scholars have successfully sought to enrich Said's compelling claim that impe-rialism fundamentally shapes Victorian narrative in sometimes unexpected ways. I use "Brother Jacob" to consider how Eliot—and perhaps other Victo-rian authors—may have anxiously, if unconsciously, contemplated the injus-tice of colonization.

While casting "Brother Jacob" as an imperial text might, at worst, distort its emphasis to suit a modern interpretation, locating it within such a context offers a compelling way of interpreting an otherwise oddly mysterious and provocative text that has received relatively little attention from contemporary academics. I also hope a specific reading of this story might further illuminate how the complicated interplay between narrative, empire, and moral discourse in mid-Victorian England emerges in other novels, from Charlotte Brontë's *Jane Eyre* (1848) to Wilkie Collins's *The Moonstone* (1868). While much has been written on the rhetorical strategies used by literary narratives to affirm imperial authority, or to work through a fear of colonial rebellion in order to confirm English supremacy, considerably less work pursues how Victorian writers may have apprehensively considered the ethics of imperial domination. Ultimately, a discussion of how the literary nemesis was persis-tently affiliated with the Empire—not only in "Brother Jacob," but in other texts as well—should productively complicate our understanding of the relationship between mid-Victorian narrative and imperial culture.

## II

Recent literary scholarship on Eliot and race tends to confine the subject to discussions of the gypsies in *The Mill on the Floss* (1860) or Jewish identity in *Daniel Deronda* (1879).[5] But a closer inspection of her work suggests that Eliot's awareness of racial difference extends beyond England's own native cultures. This is particularly evident in her 1856 *Westminster Review* critique of Harriet Beecher Stowe's *Dred* (1856), a short but compelling review which proves a useful starting point for a study of Eliot and imperialism. In Eliot's rather contradictory examination of Stowe's second major anti-slavery novel (published four years after *Uncle Tom's Cabin* [1852]), she responds to Stowe's moral passion with respect tempered by a sense of foreboding, as her writing of the review prompts her to reflect upon the inevitably violent consequences of slavery for white oppressors. She links this fear, moreover, to the literary idea of the nemesis, an association which sets the stage for further exploration of the relationship between this common nineteenth-century narrative trope and the cultural anxieties surrounding the mid-century Empire.

Eliot's review of *Dred* indicates her basic disapproval of slavery from the outset, an attitude not especially surprising amidst the ranks of those middle- to upper-class educated Victorians who prided themselves on adopting a more enlightened attitude toward slavery—abolished in Britain in 1834–than Americans. But it also contains an oblique nervousness about the implications of *Dred*'s political challenge, a vague, uneasy recognition that the consequences of racial domination will ultimately prove neither comfortable nor safe. This anxiety first surfaces in her characterization of the book's tone. Although the anti-slavery polemics of *Dred* are far more muted than in *Uncle Tom's Cabin*—the novel is suffused with despair rather than overt political anger—Eliot nevertheless describes the book as emitting an alarming, almost menacing violent charge, as if the very theme of racial injustice ignites a political fuse. "[*Dred* has] an uncontrollable power," she remarks, "and critics who follow it with their objections and reservations—who complain that Mrs. Stowe's plot is defective, that she has repeated herself, that her book is too long and too full of hymns and religious dialogue, and that it creates an unfair bias—are something like men pursuing a prairie fire with desultory watering-cans'' (325). Stowe's critique of slavery, in other words, literally burns away at its subject matter, and Eliot's charged image of an all-consuming conflagration suggests that the book's moral energy is both unavoidable and terrifying. Those readers more interested in complaining about insignificant textual details than the force of Stowe's moral and social criticism, Eliot implies, will eventually be burned by their failure to recognize the true issue at hand.

No sooner does Eliot challenge her readers to recognize the power of Stowe's subject matter, however, when she suddenly reverses her position, explicitly renouncing any interest in *Dred*'s politics. Attempting to separate her admiration of *Dred* from questions of race, she argues that her "admiration of the book is quite distinct from any opinions we may have as to the terribly difficult problems of Slavery and Abolition" (326). But this disclaimer rings weirdly dissonant, given that the rest of her review proceeds to focus on the book as an important representative of "the Negro novel" (326). *Dred*, claims Eliot, "is a novel not only fresh in its scenery and manners, but possessing that *conflict of races* which Augustin Theiry has pointed out as the great source of romantic interest—witness 'Ivanhoe'" (326, Eliot's emphasis). Eliot goes on to exempt Stowe's book from the very same aesthetic criticisms—the presence of "too much doctrine" or overt moralizing—she often levels at other novels, which further suggests that what is most important in *Dred* is precisely what she claims is irrelevant: the subject of slavery and, more generally, the consequences of racial domination.[6] Eliot's own emphasis on race—her implication that the book's portrayal of racial injustice overrides its aesthetic concerns, her rebuke of those critics who complain of the novel's "unfair bias" against slavery, and her claim that *Dred*'s moral resonances are impossible to ignore—makes it difficult to read her review as anything but a meditation on race relations.

That Eliot would even attempt to exclude the subject of race from a discussion of an anti-slavery novel suggests an ambivalent, if not openly distressed, reaction to Stowe's provocative critique of a social system that bears significant similarities to British imperial rule. Admittedly, not all omissions necessarily indicate repression. But Eliot's urgent need to clarify her appreciation of *Dred* as distinct from its politics implies that despite her aversion to slavery, she finds Stowe's call to abolish it deeply troubling. If, as Toni Morrison observes, sometimes "underscored omissions" (6) yield insights about race that are just as compelling as overtly expressed tropes and themes, in this case, Eliot's effort to excise race from her review betrays alarm at the thought that abolishing slavery may result in a moral rebalancing, a shift in power that may not favor white oppressors.

Hence Eliot implores her readers to remember that the worst part of slavery is the resentment and the violence it breeds among the subjugated, which makes the thought of granting slaves their freedom almost terrifying. The "most terribly tragic element in the relation of the two races," she says, is "the Nemesis lurking in the vices of the oppressed. [Stowe] alludes to the demoralization among the slaves, but she does not depict it; and yet why should she shrink from this, since she does not shrink from giving us a full-length portrait of a Legree or a Tom Gordon?" (327–28). The development of vice may be "terribly tragic," but Eliot also finds it threatening, and wonders why Stowe seems not to share her anxiety. Her use of the nemesis metaphor suggests that the enslaved Others will some day return to demand a moral reckoning from their self-appointed masters—not a very comforting thought in mid-century England, troubled by rebellion from dominated native Others.

Although Eliot's review of *Dred* may not stand as her most significant critical work (nor is it my version of Casaubon's key to all mythologies), it does offer one way to begin to understand the complexity of mid-Victorian attitudes toward the subject of racial equality. Eliot's rather convoluted opinion of Stowe's novel, in which she reveals both a keen affinity for Stowe's provocative moral challenge and a nagging fear of the results of that challenge, provides a compelling instance of the tensions inherent in many nonliterary mid-century discussions of race. As Catherine Hall notes, the same Victorian intellectuals who demanded freedom for slaves or additional rights for colonized subjects often betrayed a simultaneous fear of those subjects actually achieving those rights. Eliot's use of the nemesis to express this ambivalence provides an early example of the literary trope's affiliations with questions of race and power.

With "Brother Jacob," Eliot continues to associate the nemesis with race, but also situates the trope within a narrative with distinct imperial resonances. A story which satirizes popular views of the British colonies, the story's plot features a vaguely ominous, racialized nemesis character who exposes the selfish hypocrisy underlying imperial authority. If, as Eliot's review of *Dred* suggests, racial domination creates a nemesis of its oppressed subjects, then "Brother Jacob" further intimates that the nemesis's return promises a moral reckoning both just and profoundly unsettling.

### III

Most literary scholars agree that "Brother Jacob" clearly reveals Eliot's "disapproval of imperialist exploitation" (de Sola Rodstein 301).[7] Given that Eliot's fable revolves around the downfall of an unscrupulous confectioner, David Faux, who uses wildly exaggerated stories about his trip to the West Indies as a form of social leverage, there is, certainly, no question that the story satirizes the problematic ignorance which so often attends British colonialism. All too eager to believe David's outrageous tales of colonial adventure, the provincial citizens of Grimworth uncritically accept his fraud and grant him access to their top social circles. They are humiliated, however, by the unexpected appearance of David's idiot brother Jacob, whose sudden arrival in Grimworth unintentionally exposes David's—and their own—hypocrisy.

Eliot's censure of the moral logic that undergirds colonial power structures surfaces in both her description of David's attitude toward the colonies and in her representation of the unenlightened Grimworth citizens. She targets the outrageous egotism behind David's assumption that America's "chiefly black" population might render it "the most propitious destination for an emigrant who, to begin with, had the broad and easily recognisable merit of whiteness" (4), and goes on to say that perhaps his ultimate failure to achieve "a brilliant career among 'the blacks' " in Jamaica might be because " 'the blacks' . . . had already seen too many white men" and thus "did not at once recognize him as a superior order of being" (39).

But Eliot further suggests that David's misguided faith in his own whiteness is less compelling than the disturbing moral blindness revealed in Grimworth's collective willingness to embrace him. In her description of Grimworth's undoing, Eliot lampoons the ignorance of the duped citizens with an unusual vehemence, depicting them as largely responsible for their own misfortune.[8] Since the story explicitly associates Grimworth's humiliation with the town's ignorance about the colonies—the townspeople are vulnerable to David primarily because they so eagerly believe his ludicrous stories about the West Indies—Eliot's unsympathetic portrait implies a strong critique of the moral logic that underscores colonial power. For she suggests that the town's blind faith in David's patently unbelievable tales of colonial adventure exhibits a moral evasiveness far more complex than simple small-town naivete. In fact, the townspeople's eager desire to believe the most ridiculous lies about the colonies effectively transforms their provincial innocence into a problematic moral failure: a self-serving and deliberate refusal to recognize the truth about a real place with real problems.

After all, the "withered" (35), "sallow" (18), and otherwise unattractive David is not a particularly cunning villain. But he excels at selling the version of the West Indies that Grimworth wants to hear. He claims, for instance, to have "seen the very estate which had been [Mrs. Chaloner's] grandfather's property," and confirms her belief that "the missionaries were the only cause of the negro's discontent" (22). He further

> charm[s] the ears of Grimworth Desdemonas with stories of strange fishes, especially sharks, which he had stabbed in the nick of time by bravely plunging overboard just as the monster was turning on its side to devour the cook's mate; of terrible fevers which he had undergone in a land where the wind blows from all quarters at once; of rounds of toast cut straight from the bread-fruit trees; of toes bitten off by land-crabs; of large honours that had been offered to him as a man who knew what was what, and was therefore particularly needed in a tropical climate; and of a Creole heiress who had wept bitterly at his departure.
>
> (27)

By pandering to the town's desire to view the colonies as an exotic fantasy space, David becomes one of its most revered members.[9] The Grimworth citizens think of him as the "man who had been to the Indies" (31), and reward him with a thriving business and a fiancée (an engagement arranged by the girl's father, who hopes David's West Indian associations will lend their family glamour, prestige, and possibly even Jamaican rum).

The town's enthusiastic affirmation of the most preposterous stories, stories so extremely implausible that even the most provincial audience might reject them, functions as moral failure. Eliot suggests that Grimworth's eagerness to believe David serves as an evasion of the truth, a deliberate choice to avoid reality, which causes the town's ultimate undoing. As her prefatory quote from La Fontaine implies—"*Trompeurs, c'est pour vous que j'écris / Attendez vous à la pareille*"—"Brother Jacob," like any moral fable, gives its selfish and ignorant characters their just comeuppance.

From this perspective, the story reads like a relatively simple morality tale bent on challenging the complacent assumptions of British imperial ideology, a literary counterpart to the nonfictional critiques of colonial life written by some of Eliot's contemporaries. Eliot's pointed rejection of the comfortable bourgeois view of the colonies as spaces untroubled by economic difficulties or social tension parallels the nineteenth-century reports on the colonies which acknowledged their many problems. Although British citizens may have been overwhelmingly in favor of imperial expansion, imperial ideology was neither monolithic nor unchallenged. There were dissenting voices who argued for gentler governing policies and greater rights for colonized subjects, and educated middle-class readers were no strangers to regular news reports on the tragic brutality and depressed conditions of recently freed slaves in colonial territory. Hall points out that although information on the colonies was always mediated through the lens of imperialist desires and expectations, the origins of political debates over the nature and rights of colonial subjects were founded on "reports in the missionary press and in the anti-slavery press" which focused on the more troubling aspects of racial oppression, as well as "public meetings, lecture tours, fund-raising campaigns, books, pamphlets, [and] private letters designed to be read in part at missionary prayer meetings or abolitionist gatherings" (211). Such reports frequently criticized imperial administrative bodies and generally emphasized the dismal effects of colonization on the colonized. In Eliot's portrayal of the Grimworth citizens, who prefer to believe David's exotic stereotypes instead of grim, guilt-inducing truth about colonization, she shares the perspective of those nonfictional accounts of the Empire which highlighted both its bureaucratic and moral shortcomings.

Eliot's censure of the ignorant bourgeoisie, disposed to believe even the most implausible lies about the colonies, resonates even more powerfully when one recalls that her story was written in the aftermath of the Indian Mutiny, a crisis in British colonial rule that exposed the same British arrogance Eliot lampoons in "Brother Jacob." The Mutiny, a rebellion of the East India Army's native soldiers, revealed not only that the Empire was less stable than had been assumed, but, even more disturbing, that its colonized subjects were apparently far more dangerous and committed to ousting their colonizers than the British had thought possible.[10] The troubling implications of this overt challenge to imperial rule reverberated throughout England, and scathing condemnations of the Indian administration's failure to predict or quickly resolve the uprising appeared in the press with obsessive regularity. The daily papers defensively depicted the rebellious sepoys as religious fanatics or hysterics misled by the unscrupulous Tipoo Sultan, and the innocent British government as caught within an unavoidable but ineffectual series of laws and governing policies. Reports of military maneuvers and individual campaigns proved an inexhaustible source of interest in monthly periodicals. Even Eliot admitted, in a letter to Sara Hennell, that she simply wished the whole business would go away, observing that she "should be satisfied to look forward to a heaven made up of long autumn afternoon walks, quite delivered from any necessity of giving a judgment on the Woman Question or of reading newspapers about the Indian Mutinies'' (383).

Despite Eliot's professed desire to ignore the Mutiny altogether, ''Brother Jacob'''s satiric view of Grimworth's unwarranted faith in its misguided perceptions of the colonies compellingly parallels the real indictment of imperial attitudes which emerged in the press immediately after the Mutiny's outbreak. Although vitriolic attacks on the sepoys were by far the most common reaction to the Mutiny—most articles featured a blend of severe horror, fear, and calls for immediate reprisal—some periodical accounts reveal a muted but growing awareness that the sepoys were not the only contributing factor at work. In fact, in the midst of vehement, almost hysterical appeals for vengeance and retaliation in the English popular press, a faint but persistent counter-discourse also surfaced, a discourse which suggested that the complacency and ignorance of the British colonial administration were partially responsible for colonial tensions.

Like Eliot's fictional Grimworth characters, both the mid-century East India Company and the English government at home had generally exhibited a deliberate blindness to India's political reality: an indifference to social tension between colonizers and colonized and an arrogant faith in the superiority of English culture. As Patrick Brantlinger observes, a few prominent writers and politicians—namely Karl Marx and Benjamin Disraeli—felt compelled to acknowledge that this self-absorption significantly contributed to the underlying forces which shaped the rebellion. Disraeli, notes Brantlinger, ''understood Hindu and Muslim attempts to protect beliefs and customs,'' and Marx, ''in several *New York Daily Tribune* articles, . . . stressed British incomes in India, rapacious land tenure policies, and evidence that tax collectors resorted to torture'' (202). But Marx and Disraeli were not the only public figures critiquing the East India Company. Reproaching England for failing to be fully cognizant of the social tension within the Indian colonies, *Bentley's Miscellany* offered a lengthy review of German officer Leopold von Orlich's pamphlet on the Mutiny, and quoted extensively those passages which argued that the British persistently demonstrate a disgraceful indifference to their colonies. Orlich remarked,

> It would display a gross ignorance of the real condition of India to try and thrust the blame of this terrible catastrophe upon one portion exclusively. But I am not surprised at even the most senseless views and opinions, for when I returned from India I was startled at the ignorance Englishmen of all ranks displayed as to the history and administration of India. I was positively beshamed when a member of Parliament visited me one day to obtain some information respecting questions of the day relating to India, as the honourable member designed to bring them before the House.          (60)

Even though the *Bentley's* editor quickly responds that "[i]t would be premature . . . to ascribe such a military insurrection . . . solely to neglect . . ." (60),
the article does little to diminish the damaging force of Orlich's indictment
of British obliviousness. Accompanying the more virulent charges of sepoy
disloyalty in the press, then, were less favorable critiques of British government: complaints which pointed out that the East India Company knew too
little about its own people to govern them effectively.

Even *The Times of London*, which generally and overwhelmingly supported
the government throughout the Mutiny, also grumbled that the British government had failed to acknowledge colonial problems which should have been
taken seriously, and further suggested that this neglect advanced the Mutiny's
sudden violence. A lead article from June of 1857 griped that "Lord Ellenbor-
ough might have done some real service to his country had he given us
something more substantial than gloomy remarks on the intense heat of the
season, on the want of a local police sufficient to dispense with the presence
of soldiers, on the unknown character of the officer in command at Meerut,
and on the fortunate folly or malice displayed in the neglect of a certain tank
at Delhi'' (9).

Admittedly, these sort of critiques were less common than the passionate
public calls for vengeance and brutal retaliation. Complaints of British ignorance and complacency were nowhere near as severe as they might have
been, and stopped well short of condemning imperial domination. Most criticism of the East India Company during the Mutiny treated its patronizing
refusal to acknowledge the resistance of its subjects in strictly utilitarian
terms, a practical problem rather than a moral failure. Nevertheless, those
critiques which blamed the British for failing to see what was right in front
of them, and which further suggested that the Empire's view of its own
colonial subjects may have actually inflamed sepoy resentment, encouraged
a discussion of imperial politics which accommodated ethical questions. Orlich's pamphlet, for instance, depicted the Indian government's failure as a
character flaw, not a mere bureaucratic oversight. This view of the Mutiny
supported, at least to a greater degree, a moral and ethical examination of
colonial authority. Eliot's satiric depiction of the ignorant Grimworth citizens
in "Brother Jacob" might be interpreted as a literary complement to this
critique of colonial psychology.

When read as a text which offers a literary version of the nonfictional
criticisms of British ignorance that appeared in the press shortly after the
Mutiny, "Brother Jacob" becomes a reproof of the complacent, willing sub-
scription to lazy but comforting stereotypes which imagine colonized subjects

as naturally inferior to Europeans, or as glamorous, exotic Others devoid of true power or agency. Eliot's portrayal of the Grimworth townspeople as emotionally and politically invested in David's simplistic and ultimately safe representations of the colonies slyly condemns the British public for affecting a willful ignorance about the realities of colonial life.

IV

But "Brother Jacob" cannot be read as a direct political challenge to imperial ideology, for Eliot's story contains troubling ambiguities which thwart its functioning as a simple allegory about ignorant townspeople who learn a clear moral lesson. Her final observation that Jacob is "an admirable instance of the unexpected forms in which the great Nemesis hides herself" (55) implies that we are often blind to the agents of our undoing, a profoundly troubling idea in a mid-Victorian imperial world in which colonial authority and control depend on knowing where threats lie. Eliot's story both exposes the arrogance of colonial psychology and acknowledges it as a moral problem, but also betrays a decided ambivalence at the thought of being called to account for this moral failure.

While most fables feature wise and virtuous parties contrasted by bad ones (for every grasshopper there is an ant), Eliot portrays David's nemesis, his idiot brother Jacob, as threatening and possibly even dangerous.[11] Unlike the nemesis of *Silas Marner* (1861), which, as Eliot observed in a letter to John Blackwood, "is a very mild one" (170), her dubious depiction of the thuggish and stupid Jacob foregrounds the more unsettling aspects of the trope. Jacob, who remains somewhat unlikable (certainly ignoble) despite his role as moral agent, implies that the force which exposes hypocrisy is not always rational or deliberate. Even more disturbing, it is not always civilized. As a nemesis, Jacob embodies qualities which suggest that morality does not always coincide with superior intellect, and this rather disconcerting idea corresponds to a broad cultural anxiety which surfaced in England with increasing frequency after the Mutiny: that perhaps the social authority of the Empire was not, after all, based on an inherent moral and cultural superiority.

Though Jacob is English, Eliot strongly aligns elements of his character with the Victorian stereotype of the primitive—an association that encourages a reading of the literary nemesis within the wider context of mid-Victorian imperialism. Eliot not only compares him to Caliban—Jacob is as thrilled with his lemon lozenges as Caliban with Trinculo's wine (8)—but her decision to make Jacob an idiot, moreover, reveals a startling participation in an existing mid-nineteenth-century discourse which drew explicit connections between idiots and colonized natives.[12] As evidenced by popular periodical writing, doctors and scientists generally viewed idiots and colonized subjects as members of the same species, assigning them parallel physical traits and behavioral pathologies. Jacob's hyper-physicalized body invokes nineteenth-century stereotypes of Africans: his unnatural strength and pitchfork recall the phrase ''black devil,'' and his exaggerated body and face—an exaggeration also thought to be common to idiots—further resembles nineteenth-century racist representations of black features.[13] According to mid-Victorian analyses of natives and idiots, furthermore, Jacob's uncontrollable appetite is a feature shared by both groups. ''[The idiot] manifested all the characteristics of an inferior animal'' when first admitted to the Bicêtre, remarked a *Chambers' Edinburgh Journal* article on the education of idiots, noting further that his ''appetite was voracious'' (February 13, 105). This description mirrors common mid-Victorian descriptions of West Indian natives, as evidenced in the *Dublin Review*'s assertion that ''there is no difference in any of these savages. If hungry they will fawn upon you; and when filled they will desert'' (120). Jacob's unnatural craving for sweets resonates as a symptom exhibited by both idiots and colonized subjects.

But the echoes of African stereotypes in Jacob's physical person are not as compelling as Jacob's idiocy itself, which definitively echoes the intellectual and moral inferiority so often assigned to colonized peoples at mid-century and beyond. Indeed, in popular scientific analyses Victorian writers often described idiots as colonized subjects and the colonized as literal idiots, effectively collapsing the distinction between the two:

> He is that backward pupil that we sometimes see, a big hulking boy among the minors, who plods painfully through the lesson which tiny urchins make light of. Most of us have seen the great, slow, stupid fellow bending over his books, blundering and stammering, rated by the master for a blockhead, jeered at by this youngster, patronized by that, but always behindhand. Add to this picture an extra hankering after idleness, great animal spirits, overflowing good humour, and a considerable development at the back of the head, and the negro is before you: that is the negro of the West Indies. (*Cornhill Magazine* 341)

Add an overwhelming need for lemon lozenges, and this mid-nineteenth-century portrayal of a Jamaican could almost stand in for Eliot's description of Brother Jacob.

Finally, like colonized subjects, idiots were viewed as latently aggressive creatures who needed appropriate discipline to become productive, non-violent members of British society. Idiots should be made "gentle, docile, and obedient, governable by the simplest means" (21), argued the *Edinburgh Review* in 1865, corresponding to Charles Mackay's remark that "[s]o far from being miserable, morose, and dangerous in slavery, the Negro enjoyed all the pleasures that his easy and docile nature placed within his reach. If he received kind treatment, which he generally did, he loved his master, and would have done anything in his power to serve him" (*Blackwood's Magazine* 588). The drive to "reform" idiots and colonized subjects relied on precisely the same logic—and, naturally, had less to do with altruism than it did with the practical effect of deflecting their potential rebellions, especially in the case of the colonized. *Chambers' Edinburgh Journal* reported that "most idiotic children are wayward, inattentive to habits of decency, and addicted to various vicious propensities" (Sept. 11, 170). Accordingly, they must be constantly guarded for signs of violence. The view that idiots may at any time manifest a sudden aggression certainly manifests in Eliot's portrayal of the half-witted Jacob, whom she describes as "not ferocious or needlessly predatory" except "in fits of anger" (8).

In other words, either through her deliberate construction or unconscious adherence to the dominant images of mid-Victorian culture, Eliot portrays David's personal nemesis as a virtual embodiment of nineteenth-century black stereotypes, a depiction which invites broader speculation about the nature of nemesis as it relates to colonial psychology. As a kind of racialized Other, Jacob's exposure of David's thievery and generally duplicitous behavior suggests at least one possible narrative outcome to the Empire's domination of its subjects. If an idiot brother can upset the existing power dynamic by returning to brand a paragon of the community as a liar and a thief, what does that imply about the possibility—not to mention the inherent justice—of native cultures rebelling against their colonizers and responding destructively to their thievery? As Jacob's close proximity (he has been living only one town away from Grimworth) and illuminating reemergence indicate, the idea that our present-day lives are marked by a lurking retaliation close at hand adopts a more threatening cast when considered within a colonial context. David's inability to suppress his savage brother's return hints at the existence of a larger cultural narrative of colonial anxiety: the Empire's failure to repress its colonized subjects—its potential nemesis—effectively.

Not long after Eliot finished "Brother Jacob," the fear that colonial subjects would rise up and demand a moral reckoning once again became a reality, in the form of the 1865 Morant Bay uprising. Prompted by a dispute over a simple fine, "several hundred blacks marched into the town of Morant Bay" and attacked the police station in search of weapons (Heuman 3). The Jamaican colonial government's response was extraordinarily violent, and the rebellion ended in widespread death: "439 blacks and 'coloureds' were killed, 600 men and women were flogged and over 1,000 huts and houses were burnt," notes Hall (255). The event subsequently divided the English public into two opposing camps, those who wanted the governor of Jamaica prosecuted for murder and those who wanted him applauded as an English hero. Eliot's narrative of a racialized, ominous nemesis thus anticipates the real political dynamics and moral conflicts that were to trouble the Empire in its immediate future. More generally, in a culture preoccupied with maintaining control over its imperial subjects, the nemesis proved to be a suggestive literary device for raising the more troubling aspects of imperial power.

## V

If reading "Brother Jacob" as a text which aligns the literary nemesis with colonial conflict contributes to our larger understanding of the relationship between narrative and imperialism in the mid-nineteenth century, then Eliot's association of the nemesis—one of her favorite devices for exposing moral hypocrisy—with imperial themes also indicates that perhaps Victorian novelists do not always "continually reinforce[]" (Said 73) British colonial power. In fact, Eliot's satiric representation of David Faux's West Indian tales actively lampoons the self-serving use of the colonies "for relatively simple purposes such as immigration, fortune, or exile" (Said 74), which many postcolonialist readings continue to assume is the primary role of the colonies in Victorian fiction. But those Victorian novels which align the dynamics of repression and return with a moral inquiry into the nature of British imperialism endeavor to move beyond simple affirmations of imperial authority. Eliot's use of a racialized nemesis suggests a view of Victorian narrative in which some writers struggle to come to terms with a pervasive cultural ideology with extremely troubling moral implications.

This surfaces in other nemesis figures who are associated in some way with the colonies. In addition to the many characters in mid-Victorian novels who return from the far-flung reaches of the Empire in order to force a moral confrontation, from Dickens's Magwitch to George Talboys in M. E. Braddon's *Lady Audley's Secret* (1861–62), many Victorian novels feature racialized nemesis figures who resemble Eliot's Jacob. From *Jane Eyre*'s Bertha to the Brahmins in Wilkie Collins's *The Moonstone*, these nemesis characters emerge from the colonies and disrupt the complacent assumptions of English superiority which feed imperial ideology. Literary scholars often read this narrative dynamic as an extension of the Gothic: regularly interpreting Brontë's Bertha, for instance, as Jane's Gothic double, or Collins's Brahmins as reflecting the Gothic obsession with the return of the repressed.

But to view Bertha or the Brahmins as mid-Victorian versions of nemesis, whose reappearance in the story reveals the moral failure of imperial Britain (Rochester's failure as a husband and colonist, Rachel Verinder's failure to realize that the Indian jewel does not rightly belong to her), suggests the authors' respective interest in exposing the moral ruptures inherent in British imperial authority. Stephen Arata observes that fin-de-siècle Victorian narrative often expresses a fear of colonial invasion, constructing stories of "reverse colonization" where, as in H. G. Wells's *The War of the Worlds* (1898), "the colonized Other . . . returns both to haunt the culture for its sins and to threaten its destruction as a form of retribution" (109). Perhaps if fin-de-siècle fiction focuses on the returning Other as an object of fear, a figure whose potential for claiming justice is subordinated to the destruction it brings, then the mid-century nemesis of "Brother Jacob," and of some other mid-century Victorian novels, rests more precariously between the idea of justice and ruin. The use of this moral trope in the 1850s and 1860s indicates one way that Victorian writers struggled to come to terms with imperial rule and its attendant assumption of British cultural supremacy. The nemesis was not always treated as an opportunity to consider the moral implications of colonial psychology, but its persistent association with the Empire suggests that, at least for a while, it functioned as an important device for raising ethical concerns about imperial ideology.

If the mid-century nemesis became a device for considering the moral implications of imperial ideology, it was not long, however, before the moral dimensions of this critique quickly evaporated. Over the second half of the nineteenth century, Victorian narratives increasingly exhibited an intense anxiety about the stability of the Empire, an anxiety Arata identifies in the fiction of H. Rider Haggard, Bram Stoker, and Wells among others. These late-Victorian writers endorse a much more fearful view of colonized subjects who return to demand justice—or mete out vengeance. Even Collins's portrayal of the Brahmins ultimately succumbs to this fear. Although the novel initially foregrounds the inherent violence of colonialism—Herncastle, for instance, murders an Indian Brahmin for his diamond and, in chillingly casual passive voice, remarks that "[t]he Indian met his death, as I suppose, by a mortal wound" (37)—it eventually subordinates this moral critique to a more general expression of anxiety about the Brahmins themselves. Like Brother Jacob, the Indians are mysterious, uncivilized, and dangerous to British authority.

Perhaps because of real colonial rebellions like the Indian Mutiny and the Morant Bay rebellion, by the end of the nineteenth century the literary nemesis loses its attendant theme of moral accountability. In fact, those narratives featuring the colonies frequently use the nemesis to express the fear that colonial subjects are brimming with latent hostility, ready to lash out destructively at any moment. If, at mid-century, the British "imagined" (to use Benedict Anderson's paradigm) their colonies as a national nemesis, a nemesis likely to perform a function similar to a literary one, this view of the colonies at least accommodates the idea that they might be justified in resisting the Empire. But later writers evacuate the nemesis metaphor of its moral implications, investing the trope instead with imperial paranoia. Mackay's 1866 article about America's abolition of slavery, for instance, draws upon the nemesis metaphor, but completely voids its earlier moral resonances, making it a crude articulation of white fear:

> These people ["Negrophilists"], aiding the abolitionists in their unnatural war against their white brother, not for the sake of the negro, but for the sake of the Union—the great and only object of American reverence and idolatry—have had their triumph [freeing the slaves]. *And with the triumph has come the Nemesis, the black shadow of whose avenging hand creeps over the morning sky, and threatens ere noon to darken the whole hemisphere.* In liberating the negroes by the sword, the North has itself become a slave. It is bound, like a Siamese twin, to the side of the "irrepressible nigger." (582, emphasis added)

Written only one year after the Morant Bay uprising and the abolition of slavery in the United States, Mackay's picture of the ominous black shadow haunting America shows how powerfully the theme of moral accountability formerly associated with the nemesis drops out of the metaphor in the latter half of the nineteenth century. Unlike Eliot's more ambivalent portrayal of the uncivilized nemesis as something threatening but also just (Eliot's uneasy portrait of Jacob never loses sight of his moral role), Mackay employs the trope in the much more traditionally Gothic sense of the return of a ghostly repressed, using the classic Gothic patterns of domination and subordination to reinforce white authority (see Wilt). As colonial rebellion became a more likely threat, Victorian writers increasingly moved away from the idea of the moral nemesis and back toward the Gothic narrative's dynamic of repression, in which colonized subjects, promising eventual rebellion, function as shadowy and threatening Others.

This literary shift also parallels the breakdown of moral rhetoric in nonfictional anti-slavery discourses. As Hall says of written responses to the Morant Bay uprising,

> the missionary struggle to define blackness as both equal and not equal, whiteness as superior, but with patronage, kindness, and generosity to the fore, was collapsing under the combined weight of its own contradictions, its own refusal to face the uncomfortable reality that black people might choose to be different, and a new assault from elsewhere on the mutability of racial difference. The moment of the ''poor negro'' was over.                                   (249)

The complex tension exhibited by Eliot's use of nemesis metaphor, a tension which both invites and fears a moral consideration of imperialism, loses its moral dimensions as Victorian writers increasingly articulated race relations through the Gothic tropes of imprisonment and loss, creating narratives which describe colonized subjects as nemeses only in order to affirm imperial domination.

Before this reaffirmation of imperial authority in late-Victorian narratives, however, Eliot's ''Brother Jacob'' suggests that mid-Victorian narrative considered the possibility—if only briefly and somewhat indirectly—that colonial domination bore serious moral consequences. Eliot's implicit link between the nemesis trope and imperial ideology intimates to her readers that Britain's perception of itself as morally and culturally superior is inherently unstable and fundamentally vulnerable to moral criticism. This acknowledgement lends more depth to the persistent view of mid-Victorian imperial narratives as either validations of imperial authority or thoughtless expressions of imperial fear. The mid-Victorian nemesis, if only temporarily, creates in Victorian colonial narrative an opportunity to consider the moral and social ramifications of imperial rule. Perhaps it is no surprise that Eliot the moralist took this opportunity, and her portrayal of Brother Jacob metaphorically evokes the possibility of imperial failure and uneasily intimates the justice of colonial rebellion.

## NOTES

1. For Eliot's remark about the insignificance of ''Brother Jacob,'' see her journal entry for 27 Sept. 1860.

2. Welsh suggests that Eliot's use of the nemesis reveals a broad shift in Victorian perceptions of privacy in the new information age: if repressing past wrongs leaves one vulnerable to their future reappearance, then it also leaves one vulnerable to blackmail. He views "Brother Jacob" as a "light[er]" and earlier experimentation with the blackmail plot (163).

3. See Peter Allan Dale for further discussion of "Brother Jacob" as a parable: he remarks that "[t]he Fontainean epigraph invites us to the essential task demanded of readers of this kind of fiction. . . . We must read, that is, not as we read a novel, with our attention fixed on the problem of life itself, but with a view towards deciphering the *allegoresis*, the puzzle deliberately hidden within the text" (19).

4. I refer to this event as the Victorians did—as a "mutiny" rather than a struggle for political independence—because this term highlights the assumption that the uprising had little, if any, political legitimacy. As the word "mutiny" implies, the British preferred to consider the resistance an internal upheaval within international domestic space: a family rift rather than a serious political revolution.

5. See Deborah Nord. See also Reina Lewis's chapter "Aliens at Home and Britains Abroad: George Eliot's Orientalization of Jews in *Daniel Deronda*" in *Gendering Orientalism*, in which she argues that "despite the novel's generally positive portrayal of Judiasm and Marian Evans's evident desire to challenge prejudice, *Daniel Deronda* replicates many of the fundamental Orientalist tropes of difference and otherness" (192). In Susan Meyer's *Imperialism at Home*, she claims that "in *Mill on the Floss* George Eliot imagines the destructive results that attend the 'fusion' of races, [but] in *Daniel Deronda*, her last novel, Eliot envisions—and celebrates—a perhaps more ominous world in which such a destructive fusion will not occur because the races are kept separate" (157).

6. See Eliot's "Silly Novels by Lady Novelists," in which she lampoons "mind-and-millinery" novels written by women for being overly religious, or (as she says of the novel *Compensation*), "heavily dosed with doctrine, but . . . [with] a treble amount of snobbish worldliness and absurd incident to tickle the palate of pious frivolity" (306).

7. De Sola Rodstein suggests that David's job as confectioner reveals Eliot's implied disapproval of colonial enterprise through its criticism of sugar as morally and nutritionally unhealthy. Ultimately, de Sola Rodstein is less interested in Eliot's critique of imperial psychology than in the relationship between the story's fetishistic focus on sweets and Eliot's own sense of her literary authority. She argues that the themes of creation and consumption express Eliot's feelings about her recent public exposure as an author and her anxiety about the worth of literary representation.

8. Dale remarks that Eliot's exceptionally harsh tone creates "the purest expression we have in George Eliot's fiction of the ironist's perception, everywhere present in the major work but always subordinated, that people may, after all, be more ridiculous than they are lovable" (18).

9. See the colonial stereotypes in Patrick Brantlinger's *Rule of Darkness*, which mentions *LallaRookh* (1817)—a favorite text in Grimworth—as contributing "to the growing stock of stereotypic images of India" (24).

10. "[T]here was a great deal of underlying resentment about white Christian rule in a country of many other races and cultures, all of whom most probably regarded their subservience to the British as degrading," remarks Said (146).

11. Literary scholars generally agree that "Brother Jacob" fails to provide us with a clearly "good" moral force—or counterpart to David Faux—at all. Welsh notes that "[t]he story certainly has a despicable hero" (161), and James Diedrick observes that it "is the only one of Eliot's narratives that withholds sympathy for the characters" (464). Even Henry James, who preferred the story to "The Lifted Veil" (1859), found "Brother Jacob" extremely funny precisely because of its "ironic, satiric manner"—not its sympathetic view of good and evil (131).

12. Mid-period accounts of idiots often applied to them the rhetoric of slavery. *Chambers' Edinburgh Journal*, for instance, describes an idiot learning to sew as "view[ing] thread and thimble in the light of a galley-slave's chain" (11 May 1861, 304). Even more specifically, an *Edinburgh Review* article from a July 1865 describes an idiot from the American South as "intellectually dead . . . no question could arouse him . . . nothing was ever apparently noticed by him till he saw a coloured man, such as he used to see in the South, whence he came; and he seemed to recognize him with pleasure, exclaiming, 'Oh, you!' as if in dim remembrance of his former home" (23). Minstrelsy, moreover, was often an encouraged form of entertainment in the education of idiots: the *Edinburgh Review* observes that at the Earlswood asylum, for instance, the idiots there "formed a Nigger Troupe, and with blackened faces and grotesque dresses joined the attendants in a performance of great humour" (July 1865, 23).

13. The *Edinburgh Review* (July 1865) notes that while "dimensions of the head . . . nor other measurements often relied upon, can be regarded as true criteria of idiocy . . . the general peculiarities of [the idiot's] body are all abnormal" (23). See George W. Stocking's *Victorian Anthropology* for a thorough account of the rise of nineteenth-century anthropology. Early anthropologists frequently associated physicality with intellectual capability. Eliot herself, of course, was also deeply interested in phrenology, a preoccupation many literary scholars see echoed in her fiction.

# WORKS CITED

Anderson, Benedict. *Imagined Communities: Reflections on the Origin and the Spread of Nationalism.* 1983. Revised edition. London: Verso, 1991.

Arata, Stephen. *Fictions of Loss in the Victorian Fin de Siècle.* New York: Cambridge, 1996.

Brantlinger, Patrick. *Rule of Darkness: British Literature and Imperialism, 1830–1914.* Ithaca: Cornell UP, 1988.

Brooks, Peter. *Reading for the Plot: Design and Intention in Narrative.* New York: Vintage, 1985.

Burton, Antoinette. *At the Heart of the Empire: Indians and the Colonial Encounter in Late-Victorian Britain.* Berkeley: U of California P, 1998.

"The Causes of the Indian Mutiny." *Bentley's Miscellany* 43 (1858): 60–68.

Collins, Wilkie. *The Moonstone.* 1868. Ed. J. I. M. Stewart. Harmondsworth: Penguin, 1983.

Dale, Peter Allan. "George Eliot's 'Brother Jacob': Fables and the Physiology of Common Life." *Philological Quarterly* 64.1 (1985): 17–35.

de Sola Rodstein, Susan. "Sweetness and Dark: George Eliot's 'Brother Jacob.'" *Modern Language Quarterly* 52.3 (Sept. 1991): 295–317.

Diedrick, James. "George Eliot's Experiments in Fiction: 'Brother Jacob' and the German *Novelle.*" *Studies in Short Fiction* 22.4 (1985): 461–68.

"Education of Idiots at the Bicêtre." *Chambers' Edinburgh Journal.* New series, 7 (1847): 105–07, 169–70.

Eliot, George. "Brother Jacob." 1864; 1878. London: Virago, 1989.

———. "Silly Novels by Lady Novelists." *Westminster Review* (Oct. 1856): 442–61. Rpt. in Pinney 300–24.

———. "Three Novels." *Westminster Review* (Oct. 1856): 571–78. Rpt. in Pinney 300–24.

———. "To John Blackwood." 24 Feb. 1861. *George Eliot: The Critical Heritage.* Ed. David Carroll. London: Routledge and Kegan Paul, 1971. 169–70.

———. "To Sara Sophia Hennell, Richmond." *The George Eliot Letters.* Ed. Gordon S. Haight. Vol. 2: 1852–1858. New Haven: Yale UP, 1954. 382–84.

Hall, Catherine. *White, Male, and Middle-Class.* New York: Routledge, 1992.

Harris, Margaret, and Judith Johnston, eds. *The Journals of George Eliot.* Cambridge: Cambridge UP, 1998.

Heuman, Gad. *"The Killing Time": The Morant Bay Rebellion in Jamaica.* Knoxville: U of Tennessee P, 1999.

"Idiot Asylums." *Edinburgh Review,* American edition, 122 (July 1865): 19–38.

James, Henry. " 'The Lifted Veil' and 'Brother Jacob.'" *Nation* (25 Apr. 1878): 277. Rpt. in *A Century of George Eliot Criticism.* Ed. Gordon S. Haight. Boston: Houghton Mifflin Company, 1965. 130–31.

Leavis, F. R. "George Eliot." In Stang 46–55.

Lewis, Reina. *Gendering Orientalism: Race, Femininity and Representation*. London: Routledge, 1996.

Mackay, Charles. "The Negro and the Negrophilists." *Blackwood's Magazine* 99 (May 1866): 581–97.

Meyer, Susan. *Imperialism at Home: Race and Victorian Women's Fiction*. Ithaca: Cornell UP, 1996.

Morrison, Toni. *Playing in the Dark*. New York: Random House, 1992.

"The Negro in Africa and the West Indies." *Dublin Review*. New series, 7 (July 1866): 116–42.

"Negroes Bond and Free." *Cornhill Magazine* 4 (Sept. 1861): 340–47.

Nord, Deborah Epstein. " 'Marks of Race': Gypsy Figures and Eccentric Femininity in Nineteenth-Century Women's Writing." *Victorian Studies* 41.2 (1998): 189–210.

Pinney, Thomas, ed. *Essays of George Eliot*. New York: Columbia UP, 1963.

Said, Edward W. *Culture and Imperialism*. New York: Vintage, 1993.

Stang, Richard, ed. *Discussions of George Eliot*. Boston: D.C. Heath, 1960.

*The Times of London*. 30 June 1857: 9.

Welsh, Alexander. *George Eliot and Blackmail*. Cambridge: Harvard UP, 1985.

Wilt, Judith. "Love/Slave." *Victorian Studies* 37.3 (1994): 451–60.

# Recent Dickens Studies: 2000

## David Garlock

*This survey focuses on major critical studies related to Dickens's life and work that surfaced during the year 2000. The monographs and essays reviewed are grouped under familiar classificatory headings: namely, biographical studies, reference works, cultural studies, postcolonial readings, textual explication and, finally, a separate category reserved for one essay that seemed to merit its own rubric. Each capsule-sized review is intended to summarize the essential thrust of each contribution to scholarship considered. The survey also attempts to cluster these miniaturized assessments in meaningful ways, reflecting current trends that persistently destabilize, mold, re-shape, and/or calcify contemporary perceptions of text and author. The unmistakably clear image that emerges from a cacophony of critical postures and styles is of a writer and visionary whose legacy continues to fire our imaginations.*

A surveyor of recent Dickens studies should perhaps be forgiven for feeling a touch of mesmeric sympathy with Mr. Venus of *Our Mutual Friend*. After all, trafficking in "human warious" is surely no less wearisome—yet fraught with serendipity—than sifting through the scattered critical "warious" that surfaced during the year 2000. Like my fictional doppelganger, I have often stumbled upon clues and mysteries where one might have anticipated mere heaps of dust.

Disclaimers notwithstanding, taxonomic sorting (albeit makeshift) may yield unanticipated paroxysms of exhilaration, while, as Dickens's articulator of bones might have observed, some dust-enshrouded, exhumed artifacts excite more interest than others. In fact, on occasion—particularly when sifting through relatively obscure specimens of recently disinterred biographical or cultural detritus—I was inclined to wonder, with Ezekiel: "Can these bones live?"

Still, even a cursory glance at titles of recently published criticism suggests the persistent vitality that continues to comprise the greater part of current scholarship, as we embark on a new century poised to pass its own judgment on the Dickensian canon. No greater taxonomic charlatan than Mr. Venus, I have probably been as arbitrary as he in my sorting of the "warious" monographs and essays I have encountered into six bin-like categories: namely, (1) biographical studies, (2) reference works, (3) cultural studies, (4) postcolonial readings, (5) textual explication, and, finally, (6) a separate slot for an essay that I felt merited its own category.

Anyone who has ever taken on a task of this kind knows that there is a great deal of overlapping of styles and critical approaches. Current theory seems to inflect (some would say "infect") most of the critical works I have reviewed, and, as Mr. Venus would not hesitate to caution, classification is presumptive and, inherently, a slippery business.

Caveat lector!

## 1. Biographical Studies

With all of the excellent biographies available to the Dickens scholar, one might be tempted to wonder what biographical details remain unearthed. Yet, in *Charles Dickens Revisited*, part of the Twayne's English Authors Series, Robert Newsom manages to lend fresh insights into some of Dickens's major work, as he explores the ceaseless tension that will always separate (as it entangles) author, reader, and written text. His opening chapter, "Dickens and the Problem of the Author," presents a keen analysis of the familiar debate centered around traditional notions of authorship and theory-based challenges to the lionization of "great" literary figures as glorified—if sometimes desiccated—icons. According to Newsom, "Dickens tests the death-of-the-author proposition in fascinating ways" (2).

A defining aspect of Newsom's biography is his focus on the dichotomies and warring contradictions that constitute so much of the authors work and which seem to bedevil his psyche. Newsom offers a multi-layered portrayal of Dickens's divided "selves," biographically and in terms of his work. A typical example of Newsom's extrapolating a kind of self-portrait from the novels would be his describing characters in *Oliver Twist* as embodiments of various aspects of their creator's character: "Just as the Artful and Oliver embody Dickens's various selves, so too do Sikes and Nancy constitute further splittings of Dickensian selves" (57). In chapter 4, entitled "Sentiment and Skepticism," Newsom relates the conflicted mind and consciousness of the author with the warring states of mind that seem so often to dominate Victorian culture and thought, generally. Indeed, the rising tide of skepticism that overwhelmed the Victorian Age often appeared to be in conflict with the concerns and preoccupations associated with refinement of the human spirit. Dickens was acutely aware of the conflictive nature of value systems represented by cold rationality on the one hand and cherished traditional belief systems on the other. Essentially a Carlylean, Dickens veered toward the side of faith, but a faith tempered with respect for rational thought and the corrective forces of reason: "Dickens always consciously and explicitly identified himself with Carlyle and the party of the spirit" (59). Dickens's commitment to the "party of the spirit" is not without its inconsistencies, however, and Newsom exploits to advantage these complexities infusing the author's life and his creations.

In his last chapter, Newsom explores what he considers to be the crowning contradiction in Dickens—the author's attitude toward class structures and the responsibilities of civilized society. The shift from class structures based on inherited wealth and privilege toward a more egalitarian model, while it neither began nor ended with the Victorians, probably assumed a higher profile and greater acceleration during Dickens's lifetime than ever before. Once again, this major shift in structures of power and social status seems to evoke responses detectable in Dickens's life and work that are consistent only in their variability. Concurring with Ian Watt, Newsom connects the evolution of the novel as genre with the rise of a powerful and dominant middle class during the nineteenth century. On the surface, the comforts and assurances of middle-class privilege and stability are ostensibly celebrated by popular novelists of the period such as Elizabeth Gaskell and Charles Dickens—two novelists who practically define that most middle-class of genres. However, a major strength of Newsom's biography of Dickens is his eschewing facile classifications that gloss over the undercurrents defying formulaic assessment. There is more under scrutiny in Dickens than the joys and sorrows of jockeying for social standing or the rewards achievable through a responsible commitment to tranquil domesticity. Newsom concludes his biography with a concise statement alluding to the unfathomable complexities with which his author wrestles and with which thoughtful readers must engage. Mere comfort through acceptance of ordinary domestic life never emerges as quite the fulfilling goal it ought to be: "That he was never entirely comfortable himself with such a homely notion does not so much undermine its truth as point us once again to the tensions that give it life" (180).

Although not a biographical work in the strictest sense, *Dickens Redressed, The Art of "Bleak House" and "Hard Times,"* by Alexander Welsh analyzes Dickens's two major mid-career novels in biographical terms. Welsh provides evidence that Esther Summerson may have been based upon Dickens's sister-in-law Georgina Hogarth, for example, but he also maintains that *Bleak House* contains many autobiographical elements, as well: "Even if Miss Summerson's character and situation did depend upon Miss Hogarth's, the novelist has portrayed his heroine subjectively, as deeply representative of himself" (23). Welsh reads *Bleak House* and *Hard Times* as companion novels, viewing the latter as epilogue and dialogic counterpoint. Writing from a perspective that seems a far remove from "death of the author" issues, Welsh defends his reliance on biographical detail as a source of interpretation: "In order to say anything useful about *Bleak House* and *Hard Times*, naturally, I have often to infer something of the author's purposes" (xvii).

Throughout this monograph, Welsh repeatedly makes comparisons between the first-person narrator of *David Copperfield*, generally considered the most autobiographical of Dickens's novels, and Esther Summerson's narrative voice. In his explication of major events and plot complications within the novel, Welsh alludes repeatedly to the mores and values of the society in which Dickens developed his craft. For example, the plot-driving scandal of Lady Dedlock's giving birth to Esther is incomprehensible without some appreciation of the social and cultural framework that shaped the perspectives of the novelist, according to Welsh: "The whole scandal of the heroine's mother in *Bleak House* has to be seen against the background of changing conditions of class mobility and publicity in the period . . ." (63). In Welsh's view, Dickens, in the guise of his narrators, seeks to redress personal and social grievances of various kinds through the ruses and camouflages afforded by the narrative process. This take on Dickens's use of gender-crossing narrative legerdemain in speaking through Esther's narrative voice, for example, is supported by close readings of specific passages within the novel, and Welsh's argument for the autobiographical aspects of the work seldom seem strained or tortured. Nor does Welsh accept wholeheartedly a postmodernist interpretation of the dual narrative voices present in the novel: "The oppositions that the novel seeks to establish may or may not be nullified—or, latterly, deconstructed" (140).

Welsh's reading of *Hard Times*, which comprises the last three chapters of the book, considers this novel as an epilogue to *Bleak House*. First-person narrative is abandoned, and, instead, clownlike characters are portrayed in garish hues. According to Welsh, "Clowning does not permit outright identification but rather a mixture of recognition and embarrassment" (208). Hence, Dickens is no longer redressed. He is, rather, re-*dressed*. The clown makeup and harlequinesque charade permit a level of distancing that may allow for a more biting satire than *Bleak House* and a certain relinquishment of control. "Dickens clearly looks to the future instead of to the past, the completed action of the previous novel" (208). Appropriately, *Hard Times* ends in irresolution. Welsh's linking of two dissimilar masterpieces reveals that through the mediation of his art, Dickens expresses the effectiveness of satire along with its inevitable limitations. According to Welsh, the clown-figures of *Hard Times* take on a Chaplinesque character, bridging the gap between ridicule and pathos.

Short essays dealing with minutiae related to an author's life (biographical canapés?) are a special delight to the scholar when they illuminate some specific aspect of a writer's literary legacy. An example is John Bowen's informed treatment of a particularly troubling sequence of events in Dickens's life, relating a tumultuous period to the production of the short story "His Boots." In "Bebelle and 'His Boots': Dickens, Ellen Ternan and the Christmas Stories," Bowen elaborates upon the well-known fact that during the period 1862–1863, Dickens visited Ellen Ternan in France. There is a great deal of speculation about whether or not an illegitimate child resulted from this much-discussed affair, but Bowen finds interesting parallels between the "Boots" story and issues that may have been bedeviling the writer at midlife. Bowen offers a biographically based explication of what he considers "a quite complex and suggestive story" (198). He compares the protagonist to Scrooge as well as to Dickens himself, noting that at the end of this chronicle of a fall from grace and subsequent redemption, Langley of "Boots" "reenters family life and the society from which he has exiled himself" (199). While postulating a possible link between Dickens's life and the story published in the 1862 edition of *All the Year Round* is to some degree speculative, Bowen's presentation of parallels offers a potentially valuable insight into the preoccupation with illegitimacy that characterizes so much of Dickens's work.

In a similar vein, "The Traveller as Liar: Dickens and the 'Invisible Towns' in Northern Italy," by Clotilde de Stasio, employs biographical details from a variety of sources in an assessment of Dickens's view of travel and the travelogue genre. Culling evidence from letters and Dickens's *Pictures from*

*Italy*, along with other sources, de Stasio detects "a constant tension between memory and experience, dream and reality" (5). There is an element of self-mockery in the composite portrait of the Victorian traveler that surfaces in *Little Dorrit*, and which resonates throughout much of the travel literature of the period, according to this well-researched and informative essay. According to de Stasio, Dickens made a distinction between himself as a traveler and his narrative voice as a travel chronicler. For Dickens, the actual city of Milan—the geographical location—competes with the fog-enshrouded Milan of the writer's imagination, "a strange evanescent place mysteriously reminiscent of London and Bombay" (9). In other words, Dickens the traveler superimposes London upon the towns of Italy, much as Marco Polo superimposes his native Venice upon the cities of the orient in Calvino's *Le città invisibili*. I found the comparisons between travel literature and fiction, with all of their strange interconnections, quite thought-provoking. The truth-lie dynamic that pervades both genres is an underlying theme of this essay—one that is supported by many illustrative examples extrapolated from biographical details and from the fictive milieu of Dickens's imagination.

Illuminating biographical detail likewise informs "Fictional Exorcism?:Parodies of the Supernatural in Dickens," by Tore Rem. According to Rem, Dickens was intrigued by the ghost story genre and was possessed of "a genuine fascination for a real, though concealed, world beyond our control" (15). Rem argues that Dickens's humorous treatment of ghosts in his fiction was a means of allaying his fears of a phenomenon which he at least tentatively accepted. Humor, in fact, may have helped to exorcise ever-present fears, since authorial control over his fictive ghosts provided an effective means of assuaging the dread of actual ghosts, according to this view. A number of interesting facts regarding Dickens's dabbling in mesmerism, which might be seen as conflictive with his antagonism toward spiritism and astrology, are put forward to create a general portrait of a mind mired in irresolution regarding issues that dominated the media and the public imagination during the author's lifetime. Rem opines that it is a mistake to place Dickens within the tradition of conventional skepticism, and, rather, presents compelling evidence that the consummate creator of fictive ghosts left the issue of their actual existence an open question.

Another ambivalence on the part of Dickens seems to have been his attitude toward the socially conscious, activist women of his generation. Gill Gregory explores this ambiguity in "Dickens and Adelaide Procter." Adelaide Proctor, who died at the age of 38 in 1864, "both attracted and disturbed him" (36). In fact, although Dickens published 80 of Proctor's poems from 1853 to 1860 in both *Household Words* and *All the Year Round*, there seems to have been a kind of dialogic tension between her poems and some of Dickens's prose narratives appearing in the same issues of these periodicals. Dickens specifically caricatures Proctor in the 1859 Christmas number of *All the Year Round*, arraying her with all of the characteristics of the hyper-radical feminist obsessively devoted to "causes." The fact that Dickens published the poet, while seeming to ridicule aspects of her alleged zealotry, provides a fascinating insight into a mind that contained many contradictions—an aspect of Dickens and his fictive landscape that Gregory exploits profitably.

Another essay concerned with issues of gender related to Dickens's biography is "In the Marketplace: Dickens, the Critics, and the Gendering of Authorship" by Kathleen Sell-Sandoval. This essay explores the nineteenth-century proclivity toward classification of literary productions in terms of characteristics associated with gender stereotypes. Hence, prose that is lucid and clear comes to be labeled as "masculine," while excessively sentimental writing comes to be considered "feminine." Mere "popular" fiction is written by and for women; high "art" in fiction is a manly pursuit, and is, therefore, worthy of manly attention. This absurd dichotomization led to inevitable clashes, as more and more women writers began to compete with their male counterparts in a burgeoning literary marketplace. Sell-Sandoval quotes extensively from widely-read literary critics of the Victorian period, particularly from passages that are dismissive of Dickens as an author who is not to be taken seriously because his work is popular (i.e., of little worth and, hence, irremediably feminized). "One such distinction is the claim that Dickens's work is grounded in an emotional rather than in an intellectual appeal and indeed that he is incapable of such an intellectual appeal because of the quality of his mind" (231). That Dickens rose above all of this critical tumult and, in fact, exulted in his popularity is a tribute to both the author and his readers. I found Kathleen Sell-Sandoval's essay particularly interesting, because it demonstrates through her illuminating research of contemporary critical responses to Dickens's work that gender stereotyping distorts perceptions in ways that negate individual worth—a negative process that affects both men and women.

Still another essay providing valuable insights into Dickens's attitude toward women is Margaret Flanders Darby's "Dickens and Women's Stories: 1845–1848—Parts One and Two." Darby describes in considerable detail the efforts of Dickens, in collaboration with Angela Burdett-Coutts, to establish a way station and rehabilitation center for homeless prostitutes. The history of the establishment of Urania Cottage provides some telling insights into Dickens's character and the genuineness of his concerns with social issues of his day. At the same time, it is easy for us to view some of his perspectives on the plight of the "fallen woman" as quaint and prudish. While Dickens firmly believed that virtue and self-respect could be restored to a woman who had allowed herself to become degraded in the eyes of society, he also believed that a fresh start for such a woman was only viable if she was willing to emigrate. Those who are familiar with Dickens's approach to Christian doctrine will not be surprised to learn that Dickens, the philanthropist, was opposed to the oppressive, preachy tactics often associated with evangelical fervor: "He saw to it that the girls were protected from the overbearing and punitive evangelical Christianity he always hated" (75). Music and artistic surroundings were to be introduced into the lives of the social outcasts, to whom Dickens, along with his female compatriots Elizabeth Gaskell and Angela Burdett-Coutts, hoped to offer a chance at a better life. Through an incisive analysis of some of Dickens's correspondence during the period of his involvement with Urania Cottage, Darby extracts a portrait of the novelist/ philanthropist. The man who emerges appears ultimately conflicted in his attitudes toward the women he hoped to liberate from their degraded status as prostitutes. Darby makes much of Dickens's tendency to destroy correspondence received from others, while saving his own letters. She presents compelling evidence that he wished to ensure that his own perspective on his personal history—including his account of his relationship with prostitutes in the role of counselor and benefactor—be preserved intact.

The role of Dickens as philanthropist extended far beyond his interest in the plight of prostitutes. Claudia Dereli provides a telling glimpse of Dickens's self-effacing generosity in her elaboration upon a minor footnote in the life of Dickens in her insightful "Charles Dickens and a 'Bohemian' Poet: Benevolent Radicals?" In this essay, Dereli explores the relationship between Dickens and Robert Brough, a struggling London-based playwright who died at the age of 32 in 1860. Although the two men had widely differing lifestyles, they shared a number of libertarian views, including an abiding distaste for the effete aristocracy, opposition to the Crimean War, and sympathy for society's outcasts. Dickens admired Brough's work and, in fact, offered encouragement by publishing some of the young author's work in *Household Words*. When the fledgling playwright died at an early age, leaving a wife and children with inadequate means of survival, five leading London theater companies participated in a benefit night, hoping to raise money for the young widow. Dereli notes that Dickens became a trustee of the funds raised, emphasizing the popular novelists sympathetic nature and his support of the family of a marginalized, "bohemian" playwright.

During the year 2000, several interesting biographical footnotes to *The Mystery of Edwin Drood* appeared in *The Dickensian*. In "Disappearances: George Parkman and Edwin Drood," Robert Tracy theorizes that Dickens's knowledge of a famous murder case may have provided the skeletal framework for the novel Dickens did not live to finish. While Tracy readily acknowledges that *"The Mystery of Edwin Drood* is much more complex than the Parkman murder" (116), he cites a number of arresting parallels between the fictional account of Drood's murder and the case of Parkman's murder by Professor Webster of Beacon Hill in Boston, as reported in the *London Times* from 1849 to 1850. He goes as far as to suggest that the name John Jasper may be a homonym for John Webster (a bit of a stretch, perhaps). Although the connection Tracy is proposing is admittedly speculative, the similarities presented provide a revealing glimpse into a real-life case of the period, and an insight into a newsworthy subject and a fictive genre, both of which seem to have enduring appeal from one century to another.

Another essay from *The Dickensian* dealing with a *Drood* footnote is Robert Raven's "Some Observations on Charles Collins's Sketches for *Edwin Drood*" (451). Raven's central thesis is based on careful examination of sketches Charles Collins prepared for the Chapman and Hall publication of Dickens's last novel. He presents the argument that these sketches provide a valuable glimpse into the evolution of *Drood*'s plot development, and that these drawings were created prior to the actual writing of the text. Raven extrapolates most of the evidence he presents from the drawings themselves. The reproduction of these drawings that accompanies the article in *The Dickensian* makes his argument easy to follow. The succession of sketches which portray variant renderings of a single scene is quite intriguing, and provides an interesting visual window into the creatively collaborative process into which Dickens and his illustrators would often enter.

In two companion essays appearing in separate numbers of *The Dickensian,* Arthur Cox offers a detailed description of mesmerism (or Animal Magnetism) as practiced during the nineteenth century and as embraced, at least tentatively, by Dickens. In the first essay, "Magnetic Sympathy in *The Mystery of Edwin Drood*, Part I: Mr. Crisparkle Takes a Memorable Night Walk," Cox attempts to reconcile Dickens's disinclination to accept spiritism and belief in telepathy with his attraction toward mesmerism as verifiable paranormal phenomenon. According to Cox, Dickens was drawn to the emphasis on the role that sympathy played in the practice of mesmerism. His alliance with mesmerism went beyond a naïve belief in the existence of an "electromagnetic fluid" that supposedly suffuses the universe and all of life. Mesmerism of the kind with which Dickens allied himself entailed a doctrine of sympathy: " . . . he believed that where human mysteries were concerned, it was through fellow-feeling that one understands" (131). Cox relates this Dickensian cult of sympathy to the phenomenal successes with audiences for which the author was famous. For Dickens, the rapport with an audience was an exchange of sympathies that functions like an electric current, according to Cox.

In "Magnetic Sympathy in *The Mystery of Edwin Drood*, Part II: Neville Landless Sets Out on a Pilgrimage," Cox applies his research on Dickens's allegiance to certain principles of mesmerism more specifically to the plot structure of the unfinished murder mystery. In particular, Cox explores the relationship between the twins, Neville and Helena Landless, defining their connection as sympathetic in the mesmeric mode. Another example of a mesmeric bond is that between John Jasper and Neville Landless, a relationship where, according to Cox, the former "magnetises" the latter. In his concluding paragraphs, Cox employs his encyclopedic knowledge of nineteenth-century ideas about mesmeric phenomena to support his own intriguing theory of how *Drood* might have ended if Dickens had lived to unravel the mystery. One need not accept all of the premises proffered in Cox's essay to find this discussion quite fascinating in terms of the impact of a popular enthusiasm upon Dickens's life and work.

## 2. Reference Works

The year 2000 saw the publication of *The Companion to Great Expectations* by David Paroissien. This 506–page volume, number seven in a series of "companions" to Dickens's novels, provides compendious annotation, offering illuminating explication of specific passages that may be inaccessible to most readers due to changes in culture, technology, social norms, and/or the meanings of everyday words and expressions. The organization of this reference tool, patterned after the kind of textual glossing one might expect in a biblical commentary, is arranged chapter by chapter paralleling the chapter divisions of the novel, allowing for easy referencing while reading *Great Expectations* itself. Paroissien's source materials range from British Parliamentary Papers and periodicals popular during the Victorian period to such obscure documents as an unpublished diary housed in the National Library of Australia. An arbitrarily chosen example of the kind of fascinating minutiae offered in this volume is an entry expanding upon a reference to gas lighting in chapter 33 of *Great Expectations*. Typical of the entire volume, this entry provides considerable insight into the impact of gas lighting on the social conditions of London during the nineteenth century: "In industry and commerce, gas-lighting extended the working day, especially in winter; streets became safer to frequent after dark, it made possible evening classes, thus enabling adults to gain an education after a day's work, and it made it easier for dinner, until now taken around three in the afternoon, to slip into the evening" (281). For readers of Dickens's novel in 1861, familiarity with the significance of gas lighting would have been commonplace; for readers of our time, the provision of such background provides a kind of enriched texturing of the novel that would be lacking otherwise.

The organization of the material in this volume will benefit both seasoned scholars and general readers of *Great Expectations*. This venerable tome earns its name, a delightful and informative "companion" that any reader of Dickens's novel would be glad to have at his or her elbow. An added bonus to the notes and commentary is a "Hypothetical Chronology," which helps situate the events of the novel in an orderly fashion and within an appropriate historical context. Several pages of maps, based on actual maps of the period described in the novel, provide valuable assistance to readers unfamiliar with place locations within the story, affording the reader a visual representation of Mr. Jaggers's Little Britain, the terrain extending from London to Woolwich, Pip's Rochester, Miss Havisham's Uptown, etc. The bibliography is comprehensive, and, as one might expect, staggering. All in all, this impressive volume furnishes about as thoroughgoing a guide to *Great Expectations* as one could possibly hope for. Whether read straight through, or in tandem with the great novel itself, this compendium of first-rate scholarship provides a seamless blend of erudition and accessibility.

A reference work that is sure to become an invaluable resource to Dickens scholars in the future is *The Dickens Christian Reader*, edited by Robert C. Hanna. Steeped in the traditions of the King James Version of the Christian Bible, Dickens often demonstrated his love of the archaisms and quotable precepts of the 1611 translation of Scripture through allusions that pervade all of his major work. It is almost impossible to overstate the effect that the King James Version had upon the typical middle-class household in both England and America during the nineteenth century. And, although Dickens's disaffection for the excesses of evangelical zealotry is well-documented, there is no doubt that he considered himself a follower of the Christian faith. The extent of his commitment to the majesty and eloquence of the sacred writings revered by Christian believers is amply demonstrated in this compendious collection of cross references, linking specific passages in the King James Version of the Bible to specific novels and other works. In the typical college classroom of today, the professor of English literature is likely to encounter students woefully unaware—though not necessarily dismissive—of the rich literary heritage that was once taken for granted by those who had even the most superficial knowledge of biblical lore. Robert C. Hanna has compiled an easy-to-use reference work that bridges this significant cultural and historical gap.

## 3. Cultural Studies

Although it has also been admirably summarized and assessed in Michael Lund's survey in Volume 30 of *DSA*, I feel compelled to include some comments on Goldie Morgentaler's *Dickens and Heredity*, since the publication date falls within the scope of this survey. Morgantaler's study exemplifies the value of a "cultural studies" approach, offering meaningful contextualization of Dickens and the scientific predilections and presuppositions of his era. Her encyclopedic command of the history of science and its impact on the literary imagination during the nineteenth century is impressive, and she applies this knowledge judiciously. It is accepted knowledge that hereditary concerns take center stage in many of Dickens's novels. Exploring parallels between developments in the science of heredity and the development of Dickens as a novelist, Morgentaler traces the evolution of Dickens's concept of heredity, from his early acceptance of the received wisdom of his age through his eventual adoption of a more sophisticated, science-based notion of the often-inscrutable complexities impacting one's biological, psychological, and social heritage. Morgentaler's elucidation of preformationist theory provides a valuable insight into attitudes that dominated the culture of Dickens's time: "Preformation confirmed not only the existence of God, but also the substantial accuracy of biblical revelation. It enhanced and strengthened the notion of the fixity of species at the same time as it reinforced the mechanistic bias of the era'' (11). The radical departure from all notions of predestinarian fixity brought about by the revolution in scientific thought promulgated by Lyell and Darwin, among others, can be detected in Dickens's abandonment of hereditary fixity (a preformationist bias) in his later novels. Morgentaler provides ample evidence of this shift in perspective. She explores the concept of "inherited goodness" in *Oliver Twist* and, in later chapters, contrasts this with later novels that seem to portray a post-Darwinian world. Unlike Oliver, who seems to inherit goodness, and Monks, who embodies evil due to traits apparently pre-determined by birth, Miss Havisham of *Great Expectations* inhabits a world subject to Darwinian adaptive principles, independent of inherited predisposition: "The idea of not fitting, of not having adapted to one's environment, and therefore cheating and distorting the next generation—as Miss Havisham does to Estella—this appears to be a Darwinian, not a theological construct" (171). An appreciation of the interactive tension between science, theology, and literature during the nineteenth century informs much of what is written about the Victorian period. Goldie Morgentaler's unique contribution to this appreciation is her explicit examples of how dynamic shifts in focus characterizing the scientific community are reflected in the creative, evolving world of Dickens's fictive imagination.

Within a quite different context, the role of science in popular culture, as well as the incursion of scientific theory into social and political ideologies, suffuses Pam Morris's "A Taste for Change in *Our Mutual Friend*: Cultivation or Education," which is chapter 12 in an anthology of cultural studies edited by Juliet John and Alice Jenkins called, appropriately, *Rethinking Victorian Culture*. Morris traces the novel's recurrent references to dustheaps and mounds of archaic relics to the popularity of Lyell's *Evidences of the Antiquity of Man*, an immensely popular book during the period when Dickens published his last completed novel. This essay offers a reading of *Our Mutual Friend* as commentary on the social and cultural upheavals that harbingered transformation of culture and society in the 1860s. Lyell's popularizing of geological discoveries threatened the shaky foundations of biblical literalism, while Marxist theory challenged the heretofore unassailable societal infrastructures undergirding the bourgeoisie. The Veneerings and Podsnaps of the world exploit commodities, both material and human, while promoting a kind of bottom-line barrenness that affects all aspects of social and cultural life. "It is a cultural and political order that fuses an encompassing dullness with competitive savagery" (184). Language itself becomes commodified in a world obsessed with the exchange value of all human activity: "Words in *Our Mutual Friend* are shown to be commodified in a system of surplus value" (185). Morris notes that it is only the socially and culturally marginalized characters in Dickens's novel who discover the transforming power of language. For example, it is Jenny Wren and the Boffins who imaginatively transcend the baseness of a social order alien to their natural impulses. Morris juxtaposes two distinctive "opposing systems of value" that shape the plot-inciting tensions of the novel. However, according to Morris, Bradley Head-stone "is the only character the writing endows with imaginative force" (193). In a world in which the Wrayburn system of class snobbery prevails, Headstone is destined for Darwinian usurpation: "All that is left of his trajectory is for him to cast himself back into primal slime and mud" (192). Morris views Dickens's consigning Headstone and his aspirations to a miserable fate as pivotal to our understanding of a novel that ultimately challenges conventional notions regarding values undergirding our whole educational system and the aesthetic principles it embraces.

In her introductory chapter to *Scenes of Sympathy*, Audrey Jaffe describes the evolution of a kind of sympathetic consciousness which, according to her hypothesis, arose during the Victorian period in tandem with the rise of commodity culture—a culture which flourished during the century which followed the Victorian period. "Indeed, the regular recurrence of the adjective 'Dickensian' in twentieth-century descriptions of urban poverty suggests that Victorian novels more than any other form (and Dickens more than any other Victorian novelist) continue to provide the terms and images of contemporary sympathetic representation" (14). Jaffe's exploration of the shaping of a public social conscience that came to be associated with Victorian novelists begins with a chapter entitled "Sympathy and Spectacle in Dickens's 'A Christmas Carol.' " In this opening chapter, much is made of the role of spectatorship in the conversion of Dickens's archetypal wicked, old sinner. And, in an inspired explication of the reader/text dynamic, both within and outside of the tale of repentance and conversion, the relationship of the visiting spirits to Scrooge is presented as analogous to the relationship between Dickens's narrator and the readers of the text. Jaffe's allusion to the sympathetic response which Dickens sought to elicit from his readers evokes an age that was perhaps more willing than ours to believe in conversions of one kind or another—or at least willing to entertain the possibility of an awakened consciousness attainable through response to literary representation. "As a model of socialization through spectatorship, the narrative posits the visual as a means toward recapturing one's lost or alienated self—and becoming one's best self" (29). In her treatment of a tale that seems to find its own power of resurrection and renewal with each passing generation, Jaffe points out that the inherent theatricality of the "Carol" was recognized from its inception. The spirits—who do their own effective "staging" of events past, present, and future—provide for Scrooge a kind of framing device that permits a distancing perspective, while concurrently heightening awareness.

In a sense, Scrooge (as well as the reader) is "protected" by the frame, in much the same way that a contemporary audience is provided a vicarious experience through cinematic framing, while kept free from harm or physical deprivation. (One eats popcorn while being dragged through scenes of mayhem!) Jaffe quotes from Sergei Eisenstein's mid-century essay, "Dickens, Griffith, and the Film Today," in her opening paragraph, emphasizing the function of Dickensian framing as an effective means of realizing the Victorian ideal of a burgeoning commodity culture tempered with a social conscience. "An emphasis on visuality, whether literary or cinematic, promotes spectatorship as a dominant cultural activity" (27). Within the context of "A Christmas Carol," the proto-cinematic framing structure is imbued with a pragmatic utility. Through the process of "reading" the highly theatrical scenes placed before him by the spirits, Ebeneezer Scrooge becomes a kind of competent reader of his past, present, and future life. Jaffe offers an insightful explication of the way in which Dickens and his readers reconcile commodity culture with Christian virtues. In effect, everything is defined in terms of its exchange value, including the ability of a middle-class reader to employ the faculty of imagination in the process of "exchanging" his/her place with a disenfranchised, destitute person. In what is arguably one of her most brilliant insights, Jaffe relates the enduring popularity of the "Carol" to its linkage with a production economy—an economy that thrives on capitalistic demise and resuscitation, as well as the proliferation of "productions" of a spectacular variety, in seemingly limitless permutations and transformations: "With the metaphorical deaths and rebirths of Scrooge and Tiny Tim echoing its annual return, the story associates the idea of Christian renewal with its own form of production" (54).

Sympathetic representation surfaces as a recurrent theme in Marlene Tromp's *The Private Rod: Marital Violence, Sensation, and the Law in Victorian Britain.* This monograph, dealing with the theme of violence against women as depicted in the work of five Victorian writers (Dickens, Wilkie Collins, Mary Elizabeth Braddon, Margaret Oliphant, and George Eliot), opens with a chapter focusing on the relationship between Bill Sikes and Nancy, a disturbing portrait of domestic violence that came to assume a high profile in Dickens's evaluation of his own work, a significance further enhanced by his public readings of the scene in which Nancy is murdered by her enraged lover. In "A 'Pound' of Flesh: Morality and the Economy of Sexual Violence in *Oliver Twist*," Tromp argues that Dickens's portrayal of violence against a socially ostracized woman departs radically from the model

provided by the narratives found in the Newgate Calendars and in their successors, the Newgate novels, in which the victim is often depicted as being
as brutal and coarse as her victimizer. "*Oliver Twist* reconfigures this model
by exalting the woman-victim and marking her as a candidate for salvation,
rather than describing her as flawed" (38). Dickens's portrayal of those who
exist outside the framework of middle-class values and adherence to legal
codes marks a transition from the popular lurid crime novel, anticipating the
rise of the sensation novel that was to follow, enjoying an enormous vogue
in the 1860s and 1870s. In her discussion of this pivotal shift, Tromp emphasizes the ethereality of the privileged classes in *Oliver Twist* and the corollary
physical materiality of the underclass. Her explication of the role of physical
bodies and textual "bodies" is quite insightful and thought-provoking,
whether or not one totally accepts her appropriation of Lacanian theory.
Embodiments of texts, social classes, and physicality are made to correspond
within Tromp's interpretive framework. Nancy's murder is clearly seen as a
kind of watershed event within the fictive world of Dickens's imagination.
"The move to disembody privileged women also makes visible the role of
economics in the abuse of the women, as we see in Nancy's murder" (65).
In Tromp's view, *Oliver Twist* anticipates the sensation novel, a genre whose
value as an instrument of social reform has been undervalued by critics.

Another informative treatment of the cultural milieu in which *Oliver Twist*
was created is provided by Juliet John's essay "*Twist*ing the Newgate Tale:
Dickens, Popular Culture and the Politics of Genre" in *Rethinking Victorian
Culture*. John deals with ways in which this early Dickens novel employs
familiar conventions of the Newgate fiction of the 1830s and 1840s, while,
at the same time, transcending and transforming these conventions in a way
that registers the age's anxiety concerning the glorification of criminality
through glamorized portrayals of marginalized individuals and their modes
of subsistence. "Newgate Novel" was a generalized epithet used to deride a
certain class of popular fiction—lurid potboilers that found a diverse and
receptive reading public. The elitist assumption—common in Victorian society and persisting to this day—that an unbridgeable gulf must separate popular fiction from works of literary merit was, to some great extent, exploded
by the rapid rise in popularity of Dickens's novels, from the early 1830s
onward. John describes the rise in readership in the early nineteenth century in
terms of mass distribution of literary and cultural values once the proprietary
possessions of a privileged few: "Dickens's novels were, of course, formed
by, and formative in, these crucial changes in the distribution of cultural
capital" (129). John views this as a vital force in the empowerment of an

underclass, heretofore disempowered as much by their substandard tastes (for a theater dominated by sensationalism and melodrama, for example) as by their lack of economic power. Unlike most popular (hence, ''substandard'') theatrical productions, novels adhering more or less to the Newgate model were beginning to transcend and flout social and economic barriers. Generic battlelines were drawn and literary preference became politicized: ''The New-gate controversy brought home the power of the novel with such force that each of the Newgate novelists was fully conscious of the power at their disposal—none more than Dickens'' (131). John expands her argument to an explication of Fagin's role as a manipulator of fictions—a consummate storyteller. ''Fagin is conscious from the outset that fiction, drama and comic entertainment have the power to corrupt'' (132). Hence, Fagin is able to make crime look like high romance, a clear allusion to the insidious power of Newgate-style glorification of the twilight world the old villain inhabits. Death by hanging is trivialized—Fagin makes it a kind of morbid joke. Fur-ther, John describes Fagin's staging the pickpocketing scenario for Oliver's benefit as a kind of ''inverted morality play.'' The essay goes on to describe the roles of emotion and pleasure in the creation of fiction palatable to a mass readership. Dickens exploited and critiqued both, according to John. ''His texts thus emphasize the liberating as well as the imprisoning potential of the popular cultural experiences of emotion and pleasure'' (142).

Issues surrounding the experience of emotion and pleasure inform *The Spectacle of Intimacy*. This intriguing title suggests oxymoronically two con-tradictory Victorian obsessions—the privacy of home life disjunctively yoked with a kind of fetishistic voyeurism. Karen Chase and Michael Levenson explore this intriguing contradiction through a series of essays, one of which deals with Dickens's virtual overnight success with the fireside reading public in England and America, a phenomenon that captivated his attention from the 1840s onward. ''The desire to secure closed walls and then to accumulate an immensity of artifacts, a plenitude of emotions—this is a deep and widely shared impulse'' (89). In the essay ''Tom's Pinch: The Sexual Serpent Beside the Dickensian Fireside,'' Chase and Levenson exploit Dickens's sexual pun-ning in *Martin Chuzzlewit*, expanding upon the interactive roles of frustrated sexual desire and the impulse toward domesticity, recurrently meshed throughout novels intended for fireside contemplation. ''Tom plays the organ, and Dickens plays (shamelessly) on the sexual pun'' (93). In terms of Victo-rian culture's demands upon the creative life of a popular author and his thoroughly domesticated readers, the pinch is felt when private desire clashes with the exhibitionist drive toward public exposure. After all, the determinedly (as opposed to spurious) secretive life would crave a black hole of true secrecy. The obsession with privacy suggested by the Dickensian evocations of a tranquil hearth wars against the impulse to embrace a more complex milieu clammering outside the walls of domesticity. "The secrets of private life must be on display; desire compels it; and so do the conditions of publishing" (101).

The use and abuse of alcohol seems to find its way into the literature of every generation. The Victorians were no exception, and, in "Alcohol, Comedy, and Ghosts in Dickens's Early Short Fiction," David J. Greenman points out the discrepancy between serious and comic treatments of drunkenness in Dickens's early work: "At the outset of his career Dickens could obviously move freely between a serious and a comic view of excessive alcohol consumption" (12). Although this lighthearted portrayal of alcohol abuse would disappear later in the novelist's career, it is interesting to note conflictive depictions of the drunkard's lot in the early pieces cited by Greenman.

In "The 'Civil Service' and 'Administrative Reform': The Blame Game in *Little Dorrit*," Trey Philpotts makes a careful distinction between the valuable services performed by middle-class clerks (the civil servants) and the absurd policies and practices of high level governmental officials. According to Philpotts, the satirization of the Circumlocution Office in Dickens is aimed specifically at high level government departments headed by an aristocratic elite. He is not burlesquing the practices of underpaid government bureaucrats, as a modern reader might suppose, but is rather seeking to encourage the reformation of high level administrative bungling. Dickens certainly favored administrative reform, but this meant political reform more than bureaucratic reform.

As I write these words at a location approximately thirty blocks north of what was once the World Trade Center in New York, I cannot help associating my own anxiety concerning the promise and peril of the new millennium before us with Andrew Sanders's retrospective look at the link between millennial anxiety and madness that has been a part of Western culture for centuries. One of thirteen essays found in *Rethinking Victorian Culture*, "Dickens and the Millennium" provides an overview of millenarianism and its popularity in England and America during the nineteenth century. Sanders relates the eschatological fervor of Millerites and Mormons to the secularized apocalyptic rhetoric of Thomas Carlyle, and traces the history of end-of-the-world hysteria from a period preceding the French Revolution up through the religious revivals of the nineteenth century—an emphasis on last and final issues, the fires of which smolder to this day. Sanders explores Dickens's take on millenarianism and its effects in one of the writer's travel essays from *All the Year Round*, an adventure entitled "Bound for the Great Salt Lake." Based on his treatment of the subject, Sanders concludes that Dickens was quite unimpressed with the biblical literalism that informs most evocations of apocalyptic gloom. "From the evidence of his fiction, Dickens would appear to have been singularly unresponsive to millenarianist doctrine and not in the least persuaded by its urgency in the 1830s and 1840s" (84). Further proof of Dickens's lighthearted approach to the proclaimers of universal doom is evinced from the portrayal of Melchisedek Howler in *Dombey and Son*. The character's name alone is enough to elicit a smile. "Melchisedek Howler is a comic device, almost a throwaway one" (85). Siding with Carlyle, Dickens apparently saw a social apocalypse as a greater threat than any divinely ordained cataclysm. Humanly engineered apocalyptic horrors are those to be feared, according to both Carlyle and Dickens. I found Sanders's analysis and reassessment of the prophetic visions of both writers compelling and chillingly relevant.

### 4. Postcolonial Readings

Among collections of essays with a unifying theme, *Dickens and the Children of Empire*, edited by Wendy S. Jacobson, stands out as a model of coherence achieved through a clever orchestration of disparate voices. Jacobson has managed to collate and juxtapose the widely divergent viewpoints of fourteen critics in a manner that illuminates and defines contemporary postcoloniality, while offering insights into the colonialist attitudes that pervaded the British Empire during its heyday. A lecturer at Rhodes University in South Africa, Jacobson has assembled an array of critical perspectives arising, at least in part, from a diversity of national and cultural orientations. Surveying the roster of contributors, one cannot help being struck by the geographical range represented: residents of South Africa and Australia in the company of the usual preponderance of English and American academicians.

One of the most sharply focused essays in the collection is Anthony Chennells's "Savages and Settlers in Dickens: Reading Multiple Centres." Chennells articulates a mindset that envisions the British Empire as a cultural and commercial center around which the rest of the planet extends as a kind of "savage periphery" (153). Chennells provides insights into the way Dickens exploits this center/periphery model in both *Dombey and Son* and *Bleak*

*House*, quoting passages that satirize the jingoism of the period. Chennells also explores the conflictive nature of Dickens's take on the world-shaping role of an empire which he considered culturally and economically advanced. The dichotomization of center and periphery recurs thematically throughout Jacobson's collection of essays, incorporated analogically in James Kincaid's "Dickens and the Construction of the Child," in which adulthood becomes the center of life, while children exist on the marginalized periphery. Hence, children are, in a sense, like colonized vassals. They are treated as exotic, untamed, and, consequently, inferior but cute, sexually taboo and quaint little aliens. "When we invented the modern child, we made it live in another country, a country we then decided to make exotic and heartbreakingly attractive" (30). For Kincaid, Oliver Twist exists in this netherworld of alienated and exotic idealization: "Abused and mistreated, Oliver is beaten for asking for food, for being born at all" (37). Kincaid does not view all of the children in Dickens as marginalized and "colonized" by the adult world; he detects the emergence of a redeemed childhood in the character of Pip in *Great Expectations*: "He becomes not the abused child but the child of grace" (41). Kincaid explores the "colonization" of childhood by adults. According to Kincaid, through idealization, adults impose an alien exoticism/eroticism upon children that is analogous to a similar alterity imposed upon the "savage" inhabitants of unfamiliar societies and cultures. "We care for the idea of the child so deeply that the actual children before us are annoying intruders" (30). Kincaid cites evocations of childhood in Dickens that illustrate the idealization of the child as an alienated and exotic "other," outside the realm of possible empathic identification. Oliver Twist is presented as a typical embodiment of the idealized child, but Kincaid discovers in Pip a child who transcends the adult-imposed construct.

The link between the marginalized child and the marginalized natives of far-flung colonial "possessions" is brilliantly explicated in "Primitives and Wingless: the Colonial Subject as Child" by Bill Ashcroft. "In the invention of childhood itself in post-medieval society are seen the factors which make it amenable to imperial rhetoric" (185). In a similar vein, the symbolic significance of the marginalized child, "the otherness of the child" (14), provides the major theme of John Bowen's essay "Spirit and the Allegorical Child: Little Nell's Mortal Aesthetic." Although usually dismissed as an absurdly sentimentalized caricature of guileless innocence, Nell's portraiture as seen by Bowen reveals "some elements of psychological interiority and complexity" (23), particularly in her dreams. His reading of *The Old Curiosity Shop* in terms of the allegorization of the child elevates Nell's life and death to a level far above her mundane surroundings: "we need to see Nell's spirit in the context of a much wider discourse of spirit in the book" (24).

In "Dickens in Africa: 'Africanizing' *Hard Times*," also from *Dickens and the Children of Empire*, native Zimbabwean Greenwell Matsika explores parallels between the underlying values that inform Dickens's novel and recurring tropes detectable in African literature. For example, naming in Dickens takes on a level of significance not alien to the significance of naming in pre-colonial African cultures: "Naming in Dickens's novels has much the same significance as naming has in most African societies where besides conferring an identity, names are associated with special events or aspects of life and personalities" (175). Matsika elaborates upon examples from *Hard Times* in particular, a novel in which name-environment associations are perhaps even more blatant than is some of Dickens's other works. This essay also cites the tension between city life and humane values as a characteristic shared by African novels and the world of Dickens's fictive imagination: "Almost invariably in African novels the city is regarded as antithetical to basic human values" (175). Matsika cites several examples of what he terms "the process of Othering" in *Hard Times*, and he relates this trope to myths about Africa imposed by colonists. He concludes that his "Africanizing" of *Hard Times* attests to the robust vitality and relevance of Dickens's novel. "My reading of *Hard Times* is a reminder that any great novel speaks to readers coming to it in historical times and cultural contexts which may be very different from those which gave it its origins" (181).

The relationship between Pip and Magwitch provides a major focus of Grahame Smith's treatment of colonialism and childhood in "Suppressing Narratives: Childhood and Empire in *The Uncommercial Traveller* and *Great Expectations*." Smith finds interesting parallels between Dickens the traveler and Magwitch the criminal exiled and consigned to the periphery. In some sense, the journey that takes one outside the genteel and sophisticated center refines and humanizes the traveler. Smith detects qualities in the character of Magwitch that resemble the redemptive role assumed by his creator. "Magwitch is a bearer of love, as well as a cause of it in others, and it is an irony of this great novel that love should enter a center where it is often lacking from a brutalized and apparently uncivilized periphery" (52).

The ambivalence of Dickens exemplified in his portrayal of Empire and peripheries is explored incisively by Murray Baumgarten in "The Imperial Child: Bella, *Our Mutual Friend*, and the Victorian Picturesque." While critical of exploitation, Dickens and his creation Bella participate in the poeticizing of society's peripheries. Bella is the unwitting heir of Empire and its hegemonic dominance. Like the newly-affluent and mobile traveler of the age, Bella of *Our Mutual Friend* romanticizes the world beyond her ken. She is like Dickens in that she participates in the benefits of Empire while achieving a limited level of objectivity towards its flaws and culpabilities. "In the degradation of imperial to picturesque fantasies, Dickens articulates a critique of as well as a limited participation in the defining structures of his age" (62).

Ambivalence toward America, that most renegade of all the peripheral offspring of Empire, provides the major focus of three chapters in Jacobson's collection. The first of these offers a postcolonial reading of "The Wreck of the *Golden Mary*," which appeared in the Christmas issue of *Household Words* published in 1856. Lillian Nayder offers an insightful analysis of this treatment of the American Gold Rush in "Dickens and 'Gold Rush Fever': Colonial Contagion in *Household Words*." The promise of wealth and opportunity in lands peripheral to the British Empire is compromised by the inequalities and vagaries of human folly that seem to surface uninvited in all ports of call and at all social levels. Gold seems a metaphor for some elusive ideal, eternally pursued but never fully realized or even adequately comprehended by those who pursue its discovery. According to Nayder, the vessel called the *Golden Mary*, a metaphorical representation of the elusive gold available in far-flung corners of the globe, "is not an angel but a whore" (75). The romanticized, picturesque world of the periphery takes on the familiar appearance of gritty reality—a world filled with conflicts and inequalities—upon close examination.

Dickens's fluctuating attitudes toward Native Americans comprise the main focus of "Dickens and the Native American" by Kate Flint. This well-researched and informative essay chronicles changes in the novelist's viewpoint, culling evidence from *The Letters, Household Words, American Notes,* and allusions to aboriginal life in some of the novels. The Native American seems to devolve from a noble savage to a sideshow curiosity in the minds of many of Dickens's contemporaries, and this reconfiguration of the public perception seems to have been a process to which Dickens was not immune. From this and a number of other recent studies I have encountered, the composite portrait of Dickens that emerges is of a writer and social reformer who could be extraordinarily conflicted in his feelings toward those whom he hoped to benefit. The love/hate relationship with America extended to her Native inhabitants: "There is no one Dickensian Native American, just as there is no unitary Victorian version of the Native American" (103), according to Flint.

The tensions between center and periphery—a significant theme pervading Jacobson's collection of essays and informing much of current postcolonial discourse—is nowhere better articulated than in the scathing appraisals of American life and social customs Dickens himself wrote following his first visit in 1842. Robert E. Lougy relates this phenomenon to the genesis and evolution of *Martin Chuzzlewit* in ''Nationalism and Violence: America in Charles Dickens's *Martin Chuzzlewit*.'' Lougy describes the disappointments and reversals of that disastrous adventure in the New World as ''dreams nurtured and then betrayed'' (105). According to Lougy, disgusted and disillusioned British travelers were in plentiful supply during this period: ''He was by no means the first English traveler to visit America and then return home, denounce it, and make a pile of money in doing so'' (105). This essay deals with the concept of America functioning as a trope within the world of the novel, *Martin Chuzzlewit*. Dickens is appalled at the rawness and untrammeled violence that seems to pervade life in that distant periphery of civilization known as America—a vision of the American ethos he attempts to capture in the novel: ''*Martin Chuzzlewit* is in fact haunted by the ways in which violent and unconscious aggressive traits are passed on from one generation to the next'' (109). The conflict between young Martin and Elijah Pogram is essentially a debate between the staid institutions and customs of the Old World and the uncluttered, disrespectful disregard of the New World. Lougy manages to incorporate allusions to Lacan, Marx, Freud, Rousseau, and Derrida, among others, in his explication of Dickens's attitude toward social and cultural life in America as viewed through the lens of the novel. His incorporation of these major figures into his argument is brilliantly orchestrated, lacking the cut-and-paste stickiness that might vitiate the effect in a less convincing essay. Lougy exhibits a firm grasp of the social and political history with which he is dealing; his contextualization of Dickens's take on the American character enhances his treatment of the role the novelist's predilections and prejudices played in his creation of *Martin Chuzzlewit*.

The ambiguities that plagued the children of Empire is further explored by Catherine Gallagher in her well-researched essay ''Floating Signifiers of Britishness in the Novels of the Anti-Slave-Trade Squadron.'' Gallagher offers a detailed analysis of *The Cruise of the Midge*, written in 1834 by Michael Scott, explaining in detail the rationale for the existence of anti-slave-trade squadrons and the characteristics of the sailors who comprised these squadrons. This essay provides valuable insights into the significance of Britain's maintenance of a post-Napoleonic *Pax Britannica*.

## 5. Textual Explication

Textual commentary characterizes John Bowen's *Other Dickens, Pickwick to Chuzzlewit.* I have included this volume, although it has been reviewed in volume 30 of *DSA*, since the publication date falls within the scope of this essay. Current theory informs Bowen's approach to the early works discussed, and, like Newsom, he confronts the much-vexed issue of authorship and authorial authority frontally: "Like Scrooge, I am certain that Dickens is dead: to begin with" (7). Bowen's underlying premise is that the complexity of the early novels has been underrated, and he seeks to refute this notion in the chapters that follow his introduction. Devoting a chapter each to *Pickwick Papers, Oliver Twist, Nicholas Nickleby, The Old Curiosity Shop* (and *Master Humphrey's Clock), Barnaby Rudge,* and *Martin Chuzzlewit,* Bowen seeks to explore levels of subtext in the novels that may have been slighted by earlier critics. An example would be his analysis of the complex issues surrounding biological and social inheritance in *Chuzzlewit*, and the relationship between that potentially chaotic conundrum and convoluted problems of interpretation: "The task of interpretation, like that of family history, is to control issue, whether textual or bodily, but the issue of the preface, and the issues of the text, are not easily ordered or restrained" (187).

In *Rereading Victorian Fiction*, editors Alice Jenkins and Juliet John have assembled a number of essays that consciously (and, in some cases, self-consciously) apply current literary theory to some major Victorian writers. Among these essays, two deal exclusively with Dickens: "Two Kinds of Clothing: *Sartor Resartus* and *Great Expectations*" by Bernard Beatty, and "Don Pickwick: Dickens and the Transformations of Cervantes" by Angus Easson. The Beatty essay employs close readings of passages in *Great Expectations* that deal specifically with clothing worn by major characters in the novel. He links Carlylean clothes philosophy as delineated in *Sartor Resartus* with what he views as the underlying significance of articles of clothing worn by Pip, Miss Havisham, Magwitch, and Joe Gargery. Beatty draws a sharp distinction between Carlyle's Professor Teufelsdrockh, who sees clothing as essentially transparent, and Dickens's characters, for whom clothing takes on a kind of transcendent significance. "That is why clothes, like liturgical vestments, are worn in the first place. They exist to signify" (53). Beatty puts forward a rather complex explanation of how Miss Havisham's wedding garments signify both eros and agape, and of how Pip's adorning himself in clothing befitting an aristocrat suggests a denial of his finer self. Contrasting

Professor Teufelsdrockh's clothes philosophy with clothing obsessions exhibited by major characters in *Great Expectations* provides some powerful insights into distinctions between Dickens and Carlyle that Beatty wishes to highlight.

Dickens's knowledge of *Don Quixote* provides the basis for Angus Easson's essay comparing Cervantes's creation with *The Pickwick Papers*. Easson explores the picaresque genre's relationship with the development of the novel as a distinctive form, basically viewing *Pickwick* as a reworking of a tale whose popularity had not waned since the first appearance of Cervantes's hero. Easson focuses, in part, on the destabilizing subjectivity that characterizes both Pickwick and Quixote. Although Mr. Pickwick does not share the delusional characteristics of Cervantes's sad knight, Dickens distorts his surroundings in ways that suggest postmodernist instability. In some sense, Dickens reconfigures the knight errant, ultimately idealizing his quixotic hero: "He uses satire and burlesque, often enough against Pickwick early on, but he also and increasingly turns to the idealizing of Quixote generated by the reading and rewriting of Cervantes" (186).

The revitalization of a familiar *topos* also comprises the focus of Lothar Cerny's essay "Life in Death: Art in Dickens's *Our Mutual Friend*." According to Cerny, Dickens reverses the ancient "death in life" motif that pervades so much of Christian thought from the Middle Ages onward. In fact, in *Our Mutual Friend*, life is found where one might have expected death. Cerny maintains that Jenny Wren and Mr. Venus play pivotal roles in the devlopment of this theme, a controlling idea that is central to the novel. Jenny Wren's encounter with Fascination Fledgeby, which contains her summoning call to a rooftop paradise that has no relation to the cutthroat world of business and social climbing, contains a key passage that supports Cerny's "life in death" thesis. Jenny inhabits a world unknown to Fledgeby, a world shaped by her semiotic reconfiguration of stereotypical representations of life and death: "Jenny Wren changes the world above all by language, by giving new names and a new existence to people and things" (23). For Cerny, she represents the power of poetic alchemy to transform what is normally considered grotesque and imperfect into something aesthetically pleasing and morally sound. Hence, her doll-dressing functions as a metaphor for the transforming power of language. Waste and refuse become the raw materials of artistic creation, emblematic of the functional journeywork of Dickens, the novelist. This is, of course, the function of Mr. Venus, as well: "Mr. Venus resembles the divine director, who rules over his creation by naming things" (25). This revitalization through naming, the "art" of articulation, finds its antithesis in the world created by the Veneerings and Mr. Podsnap. The decorations, the veneering overlays that gild a rigidly controlled, vacuous conformity to prefabricated economic and moral systems, are contrasted with the imaginative, creative impulses required of the artist, the discoverer of beauty in imperfection. The semblance of life created by Mr. Venus suggests the work of the literary imagination. ''Symbolically it makes the world a better place'' (33).

The power to transform the familiar into something unfamiliar is an underlying theme of Nicola Bradbury's ''Dickens and James: 'Watching with My Eyes Closed': The Dream Abroad.'' Bradbury explores parallel preoccupations of the two authors. In particular, this essay provides illuminating insights into the recurrent theme of travel and the tensions that inevitably result when preconceptions conflict with actual experiences. For both James and Dickens, as well as many of the characters they create, travel to foreign lands becomes an exploration of one's inner self as much as a journey abroad: ''Both Dickens and James identify travel with psychological and even philosophical exploration'' (81). Comparing scenes in *Little Dorrit* with parallel scenes in *The Portrait of a Lady*, Bradbury relates the ''negative capability'' achieved by both novelists to their integration of plot mechanisms and the ''dream'' landscapes they fashion through the perceptions of their major characters. ''Plot chances split and reunite persons as distance heightens and interiorizes experience'' (83). The parallels Bradbury presents provide fresh insights into the works of both James and Dickens, and the thematic congruities which emerge.

''Plot chances'' and the opacity of indecipherable languages are significant components shaping the structure of Dickens's *Bleak House*. Teresa Valenti presents some novel and insightful analyses of these elements of the novel in ''The Forgotten Father in Charles Dickens's *Bleak House*.'' Offering a postmodernist reading of one pivotal event in the novel, Valenti deconstructs the typescript and contents of a letter presumably written by Captain Hawdon, Esther Summerson's father. The letter, emblematic of the thin tissues of coincidence and the opacity of written communication, reinforces the reader's awareness of the barriers (social and cultural) that exist between Esther and her illegitimate father. In the spirit of postmodernist sensibility, Valenti maintains that the letter also represents other kinds of inaccessibility: ''However, [the letter] highlights certain paradoxes relating to the acquisition of knowledge as both valuable and meaningless'' (90). The theme of contradictory, opaque and/or indecipherable writing pervades *Bleak House*, particularly in its parody of the convoluted circumlocutions perpetuated by an arcane legal system and the obscurantism perpetuated by documents written in legalese.

Valenti exploits the incomprehensibility of the letter from Esther's father, reading the contradictions and elisions in the text as emblematic of Esther's removal from social acceptance and self-knowledge. The codes that undergird social norms are encrypted in ways that intentionally exclude the social pariah. "Esther, as illegitimate hence non-existent or unacknowledged, is denied access to both the social and legal codes of knowing" (90). I found Valenti's analysis of a seemingly trivial element in a work that is notably sprawling and capacious especially compelling because she manages to incorporate so many of the novel's central issues tangential to her limited focus.

A completely different kind of decoding project informs Mark M. Hennelly, Jr.'s " 'Betwixt 'Em Somewheres': From Liminal to Liminoid in *David Copperfield*, *Bleak House*, and *Great Expectations* (Part One)." Hennelly appropriates the distinctions made between liminal and liminoid motifs in an essay by Victor Turner and applies them to three of Dickens's novels. According to Hennelly's application of Turner, the Victorian world portrayed by Dickens is a world in transition between liminal and liminoid cultures, systems of "play," or modes of perception. Since the Industrial Revolution marks a highly significant watershed for Turner, emerging capitalist societies find themselves "trapped somewhere between the liminal and liminoid" (199). "In fact, Turner's paper unintentionally provides a fascinating commentary on *Great Expectations*, particularly in suggesting that the plot dramatizes the very difficult transition (and consequent growing pains) in evolving from a liminal to a liminoid culture" (201). This essay provides numerous examples of ways in which Turner's theoretical model may be superimposed upon all three of the novels under consideration. According to Hennelly, "liminoid exclusion" of individuals with outsider status in *Bleak House* establishes this monumental work as Dickens's first great existential novel. Like many other theory-based explications, Hennelly's Turner-inspired analyses of selected passages may effectively stimulate thought and reflection, and, in many ways, serve to further enhance appreciation of the works under consideration. One need not necessarily buy into every aspect of Turner's hypotheses to benefit from the insights a Turneresque reading may offer.

An essay providing a highly particularized focus is Daniel L. Plung's "Environed by Wild Beasts: Animal Imagery in Dickens's *David Copperfield*." Plung identifies four animal species in the novel which he presents as representative of four distinct kinds of beings inhabiting a complex and stratified moral universe: song birds suggest good and innocence, lions and raptors suggest beings fallen from grace, dogs represent self-interest, and slithering animals (suggesting a primeval fall from innocence) embody irremediable evil. Plung provides many examples of animal imagery related to characters in the novel. Not surprisingly, Uriah Heep is often described in terms that evoke images associated with reptilian creatures. "Repeatedly, David reminds the reader what a slimy, slippery man Uriah Heep is, and how Uriah slithers through a protracted series of evil deeds" (220). This essay does not purport to provide an exhaustive catalogue of the animal imagery associated with the more than fifty characters in the novel; rather, it seeks to enhance our appreciation of the subtle ways in which the narrator employs commonplace (and sometimes prejudicial and erroneous) perceptions of the animal kingdom to add texture to his characterizations. "Clearly, Dickens did not intend *David Copperfield* as allegory, but, rather, as a representation of a complex human community with all its diverse personalities, behaviors, and human characteristics" (223). Plung provides a useful key to increasing our appreciation of Dickens's artistry in this most autobiographical of his novels, admirably accomplishing this without excessive theorizing and without overstating the significance of his observations.

In a class by itself is Patricia Marks's intriguing appraisal of a comic adaptation of Dickens's last and unfinished work. " 'With A Rush Retire': Robert Newell's *Edwin Drood* Adaptation" analyzes the efforts of an American writer, Robert Henry Newell, to present a humorous treatment of a thoroughly Americanized *Drood*. This version appeared in a little known American publication called *Punchinello*, and it was written in a burlesque style popular in America during the postwar period. "Newell's breezy style seems an unusual match for Dickens's novel, but such dislocation was common for post-Civil War humorists who found themselves in complex and out-of-joint times" (149). Marks presents a telling portrait of the social and cultural scene in which this adaptation surfaced. The interest that such an adaptation generated is, of course, a revealing glimpse into the enduring popularity of Dickens in America. At the same time, this literary anomaly demonstrates the degree to which Dickens furnished American culture with material for self-portraiture: "Newell's burlesque is finally less a commentary on Dickens's work or an attempt to make fun of the original than a debunking of his native social scene" (159). Marks ends her essay with a delineation of Newell's completion of Dickens's unfinished plot. The absurd and improbable denouement provided by Newell, like many other tentatively manufactured endings to Dickens's eternally open-ended mystery, attests to the enduring fascination of the original work and its originator.

## 6. Back to the Future

Is it possible that the new millennium will usher in an anti-theory backlash? Is the "death of the author" movement dead? Probably not, but Bert Hornback's "Dickens's Failure" stands poised to lead the retro revolution, even if followers are few. Hornback traces the development of Dickens's oeuvre from the early novels through his mature work, presenting as the essence of the novelist's achievement a kind of progression of consciousness designed to sensitize his vast audience while profoundly affecting the writer himself. According to Hornback, " . . . metaphysical revolution is principled character work, and most of us live shy of that kind of life" (140). Eschewing current jargon, the essay addresses—without apology—the function of the Dickens canon as a progressively demanding series of moral and social lessons: "When Dickens invented the novel of social criticism, he wanted to change things in this world" (140). As if responding to the aesthetic, linguistic, and cultural relativism that pervades so much of contemporary criticism, Hornback unabashedly trumpets a resuscitated doctrine of purposive art: "The purpose of art—like the purpose of education—is, I think, nothing more or other than to teach us to pay attention to life" (147). This call to conscience-motivated attentiveness—a kind of pleading for a secularized rebirth of sympathetic social awareness—infuses all of Dickens, according to Hornback.

He ends the essay on a somewhat dispirited note, despairing that the "message" and vision of Dickens can be comprehended by irremediably insensate general readers. Moreover, literary critics adequately attuned to the underlying wisdom that requires an attentive sensitivity are sorely lacking, even among academicians: "They are too busy with current aerobic criticism fads to pay attention to an artist like Dickens" (147).

Selah!

# WORKS CITED

Ashcroft, Bill. "Primitive and Wingless: The Colonial Subject as Child." *Dickens and The Children of Empire*. Ed. Wendy S. Jacobson. Houndsmills, Baskingstoke, Hampshire and New York: Palgrave, 2000.

Baumgarten, Murray. "The Imperial Child: Bella, *Our Mutual Friend* and the Victorian Picturesque." *Dickens and the Children of Empire*. Ed. Wendy S. Jacobson. Houndsmills, Baskingstoke, Hampshire and New York: Palgrave, 2000.

Beatty, Bernard. "Two Kinds of Clothing: *Sartor Resartus* and *Great Expectations.*" *Rereading Victorian Fiction.* Eds. Alice Jenkins and Juliet John. London: Macmillan, New York: St. Martin's, 2000.

Bowen, John. "Bebelle and 'His Boots': Dickens, Ellen Ternan and the Christmas Stories." *Dickensian* 96 (2000): 197–208.

———. *Other Dickens: Pickwick to Chuzzlewit.* Oxford: Oxford UP, 2000.

———. "Spirit and the Allegorical Child: Little Nell's Moral Aesthetic." *Dickens and the Children of Empire.* Ed. Wendy S. Jacobson. Houndsmills, Baskingstoke, Hampshire and New York: Palgrave, 2000.

Bradbury, Nicola. "Dickens and James: 'Watching with My Eyes Closed': The Dream Abroad." *Dickens Quarterly* 17 (2000): 77–87.

Cerny, Lothar. " 'Life in Death': Art in Dickens's *Our Mutual Friend.*" *Dickens Quarterly* 17 (2000): 22–36.

Chase, Karen, and Michael Levenson. *The Spectacle of Intimacy: A Public Life for The Victorian Family.* Princeton: Princeton UP, 2000.

Chennells, Anthony. "Savages and Settlers in Dickens: Reading Multiple Centres." *Dickens and the Children of Empire.* Ed. Wendy S. Jacobson. Houndsmills, Baskingstoke, Hampshire and New York: Palgrave, 2000.

Cox, Arthur. "Magnetic Sympathy in *The Mystery of Edwin Drood,* Part I: Mr. Crisparkle Takes a Memorable Night Walk." *Dickensian* 96 (2000): 127–50.

———. "Magnetic Sympathy in *The Mystery of Edwin Drood,* Part II: Neville Landless Sets Out on a Pilgrimage." *Dickensian* 96 (2000): 209–42.

Darby, Margaret Flanders. "Dickens and Women's Stories: 1845–1848 (Parts One and Two)." *Dickens Quarterly* 17 (2000): 67–76, 127–38.

Dereli, Claudia. "Charles Dickens and a 'Bohemian' Poet: Benevolent Radicals?" *Dickensian* 96 (2000): 41–44.

De Stasio, Clotilde. "The Traveller as Liar: Dickens and the 'Invisisble Towns' in Northern Italy." *Dickensian* 96 (2000): 5–13.

Easson, Angus. "Don Pickwick: Dickens and the Transformations of Cervantes." *Rereading Victorian Fiction.* Eds. Alice Jenkins and Juliet John. London: Macmillan , New York: St. Martin's 2000.

Flint, Kate. "Dickens and the Native American." *Dickens and the Children of Empire.* Ed. Wendy S. Jacobson. Houndsmills, Baskingstoke, Hampshire and New York: Palgrave, 2000.

Gallagher, Catherine. "Floating Signifiers of Britishness in the Novels of the Anti-Slave Trade Squadron." *Dickens and the Children of Empire.* Ed. Wendy S. Jacobson. Houndsmills, Baskingstoke, Hampshire and New York: Palgrave, 2000.

Greenman, David J. "Alcohol, Comedy and Ghosts in Dickens's Early Short Fiction." *Dickens Quarterly.* 17 (2000): 3–13.

Gregory, Gill. "Dickens and Adelaide Procter." *Dickensian* 96 (2000): 29–40.

Hanna, Robert C. *The Dickens Christian Reader.* New York: AMS Press, 2000.

Hennelly, Jr., Mark M. " 'Betwixt 'Em Somewheres': From Liminal to Liminoid in *David Copperfield, Bleak House,* and *Great Expectations* (Part One)" *Dickens Quarterly* 17 (2000): 199–215.

Hornback, Bert. "Dickens's Failure." *Dickens Quarterly* 17 (2000): 139–48.

Jaffe, Audrey. *Scenes of Sympathy.* Ithaca: Cornell UP, 2000.

John, Juliet. "*Twisting* the Newgate Tale: Dickens, Popular Culture and the Politics of Genre." *Rethinking Victorian Culture.* Eds. Alice Jenkins and Juliet John. London: Macmillan, New York: St. Martin's, 2000.

Kincaid, James. "Dickens and the Construction of the Child." *Dickens and the Children of Empire.* Ed. Wendy S. Jacobson. Houndsmills, Baskingstoke, Hampshire and New York: Palgrave, 2000.

Lougy, Robert E. "Nationalism and Violence: America in Charles Dickens's *Martin Chuzzlewit.*" *Dickens and the Children of Empire.* Ed. Wendy S. Jacobson. Houndsmills, Baskingstoke, Hampshire and New York: Palgrave, 2000.

Marks, Patricia. " 'With a Rush Retire': Robert Newell's *Edwin Drood* Adaptations." *Dickens Quarterly* 17 (2000): 149–68.

Matsika, Greenwell. "Dickens in Africa: 'Africanizing' *Hard Times.*" *Dickens and the Children of Empire.* Houndsmills and New York: Palgrave, 2000.

Morgentaler, Goldie. *Dickens and Heredity: When Like Begets Like.* Houndsmills, Baskingstoke, Hampshire: Macmillan and New York: St. Martin's, 2000.

Morris, Pam. "A Taste for Change in *Our Mutual Friend*: Cultivation or Education?" *Rethinking Victorian Culture.* Eds. Alice Jenkins and Juliet John: London: Macmillan, 2000.

Nayder, Lillian. "Dickens and 'Gold Rush Fever': Colonial Contagion in *Household Words.*" *Dickens and the Children of Empire.* Ed. Wendy S. Jacobson. Houndsmills, Baskingstoke, Hampshire and New York: Palgrave, 2000.

Newsom, Robert. *Charles Dickens Revisited.* New York: Twayne, 2000.

Paroissien, David. *The Companion to "Great Expectations."* East Sussex: Helm, 2000.

Philpotts, Trey. "The 'Civil Service' and 'Administrative Reform': The Blame Game in Dickens's *Little Dorrit.*" *Dickens Quarterly* 17 (2000): 14–21.

Plung, Daniel L. "Environed by Wild Beasts: Animal Imagery in *David Copperfield*." *Dickens Quarterly* 17 (2000): 216–23.

Raven, Robert. "Some Observations on Charles Collins's Sketches for *Edwin Drood*." *Dickensian* 96 (2000): 118–26.

Rem, Tore. "Fictional Exorcism?: Parodies of the Supernatural in Dickens." *Dickensian* 96 (2000): 14–28.

Robson, Catherine. "Girls Underground, Boys Overseas: Some Graveyard Vignettes." *Dickens and the Children of Empire*. Ed. Wendy S. Jacobson. Houndsmills and New York: Palgrave, 2000.

Sanders, Andrew. "Dickens and the Millennium." *Rethinking Victorian Culture*. Eds. Alice Jenkins and Juliet John. London: Macmillan, and New York: St. Martin's, 2000.

Sell-Sandoval, Kathleen. "In the Market Place: Dickens, the Critics and the Gendering of Authorship." *Dickens Quarterly* 17 (2000): 224–35.

Smith, Grahame. "Suppressing Narratives: Childhood and Empire in *The Uncommercial Traveller* and *Great Expectations*." *Dickens and the Children of Empire*. Ed. Wendy S. Jacobson. Houndsmills, Baskingstoke, Hampshire and New York: Palgrave, 2000.

Tracy, Robert. "Disappearances: George Parkman and Edwin Drood." *Dickensian* 96 (2000): 101–17.

Tromp, Marlene. *The Private Rod: Marital Violence, Sensation, and the Law in Victorian Britain*. Charlottesville: UP of Virginia, 2000.

Valenti, Teresa. "The Forgotten Father in Charles Dickens's *Bleak House*." *Dickens. Quarterly* 17 (2000): 88–93.

Van Wyk Smith, Malvern. " 'What the Waves Were Always Saying': *Dombey and Son* and Textual Ripples on an African Shore." *Dickens and the Children of Empire*. Ed. Wendy S. Jacobson. Houndsmills, Baskingstoke, Hampshire and New York: Palgrave, 2000.

Welsh, Alexander. *Dickens Redressed: The Art of "Bleak House" and "Hard Times."* New Haven: Yale UP, 2000.

# Review of Brontë Studies: The Millennial Decade, 1990–2000

## Linda H. Peterson

*The final decade of the twentieth-century saw the publication of several important biographies on the Brontës and scholarly editions of their work, most notably Juliet Barker's* The Brontës *(1994), a comprehensive account of the family's life and work; Sue Lonoff's translation and critical edition of* The Belgian Essays *(1996); Christine Alexander and Jane Sellars's* The Art of the Brontës *(1995), a collection, with commentary, of the siblings' visual work; and* The Letters of Charlotte Brontë, with a Selection of Letters by Family and Friends, *edited by Margaret Smith. In critical studies, Anne Brontë emerged as an artist in her own right, differentiated from her sisters by an allegiance to Enlightenment feminism rather than Romantic ideology; Emily Brontë became a resister, opposer, and questioner of Victorian patriarchy and its manifestations in literature and culture, rather than an isolated figure of Romantic genius; and Charlotte Brontë's fiction was increasingly read within the contexts of nineteenth-century debates over slavery, racism, colonialism, and the politics of class and gender.*

"Of writing many books there is no end": so Elizabeth Barrett Browning began her autobiography of a woman poet, *Aurora Leigh* (1857). Given the allusion to Ecclesiastes 12:12, I have often wondered whether Barrett Browning meant to lament the "vanity" and "vexation of spirit" that comes from

*Dickens Studies Annual,* Volume 31, Copyright © 2002 by AMS Press, Inc. All rights reserved.

producing too many books and the "weariness of the flesh" that studying them entails, or whether, in keeping with the larger context of the allusion, she meant to recall the final judgment of all human works, her own included, and thus hold herself to a high standard in writing. I can certainly attest to the weariness of the flesh I have felt in reading a decade of Brontë scholarship, but I can also affirm its high standards, especially in new editions of letters and juvenilia. Nonetheless, in the survey that follows, I have tried to avoid definitive judgments and instead have attempted to identify trends in Brontë studies, to recognize books that initiate or follow those trends, and occasionally to suggest issues that remain to be explored.

## Biography and Letters

The biography of the 1990s is unquestionably Juliet Barker's *The Brontës* (1994). When it appeared, it was hailed in the *TLS*—quite rightly—as "an outstanding achievement, a magnificent portrait which not only contains a wealth of important material, but is also a delight to read." The reviewer, Rebecca Fraser, noted that she found it "hard to imagine it ever being surpassed." Barker, for many years a curator and librarian at the Brontë Parsonage Museum, seems to have read every scrap of paper the Brontë family ever composed, as well as every contemporary document written to and about them. In undertaking her research, she has traveled to the sites where the Brontës lived, worked, and visited, reading local history and recreating a sense of the places as they existed at mid-nineteenth-century. Thus, in conceiving her biography, she has enlarged its geographical, historical, and cultural range by setting the Brontës' activities within regional, national, and European contexts. This biography, a massive 1003 pages including notes, is the biography not only of the past decade, but of an entire century.

How does it change our understanding of the Brontës' lives and work? The question of "lives" is relatively straightforward; more difficult, the question of "works." Certainly, the Rev. Patrick Brontë, father of three famous daughters, becomes a compelling figure in his own right. With significant literary ambition, a commitment to evangelical religion and its social causes, and a passion for educational reform, he emerges from the myth of eccentricity in family life and severity to his children to become a compassionate, hard-working clergyman who cared deeply about the poverty of his parishioners, fought hard for national education, and supported the Reform Bill of 1832. Unlike his children, who often assumed more conservative, Tory positions than he, Patrick worked *against* slavery, *for* Catholic Emancipation, and *for* a reform of the penal code. So, too, in Barker's portrait, his literary ambitions and early publications emerge for their own interest as well as for possible influences on his daughters' work, especially in his insistence on everyday realism and moral high-mindedness. In his solitude after their deaths, he stands as a deeply grieving mourner, whose "selfless pride and generosity" would "not let him diminish his daughter's portrait in order to set the record straight on himself" (798).

The son of the house, Patrick Branwell Brontë, also receives Barker's sympathetic attention, despite what seems to be overwhelming negative evidence about his talent, achievement, and mental or moral discipline. Barker documents the literary collaboration of Branwell and Charlotte in the Angrian tales, thus giving Branwell's juvenilia as much space as Charlotte's and implicitly, if not explicitly, treating the collaboration as a writers' workshop that might have led to a significant literary career. Barker also records Branwell's training as a painter and his early attempt at this profession; his entry into a new business arena (the railroad); and his continuing efforts to write poems and publish them not only in local and regional newspapers, as he managed to do, but in national periodicals such as *Blackwood's Magazine*. What Barker does not address is the issue of quality: Was anything that Branwell wrote truly excellent? I find the quoted poetry and prose mediocre at best, dull at worst. Rather than argue Branwell's ability or achievement, Barker instead casts him in the role of originator: in her view, it was a typical pattern that "Branwell initiated a new idea, dominated its early development and then, getting bored, would go off to do something else" (160). While this pattern holds true for the juvenilia written with Charlotte in 1830, it seems unlikely that, fifteen years later in 1845, when Branwell wrote to his friend Joseph Leyland that he was writing a three-volume novel, we should credit him with being "the first member of his family to tread a new path, in seeing the potential of the novel as a marketable commodity and setting about writing one for publication" (475). As Edward Chitham's evidence in *A Life of Anne Brontë* (1991) suggests, in 1840 Anne had started composing her own prose narrative, whether a novel about "Olivia Vernon" or an autobiographical predecessor to *Agnes Grey*. If anyone deserves credit for being the first "novelist" of the Brontë family, perhaps it should be Anne.

Indeed, in Barker's biography, as in many monographs of the 1990s, Anne Brontë receives much more attention—and literary credit—than she has earlier attracted. In the sisterly triumvirate, Anne assumes the role of "peacemaker" (479), soothing troubled waters when the invasive Charlotte "accidentally light[s]" upon the reclusive Emily's poetic manuscript and insists on publication. In the familial economy, Anne takes responsibility for their well-being when no one else can or will by finding herself a position as governess at Thorp Green, sticking with it for five years, and coming home only when Branwell's affair with his employer's wife (and his imminent disgrace) compel her to leave. In literary achievement, too, Anne merits independent recognition—for her creation in *Agnes Grey* of the first "plain and ordinary woman as its heroine" (503), her "far deadlier exposé of the trials of being a governess" (503), her creation of a professional woman artist as protagonist in *The Tenant of Wildfell Hall*, and her greater commitment to realism and feminist causes in both her novels.

Nonetheless, Barker's *The Brontës* is dominated by Charlotte—as it perhaps must be, given that Charlotte outlived her siblings, published more literary work, and created their first public portraits in the "Biographical Notice of Ellis and Acton Bell." Branwell, Emily, and Anne die by the end of chapter 19, "Stripped and Bereaved," and the biography continues for another nine chapters (260 pages), detailing that part of the story most readers know well: the literary success of *Wuthering Heights* and *Jane Eyre*; the subsequent publication and fame of *Shirley* and *Villette*, the afterglow in Elizabeth Gaskell's *Life of Charlotte Brontë* (1857), and the remaining years of Patrick Brontë and Charlotte's widower, the Rev. Arthur Nicholls. Charlotte's dominance—her sheer physical longevity—has other effects as well. It inevitably leads Barker to dwell more on Charlotte's literary achievement than on that of her sisters', not only because she survived them but because much more of her manuscript material—and material about her—survives. It also leads Barker, perhaps not inevitably, to attribute to Charlotte the bossy dominance of an older sister, always patronizing Anne, the youngest sibling, or moralizing about Branwell, the dissolute brother, or pushing Emily, the recluse, to show her literary ambition—despite, as Barker points out, Charlotte's own inability to survive as a governess, to stop fantasizing about a married man, or to pull herself out of serious bouts with depression in the 1840s.

Was Charlotte as dominant and domineering as Barker suggests? What motivates this reassessment of the elder sister? Although Barker's motivation puzzled me throughout much of the biography, even when the evidence against Charlotte was substantial, it finally crystallized in chapter 27, "Saintliness, Treason and Plot." The "villain" of the piece, we discover, is not Charlotte but her first biographer, Mrs. Gaskell. The "saintliness" is the false characterization of Charlotte; the "treason" and "plot" refer to Gaskell's duplicitous treatment of Charlotte's father and widower, especially in her fulsome quotation of letters that include negative portraits of parsonage life and lukewarm descriptions of Charlotte's future husband. Barker cannot seem to forgive Gaskell for her hagiographic portrait of 1857, in which Gaskell "vindicate[s] her friend by blaming her family and her upbringing in Haworth for all the critical condemnation of her writing" (796). What compels Barker in this chapter and elsewhere, in other words, is a desire to paint a fairer portrait of the entire Brontë family.

Yet Barker's success in rewriting the Brontes' *lives* leaves the question of their literary *work* more perplexing than ever. Gaskell's *Life of Charlotte Brontë*, as Linda Hughes and Michael Lund have demonstrated in *Victorian Publishing and Mrs. Gaskell's Work* (1999), was meant less as a hagiography than as an attempt to reconcile the two streams of a woman writer's life that so fascinated the Victorian public: the woman as daughter, sister, wife, and mother, and the woman as professional author. It was also, as Barker acknowledges, an attempt to explain the coarseness and brutality of the Brontës' novels to a Victorian readership unaccustomed to such productions by middle-class gentlewomen. Charlotte had recoiled in her lifetime from the harsh comments of reviewers on this issue of decorum, as had her father and husband; indeed, a primary reason for their authorizing Gaskell's biography was to silence "malignant falsehoods" against one "whose name those who knew her best but speak with reverence and affection" (780). If Gaskell answered Charlotte Brontë's critics by focusing on social isolation, regional difference, and familial tragedies in the treatment of her subject, she was taking her cue from Charlotte herself, who gave similar explanations in the biographical preface to re-issues of *Wuthering Heights* and *Agnes Grey* in 1850. And Gaskell succeeded, as the reviews of *The Life of Charlotte Brontë* quoted by Barker attest.

What Barker's monumental biography raises, then, is the abiding question of a "life and letters": To what use do or can we put the "life" in explaining the "work"? Barker intends her new account to "sweep away the many myths which have clung to the Brontës for so long" (xx), and in this myth-breaking she magnificently succeeds. Yet the Brontë "myths" include not just the tales of family life that Barker discredits but the myths of authorship that readers have formulated to explain the sisters' literary achievement. For these myths, Barker offers "the fact that they were such an extraordinarily close family" as "the key to their achievements" (xviii). While the siblings' juvenile collaboration certainly provided the equivalent of an ongoing literary workshop, and while collaborative writing has become a new means of explaining writerly production, especially in opposition to Romantic myths of individual genius, it is not clear that close family ties can adequately explain why this particular family produced three famous novelists and two (perhaps more) classics, nor why the novels of the three sisters are so different in form, tone, and ideology. After all, there were other nineteenth-century literary families, including the Stricklands, the Howitts, and the Marryats, who did not achieve the Brontës' distinction.

As Edward Chitham puts it in his new *Life of Anne Brontë* (1991), "it is the business of Brontë scholars to address" certain "key questions," including "what was the literary relation between *Jane Eyre, Wuthering Heights* and *Wildfell Hall*; and what were the attitudes of the three sisters towards each others' work" (7)? Chitham's phrasing implies that collaboration tells part of the story, but that individuation is also important. For Anne Brontë, he argues, it was essential, for "fate thrust on Anne a role she never quite transcended." As the youngest of six children and the youngest of the three famous novelists, Currer, Ellis, and Acton Bell, she was "expected to be a small-scale copy of the others" (15).

Chitham's biography of Anne, the first since Winifred Gerin's groundbreaking work of 1959, reveals Anne Brontë in her own right—not by ignoring her familial relations or her literary collaborations with Emily, but by focusing on the different life experiences that led Anne to different literary work in *Agnes Grey* and *Wildfell Hall*. Anne did not, as we often forget, attend the Cowan Bridge School with her sisters Charlotte and Emily; she was last to attend Miss Woolner's school at Roe Head, taking Emily's place only after homesickness struck her sister; and she was not included in the Belgian venture, instead leaving home for five years to work as a governess at Blake Hall and Thorp Green.

Chitham''s *Life* is less fluid that Barker's *The Brontës*—in part because he is a cautious biographer who insists on discussing the evidentiary issues before stating conclusions, in part because he frequently refers the reader to other books he has written, including *A Life of Emily Brontë* (1987). Nonetheless, his *Life of Anne Brontë* is essential to scholars working on the Brontës' novels, if only because it addresses more dispassionately the questions of collaboration, influence, and individuality. Moreover, it provides a thorough account of Anne's life as governess at Thorp Green from 1840 to 1845; a useful discussion of her poetry, including a spirited recreation of her romance with William Weightman, her father's curate; and a detailed critical reading of *Wildfell Hall* as a response to, often a rewriting of, Emily's *Wuthering Heights* and Charlotte's *Jane Eyre*. Chitham's caution and his work with T. J. Winnfrith on *Brontë Facts and Brontë Problems* (1983) help the critic see where the biographical *cruces* lie and where intextuality begins and ends.

Those readers who feel Charlotte Brontë to be underestimated in or maligned by Barker's and Chitham's biographies, both of which take a sterner view of Charlotte's personal behavior and domineering relations with her sisters than did Gaskell's *Life*, should turn to Lyndall Gordon's *Charlotte Brontë: A Passionate Life* (1994). Gordon's lucid account was somewhat overlooked in the commotion over Barker's massive book, but it shouldn't remain unread. Like Barker, Gordon seeks to release Charlotte from the ladylike image, the dutiful daughter and wife, that Gaskell created in her 1857 *Life*. But as Gordon seeks the "volcanic" life beneath "the still, grey crust" (4), she finds Charlotte's art emerging from a "dual allegiance" to—or tension between—"the burdened pilgrimage on the one hand and the free-ranging moors on the other" (25), the "obedient girl" and the "romantic enthusiast" (67). She argues that "Charlotte practised the manners of a well-bred lady—the modesty, the decorum, the reserve—and, at the same time, exploded the artifice of tameness" (83) in her writing. While these binaries may seem familiar, they are worked out with originality and admirable detail in the narrative, which keeps its focus on the life not so much to get the facts straight (as Barker often insists on doing) as to understand how Charlotte's life could have produced such magnificent art. The goal of Gordon's biography is, ultimately, about "passion and creativity" (which should not be understood solely in sexual terms) and about "the reach of words" (333).

Shorter recent biographies worth consulting include two from the British Library's "Writers' Lives" series: Jane Sellars's *Charlotte Brontë* (1997) and Robert Barnard's *Emily Brontë* (2000). Barnard, an English professor turned mystery writer, gives a lively, readable account of Emily's life and work; Sellars, former director of the Brontë Parsonage Museum, writes a more scholarly, yet admirably accessible account of Charlotte. The real attractions of these books, each just over 100 pages, are the lavish illustrations from the archives of the British Library, the Brontë Parsonage Museum, and the Brontë Society. Manuscript pages, covers of first editions, engravings of places the sisters visited, photographs of places they lived and worked, periodical illustrations of mills, factories, Liverpool and London, clothing, needlework, and other memorabilia from the parsonage, the usual (and some less usual) portraits—these well-chosen visual materials make the two volumes important, if only for contemporary contexts in teaching the novels. One only hopes that Oxford University Press will keep the volumes in print at a reasonable price so that teachers can order them for classroom use.

## Books, Monographs, and Collections

Most monographs of the last decade have appeared in special series, including Macmillan's "Women Writers," Twayne's "English Authors," Indiana's "Key Women Writers," and the British Council's "Writers and Their Work." Because such series often have a strong pedagogical component and balance a need to introduce novice readers to current scholarship with a desire to present original readings of the novels or the author's life, they reflect the critical interests of the 1980s as much as new approaches of the 1990s. As a group, these monographs give a useful map of the territory that Brontë scholarship has already explored, and they hint at new directions in which it is heading—particularly, the new attention to Anne Brontë's novels as interesting texts in their own right; the continuing dominance of feminist approaches in criticism on all three sisters; and the new connections with postcolonial, cultural, and neohistorical studies in recent criticism on Charlotte Brontë's fiction. These monographs also confirm that all three Brontë sisters have achieved canonical status, at least in the feminist canon.

## Emily Brontë

Lyn Pykett's *Emily Brontë* (1989) in the Macmillan series successfully consolidates the feminist criticism of the 1980s with her own special interest in how a Victorian woman writer locates herself within or against literary traditions (82). Pykett begins with the few known facts of Brontë's life, using them to establish the paradox of her life and work: Emily as the "brooding precocious genius" versus Emily as the "dutiful daughter of the parsonage" (2). The readings of Ellis Bell's poetry and fiction insist on the same paradox—or "complex relationship," to use Pykett's phrase—between the traditional religious sources of Emily's verse and the more transgressive Romantic influences, between realism and romance in *Wuthering Heights*, between the female Gothic and the turn to the Victorian domestic novel.

In keeping with the "series" approach, Pykett refers to most of the major criticism of the 1970s and '80s but rejects monolithic interpretations, whether the "masculinist political readings" (129) of Kettle, Eagleton, and Widdowston that make Heathcliff "the centre and raison d'etre of *Wuthering Heights*" or feminist readings like Ellen Moers's that see Brontë as a genius independent of literary traditions. Pykett argues instead for an author writing both in relationship to "traditions and views of women's writing" and in a "complex and problematic relationship, as a woman writer, to dominant masculine traditions and definitions of literature'' (121). Her greatest insight comes, I think, in treating the Gothic and domestic as structurally continuous in *Wuthering Heights* and thus showing how Brontë makes ''the domestic the source of the Gothic'' (80). Her greatest virtue comes in keeping both halves of the paradox in balance—duty and resistance, tradition and rebellion.

Steve Vine's *Emily Brontë* (1998) in the Twayne series takes Pykett's notion of a woman writer in ''complex and problematic relationship'' to dominant masculine traditions and pushes it to the extreme, seeing Emily's oeuvre as a series of acts of ''textual resistance.'' In his preface Vine notes that, for much of the past 150 years, Emily has been viewed as ''an abstruse genius'' or a ''native sibyl''; instead, following the trend of recent scholarship, he presents her as a writer ''energetically and critically'' engaged with ''questions of genre, ideology, gender, and language.''

These four terms more or less define the keynotes of Vine's chapters. In chapter 1, typically the ''biography'' chapter in the Twayne monographs, Vine uses Brontë's diary papers and *devoirs* to show how she textually resisted ''the patriarchy that surrounded her''; he carefully studies the *devoirs* for their ''ironic interventions in and commentaries on the mores and categories of nineteenth-century culture'' (x). In chapter 2 Vine mounts an argument for Brontë's Gondal fictions as self-dramatic rather than self-expressive, and then uses this ''aesthetic of self-dramatization'' in chapter 3 to discuss the ''contradictory speaking positions'' that afflict Brontë ''as a woman poet writing in a masculine literary tradition'' and ''as a dissident poet writing within an orthodox religious culture'' (xi). Similarly, in the two chapters on *Wuthering Heights*, Vine uses post-structuralist theory and Kristevan psychoanalytic theory to show the novel ''deconstructing bourgeois subjectivities and stabilities with a force of derangement and delirium.'' While all of these chapters are worth reading for their critique of prior criticism and new commentary on Brontë's work, one wonders if *every* piece of Emily Brontë's writing need be read as an act of textual resistance—whether in the *devoirs* to ''Constantin Heger's paternal and patriarchal world'' (74) or in the poems to ''the heavenly Father of orthodoxy'' (46) or in the novel to ''the constituted cultural horizons of its bourgeois readers'' (83). The odd cumulative effect is a monolithic Brontë, one who produced only texts of cultural resistance, never one who (re)produced any aspect of Victorian ideology.

Stevie Davies's two monographs, *Emily Brontë: Heretic* (1994) and *Emily Brontë* (1998) in the ''Writers and Their Work'' series, also see Brontë as a resister (as her label "heretic" implies). Davies's Brontë, however, is "complex and compound: 'contrary' in the sense that the self she articulated was riven with contradiction" (xii). In the first monograph, Davies reads this contradiction within Brontë herself—a "self-deifying author" who could write "No coward soul is mine," yet who was also a home-bound woman, afraid of strangers, physically and psychically homesick whenever forced out into the world. She also reads contradiction and complexity in Brontë's work—in the poetry, for example, that retaliates against religion as an "oppressive agent of patriarchy," yet that also is "a product of Protestantism, which ironically gave [Brontë] a legacy of power and authority to criticise its own icons and structure" (140). Expanding this notion of Protestantism as a tradition internally producing resistance to religion itself, Davies reads *Wuthering Heights* as a work of antinomianism, "an extreme form of Calvinism which asserts that God absolves his elect from obedience to natural, moral and civil law" (146). With Joseph as the Calvinist and Cathy and Heathcliff as the antinomians, the protagonists become resisters and a law unto themselves; yet their passionate attachment to each other retains "a religious dimension" that prevents us from reading the novel as merely a "romantic love-story" (159)—or, I would add, merely as an account of resistance to cultural ideologies.

Although less systematic than Vine's book and perhaps less useful as an introductory guide, Davies's treatment is more satisfying in explaining the sources of Brontë's resistance within Protestantism and thus in dealing with the complexity of Brontë's thought and expression. Moreover, as Patsy Stoneman noted in her review of Davies's earlier book, *Emily Brontë: The Artist as a Free Woman* (1988), and as is true for both new monographs, Davies's feminist approach actually presents a startling contrast to much feminist criticism of the 1970s and 1980s (and some of the '90s) that sees the nineteenth-century woman writer "as excluded and repressed by masculine culture."[1] For Davies, there is a sense of "joyous literary feud with Milton" (146), just as there is a sense of joyous and vibrant feminist creation throughout Emily's oeuvre. Also drawing on Protestant theology in this earlier book, Davies argues that *Wuthering Heights* "uniquely among mythopoeic works of fiction . . . raises the mother principle . . . to the status of deity, presenting it as the focal object of human aspiration and the final end of Emily Brontë's language of desire" (25).

In most criticism of the past decade, in other words, Emily Brontë emerges as a resister, opposer, and questioner of patriarchy and its manifestations in Victorian literature and culture. While this may be a departure from earlier myths of Emily as a Romantic genius, a solitary artist in nature's "wild workshop," it is not actually a departure from the long-standing biographical tradition of treating Emily as the most unconventional of the Brontë sisters. Emily's personal unsociability and unconventionality become, in recent criticism, a writerly resistance to Victorian social mores, cultural ideologies, and (masculine) literary conventions. The one partial exception to this generalization is Edward Chitham's *The Birth of Wuthering Heights: Emily Brontë at Work* (1998). Although Chitham, like other scholars of the '80s and '90s, rejects the romantic portrait of Emily as a brooding, untutored genius from whose head *Wuthering Heights* "must have sprung fully fledged" (87), his goal is less to cast her as a resister of patriarchy than to show her as a careful, disciplined writer whose novel emerged from a long literary apprenticeship. In so doing, Chitham's ultimate goal is to argue, following a line sketched by Thomas Winnifrith in *Brontë Facts and Brontë Problems* (1983), that Emily must have composed, if not completed, a second novel.

### Anne Brontë

If Emily Brontë has held pride of place as the most determined opponent of dominant Victorian ideologies, Anne Brontë has long been seen as the most conventional of the sisters, the youngest, least able and ambitious of the three. Not so any longer. Monographs of the 1990s present a new version of Anne, author of *Agnes Grey* and *The Tenant of Wildfell Hall*. In all of the series monographs, she becomes less acquiescent, more resistant and revolutionary.

Elizabeth Langland's subtitle to the *Anne Brontë* in the Macmillan series —*The Other One*—sounds the keynote. Because Anne is the least written about sister, overshadowed by Charlotte and Emily during her lifetime and in the subsequent 150 years of scholarship, Langland argues that feminist critics have greater need—and greater opportunity—to introduce new approaches to Anne's novels and create a case for individual achievement even in her poetry. Indeed, there is an almost missionary zeal in the new monographs on Anne, so determined her advocates seem on converting readers to the virtues of the youngest Brontë's work or condemning the skeptical for "collud[ing] with a literary and critical history" that has "underestimate[d] Anne Brontë's contribution to the novel and to poetic form" (Jay 5).

Langland's *Anne Brontë: The Other One* (1989) is perhaps the most original of these monographs, though all have original ideas to advance. Taking her cue from Anne's preface to the second edition of *The Tenant of Wildfell Hall*, "Acton Bell is neither Currer nor Ellis Bell," Langland suggests that we avoid the critical practice of assuming that she is the weak sister, that "Anne is trying to do what Emily and Charlotte are doing but that Anne cannot succeed through lack of talent" (29). Instead, according to Langland, we should read Anne Brontë's work as a self-conscious critique of her sisters' novels, especially as it "establishes alternative standards and values" (29). Langland's Anne is an Enlightenment feminist rather than a Romantic devotee—a writer influenced by William Cowper, Samuel Johnson, Hannah More, and Charles Wesley (among others) rather than the Romantic poets Byron and Shelley, whom her sisters idolized. This literary and philosophical difference, which developed while Anne was living apart from her family as a governess at Thorp Green, led her to emphasize reason, logic, and restraint in self-development rather than passion, emotion, and rebellion against conventions. It had a profound effect upon her engagement with the novel of female self-development in both *Agnes Grey* and *Wildfell Hall*: "Cultivation of the spiritual life, leading to mastery of the passions, seems to ensure a greater degree of self-determination for [her heroines] rather than an increase in self-abnegation typical of the protagonist of the female *Bildungsroman*" (106).

As evidence of Anne Brontë's individual achievement, Langland points out that Anne was one of the earliest women novelists to create a professional artist as a heroine—Helen Huntingdon in *The Tenant of Wildfell Hall* (1848)—and that, unlike her sister Charlotte, Anne did not depict the pursuit of a profession as merely marking time until marriage. Moreover, Anne's depiction of Helen's experience implicitly critiques the male brutality and violence of Emily's Heathcliff, the "foolish idealism" of Jane Eyre, who, like the young Helen, believes herself "capable of redeeming the barrenness and waste of a man's earlier life" (52), and the "disturbing masochistic way" so many of her sisters' heroines respond to "masculine aggression" (57). In Langland's reassessment, Anne Brontë's brief literary career shows remarkable progress intellectually and technically, her novels in many ways foreshadowing insights of modern feminism. Had not Charlotte suppressed *Wildfell Hall* for a decade, it would have had a far greater impact on the nineteenth-century tradition of the women's novel: in Langland's view, "it might have helped generate representations of a new kind of heroine, more spirited and independent" (54).

Whether or not one agrees with this high estimate of Anne Brontë's work, Langland's reassessment is persuasive in offering alternative literary traditions and philosophical frameworks in which to interpret Anne's poetry and fiction against those of her sisters. In its emphasis on literary achievement, social critique, and sisterly relations, her approach has also been highly influential on subsequent monographs on Anne Brontë.

Elizabeth Hollis Berry's *Anne Brontë's Radical Vision: Structures of Consciousness* (1994), in the Canadian "English Literary Studies" series, also makes the case for Anne's literary achievement, often in comparison with her sisters' work. But Berry's method is more purely formalist, an "examination of imagery [that] focuses on Brontë's antithetical method which explores social structures and their inherent dichotomies" (11). By this Berry means that Anne embeds her social commentary within "natural and spatial images" that are both material and figurative—for instance, the images of wind and storm in *Agnes Grey* that function as a critique of the Bloomfield family.

In *Anne Brontë* (1996) in the Twayne English Authors Series, Maria Frawley begins with more ambivalence than Langland about reading Anne's work within and against a familial context. Indeed, Frawley laments that "Anne Brontë has, in many ways, been condemned to be seen only as her family and friends saw her" (1). But then Frawley turns this problem into an opportunity by noting the "dilemmas of identity" that dominated Anne's life and work, dilemmas which Frawley grounds biographically in her position as youngest sister and narratively in her experiments with autobiographical genres, including the diary, journal, letter, and *bildungsroman*. Frawley's key themes emerge from what she sees as Anne's abiding interest in the "secrecy, silence, and solitude" of Victorian women and women writers—"the possibilities of autonomy and the problematics of anonymity; the interplay between public and private identities; the relationship of privacy to personhood; [and] the perplexities of human behavior and development" as "individuals continually and sometimes inexplicably re-create themselves as they interact with others" (144–45).

These themes are most revealing when Frawley interprets poems such as "Self-Congratulation," which she reads as an exploration of "the instability of selfhood" (53), or "Self-Communion," as a "process of self-discovery to an acknowledgment of a synthetic unity of selfhood" (144), or when she analyzes the complicated process of revealing and withholding personal stories in *The Tenant of Wildfell Hall*. Frawley is effective as well in her discussion of "private speech" in *Agnes Grey*. Ultimately, however, the "thematics" of "secrecy, silence, and solitude" do not resolve the critical dilemma with which Frawley begins: whether Anne's work has distinctive literary merit or has interest primarily because of its participation in a remarkable nineteenth-century family phenomenon. Like all scholars of the 1990s who write on Anne Brontë, Frawley wants to argue for the individuality of Anne's work and its literary merit; yet this goal cannot be achieved by focusing on the self-representational strategies of Anne's poems and novels without comparing them in effectiveness to those used by her sisters and other contemporary writers. In the end, if we're bound to make comparisons, I agree with Charlotte (and most nineteenth-century reviewers) that Anne's work has a "sweet sincere pathos" but that it lacks the power and energy of Emily's poetry and novel (or of Charlotte's *Jane Eyre*). In arguing Anne's case, Langland is more successful in showing Anne's distinctiveness not by attempting to demonstrate superior literary technique but by aligning her with a different literary tradition from the one her sisters embraced.

Betty Jay's *Anne Brontë* (2000), in the "Writers and Their Work" series underwritten by the British Council, argues Anne's special contribution to the nineteenth-century novel not in narratological terms but in terms of her engagement with contemporary social and political issues, especially of class and gender. Jay's three well-conceived chapters provide succinct, yet deeply informed readings of *Agnes Grey, Wildfell Hall*, and selected poetry within the contexts of Victorian social history as well as "recent theoretical debates concerning feminism, subjectivity, power and agency" (5). For scholars who want an overview of where work on Anne Brontë now stands, Jay's book provides an excellent resource.

Yet it is also an original work of criticism. While the summary of "the governess debates" of mid-nineteenth-century will be familiar to Victorianists and the discussion of Agnes Grey's ambiguous class status, equally familiar, Jay's reading of the tensions within the novel about proper womanhood—for instance, Agnes's inability to recognize the hoydenish behavior of Mary Ann Bloomfield or Matilda Murray as a resistance to Victorian gender categories different from her own or Agnes's insufficient recognition of her erotic desire for Weston—make this monograph worth reading for its new insights. So, too, Jay's reading of the textual/sexual politics of *The Tenant of Wildfell Hall* incorporates useful criticism from prior articles and books, especially Jill L. Matus's *Unstable Bodies* (1995) and Susan Meyer's "Words on 'Great Vulgar Sheets'" (1996), while advancing its own interpretation to counter Terry Eagleton's claim that the novel fails because of its "relative separation of the personal and social" (36).

If I remain skeptical about the achievement of Anne Brontë's poetry, it is largely because Jay selects only four of the best poems to bolster her argument that Anne finds in religion a recompense for emotional loss but, more importantly, self-consciously explores the limits of such spiritual recompense.

More of Anne's 60 existing poems would require consideration to make this point stick. Even then, I would wonder whether Anne's poetry is best read as a "subversively subjective project" (76) or whether it might not be better for feminist criticism to acknowledge that not all women writers wish to be subversive in all aspects of their literary careers.

## Charlotte Brontë

Charlotte, the oldest sister, has received harsher scrutiny in recent biographies and criticism—in part because she seem less subversive than Emily at a critical moment when "subversion" seems to be the key virtue, in part for her dominance over Anne and suppression of *The Tenant of Wildfell Hall*, in part for her personal and fictional acquiescence to the Victorian marriage plot. Nonetheless, Charlotte remains the subject of much admiring feminist criticism—in sheer quantity, of the most new monographs on the Brontës, in quality, of the most innovative literary and cultural studies.

We can trace the trends in criticism and scholarship by comparing the beginning and end of the decade. Pauline Nestor's *Charlotte Brontë* (1987), the first monograph in the Macmillan series to consider a Brontë sister, and Nestor's subsequent *Jane Eyre* (1992) in the Harvester-Wheatsheaf "Keytexts" series, are both firmly feminist projects, grounded in the questions of the 1970s and '80s. For *Jane Eyre*, according to Nestor, the two critical lessons the heroine must learn are "self-control and self-assertion" (50); for *Shirley*, the issue is the oppression of women and workers by a misogynistic patriarchy; for *Villette*, it is "the repression of the individual" (85). Similarly, Janet Gezari's *Charlotte Brontë and Defensive Conduct* (1992) concerns itself with repression and expression, silence and speech: the difficulty of speaking in a society that enjoins women to silence and the "strategies of defensiveness" that are an intelligent response to such conditions and powerful idiom in Charlotte's novels. Nonetheless, as Susan Fraiman noted in reviewing Gehazi's book along with Carol Bock's *Charlotte Brontë and the Storyteller's Audience* (1992), these essentially biographical-critical studies address old concerns and do not engage with emerging interests in "cultural discourses of imperialism, scientific racism, or domesticity and bourgeois subjectivity."[2]

We see a shift towards these interests—perhaps the most significant trend of the decade—first in Penny Boumelha's *Charlotte Brontë* (1990) in the

"Key Women Writers" series. Boumelha's monograph is a forthright feminist reading of Charlotte's novels and, in keeping with the goal of the series,
a reassessment of a "mainstream" woman writer in terms of the question,
"In what way can such writers be regarded as feminist?" For Boumelha
what makes Brontë's work "feminist" is not so much its revision of two key
fictional traditions, the "romance" and the *bildungsroman*, but rather
Brontë's introduction of a third "plot of desire," those things unnarratable
within existing traditions or that escape from narrative itself into what Boumelha calls "rhapsody."

Boumelha sees Charlotte's first novel, *The Professor*, as fearful of desire,
so much so that "all that would speak of desire is split off and projected,
beyond the confines of the novel, onto the unimagined narrative of Lucia"
(23); this expellation allows Brontë to resolve the tension between the traditional plots of romance and vocation "into one for both protagonists" (22).
*Jane Eyre* speaks its desire directly, as in the famous "rhapsody" when Jane
paces the third-floor attic of Thornfield Hall and dreams of women's freedom,
but desire is felt more frequently in the tension between the two traditional
plots—"sometimes seen as an opposition between Gothic and realist elements, or Romantic and realist, or fairy-tale and novel—that gives this novel
its peculiar intensity and force" (77). In *Shirley*, desire is repeatedly disruptive of plot, particularly when moments of "feminine" rhapsody stop the
"masculine" realism; but, paradoxically, according to Boumelha, this novel
more than any other depends on the traditional closure of the romance plot
in order to achieve the happiness of its two heroines, with the dissidents (the
feminist Yorke sisters, as well as the loom-breaking workers) being expelled
to the "colonies." Finally, perhaps almost predictably, in *Villette* the traditional plots of romance and vocation are repeated and "subjected to critique," with the plot of "desire" expressed in the figures of Vashti and the
nun, who represent versions of the female self not encompassed or displayed
by traditional narratives (117).

As the above summary suggests, Boumelha incorporates and extends the
feminist criticism of the 1970s and '80s in her reading of desire in Charlotte
Brontë's novels. Yet anticipating the 90's, she also introduces the "significant
social and textual issues [of] race and class" (8). She does so most successfully with *Jane Eyre*, in which she contrasts the metaphorical uses of "slavery" to represent the condition of women with the utter silence on the actual
slavery in Jamaica that underwrites Rochester's wealth and Jane's final
achievement of equality, and with *Shirley*, in which she explores the expressed

parallels between women and workers but also the "intractable problems" that Brontë's own class position created in uniting their interests.

These social and political issues become prominent—and typographically distinct—in Diane Long Hoeveler and Lisa Jadwin's *Charlotte Brontë* (1997) in the Twayne series. After their survey of the biographical and critical traditions, Hoeveler and Jadwin divide the chapters on Charlotte's novels into subsections such as "The Feminist Reclamation of *The Professor*," "Formalist Readings" and "Political Readings" of *Jane Eyre*, "The 'Woman Question'" and "Political and Religious Criticism" in *Shirley*, and "*Villette* as Critique of Women's Roles." Such divisions acknowledge both strong formalist and feminist traditions of interpreting Brontë's fiction and recent interests that New Historicism and cultural studies have brought to the table. If an attention to the spectrum of critical positions makes Hoeveler and Jadwin's book a less independent work of hermeneutics, it also makes the monograph highly useful to serious non-Brontëans who need a reliable guide to the extensive scholarship. Moreover, the final chapter, "'All Turned Up in Tumult': The Poetry and Letters," gives the best brief introduction to Charlotte Brontë's letters that I have encountered, both in terms of their publication history and in relation to Brontë's biography.

What Hoeveler and Jadwin's subsections imply (and what some of the footnotes acknowledge) is that the most innovative recent criticism on Charlotte Brontë has emerged not from monographs but from individual articles (or book chapters) addressing issues applicable to a wide range of Victorian texts—a generalization that holds true for recent criticism on Emily Brontë as well. From postcolonial studies, one thinks of Gayatri Spivak's seminal "Three Women's Texts and a Critique of Imperialism" (*CI*, 1985) or Susan Meyer's more intensive "Colonialism and the Figurative Strategy of *Jane Eyre*" (*VS*, 1990), which explores the problematic association of white women and colonized races in Brontë's novel and the disquietude (rather than political solidarity) that emerges. Or from ethnography and Irish studies, one thinks of Terry Eagleton's suggestive introduction to *Heathcliff and the Great Hunger: Studies in Irish Culture* (1995), which suggestively reads Heathcliff as an "Irish nationalist" and Edgar as "the Irish revisionist historian," or Elsie Michie's "'The Yahoo, Not the Demon': Heathcliff, Rochester, and the Simianization of the Irish'" in *Outside the Pale* (1990), which uses Victorian ethnographic studies of Irish and oriental "savages" to expose the colonial grounding of the Victorian myth of upward mobility. Or, from historical studies of the abolitionist and missionary movements, one thinks of Maja-Lisa von Sneidern's "*Wuthering Heights* and the Liverpool Slave

Trade" (*ELH*, 1995), with its discussion of the "game of bondage" that infects romantic and domestic relations in a slave culture, or of Mary Ellen Gibson's "Henry Martyn and England's Christian Empire" (*VLC*, 1999), with its readings of virtue and violence in a culture that produces men like St. John Rivers.

It is impossible to acknowledge all the important articles on the Brontës that appeared in the 1990s. (I have included a selected list of book chapters in the bibliography.) Yet recalling even some of them points to the ground-breaking work of *journal articles* in the advancement of Brontë studies. It also gives a sense a belatedness to several worthy books published during the decade: Kathleen Constable's *A Stranger within the Gates: Charlotte Brontë and Victorian Irishness* (2000), a study of Irish biographical, historical, and literary influences; the late Jerome Beaty's *Misreading Jane Eyre* (1996), an expansion of and meditation on the materials of his 1977 *Genre* article, "*Jane Eyre* and Genre"; and Firdous Azim's *The Colonial Rise of the Novel* (1993), a consideration of how the development in English fiction of "a consistent narrating [female] subject" is constructed "by the effacement of *Other* subjects" (89–90). Partial exceptions to this "belatedness of the book" are Sally Shuttleworth's *Charlotte Brontë and Victorian Psychology* (1996) and Marianne Thormählen's *The Brontës and Victorian Religion* (1999), the latter unavailable from Cambridge University Press in time for detailed consideration. Shuttleworth's book introduces a range of popular and professional discourses drawn from medical texts, scientific treatises, studies of physiognomy and phrenology, and Victorian social theory, which she labels "pre-Freudian psychology." While some aspects of this material may be familiar to Victorianists, the extensive research, the application of these pre-Freudian discourses to Charlotte Brontë's novels, and Shuttleworth's articulation of her methodology add new readings and approaches to Brontë studies.

Even so, as I read the books and many articles for this review, I came to wish that publishers of "collections" on the Brontës would redirect their energy away from volumes representing the historical range of Brontë criticism and toward volumes that assemble the best articles of a decade—rather like "The Best American Essays" or "The Best American Short Stories" published by Houghton Mifflin. Do we truly need Prentice Hall's *Critical Essays on Emily Brontë* (1997), edited by Thomas J. Winnifrith, with its repetition of critical views that have been published in many collections over the past 30 years? However knowledgeable the editor, however worthy the critics, many long dead, we have this material available to us elsewhere. Or, to pose the question differently, do we do our students pedagogical good by providing them with snippets of sixteen essays on *Wuthering Heights*, re-packaged under such rubrics as "Heathcliff's Monomania," "The Theme of Haunting," and "Love and Addiction in *Wuthering Heights*," as Greenhaven Press has done in its *Readings on Wuthering Heights* (1999)? Although one might argue that a few collections—for instance, Harold Orel's *The Brontës: Interviews and Recollections* (1997)—bring together historical material diffi-cult to find in one place, most just reprint criticism readily available else-where. After all, we now have the comprehensive four-volume *The Brontë Sisters* (1996), edited by Eleanor McNees, that includes recollections, obituar-ies, early studies, and responses to and evaluations of all the juvenilia and novels, from the time of their publication to 1993. Surely we can ask our libraries to purchase this comprehensive collection and be done with the others.

Perhaps Barrett Browning stated the inevitable: "Of writing many books there is no end." Yet might we not influence the kind of books that are published, especially collections? Given the felt need for the book as the publishing form of permanence, might we not make "permanent" instead the best *new* essays from each decade rather than reissue old work?

### Editions, Microfilm, and Bibliographic Materials

Having noted the over-production of collections of criticism, I want here to commend Yale, Oxford, and Cambridge University Presses for their publi-cation of important new scholarly editions: *The Belgian Essays: A Critical Edition* (1996), edited and translated by Sue Lonoff; *The Art of the Brontës* (1995), by Christine Alexander and Jane Sellars; and *The Letters of Charlotte Brontë, with a Selection of Letters by Family and Friends* (1995, 2000), edited by Margaret Smith. Also important during the last decade was the publication of the second volume of *An Edition of the Early Writings of Charlotte Brontë* (1991), edited by Christine Alexander.

Emily and Charlotte's Belgian *devoirs*, written during their sojourn at the school of Constantin and Zoë Heger in Brussels, provide an important link between the juvenilia and the mature novels, but until Sue Lonoff undertook this definitive critical edition, they had never before been fully published or translated. Lonoff is an ideal editor of these texts: a scholar-teacher, for many years a lecturer in Harvard's expository writing program, and a director in the Derek Bok Center for teaching, she brings not only editorial expertise but also a deep understanding of pedagogical methods, especially in the teaching of writing. Lonoff's extensive introduction discusses Heger's pedagogical principles and practice, his influence on Charlotte's (if not the resistant Emily's) style in the *devoirs*, and his long-term effect, personal and literary, on Charlotte's work. In Lonoff's view, Heger was crucial to the development of Charlotte's mature prose: the *devoirs* show us how she learned "to fuse creative and expository methods, to invent yet still accede to formal discipline" (xxiv). Lonoff makes this claim good in her commentary on Charlotte's *devoirs,* even if she leaves us with the scholarly puzzle of what Emily, who rebelled against Heger's imitative method, actually learned from her Belgian teacher.

Alexander and Sellars's collection of the Brontës' art brings together for the first time "an accurate record of their productions and aspirations as artists" (1). This beautifully-produced volume includes plates of all known drawings and paintings, and entries for each "written to tell a story—of the history of the paintings, and the way they reflect the interests and skills of the Brontës" (6). The volume also includes a helpful first chapter, "The influence of the visual arts on the Brontës," and chapters on each sibling's training and achievement as an artist. It is a book worth consulting—if not for the quality of the art itself, then for images relevant to the novels, for a sense of how fully the visual culture of the literary annuals permeated the Brontës' imaginations, and for a salutary lesson that, whatever the myths, Branwell was not an infant genius and Emily was not always "resistant" to the dominant culture.

Margaret Smith's edition of Charlotte Brontë's letters, the first volume published in 1995, the second completed in 2000, is an immense achievement, the result not only of her own devoted labor but also of extensive contributions by other scholars. Smith begins her "Acknowledgements" by recognizing the work of the late Mildred Christian, former professor of English at Newcomb College, Tulane University, who located many of the manuscripts of the Brontës' letters and made photographs of material no longer accessible (vii). Indeed, the acknowledgments are a virtual roll-call of important Brontëans who contributed editorial help and scholarly expertise to this edition, including Kathleen Tillotson, Ian Jack, Jane Sellars, and Juliet Barker (who published extracts in a popular form, *The Brontës: A Life in Letters*, 1997). Smith's edition includes a thorough history of the letters, as well as biographical sketches of the correspondents, detailed annotations of the contents, and a careful account of the provenance.

Another important completion in the last decade is Christine Alexander's second volume of *An Edition of the Early Writings of Charlotte Brontë* (1991).

The publication of reliable texts of the juvenilia has sparked popular editions, including Alexander's own *Charlotte Brontë's High Life in Verdopolis : A Story from the Glass Town Saga* (1995), with facsimile illustrations from the manuscript and drawings by Charlotte herself. As part of the Juvenile Press series, Juliet McMaster and Leslie Robertson have issued a paperback version of "My Angria and the Angrians" (1997) and McMaster et al. have edited another excerpt, "Albion and Marina" (1999), both based on the scholarly edition by Alexander. With lively illustrations (not Charlotte's) and good introductions connecting the sagas with nineteenth-century colonialism and orientalism, these texts are suitable (and suitably priced) for classroom use. My only concern is that few teachers seem to incorporate the juvenilia into their classes. If Diane Hoeveler and Beth Lau's collection *Approaches to Teaching Jane Eyre* (1993) is any indication, not one current "approach" incorporates the Glass Town or Angrian materials into practical lesson plans.

Will anyone but the most passionate devotée use Victor A. Neufeldt's *The Works of Patrick Branwell Brontë: An Edition* (1997–1999)? Clearly a labor of love, this three-volume work incorporates all the poetry and prose, published and unpublished, known to have been written by the ill-fated brother of the famous Brontë sisters. In the introduction to the first volume, Neufeldt laments that Branwell has long been mistaken and underappreciated. Quoting lines from Matthew Arnold's "Haworth Churchyard," "But some dark shadow came . . . and interposed," he tries to reverse "the tone of dismissive scorn that has bedeviled Branwell scholarship to this day" (xix), largely by accounting for the significant number of poems Branwell published in local newspapers. But this early success at placing his work does not answer the question of quality, and more skeptical readers will leave the volumes believing that Branwell was right to say, on his deathbed, "In all my past life I have done nothing either great or good." Whether or not one finds the poems interesting, Neufeldt's history of the manuscripts, including the manipulations of the notorious T. J. Wise, is fascinating stuff. See also Neufeldt's *Bibliography of the Manuscripts of Patrick Branwell Brontë* (1993) or, for the poems only, his *Poems of Patrick Branwell Brontë: A New Text and Commentary* (1990).

Finally, not quite an edition but nonetheless a useful scholarly tool, is the microfilm of *The Brontë Manuscripts: Literary Manuscripts and Correspondence of the Brontë Family from the Brontë Society Collection at Haworth Parsonage and the British Library* (1992). For those who want online access to scholarly editions of the novels, as well as the juvenilia and letters (Shake-speare Head edition), images of Patrick Brontë's paintings, and 3,000 manu-script pages from the Brontë Parsonage Museum, consult *The Brontës*, edited by Tom Winnifrith et al. and released in 1997 by Primary Source Media.

### The Afterglow: The Brontës in Popular Culture

Every Victorianist knows that the Brontës—and especially *Jane Eyre* and *Wuthering Heights*—have become common currency, authors and characters known to the general reading public. When John Sutherland wants to sell a collection of literary conundrum, he packages it under the title *Is Heathcliff a Murderer?* (1996); when, a year later, his publisher decides it's become a "cult classic," he issues another collection, *Can Jane Eyre Be Happy?* (1997)—both only having one essay on the Brontës, the rest covering other English novels. Or, when the English PhD Robert Barnard gives up teaching and turns mystery writer, he quickly pens *The Case of the Missing Brontë* (1983), years later *The Corpse at the Haworth Tandoori* (1998)—the former including a hilarious parody of Brontë scholarship, the latter having nothing to do with the Brontës beyond its setting. Even as I was finishing this review, a cable movie channel aired the 1994 classic *Jane Eyre*, starring Joan Fontaine and Orson Welles, and several other made-for-television versions regularly appear. Even people who don't read, and even people who don't speak En-glish, know Jane and Rochester, Heathcliff and Cathy.

Two books recently published analyze this remarkable phenomenon: Lu-casta Miller's *The Brontë Myth* (2001) and Patsy Stoneman's *Brontë Trans-formations* (1996). Miller's emphasis falls on the Brontës themselves, though of course she cannot separate the authors from the books they wrote, as readers have always confused and conflated them. As Miller points out, "Like *Jane Eyre*, like *Wuthering Heights*, the tragic story of the Brontë family has been told and retold time and again in endless new configurations" (x)—with famous actors playing not just Heathliff or Cathy, but Emily, not just Jane Eyre or Rochester, but Charlotte. Miller begins with Charlotte as "her own mythologiser" and continues with the biographies that followed the basic myths: "the positive myth of female self-creation" and the myth of the "martyr to duty and model of Victorian femininity" (ch. 1), especially in Gaskell's *Life* and later nineteenth-century accounts (chs. 2–4). She includes twentieth-century psychobiographies (ch. 5) and more recent fictions and feminist criticism (ch. 6). The analysis repeats itself with Emily Brontë, again beginning with Charlotte's mythologizing and Gaskell's *Life* (ch. 7), covering nineteenth-century interpretations of Emily as "a woman worthy of being avoided" (ch. 8), and ending with versions of Emily as "The Mystic of the Moors" (ch. 9). Throughout most of this history, Charlotte figures as the more appealing sister—a position that has shifted, I would argue, in recent criticism that views Emily as the "resister" and thus the heroine of modern feminism.

Patsy Stoneman's book, *Brontë Transformations*, has a different purpose (to my mind, more difficult and ambitious). Using Pierre Macherey's notion of a text not as a "creation" or "self-contained artifact," but instead as a "production" in which disparate materials are worked over and changed in the process, Stoneman views the Brontës' novels as not only "produced" by the writer but as "re-produced" by society. Thus, whereas Miller's book might be seen as an analysis of the mythologizing of the authors that occurred within biographies and criticism of the past 150 years, Stoneman's study concerns itself with the "cultural dissemination" of *Jane Eyre* and *Wuthering Heights* in multiple media and cultural institutions: plays and musicals, operas and ballets, films and television series, picturebooks and comicbooks, parodies and fictional rewritings.

Organized chronologically, as is Miller's book, *Brontë Transformations* takes us from nineteenth-century stage adaptations of *Jane Eyre*, which initially focused on its "revolutionary" aspects (7) and then shifted to "the question of proper womanhood" (33), through versions of Bertha in fiction and psychoanalysis (1892–1917), echoes of *Wuthering Heights* in Olive Schreiner's *Story of an African Farm* (1883), and the general fascination with Emily among New Woman Writers at the fin de siècle. Stoneman continues with the inter-war period and World War II, drawing on stage and early film versions as well as illustrated texts, and closes with a discussion of "the sequels syndrome," the acts of writing back or writing beyond the ending of these two Brontë novels.

What motivates these modern responses? In the case of postcolonial literature, such as Jean Rhys's *Wide Sargasso Sea* or V. S. Naipaul's *The Guerillas*, the rewritings suggest that "an order has collapsed," "the Victorian names [from *Jane Eyre* or *Wuthering Heights*] reverse or disappoint the expectations they arouse" (237), and the "others" find voice to tell their new versions of history. In some postmodernist fictions, like Jane Urquhart's *Changing Heaven*, the point seems to be the mutability of "eternal truths," the story of "how all truth is a process of endless deferral" (253). One suspects, however, that the continuing rewritings reveal our fundamental satisfaction with the Brontës' novels and the Brontë myths—and their enduring hold on readers' and writers' imaginations.

## NOTES

1. Patsy Stoneman, "Feminist Criticism of *Wuthering Heights*," *Critical Survey* 4 (1992) 150.
2. Susan Fraiman, Review of *Charlotte Brontë and the Storyteller's Audience* and *Charlotte Brontë and Defensive Conduct*, *Victorian Studies* 37 (1994) 345.

### SELECTED BIBLIOGRAPHY: THE BRONTËS, 1990–2000

#### Biographies, Letters, and Editions

Alexander, Christine, and Jane Sellars, eds. *The Art of the Brontës*. Oxford: Oxford UP, 1995.

Barker, Juliet. *The Brontës*. New York: St. Martin's, 1994.

———. , ed. *The Brontës: A Life in Letters*. London: Viking, 1997.

Barnard, Robert. *Emily Brontë*. British Library Writers' Lives. Oxford: Oxford UP, 2000.

Chitham, Edward. *A Life of Anne Brontë*. Oxford: Blackwell, 1991.

Gordon, Lyndall. *Charlotte Brontë: A Passionate Life*. London: Chatto and Windus, 1994.

Lonoff, Sue, ed. *The Belgian Essays: A Critical Edition*. New Haven, CT: Yale UP, 1996.

McMaster, Juliet, and Leslie Robertson, eds. *My Angria and the Angrians*. Edmonton, Canada: Juvenilia P, 1997.

McMaster, Juliet, and others, eds. *Albion and Marina*. Edmonton, Canada: Juvenilia P, 1999.

Neufeldt, Victor A., ed. *A Bibliography of the Manuscripts of Patrick Branwell Brontë*. New York: Garland, 1993.

———. , ed. *Poems of Patrick Branwell Brontë: A New Text and Commentary*. New York: Garland, 1990.

———. , ed. *The Works of Patrick Branwell Brontë: An Edition*. 3 vols. New York: Garland, 1997–1999.

Rosengarten, Herbert, ed. *The Tenant of Wildfell Hall.* By Anne Brontë. Oxford: Clarendon P, 1992.

Sellars, Jane. *Charlotte Brontë.* British Library Writers' Lives. Oxford: Oxford UP, 1997.

Smith, Margaret, ed. *The Letters of Charlotte Brontë, with a Selection of Letters by Family and Friends.* 2 vols. Oxford: Clarendon P, 1995, 2000.

## Monographs and Collections

Beaty, Jerome. *Misreading Jane Eyre: A Postformalist Paradigm.* Columbus: Ohio State UP, 1996.

Berry, Elizabeth Hollis. *Anne Brontë's Radical Vision: Structures of Consciousness.* Victoria, BC: English Literary Studies, 1994.

Bock, Carol. *Charlotte Brontë and the Storyteller's Audience.* Iowa City: U of Iowa P, 1992.

Boumelha, Penny. *Charlotte Brontë.* Bloomington: Indiana UP, 1990.

Chitham, Edward. *The Birth of Wuthering Heights.* New York: St. Martin's P, 1998.

Constable, Kathleen. *A Stranger Within the Gates: Charlotte Brontë and Victorian Irishness.* Lanham, MD: UP of America, 2000.

Davies, Stevie. *Emily Brontë: Heretic.* London: The Women's Press, 1994.

———. *Emily Brontë.* Tavistock, Devon: Northcote House, 1998.

Frawley, Maria H. *Anne Brontë.* New York: Twayne, 1996.

Gezari, Janet. *Charlotte Brontë and Defensive Conduct.* Philadelphia: U of Pennsylvania P, 1992.

Ghnassia, Virginia Jill Dix. *Metaphysical Rebellion in the Works of Emily Brontë.* New York: St. Martin's P, 1994.

Hoeveler, Diane Long, and Lisa Jadwin. *Charlotte Brontë.* New York: Twayne, 1997.

———. , and Beth Lau, eds. *Approaches to Teaching Jane Eyre.* New York: Modern Language Association, 1993.

Jay, Betty. *Anne Brontë.* Tavistock, Devon: Northcote House, 2000.

Knapp, Bettina. *The Brontës: Branwell, Anne, Emily, Charlotte.* New York: Frederick Ungar, 1991.

Langland, Elizabeth. *Anne Brontë: The Other One*. London: Macmillan, 1989.

McNees, Eleanor, ed. *The Brontë Sisters*. 4 vols. Robertsbridge, East Sussex: Helm Information, 1996.

Miller, Lucasta. *The Brontë Myth*. London: Jonathan Cape, 2001.

Mitchell, Hayley R. ed. *Readings on Wuthering Heights*. San Diego: Greenhaven P, 1999.

Nestor, Pauline. *Charlotte Brontë*. London: Macmillan, 1987.

————. *Charlotte Brontë's Jane Eyre*. London: Harvester Wheatsheaf, 1992.

Orel, Harold, ed. *The Brontës: Interviews and Recollections*. London: Macmillan, 1997.

Pykett, Lyn. *Emily Brontë*. London: Macmillan, 1989.

Schönberger-Schleicher, Esther. *Charlotte and Emily Brontë: A Narrative Analysis of Jane Eyre and Wuthering Heights*. New York: Peter Lang, 1999.

Shuttleworth, Sally. *Charlotte Brontë and Victorian Psychology*. Cambridge: Cambridge UP, 1996.

Stoneman, Patsy. *Brontë Transformations: The Cultural Dissemination of Jane Eyre and Wuthering Heights*. London: Harvester Wheatsheaf, 1996.

Tayler, Irene. *Holy Ghosts: The Male Muses of Emily and Charlotte Brontë*. New York: Columbia UP, 1990.

Thormählen, Marianne. *The Brontës and Religion*. Cambridge: Cambridge UP, 1999.

Vine, Steve. *Emily Brontë*. New York: Twayne, 1998.

Winnifrith, Thomas John, ed. *Critical Essays on Emily Brontë*. New York: G. K. Hall, 1997.

## Chapters in Books

Azim, Firdous. *The Colonial Rise of the Novel*. London: Routledge, 1993. Chapters on the juvenilia and Charlotte Brontë's fiction.

Bailin, Miriam. *The Sickroom on Victorian Fiction: The Art of Being Ill*. Cambridge: Cambridge UP, 1994. Chapter on Charlotte Brontë's female characters.

Cervetti, Nancy. *Scenes of Reading: Transforming Romance in Brontë, Eliot, and Woolf*. New York: Peter Lang, 1998. Chapters on voice in *Jane Eyre* and the "politics of location" in *Villette*.

DeLamotte, Eugenia C. *Perils of the Night: A Feminist Study of Nineteenth-Century Gothic*. New York: Oxford UP, 1990. Chapter on Charlotte Brontë's Gothic fiction.

Dames, Nicholas. *Amnesiac Selves: Nostalgia, Forgetting, and British Fiction, 1810–1870*. Oxford: Oxford UP, 2000. Chapter on phrenology, physiognomy, and memory in Charlotte Brontë's fiction.

Doyle, Christine. *Louisa May Alcott and Charlotte Brontë: Transatlantic Translations*. Knoxville: U of Tennessee P, 2000. Chapters on Brontë's influence on Alcott's novels.

Eagleton, Terry. "Introduction." *Heathcliff and the Great Hunger*. London: Verso, 1995.

Hinton, Laura. *The Perverse Gaze of Sympathy: Sadomasochistic Sentiments from Clarissa to Rescue 911*. Albany, NY: State U of New York P, 1999. Chapter on *Wuthering Heights*.

Levy, Anita. *Reproductive Urges: Popular Novel-Reading, Sexuality, and the English Nation*. Philadelphia: U of Pennsylvania P, 1999. Chapter on gender and literacy in *Villette*.

Matus, Jill. *Unstable Bodies: Victorian Representations of Sexuality and Maternity*. Manchester: Manchester UP, 1995. Chapter on Anne Brontë's *Agnes Grey*.

Meyer, Susan. *Imperialism at Home: Race and Victorian Women's Fiction*. Ithaca, NY: Cornell UP, 1996. Chapters on *Jane Eyre* and *Wuthering Heights*.

Michie, Elsie. *Outside the Pale: Cultural Exclusion, Gender Difference, and the Victorian Woman Writer*. Ithaca, NY: Cornell UP, 1993. Chapter entitled "'The Yahoo, Not the Demon': Heathcliff, Rochester, and the Simianization of the Irish."

Mitchell, Judith. *The Stone and the Scorpion: The Female Subject of Desire in the Novels of Charlotte Brontë, George Eliot, and Thomas Hardy*. Westport, CT: Greenwood, 1994. Chapter on female desire in Brontë's fiction.

Parkin-Gounelas, Ruth. *Fictions of the Female Self: Charlotte Brontë, Olive Schreiner, Katherine Mansfield*. New York: St. Martin's, 1991. Chapters on *Jane Eyre* and *Villette*.

Stockton, Kathryn Bond. *God Between Their Lips: Desire Between Women in Irigaray, Brontë, and Eliot*. Stanford: Stanford UP, 1994. Chapter on lesbian desire in Charlotte Brontë's fiction.

Thompson, Nicola Diane. *Reviewing Sex: Gender and the Reception of Victorian Novels*. London: Macmillan, 1996. Chapter on *Wuthering Heights*.

Wolstenholme, Susan. *Gothic (Re)visions: Writing Women as Readers*. Saratoga Springs: State U of New York P, 1992. Chapter on Charlotte Brontë's "post-gothic gothic."

## Popular Works using the Brontës

Barnard, Robert. *The Case of the Missing Brontë*. New York: Scribners, 1983.

———. *The Corpse at the Haworth Tandoori*. London: HarperCollins, 1998.

Sutherland, John. *Can Jane Eyre Be Happy?: More Puzzles in Classic Fiction*. Oxford: Oxford UP, 1997.

———. *Is Heathcliff a Murderer?* Oxford: Oxford UP, 1996.

Tully, James. *The Crimes of Charlotte Brontë: The Secrets of a Mysterious Family, A Novel*. New York: Carroll and Graf, 1999.

# Thackeray Studies, 1993–2001

*Robert A. Colby*

*This retrospective survey of Thackeray scholarship covers the period
from 1993 through 2001, taking up the record from the last survey by
Peter Shillingsburg in DSA 23 (1994), which ended with 1992. A few
earlier items omitted by Shillingsburg are added. The essay is divided
into bibliography, textual editing and reprints, publishing history of
Thackeray's works, biography and letters, criticism and interpretation
of the novels, studies of the travel writings, Thackeray as an artist,
Thackeray as editor, adaptations on film and television, and foreign
scholarship and translation. The essay concludes with forthcoming publications and some future prospects.*

When I first undertook to review scholarship on Thackeray about twenty-five
years ago, I referred to him then as "something of a colossus in the shade."[1]
He has since emerged from the shadows, but it seems safe to say by now he
will never bask in the limelight that envelops the hero of this annual. My
bibliographical searchlight over the decade since the last survey in *DSA* (1994)
prepared by Peter Shillingsburg turns up some 150 items for Thackeray,
as against over a thousand for Dickens, roughly the same proportion that
Shillingsburg found.

The literary climate obviously has shifted from the turn of the twentieth
century when Thackeray and Dickens were still twin stars among the general
reading public. In 1898 Anne Thackeray completed the editing of the Biographical Edition of her father's works, and shortly thereafter embarked on

the enlarged Centenary Biographical Edition published in 1911 in time to observe the hundredth anniversary of his birth. These years also encompass the publication of the monumental Gadshill Edition (1897–1908) intended to commemorate the centenary of Dickens's birth, which occurred a year after that of Thackeray. So vivid consequently were the two in the public consciousness that their daughters were enlisted to help sell Liberty Bonds during World War I.

Dickens obviously has zoomed ahead of Thackeray in the post-World War II boom in Victorian studies, but there has been a decided gain in the quality of scholarship on Thackeray in recent years. This generation of dissertation writers seems to have recognized that it is necessary to dig deeply to mine his riches. As a result studies lately have tended to concentrate more on context and intellectual background. There has been only one edition of Thackeray's collected works since 1911 and that is still in progress, but it has benefitted from meticulous and sophisticated methodology. The pictorial features of his works have been scrutinized more closely than heretofore. Previously ignored areas of the canon—early writings, journalism, social commentary, travel writings—are being increasingly explored. There remains a gap between the classroom and scholarship in that *Vanity Fair* is the only one of his novels widely taught, but by now it has taken its place as a part of a spectrum rather than a unique flash of brilliance.

While it is far easier to confine writings on Thackeray over the past decade in a bibliographical essay than those for Dickens within one year, Thackeray's greater versatility means that one has to cast the net wider. A challenge to the bibliographer is that the author of *Vanity Fair* turns up in books and articles on art history, humor, travel, cooking, film, and photography, among other subjects. Thackeray's cosmopolitanism also keeps one on his toes. France, which Thackeray considered his second country, continues to pay homage to him, but the alert scholar has to be prepared to track him down in Germany, Poland, Russia, the Czech Republic, Italy, Spain. Argentina—even China.

## Catching Up and Keeping Up

A recurrent lament of Thackeray scholars is the piecemeal nature of the bibliographical record which during his heyday was largely the work of amateur bibliophiles (e.g., Henry Van Duzer, Frederick Dickson, Major Lambert). There is still nothing near a comprehensive bibliography, and there probably never will be, but in recent years systematic scholarship has been applied to portions of the printed canon.

Appended to Peter Shillingsburg's *Pegasus in Harness* (1992), a study of Thackeray's relations with his publishers, is "A Census of Imprints to 1865," assembled from library and rare book catalog entries, publishers' records, and private libraries. Entries are arranged in alphabetical rather than chronological order—*The Adventures of Philip* to *The Yellowplush Correspondence*—discrete reprints and reisssues of each title accompanied by library locations and translations into European languages. (Note: *Catherine*, Thackeray's first novel, is omitted, not having reached book publication until 1869.) Shillingsburg's spade work is ploughed into the long-awaited Third Edition of the *Cambridge Bibliography of English Literature. 1800–1900* (1999), edited by Joanne Shattuck, which extends the publication record nearly to the end of the twentieth century. His entry is preceded by the longest list of Thackerayan personae ever compiled, including such obscure pseudonyms as Bashi-Bazouk, Leonitus Hugglestone, and Brian Tuggles Tuggles.

Usefully supplementing Shillingsburg's precise work on book publication is Edgar F. Harden's *A Checklist of Contributions . . . to Newspapers, Periodicals, Books, and Serial Part Issues, 1825–1864* (1996). A bonus is a list of "Possible Thackeray Illustrations" in *Punch*. Question marks still remain with this portion of the canon, as indicated by the review of this list by Richard Pearson (*VPR*, Spring 1997), who questions Harden's methodology in attribution of pieces in *The National Standard* and the *Constitutional*, the two newspapers Thackeray was connected with as Paris correspondent. Pearson has since opened fresh journalistic sources in his *Thackeray and the Mediated Text* (see below). Robert A. Colby has brought to light several anonymously published *Times* reviews of travel books attributable to Thackeray in which he sets out criteria that were to govern his own contributions to the genre (*TNL*, November 1988; May 1999),

Serving the function of the revised format of *CBEL* proscribing critical writings on major figures except for selected pre-1920 landmarks is Sheldon Goldfarb's previously unnoticed *William Makepeace Thackeray: An Annotated Bibliography, 1976–1987* (1989). Goldfarb takes up the record from John Charles Olmsted's *Thackeray and His Twentieth-Century Critics, 1900–1975* (1977). Rudimentary statistics measure the momentum of Thackeray scholarship over the past century. Olmsted comments on 850 books, articles, and dissertations (the first in 1924) from the first three-quarters of the century. Goldfarb has uncovered more than half this number (450) from the next decade, including almost as many dissertations as Olmsted. Unlike

Olmsted, Goldfarb includes foreign language items. One of his three indexes lists characters referred to. Another bonus is a list of later reprints of items in Olmsted's bibliography.

From this point one turns to the semi-annual *Thackeray Newsletter*, the only publication devoted exclusively to him (as against an annual, a quarterly, and a triennial given over to Dickens). Launched by Peter Shillingburg in 1974 at the University of Mississippi in stapled, mimeographed sheets, it continues under his editorship at North Texas State University metamorphosed into a state-of-the-art pamphlet capable of reproducing graphics with bold definition. Here are registered not only "Thackeray Studies: Recent and Forthcoming," but reports on the Thackeray Edition also under his editorship, newly discovered manuscript locations (supplementing the Colby-Sutherland census in *Costerus* in 1974), Thackerayana for sale, dramatizations, and other adaptations. Selected specific articles from *TNL* will be cited in appropriate places later in this survey.

## The Marketplace

Shillingsburg in his aforementioned *Pegasus in Harness* provides the most detailed account available of the business side of Thackeray's career as man of letters. As indicated by the title, taken from *Pendennis*, Thackeray's fictitious retrospect of his aspirations and struggles as a writer, his winged horse had its hooves on the ground. Drawing on records and contracts, as well as correspondence with publishers, Thackeray's arduous "progress" is traced from "literary dilettante" to "literary hack" to "literary tradesman." Fortunately Shillingsburg's Gradgrindian preoccupation with facts and figures is leavened by Pickwickian chapter headings ("In which old wine is put into new wineskins"; "In which it is debated whether the market rules the artist or the artist rules the market"). Shillingsburg has already dispelled the received canard that Thackeray was careless with his texts. Here is exploded the legend—disseminated notoriously by Trollope—that he was impractical and unbusinesslike. Among Shillingsburg's discoveries is that at his death Thackeray left his daughter £1,000 more than his father left him. Appendixes reproduce contracts in full.

As general editor of the ambitious Thackeray Edition under way, Shillingsburg has made significant departures from the traditional Greg-Bowers principles of copy text, owing to Thackeray's idiosyncratic punctuation, the fitful survival of his manuscripts, and lack of evidence that he had anything to do with revisions of his novels after their first editions. A succinct summary of his own theories can be found in "Editing Thackeray: a History" (*SNNT*, Fall 1995). He makes the general point that textual editors have always had to grapple with two goals not always compatible, "to be accurate, and to be useful," that is, to reconcile truth to the documentary record with reader interest. With his own procedure on Thackeray, he notes a shift in editorial goals from *product* to *process*, from "final authorial attention" to "multiple authorial intentions," meaning essentially more attention to the stages of publication. The article concludes with a review of the vicissitudes of the Thackeray Edition, now under the aegis of the University of Michigan Press after bumpy times with two other publishers.

In "Authorial Process and Textual Stability" (*Text*, 1998), Judith Fisher illustrates through a review of the edition of *The Newcomes* some of the problems Shillingsburg confronted in determining the "true text" under unstable conditions, such as errors in the manuscript, editorial intrusion, and authorial changes of mind. As she concludes, "the variants and emendations give us multiple Thackerays from which to choose."

Some stray items, not to my knowledge to be incorporated into the University of Michigan edition, have been assembled by Richard Pearson in six volumes under the general rubric *The Thackeray Library* published by Routledge/Thoemmes Press (1996). Volume I brings together *Early Fiction and Journalism*, Volume II, *Early Travel Writings*. Subsequent volumes reprint still useful secondary literature, such as Trollope's *Thackeray* in the English Men of Letters Series; Eyre Crowe's *With Thackeray in America*; Adolphus A. Jacks's *Thackeray: A Study*; Lewis Melville's pioneering biography; and Charles Plumptre Johnson's bibliography of the early writings. This set, unfortunately, has proved inaccessible.

### "Very Truly Yrs, WMT"

Thackeray is one of the few writers whose letters make as delightful reading as his novels. It has long been known that Gordon Ray tracked down many more letters since he brought out his four-volume collection shortly after the end of World War II, but he died before he got round to publishing them. This task has been taken over by Edgar F. Harden. His two-volume *Supplement to the Letters and Private Papers of William Makepeace Thackeray* (1994) adds 1,464 new letters, with close to 250 edited from manuscripts not available to

Ray who, owing to war-time restrictions, had to work from faulty transcripts. There are also 170 additional drawings. Appended are hitherto unpublished corrections by Ray to the basic volume, as well as new library locations. All in all, Thackeray's epistolary world is now expanded by 85%. Generally speaking, the new letters illuminate Thackeray's relations with his publishers more than his personal life. The early days of *Cornhill Magazine* are more fully documented. However, there are new letters to the Baxters and the Brookfields, and—bearing on his early days of struggle—from his wife Isabella before her breakdown. A discerning review by Eileen Curran (*VPR*, Spring 1997) faults some of Harden's reading and dating of texts, but Thackerayans should be grateful for his arduous labors. One might wish that these volumes were more attractively printed and less expensive.

Harden has additionally conflated Gordon Ray's collection and his own supplement into *Selected Letters of William Makepeace Thackeray* (1996), bringing together in one volume 277 letters beginning with a note to his mother when he was seven years old, ending close to his death with a note to his doctor. They are newly edited and annotated with a general audience in mind.

Since the publication of Harden's supplementary volumes, Kenneth Fielding has discovered an additional cache of previously unpublished Thackeray letters in the Ashburton Papers on deposit in the National Library of Scotland, Edinburgh, extracts of which are incorporated in "Letters of Thackeray to the Ashburtons" (*DSA* 27, 1998). These dozen or so letters span the years 1848 to 1854. Thackeray's connection with this family is evident from his dedication of *Henry Esmond* to Lord Ashburton, but these letters mainly to Lady Ashburton reveal how much their friendship meant to him over a productive but trying period during which he suffered from frustrated love for Jane Brookfield and deteriorating health. His emotional dependence on them is indicated by the title Fielding gave this correspondence in the excerpts published beforehand (*TLS*, 12 December 1997)—" 'Kind Arms to Hang on to.'"

However, one must reckon with Edgar Harden's finding in examining the originals of errors in transmission, gaps, misdating, and inadequate annotation in Fielding's texts. To set the record straight it is necessary to turn to Harden's "Remaining Portions of the Ashburton Letters" (*TNL*, November 1999). Besides corrections, Harden supplies pictorial matter omitted by Fielding.

### "Mind . . . no life of me"

As previous reviews of Thackeray studies have noted, this famous proscription by him to his daughter Anne has been breached numerous times both right after Thackeray's death and in our time. Lady Ritchie herself wrote the introductions to the Biographical Edition to counteract what she regarded as misleading "lives" that had gained currency, but it was not until Gordon Ray's massive two-volume biography (1955, 1958), based on private family papers, that Thackeray's career became known in any breadth. Biographies since then have been largely recyclings of Ray, quite possibly because he edited the letters before undertaking the biography, putting him in command of intimate primary matter that has not been substantially augmented. The supplementary letters edited by Edgar Harden, as previously noted, illuminate his writing life more than his personal or domestic affairs.

In a way, Thackeray has had his wish in that hiatuses remain in his private life that probably can never be filled. We would like to know more about his bohemian art student period in Paris (somewhat glazed over in *The Newcomes*), possibly covered in the diaries that Anne destroyed. One infers that when he wrote in a surviving diary that he had that day "spielte un gefegelte," he was not referring just to gambling and card playing. It is assumed nowadays that the bad health that plagued him during has last years went back to a bout with gonorrhea contracted in his youth—for which Gordon Ray provided medical evidence in an appendix to the *Letters*—but its etiology is indeterminable. Nor is much known about his days as a bill conveyancer or as a lawyer (alluded to in *Pendennis*). It is known that Jane Brookfield tried to blackmail Lady Ritchie after Thackeray's death, but the surviving letters to her by Thackeray leave their intimate relationship still a matter of conjecture.

All this is by way of preamble to my dissatisfaction with the latest "new" critical biography by D. J. Taylor, titled simply *Thackeray* (1999). Taylor's experience as a novelist lends color to his opening description to Thackeray's funeral, but he is deficient as a scholar and critic. Specialist reviewers have disputed his accounts of the attempted suicide of Isabella and the nature of her illness. He exaggerates Thackeray's "money mania."[2] He conjectures on no evidence that it might have been Mme. Pauline, the down-at-heels ex-governess of "Shrove Tuesday in Paris," and obvious prototype of Becky Sharp, who infected young Thackeray with a venereal disease. He has turned up new background on the failed campaign for the Oxford seat in Parliament.

Otherwise his book is mainly warmed-over Ray, plus gleanings from more recent published sources, such as the aforementioned new letters and the newly edited journals of Anne (see below). Where he really falls short is in his professed aim to "rescue" Thackeray for the general reader. His intention, he claims, is "to demonstrate that he was the greatest writer . . . of the nineteenth century. And perhaps of all time." Yet while awarding the master the palm with his right hand, he proceeds, in effect, to stab him in the back with his left. Thackeray's true greatness to Taylor lies in his early journalism, which hardly anybody has read, is mostly out of print, and was dismisssed by the author himself as "small potatoes." Following the line of the perverse *Thackeray: Prodigal Genius* by his mentor John Carey, he writes off everything after *Vanity Fair* as "the history of capitulation." With such champions, who needs detractors?

Some fresh light is cast on Thackeray's life from another vantage point in *Anne Thackeray Ritchie: Journals and Letters* (1994), which grew out of a doctoral dissertation by Lillian Shankman under the direction of Gordon Ray, who owned these documents. Shankman died with her work in an unfinished state, her Biographical Commentary and Notes left to the editorship of Abigail Burnham Bloom and John Maynard of New York University. The main interest of the book lies in the publication in full for the first time of two reminiscences by Anny (as she is called here), one dated 1864–1865, expressing her grief at the death of her father, but also recalling her childhood; the other dated 1878 and addressed to Minny's daughter Laura. These are eked out by selected letters from Anny to family and friends, as well as letters addressed to her.

Among prominent correspondents are Robert Browning, George Eliot, and Henry James, with other fellow writer such as Dickens, Trollope, and Tennyson referred to in passing. Regretably, only a few letters to W. J. Williams, editor at Smith, Elder, in connection with the Centenary Biographical Edition are reproduced of the many at Princeton still unpublished. The posthumous editors have left numerous names "unidentified." Eileen Curran, in her searching review (*VPR*, Spring 1997), points out that these texts are really memoirs, not journals; she thinks Shankman is too hard on Hester Fuller, their first editor, and corrects some of her misidentifications. Highly questionable is the tabloid psychology, for example, the "threat of unconscious incest" between father and daughter and the presumption of sibling rivalry between Anny and Minny over Leslie Stephen. Patchy as the book is, it is good to have this record of the growing pains of a maturing prodigy who inherited some of her father's literary gift.

## Works: The Long Span

The most footloose and cosmopolitan of Victorian novelists, Thackeray was a student of comparative culture. However, only in recent years has this aspect of his achievment got its due, owing in large part to an emeritus professor of German from Queen's College, Oxford, Siegbert Prawer, who came to Thackeray in retirement and initially out of his interest in illustration. *Israel at Vanity Fair* (1992), the first book of what can be regarded as a "trilogy," already praised by Shillingsburg, is an even-handed examination of Thackeray's views on Judaism, showing that though he sometimes poked fun at Jews in his novels, his scoundrels are Gentiles. Since then have appeared two more substantial books: *Breeches and Metaphysics: Thackeray's German Discourses* (1997), and *W. M. Thackeray's European Sketch Books: A Study of Literary and Graphic Portraiture* (2000).

*Breeches and Metaphysics* refers to the tailor Beinkleider in Thackeray's parodic novel *Catherine* who, with a bow to Carlyle's *Sartor Resartus*, is skilled in "breeches and metaphysics, in inexpressibles and incomprehensibles." It begins as an extended annotation of Thackeray's never published "Commonplace Book while at Weimar," and expands into the German Sketchbook that he projected but never got round to writing. With philological precision, grace, and wit, Prawer brings out the full implications of the allusions to German people, places, and events throughout the canon from *Catherine* to *Denis Duval*, including non-fictional works. Teachers who lack the time to go through its densely packed 500 pages should certainly read the chapter titled "The German Booth in Vanity Fair" before again taking up that novel. They can then turn to the concluding summation, "A Field Full of German Folk." An additional treat is the profuse illustration, both published drawings and unpublished "squiggles."

As former president of the English Goethe Society, Prawer knows his way about the literary Rhineland.[3] In *W. M. Thackeray's European Sketch Books*, Prawer displays equal familarity with Thackeray's writing on France, Italy, Austria, Belgium, Holland, Spain, Portugal, and Turkey. (The Middle East figured in *Israel at Vanity Fair.)* Here, too, names are attached to personalities, events alluded to are explained, linguistic cat's cradles are unravelled. No item in the oeuvre is untouched, even sports like "Bluebeard's Ghost,"

"Cox's Diary," "Punch in the East," and the generally neglected comic verse. Again the text is illuminated throughout with Thackeray's "candles."

Other full-length studies over this past decade have concentrated on Thackeray's thoughts on issues of his day. Following on Deborah Thomas's *Thackeray and Slavery* (1993), previously assessed by Shillingsburg, appeared Michael Clarke's *Thackeray and Women* (1995). Both books are welcome correctives to received perceptions of Thackeray as time-bound and narrow-minded in his social outlook. Thomas shows that he was as revolted by the institution of slavery as by any kind of servitude, Clarke that he was actually ahead of his time in his sympathetic understanding of the plight of women, putting him on a wavelength with George Eliot and John Stuart Mill. Clarke departs from Gordon Ray's emphasis on the influence of women in Thackeray's own life on his fiction, pointing out more the impact of his reading as well as his acquaintance with then rife controversies. One linking thread in her book is his friendship with Caroline Norton, whose marital difficulties are reflected not only in *The Newcomes*, but in *Catherine, Barry Lyndon,* and *Vanity Fair* as well. Her unearthing of an obscure tract, Judith Drake's *Essay in Defence of the Female Sex* (1696), found in Thackeray's library after his death, casts new light on Rachel Esmond. These are but examples of the original research that has gone into this readable and enlightening book.

Among recent monographs, the most intellectually impressive is John Reed's *Dickens and Thackeray: Punishment and Forgiveness* (1995). Reed is unusual among latter-day critics in bringing these one-time rivals as "Metropolitan Novelists" (David Masson's phrase) into juxtaposition, caught in the act of playing God, but mainly to show their different mental sets. While they shared Christian convictions and a common ethos, Reed demonstrates by numerous examples that their treatment of criminals and sinners was diametrically opposed: wrongdoers in Dickens's novels are usually "hunted down," whereas in Thackeray's novels they are "found out" (the title, in fact, of one of his *Roundabout Papers*). Moreover, whereas Dickens tended to separate his characters as inherently forgiving or unforgiving, Thackeray's "mixed" characters are more shaded in their moral disposition. Some may find the novel-by-novel format of the bulk of the book somewhat cramping and occasionally tedious, but the painstaking analyses are rewarding. Wider context is provided by three densely packed introductory chapters on contemporaneous moral texts, educational theory, and legal writing, Reed's main intention being to reread the two novelists in the light of secularized Christianity, with amelioration of criminals taking precedence over retribution. Hence both Thackeray and Dickens make more of self-reformation than of courts or penal institutions.

Richard Pearson's *W. M. Thackeray and the Mediated Text: Writing for Periodicals in the Mid-Nineteenth Century* (2000) is the first book-length study of the youthful journalism since Harold Gulliver's *Thackeray's Literary Apprenticeship* (1934). Pearson's aim is to show that this generally by-passed phase of Thackeray's career was not mere apprenticeship. He finds, particularly in the accounts of continental politics that Thackeray contributed during the 1830s to the London-based *National Standard* and *Constitutional* as Paris correspondent, the urbanity and wit that we associate with the novels; in other early writings he finds prototypes for some of his fictional personae. Furthermore Pearson takes a fresh look at the novels as an ongoing critique of the emergent Victorian press and mass media. *The Adventures of Philip*, the least admired of the long novels, takes on a new vitality as a recapitulation of its author's penny-a-liner days. Pearson makes the obligatory bow to Habermas's "public sphere" theory, but not at the expense of lucidity. Three appendices augment Thackeray's anonymous unread but evidently not unreadable journalistic canon. Altogether this is a deeply researched, original investigation.

To these specialized monographs can be added noteworthy introductions by the two most active Thackerayans of this generation, Peter Shillingsburg and Edgar Harden, distilling their scholarship for a more general audience, nowadays presumably the undergraduate student or the graduate student preparing for exams.

Harden's two-part survey divides at the generally accepted watershed in Thackeray's career. *Thackeray the Writer: From Journalism to Vanity Fair* (1998) intersperses biography with the works at various stages, contrasts the objectivity of *Vanity Fair* with the first-person and third-person narration of the earlier fiction. *Vanity Fair* is distinguished as "a huge leap forward, articulating a new breadth of concrete, specific human experience, and a more extended range of reference." Generous space is given to *Catherine*, still Thackeray's most widely unread novel. *Thackeray the Writer: From Pendennis to Denis Duval* (2000) extends the "quintessential" Thackerayan narrator into the later works, emphasizing cross-references between fiction and non-fiction (*Henry Esmond /The English Humorists*; *The Virginians/The Four Georges*; *Denis Duval/The Roundabout Papers*), and explicating allusions.

Shillingsburg describes his *William Makepeace Thackeray: A Literary Life* (2001) as "an introductory portrait of the author, a characterization of 'the speaker of the works,' and an account of the relation between Thackeray's life and his works.'' His introduction briefly surveys attitudes towards Thackeray by both admirers and detractors, pointing out that the latter frequently misread him or fail to probe beneath his surface. Chapters devoted to *Vanity Fair*, female characters, male characters, *The Roundabout Papers*, illustration, and memorials to the author intercalate criticism, biography, and textual history. Shillingsburg's book is unique among general introductions in recognizing the importance of the French eclectic philosopher Victor Cousin, whom Thackeray read as an art student in Paris, as a formative influence on his relativistic authorial stance.

Among shorter pieces that survey Thackeray's works, Ina Ferris, author of the Twayne monograph on Thackeray commented on in the previous bibliographical essay, has contributed ''Thackeray and the Ideology of the Gentleman'' to the *Columbia History of the British Novel*, edited by John Richetti (1994). Here the canon is reexamined in the light of the adaptation of the model of gentility from a landed society to a commercial one.

A pair of well-written essays of value to new readers are ''Thackeray's Memorials of Defeat'' (*CR*, March 1993) and ''Thackeray the Sentimental Sceptic'' (*CR*, June 1993) by Donald Bruce. The first examines the major novels as Thackeray's ''spiritual autobiography,'' with such recurrent motifs as transience, misplaced attachments, and sentimental defeats. The second illustrates ''the erosion of the old order'' mainly from *Vanity Fair*, *Pendennis*, and *The Newcomes*.

Several other articles center on particular themes. William J. Birken's ''Thackeray's Medical Fathers'' (*VIJ*, 1993) suggests that the various doctors in the novels figure as substitute fathers for the author; surprisingly, Birken sees more of Dr. Elliotson, Thackeray's personal physician, in Dr. Firmin than in Dr. Goodenough of *The Adventures of Philip*. Mark Cronin's ''Henry Gowan, William Makepeace Thackeray, and the 'Dignity of Literature' Controversy'' (*DQ*, June 1993) traces Dickens's presumed caricature of his rival in *Little Dorrit* to clashing attitudes between the two over the profession of authorship. Further related to the anatomizing of social affectation, Brian Mcluskey's ''Fetishizing the Flunkey: Thackeray and the Uses of Deviance'' (*Novel*, Summer 1999) illustrates from the fiction and nonfiction how Thackeray's dressing of servants ''allows him to analyze the interdependence of sexual and commodity fetishism.'' As for relations with fellow writers, Robert P. Fletcher in '' 'The Foolishest of Existing Mortals': Thackeray, 'Gurlyle,' and the Characters of Fiction'' (*Clio*, Winter 1995) contends that while these two were initially compatible as exposers of cant, they grew apart—Carlyle "scapegoating" fiction in favor of historical fact, Thackeray remaining sceptical of all attempts at verbal representation of truth. On another distinguished contemporary, Elizabeth Langland in "Dialogue, Discourse, Theft, and Mimicry: Charlotte Brontë Rereads Wiliam Makepeace Thackeray" (in *Understanding Narrative*, ed. James Phelan and Peter Rabinowitz, 1994) invokes the fashionable theorists Bakhtin, Kristeva, and Foucault, among others, to demonstrate how in *Shirley* Brontë converts and subverts Thackerayan "tropes" such as "the stylization of woman as mermaid and the posture of woman as wife." In "A Good Woman on Five Thousand Pounds: *Jane Eyre, Vanity Fair* and Literary Rivalry" (*SEL*, Autumn 1995), Richard A. Kaye contends that, despite his admiration for *Jane Eyre*, Thackeray saw in Brontë a "formidable rival," and makes the ingenious but unprovable conjecture that Becky's famous "five thousand pounds a year" is a sly allusion to the sum Jane kept back from her inheritance as sufficient to support her for life.

## Individual Works: Before Becky

To the Collected Works underway at the University of Michigan Press, which has given us definitive editions notably of *Vanity Fair, Pendennis, Henry Esmond, The Newcomes,* and *The Yellowplush Papers,* can now be added *Catherine* (1999), which I have argued (in *Thackeray's Canvass of Humanity*) contains the Thackerayan canon *in ovo*. This text had its inception as a doctoral dissertation at the University of Canada, British Columbia, by Sheldon Goldfarb, who served as its editor for Michigan. *Catharine* is unique among Thackeray's completed works in never having been published in book form during his lifetime, so that Goldfarb had to use for his copy text the *Fraser's* serial (May 1839–February 1840), correcting its errors in his textual apparatus. Thackeray's illustrations in *Fraser's* are reproduced, with the addition of "The interview of Mr. Billings with his father," printed for the first time from the original in the British Library. An appendix reproduces the newspaper accounts of the Hayes murder that Thackeray worked from, together with an account of a similar contemporaneous case from *Bell's Life* of 1837. Another appendix quotes contemporaneous newspaper notices during the serial run of *Catherine,* some of them surprisingly favorable. This being the only edition presently in print, it is unfortunate that its price confines it to university libraries.

In *Thackeray's Canvass of Humanity* I wrote that because of the strands of parody woven through this "novel on novels," it could have been subtitled "Fraser's Prize Novels." In "Sources of Parody in Thackeray's *Catherine*" (*DSA* 1994), Thomas McKendy takes up this suggestion by pinning down precisely the then popular romances that "Ikey Solomons" spoofed, including Ainsworth's *Rookwood*; Bulwer's *Paul Clifford*, *Ernest Maltravers*, *Eugene Aram*, and G. P. R. James's *The Robbers*.

*The Luck of Barry Lyndon*, Thackeray's second novel, has also been added to the Michigan Collected Works, under the editorship of Edgar Harden (1999). There being no extant manuscript, the *Fraser's* serial of 1844 serves again as copy text, emended to correct errors detected by the editor, and compared with the three subsequent abbreviated book editions published during Thackeray's lifetime. "Luck" remains in the title, though it was changed to "Memoirs" in 1856. Harden has restored the original notes by Fitzboodle, the nominal editor of Barry's memoir, which were truncated in book editions, but indicates that confusion remains as to how much of Fitzboodle's presence Thackeray intended to retain.

The continuing impact of Stanley Kubrick's film version of 1975 has made *Barry Lyndon* the most discussed Thackeray novel after *Vanity Fair*, though there is no evidence that it is much taught. A published symposium on the film that appeared on its twentieth anniversary will be commented on in my section on Performance.

Two excellent critical pieces on the novel itself are Robert P. Fletcher's " 'Proving a thing even while you contradict it': Fictions, Beliefs, and Legitimation in the Memoirs of Barry Lyndon, Esq." (*SNNT*, Winter 1995), and John Watson's "Thackeray's Composite Characters: Autobiography and 'True History' in *Barry Lyndon*" (*AUMLA*, May 1997). Fletcher's is a narratological approach, making the boastful Barry a kind of surrogate for the author by undermining the "common sense distinction between truth and fiction." Watson's is more of a source study, showing how Thackeray melded and modified his sources, both factual and fictional. He finds in this mock memoir a blend of autobiography and fiction; some of the characteristics of his wife Isabella are in Lady Lyndon, while Barry's mother unites his own mother and his mother-in-law.

The only commentary on the early satires that I have come upon is Rowland D. McMaster's "*Rebecca and Rowena* and Bakhtin" (*CVE*, October 1993) which draws on Bakhtin's concepts of carnival and polyphonic discourse to bring out how Thackeray's "weaving" between optimism and pessimism, high-flown rhetoric and deflation anticipates devices employed in more complicated ways in the novels.

A dissertation by Gail David Sorensen, ''A Scholarly Edition of Three Thackeray Christmas Books: *Mrs. Perkin's Ball, Our Street, Dr. Birch and His Young Friends*'' at the University of Alberta (*DAIA*, Feb. 1997) has yet to see publication.

## ''The Bustling Place . . . ''

Advanced scholarship on Thackeray's best-known novel has been made accessible lately to students thanks once more to that familiar duo Peter Shillingsburg and Edgar Harden.

Despite its popularity, *Vanity Fair* was added to the Norton Critical Editions only in 1994. An advantage of the delay is that its editor Peter Shillingsburg was able to transfer the text he established for the Collected Works in 1989 (then under the aegis of Garland Press) with the addition of the explanatory notes from the *Annotations* to selected works published by Garland under the editorship of Edgar Harden. All of the original illlustrations—initials, vignettes, plates—are reproduced, including the cover design for the monthly parts. Background materials include the famous reviews by George Henry Lewes and Elizabeth Rigby. Among documents are an advertisement in *Punch* for July 12, 1845 of ''a situation as Governess in a gentleman's family residing in the country,'' and a description of a model governess by Maria Edgeworth. Various twentieth-century critical approaches are sampled.

Edgar Harden's monograph on *Vanity Fair* in the Twayne Masterworks Series (1995) utilizes the Garland ''standard critical edition'' for its quotations. There are two sections: Historical and Literary Context, including Critical Reception; A Reading, which covers its panoramic structure, its emergence as a serial in monthly parts, the personality of the narrator, and Thackeray's writing style.

The critical mills grind on. There are still titillating titles like ''Kiss Me Stupid: Sexuality and *Vanity Fair*,'' ''Female Sexuality and Triangular Desire in *Vanity Fair*,'' and ''The Seductivenss of Female Duplicity in *Vanity Fair*''; but a substantial number of articles view Becky as more than a ''spice girl'' and probe to the thought behind the author's Harlequin mask.

''The Implied Theology of *Vanity Fair*'' (*PQ*, Winter 1998) by J. Russell Perkin expands on the implications of Ecclesiastes and *The Pilgrim's Progress* that inspired the title, affirming that the religion expounded in the novel is closer to Augustinian orthodoxy than the Broad Church position with which

Thackeray is sometimes identified. "Middle Class Life in *Vanity Fair*" (*English*, Spring 1994) by John Peck contends that while Thackeray brilliantly portrays social change and the rise of the middle class here, he was at heart contemptuous of this class. Peck seems to me to exaggerate the ridicule of Dobbin, the one character whom Thackeray admires unequivocally.The audience is central to Kate Flint's "Women, Men, and the Reading of *Vanity Fair*" (in *The Practice and Representation of Reading in England*, ed. James Raven, Helen Small, and Naomi Tadmor, 1996). Flint points out how books read by various people in the novel illuminate their characters. She detects chauvinism on the part of the author who seems to her to favor men over women as his model reader. She also refers to his jibes at French fiction, without noting that he admired some of it (notably the novels of Charles de Bernard) for its frankness. In "Reading the Long Way Round . . ." (*YES* 1996), John Schad sees the essence of Thackeray's narrative method as "circumvention," with Becky's late wanderings serving as a metaphor for the "circularity" of structure in *Vanity Fair*. The search for Becky's models continues. John Frazee in "The Creation of Becky Sharp . . ." (*DSA* 1998) offers convincing evidence for two notorioius kept women of the Regency Period—Mary Anne Clarke, mistress of the duke of York, and Harriet Wilson, mistress of the marquess of Hertford (prototype of Lord Steyne), both of whom left memoirs.

Several articles relate graphic features to interpretation. Patricia Marks's " 'Mon Pauvre Prissonier': Becky Sharp and the Triumph of Napoleon" (*SNNT*, Spring 1996), with reference particularly to the famous initial depicting Becky in the garb of the Emperor looking out from a promontory, documents in detail how she becomes a female Napoleon, exemplifying the "carrière ouverte aux talents." Lisa Jadwin's "Clytemnestra Rewarded: The Double Conclusion of *Vanity Fair*" (in *Famous Last Words: Changes in Gender and Narrative Closure*, ed. Alison Booth, 1993) juxtaposes the two concluding plates of the novel—"Virtue Rewarded . . . ." and "Becky's Second Appearance in the Character of Clytemnestra"—both of which show her framed by a curtain and separated by a proscenium arch, emphasizing her duality and her role as poseur. Christopher Coates's "Thackeray's Editors and the Dual Text of *Vanity Fair* (*W & I*, Jan.–March 1993) reminds us of its connection with *Punch*, although it did not appear there, and urges that we read it in the way its first readers did, as pictures interrupted by text.

*Vanity Fair* also figures prominently in a special issue of *Cahiers Victoriens et Edouardiens*, to be discussed in my later section on Thackeray Abroad.

## Henry Esmond

To judge by the reduced level of publication during the period covered in this essay, this historical romance that was Thackeray's most prestigious book during his lifetime seems to have been displaced from its once prominent place in college curricula. More recent criticism has veered from what had been a favorite sport of deconstructing Henry. What is left unsaid, but implied, according to Laurence Lerner in "The Unsaid in *Henry Esmond*" (*ES* April 1995) is Rachel's sexual attraction to Henry and her jealousy of her daughter Beatrix. In a discursive and rambling article "Visual Thinking and the Picture Story in *The History of Henry Esmond*" (*PMLA*, May 1998), Robert Fletcher draws on E. H. Gombrich's psychology of perception and Walter Benjamin's cultural criticism in an attempt to establish a comparison between *Esmond* as a *bildungsroman* and "the pictorialized sketches and tableaux by which its story unfolds." Terry Tierney's narratological approach in "Henry Esmond's Double Vision" (*SNNT*, Winter 1992) views the hero as "a man who has learned to live with contradictions" as he tries to reconcile his young self (as recalled in the third person) with his older self (conveyed in the first person).

*Esmond* is utilized by Peter Shillingsburg in his *Pegasus in Harness* as a case study exemplifying the variety of contexts—the sociology of the marketplace, publishing conditions, autobiography—in which a novel by Thackeray has to be studied. He finds fallacies in more narrowly focussed modern interpretations.[4]

## Pendennis and After

Writing on Thackeray's most autobiographical novel which during the "momism" fad of the 1950s attracted some readers is now scant. Mark Cronin in the "The Rake, The Writer, and *The Stranger*: Textual Relations between *Pendennis* and *David Copperfield*" (*DSA* 1995) postulates, on the basis of parallels between the Pendennis-Helen-Laura and the Steerforth-Mrs. Steerforth-Rosa households, that *David Copperfield* was deliberately modelled on *Pendennis*, which had begun its run six months earlier. Actually, apart from an incident in common in which the two heroes attend performances of Kotzebue's *The Stranger*, Cronin brings out more differences than similarities between the two novels. In "Thackeray's Treatment of Writing and Painting" (*NCF*, June 1992), Laura Fasick concludes that, unlike the idealization of the artist J. J. in *The Newcomes*, the view of authorship represented by Arthur

Pendennis is a cynical one. What about Pen's growing engagement with humanity as *Pendennis* progresses, and his eventual maturing into the chronicler of the Newcome family?

*The Newcomes*, the most beloved of Thackeray's novels during his lifetime, has emerged from neglect with a scholarly edition and several cheaper reprints now available. Since about two-thirds of the manuscript of *The Newcomes* has survived, Peter Shillingsburg, the editor of the text produced in the Collected Works published by the University of Michigan Press, has been able (as he was not able to do with *Vanity Fair* and *Pendennis*) to track Thackeray's workmanship. The growth of this masterpiece can be traced through revisions, additions of matter in some places, transference of passages here and there, and various afterthoughts. The last appendix reprints an alternative version of number 6 (chaps. XVIII-XX), which differs from manuscript to book. A bonus of this edition is the historical introduction by Rowland McMaster, whose monograph *Thackeray's Frame of Reference: Allusion in The Newcomes* (1991) has been widely praised.

For teaching purposes there is the attractive World's Classics paperback (1995). This is not a modern text, being based on the Oxford Thackeray of 1908 edited by George Saintsbury, but it is judiciously introduced by Andrew Sanders, and its Explanatory Notes incorporate those prepared by Rowland McMaster for the Garland *Annotations*, plus additions and corrections by Sanders. There is also a reprint by Penguin Books (1996), with an introduction by David Pascoe, but without illustrations.

Oddly, since D. J. Taylor generally denigrates Thackeray's late works, *The Newcomes* is the one novel he discusses at any length in his biography. He treats it with respect, but complains of its "creeping emollience," whatever that means. He also repeats what one had hoped was the by now discredited disparagement of the Colonel as overly sentimentalized and of his death scene as mawkish—the very episode where George Saintsbury believed that Thackeray had reached a "Shakespearian pitch."

Thackeray's last two completed novels have elicited one substantial article each. "Farcical Process, Fictional Product: Thackeray's Theatrics in *Lovel the Widower* (*VLC* 1998) by Anne Layman Horn stresses the air of improvisation in this wistful trifle that Thackeray adapted from his privately produced play. Horn describes its "informal conversation with the reader," akin to a stage farce and a reversion to Thackeray's earlier magazine mode. John Peck's "Racism in the Mid-Victorian Novel: Thackeray's Phillip" (in *Varieties of Victorianism*, ed. Gary Day, 1998) displays wide reading in the literature surrounding the partially autobiographical *The Adventures of Philip*, but leaves the question of its author's attitude towards the character of Wolcomb in particular and blacks in general unresolved.

Among the contrasts in the literary fortunes of Thackeray and Dickens—whereas the unfininished *Edwin Drood* has had numerous "completions"—nobody has made the attempt for the half-told *Denis Duval* for which Thackeray left behind detailed notes on how it was to conclude. Dickens himself wrote of *Denis* in his obituary tribute to Thackeray in *Cornhill*: "I believe it to be much the best of his works." He also felt that because the end was anticipated in the beginning, "there is an approach to completeness in the fragment."

## Thackeray's Travels

Of Thackeray's three full-length travelogs, *The Irish Sketch Book* has been the most frequently reissued. More nuanced readings in recent years have tended to reverse earlier charges that Titmarsh (his travelling name) carried over English stereotypes of their Irish neighbors. John A. Gamble in his scholarly introduction to a reprint by the Bickerstaff Press (1985) contends to the contrary that his view of Ireland "while controversial was founded on well assembled facts," that he was genuinely touched by the poverty of the peasantry, and deplored religious intolerance on the part of Catholics and Protestants. Gamble refers to an "original preface" suppressed by Chapman and Hall because of its open opposition to the English government in Ireland. This preface seems to have disappeared.

Pretty much in the same vein is Kenneth L. Brewer's "Colonial Discourse and William Makepeace Thackeray's *Irish Sketch Book*" (*PLL*, Summer 1993), which draws on the theories of Edward Said and Jürgen Habermas, argues that Thackeray was critical of the "positional superiority" (Said's term) adopted by the English, and that he even accuses the English of seeing the Irish through "a drunken haze." He concludes that Thackeray's hope for the future of Ireland lay in the development of a middle class to counter the prejudiced viewpoints of Catholic aristocracy and Protestant peasantry. Thackeray's visits of course came before the potato famine and in the midst of the disruptive nationalist movement led by O'Connell.

The deft blend of the verbal and the pictorial in *The Irish Sketch Book* is informatively discussed by Donncha Ò Muirthe in "W. M. Thackeray and the Daguerreotype" (*History of Photography*, Spring 1998). Ò Muirthe praises the book as "unsentimental, perceptive, humorous," a refreshing reaction from previous Romantic-minded visitors who revelled in the picturesque beauties of Erin. This article is original in singling out Thackeray as "among the first to apprehend the documentary potential of photograpy," citing specifically his mention of the daguerreotype in the chapter on the Killarney races.

*Notes of a Journey from Cornhill to Grand Cairo*, Thackeray's account of his Middle East journey during the fall of 1844, has especially subjected him to accusations of ethnocentrism and racial prejudice. I can recall a publisher turning down the offer by a colleague to edit a reprint of this book on the grounds of its alleged anti-semitism. Scholars, notably Siegbert Prawer, have since pointed out that what seem like attacks on Judaism, particularly in the Jerusalem chapter, are really protests against the atrocities and harsh vengeance recounted in the Old Testament. What Thackeray essentially inveighed against was bigotry, which he found not only in Judaism but in the other religions as well that contended for the dominance of the Holy City—Catholicism, Protestantism, Eastern Orthodoxy, and Islam.

Especially welcome therefore is the handsome reissue of what arguably is Thackeray's greatest travel book by the Cockbird Press of East Sussex (1991). The authoritative introduction by Sarah Searight, a historian of the Middle East, recovers the turbulent rivalry in this region, alluded to by Thackeray, among the British, French, and Russians in the Ottoman Empire during these years preceding the Crimean War. Searight's notes elucidate specific people and events. The book is lavishly illustrated. Thackerayans will regret that so few of his original drawings are included, but their absence is more than made up for by the beautiful reproductions, selected by the art historian Briony Llewellyn, of prints and water colors from the Victoria and Albert Museum depicting the region. These include the work of contemporaneous artists like David Roberts, John Frederick Lewis, and William Müller, who may very well have influenced Thackeray. For such a de luxe production the book is remarkably inexpensive.

A substantial set of drawings originally intended for *Cornhill to Grand Cairo* but never published has been discovered at the Huntington Library. These will be discussed in the section on Illustration.

Thackeray travelled in his mind before he set out on his own. "Thackeray and Russia" by Robert A. Colby (*TNL*, May 1996) points out how, in a newly attributed anonymous review in the *British and Foreign Review* of January 1839 of three accounts by British visitors to the court of St. Petersburg, Thackeray anticipates both the social satire in *Vanity Fair* and his stance in the travel books that preceded it.

## Ut Pictura Poesis

From his schooldays on, Thackeray's hand was as busy as his eye and brain. Throughout his life he was a compulsive drawer, in letters, in margins of his books, in albums, meant to be seen only by family and friends. It is now recognized that the graphic element in Thackeray's oeuvre is inseparable from the verbal, but because much of this work is unpublished and his designs for his professional illustration were finished by others in a variety of techniques, this phase of his creativity has proved elusive. There has been no technical study since John Buchanan-Brown's *The Illustrations of William Makepeace Thackeray* (1979), apart from brief commentaries on illustrations by Nicholas Pickwood for the established texts of *Vanity Fair* (1989), *Pendennis* (1991), and *Flore et Zéphyr* (1989). Scholarship lately has concentrated on the relationship between text and picture.

Victor R. Kennedy's stimulating "Pictures as Metaphors in Thackeray's Illustrated Novels" (*MSA* 1994) pinpoints several stylistic elements from nineteenth-century caricature in Thackeray's pictorial initials, vignettes, and full-page plates: exaggeration, allusive elements from political satire, and a "personal repertoire of iconic symbolism, integrated with his ironic narrative voice." Visual metaphor, Kennedy contends, sometimes extends verbal metaphor, sometimes comments on a situation. At times Thackeray illustration alerts the reader to an event the significance of which becomes clear later; at others it reveals a truth the narrative does not make plain. Kennedy's pictorial examples are from *Vanity Fair, Pendennis*, and *The Adventures of Philip*.

Related in approach is Judith L. Fisher's "Image Versus Text in the Illustrated Novels of William Makepeace Thackeray" (in *Victorian Literature and the Victorian Visual Imagination*, edd. Carol T. Christ and John O. Jordan, 1995). For Fisher, changes in the mode of illustration in Thackeray's novels reflect a shift in mid-century from the "speaking pictures" of the Cruikshanks and "Phiz" to a style from a genre painting that subordinated image to text. For Thackeray, she emphasizes, image and text were a "self-conscious dialogue"; his most successful graphics do not really illustrate the text but "create alternative story lines, presenting counter voices to his narration." Fisher's article is accompanied by plates from *Vanity Fair* and *Pendennis*.

Alison Bycrly's " 'The Masquerade of Existence': Thackeray's Theatricality" (*DSA* 1994; reprinted in Byerly's *Representation and the Arts in Nineteenth-Century Literature*, 1997) investigates Thackeray's pictorial art and art criticism as reflection of his stance as a novelist. "Visual art seems to present a peculiar paradox in Thackeray's work," she writes. "His novels are insistent warnings against the seductions of appearance; illustrations, as visual reproductions of aspect, would seem to belong to the realm of illusion." The art criticism, Byerly continues, is intended to emphasize the kind of realism that visual art can achieve, and Thackeray's espousal of "mediocre" (what we call "genre") art is related to his contempt for theatricality in painting, the "sham sublime," in his words. A later article by Byerly, "Effortless Art: The Sketch in Nineteenth-Century Painting and Literature" (*Criticism*, Summer, 1999) concentrates on Dickens's *Sketches by Boz* and Thackeray's *Paris Sketchbook*. Both novelists, she concludes, were attracted to sketch art for its authenticity, spontaneity, and air of leisurely observation, "rendering the 'real' more artistic and palatable while rendering 'art' more realistic and marketable."

Bearing more on Thackeray's independent efforts is D. J. Taylor's "A Scrapbook of Ghosts: Thackeray's Lost Career as an Artist" (*TLS* 24 Sept. 1999). Taylor came upon unpublished early drawings by Thackeray in the collection of the art dealer William Drummond of London, some of which are reproduced in his biography. David S. Kerr's *Caricature and French Political Culture, 1830–1848* (2000) recovers the political milieu surrounding the "citizen-king" Louis Philippe made into an object of lampoon in newspapers by Philipon, Daumier, and others who influenced Thackeray during his Paris days. Kerr quotes from Thackeray's "Caricature and Lithography in Paris," one of the essays in the *Paris Sketchbook*. His book is profusely and delightfully illustrated, including a number of versions for the caricature of Louis Philippe as a pear that Thackeray imitated.

A unique view of Thackeray at work with pencil, sketch pad, and watercolor brush is afforded by "Thackeray's Drawings for Cornhill to Cairo in the Huntington Library" (*HLQ*, Winter 1994) by Robert R. Wark. Wark, a member of the curatorial staff at Huntington, describes a set of sixty drawings, most of them mounted in a scrapbook of unknown origin and provenance, related to *Notes on a Journey from Cornhill to Grand Cairo*. Wark's appreciative account points up Thackeray's preoccupation with "people, habits, dress, dwellings, and on commoners rather than upper class." We are reminded that the Middle East had attracted artists before Thackeray, notably David Roberts, William Müller, and John Frederick Lewis, whom Thackeray refers to in a chapter of his book. Wark finds the closest conection between Thackeray and Lewis in "their dignified, even monumental depiction of Arab men, sometimes singly, sometimes in groups." The article is generously illustrated with black-and-white reproductions, only a few of which appeared in the book. One of them proves to be a version of a plate depicting a top-hatted gentleman in an alcove (self-portrait of the artist?) observing a bazaar. This originally appeared as a frontispiece to Charles Addison's *From Damascus to Palmyra: A Voyage to the East* (1838) for which Thackeray supplied seventeen lithographs anonymously at the invitation of the publisher Richard Bentley.

My own subsequent study of these drawings in color at the Huntington Library confirms that Thackeray was indeed intent on supplying "familiar views of the East . . . faithful transcripts of Oriental life," as he indicates at the beginning of the Smyrna chapter of his book on the Middle East. Among these are street scenes of Athens, Smyrna, Constantinople, among other cities; closeups of Arab, Turkish, Hebrew, and Egyptian men and women; beggars and animals caught sleeping. However, many other sketches indicate that the artist took equal interest in the churches, monuments, and landscapes that he professed to scorn. In these he was precise with rendering of architectural detail, with shading, with such technical matters as distancing and perspective. Included in this collection are panoramic port scenes; one landscape, conjecturally of Jerusalem, foregrounded by a desert, resembles an illustration from David Roberts's *The Holy Land*. The employment of water color in many of the drawings, and of color-coding in others, suggests that Thackeray conceived what proved the last of his travel books as a *livre de peinture*. The Huntington collection certainly extends his range as an artist.

### "Thorns in the Cushion"

"As an author who has written long, and had the good fortune to find a very great number of readers, I think I am not mistaken in supposing that they give me credit for experience and observation . . . and having heard me soliloquize with so much kindness and favour, and say my say about life, and men and women, they will not be unwilling to try me as a Conductor of a Concert, in which I trust many skilful performers will take part." So Thackeray addressed his unknown readers of the newly launched *Cornhill Magazine* in January 1860. Thackeray started his career with "magazinery," and, as Richard Pearson reminds us in *Thackeray and the Mediated Text*, never entirely left it behind him. In his early years he had the misfortune of the co-proprietorship of two unsuccessful newspapers, and he tried in vain to secure a magazine editorship, notably of the *Foreign Quarterly Review*. It was not until three years before his death that he realized his ambition to head, as he confided in a letter to his publishers Bradbury and Evans early in 1844, "a slashing, brilliant, gentlemanlike, sixpenny aristocratic literary paper."

It turned out to be a shilling monthly, middle-class family-oriented magazine divided between literature and the actual world. The editorship of *Cornhill Magazine*, to which its publisher George Smith counted on Thackeray's reputation to lend luster, was the crowning accolade of Thackeray's sunset years. However, this editorship, which at first revitalized Thackeray's then waning spirits, eventually proved vexatious, as documented by Robert A. Colby in "Goose Quill and Blue Pencil: The Victorian Novelist as Editor" (in *Innovators and Preachers*, ed. Joel H. Wiener, 1985). In this essay Thackeray is considered alongside William Harrison Ainsworth, Charles Lever, and Anthony Trollope, all popular novelists who, unlike Dickens, failed as editors. In Thackeray's case, he chafed under the drudgery of routine editorial burdens, proved absentminded in handling correspondence, was involved in delicate matters of censorship (sometimes with friends), and found it painful to deal with contributors. Excerpts quoted from a sheaf of unpublished letters in the Beinecke Library at Yale, titled "Thorns in the Cushion" (after one of the Roundabout Papers), reveal tugs at the heartstrings endured by Thackeray, what he called "the arguement ad misericordium," from various would-be writers—indigent widows, a down-at-the-heels Eton graduate, even a hint from an unmarried teacher (addressed to "friend of Charlotte Brontë") that she could be available to "Mr. Batchelor" as more than a contributor.

A kind of addendum to "Goosequill and Blue Pencil" is Colby's " 'Into the Blue Water': The First Year of *Cornhill Magazine* under Thackeray" which heads off a two-part Special Issue of *Victorian Periodicals Review* under the editorship of Barbara Quinn Schmidt devoted to *Cornhill* (Fall 1999; Spring 2000). On the basis of newly published letters this article establishes that Thackeray's initial year at the helm of *Cornhill* was a relatively euphoric one, showing him inviting eminent contributors (including Garibaldi, who evidently did not respond), and exerting control over the design and contents of the magazine. The letdown began with the failure of *The Adventures of Philip* and resultant decline of sales, although Thackeray remained an active contributor after resigning the editorship, until his death.

Other articles in this issue take up various aspects of Thackeray's influence, In "Theatre, Journalism, and Thackeray's 'Man of the World' Magazine," Anne Horn sees Thackeray's role of author-editor displayed in his choice of contributors and by the slant of articles he selected as "the journalistic equivalent of the Victorian actor-manager." Rosemary Scott in "Poetry in the *Cornhill Magazine*: Thackeray's Influence" points out that while the editor was eager to include poems in each issue, his choice was governed by moral as well as literary considerations. Scott focusses on forgotten poems, omitting to mention that Tennyson's "Tithonus" originally appeared in *Cornhill*, as well as posthumously published verses by Charlotte and Emily Brontë—easy to ignore, inasmuch as the *Wellesley Index* excludes poetry. Andrew Maunder's more socio-economically oriented " 'Discourses of Distinction': The Reception of the *Cornhill Magazine*, 1859–60," based on an examination of contemporary reviews, concludes that the endeavor of Smith and Thackeray to cross "the boundary of elite and contemporary culture" was interpreted by some of the more high-brow journals as pandering to hoi polloi.

The second *Cornhill* issue of *VPR* begins with "Thackeray as Editor and Author: *The Adventures of Philip* and the Inauguration of the *Cornhill Magazine*," in which Judith L. Fisher inquires why in his dark, last completed novel Thackeray "is skeptical about religion, British manners, and the bourgeois values which he himself had promoted." Her answer involves her in a pointed analysis of the central issues explored in the novel—the decay of the old gentlemanly ideal (represented by Philip's father Dr. Firmin and the earl of Ringwood) and the rise of "a market-place economy" (embodied in Philip and his mentor Arthur Pendennis). Jennifer Phegley's "Clearing Away 'The Briars and the Brambles': The Education and Professionalization of the *Cornhill Magazine*'s Women Readers" argues that the magazine went beyond "offering light-weight entertainment for its female readers," as alleged by some scholars, in its effort to educate women in serious issues of the day and prepare them to take responsible positions in society. Phegley emphasizes the blending of fact and fiction in the contents of *Cornhill* and the inclusion of novels featuring educated women—notably George Eliot's *Romola* and Elizabeth Gaskell's *Cousin Phyllis*.

Two of the articles in this issue center on the career of Thackeray's daughter after his death: "Extending the Parameters of the Text: Anne Thackeray's Fairy Tales in the *Cornhill Magazine*," by Caroline Sumpter; "The *Cornhill Magazine* and the Literary Formation of Anne Thackeray Ritchie," by Helen Debenham. Anne made her literary debut in *Cornhill Magazine* under her father's editorship with an essay "Little Scholars," and shortly after her first novel, *The Story of Elizabeth*, appeared there. Reminiscing from the perspective of its jubilee year (January 1910), Lady Ritchie recalled: "the old days of the 'Cornhill Magazine' convey an impression of early youth, of constant sunshine associated with the dawn of the golden covers, even though it was in the winter when it first appeared.'' Her father had spared her his tribulations.

## Performance

In ''Thackeray and Dickens on the Boards'' (*Dramatic Dickens*, ed. Carol Hanbery MacKay, 1989), a retrospect of their stage history over the Victorian Age and early twentieth century, Robert A. Colby pointed out that while Dickens was conspicuous ''on the boards as well as between them,'' in his own words, from the outset of his career, Thackeray did not loom as a stage presence until the last decade of the nineteenth century. It was then mainly with *Vanity Fair*, but there were attempts also at *The Rose and the Ring*, *Henry Esmond*, *Pendennis*, and *The Newcomes*. However, whereas Dickens in general was coarsened and sensationalized by hacks, Thackeray fell into the more refined hands notably of Langdon Mitchell who was schooled in the comedy of manners. His elegant if superficial *Becky Sharp* was watered down into the RKO film of 1934, memorable mainly for Miriam Hopkins as Becky and for introducing technicolor.

The later twentieth century similarly has seen the omnipresence of Dickens on screen and television with Thackeray lagging far behind. Dickens for the most part has been reduced and over-literalized in these mass media, but Thackeray has fared worse. Stanley Kubrick's film *Barry Lyndon* continues to be a cult favorite, most recently in four papers titled ''Film Forum: *Barry Lyndon*'' (*ECL* 1995). Frank Cossa's ''Images of Perfection . . . .'' finds in the film a moral significance ''removed from Thackeray's own parodic conception of Barry'' in its representation of the decline of eighteenth-century aristocracy. John Engell's ''*Barry Lyndon*, A Picture of Irony'' in pretty much the same vein interprets Kubrick's intention as depicting a world ''in which power appears to be everything . . . exercised . . . through violence, money and sex.'' For Jeffrey L. L. Johnson in ''The Eighteenth Century Ape: *Barry Lyndon* and the Darwinian Pessimism of Stanley Kubrick,'' Thackeray's mock hero becomes a version of Gilbert and Sullivan's monkey shaved. The concluding essay by Elise F. Knapp and James Pegoletti, ''Music in Kubrick's *Barry Lyndon*: A Catalyst to Manipulate,'' closely analyzes the accompanying score which includes compositions by Handel and Schubert, as a series of motifs punctuating transitions in Barry's fortunes and reinforcing the basic melancholy of the screenplay.

Clearly the film version of *Barry Lyndon* is taken seriously by its admirers. Cossa contends that friends and foes alike concede its painterly beauty. None of these critics seems to have objected to its glacial pace and witless script or the sullen perfunctory portrayal by Ryan O'Neal of Thackeray's boisterous, self-aggrandizing scapegrace. Nor do they account for why Kubrick chose this rollicking tongue-in-cheek satire as a vehicle for his entropic world vision. It is appropriate that they refer to the film as "Kubrick's *Barry Lyndon.*" Certainly it isn't Thackeray's.

The Manager of the Performance is largely absent also from the latest BBC six-part television version of *Vanity Fair* which ran during the fall of 1998 (1999 in the United States). Its adapter Andrew Davies, who did so skillful a job with George Eliot's *Middlemarch*, accomplished the remarkable feat of making one of the world's most sparkling novels dull and plodding. Thackeray's panoramic "cynical and sentimental history" is confined here mainly to interiors and head-to-head dialogues, giving the whole a claustrophobic effect. There were some good performances in supporting roles, but Natasha Little as Becky was pretty (which Becky was not), bland, and charmless while Frances Gray as Amelia was caught too frequently in teary, unflattering close-ups. Footage which might have been given to more of the book was wasted on battle scenes (which Thackeray assiduously avoided) and, worse, hand-to-hand combats, giving no sense of the field of Waterloo. The arbitrarily altered ending showing the reunited Becky and Jos beaming on the newly married Amelia and Dobbin belonged in the Hallmark Playhouse. As usual with BBC productions, there was accompanying hoopla, a reissue of the Penguin paperback illustrated with stills from the production, and a *Radio Times* booklet, *Behind the Scenes of the BBC Vanity Fair*. According to the *Radio Times*, Natasha Little, the Becky, originally auditioned for the role of Amelia, for which she may have been better suited.

Radio still seems to be a viable medium in England for disseminating literary clasics. Donald Hawes reports intermittently on broadcasts of both Thackeray and Dickens in the *Thackeray Newsletter*. In the issue in which he unfavorably reviews the television version described above (May 1999), he praises an adaptation by Ellen Dryden of *The Rose and the Ring* on BBC Radio 4 in two one-hour parts on January 3 and 10, 1999, which starred Prunella Scales as Fairy Blackstick and Maureen Lipman as Gruffanuff.

### Thackeray Abroad

With the demise of the UNESCO sponsored *Index Translationum*, it has become virtually impossible to keep track of translations of Thackeray's works. From the University of Malaga comes "Reception and Translation as Instruments of Cultural Mediation: *Vanity Fair* in Spain" by Marcos Rodríguez Espinosa (1997). An addendum to the listing of this item in my source (*TNL*, Nov. 1998) states that a translation "is being published" by Editorial Catedra in Madrid. A Chinese friend informs me that *Vanity Fair*, translated by Yang Bi as *Ming Li Chang*, has been reissued in Beijing in the Foreign Classics in Chinese Translation Series. I gather that this version has no illustrations. There are undoubtedly more foreign translations, but they have not surfaced. In a bookshop of the Orsay in Paris I came upon an undated translation into French of *The Yellowplush Papers* (*Mémoirs d'un valet de pied*) credited to William L. Hughes. From its typography I judge it to be a reproduction of a nineteenth-century version. *The Paris Sketchbook* was published by Editions de Paris in 1997 as *L'Album Parisienne*, but according to report it is already out of print.

However, critical writing on Thackeray still flourishes in France, which he regarded as his second country, with a great part of *Cahiers Victoriens et Edouardiens* October 1993 devoted to him. A veteran French Thackeray scholar Maurice Chrétien heads off this issue with a sensitively written essay "De Finibus," the title of one of Thackeray's *Roundabout Papers* serving to characterize his avoidance of closure in his fiction, suppressing boundaries between the imaginary and the real, carrying characters over from novel to novel, and achieving continuity "by transforming linear time into a cycle where the end becomes the beginning." The other three articles are centered on *Vanity Fair*, going over familiar ground from various angles. Max Véga-Ritter, the editor of the *Cahiers*, also not new to Thackeray studies, explores the theme of "Manhood in *Vanity Fair*." Véga-Ritter points out that while *Vanity Fair* is unique among Thackeray's novels in being dominated by female characters, relations between men are important—such as Dobbin's admiring in George the manhood he feels lacking in himself. There are also variations on love rivalries (Dobbin/George; Sir Pitt/Rawdon; Lord Steyne/ Count de la Marche). The focus of "*Vanity Fair* ou l'illusion comique" by Sarah Thornton is the theatrical "fakery" by which Thackeray subverts the conventions of the popular novel and involves the reader as audience. Alain Jumeau's "Le dialogue entre le texte et l'image au chapitre 67 de *Vanity Fair*" is a close study of six of the illustrations in the novel (including "The letter before Waterloo," "Becky's second appearance in the character of Clytemnestra," and the concluding picture of the children returning their dolls to their box) to reveal "ironies, tensions, and even conflicts between text and images which modify our perception of the novel."

Previously Sarah Thornton contributed two articles on Thackeray to an earlier issue of *Cahiers*. "Icones et Iconoclasmes . . ." examines the "adoration excessive des textes" by social-climbing characters in the novels—among them Burke's *Peerage*, which becomes an object of veneration, and romantic novels through which false images are mistaken for reality. " 'Blind Love and Unbounded Credit' . . . " (*CVE*, April 1992) centers on one motif recurrent in *Vanity Fair*, the dispelling of romantic visions by monetary realities. In another French critical journal *Q/W/E/R/T/Y* (October 1992) appears still another piece by Thornton, "Becky Sharp: Le Clignotement [Flickering] d'une présence . . . ," an extended comparison of Becky with Valérie Marneffe, the unscrupulous demi-mondaine of *Cousine Bette*, who has frequently been suggested as one of Becky's literary sisters, though evidence is lacking that Thackeray knew the Balzac novel.

There are signs of activity in other European countries, of which only a short account can be provided here.

Thackeray is considered along with Scott and Dickens in an article by a German scholar Werner Wolf, "Die Domestizierung der Geschichte. . ." that appears in a Berlin journal (*Archive für das Studium der Neuren Sprachen und Literaturen* 1994). From Russia there are: " 'Literaturnost' Tekkereia" (*Isvestia Akademii Nauk*, Moscow, Sept.–Oct. 1998); "Dukhovnoe i mirskoe v 'metaforicheskoi temé' dorogi v 'Puteshestvii pilgrima D Baníana i 'Iarmarke tschcheslaviia U. Tekkereia" (*Filologicheskie Nauki* 1993); and "Tvorchestvo Tekkereia v mirovom literaturnom protesse" (*Filologicheskie Nauki* 1991). The titles translate roughly as "The 'Literariness' of Thackeray"; "Spiritual and Worldly in the Metaphoric Theme of *Pilgrim's Progress* by Bunyan and *Vanity Fair*"; and "The work of Thackeray in the World's Literary Process." The contents I leave to those who are more polyglot than I.

From Poland, by happy chance, the one pertinent article in the Cracow journal *Slavia Orientalis* (No.2, 1993) is in English—"Leo Tolstoy's Early Works and the Novels of Dickens and Thackeray" by Antoni Semczuk. This short essay is an original investigation of the influence of Thackeray on the author of *War and Peace* which, as Semczuk points out, has been neglected, while that of Dickens has been much studied. We learn that Tolstoy read *Vanity Fair* and *Pendennis* first in Russian translation, then in English, and later read his other major works. Generally Tolstoy admired Thackeray's "morally responsible attitude towards literature." Semzuk detects the influence of *Vanity Fair* particularly in Tolstoy's *Sevastopol in May* and in *Two Hussars*, which employs the puppet device. Turning up on the online version of *ABELL* is "W. M. Thackeray's *The Rose and the Ring* in Poland Betwixt Translation and Adaptation" by another Polish scholar, Monika Adamczyk-Garbowska, contributed to a festschrift published by the Maria Curie Sklowska University Press in Lublin (1997). A Czech translation of selected works of Thackeray, centered at Charles University in Prague, which was described by Lidmila Pantucková some years ago (*SNNT*, Spring-Summer 1981), has, according to latest report, ceased publication.

From this evidence one judges that Thackeray is global.

### "Come children, let us shut up the box and the puppets. . . . "

This being a millenial as well as a decennial retrospect, some kind of coda seems in order. It will have been observed that, as against the legion of Dickensians, much of the scholarship on Thackeray lately has been undertaken by a few devotees. The major advances have been in textual editing and socio-cultural context. Criticism has tended to concentrate on about a dozen titles from Thackeray's vast canon. There is a backlog of unpublished dissertations, but with a perceptible pattern of young scholars deserting Thackeray after publishing an article or two based on their dissertations, it is difficult to project the future of scholarship on him.

A previous report on the University of Michigan Thackeray Edition (*TNL*, May 1998) indicates as volumes under way *The Adventures of Philip*, edited by Judith L. Fisher; *The History of Samuel Titmarsh, The Knights of Borsellen, The Second Funeral of Napoleon,* and *Sultan Stork*, edited by Maura Ives; *Punch's Prize Novelists, The Book of Snobs, English Humourists of the Eighteenth Century,* and *The Four Georges*, edited by Edgar Harden. The uncompleted gem *Denis Duval* would be a fitting capstone to the edition. The three travel books still need annotation and elucidation. There is still the virtually untapped reservoir of short fiction, satire, social commentary, and cultural criticism that D. J. Taylor, Richard Pearson, and Siegbert Prawer argue are mature, not merely apprentice, work. Neither has Thackeray received due recognition as the master that he was of light verse. In the area of the marketplace, Judith L. Fisher's *Thackeray's Narrative Skepticism and the "Perilous Trade" of Authorship* is scheduled for publication by Ashgate in 2002. In a letter to me, the London art dealer William Drummond reports that he hopes to write about Thackeray and his early times on the basis of a collection of more than 100 drawings from Thackeray's days as a struggling artist—a breakthrough much to be anticipated.

In the twenty-first century, it can confidently be affirmed that although Thackeray is no longer grappling at the top of the tree with Dickens, his major status among Victorian novelists is secure—even in our loose canon. The faithful remnant of Thackerayans can be bolstered by the esteem in which he was held by his contemporaries who shared the top rung with him—Dickens, Trollope, George Eliot, and Charlotte Brontë. The last word, however, comes from a lesser fellow novelist, Amelia Edwards. In "From a Past Contemporary: Three Victorian Novelists," in the *Contemporary Review* of August 1994, which reprints Edwards's article "The Art of the Novelist," that had appeared exactly a century before, she wrote: "Dickens depicted his fellow-men as they are not; Trollope presents them as they appear to the world; Thackeray reads them through and through."

## Addenda

The following items came to my attention after my essay went to press:

Dames, Nicholas. "Brushes with Fame: Thackeray and the Work of Celebrity," *NCL* 56 (June 2001), 23–51.

Points out how Thackeray anticipates the mechanism of twentieth-century instant celebrity.

McAuliffe, John. "Taking the Sting out of the Traveller's Tale: Thackeray's *Irish Sketch Book*." *Irish Studies Review* 9 (2001), 25–40.

Stresses that Titmarsh is a "narrative voice" rather than Thackeray speaking for himself, and the *Irish Sketch Book* has a novelistic aspect.

Sorel, Edward and Nancy Caldwell Sorel. "Incident Report. William Makepeace Thackeray and James T. Fields," *Atlantic Monthly* 287 (2001), 87.

Relates to the Boston publisher who invited Thackeray to come to America to lecture, and was among his hosts during his successful tour.

# NOTES

1. "William Makepeace Thackeray," *Victorian Fiction. A Second Guide to Research*. Ed. George H. Ford (New York: Modern Language Association, 1978) 114–42.

2. See in particular the reviews by Catherine Peters, *Times (London) Literary Supplement* 1 Oct. 1999: 12; John Sutherland, *London Review of Books* 20 Jan. 2000: 35–36; Brooke Allen, *The New Criterion* Jan. 2001: 19–28.

3. In this capacity Prawer published a pamphlet, *Thackeray's Goethe: A "Secret History"* in *The Publications of the English Goethe Society* 67 (1992).

4. There is in addition the cryptically titled "How Do I Love Thee? Hmmmm . . . ? The Love Story in *Henry Esmond*" in *Publications of the Arkansas Philological Association Spring 1999.*

5. In compiling this review essay I want to acknowledge the assistance of Vineta Colby; Donald Stone of the English Department of Queens College and the Graduate Center, CUNY; Serge Gleboff of the Slavic and Baltic Division, New York Public Library; and Zhu Hong, who teaches Chinese literature in translation at Boston University.

## ABBREVIATIONS

ABELL.  *Annual Bibliography of English Language and Literature.* English Association.

AUMLA.  *Australia University Modern Language Association Publications.*

CR.  *Contemporary Review.*

CVE.  *Cahiers Victoriens et Edourdiens*

DQ.  *Dickens Quarterly*

DSA.  *Dickens Studies Annual.*

EC.  *Essays in Criticism.*

ECL.  *Eighteenth-Century Life.*

HLQ.  *Huntington Library Quarterly.*

MSA.  *Metaphor and Symbolic Activity.*

NCF.  *Nineteenth-Century Fiction.* (Title later changed to *Nineteenth-Century Literature)*

PLL.  *Papers on Language and Literature.* Southern Illinois University at Edwardsville.

PMLA.  *Publications of the Modern Language Association of America.*

PQ.  *Philological Quarterly.*

TLS.  *Times (London) Literary Supplement.*

TNL.  *Thackeray Newsletter.*

VIJ.  *Victorian Institute Journal.*

VLC.  *Victorian Literature and Culture.*

VPR.  *Victorian Periodicals Review.*

WI.  *Word and Image.*

YES.  *Yearbook of English Studies.*

# Ten Years of Gaskell Criticism

### *Susan Hamilton*

*This essay offers an extended look at the new materials for Gaskell
scholarship, paying particular attention to Gaskell's emergence as the
newest "celebrity author" in Britain's ever-expanding heritage industry. It examines relations between the celebrity author and the object
of literary-critical analysis, with a look at the critical work shaping
Gaskell criticism over the past ten years, particularly the impact of such
feminist engagements with Gaskell as those offered by Hilary Schor and
Deirdre D'Albertis. It also calls for a move away from the preoccupation with Gaskell's canonical status, arguing for the need to reconceptualize such key paths through her work as feminist and material
scholarship if they are to remain productive.*

It is now a critical commonplace in Gaskell scholarship to note the deep
divisons, amounting almost to chasms, that have long characterized Gaskell's
critical reception. Those divisions separated Gaskell the "social problem"
novelist from Gaskell the gentle novelist of the small concerns of middle-
class domestic life, and are now routinely understood to be, at the very least,
resolutely old-fashioned. Increasingly too, those divisions are more explicitly
approached as the very stuff of what makes Gaskell a compelling figure for
critical analysis. Victorian ideology of separate spheres no longer overtly
demands the separation of the engaged social commentator from the sympathetic domestic storyteller, if indeed it ever did. But, though Gaskell is no
longer subject to Lord David Cecil-like affection for her feminine sensibility,

*Dickens Studies Annual,* Volume 31, Copyright © 2002 by AMS Press, Inc. All
rights reserved.

a look at the past ten years in Gaskell criticism suggests that we are still grappling with the inheritance of a tradition that saw her work as formally and aesthetically incoherent and ideologically overdetermined. The past ten years have seen an important shift towards seeing such inconsistencies as the traces of larger cultural processes, but Gaskell scholarship *as a discrete field* is as variable, wide-ranging, and bitty as ever. What has changed dramatically is the sheer size of the field. There is a boom in the Gaskell industry, fuelled largely by the Gaskell Society whose journal and website have substantially reshaped how we see Gaskell as a figure for study.

I have divided this essay into three sections. I begin with an extended look at the new materials for Gaskell scholarship made available over the past ten years, including new editions of the novels, biographies, letters, and the appearance of Gaskell in cyberspace. These new materials point to the different ways in which Gaskell has been canonized, both as a literary author and as a valuable new product in England's ever expanding heritage industry. They also indicate a compelling conundrum. Gaskell's canonization has not been a formal or aesthetic one. Rather, it is remarkably personality-based. Where Gaskell's literary output has long raised critical questions of categorization, labelling, and perhaps of worth, for academic readers, her emerging status as a twenty-first century ''celebrity'' author, complete with a BBC production of *Wives and Daughters* and a central place in Cheshire's tourism industry, suggests that the ambivalence and equivocation that has too long dogged her critical reception does not shape her ''public,'' non-academic reputation. The second section of this essay discusses this new infrastructure for Gaskell scholarship. The relations between the celebrity author and the object of literary-critical analysis is followed, in the third section, by a look at some of the critical work shaping Gaskell criticism over the past ten years. This examination is necessarily selective, though I have focussed on work that seems to me to be most valuable, offering fresh looks at Gaskell's texts, and suggesting new avenues for future investigation.

The change in Gaskell's stature as a Victorian novelist is best seen in the massive expansion in the paperback market for her work. The past decade has seen an almost complete refashioning of the materials for scholarship and teaching in the form of new editions of many of Gaskell's texts. Writing in the *Gaskell Society Journal*, Shirley Foster notes that ''[I]f publishers are the ultimate determinants of a writer's status, now Gaskell has truly been 'canonised' along with George Eliot, Dickens and the Brontës, whose works were previously prioritized over hers by the major publishing houses''(*GSJ* 14 2000). Four paperback editions of *North and South, Cranford,* and *Mary*

*Barton*, and three new editions of *The Life of Charlotte Brontë*, indicate the increase in Gaskell paperback production. Foster usefully compares Penguin, Everyman, and Oxford World Classics editions in her article. Though I will not reproduce her substantial analysis here, I will draw attention to her discussion of the new Penguin editions that have appeared. These editions of *Mary Barton* (edited by Macdonald Daly), *North and South* (edited by Patricia Ingham), *Ruth* (edited by Angus Easson), *Sylvia's Lovers* (edited by Shirley Foster), *The Life of Charlotte Brontë* (edited by Elizabeth Jay), and *Wives and Daughters* (edited by Pam Morris) are part of a larger Penguin marketing strategy intended to increase academic and non-academic readership. They offer new introductions, ranging from the aggressively theoretical to the more traditional take on contextual information for reading. A planned new edition, *Gothic Tales* (edited by Laura Kranzler, to appear in 2001) suggests that the paperback market is also awakening to the value of Gaskell's shorter texts.

Everyman too has issued new, annotated editions of *Mary Barton* (edited by Alan Shelston), *North and South* (edited by Jenny Uglow, with notes by Graham Handley), *Life of Charlotte Brontë* (introduced by Jenny Uglow with additional materials by Graham Handley), and *Cranford and Mr Harrison's Confessions* (edited by Graham Handley). All include a new section on "Elizabeth Gaskell and her Critics," offering critical reviews of the specific work from the Victorian period to the present. Oxford World Classics has also put out new editions or reissues of *Cranford* (edited by Elizabeth Porges Watson), *Mary Barton* (edited by Edgar Wright), *The Life of Charlotte Brontë* (edited by Angus Easson, to appear in 2001), and *North and South* (edited by Easson and introduced by Sally Shuttleworth). Unfortunately, much of what was a nearly comprehensive World Classics list of Gaskell's short stories are now out of print, including *The Moorland Cottage and Other Stories*, *My Lady Ludlow and Other Stories*, *A Dark Night's Work*, *Lois the Witch*, and *The Manchester Marriage*—all of which are available only in expensive, library-bound editions from Classic Books.

Much of the gap in publishing Gaskell's short stories has been taken up by electronic publishing, notably in the nearly complete, if somewhat editorially uneven, e-text collection produced by Mitsuharu Matsuoka, webmaster of The Gaskell Web. Matsuoka's impressively large e-text archive includes all of the expected novels, the Brontë biography, *Cousin Phillis*, *The Moorland Cottage*, *My Lady Ludlow*, *A Dark Night's Work*, and forty-five short stories. The e-texts are presented with a minimum of editorial fuss, with the briefest of bibliographical information provided. A title here and there is linked with a relevant article in the *Gaskell Society Journal*. Other stories are contextualized with a note from Uglow's biography or reproduce A. W. Ward's notes from the 1906 Knutsford edition of her works. Still other e-texts of the short stories include reproductions of paintings, some of the George Du Maurier sketches that accompanied original publication, or amateur photographs of such story settings as Sawley, Pendle Hill, and the well of Pen Morfa. The Gaskell e-text archive shares many of the benefits of such collections, making difficult-to-access material readily available. But it does not escape all of the disadvantages endemic to electronic publishing. Material is presented in a very stripped down context or is erratically ornamented with photographs, drawings, and notes. Reading a relatively short story from the screen, or producing a hardcopy for reading, makes sense when so many of the stories are hard to access. But the advantages of electronic publication for the novel reader is harder to gauge when the e-text edition offers no new editorial content. Clearly, the varying editorial content is as much a consequence of the calls on Professor Matsuoka's time as it a question of the availability of materials. The labor required to produce an electronic archive such as this is prodigious, and the no-frills product is a welcome complement to the print editions of Gaskell's work.

To underscore the degree to which this once "minor" writer has been conferred with solidly "major" status in the publishing leagues, the deluge of material addressing the Gaskell reader, whose desires are as biographical as they are critical, is truly phenomenal. Having long relied on Chapple and Pollard's authoritative 1966 edition of the letters, we now can turn gratefully to the reissue of Chapple and Pollard's *The Letters of Mrs Gaskell* (Mandolin Press, 1997). The paperback reissue of this invaluable resource is particularly joyful for all those many readers who, unable to find secondhand copies of their own, were obliged to read Gaskell's wonderfully chatty, hilarious, clever letters in library copy, deprived of that truly intimate contact that only book ownership can confer. Gaskell would certainly sympathize with the impulse, rejoicing "it is a pleasure to me to have what I like so earnestly of *my own*"(*Letters*, nos. 73, 130) when she acquired her copy of Tennyson's *In Memoriam*. Enriching our understanding of the complexity of Gaskell's life—her writing, familial, personal, and professional concerns—are Jenny Uglow's compelling *Elizabeth Gaskell: A Habit of Stories* (Faber and Faber, 1993), John Chapple's biographical study, *Elizabeth Gaskell: The Early Years* (Manchester UP, 1997), Chapple and Anita Wilson's *Private Voices: The Diaries of Elizabeth Cleghorn Gaskell and Sophia Isaac Holland* (Keele UP, 1996), Anna Unsworth's *Elizabeth Gaskell: An Independent Woman* (Minerva

Press, 1996), and most recently Chapple and Alan Shelstone's *Further Letters of Mrs Gaskell* (Manchester UP, 2001). Felicia Bonaparte's *The Gypsy-Bachelor of Manchester: The Life of Mrs. Gaskell's Demon* (UP of Virginia, 1992) offers a decidedly untraditional biography, reading the entirety of Gaskell's textual output as "one continuous metaphoric text"(10) that can reveal the "inner" Gaskell who was always in conflict with the outer, respectable Mrs. Gaskell. Bonaparte reads textual imagery as ways in which Gaskell "could tell the world those truths she wanted not to know herself "(11).

Further evidence of the substantial increase in scholarly activity around Gaskell is the publication of a crucial new bibliographical work, Nancy Weyant's *Elizabeth Gaskell: An Annotated Bibliography of English-Language Sources, 1976–1991* (Scarecrow P, 1994). Listing 339 sources including 28 masters theses and senior honors theses, Weyant's bibliography supplements Robert L. Selig's *Elizabeth Gaskell: A Reference Guide* (G.K. Hall, 1977) and Jeffrey Egan Welch's *Elizabeth Gaskell: An Annotated Bibliography, 1929–1975* (Garland, 1977), and is the first Gaskell bibliography to make use of such computer database developments in bibliographic studies as OCLC and RLIN, as well as traditional resources such as *Humanities Index, Women's Studies Abstracts, Comprehensive Bibliography of Victorian Studies*, etc. Weyant's bibliography excludes book reviews, and she has developed a "quantitative criterion" in her selection process, which excludes all sources that mention Gaskell merely in passing or which offer only a short, two- or three-page consideration of her work. Noting that Welch's bibliography, which spanned forty-six years, identified 237 secondary sources and 78 primary works, Weyant points to the larger number of publications and dissertations identified in her bibliography despite its shorter, fifteen-year time span. Weyant plans a follow-up Gaskell bibliography with Scarecrow Press that will bring the annotated bibliography of English-language sources up to the end of 2000.

Connected to this vast outpouring of interest in Gaskell's life is a phenomenon that is both scholarly resource and celebrity cult. The Gaskell Society was formed from a literary lunch celebrating the 175th anniversary of Elizabeth Gaskell's birth in September 1985. Based in Knutsford, with branches in the United States, Italy, and Japan, the Gaskell Society produces an annual scholarly journal, the *Gaskell Society Journal*, and a newsletter with information on meetings, visits to places associated with Gaskell and her fiction, and an annual conference. Offering the inevitable (if often convenient) links to commercial book and video sellers, along with the tourist information site of

Knutsford, the Gaskell Society site embodies the spirit of celebration of Gaskell's life that has been the engine of the booming publishing and televison interest in this author. It also underscores the link between commercialization and canonization in Gaskell's move into the cultural high stakes league, in much the same way that the number of hits in an MLA web search lets us know something of the volume of critical activity, and so the critical cachet, of a figure like Gaskell. Though author-ranking is less and less an integral element of academic engagements with writers like Gaskell, the Gaskell Society, its journal, and its web page, speak to the vital role that such ranking plays in both non-academic and commercial circles. The Gaskell of cyberspace is a first-rate, sparkling personality available for downloading. Her status as a personable, canonical author grows increasingly more secure.

What is also important to note here is the considerable role that the Society has played in facilitating Gaskell scholarship, on the Net as well as in paper. The *Gaskell Society Journal*, a good portion of which is now available online, published nearly one-half of all articles on Gaskell put out in the last ten years. The articles themselves tend, overall, to be methodologically conservative or traditional. In the journal's early days, it relied for its critical heft on the contributions of scholars, like Chapple, Easson and Shelston, whose work as a whole focussed on Gaskell's life or was strongly associated with the editing of Gaskell's novels and the production of her letters. Among the many recent articles worth noting are Terry Wyke's thoroughly researched "The Culture of Self Improvement: Real People in *Mary Barton*"(*GSJ* 13 1999), which offers a fascinating introduction to the many working-class botanists, singers, and "self-improvers" that dot Gaskell's first novel, and Patsy Stoneman's "*Wives and Daughters* on Television," (*GSJ* 14: 2000) on Andrew Davies's adaptation of the novel, exploring what she contends are largely unexamined notions of "faithfulness" in English reviewers' responses to the program. It is an article that particularly suits its cyberspace venue, examining as it does the interplay between the media forms of popular culture, the product that is the "historical drama," and the material text that launches it. The journal can have the somewhat chatty tone of its newsletter forerunner, especially in its "Notes" and "Reports" section where discussions of the Gaskell listserve are equally at home with updates on Gaskell's letters. But there can be no dispute that the Society is singularly responsible for raising Gaskell's profile in both academic and non-academic reading circles.

Writing ten years ago, Hilary Schor noted the general unwillingness in Gaskell scholarship "to look for the *un*conventional ending, or what D.A.

Miller has called the "discontents of narrative" (350). Identifying this unwillingness as a pervasive tendency in Gaskell criticism, Schor ended her critical history with a call "to think more deeply about [Gaskell's] patterns of reading, references to contemporary writers, her responses to the literary marketplace, [and] the dense questions of intertextuality that have gone unexplored" (361). Schor calls to put Gaskell on the map in a way that is informed by interdisciplinary, cultural studies approaches to Victorian material. In many ways, Gaskell scholarship over the past ten years is still in the process of responding to many of Schor's calls, though important studies, including one by Schor herself, go some way to answering them. But, in contrast to the moves in publishing and internet circles, much of the most innovative and provocative academic work on Gaskell does not set out to deal comprehensively with Gaskell's writing in the way that Schor's essay imagined, but picks and chooses those elements in Gaskell's work that prove compelling to broader concerns.

Feminist and a newly revitalized materialist criticism in the 1970s and 1980s found Gaskell *in her entirety* a politically and ideologically compelling figure for criticism that had moved resolutely away from a narrowly formalist practice, which had solidified Gaskell's minor status on the basis of perceived ideological ambivalence and aesthetic disarray. Much of the critical energy behind that '70s and '80s criticism has now moved into a cultural studies/ materialist critical practice that turns to Gaskell for the very ambivalences that once banished her from the great formalist canon. The result is a field of critical enquiry in which authors *as authors* often do not attract sustained critical interest. When read, Gaskell is often but one corner of a larger field of enquiry. Important studies like Christine L. Krueger's *The Reader's Repentance: Women Preachers, Women Writers, and Nineteenth-Century Social Discourse* (U of Chicago P, 1992), which offers a substantial reading of Gaskell's work, Amanda Anderson's *Tainted Souls and Painted Faces: The Rhetoric of Fallenness in Victorian Culture* (Cornell UP, 1993), which treats *Mary Barton* and *Ruth*, Elsie B. Michie's *Outside the Pale: Cultural Exclusion, Gender Difference and the Victorian Woman Writer* (Cornell UP, 1995), Mary Poovey's *Making a Social Body: British Cultural Formation, 1830–1864* (U of Chicago P, 1995) and Elizabeth Langland's *Nobody's Angels: Middle-class Women and Domestic Ideology in Victorian Culture* (Cornell UP, 1995) are among the studies that take up Gaskell's work in relation to the larger critical project of their texts.

Articles by Tim Dolin, Andrew H. Miller, Christine L. Krueger, among others, similarly find in selected Gaskell texts the materials to launch broader

404 DICKENS STUDIES ANNUAL

critical projects. Tim Dolin's elegantly written, *"Cranford* and the Victorian Collection,'' explores the gendering of the Victorian collection—comprising definitions, descriptions, and categories of things. Taking as his starting point the formal looseness of Gaskell's novella, Dolin finds in the full range of Victorian collecting—from public museums, scientific exhibitions and market halls to miscellanies, bric-a-brac, and the jumble of overstuffed interiors—a lens by which to refocus discussions of the novel's structural play. At a time when women could not, he argues, constitute their own stories, and when women's collections were ''virtually invisible as a cultural pursuit because . . . considered meaningful only within the home''(188), *Cranford* embodies a ''fantasy of the social and political empowerment of women alone and . . . is at the same time a caricature of (comfortable middle-class female) everyday life in Victorian England, devoted to the filling-in of time''(195). Dolin's text reaches out to Victorian genre painting and the Great Exhibition, to ''relationships between men and the imperative of classification and history, narrative order and development''(202), to rest finally on the ways in which *Cranford* ''highlights the complex negotiations throughout Victorian fiction between private enclosures and public realms, domestic and public spaces''(203). Though the conclusion returns to many themes common to Gaskell criticism, the route taken to those conclusions suggests the ways in which *Cranford* signifies differently when approached as an instance of a larger cultural phenomenon rather than conceived as one element in an author's output.

Andrew H. Miller's ''Subjectivity Ltd: The Discourse of Liability in the Joint Stock Companies Act of 1856 and Gaskell's *Cranford*,'' similarly approaches Gaskell's novella as a gateway to a broader cultural concern. In a superb essay, Miller argues that Gaskell's representation of women in *Cranford* ''permits us to extend our consideration of the implications of the discourse of liability''(141). Offering a lucid, succinct history of the emergence of limited liability and the remapping of notions of moral versus economic liability across increasingly distinct public and private spheres, Miller turns to *Cranford* as a text recording the two dominant ethical attitudes, and the effects on structures of subjectivity, in the ''discourse of liability.'' The essay is a tour de force, skillfully blending analysis of the dense historical documents with a reading of the text as an inscription of shifts in Victorian subjectivities.

Christine L. Krueger's trilogy of articles on Gaskell takes as its starting point the problem of women's authority within a post-structuralist view of history that seemingly denies the possibility of agency. If Victorian women needed to disrupt histories offered by their culture's dominant discourses, to weaken the patriarch plots that defined their lives, they needed also to retain the authority to offer a "counter-representation" of women's history. Reading Gaskell's Lady Ludlow as a female paternalist, Kruger argues that it is through such figures that Gaskell explored the power of privileged women within a patriarchal culture while also examining the contradictions to patriarchal ideology such figures represented. Krueger's " 'Speaking Like a Woman': How to Have the Last Word on *Sylvia's Lovers*" is particularly evocative, reading the novel as seeking to critique dominant ideologies at the same time as it strives to represent women's histories in a coherent and politically meaningful way. Krueger locates the novel, written just after the *Life of Charlotte Brontë*, at a key juncture in Gaskell's career, one that has been seen as a radicalizing moment in Gaskell's life, both aesthetically and politically. Krueger approaches the novel as profoundly despairing over women writers's ability to represent women when "the very conventions governing historical writing served to silence and discipline them"(139). Krueger's analysis does not always root itself firmly enough in the materials of women's history writing of this period, with brief allusions to Caroline Norton having to bear a significant interpretative burden. But the attention to Gaskell's novel is consistently thoughtful and attuned to the ways in which it serves as her "wrongs of woman" novel.

Of the many excellent articles published on Gaskell in the last ten years, several indicate dominant patterns in the scholarship or have had a substantial impact on shaping the kinds of questions that get asked about Gaskell. Earlier feminist engagement with Gaskell has produced a second generation of feminist readings of her work intent on refining and extending the questions of gender (though rarely of sexuality) brought to Gaskell's texts. John Kucich's "Transgression and Sexual Difference in Elizabeth Gaskell's Novels" in many ways marked the beginning of an approach to Gaskell's work that sought to complicate the recent insights of feminist criticism. Kucich argues that gender analysis of Gaskell, focussing on sexual conflict in her work, has obscured the ways in which her system of sexual difference is itself a site of ideological cooperation, and further argues that this system of difference shapes and limits Gaskell's imagining of challenges to, and transgressions against, middle-class ideology more largely. In order to examine the ideological uses of her sexual system, Kucich turns to instances of "sexual disorder" in Gaskell, noting her "frequent inversion of her protagonists' sexual identity"(188). Where such inversions have too simplistically been seen as challenges to patriarchy and read as forms of sexual liberalization, Kucich insists that such sexual liberalizations repeat the Victorian cult of domesticity. His examples of sexual disorder in Gaskell's fiction, most notably *Cranford*, perform different work than the "softening" of a Mr. Thornton or a "strengthening" of a Mary Barton has been argued to do in much feminist criticism. For Kucich, they operate as signs of abnormality, not forms of sexual liberation. Drawing on Nancy Armstrong's work in *Desire and Domestic Fiction*, Kucich argues that the "fundamental project of [Gaskell's] novels is to clarify middle-class consciousness by correctly dividing ethical transgression along sexual lines"(196). Though Kucich does not question the heteronormative structure of sexual disorder, his article asks feminist criticism to extend its celebratory recuperative work and complicate its readings of gender in Gaskell's work, a request answered by later critics like D'Albertis.

In a different approach to the question of feminist canon building, of texts and critical concepts, an early essay by Deanna L. Davis, "Feminist Critics and Literary Mothers: Daughters Reading Elizabeth Gaskell," queries the terms by which Gaskell has been ambivalently located in a feminist canon concerned, not with aesthetic uneveness or class ambivalences, but with a search for a "female tradition." Using Harold Bloom's concept of the anxiety of influence and Chodorow's work on the reproduction of mothering, Davis argues that Gaskell is an uncomfortable figure for feminist criticism: "Women writers whose lives illustrate the limitations of being a woman are much too close in spirit to a restricting mother to be embraced"(514). For Davis, Gaskell's work is important as a site through which feminists now can begin rethinking the balance between self-care and self-sacrifice in women's lives, particularly their lives as mothers. Davis explores Gaskell's "distinction between biological and social mothering"(528), though claiming her as a "literary mother and as a creator of mothering heroines"(531). Her reading of Gaskell does not mythologize the author, asking us to see her as a figure who does not fundamentally challenge nineteenth-century cultural expectations of women, and yet in whose heroines—so often in the process of psychological breakdown at the same time as they open up fields of action—we can read the cost of both stasis and change.

Audrey Jaffe's "Under Cover of Sympathy: *Ressentiment* in Gaskell's *Ruth*," points to a gap in Kucich's argument about transgression in its exploration of sympathy for the transgressive in Gaskell's work. Jaffe's key revision is to posit that sympathy for the "fallen," far from expressing fear of contamination, acknowledges "the marginality those with limited social power perceive in themselves"(58). Starting with an overview of the critical reception of sympathy in Gaskell, Jaffe explores the change in our under-standing of the ideological work of sympathy when our critical attention shifts away from the figure of Ruth towards Benson. Jaffe argues that emphasis on identity as a gendered category in Gaskell's work has obscured attention to the novel's uneasy awareness of middle-class identity as constructed rather than natural. Expanding our reading of identity in *Ruth*, Jaffe argues that sympathy is "a way of expressing feelings about, and gaining distance from, an unstable social position"(58). The essay offers a concise, economical reading that usefully brings class and gender together.

Dorice Williams Elliott's "The Female Visitor and the Marriage of Classes in Gaskell's *North and South*" addresses an oversight in the critical literature on Gaskell's second industrial novel, locating *North and South* within nine-teenth-century debates on female visitors to the poor. Within this framework, Elliott argues that the cultural work of the novel, particularly aspects of its structure that have been deemed troubling like the happy ending, is to provide a new model of social relations that is neither rural paternalism nor based on the industrial cash-nexus. Elliott extends Bodenheimer, Schor, and Gallagh-er's earlier work, suggesting that the debates on female visiting are a crucial context for assessing the novel's reconstruction of women's plots. Elliott's careful reading, particularly of the specific kind of challenge that Margaret's visits to the industrial poor and her concern to learn working-class speech represent, is most persuasive. This is an essay that claims Gaskell as an innovator who challenges Victorian social codes and structures. As such, it reveals the degree to which even those articles that seek to move past concerns with Gaskell's status, to a critical engagement with what her novels can tell us about Victorian culture, participate in the ongoing tussle to categorize Gaskell politically, a tussle in which she is endlessly remade as a now conser-vative, now progressive, writer on class and gender.

The substantial number of single-author studies produced in the past decade speaks to the continuing role that feminist criticism plays in enlivening Gas-kell studies. Gaskell has benefitted from the recuperative, and enduring, spirit of an earlier feminist critical practice that aims to grapple with Gaskell in her entirety. These new studies, among them Terence Wright's *We Are Not Angels* (Macmillan, 1995), Kate Flint's *Elizabeth Gaskell* (1995) in Northcote House's "Writers and Their Work" series, Jane Spencer's *Elizabeth Gaskell* (Macmillan, 1993), Linda K. Hughes and Michael Lund's *Victorian Publish-ing and Mrs. Gaskell's Work* (UP of Virginia, 1999) and most notably Hilary Schor's *Scheherezade in the Marketplace: Elizabeth Gaskell and the Victorian Novel* (Oxford UP, 1992) and Deirdre D'Albertis's *Dissembling Fictions:*

*Elizabeth Gaskell and the Victorian Social Text* (St. Martin, 1997), offer valuable reinterpretations of Gaskell, reshaping our reading of her work and her place in Victorian culture in important new ways. In all of these studies, gender is the central category of analysis, reaffirming the degree to which interest in Gaskell as an author is very much a feminist concern.

The Mrs. Gaskell at the center of Hughes and Lund's study is a familiar enough figure in Gaskell scholarship now, someone who subverts and bridges, whose work is formally innovative yet still readable through recognized forms. In an accessible and leisurely exploration of Gaskell's novels and biography, Hughes and Lund argue that Gaskell's knowledge of book production, the business of publication, and the nature of reception, allowed her to see the "unclaimed spaces in the literary industry" and occupy them. The book is divided into five chapters, each considering a particular aspect of Gaskell's relation to the publishing industry, broadly defined. The first, on *Wives and Daughters,* reads that last incomplete text for what it can tell us about Gaskell's cultural authority. In many ways, the argument's conclusions are not new; Gaskell is seen to acquire cultural standing by "abnegating claims to authority or appearing to submit to the conventions of feminine domesticity"(18). What is distinctive is Hughes and Lund's reading of the serial form of the novel as a site for inscribing the value of slow steady change and representing the female body. The other chapters are similarly organized around questions of the publishing formats Gaskell used in her writing, connecting these formats to the kinds of opportunities they represent for Gaskell and so to the larger cultural work of her texts. Hughes and Lund argue, for example, that the fallen woman in Gaskell's work functions differently in the different publishing formats she used in writing about this figure. In the boldest chapter of the book, on *North and South*, the very real contribution that Hughes and Lund's distinctive emphasis on serial format can make to Gaskell scholarship is most satisfyingly fulfilled. Tackling the traditional reading of *North and South* as a failure in serial-part publication, Hughes and Lund argue that Gaskell's "conception of the nature of a single part and the relationship of successive parts departed from a standard that Dickens had established"(97). The authors show that interpretations of Dickens's "success" and Gaskell's "failure" are shaped by gender, demonstrating that masculinist concepts of plot have overly determined our understanding of the serial form. Occasionally, and most overtly in this chapter, Hughes and Lund's book seems enmeshed in biological conceptions of gender that mar the readings they offer in an otherwise consistently elegant, materially rich study. Is it really still possible to argue that "the serial novel's intrinsic form more closely approximates female than male models of pleasure''(99), embodying not tumescence and detumescence, but incipience, repetition and closure? The implication of Hughes and Lund's model is that Gaskell's "failure" in *North and South* can be recuperated only in a period (our own presumably) when a female model of textual pleasure is celebrated. The conceptual conflict between a materialist study of serial part publication and an ahistorical analysis of gender and sexuality threatens to topple the contribution to Gaskell scholarship that attention to the publishing history of the texts offers.

Schor's *Scheherezade in the Marketplace* is the single most important contribution to Gaskell scholarhip in the past decade. One indicator of its influence is that many of its critical readings of Gaskell's work now so thoroughly suffuse Gaskell criticism that it is occasionally difficult to do justice to its originality eight years after its publication. Building on the key feminist rereadings of Gaskell that appeared in the 1980s, Schor takes as her primary focus "the specific struggle of the woman writer with the literary plots she has inherited, and the forces of the marketplace she must confront; . . . with the ways in which Scheherezade may have had to reimagine her own career''(4). Schor's beginning assumptions are crucial: "that Gaskell was intensely interested in publication and in acquiring a public voice, and that her attempt to write the fiction of those denied a voice within Victorian society led her to an awareness of her own silencing''(5). The experiments with literary form that characterize Gaskell's oeuvre are read, in Schor's work, as ways in which the author examined the central stories of her own culture, particularly those stories that inscribed women as silent others. Grappling with some of the assessments or presumptions that have tended to domesticate and marginalize Gaskell's work, Schor argues that Gaskell "came to her most radical challenges to the conventions of literary plotting"(5) in her attempts to rewrite the conventions of a woman's story. Schor's book is divided into three sections, all of which concentrate on Gaskell's novels rather than the short stories or the Brontë biography. The first section on *Mary Barton* and *Ruth* sees these novels as the products of Gaskell's literary apprenticeship, particularly her coming to terms with the romantic inheritance of Wordsworth. The second section deals with the problem of publishing and the marketplace, particularly the influence of Dickens on Gaskell. The third section focusses on more formal concerns, the problem of closure and narrative relativism, connecting these to Gaskell's growing awareness of women novelists and the cultural force of Darwin and others. Each of the three sections brings together discussions on Gaskell's experimentation with the conventions of narrative, the real conditions of Gaskell's publishing, and the range of authorial questions that concerned her in their writing.

What is attractive about Schor's work is her sense of participation in a dialogue about Gaskell. She approaches her study as a contribution to an ongoing academic community discussion, building on work that has gone before. The study is strongly indebted methodologically to, and richly extends, the important work of Rosemarie Bodenheimer in the *The Politics of Story* and Catherine Gallagher in *The Industrial Reformation of English Fiction*. In Schor's strongest set of readings, she traces Gaskell's coming to authorship through the experience of writing about the powerlessness of the workers in *Mary Barton*, complicating the now familiar reading of that text as one which forwards a critique of language and received plots through her careful attention to the letters Gaskell wrote around its publication. Noting the gap between Gaskell's reluctance to be known as author of the novel and her skillful actions as an author wanting to be published successfully, Schor argues that Gaskell is ''an author intensely interested with questions of literary authority''(26), particularly maternal authority. Here Schor is careful to historicize what has been a common psychoanalytic move in feminist theory, that sees in maternal language a power to disrupt phallocentric authority and generate challenging textual disruptions to form, in order to claim a specifically political authority to Gaskell's maternal watching over. ''More than a maternal, slippery language,'' she argues, '' . . . Gaskell describes something like a maternal plot: an alternate structure of power, an alternate family, an alternate England''(34) .

Like Schor's, Deirdre D'Albertis's *Dissembling Fictions* starts with an assertion that Gaskell sought publicity, a public voice. Her book reads against those feminist recuperations of Gaskell that, in D'Albertis's view, overemphasize female community and maternal self-sacrifice in Gaskell's work. Like Schor, D'Albertis reads for the fissures in Gaskell's plots, exploring the ''unremarked upon 'Other' Gaskell as a necessary . . . complement to the seraphic portrait of a novelist as guileless, ignorant and unself-aware''(12). D'Albertis starts from a conventional enough place in Gaskell criticism, the lack of integration of political and domestic plots that had long been thought to mar her work, and reads that incoherence as traces of a larger instability in Victorian social discourse. Using the work of critics like Deborah Epstein Nord on the Victorian street, John Kucich on transgression in Victorian fiction, Schor and Gallagher, D'Albertis offers rich, gripping interpretations of many of Gaskell's key texts. Her work on Gaskell's Brontë biography (which also appeared as an important article in *Victorian Studies*) and *Sylvia's*

*Lovers* strikes me as particularly powerful. Though D'Albertis has a tendency to overstate the newness of her approach and to overwrite her points, her readings are richly evocative, often galvanizing, offering her readers a judicious balance between useful synopses of the larger social discourses she sees framing Gaskell's works and sharp, smart, up-close analysis of specific elements of those texts. Her last chapter on Gaskell and feminist historiography tackles what she sees as the central "myths" in feminist literary historiography, particularly the myth of the happy family and the importance of the mother in feminist canon building. But it also exposes D'Albertis's investment in being a critical maverick, and the shaky ground that such an investment can lead her to occupy. D'Albertis point in her last chapter is "not to discredit categories of analysis dependent upon the family as a system, but rather to question the exclusivity and the narrowness of those categories as they have been constructed and applied to Gaskell."(176) She urges the introduction of a "dynamic of conflict" into our picture of Gaskell, and an embrace of conflict in feminist historiography itself. Here, D'Albertis's penchant for forceful position-taking leads her to misrepresent the critical investments of feminist historiography and theory more generally, a field that is consciously grappling with its central terms of reference. Though I would agree that Gaskell criticism has been slow to take up the recent challenges of feminist theory, and indeed that feminist *literary* historiography could be better informed by debates in feminist historiography on agency and subjectivity, any reading of recent feminist theory on race, nation, and sexuality indicates that conflict is the often exhilarating modus operandi of most participants in this field. To suggest otherwise is to contort the field in the name of inflating one's own critical position with more newness than may be the case.

Taken together, Schor's and D'Albertis's books are important revisions of Gaskell and her place in Victorian culture, and point to new directions for critical engagement with this author. Their work is particularly important for the ways in which it takes up the question of "personality" through a careful study of Gaskell's relation to publicity. These works reconceptualize what it means for an author to be a celebrity in such a way as not to feed Gaskell's "celebrity" status now, but to produce analyses of her work that encourage us to think Gaskell through differently. As we know, Gaskell was much lionized in her day; a study exploring the relation between the Victorian machinery of literary celebrity and Gaskell's attempts to shape a public voice for herself would yield valuable insights. Gaskell's short stories, in particular, need to be considered alongside of her negotiations of the literary marketplace, the construction of her literary authority, and the kinds of formal and aesthetic questions they raise.

The past ten years have shown conclusively that feminist criticism has a strong hold on Gaskell, and is almost singularly responsible for her increased visibility in Victorian studies. As feminist criticism of her work shifts past its focus on gender identity and politics within a heteronormative framework, moving into the area of sexuality and queer studies, its claims on Gaskell will enrichen. Materialist criticism of her work, too, has grown beyond a somewhat narrow attention to class relations in the social problem novel to include considerations of publishing format and some work on Gaskell's engagement with social movements of her day, including the nascent feminist movement. Further consideration of Gaskell that brings together this scholarship with the new work on social movements, on nation and state, would be a welcome addition.

In the "Epilogue" to their study, Hughes and Lund quote Anne Thackeray Ritchie's preface to an 1891 edition of *Cranford*: "It remains for readers of this later time to see how nobly she held her own among the masters of her craft"(164). The criticism of the last decade has often shared Ritchie's concerns. But it also highlights which roads have been too well travelled in Gaskell criticism, and the need to reconceptualize key paths through her work if they are to remain productive. Years of Gaskell criticism demonstrate beyond any question that many past assessments are as important now, not for what they can tell us about Gaskell and Victorian culture, but as valuable documents in the history of literary critical practice. The constant reconsideration of Gaskell's status, begun in 1865 by those who wrote her obituaries and reviewed her literary career, now threatens to bog down criticism of this vital figure in a repetitious return to past literary historical debates. Too much of recent Gaskell criticism frames its entry through these terms, impeding its movement towards new frameworks for discussion. Schor gestured towards some of those frameworks ten years ago, and it is telling of the degree to which questions of canonicity have shaped Gaskell research that so many of them remain to be taken up, despite their heightened visibility in Victorian studies overall. There is still much room to maneuver in Gaskell studies, opportunity for reshaping her relevance for us today. And that is, perhaps, what is finally of most importance.

# WORKS CITED

Anderson, Amanda. *Tainted Souls and Painted Faces: The Rhetoric of Fallenness in Victorian Culture*. Ithaca, NY: Cornell UP, 1993.

Bonaparte, Felicia. *The Gypsy-Bachelor of Manchester: The Life of Mrs. Gaskell's Demon.* Charlottesville: UP of Virginia, 1992.

Chapple, John and Alan Shelstone. *Further Letters of Mrs Gaskell.* Manchester: Manchester UP, 2001.

Chapple, John and Arthur Pollard. *The Letters of Mrs Gaskell.* Manchester: Mandolin Press, 1997.

Chapple, John. *Elizabeth Gaskell: The Early Years.* Manchester: Manchester UP, 1997.

Chapple, John and Anita Wilson. *Private Voices: The Diaries of Elizabeth Cleghorn Gaskell and Sophia Isaac Holland.* Keele: Keele UP, 1996.

D'Albertis, Deirdre. " 'Bookmaking Out of the Remains of the Dead': Elizabeth Gaskell's *The Life of Charlotte Bronte.*" *Victorian Studies* 39.1 (1995): 1–31.

———. *Dissembling Fictions: Elizabeth Gaskell and the Victorian Social Text.* New York: St. Martin's, 1997.

Davis, Deanna L. "Feminist Critics and Literary Mothers: Daughters Reading Elizabeth Gaskell." *Signs* 17.3 (1992): 507–32.

Dolin, Tim. "*Cranford* and the Victorian Collection." *Victorian Studies* 36.2 (1993): 179–206.

Elliott, Dorice Williams. "The Female Visitor and the Marriage of Classes in Gaskell's *North and South.*" *Nineteenth Century Literature* 49 (1994): 21–49.

Flint, Kate. *Elizabeth Gaskell.* Plymouth, UK: Northcote , 1995.

Foster, Shirley. "Gaskell in Paperback." *Gaskell Society Journal* 11 (1997). www.lang.nagoya-u.ac.jp/'matsuoka/EG-Journal.html

Hughes, Linda K. and Michael Lund. *Victorian Publishing and Mrs. Gaskell's Work.* Charlottesville: UP of Virginia, 1999.

Jaffe, Audre. "Under Cover of Sympathy: *Ressentiment* in Gaskell's *Ruth.*" *Victorian Literature and Culture* (1993): 51–65.

Krueger, Christine L. *The Reader's Repentance: Women Preachers, Women Writers, and Nineteenth-Century Social Discourse.* Chicago: U of Chicago P, 1992.

———. " 'Speaking Like a Woman': How to Have the Last Word on *Sylvia's Lovers.*" In *Famous Last Words: Changes in Gender and Narrative Closure.* Ed. Alison Booth. Charlottesville: UP of Virginia, 1993. 135–53.

———. "The 'female paternalist' as historian: Elizabeth Gaskell's *My Lady Ludlow.*" In *Rewriting the Victorians: Theory, History and the Politics of Gender.* Ed. Linda Shires. London: Routledge, 1992. 166–83.

————. "Witnessing Women: Trial Testimony in Novels by Tonna, Gaskell and Eliot." In *Representing Women: Law, Literature and Feminism.* Ed. Susan Sage
Heinzelman and Zipporah Batshaw Wiseman. Raleigh, NC: Duke UP, 1994.
337–55.

Kucich, John. "Transgression and Sexual Difference in Elizabeth Gaskell's Novels."
*Texas Studies in Literature and Language* 32.2 (1990): 187–213.

Langland, Elizabeth. *Nobody's Angels: Middle-class Women and Domestic Ideology
in Victorian Culture.* Ithaca, NY: Cornell UP, 1995.

Michie, Elsie. *Outside the Pale: Cultural Exclusion, Gender Difference and the Victorian Woman Writer.* Ithaca, NY: Cornell UP, 1995.

Miller, Andrew H. "Subjectivity Ltd: The Discourse of Liability in the Joint Stock
Companies Act of 1856 and Gaskell's *Cranford.*" *English Literary History* 61
(1994): 139–57.

Poovey, Mary. *Making a Social Body: British Cultural Formation, 1830–1864.* Chicago: U of Chicago P, 1995.

Schor, Hilary M. "Elizabeth Gaskell: A Critical History and a Critical Revision."
*Dickens Studies Annual* 19 (1990): 345–69.

————. *Scheherezade in the Marketplace: Elizabeth Gaskell and the Victorian Novel.*
Oxford: Oxford UP, 1992.

Selig, Robert L. *Elizabeth Gaskell: A Reference Guide.* Boston, MA: G.K. Hall, 1977.

Spencer, Jane. *Elizabeth Gaskell.* London: Macmillan, 1993.

Stoneman, Patsy. "*Wives and Daughters* on Television." *Gaskell Society Journal* 14
(2000). www.lang.nagoya-u.ac.jp/'matsuoka/EG-Journal.html

Uglow, Jenny. *Elizabeth Gaskell: A Habit of Stories.* London: Faber and Faber, 1993.

Unsworth, Anna. *Elizabeth Gaskell: An Independent Woman.* London: Minerva
Press, 1996.

Welch, Jeffrey Egan. *Elizabeth Gaskell: An Annotated Bibliography, 1929 -1975.* New
York: Garland, 1977.

Weyant, Nancy. *Elizabeth Gaskell: An Annotated Bibliography of English-Language
Sources, 1976–1991.* Metuchen, NJ: Scarecrow, 1994.

Wright, Terence. *Elizabeth Gaskell, 'We Are Not Angels': Realism, Gender, Values.*
London: Macmillan, 1995.

Wyke, Terry. "The Culture of Self Improvement: Real People in *Mary Barton.*"
*Gaskell Society Journal* 13 (1999): 85–103.

# INDEX

415